Ancient Near Eastern History and Culture

William H. Stiebing, Jr.
University of New Orleans

Longman

New York San Francisco Boston
London Toronto Sydney Tokyo Singapore Madrid
Mexico City Munich Paris Cape Town Hong Kong Montreal

Vice President and Publisher: Priscilla McGeehon
Acquisitions Editor: Erika Gutierrez
Executive Marketing Manager: Sue Westmoreland
Supplements Editor: Kristi Olson
Media Editor: Patrick McCarthy
Production Manager: Joseph Vella
Project Coordiantion, Text Design, and Electronic Page Makeup: Electronic Publishing Services Inc., NYC
Cover Design Manager: John Callahan
Cover Designer: Laura Shaw
Cover Photo: Corbis, Inc.
Photo Researcher: Photosearch, Inc.
Manufacturing Buyer: Alfred Dorsey
Printer and Binder: Phoenix Color Corp.
Cover Printer: Phoenix Color Corp.

Library of Congress Cataloging-in-Publication Data
Stiebing, William H. Jr.
    Ancient Near Eastern history and culture / William H. Stiebing, Jr.--1st ed.
      p. cm.
    Includes bibliographical references and index.
    ISBN 0-321-06674-X
      1. Middle East--History--To 622. I. Title.

DS62.2 .S65 2003
939'.4--dc21

                            2002067543

Copyright © 2003 by Addison Wesley Longman, Inc.

All rights reserved. No part of this publication may be reproduced, stored in a retrieval system, or transmitted, in any form or by any means, electronic, mechanical, photocopying, recording, or otherwise, without the prior written permission of the publisher. Printed in the United States.

Please visit our website at http://www.ablongman.com

ISBN 0-321-06674-X

3 4 5 6 7 8 9 10—PHX—05 04

Dedicated to

Ann— My Wife, Best Friend,

and Fount of Inspiration

Brief Contents

Detailed Contents vii • *List of Tables, Figures, Maps, and Documents* xi
• *Preface* xv • *Acknowlededgments* xvi

CHAPTER 1
Introduction 1

CHAPTER 2
The Dawn of Civilization in Western Asia 29

CHAPTER 3
The First Mesopotamian Empires 65

CHAPTER 4
Egypt to the End of the Old Kingdom 103

CHAPTER 5
The Rise and Fall of the Egyptian Middle Kingdom 139

CHAPTER 6
The Era of Egyptian Greatness 162

CHAPTER 7
The End of the Bronze Age 193

CHAPTER 8
Recovery and Transformation (c. 1100–745 B.C.E.) 223

CHAPTER 9
Mesopotamian Supremacy 263

CHAPTER 10
The Persian Empire 293

CHAPTER 11
The Legacy of the Ancient Near East 323

Glossary 329 • *Chronological Chart* 334 • *Index* 336

Detailed Contents

List of Tables, Figures, Maps, and Documents   xi

Preface   xv

Acknowledgments xvi

CHAPTER 1
INTRODUCTION   1

Studying the Ancient Near East   1
What Is the "Near East"?   1
The Nature of Historical Study   3
Antiquity's "Clues"   4

**Creating a Chronology
for the Ancient Near East   6**
A Note on Chronological Terminology: B.C.E./C.E.
vs. B.C./A.D.   6
Absolute and Relative Chronology   6
Sources for Ancient Near Eastern Chronology   8

Prelude: Near Eastern Prehistory   10
The Origins of Sedentary Life
(c. 10,500–8300 B.C.E.)   10
Early Agricultural Communities in
Southwest Asia (c. 8300–6000 B.C.E.)   13
The Development of Complex Societies in
Southwest Asia (c. 6000–3700 B.C.E.)   19
Early Cultures of the Nile Valley
(c. 8000–3500 B.C.E.)   22
Major Social, Economic, and Political
Developments of the Neolithic Age   23

CHAPTER 2
THE DAWN OF CIVILIZATION
IN WESTERN ASIA   29

**The Emergence of Mesopotamian Civilization
(c. 3700–3000 B.C.E.)   29**
The Urban Revolution   29
The Development of Cuneiform
Writing   33
The People of Mesopotamia   37
The Origins of Elam   39

**The Mesopotamian Early Dynastic Period
(c. 3000–2330 B.C.E.)   40**
An Era of Independent City States   40
The "Royal Tombs" of Ur   44

**Mesopotamian Culture During the Early
Dynastic Era   46**
Religion and World View   46
The Development of Kingship   50
Economy and Society   51
Education, Literature, and the Arts   53
Science, Technology, and Warfare   55

**Urbanization in Other Areas of Western Asia
c. 3300–2300 B.C.E.   58**
Early Bronze Age Syria and Palestine   58
Early Bronze Age Anatolia and
Iran   60

Every chapter ends with *Suggestions for Further Reading and Information (Internet Links* and *Books and Articles)* and *Notes*

CHAPTER 3
THE FIRST MESOPOTAMIAN EMPIRES 65

The Akkadian Empire (c. 2334–2193 B.C.E.) 65
Sargon of Agade (c. 2334–2193 B.C.E) 65
Divine Kingship 68
Administration of the Empire 71
The Empire's Collapse 72

**The Third Dynasty of Ur
(c. 2112–2004 B.C.E.) 75**
Ur's Rise to Power 75
Shulgi's Reforms 77
The Fall of Ur 78

**Persian Gulf and Central Asian
Civilizations 79**
Dilmun, Magan, and Meluhha 79
The Oxus Civilization 84

**The Old Babylonian Period
(c. 2000–1595 B.C.E.) 85**
The "Interregnum" After the Fall of Ur 85
Hammurabi and His Rivals 87
Old Babylonian Cultural Developments 90
The End of Hammurabi's Dynasty and
the Rise of the Hittites 94

The Emergence of New Peoples 95
Indo-Europeans 95
Hurrians and the Mitanni 97
Kassites 98

CHAPTER 4
EGYPT TO THE END OF THE OLD KINGDOM 103

The Late Predynastic Era (c. 3500–3000 B.C.E) 103
The Geography of Egypt and Nubia 103
The People of the Nile Valley 105
Prelude to Civilization: The Naqada II
Period 105

**The Formation of the Egyptian State
(c. 3050–2686 B.C.E.) 108**
The Process of Unification 108
The Development of Egyptian
Writing 110
The Early Dynastic Period (Dynasties 1 and 2)
112

Major Elements of Egyptian Culture 114
Ma'at 114
Divine Kingship 115
Burial and the Afterlife 117
Religion and Ritual 119

**The Old Kingdom
(Dynasties 3-6, c. 2686-2180 B.C.E.) 123**
Djoser and the First Pyramid 123
The Zenith of Royal Power: The Fourth Dynasty
(c. 2613-2498 B.C.E.) 126
The Latter Part of the Old Kingdom: Dynasties 5
and 6 (c. 2498-2180 B.C.E.) 130
Early Egyptian Society and Culture 131

CHAPTER 5
THE RISE AND FALL OF THE EGYPTIAN MIDDLE KINGDOM 139

**The First Intermediate Period: Dynasties 7–11a
(c. 2180–2040 B.C.E.) 139**
Where is Ma'at? 139
The Intermediate Period's Effects 140

**The Middle Kingdom: Dynasties 11b–13a
(c. 2040–1720 B.C.E.) 143**
The Establishment of the Middle Kingdom 143
The Impressive Twelfth Dynasty 146
Cultural Developments During the Middle
Kingdom 148

**The Second Intermediate Period: Dynasties
13b–17 (c. 1720–1540 B.C.E.) 152**
The Onset of the Second Intermediate
Period 152
The Kingdom of Kush (Upper Nubia) 153

Hyksos Rule and the Dynasty at Thebes:
Dynasties 15 and 17 (c. 1650–1540 B.C.E.)
153
Hyksos Relations with the Levant   156
Egyptian and Levantine Contacts with the
Minoan Culture of Crete   158

CHAPTER 6
THE ERA OF EGYPTIAN
GREATNESS   162

The Beginning of the Egyptian New Kingdom
(c. 1550–1479 B.C.E.)   162
The Early Eighteenth Dynasty   162
The "Royal Heiress" Theory   164

Hatshepsut and Thutmose III
(c. 1479–1425 B.C.E.)   165
Hatshepsut's Seizure of Power   165
The Sole Rule of Thutmose III   168

The Egyptian Empire at Its Height
(c. 1425–1350 B.C.E.)   169
The Reigns of Amenhotep II and
Thutmose IV   169
Amenhotep III, "The Magnificent"   170
The New Egyptian Army   173
Late Bronze Age Canaan (Palestine
and Coastal Syria)   174
Relations with the Aegean
Kingdoms   176

Akhenaton and the Amarna Period
(c. 1350–1334 B.C.E.)   178
Controversies of the Amarna Age   178
Did Akhenaton Have a Co-Regency
With His Father?   179
The Beginning of Amenhotep IV's Reign   180
Akhenaton's Religion   181
The Revolution's Denouement   185

The End of the Eighteenth Dynasty
(c. 1334–1293 B.C.E.)   187
Tutankhamun and the Restoration of Amun   187

The Reigns of Ay and Horemheb,
(c. 1325–1293 B.C.E.)   188

CHAPTER 7
THE END OF THE BRONZE AGE   193

The Zenith of Hittite Power
(c. 1344–1180 B.C.E.)   193
Revival and Extension of the Hittite
Empire   193
Hatti's Showdown With Egypt   195
Achaeans and Trojans in Hittite Texts?   198

Hittite Culture   199
Economy, Society, and Government   199
Religion   201
Languages and Literature   203

The Twilight of the Egyptian Empire
(c.1293–1150 B.C.E.)   205
The Empire's Final Flash of Greatness   205
Invasions of the Sea Peoples   208

The Collapse of Bronze Age Societies in the
Eastern Mediterranean   212
The Mycenaean Kingdoms   212
The Demise of the Hittite Empire   213
The End of Egyptian Power   215
The Decline of Assyria and Babylonia   215
What Caused the Collapse?   217

CHAPTER 8
RECOVERY AND
TRANSFORMATION
(C. 1100–750 B.C.E.)   223

Mesopotamia and Egypt   223
Assyria and Babylonia   223
The Third Intermediate Period in Egypt   225

Anatolia   227
The Kingdom of Urartu   227
The Phrygian and Neo-Hittite Kingdoms   229

Syria   230
  The Aramaeans   230
  The Phoenicians   233

Early Israel   241
  The Emergence of Israel   241
  The Formation of the Israelite State
    (The United Monarchy)   244
  The Kingdoms of Israel and Judah   248

Other Small States of the Southern Levant   251
  The Philistines   251
  Ammon, Moab, and Edom   253
  Small Kingdoms and Confederations in
    Arabia   256

CHAPTER 9
MESOPOTAMIAN SUPREMACY   263

**The Height of Assyrian Dominion
  (744–627 B.C.E.)   263**
  Reestablishment and Expansion of Assyrian
    Power (744–681 B.C.E.)   263
  The Empire at Its Zenith (680–627 B.C.E.)   268

Neo-Assyrian Society and Culture   272
  The King, Crown Prince, and Queen   272
  Non-Royal Social Classes   274
  The Army   275
  Administration of the Empire   276
  Art, Literature, and Science   277

**The Neo-Babylonian (or Chaldean) Empire
  (625–560 B.C.E.)   279**
  Destruction of Assyria (627–605 B.C.E.)   279
  Formation of the Neo-Babylonian and
    Median Empires   280
  Nebuchadnezzar's Babylon   281
  The End of the Neo-Babylonian Empire   284

The Emergence of Biblical Monotheism   286
  The Triumph of the Reform Movement   286
  The Babylonian Exile   288

CHAPTER 10
THE PERSIAN EMPIRE   293

**The Origins and Growth of the Achaemenid
  Empire   293**
  The Fluorescence of the Lydian Kingdom
    (c. 685–547 B.C.E.)   293
  The Creation of the Persian Empire   294

The Persian Empire at Its Height   299
  Crisis and Restoration   299
  Reorganization of the Empire   301
  Wars With the Greeks   303

Persian Culture   305
  The King and Court   305
  The Persian Army   307
  The Religion of Zoroaster   308
  Persian Architecture and Art   310

Judah During the Persian Period   313
  The Restoration of Judah   313
  Religious Developments During the Persian Era
    315

The End of the Achaemenid Persian Empire   318
  Decline of the Empire (424–330 B.C.E.)   318
  Conquest by Alexander the Great   319

CHAPTER 11
THE LEGACY OF THE ANCIENT
NEAR EAST   323

Food, Drink, and Animals   323

Mathematics and Science   324

Language and Literature   325

Music, Art, and Architecture   326

Religion and Speculative Thought   327

Glossary   329
Chronological Chart   334
Index   336

List of Tables, Figures, Maps, and Documents

Tables

Table 1.1: Chronology of the Earliest Mesopotamian Cultures   19

Table 2.1: The Chronology of Early Sumer   29

Table 3.1: Chronology of the Akkadian Period and the Third Dynasty of Ur   68

Table 3.2: Chronology of Hammurabi's Dynasty   88

Table 4.1: Chronology of the Egyptian Predynastic and Early Dynastic Periods   106

Table 4.2: Chronology of the Egyptian Old Kingdom (Dynasties 3–6)   133

Table 5.1: Chronology of the First Intermediate Period, Middle Kingdom, and Hyksos Era   140

Table 5.2: Chronologies of the Middle Minoan and Late Minoan I Periods in Crete   158

Table 6.1: Chronology of the Eighteenth Dynasty   163

Table 7.1: Probable Chronology of the Hittite New Kingdom or Empire   193

Table 7.2: Chronology of the Nineteenth and Twentieth Dynasties   205

Table 8.1: Chronology of Assyrian Kings 911–745 B.C.E.   224

Table 8.2: Chronology of the Rulers of Israel and Judah, c. 1027–750 B.C.E.   248

Table 9.1: Chronology of the Neo-Assyrian and Neo-Babylonian Kings   264

Table 9.2: Chronology of the Last Kings of Israel and Judah, 747–586 B.C.E.   286

Table 10.1: Probable Chronology of the Median, Lydian, and Persian Rulers   295

Figures

Figure 1.1: An Illustration of Stratification at an Archaeological Site   7

Figure 1.2: The Pre-Pottery Neolithic A Tower at Jericho c. 7500 B.C.E.   14

Figure 1.3: Plaster Statues from Ain Ghazal, Jordan   15

Figure 1.4: Schematic Reconstruction of Çatal Hüyük, Level VI c. 6000 B.C.E.   17

Figure 1.5: Reconstructions of Two "Cult Centers" or "Shrines" at Çatal Hüyük   18

Figure 2.1: Reconstruction of the White Temple and Platform at Uruk c. 3200 B.C.E.   33

Figure 2.2: The Development of Cuneiform Writing   35

Figure 2.3: The Stele of Eannatum of Lagash ("The Stele of the Vultures")   44

Figure 2.4: Reconstruction of a Lyre from One of the "Royal Tombs" of Ur c. 2600–2500 B.C.E.   55

Figure 2.5: The So-Called "Ram in the Thicket" from One of the "Royal Tombs" of Ur c. 2600–2500 B.C.E.   56

Figure 2.6: Four-Wheeled Chariots and Infantry Attack an Enemy c. 2600–2500 B.C.E.   58

Figure 3.1: Bronze Head of an Akkadian King   67

Figure 3.2: The Victory Stele of Naram-Sin   70

Figure 3.3: A Reconstruction of the Ziggurat and Temple of Nanna, the Moon God, at Ur   76

Figure 3.4: Indus Seals with Brief Inscriptions in the Undeciphered Indus Script   82

Figure 3.5: Hammurabi's Law Stele   89

Figure 4.1: The West Bank of the Nile at Luxor in Upper Egypt   104

Figure 4.2: Part of the Enclosure Wall of Djoser's Step Pyramid   107

Figure 4.3: The Most Common Ancient Egyptian Crowns   108

Figure 4.4: The Narmer Palette   109

Figure 4.5: Examples of Egyptian Hieroglyphic Writing   111

Figure 4.6: Pharaoh Making Offerings to a God   117

Figure 4.7: The Temple of Isis at Philae   122

Figure 4.8: The Step Pyramid of Djoser at Saqqara   124

Figure 4.9: The Sides of the Great Pyramid Today   127

Figure 4.10: The Great Sphinx and the Great Pyramid   129

Figure 5.1: Weighing the Heart against *Ma'at*   143

Figure 5.2: Middle Kingdom Model of a Contingent of Nubian Archers   144

Figure 5.3: Reconstruction of Mentuhotep II's Mortuary Temple at Deir el-Bahri, Thebes   145

Figure 5.4: Portrait of Senusret III   148

Figure 5.5: Late Old Kingdom (Dynasty 6) and Middle Kingdom Nobles' Shaft Tombs at Aswan   149

Figure 5.6: Examples of *Shabti* Figurines   150

Figure 6.1: Amun Confirming Hatshepsut As King   166

Figure 6.2: The Mortuary Temple of Hatshepsut at Deir el-Bahri, Thebes   167

Figure 6.3: The Colossi of Memnon (Amenhotep III) at Thebes   171

Figure 6.4: Amenhotep III's Papyriform-Columned Court at the Luxor Temple, Thebes   172

Figure 6.5: The Battle of Qadesh   174

Figure 6.6: The Development of the Alphabet   177

Figure 6.7: Statue of Akhenaton from the Aton Temple, Thebes   180

Figure 6.8: The Aton Blessing Akhenaton and Nefertiti While They Play with Their Daughters   183

Figure 6.9: The Solid Gold Inner Coffin of Tutankhamun   189

Figure 7.1: Bas-Relief of A Hittite Warrior God   201

Figure 7.2: Central Group of Deities in Chamber A at Yazilikaya   202

Figure 7.3: A Hittite Royal Seal Impression   204

Figure 7.4: The Great Hypostyle Hall of the Temple of Amun at Karnak   206

Figure 7.5: The Facade of the Great Temple of Ramesses II at Abu Simbel   207

Figure 7.6: The Abu Simbel Temples on the Shore of Lake Nasser   208

Figure 7.7: Land Battle Against the Sea Peoples   211

Figure 8.1: A Relief from Kalhu Depicting Asshurnasirpal II and His Forces Attacking a City   225

Figure 8.2: Urartian Bronze Cauldron   228

Figure 8.3: Fragments of an Aramaic Stele at Dan   232

Figure 8.4: Eighth-Century B.C.E. Assyrian Relief   234

Figure 8.5: An Assyrian Depiction of Phoenician Biremes   238

Figure 8.6: Plans of Tenth-Century B.C.E. Gates at Gezer, Hazor, and Megiddo   247

Figure 8.7: Ninth-Century B.C.E. Life-Size Limestone Head of an Ammonite King   254

Figure 9.1: Reconstruction of the Citadel of Dur-Sharrukin   266

Figure 9.2: Sennacherib's Assault of the Judean City of Lachish   268

Figure 9.3: The Dying Lioness   278

Figure 9.4: Babylon at the Time of Nebuchadnezzar (604–562 B.C.E.)   282

Figure 9.5: Reconstruction of Babylon's Ishtar Gate   284

Figure 10.1: Relief and Inscription of Darius I at Behistun   300

Figure 10.2: Plan of Persepolis   311

Figure 10.3: Doorway of the Gate of All Lands   312

Maps

Map 1.1: The Near East—Ancient Place Names and Modern State Borders   2

Map 1.2: Near Eastern Sites of Incipient Cultivation and Early Plant and Animal Domestication   12

Map 2.1: Major Urban Centers of Southern Mesopotamia   30

Map 2.2: The Near East in the Third and Second Millennia B.C.E.   40

Map 3.1: The Akkadian Empire at Its Greatest Extent (Under Naram-Sin) and the Empire of the Third Dynasty of Ur   69

Map 4.1: Ancient Egypt   113

Map 5.1: Egypt During the Latter Part of the Second Intermediate Period   154

Map 6.1: Remains of Ancient Thebes   164

Map 6.2: The Egyptian Empire c. 1425 B.C.E.   169

Map 7.1: The Hittite Empire at its Greatest Extent (c. 1322–1220 B.C.E.)   194

Map 7.2: Migrations at the End of the Bronze Age (c. 1200–1100 B.C.E.)   214

Map 8.1: Major Phoenician Colonies of the Ninth Through Seventh Centuries B.C.E.   237

Map 8.2: The Kingdoms of Israel and Judah at the Time of Omri (c. 885–874 B.C.E.)   250

Map 8.3: Kingdoms and Confederations in First Millennium B.C.E. Arabia   257

Map 9.1: The Assyrian, Neo-Babylonian, and Median Empires at Their Greatest Extent (671–655 B.C.E.)   271

Map 10.1: The Achaemenid Persian Empire   298

Documents

Document 2.1: Excerpts from the *Sumerian King List*   42

Document 3.1: The Birth Legend of Sargon   66

Document 3.2: A Lamentation Over the Destruction of Ur   80

Document 3.3: Selected Laws from Hammurabi's Stele   92

Document 4.1: Examples of the Pyramid Texts   125

Document 4.2: The Diagnosis and Treatment of Two Injuries   134

Document 5.1: Dispair over Life in a World without Ma'at   142

Document 5.2: Some Magical Funerary Texts   151

Document 5.3: The War Between Kamose and the Hyksos   157

Document 6.1: The Hymn to the Aton   184

Document 6.2: Prayers to Akhenaton   185

Document 7.1: The Treaty between Hattusilis III and Ramesses II   197

Document 7.2: Merneptah's Victory Stele   209

Document 8.1: The Assyrian Account of the Battle of Qarqar   226

Document 8.2: The Victory Stele of Mesha, King of Moab   255

Document 9.1: Sennacherib's Siege of Jerusalem   269

Document 10.1: The Cyrus Cylinder   296

Document 10.2: Elephantine Papyri Concerning the Egyptian Temple of Yaho (Yahweh)   316

Preface

This book is intended as a general introduction to the history and culture of the ancient Near East for both students and interested lay persons. For many years, those looking for such a book had to choose between relatively detailed individual histories of various areas (e.g., Egypt, Mesopotamia, Anatolia, ancient Israel) or one or two very broad general surveys that lacked substance and detail. In recent years, though, several works that attempt to rectify this problem have appeared. Unfortunately, while each of these books has good points, none of them is completely satisfactory. So, the present book will attempt to steer a middle course between the detail exhibited by some works and the excessive brevity of others.

A society's cultural expressions are rooted in its environment, experiences, and relationships with other cultures—that is, in its history. So both a factual narrative of events and a description of the basics of individual cultures is necessary. This book's arrangement follows the divisions into periods, kingdoms, or empires generally used in Near Eastern political history, and descriptions of society and culture will be linked to those political narratives. This combination of factual narrative and broader discussion of culture will allow students and general readers to get a rounded introduction to the subject of ancient Near Eastern history. It will also allow instructors to concentrate on either political history or social-cultural history, knowing that whatever the emphasis in class, their students will have been introduced to both aspects of the subject. There is also an emphasis on problems and areas of uncertainty to help readers understand how evidence is used by historians, archaeologists, and other scholars to create interpretations. This aspect will also help them understand that often, several different interpretations of the same evidence are possible.

To allow readers to get at least a small sampling of the variety of written sources surviving from the ancient Near East, each chapter except the first (on prehistory) and the last (the Near East's legacy) contains quotations from several different types of documents. Notes are included for those interested in pursuing important points or problems. Unusual words or terms are defined when they first occur. Those printed in boldface type indicate that they are listed and defined in the glossary at the end of the book. A list of recommended web sites, books, and articles has been included at the end of each chapter. Maps, illustrations, and chronological tables have also been included to help the reader more clearly visualize and understand the ancient Near Eastern world.

Since this history covers a wide variety of cultures and languages, I need to add a word or two about the spelling of names and foreign words. The languages spoken in the ancient Near East had sounds that do not exist in English. For example, most of the ancient Near Eastern languages had a sound like an English "h," but they also had a more guttural sound like the "ch" in German words such as *ach*. Specialists usually use an "h" with a curved line under it to represent this German "ch" sound. However, most readers would not realize what sound was indicated by this special symbol, or the differences in sound between an "s" and an "s" with a dot under it (used to represent a sound like "ts") or an "s" with a little "v" over it (used to represent the "sh" sound). So, I have generally used simplified spellings: a plain "h" for the variety of "h" sounds, a simple "s" for all of the "s" sounds, etc. But even this rule has not been followed invariably. For example, the name of the principle Assyrian god (and of Assyria's most ancient capital city) is written three different ways in English: Assur, Ashur, or Asshur. To be consistent with other words in which I transliterated the "sh" sound with "s," I should have chosen "Assur." However, I used "Asshur" because it conveys to the reader both the correct pronunciation and the doubled consonant of the original. Rather than adopt a consistent transliteration from the original languages, I have tried to use the forms of the names most commonly found in other works or the transliterations that are easiest to read and pronounce. (After looking at some of the names and foreign words in this book, many readers may question that last sentence, but I assure them that if I had used the correct scholarly transliterations, the situation would have been far worse.) In cases where names were well known in another form (usually Greek or Hebrew), I have generally used the English forms of those ancient versions of the names. Thus, I refer to Sennacherib rather than Sinahheeriba (or the more scholarly form which would have the curved lines under the "h"s and various diacritical marks over some of the vowels) or Hadadezer rather than Hadad-idhr (in which the "dh" would be pronounced like the "th" in "the"). An exception to this rule about using Greek or Hebrew versions when they are available is my spelling of most Egyptian names. Egyptologists are divided, with some using Greek forms of the names such as Sesostris or Amenophis while others write the same names as Senusret (or Senwosret) and Amenhotep, spellings derived from the Egyptian hieroglyphs. Most American Egyptologists fall into the second camp, so I have used the most common forms of the spellings derived from the hieroglyphic inscriptions. I have tried to provide alternate forms of names, so hopefully readers will recognize the names of individuals mentioned here when they run across them in a different form in other works.

William H. Stiebing, Jr.
New Orleans, Louisiana

Acknowledgments

A work like this one cannot be produced without the help of many people. I would like to thank Jay O'Callaghan for initiating this project at Longman Publishing Company and giving it his full support. My editor, Erika Gutierrez, has also been extremely helpful and encouraging. Production Editor, Shannon Egan, did an excellent job overseeing the copyediting and scanning of the manuscript. The reviewers who read this work in various stages of completion have supplied many valuable comments and suggestions; clearly they have helped make this book better than it would have been otherwise. They are: Pamela Barmash, Washington University; Oded Borowski, Emory University; Henry E. Chambers, California State University; Marc W. Chavalas, University of Wisconsin; Marc Cooper, Southwest Missouri State University; Judy E. Gaughan, Colorado State University; William J. Hamblin, Brigham Young University; Robin J. DeWitt Knauth, Lycoming College; Kathryn E. Meyer, Washington State University; Gladys Frantz-Murphy, Regis University; John Robertson, Central Michigan University; Ronald H. Sacks, North Carolina State University; Mathew W. Waters, University of Pennsylvania; Edwin Yamauchi, Miami University; and Jonathan R. Ziskind, University of Louisville. Thanks are also due Aidan "Toni" Khalifah whose expertise and help were invaluable on the trip to Egypt during which I took many of the photographs that appear in this work. I am also grateful to my students at the University of New Orleans, who used parts of the manuscript in class and provided important feedback. Of course, any deficiencies that remain are my own fault and exist in spite of the best efforts of all these people. Finally, I must express the huge debt of appreciation I owe to my wife Ann. She has consistently supported my efforts, accompanying me to museums and trudging over archaeological sites, reading chapters to make sure they are understandable to lay readers, and providing the love and grounding without which I would have difficulty functioning. More than she may ever realize, whatever value this work has is due, in large part, to her.

1

Introduction

STUDYING THE ANCIENT NEAR EAST

What Is the "Near East?"

This book is an introduction to the ancient history and culture of an area scholars of antiquity call the Near East. This large territory includes **Asia Minor** (Turkey), the **Levant** (Syria west of the Euphrates, Lebanon, Israel, and Jordan), Egypt, portions of northwestern Arabia, **Mesopotamia** (the area between the Tigris and Euphrates rivers that includes Syria east of the Euphrates and Iraq), and the Iranian plateau. It extends from the Aegean and Mediterranean Seas on the west to Afghanistan and Pakistan on the east; from the Black Sea, Caucasus Mountains, Caspian Sea, and Turkmenistan on the north to the first Nile **cataract**, Arabian Desert, and Persian Gulf on the south. This is an area almost as wide as the continental United States and much larger than Europe (see Map 1.1). It naturally has much diversity in terrain, climate, and culture.

This large region has at times been called by several other names: the ancient Orient, the Middle East, or western Asia and Egypt. From the fifteenth through eighteenth centuries when European nations were just "discovering" the lands and cultures of China, Japan, India, and Southeast Asia, the term "Orient" or "East" generally referred to the region we are calling the Near East. Even during the nineteenth and early twentieth centuries, the "Orient" in the name of the famous Orient Express train referred to Turkey, since Istanbul was its final destination. The Christmas carol "We Three Kings of Orient Are" alluded to **magi** traveling from Persia or Mesopotamia, not from China or Japan. As the more distant Asian lands became better known, they became the "Far East" and the old Orient or East became the "Near East."

"The Middle East" is a term developed in the twentieth century to designate most of the area that formerly had been the Ottoman Turkish Empire. It usually includes the countries of Asia west of Afghanistan and Pakistan. Thus, it corresponds generally with the area covered in this book. However, the term is also often applied to those lands that are primarily Islamic in culture. When used in this way, it excludes Israel, but includes Afghanistan, Pakistan, and Egypt. Sometimes, the term even includes the other Muslim nations of North Africa (Libya, Tunisia

1

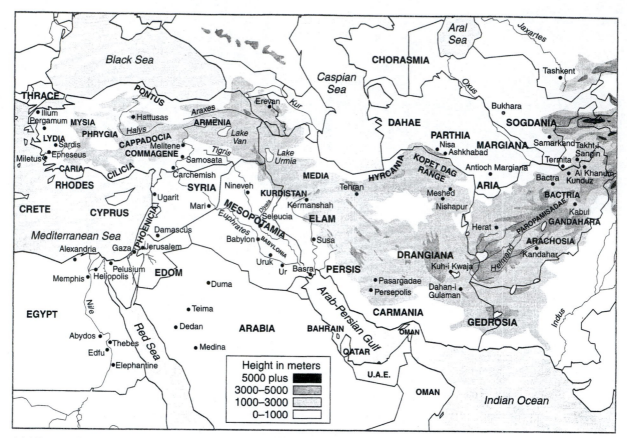

MAP 1.1   The Near East—Ancient Place Names and Modern State Borders

Source: Amélie Kuhrt, *The Ancient Near East, c. 3000–330 BC.* (London: Routledge, 1995), vol. 1, Map 1, pp. 2–3.

and Morocco). This dual meaning might make it useful for modern political analysis, but "Middle East" is too ambiguous a designation for use by historians. So, although news reporters, politicians, and political scientists have adopted the use of "Middle East," scholars studying ancient civilizations generally have not.

In recent decades, American schools have been providing better coverage of African states and civilizations. As part of that emphasis, educators have stressed Egypt's position in Africa and its role as an African culture. Also, ancient Egypt was more self-contained and its culture more parochial than the other Near Eastern nations. Thus, some scholars have preferred to speak of western Asia and Egypt rather

than the Near East. Geographically, that terminology is correct. However, in antiquity, Egypt was related economically, diplomatically, and to a degree, culturally, to the societies of western Asia. While it also had similar connections with Nubia to the south and lesser ones with Libya to the east, it had few affiliations with the rest of Africa. Most students of ancient cultures have continued to consider ancient Egypt an integral part of the Near East. Furthermore, the designation "Near East" is shorter and less cumbersome than "western Asia and Egypt." Therefore, the Near East has remained a viable scholarly designation for the region even though it includes parts of two continents and its outer boundaries are somewhat fluid.

In ancient times, trade routes crisscrossed the Near East, keeping the various cultures and civilizations of the area in touch with one another. In addition, there was extensive trade and contact with other cultures on the fringes of the Near East. Urban civilizations that developed in south-central Asia and the Indus Valley maintained trade relations with Mesopotamia in the third and second millennia B.C.E. as did Persian Gulf cultures around Bahrain, Qatar, and Oman. The Nubians not only traded with Egypt, but often were subjects of the Egyptian Empire. For a time, they even reversed the situation and became Egypt's masters. The Aegean civilizations that developed in Crete and mainland Greece not only had close relations with the peoples of Asia Minor, but also carried on extensive trade with Egypt, Cyprus, Palestine, and Syria. Thus, though most of these neighboring areas and cultures are not usually considered part of the ancient Near East, we will have to give some attention to them in this work.

The Nature of Historical Study

Many people mistakenly believe that historical study is primarily a matter of learning facts about the past. Perhaps in school these individuals had to learn the names of the U.S. presidents in order, or memorize other lists of historical names and dates. However, such "facts" are not history; they are just the building blocks of history. In the words of Mary Lynn Rampolla, "The historian's goal is to acquire insight into the ideas and realities that shaped the lives of men and women of earlier societies."[1] Or, to put it more briefly, historians seek to *understand* and *explain* the human past. The words used in that statement are important, for understanding and explanation consist of much more than just determining the "facts." Historical study involves not only learning *what* happened, but *why* it happened, *how* it happened, and to *whom* it happened. The historical approach is rooted in this attempt to satisfy our curiosity about past events and societies by solving puzzles and answering questions. Certainly, historians need to find the answers to factual questions about "who," "what," "where," and "when." But they also seek to learn the answers to "why" and "how." Without some understanding of their context, causes, and connections to one another, historical "facts" are just worthless bits of information, useless except in trivia games.

It should be noted that others besides historians seek to understand and explain past events. Some anthropologists study vanished cultures in order to understand how cultures, civilizations, and states begin and develop. Sociologists often analyze earlier societies to obtain comparative data. Economists also frequently use examples and comparisons drawn from the past. Furthermore, today, historians utilize the methods and insights of all of these social sciences in their study of the past. So what sets history apart from these other disciplines? The answer is history's concern with the unique aspects of past events and cultures and with their change and development through time.

Traditionally, when anthropologists, sociologists, and economists studied past cultures, they usually sought to find constants. They were trying to isolate universal elements that occur in all cultures and societies, and they hoped that they would be able to formulate general laws of cultural, social, or economic development. On the other hand, historians noted the distinctiveness and individuality of the events, people, and cultures of the past. However, the distinctions between the methods and goals of these various fields of study have tended to become blurred in recent years. Even in earlier times, historians generally recognized the importance of recurring tendencies throughout history, though few would have considered them "laws." It is the common components (human nature, emotions, motivations, patterns of organization) that we share with past individuals and cultures that allow us to at least partially comprehend them. However, historians must also be constantly aware of the particular, singular aspects and contexts of past events.

The common expression (borrowed from the Greeks) that "history repeats itself" is not really true. Every historical event happens only once and is bound to a particular place, particular ideas and customs, and a particular time.[2] Historians are aware that this unique, unrepeatable nature of the past makes it impossible for them to ever *completely* understand or explain it. We must rely on the records of those who were there, or on later stories based on accounts of those who were there, and on the physical remains that survive from the past. All of this material, of course, requires interpretation. Nevertheless, we seek as best we can to comprehend the past on its own terms, trying to avoid reading our own customs, values, and ideas into bygone times and places.

Time also has a necessary role in historical analysis. Historians seek to understand and explain human behavior and its results in the context of time. We must always be cognizant of change and progression, for, like the present, the past was dynamic. An early Greek philosopher made this point when he said that "you cannot step twice into the same river, for fresh waters are ever flowing in upon you."[3] Obviously, rivers are always moving and changing. But people also change and develop, not only from year to year, but also moment to moment. Nothing in this world is static; everything is constantly in process. Historians seek to comprehend and describe how past events, institutions, societies, and even individual human personalities and ideas evolved out of, or were influenced by, what went before and how they, in turn, affected what followed.

The perceptive reader will have recognized that there is an irreducible subjective element in such historical study. No matter how hard the historian tries to be objective, he or she cannot totally avoid the influences of our modern culture. Like past events, we are the products of our own time and our own society that shape the way we understand the world, including its past. Furthermore, the past cannot be repeated, so there is no way to be certain that one has properly understood it or correctly explained it. Even so-called "facts" about the past are not totally unquestionable. Historical "facts" are only interpretations of evidence that are accepted by almost all historians.

However, the truism that historical study can never be totally objective should not lead to the mistaken belief that all views about the past are equally valid. It is correct that no historical interpretation is absolutely true and unchangeable. But some views about the past are better than others, and *some* are almost certainly wrong. For example, some people claim that early human accomplishments were inspired or actually created by ancient visitors from outer space. However, the evidence adduced for such ancient astronauts cannot withstand close scrutiny.[4] Instead, many different types of evidence support the less romantic view that earthlings developed their own civilizations and built their own monuments. So we can (and should) judge historical constructs to be better or worse, probable or unlikely, depending on how well or poorly they explain the available evidence.

In the past, historians have argued whether historical study should be classified as a science or an art. However, it doesn't really seem to be either, though it has elements of both. Perhaps the best category for historical study is not science or art, but detective work. Like detectives, historians of the ancient world must develop logical explanations of past events using only incomplete bits of evidence or clues. They must gather all the evidence they can, striving to understand its original contexts, purposes, and limitations. Then, from the fragmentary evidence, they must carefully and imaginatively arrange the events into a meaningful pattern.[5]

Furthermore, historians, like detectives, frequently disagree about what is the most logical reconstruction of events, especially when the evidence is sparse. Sometimes a new piece of evidence will show that even a generally accepted reconstruction is wrong (or very unlikely). So, in the material that follows, areas of disagreement will be noted frequently and conflicting reconstructions or interpretations mentioned. In contradiction to the view of history as a recitation of "facts," such controversies are a necessary part of historical study.

Antiquity's "Clues"

Historians studying ancient times usually must work with material from two different sources: archaeology and written texts. When we referred above to disciplines other than history that study the past, we did not mention archaeology. Archaeology is a field of study distinguished by its methodology and the specific things it studies. Archaeology attempts to reconstruct the human past through the discovery and analysis of its material remains or **artifacts**. Anything that has been made, altered, or used by humans or which owes its position in space to humans is an artifact. Buildings, pottery, and metal tools are examples of artifacts. However, so too are sea shells that people carried away from a beach, or natural stones that they piled on top of graves or hurled at animals or enemies. Careful analysis of such remains provides important information about vanished cultures that can be used by scholars in many different fields, especially in anthropology and history. Historians use archaeological evidence primarily to supplement and test their written sources. Archaeology also has provided historians with long-lost texts such as ancient inscriptions, clay tablets, and papyrus scrolls.

Archaeological evidence is valuable, but written material is at the heart of any historical investigation. In fact, the appearance of written records is used to distinguish the historical era proper from prehistory. However, texts from the past are like statements that witnesses and suspects make to modern detectives. They often provide the clearest and best evidence for a reconstruction of past events. However, a good detective knows that some of his witnesses may be mistaken, lying, or telling only part of the truth. In the same way, historians must carefully analyze their textual evidence to determine its relevance and its reliability.

Much of the written evidence historians of ancient times must use is the equivalent of what our legal system calls "hearsay." It comes from writers who lived long after the events that they relate and contains much local folklore and tradition that may or may not be accurate. Probably the best-known example of such "hearsay" evidence would be the narrative portions of the Bible. Other examples can be found in the works of ancient historians such as Herodotus and Josephus. Furthermore, sometimes the level of "hearsay" between the "witness" and the original event is even greater than in the examples just men-

tioned. The writings of some ancient authors survive only in quotations from their work by other ancient figures. The history of Egypt written by Manetho, an Egyptian priest of the early third century B.C.E., is known only through such quotations. The same is true for the work of the Hellenistic Babylonian priest, Berossus. Thus, not only were these authors writing long after the events they were describing, but we also have the added problem of trying to decide whether or not they were quoted correctly. Obviously, the historian has to analyze such sources with great care and seek independent substantiation of their testimony.

Even writings that are contemporary with the events they describe must be carefully scrutinized for bias or possible distortions of the truth. Royal inscriptions and chronicles may lie or exaggerate in order to glorify the ruler. The author of a personal letter may have misunderstood or misrepresented contemporary events. Some texts may describe ideals more than reality. Because of these limitations, the most reliable information often comes from analysis of writings that were not intended to provide historical data. Personal business records, lists of temple personnel, transcripts of court suits, and other "nonhistorical" documents may provide the historian with valuable clues about the times and societies in which they were produced. Occasionally, such materials also provide information about major historical figures or events.

The greatest difficulty faced by the historian of the ancient Near East, however, is the spotty nature of the evidence. Only a small portion of the material that once existed now survives, and only a portion of that surviving material has been recovered for study. The "clues" we have are often very inadequate. Nevertheless, by painstaking testing, analysis, and correlation of the evidence provided by archaeology and written sources, historians have been able to plausibly reconstruct the ancient Near Eastern world. Naturally, this construct is only tentative. At any time, the discovery of new evidence could change it. Also, changes in historians' assumptions, concerns, and interests constantly lead them to seek out new evidence or to ask new questions of old evidence. Thus, the process of discovering and explaining the past never ends.

CREATING A CHRONOLOGY FOR THE ANCIENT NEAR EAST

A Note on Chronological Terminology: B.C.E./C.E. vs. B.C./A.D.

It has long been customary in the West to date events in relation to the supposed date for the birth of Jesus of Nazareth or Jesus Christ as he is called by Christians. (It should be noted that "Christ" is not part of Jesus' name. It is a title derived from the Greek word *christos*, which translates the Hebrew word *mashiah*, messiah, or "anointed one.") Actually, scholars are not exactly certain when Jesus was born, but the date we use for chronological purposes was calculated in the early sixth century by a monk named Dionysius Exiguus. As a Christian, Dionysius believed that the most important event in history had been the birth of Jesus. So, he decided to date succeeding events in relation to that date. Just as the reigns of kings and emperors were dated from the time they ascended to the throne, so the years since the birth of Jesus would be designated as if he were a reigning monarch—*anno Domini* ("the year of the Lord," abbreviated A.D.) 1, A.D. 2, and so forth. Events before the birth of Jesus later came to be designated B.C., "before Christ."

Today, many people fail to recognize the use of B.C. and A.D. as statements of Christian faith. To date events B.C. or A.D. is to profess one's faith that Jesus of Nazareth is the Messiah, the Savior sent by God. This fact did not cause much of a problem in the Middle Ages and early Modern Period, because the vast majority of Westerners were Christians. Today, there are many more non-Christians in Western countries than there were in earlier times. Because of this, some non-Christian scholars began using neutral chronological terminology that did not force Jews, Muslims, Hindus, and others to reference Jesus as Christ whenever they read or wrote a date. Today, many Christian scholars also use this neutral terminology. Instead of B.C. and A.D., these scholars date events as occurring B.C.E., "before the common (or Christian) era," or C.E., (year X of) "the common (or Christian) era." The "common" or "Christian" era refers to the epoch that began with the birth of Jesus as calculated by Dionysius Exiguus. Thus, 1250 B.C.E. is the same year as 1250 B.C., and 100 C.E. is the same year as A.D. 100.

In the interest of inclusiveness and fairness, this book will use the neutral designations B.C.E. and C.E. in place of B.C. and A.D.

Absolute and Relative Chronology

Since historians attempt to understand the development and change of cultures and institutions through time, chronology is important. We usually think of chronology in terms of dates—the U.S. Declaration of Independence was adopted on July 4, 1776, or Columbus first landed in the New World in 1492. However, such dates are examples of only one type of chronology, known as **absolute chronology**. Absolute chronology counts years from a specific point of reference. The dates 1776 and 1492, for example, are based on the supposed date for the birth of Jesus of Nazareth. We are used to such precise dates for events in our own time, and we would like to have them for events in the past. However, it is often difficult to date events that occurred more than 400 or 500 years before the time of Jesus with such precision. And for the prehistoric period, the time before the development of writing, precise absolute dates for human events are impossible.

Many events and periods of antiquity can be dated only in terms of their order or sequence. We call this type of dating "**relative chronology**." This is the kind of chronology usually produced by archaeological excavations. As archaeologists uncover ancient settlements, they usually find the remains of buildings constructed atop the vestiges of still earlier structures, layer upon layer. The sequence of a site's layers of remains or strata is known as its stratification, and the analysis of stratification is called **stratigraphy**. The material in the layer at the bottom of a mound is earlier than that in the layers above it. Pits dug into a site are later than the layers they cut through. We may not know exactly when any one of the layers was created, but their sequence allows us to place the objects they contain in proper chronological order in relation to one another. The only time that this "law of superposition" is not true is when there has been disturbance of the original layers. For example, if someone digs a deep pit and piles the excavated debris on top of the ground surface nearby, the earlier material from the bottom of the pit will wind up above material from the time the pit was dug. Also, objects from the time when the pit was dug may fall into the pit and wind up at the same depth as objects of much earlier date. Therefore, it is very important that the archaeologist recognize such disturbances in determining the stratigraphical history of a site (see Figure 1.1).

Archaeologists can extend a stratigraphical sequence from one mound, or **tell** (the Arabic term for a mound), to entire cultural regions by comparing the assemblages found in the layers of one mound with those of others in the region. An archaeological **assemblage** is a group of objects found in association with each other, thought to be contemporaneous and belonging to one group of people. For example, if archaeologists uncover certain types of pottery,

weapons, and other artifacts in Stratum 2 (counting from the top) of one mound and an assemblage of the same types of artifacts in Stratum 6 of another mound, they can assume that these two strata are roughly contemporaneous. Such comparisons allow them to create sequences of cultural phases or periods (defined by their archaeological assemblages) for entire cultures.

Fortunately, archaeological assemblages and sequences can often be provided with generalized absolute dates by noting relationships with Egypt or Mesopotamia (and later with Greece, Rome, and other areas). Scholars have developed at least an approximate absolute chronology for areas that had many written texts, including king lists and astronomical observations (see the next section). So, Palestinian objects found in Egypt and Egyptian and Mesopotamian objects found in Palestinian archaeological deposits allow us to provide approximate dates for the Palestinian archaeological assemblages and sequences.

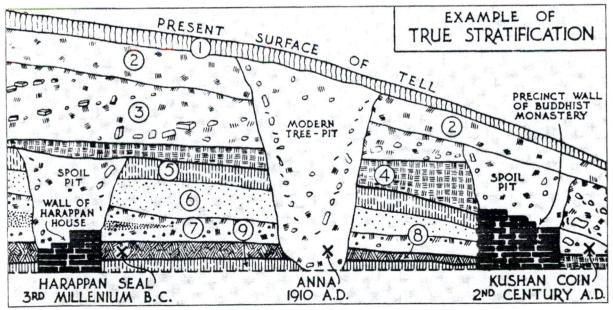

FIGURE 1.1   An Illustration of Stratification at an Archaeological Site

Source: From Mortimer Wheeler, *Archaeology from the Earth.* (Oxford: Oxford University Press).

Furthermore, over the past half century, science has provided archaeologists with additional ways to date the past. The best-known and most useful of these scientific dating techniques is **radiocarbon dating** (also known as **carbon-14 dating** or ^{14}C dating) developed by physicist Willard Libby just after World War II. All living things contain carbon, and it was learned that a very small but fixed proportion of that carbon is the radioactive isotope of carbon, ^{14}C. As long as an organism is alive, the proportion of radioactive carbon it contains remains constant. However, when an organism dies, it ceases to receive new carbon-14, and the radioactive carbon it already contains gradually decays into nitrogen. So the proportion of carbon-14 to normal carbon decreases as time passes. It takes 5,730 years, plus or minus 40 years, for half of the radioactive carbon in an object to become nitrogen, another $5,730 \pm 40$ years for half of the remaining ^{14}C to decay, and so on. Scientists determine the percentage of radioactive carbon remaining in organic material found in archaeological deposits and compare it with the percentage in presently living organisms. They then can calculate how long the ^{14}C has been decaying and thus, how long ago the organism in question died. This dating method can provide at least general absolute dates for organic objects up to approximately 70,000 years old.[6]

Dendrochronology, or tree-ring dating, is another scientific dating method that has proved useful to archaeology. Trees add a ring every year and the width of the rings varies according to climatic conditions. Scientists can compare groups of wide and narrow rings in recently cut trees with those in old stumps and beams from the same area to create tree-ring sequences extending far backward in time. In England and the southwestern United States, such sequences stretch back more than six thousand years. They have been particularly useful as indicators of periods of climatic change and as a means of correcting radiocarbon dates. By testing selected rings from these tree-ring sequences, scientists can determine whether the radiocarbon date deviates from the true date and if so, by how much. The ratio of carbon-14 to normal carbon has varied over time, so our calculations based on the present-day ratio of carbon iso-

topes were bound to produce somewhat inaccurate dates for earlier material. Today, based on radiocarbon testing of tree rings, scientists have constructed charts showing the amount of deviation between radiocarbon dates and actual absolute dates. They use these charts to correct radiocarbon dates to more accurately reflect the true age of tested objects up to 5,000 to 6,000 years old.

Scientists have also developed other methods for dating archaeological remains. Fission-track dating uses microscopic evidence of the fission of trace amounts of a uranium isotope to date glass and inclusions in clay. Archaeomagnetic or paleomagnetic dating obtains dates by comparing the magnetic orientation of particles in clay ovens, burned walls, and other fired materials with past positions of the earth's magnetic pole. **Obsidian** hydration dating determines when a tool made of this volcanic glass was last used by measuring the amount of water its surface layers have absorbed. And thermoluminescence dating determines when clay objects were last fired by measuring the amount of light emitted when they are subjected to high heat. These dating techniques have all been useful, but none is as widely used or is as accurate as corrected radiocarbon dating.

Sources for Ancient Near Eastern Chronology

The chronological framework for ancient Near Eastern history has been developed through careful analysis of many different types of material. Some, like lists of rulers derived from Hittite documents and various texts found at Ebla, Aleppo, and other Syrian cities, provide only relative chronologies. Fortunately, though, absolute dates can be determined for several events mentioned in ancient Mesopotamian and Egyptian sources. Trade, diplomatic relationships, and other connections between the various Near Eastern peoples then make it possible for scholars to date other areas by means of the Mesopotamian and Egyptian chronologies.

However, almost all of the absolute dates on which we rely are derived from astronomical observations mentioned in Egyptian or Mesopotamian texts. This fact makes our chronologies less precise than one might think. Most astronomical phenomena recur in cycles. Often the cycles are short enough that two or three different dates are possible for an astronomical event mentioned in an ancient text. Other questions arise due to gaps in the records, uncertainty about the length of some kings' reigns, the possible overlapping of some reigns, and similar problems.

The ancient Mesopotamians not only created various king lists, they also kept lists of year names or designations. In early Mesopotamia, each year was given a specific name such as "the first conquest of Ebla." These names were used to date documents, and lists of them formed a fixed chronology for the area. In later Assyria, there was a *limmu* official for each year whose name was used as the year name. The Assyrian *limmu* lists served the same function as earlier year-name lists. Unfortunately, there are gaps between the various year lists. Specialists have reconstructed ancient Mesopotamian chronology from the surviving king and year lists, historical chronicles, inscriptions, and several synchronisms (indications of events that occurred at the same time or of persons who were contemporaries). A reference to a solar eclipse that occurred in 763 B.C.E. allows us to provide firm dates for Assyrian rulers and events back to almost 1000 B.C.E. and for the later Neo-Babylonian and Persian Periods. However, Mesopotamian chronology for the second and third millennia is uncertain. Observations of movements of the planet Venus made near the end of the First **Dynasty** of Babylon yield several possible dates. Thus, the beginning of Hammurabi's reign is dated 1848, 1792, or 1728 B.C.E. by different scholars. There also is a gap of unknown duration between the end of the First Dynasty of Babylon (Hammurabi's dynasty) and the beginning of Kassite rule, and between the end of the Akkadian Empire and the rise of the Third Dynasty of Ur. This means that dates for early Mesopotamia can vary by as much as 200 or 300 years.

The basic framework for Egyptian chronology is its dynastic sequence. This arrangement is based on the Hellenistic work of Manetho. However, as previously mentioned, Manetho's history is known only from excerpts included in the writings of later indi-viduals. The ancient Egyptians also made some king lists, one or more of which Manetho probably used to write his history. Unfortunately, only a few fragmentary examples of these lists survive. These include the Turin Royal Canon, a fragmentary list known as the Palermo Stone, the Royal List of Karnak, the Saqqara Table of Kings (on the wall of a tomb) and the Abydos Table of Kings (on the walls of a temple). We must compare the information found in the excerpts from Manetho with that derived from these surviving king lists, and check both against inscriptions and other documents. In this way, scholars have reconstructed the probable sequence of Egyptian rulers and the approximate lengths of many of their reigns.

Just as in Mesopotamian chronology, absolute dates for ancient Egypt are derived from textual references to astronomical events. Early in their history, the Egyptians created a civil calendar that began with the start of the Nile's flood, or **inundation**. They also soon observed that after a period of invisibility, the star Sirius (Sopdet to the Egyptians, Sothis in Greek) reappeared at about the same time that the inundation commenced. However, the civil calendar was only 365 days long while the actual solar year is about $365\frac{1}{4}$ days long. So, the calendar gradually got out of synchronization with the seasons of the solar year. Only once in every 1,460 years did the rising of Sirius actually take place on the first day of the civil year. Ancient accounts indicate that this event occurred in 139 C.E. This reference allows us to calculate the possible absolute dates for Egyptian references to the calendar dates for the rising of Sirius in the seventh year of Senusret III (Dynasty 12) and in the ninth year of Amenhotep I (Dynasty 18). These calculations indicate that the seventh year of Senusret III fell between 1876 and 1864 B.C.E., with 1872 B.C.E. being the most probable date. From this date, scholars can calculate the dates for the reigns of the rest of the Middle Kingdom **pharaohs** and provide approximate dates for those of earlier dynasties. A similar calculation indicates that the date for the ninth year of Amenhotep I probably fell in 1537 or 1517 B.C.E. Thus, the inception of Amenhotep I's dynasty (the Eighteenth) is usually placed around 1570 or 1550 B.C.E. From this date, other New Kingdom dates can be worked out.

The Egyptians also used a lunar calendar for determining the times for religious festivals. A series of lunar observations recorded during the reigns of Thutmose III and Ramesses II provides another possible way to date New Kingdom reigns. However, depending on where in Egypt one assumes the observations were made, the date for the beginning of Thutmose III's reign could be 1504, 1490, or 1479 B.C.E. In recent years, most Egyptologists have come to support the 1479 B.C.E. date, making 1550 B.C.E. the most likely date for the beginning of the Eighteenth Dynasty. Similarly, Ramesses II could have come to the throne in 1304, 1290, or 1279 B.C.E., with the evidence favoring 1279 B.C.E.

Thus, pre-first millennium B.C.E. absolute dates for both Mesopotamia and Egypt are not certain. Yet these are the dates on which the chronologies for other areas must be based. This history of the ancient Near East will use the absolute dates generally deemed most probable. Nevertheless, most of these "absolute" dates will be preceded by **c.** (an abbreviation for *circa*, meaning "about") or by the word "approximately," "around," "about," "roughly," or some other expression of uncertainty.

PRELUDE: NEAR EASTERN PREHISTORY

The Origins of Sedentary Life (c. 10,500–8300 B.C.E.)

Though human beings emerged on earth some 2.5 to 3 million years ago, settled life, agriculture, civilization and history are all relatively recent. These developments have all taken place within the past 13,000 years. By that time, our species, *Homo sapiens sapiens* (doubly-wise human), had spread throughout the world and totally replaced earlier human species. Today scholars hotly debate the origins, movements, and interconnections of various early types of humans represented in the fossil record.[7] However, fascinating as these arguments are, they are beyond the scope of this book. Our story begins at the end of the last Ice Age when the human way of life began to undergo momentous changes.

Following the ideas of archaeologist V. Gordon Childe, many scholars once believed that the change to our present-day climate around 8000 B.C.E. led Near Eastern peoples to domesticate plants and animals. According to this theory, as deserts spread in Africa and southwest Asia, people, animals, and plants were forced into closer contact in smaller areas (oases or river valleys). The need for new food sources and the proximity of wild varieties of grain, sheep, goats, pigs, and other animals prompted humans to begin the Neolithic (or Agricultural) Revolution. This "oasis hypothesis" had to be abandoned when archaeologists discovered that the wild ancestors of wheat and barley were not native to the river valleys or oases. Moreover, in the 1950s, Robert Braidwood's excavations at Jarmo and other sites in the hill country of northern Iraq suggested that the Near East's earliest agricultural villages had developed in the "hilly flanks" of the fertile crescent, not in the oasis zones. Finally, scholars learned that agriculture developed before the modern deserts and oases appeared. Therefore, Childe's theory has been discarded, and with it, the notion that agriculture made settled life possible. We now know that sedentary occupation *preceded* the development of agriculture, and that the entire process stretched over hundreds of years. "Revolution" may be the wrong word to describe it.

According to climatologists, as the glaciers covering much of northern Europe, Asia, and North America began retreating around 15,000 years ago, climates around the world began fluctuating wildly. Over the next few thousand years, temperatures and sea levels gradually rose. Many Ice Age species, such as the woolly mammoth, saber-tooth tiger, and giant ground sloth, became extinct. The continents began to assume their present shapes as seas covered continental shelves and land bridges in various areas, including the one between Asia and North America. The rising waters also cut off some peninsulas such as Britain and Japan, turning them into islands. Major rivers such as the Nile and the Mississippi filled their valleys with silt and created expansive deltas. Rainfall across North Africa and southwest Asia was higher than it had been during the Ice Age and much higher than it is now. The area that is now the Sahara Desert was covered with grasslands and shallow lakes supporting herds of giraffes, hippopotami, and other animals. Forests and dense stands of wild cereal grasses gradually replaced the former dry steppe grasslands in Syria and the Levant.

The Natufian culture that emerged in Palestine and southern Syria around 10,500 B.C.E. developed a new subsistence pattern to exploit these environmental changes. Some Natufians continued to live in caves, but others settled on riverbanks, lake shores, and in areas that later would be deserts. Abundant wild food supplies allowed the Natufian people to become sedentary and gradually increase the size of their groups. While remaining hunters, fishers, and gatherers, the Natufians lived in fairly large settlements ranging in size from around 5,400 to 10,800 square feet (500 to 1,000 square meters). The larger sites such as Munhatta in Israel probably had a population of between 150 and 250 people who seem to have occupied the sites year-round. Natufian settlements contained rows, and later, clusters of circular or oval huts. The lower portions of the huts' walls were made of undressed stone, while the upper portion probably consisted of a framework of wood and animal skins. The floors were often partially recessed into the earth and sometimes contained mud-plastered storage pits.

Storage facilities are a new feature suggesting that the Natufians intensively gathered wild barley and emmer wheat as well as acorns and other nuts to supplement their hunting of gazelles, deer, wild cattle, goats, and pigs. This idea is supported by finds of numerous stone grinding mortars and pestles, as well as the earliest-known sickles (consisting of small flint blades set into wood or bone handles). Since gruel or porridge made from grain is not very appetizing, especially when meat dishes were still widely available, some scholars have argued that early peoples used grain primarily to make beer.[8] However, whether to make gruel, beer, or bread, the evidence suggests that some Natufian communities gathered large amounts of grain.

Several groups of Natufians not only became permanently settled, but probably began practicing **incipient cultivation** and engaged in **incipient herding** of animals. That is, near their settlements, these groups planted wild grains from seeds they had collected, in some cases probably from places fairly distant from the settlements. At Tell Abu Hureyra in Syria (see Map 1.2), the villagers seem to have driven wild gazelles into stone enclosures near the site, then killed them. In time, the people may have begun to keep some of the animals alive within the pens for later use. There is clear evidence that the Natufians had domesticated the dog by about 10,000 B.C.E., but it seems to have remained the only fully domesticated animal for at least two thousand years.

Natufian sites have also produced evidence of growing trade in marine shells, gemstones, obsidian, and other goods, which probably included salt. Robert Wenke has noted that "with the increased importance of wild cereals in the diet, salt probably became for the first time a near necessity: people who eat a lot of meat get many essential salts from this diet, but diets based on cereals can be deficient in salts."[9] Salt became an increasingly important trade commodity over time.

There are indications that the luxury items obtained through trade were not evenly distributed throughout the population, so differences in social rank and status probably existed. Such social stratification and some kind of leadership for the larger Natufian communities would naturally be suspected on the basis of ethnographic analogy. However, Natufian burials provide more direct evidence. Most of the dead were unaccompanied by grave goods, but a few were buried with luxury items such as beaded headdresses, necklaces, pendants, or belts made of shells, bone, and various kinds of stone.

The Natufians usually buried their dead under house floors and at cave entrances, but customs differed from place to place. At Nahal Oren on Mount Carmel (see Map 1.2), large limestone mortars were placed in the graves, their pierced bottoms at the level of the corpse while their uppermost portions protruded above the earth filling. These stones seem to

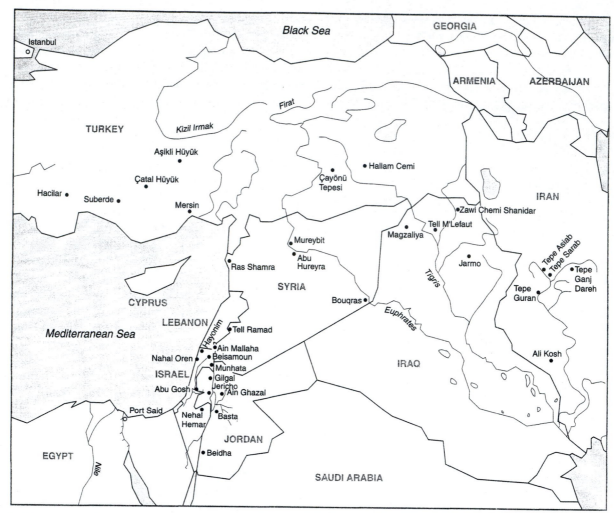

MAP 1.2   Near Eastern Sites of Incipient Cultivation and Early Plant and Animal Domestication

Source: C. C. Lamberg-Karlovsky and Jeremy A. Sabloff, *Ancient Civilizations: The Near East and Mesoamerica,* 2nd ed.
(Prospect Heights, IL: Waveland Press, 1995), p. 50.

have linked the living with the dead. Traces of burn-ing on top of the graves suggest a special rite, perhaps funeral meals. The heads of the dead at Ain Mallaha (see Map 1.2) were wedged between two stones and their extremities covered with large stones as if intended to keep them in the graves. At some late sites, the heads had been removed from adult bodies before burial. Some scholars think these various bur-ial practices indicate that the Natufian people had a

cult of ancestor worship. At the least, they show that the Natufians had developed some concepts about the meaning and nature of death.

What seems to be nonutilitarian art is another feature of Natufian settlements. These people deco-rated bone and stone objects with incised geometric patterns. They also created three-dimensional carved figurines of animals and humans, especially women. It is usually assumed that the statuettes have religious significance—for example, the female figures may have been representations of the "Mother Goddess." It has also been suggested that the carved designs may have reflected a growing sense of group identity (symbols designating nascent clans or tribes), while the beaded necklaces and ornaments indicated differences in rank or status within the group.

Early Agricultural Communities in Southwest Asia (c. 8300–6000 B.C.E.)

At the end of the Natufian Period, regional variations of the culture developed in different parts of Palestine and southern Syria. At about the same time, related village cultures emerged in northern Syria, Asia Minor, and in the hills north and east of Mesopotamia. The appearance of these village cultures marks the beginning of the Neolithic Period (or "New Stone Age").

The climate in southwest Asia began to turn cooler and drier (especially in the summers) around 8300 B.C.E., though not permanently, as once believed. This climatic change, known as the Younger Dryas, lasted about a millennium. It probably helped trigger the "Agricultural Revolution," but not exactly in the way Childe had hypothesized. As we have seen, groups of Natufians were already living in permanent or semipermanent settlements and were probably practicing incipient cultivation of wild grains by 9000 B.C.E. Also, their population had been slowly growing. The increasing seasonal aridity after approximately 8300 B.C.E. and the more populous communities made it much more difficult for semisedentary or sedentary groups to continue to support themselves by intensive hunting and gathering. Many Natufian settlements were abandoned, and the descendants of their inhabitants seem to have become mobile hunters and gatherers once more. Others probably adapted by storing more food for use in the summer, but in order to stay near their stored supplies, they likely became even more sedentary. Some communities began to experiment with various wild grains, first selecting those that were best suited to the local environment, then eventually mixing different varieties to produce hybrids that could grow in diverse environ-

ments. Thus, at the beginning of the Neolithic Period, the descendants of the Natufian people domesticated plants and became the first genuine agriculturalists.[10] Knowledge of agriculture gradually spread through western Asia and eventually to Egypt. However, though the Levant was probably the earliest site of agricultural development, it was not the only one. At slightly later times, agriculture seems to have developed independently in East Asia, sub-Saharan Africa, New Guinea in the Pacific, and Mesoamerica in the New World. As anthropologist Robert Wenke points out, "The fact that domestication appeared independently in many different environments at many different times and involved scores of plant and animal species, however, suggests that climatic changes alone do not entirely explain the origins of agriculture."[11]

In the Levant, the Natufian-derived cultures of the period from c. 8300 to 7500 B.C.E. are generally labeled "Pre-Pottery Neolithic A" (PPNA). While most PPNA communities continued to have fewer than 200 inhabitants, a few were much larger. Tell Mureybit on the Euphrates in Syria and Jericho near a spring in the Jordan Valley (see Map 1.2) each probably had hundreds of occupants (in the case of Jericho, possibly as many as a thousand). Jericho is clearly the most important PPNA site. Its small Natufian settlement developed into a large PPNA village of circular mud-brick huts with stone foundations spread over an area of some eight to ten acres. Jericho's inhabitants protected their settlement with a 28-foot-wide ditch and a stone wall 5 to 10 feet thick. Archaeologist Kathleen Kenyon dug only small portions of the mound down to the Pre-Pottery Neolithic A strata. Nevertheless, in her three major trenches on the north, south, and west sides of the mound, she found segments of wall, some surviving to a height of about 2.5 meters (over 8 feet). Presumably, these defenses surrounded the entire site. Attached to the inside of the wall on Jericho's western side was a massive circular stone tower about 33 feet in diameter and 28 feet high (see Figure 1.2). The tower was solid except for a steep internal 22-step staircase leading to the top. Kenyon believed that the ditch, wall, and tower were designed for defense against human enemies. The walls also could have been meant to keep

FIGURE 1.2   The Pre-Pottery Neolithic A Tower at Jericho c. 7500 B.C.E.

The square hole in the center of the tower's top is the entrance to the internal stairway.
Source: University College of London Institute of Archaeology Library.
Photo: Peter Dorrell, UCL.

much manpower and time to build. They indicate that PPNA Jericho must have had a strong, organized system of leadership. Study of faunal remains from Jericho's PPNA layers reveals that wild animals were still being hunted, and there is little evidence of animal domestication. However, archaeologists have uncovered traces of domesticated barley and wheat, and carbonized remains of figs and lentils may indicate that they also were domesticated. These crops, produced in abundance in the oasis around Jericho's spring, must have represented the settlement's primary wealth, though trade of salt, bitumen, and other products from the Dead Sea probably contributed as well.

The succeeding period (c. 7500 to 6000 B.C.E.) in the Levant is called Pre-Pottery Neolithic B (PPNB). Agriculture greatly progressed during this era, and sites were located in a variety of regions, including areas now very arid such as the **Negev** in Palestine, the Transjordanian plateau, and southern Sinai. This occupation pattern and other evidence indicates that the dry weather of the Younger Dryas had ended. In fact, rainfall amounts in PPNB were not only greater than during PPNA, but probably also greater than at present.

In the early 1980s, a large PPNB agricultural village, first occupied around 7250 B.C.E., was excavated at Ain Ghazal near Amman, Jordan. While initially about the same size as Jericho (approximately 10 acres), Ain Ghazal grew throughout the seventh millennium B.C.E. It doubled its original size by about 6500 B.C.E. and tripled it by c. 6000 B.C.E. Even if all of the site was not occupied at the same time, Ain Ghazal probably had one of the largest populations in the Near East. Its stone buildings were generally rectangular rather than circular, had plastered floors, and seem to have varied in size (possibly indicating disparities in wealth). Though its inhabitants had herds of goats and grew domesticated wheat, barley, peas, lentils, and chick peas, half of their diet still consisted of wild game and plants (mostly pistachios, almonds, and figs).

The best-known finds from Ain Ghazal are a series of human statues made of lime plaster modeled over reed and grass cores (see Figure 1.3). Details of

out wild animals, though they seem to be much larger than necessary for that purpose. Others have suggested that the walls may have been created to protect the settlement against mudslides and seasonal flooding. The purpose of the tower, though, is puzzling. Since it was on the inside of the wall, it would not have been very useful in warfare except as a lookout post. Thus, some think the tower may have had a religious or social function rather than a military one.

Whatever their intended use (and they might have served more than one purpose), these monuments took

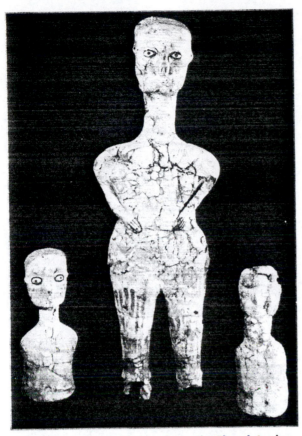

FIGURE 1.3   Plaster Statues from Ain Ghazal, Jordan

These statues are c. 6500 B.C.E.

Source: University College of London Institute of Archaeology Library.
Photo: Peter Dorrell and Stuart Laidlow, UCL.

Smaller clay figurines, usually of animals and women, may also have been used in magic rituals.

Another indicator of seventh millennium B.C.E. religious beliefs, possibly ancestor worship, are caches of human skulls, often plastered and decorated. The practice of removing heads from bodies and burying them separately had existed in the PPNA era. However, at Ain Ghazal, Beisamoun, Jericho, and Tell Ramad (see Map 1.2) skulls now were made more lifelike by covering them with plaster modeled into human features. Imbedded seashells often were used for eyes. One skull found in the Nahal Hemar cave had bitumen on top, possibly representing hair.

In the Zagros Mountain region to the east of Mesopotamia and in **Anatolia**, people were taking similar steps towards domestication of plants and animals. Zawi Chemi, a site in northeastern Iraq (see Map 1.2), has provided evidence that sheep were probably domesticated in the Zagros region as early as c. 8400 to 8000 B.C.E. Finds at Asiab, Ganj Dareh, and Ali Kosh, other early eastern Zagros sites, show that sheep and goats definitely had been domesticated there by the early part of the eighth millennium B.C.E. The inhabitants of these villages also planted emmer wheat and two-row hulled barley, which are not native to the area, while continuing to gather wild einkorn wheat and other wild grasses and legumes. Braidwood's excavation at Jarmo showed that by the time this small village arose around 6700 B.C.E., both types of wheat (emmer and einkorn) had been domesticated in the Zagros region, two-row barley was in the process of being domesticated, and pigs had been added to the list of domesticated animals. Also, the earliest pottery vessels yet known in the Near East were made at Ganj Dareh around 7000 B.C.E. (Soon afterward, the use of pottery seems to have developed independently at Jericho and several other sites.)

In **Anatolia**, archaeologists have uncovered the remains of a 100- to 200-hundred-person settlement that was occupied from about 7300 to 6500 B.C.E. at Çayönü Tepesi. Like contemporary villagers, Çayönü's inhabitants consumed both wild and domesticated plants and eventually supplemented their hunting

the faces and garments were painted on the plaster, and eyes were often made of inlaid shells with painted dots in the center. These sculptures are relatively large, some about three feet high. Similar PPNB plaster statues are known from Jericho and a cave in Nahal Hemar in the Judean desert. However, the examples from Ain Ghazal are more numerous and better preserved than the others. Such statues seem to have been religious in nature and, according to excavator Gary Rollefson, they probably reflect "a sophisticated system of public ritual and ceremony."[12]

with herds of domestic sheep, goats and pigs. They also created some implements and jewelry by cold hammering native nuggets of copper. Archaeologists have excavated other early agricultural villages in Asia Minor at Hacilar, Suberde and, recently, Navali Cori near Çayönü. Anatolia was probably also the site of the earliest domestication of cattle around 7000 B.C.E.

The best-known Neolithic site in Asia Minor is Çatal Hüyük in the foothills of the Taurus Mountains. It was continuously occupied between about 6500 and 5600 B.C.E. At its zenith (c. 6000 B.C.E.), it covered more than 30 acres and had 4,000 to 6,000 inhabitants. It was, as far as we know, the largest site of its time, many times larger than most Neolithic villages. The population seems to have utilized at least some irrigation to grow domesticated varieties of wheat, barley, peas, and lentils. They also had herds of domesticated cattle that probably provided milk, yogurt, butter, and cheese to the diet in addition to beef. Hunting and gathering also continued, supplying extra meat (and skins), wild walnuts, berries, pears, crab apples, grapes, figs, and pomegranates, all native to the area.

Çatal Hüyük's economy flourished because of craft industry and trade in addition to agriculture and cattle herding. Semispecialized craftsmen produced woven cloth and rugs, clay and stone statuettes, flint and obsidian tools, carved objects of bone or wood, and lead (and in the later levels, copper) pendants and beads. It is likely that these artisans were still primarily farmers who worked only part-time at their other crafts. The people of Çatal Hüyük also used handmade pottery vessels, but these are simple enough that they probably did not require specialized craftsmen for their manufacture. Furthermore, just as Jericho probably prospered in part because of access to trade commodities from the Dead Sea, much of Çatal Hüyük's wealth probably derived from nearby deposits of obsidian. Neolithic people highly prized this lustrous dark volcanic glass that they could use to make beautiful tools and ornaments. Obsidian formed one of the staples of early trade in the Near East, and Çatal Hüyük seems to have been a center for its distribution.

Çatal Hüyük was not walled like Jericho. Instead, its mud-brick houses were joined to one another by common walls and had no entrances on the ground floor. The outer house walls presented an unbroken barrier to humans or wild animals who sought entrance (see Figure 1.4). Residents must have entered the town by means of ladders that could quickly be pulled up if enemies threatened. Even inside the settlement, ladders were used to enter houses from the courtyards around which many of them were grouped or to reach a house's upper stories. There were no streets—residents moved across the rooftops, which probably were also used for a variety of social and economic activities.

The inhabitants buried their dead in family graves beneath the floors or plaster platforms within their houses. Bodies were probably placed on platforms outside the settlement until the flesh was stripped away by birds and insects. Then the bones were wrapped in cloth, woven mats, or baskets and deposited in the graves. Most burials contained no burial goods, but some included jewelry, weapons, and other personal items. Evidence from the burials indicates that the average lifespan of the residents of Çatal Hüyük was short—34.3 years for men and 29.8 years for women. Few people lived more than 40 years, though a small number reached the age of 60 or more. Only slightly more than half of the average 4.2 children born per family managed to survive infancy.

The site has also provided extensive information on Neolithic religious belief systems and cultic practices. At least 40 of the 139 excavated rooms may have been used as cult centers or shrines. Such a concentration of cult centers suggested to their excavator, James Mellaart, that this portion of the site had been the sacred quarter.[13] The shrines contained modeled plaster bull heads and bulls' horns inset into plaster benches or into the sculptured heads (see Figure 1.5). Shrines were also decorated with modeled plaster rams' heads, elaborate wall paintings, and plaster bas-reliefs. The paintings and reliefs often depicted hunting scenes, vultures attacking headless human bodies (see Figure 1.5a), or females ("goddesses"?) giving birth to rams or bulls (see Figure 1.5b). Thus, the contents of these structures seem to suggest that religious beliefs centered around animal and human fertility (birth) and death.

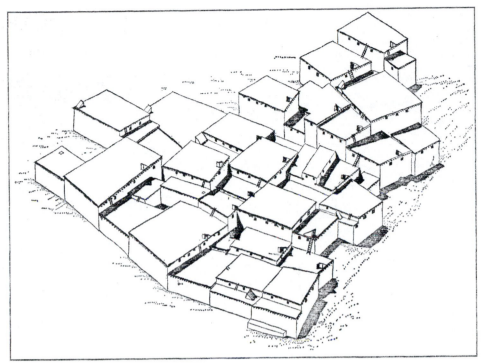

FIGURE 1.4   Schematic Reconstruction of Çatal Hüyük, Level VI, c. 6000 B.C.E.

Source: From Marija Gimbutas, *The Civilization of the Goddess.* (San Francisco: Harper).
Photo: General Research Division, New York Public Library, Lenox and Tilden Foundations.

There were also burials under the platforms of the shrines, but these bodies were treated differently from those in private houses. Red ochre usually had been washed over the bones, and sometimes the skulls had been removed and placed on platforms or against the walls (see Figure 1.5a). The shrine burials also contained valuable obsidian, polished stone, bone, and metal objects. Possibly these burials indicate the existence of a class of priests at Çatal Hüyük who naturally might be buried in the communal worship places where they performed cultic rites. Or these burials may contain the remains of the community's leaders. Another possibility is that each family conducted its own religious rites and that the numerous "shrines" are not community cult centers, but rather just the houses of the town's wealthy elite. Excavation of other portions of the mound would undoubtedly clarify this issue. However, the recent discovery of what has been called a large seventh mil-

lennium "temple" at Navali Cori suggests that Mellaart's view that Çatal Hüyük had communal cult centers (and possibly priests) is correct.

After about 6500 B.C.E., pottery use spread across the Near East, becoming universal at village sites by about 6000 B.C.E. Because pottery is cheap and easy to make compared to stone or wooden vessels, it became the most common artifact found at ancient sites. It is easily broken, and the broken pieces (called **sherds**, potsherds, or shards) cannot be reused, so they are discarded. Though whole pottery vessels are fragile, broken sherds, once buried in debris, last for thousands of years. Moreover, the shape and decoration of pottery vessels were modified more frequently than those of other artifacts and, due to their fragility and changes in style, pottery vessels were not generally passed down generation after generation as heirlooms. Thus, more than any other artifact, archaeologists use pottery shapes, decoration, and technique of manufacture to

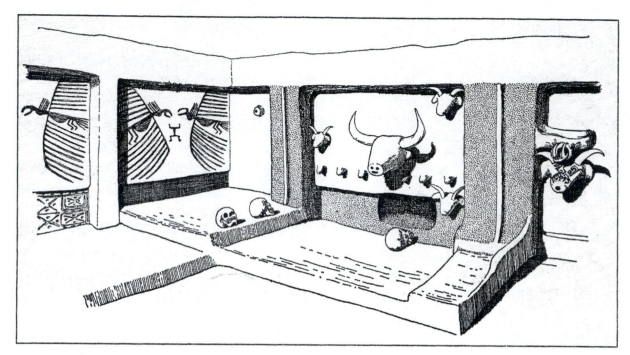

FIGURE 1.5
Reconstructions of Two "Cult Centers" or "Shrines" at Çatal Hüyük

These reconstructions show the importance of bulls, rams, birth, and death.

Source: From James Mellaart, Çatal Hüyük: A Neolithic Town in Anatolia. (New York: McGraw-Hill).

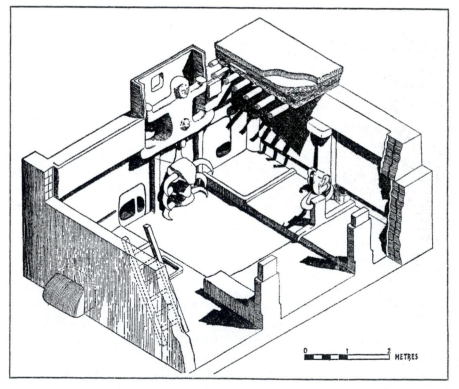

identify and date archaeological assemblages from ancient cultures.

The widespread use of pottery after c. 6500 to 6000 B.C.E. shows the increasingly sedentary nature of Near Eastern societies in the latter part of the Neolithic period, for pottery is too fragile and too heavy to be of much use to nomadic groups. Its rapid spread also suggests the growing need for watertight containers (for storing, carrying, cooking, and consuming food or drink) in sedentary agricultural communities. By the end of the seventh millennium B.C.E., most of the plants and animals that would later be utilized throughout the Near East had been domesticated. Also, agriculture and pottery use had expanded westward through Greece to much of Europe and eastward to Pakistan and Central Asia. Around 6000 B.C.E., complex and distinctive pottery styles made on a slow wheel (a wooden slab on a peg that could be turned by hand) began to appear. The spread of these styles over wide areas suggests that some societies were beginning to develop political and economic structures more complex than those of individual villages.

The Development of Complex Societies in Southwest Asia (c. 6000–3700 B.C.E.)

Major advances now began to occur in Mesopotamia as people slowly developed crops and animals that could withstand the heat and aridity of the plains and lowlands between the Tigris and Euphrates rivers. A series of chronologically overlapping cultures, primarily distinguished by their characteristic pottery styles, gradually spread over Mesopotamia. These cultures, named after the sites where they were first noted, are the Hassuna, Samarra, and Halaf in the north, and the Ubaid in the south (see Table 1.1).

The Hassuna culture (c. 6000 to 5500 B.C.E.) was characterized by small villages averaging between 100 and 200 inhabitants each. Houses consisted of several rooms grouped around a central courtyard. A few vessels (possibly containing food and water) were buried with the dead, suggesting belief in some kind of existence after death. There were not very many luxury

TABLE 1.1
Chronology of the Earliest Mesopotamian Cultures

Date B.C.E.	North	North-Central	South
6000	Hassuna		
5500		Samarra	Ubaid 0 (Awayli or Oueili)
	Halaf	Halaf	Ubaid 1 (Eridu)
5000			Ubaid 2 (Hajji Muhammad)
			Ubaid 3
4500	Ubaid		Ubaid 4
4000			

goods, few indications of significant differences in wealth or status, and no evidence of temples or administrative centers. However, the distribution of Hassuna painted ware across northern Mesopotamia connects these independent agricultural villages to one another. One explanation of the relationship is that "the integration of these villages was based on a tribal organization structured by kinship."[14]

Toward the end of the Hassuna Period, the Samarra culture (c. 5600 to 5300 B.C.E.?) developed across north-central Mesopotamia. Some think it originated in Iran, for the designs on its pottery (painted geometrical designs and stylized animals) are similar to some found at several Iranian sites. Samarran sites, especially Tell es-Sawwan (a site on the Tigris about 60 miles north of Baghdad), provide evidence for trade and a high level of craftsmanship in making pottery and other artifacts. Possibly some specialization existed in several of the crafts. A few graves contained objects made of alabaster, turquoise, carnelian, greenstone, and copper, probably indicating some differentiation in status and wealth.

In addition to food crops, the Samarran people grew flax (linseed) for making linen and oil. This culture seems to have been the first to depend on irrigation to grow its crops, for the area it occupied probably could not have supported **dry farming** (agriculture based on rainfall alone). The practice of irrigation is also indicated by the large size of the flax seeds found at Samarran sites and by the fact that at Choga Mami (east of Baghdad, on the border with Iran) archaeologists found traces of irrigation canals that probably belong to this period. The Samarrans used large sun-dried molded mud-bricks to build buttressed rectangular houses and, at Tell es-Sawwan at least, a fortification wall. They also constructed buttressed T-shaped storage buildings similar in appearance to later Sumerian T-shaped temples. These storage buildings seem to have been communal, suggesting that seed, grain, and probably fields were owned by the entire community.

The little-known Halaf culture (c. 5500 to 4800 B.C.E.) succeeded that of Hassuna in the north and eventually replaced the Samarra assemblage in north-central Mesopotamia. It spread over a much wider area than its predecessors, occupying a wide band from southeastern Turkey through northern Syria and northern Iraq. Its settlements, which perhaps should be called small towns rather than villages, were not normally built on top of previous ones, and Halaf buildings were usually circular instead of rectangular. This discontinuity has suggested to some scholars that the Halaf culture was the product of newcomers to the area. Others trace its origins to the area of northern Mesopotamia later called Assyria.

Some of the Halaf circular structures (called *tholoi*) had rectangular extensions once thought to be entrances. Archaeologists found burials under some *tholoi* and female figurines scattered outside them. This led to the view that these buildings must have been used for religious rites. However, more recent excavations have indicated that most of the *tholoi*

were probably household dwellings and that the rectangular extensions were usually storerooms rather than entrance halls.

The most characteristic remains of the Halaf culture are its ceramic wares that were skillfully decorated with intricate geometric designs in glossy red, black, and white paint. The consistent excellence of Halaf pottery and analysis of its clay and designs indicate that it was made by specialists in only a few production centers. It was distributed not only over the large area of the Halaf culture itself, but because of its quality and beauty, it was also traded over even greater distances. Some scholars see the existence of regional centers for pottery manufacture as evidence for a tribal organization of Halaf society under the leadership of chieftains. However, at present there is not enough evidence for scholars to be certain about the Halaf culture's social organization.

The first-known culture to occupy southern Mesopotamia was the Ubaid (c. 5500 to 3700 B.C.E.). It seems to have arisen about the same time as the Halaf culture of northern Mesopotamia, though it is possible that the earliest occupation levels in the south are deep beneath alluvial silt and have not yet been found. The earliest settlement discovered so far in the lower Tigris and Euphrates valleys was at Tell Awayli (or Tell Oueili as it is spelled by its French excavators) near later Larsa. Finds from the lowest levels of this site have affinities with both the earlier Samarra culture to the north and the later Ubaid culture of the south. This fact suggests that the Ubaid culture was not brought to Mesopotamia from Iran or some other foreign area as once thought, but rather developed in southern Mesopotamia from Samarran antecedents. Thus, the excavators of Awayli have dubbed its earliest assemblages "Ubaid 0" since the designation "Ubaid 1" had already been used.°

The southern portion of Mesopotamia was not an ideal environment for agricultural settlements. Rain-

---

°Ubaid 1 was used to designate the Eridu assemblage that previously was the earliest known in southern Mesopotamia, and Ubaid 2 was adopted for the cultural phase previously called Hajji Mohammad.

fall was sporadic and insufficient for agriculture. There were no metal ores or precious stones for luxury goods or trade and no hardwood trees or stone for construction materials. The summers were almost unbearably hot, while the winters were very cold. The Tigris and Euphrates rivers have unpredictable spring floods due to melting snow in the mountains of eastern Anatolia where these waterways originate. These floods not only could destroy settlements near them, but they came when crops were ripening, not during the planting season. Moreover, large portions of southern Mesopotamia were covered with lakes and marshes produced when the rivers flooded their banks. These marshes were ideal breeding grounds for mosquitoes and other insects. Many scholars consider the eventual emergence of civilization in these hostile circumstances a perfect illustration of Arnold Toynbee's theory that social institutions and civilization developed as a response to severe environmental challenges.[15] According to this view, the cultures of northern Mesopotamia experienced less stress and were able to thrive without moving beyond a tribal village level of organization. In contrast, the daunting challenges of life in southern Mesopotamia spurred the inhabitants to develop more centralized administrative and religious systems and a much more complex society in order to overcome the hostile environment.

The early Ubaid people seem to have first settled along the river banks, especially those of the slower-flowing Euphrates, building houses of reeds and mud-brick and utilizing the irrigation from the rivers to grow their crops. As their irrigation techniques improved, they were able to control the rivers a bit more. Their canals watered areas further from the river channels, making more land suitable for occupation. The gradual growth in the size and number of Ubaid settlements shows that population was increasing. Tell Awayli (Ubaid 0) was quite small, but during the Ubaid 1 phase, Al-Ubaid, the type-site for the culture, probably housed at least 750 people. At the same time, Eridu, with a probable population of 2,000 to 4,000, likely was already a town with a temple-centered administration. By the later stages of the Ubaid

Period, many towns and several small cities dotted the countryside.[16] This population growth raises the common "chicken or egg" cause-and-effect question which cannot be answered. Did the Ubaid Period's population growth result from more land being made available for agriculture by improved irrigation technology? Or, did having extra mouths to feed stimulate the improvement of irrigation techniques so that more land could be occupied?

In the earliest levels of Eridu (Ubaid 1), archaeologists uncovered a building with an altar-like platform within a deep recess. In the center of the room, they found a similar structure with traces of burning on it, suggesting that it was an offering table (an altar for burnt offerings). The excavators' interpretation that this structure was a temple is borne out by the fact that not only does it have key features of later Mesopotamian temples, but also that ten later prehistoric temple-like structures were built directly above this one. These buildings have the same form as those built on the same spot in historical times that written accounts definitely indicate were temples. Thus, the place where these temples stood seems to have been considered sacred for more than a thousand years. Surrounding Eridu's Ubaid 1 temple were the houses of the wealthy elite. Beyond them were the houses of craftsmen and then the houses of farmers and herders. This settlement pattern suggests that in early Ubaid times, the temple had already become the center of economic and social activity that it would clearly be by the end of the era.

With the advent of the Ubaid 3 phase around 4800 to 4700 B.C.E., Ubaid culture expanded into northern Mesopotamia, reaching as far as northern Syria and southeastern Anatolia. Ubaid 3 painted pottery replaced the Halaf style, and Ubaid-style temples, now much larger and standing upon raised platforms about three feet high, began to be built in the north as well as the south. Ubaid cultural elements (largely pottery styles) also spread eastward into Khuzistan (an area of southwestern Iran also known as Susiana after its largest settlement, Susa) and southward into areas of Arabia, Bahrain, and Qatar. Some Ubaid pottery reached as far as the

United Arab Emirates and Oman. It is probable, though, that this Ubaid expansion into distant areas consisted of cultural influence, not population movements or conquest. In each area, local elements were mixed with the Ubaid influences from southern Mesopotamia. Khuzistan (or Susiana), for example, already had irrigation-based agriculture, was densely populated, and had several large settlements besides Susa before coming under Ubaid influence during the last half of the fifth millennium B.C.E. Though it copied some Ubaid features such as pottery forms and decoration, Khuzistan maintained its own cultural identity. Also, in Level XIII at Tepe Gawra in northern Mesopotamia (Ubaid 3 Period), archaeologists noted a complex of three Ubaid-style temples, but burials and painted mother-goddess figurines were of local types which were quite different from those of southern Mesopotamia. Likewise, analysis of the clays of Ubaid pottery found at sites along the Persian Gulf shows that these wares were most likely made in the area around the southern Mesopotamian towns of Ur and Eridu. Thus, these vessels were imports and evidence of trade, rather than indicators that Ubaid people had colonized areas along the Persian Gulf.

By the latter part of the Ubaid Period, settlements in southern Mesopotamia and Khuzistan ranged from small villages to towns and a few small cities. In Khuzistan, the sites were probably already beginning to be organized into networks in which small- and medium-sized sites were linked economically and politically with a larger 2,000- to 5,000-person community nearby. The Mesopotamian sites were still rather evenly spaced across the countryside, suggesting that no network organization existed there yet. However, all of the major Mesopotamian settlements had centrally located temples and probably had become regional "ceremonial centers." These sites also had large storage buildings suggesting some sort of central administration and differences in residences and burials that indicate growing social stratification. The increasingly complex societies of the Ubaid era in southern Mesopotamia and southwestern Iran formed the foundation for the Urban Revolution that would follow.

Early Cultures of the Nile Valley (c. 8000–3500 B.C.E.)

The people living on the edge of the Nile Valley in southwest Egypt may have practiced incipient herding of cattle as early as c. 8000 B.C.E. and seem to have begun domesticating them by c. 7000 to 6000 B.C.E. Cattle domestication in this area may have occurred as early as, or earlier than, it did in Asia Minor, though the existence of domesticated cattle in Asia Minor by about 6500 B.C.E. is much more fully documented. It also appears that the Egyptians began using pottery about 7000 B.C.E., possibly as early as the peoples of the Zagros area east of Mesopotamia. By c. 6200 to 5900 B.C.E., Egyptian groups were creating villages containing as many as 14 family units each. However, archaeologists have recovered few plant remains from these sites, so it is not certain that their occupants were agriculturalists. Around 6000 B.C.E., Egyptians definitely were gathering wild sorghum for food, but true farming does not seem to have become common in the Nile Valley until long after its appearance in the rest of the Near East. The inhabitants dwelling near the Nile continued to live largely by fishing supplemented with hunting and gathering into the fifth millennium B.C.E.

The earliest known town in Egypt developed c. 5000 B.C.E. at a site called Merimde on the western edge of the Delta, about 15 miles northwest of Cairo. This part of the Nile Valley, the Delta area north of Cairo, was known in antiquity as **Lower Egypt**. **Upper Egypt** was the long thin portion of the Nile Valley from the first cataract to the beginning of the Delta. Merimde also produced the earliest conclusive evidence of true farming within Egypt. The inhabitants of this unwalled Lower Egyptian town first lived in shelters made of reeds. Later they built oval houses of wickerwork (rushes woven between sticks) and engaged in trade with both Palestine and Upper Egypt. It was probably through contacts with Palestine that Egyptians learned to cultivate barley and wheat. Not long after its appearance at Merimde, farming was also being practiced in the Faiyum Oasis just west of the Nile.

The practice of growing cereal crops and domesticating animals gradually spread through the Delta and then up the Nile. By about 4000 B.C.E., farming villages existed throughout Egypt. Fishing and fowling seem to have remained important occupations in these villages, while hunting gradually gave way to the raising of sheep, goats, cattle, and pigs. Gathering was totally replaced by farming. Although agriculture became common to both areas, the cultures of Lower and Upper Egypt remained distinct. Archaeologists designate the early cultural assemblages of the Delta "Merimde," and those in the Faiyum are called "Faiyum A." The Upper Egyptian culture of this time (c. 5000 to 4000 B.C.E.) is known as "Badarian" after Badari, the site where it was first discovered. The Merimde culture in the north was succeeded around 4000 B.C.E. by one called Omari A, while the Badarian assemblages of Upper Egypt evolved into those known as Naqada I (or Amratian). During this time, pottery became better fired and for the first time, carved stone vessels, known earlier at Merimde, appeared in the south. However, tools and weapons were still made almost entirely of wood, stone, and bone. One of the biggest differences between the northern and southern Egyptian cultures was their burial practices. The Omari people buried their dead in graves dug within their villages, possibly under the floors of their huts. The Naqada I groups buried their dead in cemeteries in the desert outside of their villages and towns. The successors of these dual cultures persisted until about 3200 to 3150 B.C.E. when Egypt attained a degree of cultural unity during the latter stages of the Naqada II Period (see Chapter 4).

Major Social, Economic, and Political Developments of the Neolithic Age

As we have seen, the most important socioeconomic development of the Neolithic Period was the Agricultural Revolution. By 4000 B.C.E., sedentary agricultural societies existed throughout the Near East. Few communities in the region still lived by hunting, fishing, and gathering, though some continued a seminomadic existence while herding domesticated animals (mostly sheep and goats). Agriculture led to a large increase in population (probably due mainly to the higher birthrate of sedentary groups). Long-distance trade became common, allowing groups in Palestine or Mesopotamia to have access to Anatolian obsidian and beautiful **lapis lazuli** from Afghanistan. Meanwhile, people living in the mountains could have jewelry made from seashells from the Mediterranean or the Persian Gulf. Society also benefited from the many technological advances of this era. Neolithic people learned to make strong houses of mud-brick or stone. They learned how to spin thread from flax and wool and weave it into cloth for garments, sacks, sails, and other useful items. In time, they created spindles and looms to do this job more efficiently. They created pottery vessels, learned to fire them in ovens, and toward the end of the era, developed the pottery wheel that allowed them to mass-produce utilitarian wares. The creation of efficient ovens not only resulted in hard, impermeable pottery, but also in better food products such as bread and beer. By the latter part of the Neolithic Period, many groups were able to make ovens hot enough to melt copper, allowing them to mold copper tools and ornaments. Thus, the last phases of the Neolithic Age are sometimes called the Chalcolithic (Copper/Stone) Period. Neolithic people also developed irrigation techniques that allowed agriculture to spread to some areas with too little rainfall for dry farming.

Unfortunately, these developments had some negative side effects. Larger communities of people living in close quarters increased the incidence and fatality rates of infectious diseases. Moreover, reliance on agriculture seems to have greatly reduced dietary variety, which also impacted health. Studies of skeletal remains have indicated that Neolithic agriculturalists often suffered from malnutrition (mostly due to lack of meat protein and vitamin and mineral deficiencies). They had badly worn and abscessed teeth (from bits of sand and stone in their stone-ground grain) and a shorter and less robust stature than their hunter-gatherer predecessors. Women's spines and big toes were often permanently deformed and arthritic from the many hours they spent on their knees with bent backs and sharply flexed toes while grinding grain. These various health problems resulted in a decreased life expectancy and an overall reduction in quality of life for Neolithic agricultural populations.

The latter part of the Neolithic Period also saw the advent of labor specialization and a hierarchically organized social system. The archaeological evidence suggests that by the end of the Ubaid Period, there were separate groups of skilled potters, tool makers, priests, and other specialists in large settlements in Mesopotamia and Khuzistan. Along with specialization came the growth of a privileged ruling class that managed to control most of the society's wealth from both agriculture and trade. Exactly how class distinctions developed and how some individuals were able to make themselves into a wealthy and powerful elite is unknown.[17] Some scholars think that class differences were the natural outgrowth of an enlargement of the concept of private property during the sixth millennium. Before that time, there likely was individual ownership of personal ornaments and small objects, but most villages probably held land, tools, and produce in common. In the Late Neolithic Period, the investment of time and effort in building houses, irrigating fields, and storing food seems to have created a broader idea of private ownership. Since some individuals were better than others at what they did (farming, weaving, making pottery, trading, etc.), they produced more wealth that they could claim as their own, and thus, they became members of an affluent elite.

Other scholars argue that a privileged class of priests was the first to emerge because of society's desire for divine help with agricultural processes. The goodwill of deities who control nature was obviously important to early societies, and in Mesopotamia, by the latter stages of the Ubaid Period, towns seem to have been temple-centered. This suggests to some that priests who controlled the religious rites had become dominant.

On the other hand, most Late Ubaid towns and small cities seem to have had defensive walls. This situation presents a stark contrast between the Ubaid era and previous periods. With the exception of towns such as Jericho and Çatal Hüyük, most pre-Ubaid settlements did not have elaborate provisions for defense. So, some anthropologists have hypothesized that larger populations and increased competition for land and luxury goods resulted in more conflict within individual settlements as well as raiding, looting, and fighting between settlements and societies. Such conflict probably created a need for stronger internal administration and ways to defend fields, stored agricultural surpluses, and other wealth. This need, in turn, would have brought about an increase in the power of local chieftains and capable warriors. According to this theory, the creation of large sedentary populations concentrated in clustered towns and cities eventually led to organized warfare and to governments dominated by kings and a military elite.

As is usually the case, there probably is some truth in each of these theories about the development of differences in class status, wealth, and power. The rise of wealthy, propertied individuals, priests, secular authorities and military leaders seems to have been taking place simultaneously. Moreover, the factors producing these elite factions were not only interrelated, but operating in ways that mutually supported and strengthened one another.

Finally, many scholars believe that the various changes of the Neolithic Period resulted in a lowered status for women. In hunting-gathering bands, men and women share in food production—men usually hunting animals while women do most of the gathering of plant foods. Such groups are almost always quite small, usually consisting of only 15 to 40 people, often members of a single extended family. In these groups (which most anthropologists label "band societies"), all of the adult members usually have roughly equal status and material resources. The change to a sedentary lifestyle and reliance on agriculture changed such egalitarian groups. Some scholars have argued that initially, the Agricultural Revolution actually elevated the position of women within society. Relying principally upon the widespread occurrence of female "fertility" figurines, these scholars believe that early Neolithic agricultural groups saw a mother goddess as the source of life and women as her human counterparts. Thus, supposedly, early farming cultures accorded women very high rank, possibly even becoming **matriarchies**—societies ruled by women.[18] Whether or not a "prehistoric matriarchy" ever existed (and the available evidence doesn't allow us to settle this issue), it is clear that by the time written records emerge in the Near East, women not only didn't rule, they were no longer even equals. Society was **patriarchal**, with men controlling the family, property, and the state. A possible reason for the change in women's status was the fact that sedentary life required them to spend more time bearing and raising children. In nomadic societies, the hard work performed by a woman (from gathering food to carrying gear when on the move) usually results in her having children several years apart. Why this is true—whether it is planned or due to biological changes that reduce fertility for a time (such as breast feeding) or caused by natural abortions brought on by hard work—is unknown. However, the intervals between the pregnancies of sedentary women are much shorter. Their higher birthrate gradually led to population increases, though the higher infant mortality rate of early agricultural societies kept the population from growing too quickly. Pregnancy, delivery, and caring for infants limited the time women could spend in the fields, though they still worked at home grinding grain and preparing food. The introduction of the plow at the end of the Ubaid Period or early in the following Uruk era simply compounded the problem, for it was too heavy for most women to control. Thus, women living in villages and towns ceased being equal partners in food production and became primarily concerned with childbirth and child care.

Though the role of women as mothers was extremely important, it was not as highly valued by society as the more "productive" occupations of men. Thus, the status of men grew as that of women declined. Also, during the process of animal domestication, people probably became aware of the male's role in producing offspring. This knowledge seems to have reduced an earlier awe of females as "life givers." In some places, in fact, men's sperm began to be thought of as the true source of life, which was just implanted in female receptacles. Finally, as strife between groups increased, male warriors became increasingly important. For these and possibly other unknown reasons, by the advent of writing, males dominated Near Eastern households and societies.

SUGGESTIONS FOR FURTHER READING AND INFORMATION

Internet Sites about the Ancient Near East

Abzu: Guide to Resources for the Study of the Ancient Near East: http://www.oi.uchicago.edu/oi/dept/ra/abzu/abzu.html

Internet Ancient History Sourcebook: Ancient Near East: http://www.fordham.edu/ halsall/ancient/asbook1.html

The History of the Ancient Near East Electronic Compendium: http://www.maxpages.com/ribbentrop

The Oriental Institute of the University of Chicago (information on Anatolia, Egypt, Mesopotamia, the Levant, Cyprus, and Persia): http://www.oi.uchicago.edu/OI/OI_TOC.html

Books and Articles

General Works on the Ancient Near East

Beyerlin, Walter, ed. *Near Eastern Religious Texts Relating to the Old Testament*. Philadelphia: Westminster Press, 1978.

Bienkowski, Piotr, and Alan Millard, eds. *Dictionary of the Ancient Near East*. Philadelphia: University of Pennsylvania Press, 2000.

Burney, Charles. *From Village to Empire: An Introduction to Near Eastern Archaeology*. Oxford: Phaidon, 1977.

Caubet, Annie, and Patrick Pouyssegur. English translation by Peter Snowdon. *The Ancient Near East*. Paris: Finest SA/Editions Pierre Terrail, 1998.

Collon, Dominique. *Ancient Near Eastern Art*. London: British Museum Press, 1995.

Coogan, Michael, ed. *The Oxford History of the Biblical World*. London and New York: Oxford University Press, 1998.

Dunstan, William E. *The Ancient Near East*. New York: Harcourt Brace College Publishers, 1998.

Edwards, I. E. S., et al., eds. *The Cambridge Ancient History.* 3rd ed. Vols. 1–4. Cambridge: Cambridge University Press, 1970.

Freedman, David Noel, ed. *The Anchor Bible Dictionary.* 6 vols. New York: Doubleday, 1992.

Gibson, McGuire, and Robert D. Biggs, eds. *The Organization of Power: Aspects of Bureaucracy in the Ancient Near East.* 2nd ed. Chicago: Oriental Institute of the University of Chicago, 1991.

Hallo, William W., and K. Lawson Younger, Jr., eds. *The Context of Scripture.* Vol. 1: *Canonical Compositions from the Biblical World.* Leiden/New York/Cologne: Brill, 1997.

Hallo, William W., and William Kelly Simpson. *The Ancient Near East: A History.* 2nd ed. New York: Harcourt Brace College Publishers, 1998.

Klengel, Horst. *Syria 3000 to 300 BC: A Handbook of Political History.* Berlin: Akademie Verlag, 1992.

Knapp, A. Bernard. *The History and Culture of Ancient Western Asia and Egypt.* Chicago: The Dorsey Press, 1988.

Kuhrt, Amélie. *The Ancient Near East, c. 3000–330 BC.* 2 vols. London and New York: Routledge, 1995.

Lesko, B. S., ed. *Women's Earliest Records from Ancient Egypt and Western Asia.* Atlanta: Scholars Press, 1989.

Matthews, Victor H., and Don C. Benjamin. *Old Testament Parallels: Laws and Stories from the Ancient Near East.* New York: Paulist Press, 1991.

Mazar, Amihai. *Archaeology of the Land of the Bible, 10,000–586 B.C.E.* New York: Doubleday, 1990.

Meyers, Eric M., ed. *The Oxford Encyclopedia of Archaeology in the Near East.* 5 vols. New York/Oxford: Oxford University Press, 1997.

Pritchard, James B., ed. *Ancient Near Eastern Texts Relating to the Old Testament.* 3rd ed. Princeton, NJ: Princeton University Press, 1969.

Saggs, H. W. F. *Civilization Before Greece and Rome.* New Haven, CT: Yale University Press, 1989.

Sasson, Jack M., ed. *Civilizations of the Ancient Near East.* 4 vols. New York: Scribner's, 1995.

Snell, Daniel C. *Life in the Ancient Near East, c. 3100–332 B.C.E.* New Haven, CT: Yale University Press, 1997.

Von Soden, Wolfram. *The Ancient Orient: An Introduction to the Study of the Ancient Near East.* Translated by Donald G. Schley. Grand Rapids, MI: Eerdman's, 1994.

History, Archaeology, and Chronology

Aitken, M. J. *Science-Based Dating in Archaeology.* New York: Longman, 1990.

Appleby, Joyce, Lynn Hunt, and Margaret Jacob. *Telling the Truth About History.* New York: W. W. Norton & Co., 1994.

Aström, Paul, ed. *High, Middle or Low? Acts of an International Colloquium on Absolute Chronology Held at the University of Gothenburg, 20–22 August, 1987.* Gothenburg: 1987–1989.

Bietak, Manfred, ed. *High, Middle or Low? Acts of the Second International Colloquium on Absolute Chronology: The Bronze Age in the Eastern Mediterranean.* Vienna: 1992.

Ehrich, Robert W. *Chronologies in Old World Archaeology.* 3rd ed. 2 vols. Chicago: University of Chicago Press, 1992.

Fagan, Brian M. *Ancient Lives: An Introduction to Archaeology.* Upper Saddle River, NJ: Prentice Hall, 2000.

Greene, Kevin. *Archaeology: An Introduction.* Philadelphia: University of Pennsylvania Press, 1995.

Haddock, B. A. *An Introduction to Historical Thought.* London: Edward Arnold Publishers, Ltd., 1980.

Hodder, Ian. *The Archaeological Process: An Introduction.* Malden, MA: Blackwell, 1999.

Lichtman, Allan J., and Valerie French. *Historians and the Living Past: The Theory and Practice of Historical Study.* Arlington Heights, IL: AHM Publishing Corp., 1978.

McIntosh, Jane. *The Practical Archaeologist: How We Know What We Know About the Past.* 2nd ed. New York: Facts on File, 1999.

Morley, Neville. *Writing Ancient History.* Ithaca, NY: Cornell University Press, 1999.

Peregrine, Peter N. *Archaeological Research: A Brief Introduction.* Upper Saddle River, NJ: Prentice Hall, 2001.

Pollard, A. M, and D. R. Brothwell, eds. *Handbook of Archaeological Science.* Bognor Regis, West Sussex, UK: John Wiley & Sons, 2001.

Renfrew, Colin, and Paul Bahn. *Archaeology: Theories, Methods, and Practices.* 3rd ed. London and New York: Thames and Hudson, 2000.

Rosen, A. M. *Cities of Clay: The Geoarchaeology of Tells.* Chicago: 1986.

Sharer, Robert J., and Wendy Ashmore. *Archaeology: Discovering Our Past.* 2nd ed. Mountain View, CA: Mayfield, 1993.

Tholfsen, Trygve R. *Historical Thinking.* New York: Harper and Row, 1967.

Near Eastern Prehistory

Banning, E. B. "The Neolithic Period: Triumphs of Architecture, Agriculture, and Art." *Near Eastern Archaeology* (formerly *Biblical Archaeologist*), vol. 61, no. 4 (1998), pp. 188–237.

Bar-Yosef, Ofer. "The Natufian Culture of the Levant, Threshold to the Origins of Agriculture." *Evolutionary Anthropology*, vol. 6, no. 5 (1998), pp. 159–177.

Bar-Yosef, Ofer and F. Valla, eds. *The Natufian Culture in the Levant*. Ann Arbor, MI: International Monographs in Prehistory, 1991.

Bogucki, Peter. *The Origins of Human Society*. Malden, MA: Blackwell Publishers, 1999.

Fagan, Brian M. *World Prehistory: A Brief Introduction*. 4th ed. Upper Saddle River, NJ: Prentice Hall, 1999.

Feder, Kenneth L. *The Past in Perspective: An Introduction to Human Prehistory*. 2nd ed. Mountain View, CA: Mayfield, 2000.

Gebauer, A. B., and T. D. Price, eds. *Transitions to Agriculture in Prehistory*. Madison, WI: Prehistory Press, 1992.

Henrickson, Elizabeth F., and Ingolf Thuesen. *Upon this Foundation: The Ubaid Reconsidered*. Carsten Niebuhr Institute of Ancient Near Eastern Studies, Publication 10. Copenhagen: Museum Tusculanum Press, 1989.

Henry, Donald O. *From Foraging to Agriculture: The Levant at the End of the Ice Age*. Philadelphia: University of Pennsylvania Press, 1989.

Lamberg-Karlovsky, C. C., and Jeremy A. Sabloff. *Ancient Civilizations: The Near East and Mesoamerica*. 2nd ed. Prospect Heights, IL: Waveland Press, 1995.

Maisels, Charles Keith. *The Emergence of Civilization: From Hunting and Gathering to Agriculture, Cities, and the State in the Near East*. London and New York: Routledge, 1990.

Moore, A. M. T., G. C. Hillman, and A. J. Legge. *Village on the Euphrates: From Foraging to Farming at Abu Hureyra*. New York: Oxford University Press, 2000.

Nissen, Hans J. *The Early History of the Ancient Near East, 9000–2000 B.C.* Translated by Elizabeth Lutzeier, with Kenneth J. Northcott. Chicago: University of Chicago Press, 1988.

Oates, David, and Jane Oates. *The Rise of Civilization*. Oxford: Elsevier Phaidon, 1976.

Özdogan, Mehmet, and Nezih Basgelen, eds. *Neolithic in Turkey: The Cradle of Civilization. New Discoveries*. vol. I: Text, vol. II: Plates. Istanbul: Arkeoloji Ve Sanat Yayinlari, 1999.

Redman, Charles L. *The Rise of Civilization: From Early Farmers to Urban Society in the Ancient Near East*. San Francisco: W. H. Freedman, 1978.

NOTES

1. Mary Lynn Rampolla, *A Pocket Guide to Writing in History*, 3rd ed. (Boston and New York: Bedford/St. Martin's, 2001), p. 1.

2. See Trygve R. Tholfsen, *Historical Thinking* (New York: Harper and Row, 1967), pp. 276–279, and Richard Marius, *A Short Guide to Writing About History* (New York: Longman, 1998), pp. 4 and 8.

3. Heraclitus of Ephesus (c. 500 B.C.E.), fragments 41 and 42 in John Burnet, *Early Greek Philosophy*, 4th ed. (London: A. & C. Black, 1930), p. 136.

4. See William H. Stiebing, Jr., *Ancient Astronauts, Cosmic Collisions and Other Popular Theories About Man's Past* (Buffalo: Prometheus Books, 1984), pp. 81–106, and Kenneth L. Feder, *Frauds, Myths, and Mysteries: Science and Pseudoscience in Archaeology*, 3rd ed. (Mountain View, CA: Mayfield, 1999), pp. 184–215.

5. See Carol G. Thomas and D. P. Wick, *Decoding Ancient History: A Toolkit for the Historian as Detective* (Englewood Cliffs, NJ: Prentice Hall, 1994), and Richard Marius (1998), p. 11–12.

6. Radiocarbon tests are actually run several times on different samples and then analyzed statistically. The "date" given is actually the mean of the dates obtained from testing the several samples. The "plus or minus" number after a date indicates one standard deviation from that mean date. There is a two out of three chance that the correct date falls within one standard deviation from the mean. Thus, a C-14 date of 1570 ± 50 B.C.E. means that there is a 67 percent likelihood that the correct date of the tested sample is between 1620 and 1520 B.C.E.

7. For a full summary of the issues and theories, see Robert J. Wenke, *Patterns in Prehistory: Humankind's First Three Million Years*, 4th ed. (London and New York: Oxford University Press, 1999), pp. 160–267. For opposing views on the relationship of Neanderthals to modern humans, see Joao Zilhao, "Fate of the Neanderthals," *Archaeology*, vol. 53, no. 4 (July/August 2000), pp. 25–31, and Jean-Jacques Hublin, "Brothers or Cousins?," *Archaeology*, vol. 53, no. 5 (September/October 2000), pp. 49–54.

8. S. H. Katz and M. M. Voigt, "Bread and Beer: The Early Use of Cereals in the Human Diet," *Expedition*, vol. 28, no. 2 (1986), pp. 23–34.

9. Wenke (1999), p. 293.

10. For a more complete discussion of the Natufian culture and the beginnings of agriculture, see Ofer Bar-Yosef, and F. Valla, eds., *The Natufian Culture in the Levant* (Ann Arbor, MI: International Monographs in Prehistory, 1991); Ofer Bar-Yosef, "The Natufian Culture of the Levant, Threshold to the Origins of Agriculture," *Evolutionary Anthropology*, vol. 6, no. 5 (1998), pp. 159–177; C. C. Lamberg-Karlovsky and Jeremy A. Sabloff, *Ancient Civilizations: The Near East and*

Mesoamerica, 2nd ed. (Prospect Heights, IL: Waveland Press, 1995), pp. 41–61; and Robert J. Wenke (1999), pp. 268–304.

11. Wenke (1999), p. 288.

12. Gary Rollefson, "'Ain Ghazal," in David N. Freedman, editor-in-chief, *The Anchor Bible Dictionary* (New York: Doubleday, 1992), vol. I, p. 132. See also Rollefson's "Ritual and Ceremony at Neolithic 'Ain Ghazal (Jordan)," *Paléorient*, vol. 9, no. 2 (1983), pp. 29–38.

13. James Mellaart, *Çatal Hüyük: A Neolithic Town in Anatolia* (New York: McGraw-Hill, 1967), pp. 77–130.

14. Lamberg-Karlofsky and Sabloff (1995), p. 98.

15. Arnold Toynbee, *A Study of History*, abridgment of vols. I–VI (London: Oxford University Press, 1947), pp. 111–118.

16. For the data from surveys of southern Mesopotamian sites, see Robert McC. Adams, *The Evolution of Urban Society* (Chicago: Aldine, 1966), and R. McC. Adams and H. Nissen, *The Uruk Countryside* (Chicago: University of Chicago Press, 1972).

17. For a discussion of the various theories about the development of classes and community organization, see Charles L. Redman, *The Rise of Civilization: From Early Farmers to Urban Society in the Ancient Near East* (San Francisco: W. H. Freeman, 1978), pp. 201–213; Hans J. Nissen, *The Early History of the Ancient Near East, 9000–2000 B.C.*, translated by Elizabeth Lutzeier, with Kenneth J. Northcott (Chicago: University of Chicago Press, 1988), pp. 58–61; and Charles K. Maisels, *The Emergence of Civilization: From Hunting and Gathering to Agriculture, Cities and the State in the Near East* (London and New York: Routledge, 1990), pp. 203–220.

18. For example see Marija A. Gimbutas, *Goddesses and Gods of Old Europe, 6500–3500 B.C.: Myths and Cult Images*, updated ed. (Berkeley: University of California Press, 1990), and *The Living Goddesses* (Berkeley: University of California Press, 1999). Also see Lucy Goodison and Christine Morris, eds., *Ancient Goddesses: The Myths and the Evidence* (Madison: University of Wisconsin Press, 1999).

2

The Dawn of Civilization
in Western Asia

THE EMERGENCE OF
MESOPOTAMIAN CIVILIZATION
(c. 3700–3000 B.C.E.)

The Urban Revolution

Around 3700 B.C.E., the Ubaid culture in southern Mesopotamia evolved into that of the succeeding Uruk Period (c. 3700 to 3300 B.C.E.). The Uruk culture, in turn, developed into that of the Jemdet Nasr era (c. 3300 to 3000 B.C.E., see Table 2.1). During

TABLE 2.1
The Chronology of Early Sumer

The Uruk Period	**3700-3300 B.C.E.**
Early Uruk	3700-3500 B.C.E.
Late Uruk	3500-3300 B.C.E.
The Jemdet Nasr Period	**3300-3000 B.C.E.**
The Early Dynastic Period	**3000-2330 B.C.E.**
Early Dynastic I	3000-2700 B.C.E.
Early Dynastic II	2700-2500 B.C.E.
Early Dynastic III	2500-2330 B.C.E.

these periods, population increased much more rapidly than in previous eras, and many new settlements appeared in the south.

In part, the relatively sudden growth in the number and size of southern Mesopotamia's settlements during the fourth millennium B.C.E. was made possible by an increase in the available land suitable for farming. It was once thought that the Persian Gulf had reached far inland in antiquity and that the most southern portions of Mesopotamia were built up after 6000 to 5000 B.C.E. by soil deposition from the Tigris and Euphrates rivers. Then, in 1952, a geological study indicated that most of the rivers' silt was being deposited before reaching the Persian Gulf, and that the whole area is sinking at a rate that just about equals that of the deposition of silt. Thus, the study argued, in antiquity, the head of the Gulf probably was about where it is now, or even a bit further south.[1] However, studies of cores taken from the bottom of the Persian Gulf in the 1960s and estimates of the higher sea levels of prehistoric times have supported the earlier view.[2] While there is still some disagreement over this issue, it is likely that from about 5000 to 2500 B.C.E., the Persian Gulf reached almost to Ur, Eridu, and Lagash (Map 2.1). Around 3700 B.C.E., the

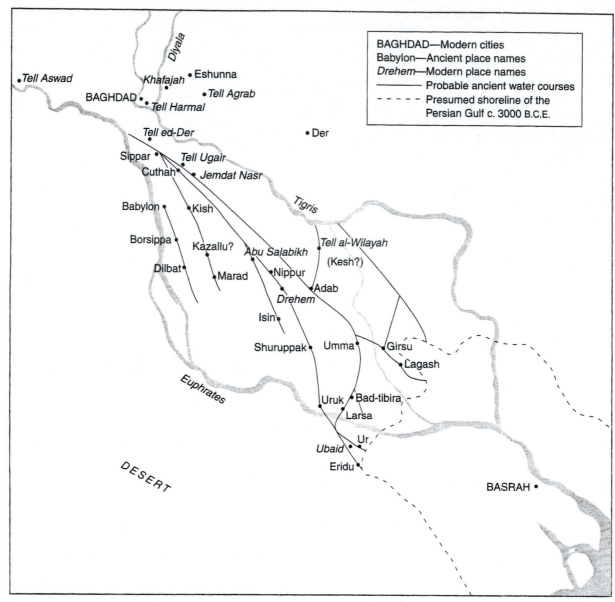

MAP 2.1   Major Urban Centers of Southern Mesopotamia

Source: Charles Keith Maisels, *The Emergence of Civilization: From Hunting and Gathering to Agriculture, Cities, and the State in the Near East* (London and New York: Routledge, 1990), Map 5.2.

region's weather seems to have become drier, and it was probably this change, rather than the slower process of silt being deposited in the Gulf, that made more land available for settlement in a relatively short time. The cores from the Gulf show less mineral content and more organic material from this time, indicating that the rivers flowed more slowly and carried less water than they did previously. The lower levels of the Tigris and Euphrates meant less overflow and flooding, allowing most of the extensive marshes and swamps that probably had covered much of southern Mesopotamia in earlier times to gradually drain and dry up. But for a time, there still would have been small streams and ponds that allowed farmers to grow crops with natural irrigation.

A new feature of this era was that while new villages continued to be created, the growing population became more disproportionately concentrated in towns and small urban centers. Towns (with a minimum of 1000 to 2000 inhabitants) are usually four or five times larger than villages. A small urban area (containing at least 5,000 people) is normally twice as large as a typical town and more than 20 times larger than most villages. During the Uruk and Jemdet Nasr periods, while the number of southern Mesopotamian villages increased from about 17 to 124, towns multiplied from 3 to 20, and small urban centers from 1 to 20.[3] By c. 3000 B.C.E., there was also at least one large city in the south—Uruk, the type site for the Uruk Period. The population of Uruk (called Erech in the Bible) grew from about 10,000 people to around 40,000 to 50,000 during the fourth millennium B.C.E.

A high density of population is not the only criterion for urbanism, and Uruk exhibited other urban characteristics, as well. It had monumental temples, and these testify to the existence of agricultural surpluses, a concentration of wealth, and strong leadership or governmental organization. Also, the diversity in size, construction, and decoration of Uruk's houses indicates differentiation of the population, probably as a result of occupational specialization and class distinctions. There is also much evidence of long-distance trade for metal, stone, and other raw materials. Moreover, Uruk seems to have been the hub of a regional economic system, a characteristic feature of later cities. While Uruk was vastly increasing its size, many of the small villages closest to it were abandoned, suggesting that Uruk's growth was mainly due to migration from the countryside into the city. On the other hand, villages and towns a bit further away became economically (and probably politically) linked to Uruk. Meanwhile, similar developments, but on a slightly smaller scale, were taking place at other Mesopotamian sites such as Eridu, Ur, Umma, Shuruppak, and Nippur (see Map 2.1). As these cities grew, they seem to have organized older or newly created villages and towns into urban-centered economic and political complexes. V. Gordon Childe called this era when cities and urban institutions began to develop and flourish "The Urban Revolution."

One of the characteristic artifacts of the Late Uruk period (c. 3500 to 3300 B.C.E.) was an ugly gray bowl with an angled or beveled rim. These beveled-rim bowls all were about the same size, and potters seem to have mass-produced them by pressing sheets of clay into molds. The resulting vessels were so coarse and crudely made that they would not hold liquids, yet at some sites they comprise more than 75 percent of the excavated pottery. Hans Nissen has argued that these bowls served as standard measuring devices and were handed out filled with grain to those receiving daily rations.[4] The beveled-rim bowls may be evidence for the existence of a standardized system of weights and measures and a **redistributive economy** like that of the later Sumerian city-states. This type of economy is a managed system in which production is controlled by a central institution (such as a temple or the government) which collects goods and products and then doles them out to workers or dependents according to rank, need, or other criteria. Like the Ubaid culture before it, the Uruk urban culture expanded beyond the confines of southern Mesopotamia. Characteristic pottery, architecture and other features of the Late Uruk Period have been found at sites as distant as northern Iran, southeastern Turkey, and Egypt. While some of the Uruk-style objects found outside of southern Mesopotamia were probably due to trade (as was the spread of Ubaid pottery), at many sites, something more was almost certainly involved. Finds of many beveled-rim bowls (which clearly were not desirable trade objects) suggest the spread of the redistributive economic system. Furthermore, people as well as concepts and objects seem to have been streaming out of lower Mesopotamia. Carchemish, Samsat, and Hassek Hüyük in southeastern Turkey, Habuba Kabira and nearby sites in Syria, Tell Brak, Nineveh, and several other sites in northern Mesopotamia, and Godin Tepe and other sites in northwestern Iran probably contained settlements of southern Mesopotamian emigrants. Several of these Uruk "colonies" were cities containing at least 5,000 people that had often been founded on virgin soil or had totally replaced the remains of earlier occupants. For the most part, their artifactual repertoire reflects that of Uruk, while few elements of the local cultures were present. At some sites, the Uruk people settled within already existing local communities. Nevertheless, even in these cases, the Uruk colonies usually remained culturally distinct, and sometimes, as at Godin Tepe in northern Iran, the colonists built walls around their quarters to separate them from the precincts of the natives.

The reason why this Uruk expansion took place is not known. One suggestion is that the colonies were trading posts created because of the southern Mesopotamians' need to secure raw materials and to control trade.[5] Others argue that these settlements resulted from political expansion through territorial conquest.[6] Whatever the reasons for their creation, most of these colonies existed for only about a century or so, and none lasted more than 150 years. Generally, the areas where the colonies had been situated continued their older cultural practices as if this interlude had never occurred. Close contacts between northern Mesopotamia and northern Syria on the one hand, and alluvial Mesopotamia on the other, did not resume until the Early Dynastic Period after c. 3000 B.C.E.

In addition to urbanization, three other characteristic features of later Mesopotamian civilization emerged around 3600 B.C.E.: the construction of monumental temples on high platforms, **cylinder seals**, and texts written on clay tablets. Uruk Period temples, typified by the examples excavated at Uruk and Eridu, evolved from those of the Ubaid Period. These structures usually consisted of a long central room containing an altar and offering table with several smaller rooms opening off the two long sides. The exteriors of the temples had many buttresses, creating an inset-offset paneled effect, and they were often decorated with mosaics of painted clay cones or "nails" set into their surfaces. Earlier temples had been built on low brick or stone platforms, and when a new temple was constructed on the same site, its platform usually incorporated the ruins of its predecessors. By the Jemdet Nasr Period, after centuries of building and rebuilding on the same sites, temple platforms became significant monuments in their own right, raising the temples high above the cities' other structures (see Figure 2.1). This process would continue into the Sumerian Early Dynastic Age and would eventually result in the stepped, pyramid-like structures known as **ziggurats** on which major Mesopotamian temples would stand in later times.

The cylinder seal also seems to have been introduced during the Late Uruk Period. For centuries, inhabitants of the Near East had produced stamp seals which were small pieces of stone with a flat circular or square surface bearing a carved design. Stamp seals were used to make impressions on clay objects to indicate ownership, to magically protect property, and to prevent tampering. However, around 3600 B.C.E., people in the city of Uruk began using a new type of seal. The design for this seal was carved on the outer surface of a cylinder of stone or metal usually one to two inches long and one-half to three-fourths of an inch in diameter. A hole was drilled lengthwise down the center of the cylinder so a string could be passed through it, allowing it to hang around the neck. It could also be mounted on a metal or wooden axle. Such cylinder seals would be rolled across damp clay surfaces, leaving impressions of their carved designs. Though some Mesopotamians continued to use stamp seals on occasion, cylinder seals were found to be more efficient. The design on a

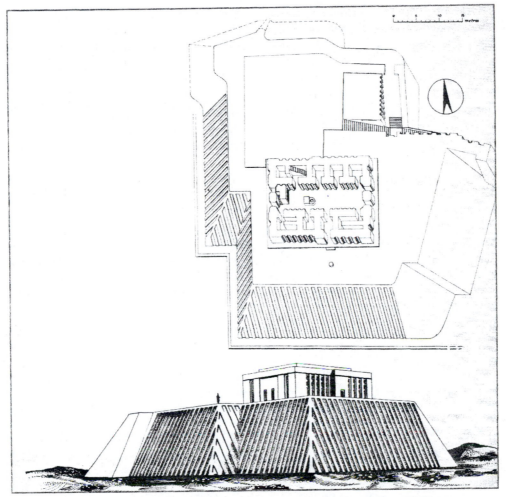

FIGURE 2.1   Reconstruction of the White Temple and Platform at Uruk c. 3200 B.C.E.

Source: From M.E. Mallowan, *Early Mesopotamia and Iran.* (London: Thames & Hudson, Ltd.).

cylinder seal could be rolled out continuously, covering (and thus securing) a larger area than a stamp seal. By the end of the Uruk Period (c. 3300 B.C.E.), the use of cylinder seals had spread to other southern Mesopotamian sites and to Uruk colonies elsewhere. Examples from this time have also been found at other sites in Iran, Syria, and Egypt. The cylinder seal remained a hallmark of Mesopotamian culture throughout ancient times.

The Development of Cuneiform Writing

The earliest known written texts in Mesopotamia were found in Level IV at Uruk and date to about 3600 to 3500 B.C.E. They consist of cushion-shaped lumps of clay with drawings of objects and numerical symbols that had been scratched into their surfaces with a pointed object while the clay was still damp.

Since many of the drawings were pictures of recognizable things (donkeys, cows, grain, fish, etc.) they have been designated **pictographs** or "picture writing." However, some of the signs (for example, those for sheep, wool, garment, perfume, and the numerals) seem to be arbitrary symbols for words or ideas rather than pictorial representations of physical objects. Furthermore, there are representations of wild animals (such as lions) that would not normally appear in record-keeping texts, so possibly those signs were being used for similar-sounding words or related ideas. Many scholars prefer to characterize the signs on these texts as logograms (signs used to represent words) or **ideograms** (signs used to represent ideas, also called ideographs). Such ideographic texts became more common during the following Jemdet Nasr Period (c. 3300 to 3000 B.C.E.). The importance of the appearance of writing has led some scholars to use the term Protoliterate ("first writing") Period for the time from the latter part of the Uruk through the Jemdet Nasr eras. Students of early writing once thought that some brilliant inhabitant of Uruk had invented the ideographic writing system from scratch, but we now know that it had antecedents. Furthermore, similar writing systems developed in northern Mesopotamia, Syria, Iran, and Egypt at about the same time as (or possibly even a little earlier than) writing's appearance in southern Mesopotamia.

As early as the Late Paleolithic Period, humans seem to have kept track of the movements of the sun and moon and made primitive calendars by cutting various kinds of grooves into pieces of bone. Soon after the beginning of the agricultural revolution, someone (probably in the Zagros region) developed a method for keeping track of possessions, trade, debts, or other transactions by using small, various-shaped pieces of clay (called tokens) to represent some commodities and numbers. The use of clay tokens, mostly cones, disks, spheres, and other geometrical shapes, spread over much of the Near East. Archaeologists have found sixth through fourth millennium B.C.E. examples at sites from the Indus River to southwestern Turkey, with the greatest concentration occurring in western Iran and Mesopotamia.

Egyptians do not seem to have adopted the token system, though a few early examples were found at Khartoum in southern Nubia.

In the fourth millennium B.C.E., people began to seal the tokens in hollow clay balls (called *bullae*) whose outer surfaces bore impressions corresponding to the shapes and number of the tokens they contained. Sometimes these *bullae* were also impressed with the images from stamp or cylinder seals. The practice of impressing token shapes on *bullae* probably inspired the Late Uruk Period idea of drawing the shapes on convex cushion-shaped clay tablets and dispensing with the tokens themselves.[7] Many new pictographic representations of animals and other objects were added at this stage of writing's development, but many of the early ideograms continued to be drawings of the old tokens (see Figure 2.2).

Archaeologists have uncovered late fourth millennium ideographic tablets not only at Uruk, but also at Susa and several other western Iranian sites, at Nineveh and Tell Brak in northern Mesopotamia, and at Habuba Kabira in Syria. Two early tablets found at Tell Brak in 1984 depict the complete figures of animals (a goat and a sheep) while on the tablets from Uruk, only the animals' heads are drawn. Some scholars think these northern Mesopotamian/Syrian ideographic texts are earlier and more primitive than those of southern Mesopotamia. Likewise, the fact that ideographic tablets have been found not just in Susiana, but over a wide area of Iran reaching as far east as Afghanistan has led some scholars to conclude that Proto-Elamite writing (as the Iranian script is called) was developed in Iran rather than being derived from southern Mesopotamia. Additionally, around 3000 B.C.E., the Egyptian hieroglyphic writing system was also being created (see Chapter 4). As has been mentioned, there is evidence of Uruk Period objects in Egypt, and Egyptian objects were found at Habuba Kabira and at contemporary sites in Palestine. Since there was contact between Iran, Mesopotamia, and Syria, between Egypt and Syria (and possibly between Egypt and Mesopotamia), it is likely that information about early experiments with writing was passed back and forth, stimulating parallel developments. Thus, as

Token	Ideograph	Sumerian (signs rotated 90°)	Old Babylonian	Neo-Assyrian	Value (WORD; syllable)	Ideographic meaning
			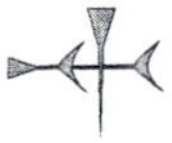	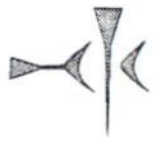	TI; ti	Arrow; Life
	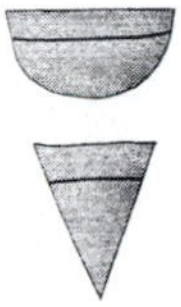	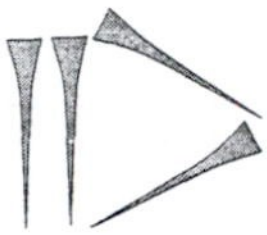			NINDA, NIG, GAR; sha, nik, niq, gar	(Bowl of) Food; Bread; Treasure; to put or place
	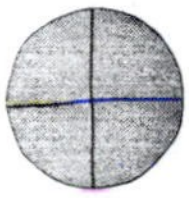	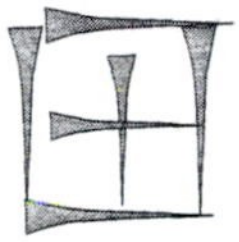	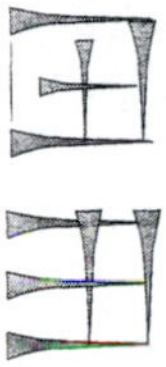	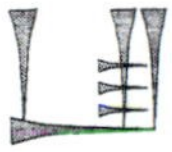	UDU, LU; lu	Sheep; Fat
	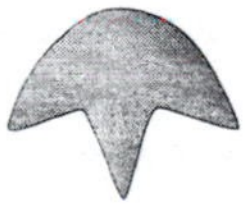	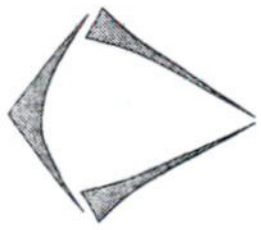		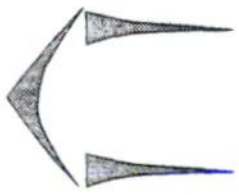	AB; ab, lid, lit, rim	Cow
					KUR; kur, qur, mat, mad, shad, shat, sad, sat, nad, nat, lad, lat	Mountain; Country

FIGURE 2.2   The Development of Cuneiform Writing

Source: Courtesy of the author.

Assyriologist C. B. F. Walker remarked, "It is beginning to look as if we should think in terms of the invention of writing as being a gradual process, accomplished over a wide area, rather than the product of a single Sumerian genius."[8]

The earliest ideographic writing seems to have been used essentially to keep economic records, though archaeologists have also found a few tablets containing lists of signs (probably for training scribes). There is no way to determine the language spoken by those who made these ideographic tablets, for the drawing of a human head conveys the same idea in any language, whether the word for it is "head"(English), *sag* (Sumerian), or some other term. However, during the Jemdet Nasr Period (c. 3300 to 3000 B.C.E.), southern Mesopotamian scribes began using their drawings not only as ideograms for words or ideas, but also as symbols for the *sounds* of the words or ideas they represented. The signs thus became syllabic, and could be used to write any word in the spoken language, even words which could not be conveyed by a picture. For example, "life" cannot be depicted, but the picture of an arrow began to be used for the word "life" (see Figure 2.2). Both words were pronounced "tee" (*ti*) in Sumerian, so the arrow sign could be used not only for the *words* "arrow" and "life," but also just for the sound "tee" in any other word. The drawing of a head could be used not only as an ideogram for the word "head" or as a symbol for its sound "sag," but also for the similar sounds "sak" and "saq." Moreover, sometimes the same sign could be used for two or more words that were pronounced differently, and those words could add to the possible syllables the sign was used to represent. These various features allow scholars to recognize that by the time Mesopotamian writing became syllabic, the language being written was Sumerian.

The Sumerian tongue was especially well suited for the development of syllabic writing from an ideographic system. Sumerian largely consisted of monosyllabic words and had many homophones (i.e., words with the same sound but different meanings). Homophones include words like "pear" and "pare" in English

and the Sumerian words *ti* ("arrow" and "life") and *gu* ("ox"and "thread"). In fact, the Sumerian language had so many homophones that it probably used some additional feature such as vocal tone or pitch to distinguish between similar-sounding words. (We can never know this for certain, of course, since Sumerian ceased to be spoken more than 3,500 years ago.) To distinguish in writing between words that might be confused with one another or misunderstood, the Sumerians added signs called **determinatives**. For example, the sign for *gish* ("wood") would be placed before words for objects made of wood; the sign for *dinger* ("god") would be placed before names of deities; or the sign for *kur* ("mountain" and "country") would be placed before the names of mountains, geographical regions, or nations.

Soon after they started drawing ideographic signs on tablets, Mesopotamian scribes began stylizing them, replacing curved lines with straight ones which were easier to make on clay. Eventually, they stopped *drawing* the signs altogether, and instead, began impressing the lines into the clay with a reed or wooden stylus cut on an angle. The blunt shape of the stylus' tip produced the characteristic wedge-shaped impressions that led early scholars to call Mesopotamian writing **cuneiform** (from the Latin word for wedge, *cuneus*). For reasons still not fully understood, at some time during the Early Dynastic Period, the direction of cuneiform writing changed from columns running top to bottom, right to left, to lines running left to right, top to bottom. At the same time, the signs were all rotated 90 degrees, reading sideways instead of vertically (see Figure 2.2).[9]

Eventually, those Mesopotamians who spoke a **Semitic°** language modified the cuneiform writing system to record their own speech (which we call **Akkadian**). These people read the ideograms in their own language rather than as Sumerian words, so they often created additional syllabic values for the signs based on their pronunciation in Akkadian. For example, the Akkadian word for "mountain" was *shadû* and

---

°It should be noted that throughout this work that the words "Semitic" and "Semite" (as well as "Indo-European," "Indo-Iranian," or "Aryan") are linguistic terms, not racial or ethnic ones.

for "country" was *mâtu*. So the sign for "mountain" or "country" (*kur* in Sumerian) came to be used not only for the syllables "kur" and "qur," but also for "shad," "mat," and similar sounds (see Figure 2.2).

As time passed, the signs evolved to look less and less like the pictures from which they originated. They became simply standardized symbols that could be ideograms representing one or more words or ideas, determinatives to help the reader understand the following sign(s), or one or more possible syllables. This complicated system with its hundreds of signs, each with several possible meanings, was too difficult for most people to learn, so literacy was generally limited to a small scribal class.

The People of Mesopotamia

Since the earliest syllabic texts of southern Mesopotamia were written in Sumerian, most scholars assume that Sumerian was also the language of the people who created the ideographic texts of Late Uruk and early Jemdet Nasr times. However, there is still some disagreement about whether the Sumerians were in Mesopotamia *before* the Late Uruk Period. Some experts have claimed that the Sumerians were newcomers to Mesopotamia who arrived only c. 3600 B.C.E., just before writing began.[10] The most important evidence for this view comes from study of the Sumerian language. The Sumerian words for the Tigris (*idiglat*) and Euphrates (*buranun*) rivers and for many of southern Mesopotamia's most important cities (including Eridu, Ur, Larsa, Isin, Lagash, Nippur, and Kish) do not seem to be Sumerian. Also, many of the basic words for agriculture (such as the words for plow, furrow, date palm, farmer) and craftsmen (such as metalworker, potter, carpenter, mason) seem to be non-Sumerian. Thus, these scholars argue, the Sumerians must have found agriculture, crafts, and cities already well established when they arrived. Since the first settlements in southern Mesopotamia were created during the Ubaid Period, and the earliest cities arose during the Uruk Period, the Sumerians could have come to Mesopotamia no earlier than the latter part of the Uruk era.

The primary Sumerian contribution to the development of Mesopotamian civilization supposedly was the creation of writing (or at least, of syllabic writing), though some think they may also have been responsible for the introduction of cylinder seals and a few other cultural elements. However, supporters of this theory of a relatively late Sumerian immigration into Mesopotamia do not agree on the location of the original Sumerian homeland. The Sumerian language is unrelated to any other known at present, so it does not provide any hints about their roots. Some scholars suggest that the Sumerians arrived by sea from the Persian Gulf, placing their origins somewhere to the south or east of Mesopotamia. Others argue for movements from the north near the Caspian Sea or overland from Iran to the east.

The opposing view holds that the Sumerian presence in Mesopotamia goes back to the beginning of the Ubaid Period (c. 5500 B.C.E.) or earlier.[11] Proponents of this idea rely principally on the fact that there is no archaeological evidence for a new group of settlers in southern Mesopotamia after the beginning of the Ubaid Period. The Ubaid material culture developed gradually into that of the Uruk Period, which in turn evolved into that of the Jemdet Nasr era, which blossomed into the Early Dynastic Sumerian culture. Continuity in temple architecture and worship from the Ubaid era into Sumerian times (especially evidenced by the long succession of temples built on top of one another at Eridu) also suggests a continuity in population. Supporters of the Ubaid = Sumerian thesis note that about a thousand years separate the beginning of the Uruk Period from the Sumerian texts of Early Dynastic (ED) times and almost the same amount again between ED I and the Ur III period from which most of our knowledge of Sumerian syntax and grammar comes. Linguists' failure to recognize etymologies for place names and words created during the early Uruk era or the even earlier Ubaid Period is understandable.

The problem of Sumerian origins probably cannot be solved given the limited evidence at our disposal. However, a view that has much to commend it is that ancestors of the Sumerians (possibly from western

Iran), Semites, and speakers of other languages all were present in southern Mesopotamia during the Ubaid and Uruk Periods. There must have been a constant stream of immigrants into alluvial Mesopotamia during those eras, especially during the Uruk Period. Most of these newcomers probably spoke isolated languages belonging to none of the known language families. Once in Mesopotamia, not only did these various groups adopt a common material culture, but their languages likely also contributed to the Sumerian tongue. As Jerrold Cooper put it, "All of the qualities that we might want to call 'Sumerian' emerged and developed only after they were settled in Babylonia and in close contact with other ethno-linguistic groups."[12]

Speakers of a Semitic language probably were part of the Mesopotamian population from very early times. The earliest syllabic Sumerian texts already have Semitic loanwords. Moreover, many of the personal names in Early Dynastic tablets from Shuruppak in the south and most of the scribes listed on those from Abu Salabikh in central Mesopotamia have Semitic names. Finally, although the texts from Abu Salabikh are written in Sumerian, they use Semitic words for various numbers as well as for grammatical elements such as "and" and "in." These facts provide reasons to accept the tradition in the later *Sumerian King List* (covered further in the following section) that many members of the semilegendary First Dynasty of Kish had Semitic names.° Thus, it is likely that at least by the end of the fourth millennium B.C.E. (and possibly much earlier) most of the inhabitants of central and northern Mesopotamia and some people in southern Mesopotamia spoke a Semitic language. Scholars call this language "Akkadian" after the later city of Akkad (written Agade in Sumerian), capital of the Semitic-speaking Sargon of Agade (c. 2334 to 2279 B.C.E.).

The old idea of early and relatively constant strife between the Akkadians north of Nippur and the Sumerians in the south is almost certainly false. This idea derived in large part from erroneous assumptions that all early Semites were nomads and that nomadic and sedentary groups were always enemies. However, there is no textual evidence indicating that Akkadian speakers ever were nomadic or that, as a group, they were enemies of the Sumerians. In fact, as we have seen, the *Sumerian King List* indicates that some "Sumerian" cities had dynasties of rulers in which kings with Semitic names were preceded and followed by monarchs with Sumerian names. In at least one instance, such a succession is known to be due to marriage between a Sumerian-speaking king and an Akkadian-speaking queen. As Daniel Snell has pointed out, in early Mesopotamia, ". . . as today, pure ethnic groups and cultures existed only in the minds of certain observers, not in reality."[13]

Both Sumerian speakers and Akkadian speakers lived in the extreme southern portion of Mesopotamia and seem to have been distinguished from one another only by language. There is also no difference between the material culture of the predominantly Akkadian-speaking population of the Baghdad-to-Nippur region (the area called "Akkad" by many scholars) and the largely Sumerian speakers to their south. In fact, as Amélie Kuhrt has pointed out, the later designation "Sumer and Akkad" for the territory from around Baghdad to the Persian Gulf may not refer to two clearly defined geographical and cultural areas, as often assumed, but rather to "the linguistic, cultural and political diversity of the area."[14] Despite their different languages, the peoples of Mesopotamia seem to have shared the same governmental concepts, religious ideas, social structure, and other cultural traditions first developed in the south. So, throughout this work, the terms "Sumerians" or "Akkadians" should not be understood as cultural terms, but simply as a shortened form of "Sumerian-speaking people" or "Akkadian-speaking people." At first, Akkadian speakers used Sumerian for keeping their records, but around 2330 B.C.E. they adapted the cuneiform script to write Akkadian. In time, certainly no later than c. 2000 B.C.E., Akkadian had developed two dialects that would persist through

---

°In fact, out of 22 names listed in this "Dynasty" (which is probably not a single family, but rather just a succession of rulers), 12 are Semitic, 6 are Sumerian and 4 are of unknown origin.

later periods: Assyrian in northeastern Mesopotamia and Babylonian in the central and southern regions.

Remnants of non-Semitic, non-Sumerian groups were also part of the Mesopotamian population. The Sumerians called them Subarians. Some cuneiform specialists have identified what they think is the Subarian language in some place names and a few magical incantations that cannot yet be understood. The Subarians seem to have been concentrated primarily in northern Mesopotamia, for Sumerian texts often refer to the area north of Babylon as Subar (Subartu in Akkadian). However, some lived in southern Mesopotamia, as well. Whether Subarian was a single language or a term used to group together several different non-Semitic and non-Sumerian languages is not yet certain. It is clear, though, that some people speaking one or more languages that were not Sumerian, Semitic, or Indo-European continued to live within Mesopotamia into the Early Dynastic Period.

All of these different groups of people—Sumerians, Akkadians, and "Subarians"—contributed to the creation of what is generally called "Sumerian" civilization. The great Assyriologist H. W. F. Saggs is almost certainly correct when he asserts that the so-called "Sumerians"

> . . . were in reality a blend of peoples, speaking at least two or perhaps more languages, who had long since ceased to be distinct ethnic groups. . . . The civilization which bloomed in the third millennium was a joint achievement of peoples, who, within the constraints of their local ecology, all shared the same basic concepts and the same way of life.[15]

The Origins of Elam

Another civilization, in close contact with and strongly influenced by that of Mesopotamia, arose in the Khuzistan/Susiana area of western Iran during the Jemdet Nasr Period. Scholars have labeled this culture "Proto-Elamite" because it seems to be ancestral to the later Elamite state. As we have seen, there had been close contacts between southern Mesopotamia

and Khuzistan during the Ubaid and Uruk Periods. Urban-centered economic and political networks probably developed in this part of western Iran even earlier than in Mesopotamia. Also, Proto-Elamite writing had appeared at Susa and other sites almost as early as the first Mesopotamian ideographic texts of the Late Uruk era.

Presumably influenced by the Uruk expansion that had reached into Iran, the Proto-Elamite culture seems to have established colonies of its own across Iran between c. 3300 and 3000 B.C.E. At Tepe Yahya and other Iranian sites hundreds of miles away from Susiana, archaeologists have uncovered specialized types of pottery (including beveled-rim bowls), cylinder seals, and Proto-Elamite tablets like those of Susa. These artifacts undoubtedly indicate the spread of the systems of economic, social, and political control developed in southwestern Iran and southern Mesopotamia during the Uruk Period. However, it is not known whether these complex interrelated structures were introduced to other parts of Iran by conquest, merchant colonies, or less direct processes of diffusion.

Trade and other contacts between Khuzistan and southern Mesopotamia continued to result in shared concepts and developments, including (probably c. 3000 to 2500 B.C.E.) the transformation of the ideographic Proto-Elamite script into a syllabic one similar to that used for Sumerian. The new script was utilized to write Elamite, a language which doesn't belong to any of the major language families, though some scholars think it possibly is related to Dravidian, the prehistoric language of Pakistan and northwest India that is still spoken in southern India today. The centuries following 3000 B.C.E. also saw the creation of a relatively strong Elamite kingdom that stretched from the Caspian Sea to the Persian Gulf, and eastward to the great deserts of Iran. Unlike the independent city-states of Sumer (covered in a later section), the Elamite state was a federated kingdom eventually binding together the originally separate political entities of Awan (Susiana), Shimashki (the area north of the Susiana Plain), and Anshan (the later region of Fars, southeast of Susiana) (see

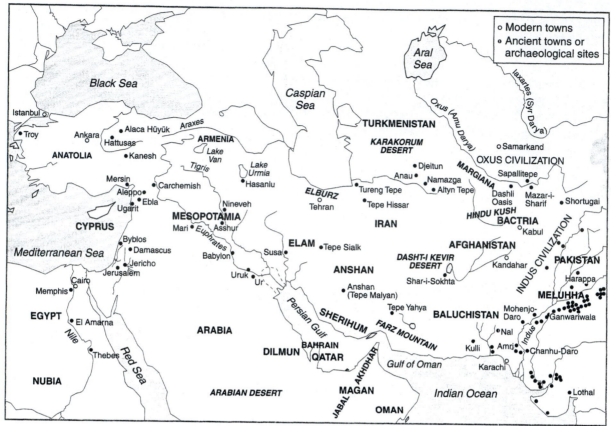

MAP 2.2 **The Near East in the Third and Second Millennia B.C.E.**

Source: Georges Roux, *Ancient Iraq*, 3rd ed. (New York: Penguin Books, 1992), pp. 516–517.

Map 2.2). At different times, each of these regions gained power over the entire federation and the capital shifted accordingly.

The area of Elam was always important to the Mesopotamian economy. It had natural resources (including metals, stone, and wood) that Mesopotamia needed. Through it passed the trade routes to Afghanistan and other eastern regions from which Mesopotamia obtained lapis lazuli, tin, and other products. From at least the start of the Early Dynastic II Period (c. 2700 B.C.E.) to the rise of the Persian Empire (539 B.C.E.), the Elamites would remain trade partners, rivals, and often enemies of the numerous successive Mesopotamian states.

THE MESOPOTAMIAN EARLY DYNASTIC PERIOD (c. 3000–2330 B.C.E.)

An Era of Independent City-States

As we have noted, the culture of southern Mesopotamia was shared by people speaking several different languages. Most of the rulers, the upper classes and the language of the texts, though, were Sumerian. Therefore, the history and culture of the Early Dynastic Period is usually classified as "Sumerian." Until the beginning of the Early Dynastic I (ED I) Period (c. 3000 to 2700 B.C.E.), cities had been largely confined to southern Mesopotamia and Elam. However, during ED I, urbanism spread to the Diyala basin northeast of Baghdad and to northern Mesopotamia. In the Diyala area, ten cities developed, including Eshnunna, Tutub (Khafaje), and Tell Agrab (see Map 2.1). In addition, 19 towns and 67 villages have been located in the Diyala area by archaeological surveys. In northern Mesopotamia, Asshur, Tell Taya, Tell Khuera, and Mari grew into moderate-sized cities. All of these central and northern sites exhibit strong Sumerian cultural influence.

Urbanism continued to progress in the south, as well. By the latter part of the Early Dynastic Period, about 80 percent of the southern Mesopotamian population lived in cities that covered more than 100 acres. While Uruk's large population of 40,000 to 50,000 was unique at the beginning of the third millennium, by about 2500 B.C.E., most of the major Mesopotamian cities contained at least 20,000 to 30,000 people; by that time, a few were approaching the size of Uruk.

Though Sumerian texts from the ED I Period can be read, they are all economic or lexical in nature and provide almost no historical information. Occasional historical inscriptions appeared during the ED II Period (c. 2700 to 2500 B.C.E.) and they became more plentiful in ED III times (c. 2500 to 2330 B.C.E.). Material remains uncovered by archaeologists also throw some light on the Early Dynastic era. In addition, the later *Sumerian King List*, as well as various epics, legends, and religious myths contain information historians can use to understand the early development of the Sumerian states. However, scholars must exercise caution when trying to draw historical information from these later literary sources.

The *Sumerian King List* utilized earlier individual lists from several Sumerian cities, but it was not compiled until about 2120 B.C.E. By that time, large kingdoms or empires had been created in Mesopotamia, so the author of the *King List* assumed that the gods always intended that there be only one ruler on earth at any given time. Thus, the compiler of this work listed the kings of various Sumerian cities as well as those of Mari (in northwestern Mesopotamia), the foreign cities of Awan (the first capital of

Elam), and Hamazi (a place somewhere in the hills to the northeast of Mesopotamia) in the order in which they are supposed to have dominated the world (see Document 2.1). Besides the impossibly long reigns of the mythical or legendary pre- and early post-Flood rulers, historians have other good reasons for questioning the accuracy of some aspects of the *Sumerian King List*. The list omits the names of monarchs such as Mesilim (or Mesalim) who titled himself "King of Kish" on several inscribed objects found at Lagash and Adab. These finds suggest that he controlled a considerable amount of territory around the end of ED II or the beginning of ED III (c. 2600 to 2500 B.C.E.). A-annepadda, who according to inscriptions was the son and successor of Mesannepadda, presented as the first king of Ur's First Dynasty in the *King List*, is also not listed. In addition, the list does not include Lagash or any of its dynasties, though texts make it clear that Lagash was a powerful city-state in the ED III era. Finally, while each of the cities and dynasties listed in the *Sumerian King List* may have had great power and status in Sumer for a while, it is unlikely that any of them actually controlled all of southern Mesopotamia for more than very brief periods of time. There are indications, for instance, that the "first" dynasties of Kish, Uruk, and Ur, placed in succession in the *King List*, in fact were partly contemporaneous, overlapping one another. In many cases, the kings who supposedly ruled over the entire land of Sumer were probably only "first among equals."

The later evidence suggests that, unlike the Egyptians or the Elamites, the Sumerians did not create a centralized state. Rather, many autonomous city-states developed, each controlling the fields, smaller towns, and villages surrounding it. As in later times, rivalry over land, canals, and other resources often must have led to warfare between these small states and to temporary conquest of one city-state by another. Kish was probably the first city-state to achieve some preeminence in southern Mesopotamia by forcing several of the other cities to become its vassals.

According to the *Sumerian King List*, Kish was the first city on which "kingship was lowered from

DOCUMENT 2.1

Excerpts from the *Sumerian King List*

Some scholars date this work to the reign of Utu-hegal, a king of Uruk (c. 2123 to 2113 B.C.E.), who freed southern Mesopotamia from domination by the Guti about a century after the collapse of the Akkadian empire. Others think it was composed around 1900 B.C.E. The author used king lists from various cities as well as material derived from myths and epics to produce a list of dynasties supporting his view that the gods had always intended Mesopotamia to be united under one king. The following excerpt begins after the mythological pre-Deluge preamble.[16]

After the Flood had swept over (the earth) (and) when kingship was lowered (again) from heaven, kingship was (first) in Kish. . . . Kalibum ruled 960 years; Qalumum ruled 840 years; Zuqaqip ruled 900 years; Atab ruled 600 years; [Mashda, son] of Atab ruled 840 years; Arwi'um, son of Mashda, ruled 720 years; Etana, a shepherd, he who ascended to heaven (and) who consolidated all countries, became king and ruled 1,560 (var.: 1,500) years; Balih, son of Etana, ruled 400 (var.: 410) years; . . . Ilku' ruled 900 years; Ilta-sadum ruled 1,200 years; En-men-barage-si, he who carried away as spoil the "weapon" of Elam, became king and ruled 900 years; Aka, son of En-men-barage-si, ruled 629 years. Twenty-three kings (thus) ruled it for 24,510 years, 3 months, and 3½ days.

Kish was defeated in battle (lit.: was smitten with weapons), its kingship was removed to Eanna (sacred precinct of Uruk).

In Eanna, Mes-kiag-gasher, the son of the (sun) god Utu, became high priest as well as king, and ruled 324 years. Mes-kiag-gasher went (daily) into the (Western) Sea and came forth (again) toward the (Sunrise) Mountains; En-me-kar, son of Mes-kiag-gasher, he who built Uruk, became king and ruled 420 years; the god Lugal-banda, a shepherd, ruled 1,200 years; the god Dumu-zi, a SHU-PESH-fisherman—his (native) city was Ku'a(ra),—ruled 100 years; the divine Gilgamesh, his father was a *lillu*, a high priest of Kullab, ruled 126 years; Ur-Nun-gal (var.: Ur-lugal), son of Gilgamesh, ruled 30 years; Utul-kalamma, son of Ur-nun-gal (var.: Ur-lugal), ruled 15 years; Laba[h. . .]ir ruled 9 years; En-nun-dara-Anna ruled 8 years; . . . .

Uruk was defeated in battle, its kingship was removed to Ur.

In Ur, Mes-Anne-pada became king, ruled 80 years; Mes-kiag-Nanna became king, ruled 36 years; [Elulu ruled 25 years; Balulu ruled 36 years. Four kings (thus) ruled it for 177 years. Ur was defeated in battle].

heaven" after the Flood (the event that seems to separate mythological events from legendary ones in Mesopotamian lore). Kish's early dominance is also suggested by the fact that as early as the beginning of ED III, Mesopotamian rulers adopted the title "King of Kish" as a claim to supremacy over all of Sumer.

The earliest king known from actual inscriptions is Enmebaragesi, a ruler of Kish. According to the *King List*, he conquered Elam and had a reign of 900 years. Though the *King List* fancifully gives Enmebaragesi (En-men-barage-si in the translation shown in Document 2.1) an impossibly long reign, two Early Dynastic II inscriptions show that he was a real person. There also may be truth in the claim by the Tummal Text, a later document describing reconstructions of a shrine in Nippur, that Enmebaragesi built Nippur's first temple of Enlil. Though the temple of the goddess Inanna at Nippur goes back to the Uruk Period, there is no evidence for an Enlil Temple there before ED II.

Enmebaragesi's son Agga (or Aka) was the last ruler of the First Dynasty of Kish according to the *King List*. A later epic poem described a conflict between this King Agga and Gilgamesh, King of Uruk. Gilgamesh, who was a semidivine hero of several Sumerian epics, is also named in the *King List* where he is the fifth king of the First Dynasty of Uruk. However, because the *King List* claims that kingship over Sumer passed to Uruk only after the end of Kish's First Dynasty, and because all of these early kings are given fantastically long reigns, it dates Gilgamesh more than a thousand years after Agga. Since Enmebaragesi was a real person, many scholars are convinced that Gilgamesh and Agga were real as well and that their dynasties overlapped considerably rather than being successive. Their historicity also seems to be indicated by the Tummal Text, which makes Gilgamesh a younger contemporary of Mesannepadda, a ruler of Ur known from seal impressions and dedicatory inscriptions. Mesannepadda was the first king of the First Dynasty of Ur according to the *King List*. Unfortunately, even if Sumerologists find an inscription of the historical figure behind the Gilgamesh legends, they may not recognize it. Gilgamesh is probably an epithet rather than a real name; it seems to mean "heroic ancestor."

Besides Gilgamesh, the *King List* names at least two other divine beings as members of the First Dynasty of Uruk—Gilgamesh's immediate predecessors, Dumuzi and Lugalbanda. In addition, Enmerkar (En-me-kar in Oppenheim's translation), predecessor of Lugalbanda as king of Uruk in the *King List*, became the hero of two later epics and a character in two others which center on the deeds of Lugalbanda. Thus, some historians refer to the ED II Period as Mesopotamia's "Heroic Age," an era whose people and events became the stuff of later myths, legends, and epic poems.

In the Early Dynastic III era, longer and more numerous inscriptions allow historians finally to be able to recognize the historicity of many more Sumerian rulers and events. In one case, they even enable us to recount the history of a long-standing border dispute between Lagash and Umma. During the late ED II era, the two city-states had expanded their territories until there was only one small piece of open country° left between them. Both cities, of course, laid claim to that land. Either because both Umma and Lagash were his vassals or simply because of his power and prestige, Mesilim of Kish arbitrated this dispute. He apparently decided that Umma should cultivate the field, but give a portion of its produce to Lagash. Umma seems to have resented this ruling, and a few generations later, it repudiated the agreement and stopped making its required payments. Naturally, this action precipitated war with Lagash. Eannatum, ruler of Lagash (c. 2430 B.C.E.), defeated Umma (see Figure 2.3), reinstated the original agreement, and imposed an additional tax on the conquered city-state. He also claims to have driven out the Elamites who were occupying parts of Sumer and then subdued Elam itself, destroying Susa and several other Elamite cities.

Eannatum's successors, though, had difficulty maintaining the supremacy he had achieved. Umma continued to violate the original agreement and began diverting water from one of the irrigation channels used by both cities. Then, after another victory by Lagash, Umma revolted against Eannatum's grandson (or great grandson), killed him, and ended the dynasty. Umma now had the upper hand.

Lagash began experiencing internal turmoil that led a new ruler, Uruinimgina (formerly read as Urukagina), to undertake extensive legal reforms. His proclamation contains the first recorded use of the Sumerian word *amargi* (literally, "return to the mother"), a term meaning "release," "freedom," or

---

°The Sumerian word for "open country," "uncultivated field," or "plain" was *edin*. Originally this word seems to have been used for all of the land between the Tigris and Euphrates rivers. It probably is the source of "Eden," the biblical name for the earthly paradise formed at the beginning of creation.

FIGURE 2.3   The Stele of Eannatum of Lagash ("The Stele of the Vultures")

The image depicted on the stone slab is of Eannatum's army triumphing over Umma.

Source: Louvre, Paris.

Photo: H. Lewandowski/Réunion des Musées Nationaux/Art Resource, New York.

"liberty."[17] Uruinimgina reduced taxes and sought to end the exploitation of the poor, orphans, and widows. He returned to the gods temple lands seized by previous rulers, and prevented nobles and government officials from confiscating commoners' domestic animals and property. He also ended a custom in which officials had "shared" in the profits and wages of craftsmen, probably by collecting kickbacks or bribes. Though Uruinimgina ended these and other abuses that had occurred before he came to power, he was unable to restore Lagash's military power.

The reforming *ensi's* rule came to an end when Lugalzagesi, ruler of Umma (c. 2340 to 2316 B.C.E.), attacked and destroyed Lagash. Lugalzagesi also conquered several other Sumerian city-states, including Uruk, which he made his capital. He then tried to build an empire stretching into northern Mesopotamia and Syria. However, he was unable to realize his hopes for a lasting empire, for he was defeated and overthrown by Sargon, the upstart Semitic ruler of a new city called Agade. Sargon's rise marked the end of the Early Dynastic Period and the beginning of the first true Mesopotamian empire.

The "Royal Tombs" of Ur

While excavating the remains of ancient Ur in the 1920s, Leonard Woolley uncovered 16 elaborate tombs consisting of one to four chambers constructed entirely of stone or of stone and brick. They appear to date from the end of the Early Dynastic II Period or the very beginning of ED III,, c. 2600 to 2500 B.C.E. Four inscriptions found in the tombs designated certain individuals as royalty—Meskalamdug and Akalamdug were given the title *lugal* ("king"), while Ninbanda and Puabi (formerly known as Shubad) were called *nin* ("lady" or "queen"). However, these "kings" were not among those from Ur listed in the *Sumerian King List*. Nevertheless, Woolley interpreted the tombs as the burial places of Ur's early royalty.

The so-called "Royal Tombs" were quite different from the approximately 2,000 other burials excavated at Ur. A typical commoner's grave was about four- to twelve-feet deep and contained a single body either wrapped in reed mats or lying in a coffin of wood, reeds, or clay. A few personal objects, such as jewelry, a knife, a pin, or a cylinder seal, were often placed with the body. Other offerings (usually weapons, tools, and vessels originally containing food and drink) were deposited elsewhere in the grave. In contrast to these simple graves, workers built the vaulted or dome-roofed chambers of the "Royal Tombs" at the bottoms of large pits about 40 feet long, 30 feet wide and 30 feet deep, entered by sloping ramps. The principal occupants of these tombs were buried not only with many precious objects of gold, silver, bronze, lapis lazuli, shell, and inlaid wood , but also with the bodies of from 3 to 74 guards and attendants.

The bodies of the sacrificial victims showed no signs of violence and were usually arranged in orderly rows with small cups next to, or in the hands of, the corpses. It seems that the "king" or "queen" had been placed in a tomb's main chamber with a collection of precious objects and often with two or more personal attendants positioned by the bier. Then the door to the chamber had been sealed. The other individuals stood in the corridor outside the main burial chamber, soldiers at attention, female attendants wearing fine garments and special gold, silver, and jeweled head-dresses, and musicians playing harps and lyres. Chariots and/or wagons laden with precious offerings had been backed down the sloped ramp, the donkeys or oxen harnessed to them guided by grooms. Then, each person seems to have consumed a poisoned beverage and composed him- or herself to await death, though the musicians may have continued playing as long as possible before slumping over their instruments. Officiants killed the draft animals whose bodies often fell on top of those of their grooms. Earth was then shoveled over the roofed chambers, open areas of the pit, and the access ramp. Archaeologists have found no comparable burials, royal or otherwise, anywhere else in Mesopotamia, except possibly at Kish. There, in the 1920s and 1930s, excavators uncovered several early tombs each containing up to three wheeled vehicles and burial goods similar to those in Ur's "Royal Tombs." However, there are no indications that sacrificed attendants accompanied these burials.

Several scholars have agreed with Woolley that these sepulchers at Ur contain royal burials, probably belonging to a dynasty that ruled Ur just before the start of the First Dynasty of Ur that is listed in the *Sumerian King List*.[18] The slightly earlier god-kings of Egypt's First and Second Dynasties practiced human sacrifice in conjunction with their burials (see Chapter 4), so possibly the early rulers of Ur (and maybe also of Kish and other cities) chose to copy that custom. Some scholars see a reference to this practice in a badly preserved Sumerian epic, *The Death of Gilgamesh*, in which Gilgamesh possibly takes his attendants with him to the grave. However, the passage is too damaged to be sure about its meaning. Whatever the truth about this fragmentary epic, it is clear that several early city-state rulers named in the *Sumerian King List* were worshiped as gods in later times. Gilgamesh, for example, became an underworld deity. Perhaps, like the Egyptians, the Early Dynastic II Sumerians believed that their kings were divine or semidivine beings who could magically enable their retinues to continue to serve them in the next world.

From the beginning, many scholars questioned Woolley's designation of the Ur sepulchers as "Royal Tombs." The fact that three-fourths of the tombs lack royal inscriptions is surprising. Even though all but two of the main chambers had been at least partially plundered in antiquity, the shafts and outer corridors were not disturbed and still contained many valuable objects. If these articles had once belonged to kings or queens, one would expect some of them to have inscriptions saying so. Moreover, most of the objects inscribed with names (usually cylinder seals) were not clearly linked with the principal burials in the tombs where they were found. In fact, there were *two* inscriptions of Meskalamdug, one designating him as king and the other only as "Hero of the Good Land." Neither was with a main burial in a tomb chamber. The cylinder seal inscribed "King Meskalamdug" was found above a chamber containing a female occupant. The "hero" inscription was found in a grave containing precious objects of gold and **electrum** (an alloy of gold and silver) dug into the shaft of one of the largest tombs. Thus, the inscribed objects might represent burial offerings given *by* the named individuals rather than being possessions of the people in the tombs.

The various unusual features of these burials at Ur have led some scholars to argue that they represent sacrifices of "substitute" kings and queens connected with Sacred Marriage fertility rites or possibly with propitiation rituals performed during times of crisis or disaster. However, since the Sacred Marriage ceremony took place every year, why are there only 16 "royal" tombs? Also, why is the principal occupant of each tomb *either* a man or a woman rather than a couple, as we might expect? Moreover, there are no textual indications that the participants in the Sacred Marriage rites were killed. While the later Assyrians seem to have killed substitute kings as part of atonement rites at times of acute crisis, there is no proof that this practice goes back to early Sumer. There is a known instance of the substitute-king rite in Isin around 1860 B.C.E., after the collapse of the Sumerian Ur III empire (see Chapter 3). So, it is possible that these mass burials could represent an extraordinary reaction to a series of extreme crises or natural disasters during the Early Dynastic era. Five later tombs at Ur from around 2200 to 2100 B.C.E. also contained multiple interments of up to 20 bodies, all buried at the same time. So it is also possible that mass burials do not represent a general Sumerian practice, but rather an early custom peculiar to Ur, perhaps associated with individuals who had held some high rank in the cult of Nanna, Ur's patron god.[19] The meaning of the "Royal Tombs" of Ur remains a mystery that probably will not be solved without new archaeological discoveries and/or a better understanding of early Sumerian texts.

MESOPOTAMIAN CULTURE DURING THE EARLY DYNASTIC ERA

Religion and World View

There seems to have been a common **pantheon** throughout most of Mesopotamia during the Early Dynastic Age. However, like the later Classical Greeks, Mesopotamians believed that each city-state had one of the major deities as its patron. Supposedly each divine patron had founded his or her city and continued to look after its interests. Thus, the patron god received the preponderance of a city's religious offerings and worship, usually at its largest temple. The Sumerian gods continued to be worshipped in later Mesopotamia, though the deities often were given Akkadian names and the identity of the head of the pantheon changed as new cities or areas rose to prominence.

Mesopotamian deities were anthropomorphic, capable of exhibiting not only human virtues such as wisdom, courage, and loyalty, but also human faults such as anger, lust, and dishonesty. They were, of course, immortal, and had supernatural strength as well as control over the natural world. An (Anu in Akkadian), the patron-god of Uruk, was the god of the sky and originally the father and ruler of all the gods. Probably early in the Early Dynastic II Period, for unknown reasons, An's primary position in the pantheon was usurped by Enlil, patron of Nippur and god of the air. Though never attaining much political power, Nippur became a holy city for all Sumerians, and Enlil was thought to be not only king of the gods,

but the deity who chose and empowered all earthly rulers. In later times, Enlil was supplanted successively by Marduk, god of Babylon, and Asshur, the Assyrian national god. Close to An and Enlil in power was Eridu's patron deity, Enki (Ea in Akkadian), god of freshwater streams, springs, and lakes as well as the *abzu* (or *apsu*), the subterranean freshwater ocean on which the earth supposedly floated. Enki was also associated with wisdom, science, craftsmanship, and magic. Ur's deity, Nanna (Sin), the moon god who controlled time and human destiny, and Sippar's patron, Utu (Shamash), god of the sun and of justice, were also major male divinities. The principal female deities were Ninhursag, regarded as the mother of the gods, and Inanna (the Akkadian Ishtar), goddess of beauty, carnal love, and fertility.

Mesopotamians believed that humans had been created to serve the gods, so the building and repair of temples was one of the primary duties of rulers. Every day, priests and priestesses clothed the divine cult statues housed within each city's temples and provided the gods with food in the form of burnt offerings and drink in the form of libations poured into the ground. These regular offerings and the rites for special events were accompanied by prayers, hymns, and dancing performed by temple musicians, singers, and other personnel. During the more public rituals connected with holidays or festivals, the general population participated in the services, probably through processions, responses, chants, and singing. If people neglected their religious offerings or angered a deity in any way, disaster would ensue. But regular offerings to the temples, observing taboos and ritual requirements, and performance of the daily rites were supposed to keep the gods happy and willing to give good things to humanity. In addition, Mesopotamians held that the gods generally were pleased when humans led virtuous lives—obeying laws, telling the truth, showing compassion to the downtrodden, and performing charitable deeds. Nevertheless, the gods' motives and actions were not always understandable or predictable. If deities did become enraged, special atonement rites would hopefully soothe their anger and make them friendly once more. In later times, some propitiation rituals probably included the appointment and slaying of a substitute king (and possibly also a queen), but it is not known whether that tradition goes back to the Sumerians.

To try to understand the will of the gods, the Mesopotamians used several methods of **divination**—reading or interpreting divine omens or portents. The most important Mesopotamian method of divination from Early Dynastic times onward was extispicy in which a young ram was sacrificed and its liver (or occasionally other organs) examined. Spots, folds, or other unusual features meant different things depending on where they were located. Other early methods of divination included observing the pattern made by oil when poured on water or the behavior of smoke rising from burning incense. One or more of these divination procedures was used before all major undertakings such as building temples, embarking on military campaigns, or performing special religious rites. Later types of divination include noting events associated with chance happenings or unusual natural phenomena (especially in the heavens), interpretation of dreams, and observation of the activities of birds.

The occasionally incomprehensible and capricious nature of the Mesopotamian gods almost certainly was due in part to the difficult and undependable Mesopotamian environment. The levels of the Tigris and Euphrates, fed by rainfall and melting snow in the mountains of eastern Anatolia, were unpredictable. Sometimes the rivers were too low, making it impossible to irrigate all of the fields. At other times they were too high, resulting in disastrous floods that destroyed crops, settlements, and lives. Furthermore, Mesopotamia was always open to invasion by peoples from the mountains to the north and east or from the desert fringes on the west. Additionally, the rivalry and almost constant conflict between their city-states contributed to the early Mesopotamians' sense of instability and insecurity. Both nature and history taught Mesopotamians that the gods who controlled the world were not always beneficent or understandable. Early Dynastic and later Mesopotamians also came to affirm the existence of many demons that constantly tried to cause harm to human beings.

Because of these beliefs, ancient Mesopotamian thought is often characterized as pessimistic. Sumerians and their successors seem to have cultivated an attitude of acceptance and resignation. They prayed for prosperity and blessings, but were not unduly surprised if instead, they experienced hardship and afflictions. Their fatalistic outlook was also displayed in their conception of the afterlife. If the "Royal Tombs" of Ur were for real kings and queens, then the Early Dynastic II Sumerians may have believed that their (divine?) rulers had some sort of glorious afterlife in which they would continue to be served by their courtiers and attendants. However, if this belief ever existed, by the end of the ED III Period, it had changed. Written sources indicate that Sumerians believed that the dead—rulers and commoners, rich and poor, good and bad alike—all went into a somewhat bleak underworld called "The Land of No Return." To reach this land, the spirits of the dead had to be ferried across a fearsome river by a boatman to whom they owed a payment. Family members buried their dead (sometimes in cemeteries and sometimes in graves beneath house floors) with offerings of food and drink to maintain them until they reached their destination. Families sometimes also included a few favorite objects that the dead person might use in the underworld. Some of the burial offerings were probably also intended to be used as payments to the boatman and various deities and demons.

Though there were contradictory ideas about what existence in the netherworld was like, it was generally agreed that no one wanted to go there. One dirge indicates that the sun goes through the underworld during nighttime on earth and that the moon spends one day a month there. It also claims that Utu, the sun god, judged the dead and presumably, provided a better existence for the good than the bad. On the other hand, another work describes the misery and despair of a dead individual who knows he cannot return to the world of the living and is painfully aware of the sorrow and hardship his death has brought to his family and friends. Also, despite the claim that the sun illuminates the underworld each night, other texts leave the impression that it was mostly a gloomy place. The later *Epic of Gilgamesh* reflects this tradition when it describes the netherworld as a place of darkness whose inhabitants eat dust and clay.

Their fatalistic attitude does not mean that Sumerians were always despondent, though. They seem to have enjoyed playing games, for game boards and "toys" were among the offerings in the "Royal Tombs" of Ur. Moreover, Mesopotamian uncertainty and insecurity about the future led them to treasure each moment in this life. They seem to have developed strong bonds of friendship, but cherished even more their family relationships. According to a Sumerian proverb, "Friendship lasts a day; kinship endures forever."[20] People were advised not to become too attached to things, for "possessions are sparrows in flight which can find no place to alight."[21] Instead, family was a person's true treasure: "The wife is a man's future; the son is a man's refuge; the daughter is a man's salvation."[22] (The final line of this proverb, "the daughter-in-law is a man's devil,"indicates that conflicts between "in-laws" is not a recent phenomenon.) Mesopotamians especially loved and prized children, for they thought that descendants were a person's only real immortality. Families usually had at least five or six children, but unfortunately, only about half of them survived to puberty.

Like other aspects of their religion and world view, Sumerian creation stories and **cosmology** remained basic to later Mesopotamian thought. Several somewhat contradictory accounts, probably derived from the traditions of different city-states, described how this world and its gods came into being. In these stories, creation takes place in three distinct ways: through sexual intercourse between deities, through gods molding figures out of clay by hand, or through the power of the divine word. Most of the gods were thought to have been created through the first method (sex), though the myths sometimes differ about who begat whom or what. For example, what seems to be the oldest creation story stated that Nammu (the primeval ocean) by herself produced Enki (fresh water and the *abzu* on which the earth floats), An (heaven) and Ki (earth). An and Ki mated and begat Enlil (air) and all the earth's vegetation before Enlil separated them. Other stories regard Enki as a son of An rather than of Nammu, and Enlil was not always regarded as a child of An. Also, as we shall see, another myth credited growing things

to the union between Dumuzi and Inanna rather than to An and Ki.

Another creation story known essentially from its early Babylonian epic version probably also had Sumerian roots.[23] It claims that the gods were begotten by a union of the male Abzu (the fresh-water ocean) and female Tiamat (the salt-water ocean). Abzu decided to destroy the gods, but Enki killed him, thus becoming ruler of the fresh waters. However, Tiamat was enraged at Abzu's death and planned to exterminate her divine children. A council of the gods chose one of their number (Enlil according to the Sumerians, Marduk according to the Babylonians) to meet the chaotic watery goddess in battle. He defeated Tiamat, cut her carcass in two and used one half as a dome over the sky and the other half as the surface of the earth.

Thus, Mesopotamians seem to have envisioned the sky (An) and earth (Ki) separated by air (Enlil). The earth, which included the underworld beneath it, was described as having four corners (like a rectangular field) and it floated upon a body of fresh water called *abzu*. Outside of and presumably surrounding the universe was Nammu, the primeval ocean. The other creation story in which a chaotic foe had to be defeated and killed produced a slight variation in this conception of the universe. The flat earth that floats on, and is surrounded by, the fresh water ocean (*abzu*) is half of Tiamat's body. Her breasts are the mountains, her insides became the salt water seas, her spittle results in clouds and rain, and from her eyes flow the Tigris and Euphrates rivers. Beneath the surface of the earth (and presumably beneath the thin layer of fresh water on which the earth floats) is the underworld. The other half of Tiamat's body forms a dome enclosing the sky and earth, holding back the primordial sea in which the spherical world floats like a bubble.

It was generally believed that human beings had been created in the image of the gods. They were molded out of clay (mixed with a god's blood in some versions). The divine "potter" was a mother goddess in some accounts and Enki, god of fresh waters, in others. "Enki and the World Order," the best-known story of creation by divine utterance, glorifies Enki's unquestioned commands by which all aspects of the civilized world were organized and their fates decreed.

Sumerian creation stories and cosmology not only influenced that of later Mesopotamians, but also became basic to the mythology of many other parts of the Near East. They were borrowed by Hurrians, Hittites, and Canaanites. Two separate creation stories ultimately derived from Mesopotamia can be found in the biblical Book of Genesis. The earlier of the two accounts (Genesis 2:4b–25, placed second in the Bible by later editors) envisions an anthropomorphic deity shaping man from clay. God also plants trees and other vegetation to make a garden in a place called Eden that is watered by four rivers, two of which are the Tigris and the Euphrates. The other creation story in Genesis (1:1–2:4a), a demythologized version of the conflict between the creator and a sea monster, has God create the universe by his words alone. Like Mesopotamian cosmology, this account envisions the earth floating on water and surmounted by a solid dome of sky (the "firmament") that holds back "the waters above the firmament." Moreover, the word *tehom* in this account, usually translated "the deep," is the Hebrew linguistic equivalent of Akkadian "Tiamat." Other Bible passages show that the ancient Israelites knew and generally accepted the older version of this story in which creation takes place only after God fights and kills a chaotic sea monster or dragon.[24]

The order and harmony of the created world, civilization and human society were supposed to be preserved by divine properties, powers or norms called *me* (a plural noun pronounced "may"). Every activity, office, institution, piece of equipment, and even each attitude and belief was thought to have its own perfect plan or design. The *me* seem to have been the divine powers or rules that allowed these ideal models to be implemented or realized in the world. The *me* were thought to be held by An or Enlil, though on occasion, other deities could possess them. One story tells how Inanna tricked her father, Enki, into giving her these divine regulatory powers and succeeded in taking them from his city, Eridu, to her temple in Uruk.

Another Sumerian myth that spread through the Near East and beyond is the account of the Deluge or Great Flood. So far, archaeologists have found only one damaged tablet relating this story, but enough survives to indicate that it is the source of the later Mesopotamian accounts from which the biblical story of Noah's flood probably ultimately derives. Some scholars believe that this Sumerian story of a flood that covers the entire earth was inspired by a real (though smaller) flood that took place in prehistoric times. Leonard Woolley and other excavators in the 1920s and 1930s found flood deposits at several Mesopotamian cities that they thought represented a flood that had covered most of southern Mesopotamia (the Sumerians' world).[25] However, later study showed that the various flood layers belonged to different times. They represented several *local* floods of limited extent that had almost certainly not covered most of Mesopotamia.[26]

Recently, it has been suggested that a great flood that created the Black Sea around 5,000 B.C.E. might have given rise to various flood stories in the ancient world. The rising water level of the Mediterranean overtopped and broke through a natural dam blocking the Bosporus Strait and flooded the valley and freshwater lake beyond, areas now at the bottom of the Black Sea.[27] While it is possible that some such real event lies behind the Deluge traditions, it is more likely that the early Mesopotamians developed their story from their experience of many smaller but nevertheless devastating local floods within Mesopotamia. Whatever the inspiration for the Mesopotamian story, it became the ultimate source for several later Near Eastern flood traditions, which in turn probably inspired the biblical story and various Greek flood accounts, including that of Deucalion's Flood.

In addition to their daily religious rites, Sumerians had special festivals and rituals throughout the year. One of the most important of these rituals was the Sacred Marriage ceremony. This rite, probably performed in every major city-state during the New Year celebration, was thought to guarantee fertility for the land, its people, and animals. Originally, the citizens of each city appear to have believed that their patron god or goddess was responsible for all aspects of the city's well-being, including fertility. Each year, the people held two *Akiti* festivals (*Akitu* in Akkadian) at the time of the equinoxes. The first took place around September 20th, the time for planting seed, while the second was held around March 20th, the time of the barley harvest. Eventually, these two festivals were reduced to one and fused with the New Year celebration that came in the spring around the same time as the second *Akiti* festival. During the combined New Year/*Akiti* celebration, a sacred "marriage" (actually a ritual sexual mating) took place to magically ensure fertility. For this rite, a male or female citizen (depending on the sex of the city's main deity) was chosen to be the deity's lover. Some scholars think that a priest or priestess portrayed the deity and that a real sexual union took place, while others think that the city's representative merely spent the night in a ritual bedchamber with the deity's statue, the "mating" taking place magically.

By the latter part of the Early Dynastic Period, Sumerians no longer believed that the Sacred Marriage took place between a city-state's patron deity and a city representative. Instead, they had come to believe that this rite reenacted the sexual union between Dumuzi (Tammuz in Semitic languages), god of vegetation and protector of herds and flocks, and Inanna (Ishtar), goddess of sexual passion and fertility. ED III and later Mesopotamians explained nature's seasonal cycles through a myth describing Inanna's journey to the underworld and how her release was secured only by having Dumuzi take her place for half the year and his sister Geshtinanna (goddess of vines) for the other half. Possibly the rise of this myth and the change in the Sacred Marriage ritual was due in large part to the development of kingship and the full attainment of male domination within Sumerian city-states.

The Development of Kingship

Various Sumerian myths and epics describe situations in which decisions were made by an assembly rather than by a king; the Sumerian word *unken* ("assembly") occurs in the earliest readable Sumerian tablets. These facts have led some scholars to argue that in the ED I era and earlier, Mesopotamian city-states had a kind of "primitive democracy" in which they were

governed by a two-house conclave consisting of a council of elders and an assembly of all free citizens.[28] The assembly supposedly acted by consensus, though giving more weight to the opinions of the elders, and chose a temporary leader to carry out its will. This leader, who seems to have been called *en* (a term that also occurs in the earliest texts), could be either male or female, and had both secular and religious authority. One of the duties for which an *en* was chosen was to mate with the city god or goddess during the Sacred Marriage ceremony.

As conflicts between cities increased, it is thought that male war leaders began to monopolize the position of *en* and hold it for longer periods of time, producing its later meaning of "lord." Women lost the opportunity to be elected *en* and eventually even ceased to be included in the assembly. Once the *en* was always male, his partner in the Sacred Marriage always had to be female. Thus, the Dumuzi-Inanna myth probably replaced those of various city gods as the basis for the fertility rite. In the ED II–III and later Sacred Marriage rites, the city-state ruler (who by then was always male) played the part of Dumuzi making love to Inanna. By the beginning of ED III at the latest, the male rulers had managed to make their position hereditary, introducing the principle of dynastic succession. They also reduced the role of the assembly until it became only an advisory body that was often ignored.

In addition to "primitive democracy" within individual cities, some scholars also argue that during the "Heroic" ED II Period, representatives of all the city-states met at Nippur and dealt with common problems. Scholars sometimes call this organization of city-states the Kengir League, using the native Sumerian word for Sumer (KI-EN-GIR or *Kengir*). The city-state delegates on occasion probably elected a common war leader to protect the area against outside threats. This practice, in turn, led to dominance of the confederation at various times by leaders of powerful city-states such as Kish, Uruk, and Ur. This theory is based on statements in later mythological texts that the ruler of all Mesopotamia was nominated by his own city-god and elected by an assembly of the gods at Nippur. "Since to a Sumerian, city and god were synonymous, the 'council of the gods' would have been equivalent to a council of cities."[29] Such meetings at Nippur are also indicated by the fact that Nippur, though it was the city of Enlil, king of the gods, did not produce its own powerful dynasties and did not contend for political dominance with other major Sumerian cities. It became essentially a religious center whose shrines were supported by other city-states, especially those trying to establish supremacy over all of Sumer.

Originally city-state leaders seem to have been priest-kings (or possibly even divine beings) who lived within the temple complex of the city's main god. As we have seen, *en* was probably the earliest title for a city's leader. However, two other titles, *ensi* and *lugal*, gradually began to be used, and the differences between them are not always clear. By the Early Dynastic III Period, priestly and secular roles and the titles for them had been differentiated. *En* seems to have become a priestly title, used for individuals having only religious duties. *Lugal* (literally "great man") developed into an essentially secular title, the closest equivalent to our word "king." During the latter part of the Early Dynastic Period, the term *lugal* seems to have been reserved for a powerful ruler who had other city-state rulers as his vassals. The other title, *ensi* ("steward"), probably originally had been used for the person who organized and directed seasonal agricultural activities, but it came to mean "governor." It was usually used in late ED III to designate a subordinate city-state ruler, the vassal of a *lugal*.

We have seen that Early Dynastic II Mesopotamians possibly considered their kings to be divine or semidivine. If, in early times, Mesopotamians did have this belief, they seem to have given it up by early- or mid-ED III, c. 2500 to 2400 B.C.E. None of the historical inscriptions of ED III rulers designate them as gods. In fact, even the few inscribed objects of "kings" and "queens" found in the ED II (or possibly very early ED III) "Royal Tombs" of Ur do not have the determinative for "divinity" preceding the personal names. Early Dynastic III and later Mesopotamian rulers (with a few clear exceptions that will

be discussed in Chapter 3) seem to have considered themselves only stewards or viceroys of their city-gods rather than gods themselves. The king was a "shepherd" chosen by the city's divine patron to look after his or her people. He was the gods' representative to humans, exercising the *me* of kingship to implement the divine laws that maintain social order and make civilized life possible. He was also the people's representative before the gods, playing an important role in major religious festivals (especially as the male figure in the Sacred Marriage ceremony) and in atonement rites when the gods were angry.

As kingship became increasingly more secular, rulers began living in administrative centers apart from the temples. Archaeologists have uncovered late ED II and early ED III examples of such palaces at Eridu, Kish, and Mari. Though the city ruler, whether called *lugal* or *ensi*, no longer directly participated in daily cultic activities, he remained responsible to the gods for the overall administration of the city's temples and their estates, as well as other aspects of city life. He was clearly more powerful than the priests, nobles, or other groups within the city. In fact, some of the statements in Uruinimgina's inscriptions indicate that one or more of the preceding rulers of Lagash had been powerful and ruthless enough to take temple lands and animals for themselves. To maintain the ruler's close relationship to the gods (and his control over the temple establishments), he usually appointed his daughters and sons (other than the crown prince) as the high priestesses and priests for the city's main deities. The ruler's wife, called *nin* ("lady" or "queen"), also played an important role in civic and religious affairs. The wife of the *ensi* of Lagash, for example, managed the temple of a goddess at Girsu, a nearby town that was the city-state's religious center. Possibly the queen's prominence was a holdover from earlier times when women as well as men had been able to serve as *en*.

Economy and Society

According to Sumerian theory, all of a city-state's land belonged to the city's patron deity, and many modern scholars once accepted this theory as fact. However, it is now known that though temples possessed major estates, most of the land in any given Sumerian city-state was privately owned. The ruler and his family owned the largest segment of private land, with the upper classes or nobles (members of the bureaucracy, priests, and soldiers) also having extensive land holdings. All of the produce from one section of each of these large estates was reserved for the landowner. These fields were worked by semifree dependents who, in exchange for their labor, could farm small plots elsewhere on the estates to support themselves and their families. Some of these "serfs" or their ancestors probably had been forced into their dependent status by royal or temple land seizures. Others likely had become part of this semifree class through poverty, recent immigration into the city-state, or a chance misfortune. Kings and temples also set aside a portion of their estates for use by administrative personnel, artisans, and other workers as recompense for their labor. Thus, these two segments of the large estates were managed much like the medieval manors of western Europe. The remainder of temple and state holdings were simply rented out to tenants in exchange for a portion of the crop.

Free peasants, who made up about half of a city-state's population, farmed small plots of land owned by their extended families. Such land was passed down in a family from generation to generation. It could be sold, but only with family approval by a family member designated by his kin. Often, other members of the family acted as witnesses to the transaction to indicate their consent. The main crops Mesopotamian farmers grew were barley and wheat, but they also had orchards of fruit trees that produced nuts, dates, pomegranates, lemons, mulberries, and other fruits.

Though most of a city's economy was based on agriculture, animal husbandry was also important. Animals probably grazed along the edges of cultivated fields, on uncultivated land, and in fields left fallow for a season. Sheep and goats were the most common animals raised, though cattle, pigs, and ducks were kept, as well. These animals were most likely herded, fed, and cared for by children who were not yet old enough to engage in other farm labor. Many farmers

also kept oxen and donkeys to pull plows and perform other necessary work in the fields. Even small farms also seem to have had small pools or ponds stocked with carp and other fish. The fish from these ponds, as well as milk, cheese, and duck eggs supplied most of the animal protein in the diet. Most people got to eat meat only on the rare occasions when they sacrificed an animal during a religious ceremony.

Trade also played a significant role in the Sumerian economy. It is not clear, however, whether most artisans and merchants were independent agents working for themselves or retainers who worked only for the temples or kings. Certainly, some of them must have been attached to the divine and royal establishments, but many (if not most) of them were probably in business for themselves. During the ED III Period, Mesopotamians traded with areas along the Persian Gulf and seem to have made contact with the fledgling civilization of the Indus Valley. They also probably exchanged bitumen, agricultural products, and textiles for gold, silver, copper, lead, stone, timber, spices, and resins from Iran, Syria, and Asia Minor. They also may have obtained gold from Egypt. While most of this trade was done by barter, the long, slow transition to a "money" economy began to take place through the use of some precious metals, particularly silver, for payment.

Early Mesopotamian society consisted of four groups. We have already mentioned the first three: nobles, commoners (including free farmers, merchants, and artisans), and semifree dependents. The fourth class was slaves. Slavery seems to have existed in Mesopotamia and Elam from at least the Late Uruk and Jemdet Nasr Periods when bound captives begin to be depicted on various objects. Most (though not all) slaves were prisoners of war, and ED III tablets indicate the foreign origin of many of them. Most of these foreign slaves probably came from conflicts with Elam or the tribes living in the Zagros Mountains. However, some slaves were fellow Mesopotamians captured during wars between city-states. Individuals could be enslaved for certain legal or religious offenses, and fathers could sell their children to pay off debts. However, children sold for debt became free again after three years. A slave could borrow money and buy his or her freedom, and if a slave married a free person, any resulting children were free. Generally only temples, palaces, and the rich owned slaves; slave-labor was not responsible for most of the work within Sumerian society.

There was also little or no market for hired labor in early Sumer, for those artisans or workers who were not attached to the palace or temple seem to have worked in family businesses or enterprises. When the government or religious establishment needed workers to erect walls or buildings, dig or deepen canals, or perform other tasks, they resorted to **corvée** labor. This term refers to temporary forced labor which citizens had to perform for the state. It was an obligation, like taxes, though it was paid with work rather than with goods or money. The Early Dynastic Mesopotamians subjected women and children, as well as men, to such forced labor.

From at least the Early Dynastic III Period onward, Mesopotamian society was patriarchal and only a male could become *en, ensi* or *lugal*. In Lagash, it was even decreed that a woman who spoke disrespectfully to a man would have her mouth smashed with a baked brick. However, women did serve in the temples as priestesses and, as mentioned above, the wife of the city ruler seems to have had some administrative responsibilities and power. Sumerian had a dialect called *emesal*, "women's language," which was used for cultic and love poetry, and almost all Sumerian love poetry was written from the female perspective. Texts confirm the existence of at least one female physician and a female scribe, so at least some women (probably from upper class families) learned to read and write. Free women could legally make contracts, they could serve as witnesses in court, and they could buy and sell land. They were free to participate in commerce and they seem to have dominated some professions, such as weaving woolen cloth. It is likely, though, that most of the women in nonagricultural jobs (such as weaving) were family members working in family businesses directed by males.

Marriages were monogamous, though males who could afford it might also have had concubines in addition to a wife. Fathers usually arranged marriages for their children as business deals or alliances between families; the terms of a betrothal were normally spelled out in a contract. But cultic love songs suggest that occasionally, surreptitious premarital courtship and wooing (including sex) may have occurred. A proverb also indicates that some unions were entered into freely, for it counsels a young man to "marry a wife according to your choice."[30] But if a marriage turned out badly, an unhappy wife had little recourse, while a husband could divorce his wife on relatively trivial grounds.

Education, Literature, and the Arts

Schools seem to have been developed along with writing in order to make the cuneiform system intelligible to others and to ensure its survival. Among the earliest ideographic tablets were several consisting of lists of signs, which must have been intended for study and memorization by future scribes. Like writing itself, the earliest Mesopotamian schools were created for use by temple personnel. But as the administration of Sumerian towns became more secular, so too, did the educational system. By c. 2500 B.C.E., most major city-states must have had secularly managed schools for training the thousands of scribes and officials that we know existed at that time.

The Sumerian school, known as the *edubba* ("Tablet House"), taught not only reading and writing, but all the knowledge and skills that leaders, officials and bureaucrats needed for the religious and secular administration of the state. Like the modern university, the scribal school became a center for the creation of new learning and culture while also preserving and disseminating the knowledge and traditions of the past. The head of a Sumerian school was called the equivalent of "professor" (or "expert") and was also known as the "school father." His faculty consisted of at least one assistant professor (the "big brother"), instructors of various subjects such as drawing and Sumerian, and individuals in charge of attendance and discipline. These teachers were paid salaries (though we don't know whether they came from public funds or privately paid tuition) and also occasionally received extra monetary gifts (or bribes) from their students' parents. Students—the children of city officials, temple administrators, and other wealthy and influential individuals—were known as "school sons," while alumni were called "school sons of past days." These terms and other indications in the texts make it likely that only boys attended school. However, since documents mention at least one female scribe and a female physician, and since some temple administrations were headed by queens and high priestesses, at least some females likely were literate. Bright girls from highly placed families may have acquired an education from family members or private tutors.

Pupils attended school from sunrise to sunset. They learned primarily by copying and memorizing lists of words (arranged by categories such as names of trees and reeds, animals, cities, stones and minerals, etc.), tables of weights and measures, mathematical tables and problems, and Sumerian grammatical forms. When these basics had been mastered, they moved on to copying and studying literary works, various types of legal documents, and practical problems dealing with wages, surveying, and construction. Corporal punishment was meted out for most infractions. Students were beaten with a cane for making mistakes in their schoolwork or for producing a sloppy tablet and for misbehavior such as being late for school, wearing improper clothing, or speaking or standing without permission. Upon the completion of their education, the alumni became governmental officials, priests, military officers, sea captains, supervisors, foremen, accountants, public scribes, and other members of their city-state's wealthy and powerful "professional" class.

Studying, copying, and redacting literary works was one of the primary tasks of senior students and teachers in the schools. The Sumerians probably first began to commit such literature to writing around 2500 B.C.E. at the beginning of the Early Dynastic III Period. A few early mythological texts from around 2400 B.C.E. have survived, but most examples of Sumerian literature come from copies made after 2000 B.C.E. However, linguistic features of these texts indicate that the bulk of them were composed much earlier, probably during the Early

Dynastic Period. They include myths, hymns, lamentations, heroic legends or epics, proverbs, and historiographic texts. These Sumerian literary works formed the basis for the later Mesopotamian literature in the Akkadian language.

Some Sumerian literary works, such as hymns and lamentations, may have been used during worship in the temples, though most literature, including "religious" works such as myths and even hymns, seems to have been composed in the schools. The vast majority of Sumerian literary compositions are in poetry, and it is likely that most of them (myths and epics as well as hymns and lamentations) were originally meant to be sung. A figure known as the *nar* ("minstrel") is often mentioned in addition to the scribe, and such bards probably played an important role in the creation and popularization of both religious and secular compositions.

Among the secular literary works, pride of place belongs to the epic tales that were probably meant to be sung at royal courts during feasts or other celebrations. The nine surviving epics relate heroic stories about early semidivine kings of Uruk—Enmerkar, Lugalbanda, and most importantly, Gilgamesh, the protagonist of five of the poems. The Sumerian Gilgamesh stories (*Gilgamesh and Agga of Kish*, *Gilgamesh and the Bull of Heaven*, *Gilgamesh and the Land of the Living*, *Gilgamesh, Enkidu and the Nether World*, and *The Death of Gilgamesh*) established him as hero par excellence throughout Mesopotamia. They were later reworked into an Akkadian epic (see Chapter 3) that in turn spread his fame over the entire Near East.

We can only surmise about the music that accompanied Sumerian epics, hymns, and other songs. Leonard Woolley, excavator of Ur, poured plaster into hollow spaces while excavating the "Royal Tombs" and thus preserved the forms of several harps and lyres whose wooden parts had decayed. Some of these instruments have been reconstructed (see Figure 2.4). From them, musicologists can draw some conclusions about how harps and lyres were tuned and the note ranges available to the musicians who played them. The early Mesopotamians also used

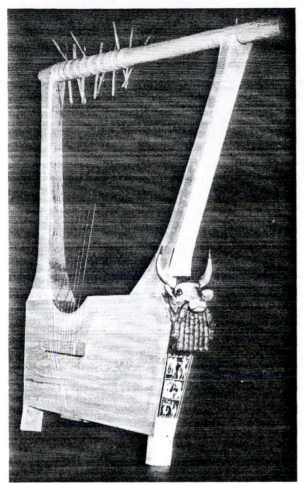

FIGURE 2.4   Reconstruction of a Lyre from One of the "Royal Tombs" of Ur c. 2600–2500 B.C.E.

Source: University of Pennsylvania Museum, Philadelphia.

Photo: Courtesy of the University of Pennsylvania Museum (Neg # 58-139-328).

viduals in prayer. These statues ranged in height from about ten inches to almost two-and-a-half feet. Worshipers placed them before cult images in temples so that magically, they could constantly venerate the deities. Sculptors also created excellent bas-relief carvings on stelae, bowls, vases, and plaques, and delicate drilled figures on cylinder seals that resulted in raised images when the seal was rolled over clay. Mesopotamian goldsmiths and jewelers were especially skillful, beating or pressing sheets of gold or electrum over wooden carvings to make ceremonial helmets or other objects. One of the most beautiful examples of their work is the so-called "Ram in the Thicket" from one of the "Royal Tombs" of Ur (see Figure 2.5). This composite sculpture, actually one of a pair found in the tomb, represents a he-goat (not a ram) tethered to the Tree of Life. The goat's head and legs, and the tree were wood covered with thin sheets of gold secured by a thin layer of bitumen. The horns, ears, "beard" and hair around the shoulders were carved from lapis lazuli. The body was wood covered with a thick layer of bitumen that glued a plate of silver to the belly and many pieces of carved shell to the sides and back. Jewelers also made gold and lapis lazuli bulls' heads to adorn harps and lyres and created many beautiful and delicate necklaces, earrings, ceremonial headdresses, and other articles of personal adornment from gold, silver, lapis lazuli, carnelian, topaz, and other stones. Still other artisans decorated harps, lyres, and other wooden objects with patterns and scenes made of inlaid ivory, colored stone, shell, and lapis lazuli (see Figure 2.4 in this section and Figure 2.6 in the following section).

Science, Technology, and Warfare

As in almost all other fields of endeavor, later Mesopotamian advances in science and technology grew from Early Dynastic roots. The Sumerians developed a mathematical system based on 60 (the sexagesimal system), but which used the factor 10 as well. Because of this system, Mesopotamians tended to order things in units of 6, 12, or 60, or in numbers evenly divisible by 60. Thus, they divided circles into

drums, tambourines, and reed or metal pipes to accompany their songs and dances.

Early Dynastic Mesopotamians proved themselves to be very skilled in other art forms, as well. They produced some sculpture in the round, though such statues were usually fairly small (probably due to the lack of native sources of stone, wood, or metal). Despite the need to import all stone, sculptors created many votive "reverence statues" depicting indi-

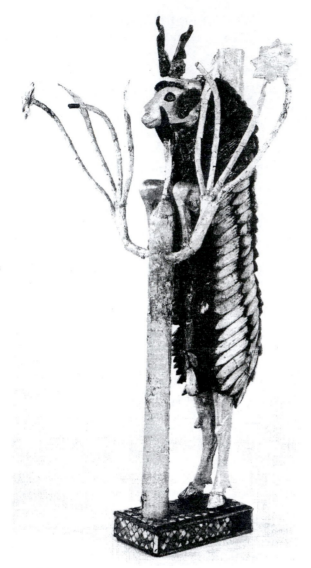

FIGURE 2.5   The So-Called "Ram in the Thicket" from One of the "Royal Tombs" of Ur c. 2600–2500 B.C.E.

The "Ram in the Thicket" is actually a he-goat in a Tree of Life.
Source: Courtesy of the Trustees of the British Museum, London.

time by water clocks—cylindrical or prism-shaped vessels from which water dripped at a steady rate.)

The flexibility of the sexagesimal system of numeration and the positional notation system developed to write it allowed later Mesopotamian mathematicians to create tabulations of reciprocals, squares, square roots, cubes, cube roots, and the sums of squares and cubes. These tables were used to help solve various types of equations and calculations of area and volume.

Belief that the sun, moon, and stars were gods and that what happened in the observable skies predicted or influenced what happened on earth, led the Mesopotamians to study the heavens. Their careful observations gradually led to the development of astronomical texts listing movements of various heavenly bodies, then to relatively accurate predictions of lunar and solar eclipses, and ultimately, to the creation of the astrological zodiac. Though these developments came later (in the case of the zodiac, much later) than the Early Dynastic Period, early Mesopotamians had already learned enough to realize that their calendar of 12 lunar months of 29 or 30 days each was about 11 days short of the solar year. So every so often, when the two got far enough out of kilter, scholars advised the ruler to add an extra month or two to the official year to bring it back in line with the solar year. In later times, Mesopotamian astronomers would develop a formula for adding intercalary months that would allow the lunar and solar calendars to be kept in agreement automatically.

Mesopotamian medicine, like astronomy, included a mixture of religious and scientific elements. Mesopotamians believed that illness was caused by demons or black magic or was sent by the gods as punishment for some sin of omission or commission. Therefore, the primary way to cure a disease was to have a *bâru* priest (diviner) identify the responsible supernatural agent. Then, an *âshipu* priest (exorcist) would remove it through magical rites and incantations if it proved to be demonic, or placate it through prayers and sacrifices, if divine. On the other hand, without denying the efficacy of magic, the *asu* (physician) took a more rational and empirical approach to medicine. As early as the latter part of the Early Dynastic period,

360 degrees, each of which could be broken into 60 minutes. The day, which began at sunset, was partitioned into 12 "double hours" of 60 "double minutes" each. We still use these divisions of circles and time. (Mesopotamians usually measured the divisions of

such physicians compiled lists of prescriptions describing the necessary ingredients and procedures for making various salves and poultices to be applied externally and medications to be taken internally. Experience seems to have shown that these prescriptions were effective against certain ailments.

Early Mesopotamia's technology, the application of knowledge to practical purposes, was also impressive. Two areas of Mesopotamian achievement have already been mentioned, metallurgy and irrigation. Around 3000 B.C.E., Near Eastern metal smiths had discovered that mixing small amounts of tin, arsenic, or other metals with copper made the final product much harder. The new alloy, bronze, could be poured into open or closed molds for casting tools, weapons, sculpture, or jewelry, or hammered into sheets and then shaped. We don't know where this discovery was first made, but it quickly spread throughout the region. Bronze use became so widespread that archaeologists generally use the term "Bronze Age" to designate the period following c. 3000 B.C.E. in the Near East. Mesopotamia was no exception. Throughout the third millennium, its people were in the forefront in using and improving the techniques for producing and working bronze and other metals.

Mesopotamian irrigation and agricultural technology also advanced during the third millennium B.C.E. As city-states grew larger and increased in number, a much more complex system of canals, levees, dams, weirs, and reservoirs became necessary. Mesopotamian engineers developed the extensive knowledge and skills needed for planning, mapping, surveying, constructing, and leveling these essential irrigation works. Technology was also applied to the improvement of agriculture. Some plows were equipped with bronze-covered points, called "the tongue of the plow," enabling them to cut more deeply into the ground. Another type of plow (used after the ground had been tilled, pulverized and raked), had a funnel just behind the blade that automatically deposited seeds into the new furrows. Farmers learned to plant a belt of date palms or other trees along the edges of their gardens. These trees protected the more delicate lettuce, turnips, chick-peas, lentils, onions, garlic, and other vegetables from being scorched by the sun or dried out by the wind. Mesopotamian agriculturalists also developed systematic methods for producing abundant yields of grain. Teachers compiled these procedures into a farm manual or "farmer's almanac" from which their pupils could learn how to successfully manage large estates.

Among the many other early Mesopotamian technological accomplishments are creation of the first-known true arches, barrel-vaults, and domes. They produced and dyed large amounts of woolen cloth, using spindles to spin the wool, horizontal and vertical looms to weave it into cloth, and alkaline solutions and foot stomping to make it thicker and more compact. They also produced textiles from flax and linen. Finally, they supplemented human and animal transport with sledges, two- and four-wheeled wagons, boats, and ships. The wheel, in particular, seems to have been a Mesopotamian invention, appearing for the first time in the Early Dynastic Period.

Most of these technological advances made life easier or better. However, some technology received military applications that made warfare more efficient and more deadly. Bronze axes, daggers, swords, spearheads, javelins, and arrowheads were more lethal than the copper or stone weapons that preceded them. The Mesopotamians also seem to have been the first to develop and use the composite bow made of wood strengthened by bands of sinew and/or horn. Such bows were difficult to make, but they were much stronger and more accurate than regular bows. Early Dynastic infantrymen not only used such weapons, but they also were protected by leather or bronze helmets and large bronze-studded rectangular shields that covered their bodies from neck to ankle (see Figure 2.3). Soldiers are also shown wearing capes that appear to be studded with metal disks (see Figure 2.6). They attacked in a phalanx formation—rows of men marching in straight lines, shields in front, and spears protruding between the shields (again, see Figure 2.3).

In addition to the infantry, early Mesopotamian armies could assault the enemy with two- or four-wheeled chariots, each pulled by four donkeys. The wheels on these chariots were made of two solid wooden semicircles or three boards held together by

FIGURE 2.6 Four-Wheeled Chariots and Infantry Attack an Enemy c. 2600–2500 B.C.E.
This well-preserved example of inlay technique is from the "Standard of Ur" found in the "Royal Tombs" at Ur.
Source: Source: Courtesy of the Trustees of the British Museum, London.

struts nailed across them. They had metal rims, sometimes with studs to provide traction. The two-wheeled chariots carried only one warrior, but the larger four-wheeled vehicles had room for a driver and a warrior (see Figure 2.6). The larger chariots were also equipped with a quiver of javelins. Because they did not have strong, fast animals to pull them, even the two-wheeled chariots were relatively slow, cumbersome, and probably difficult to steer. Nevertheless, they were faster than a man on foot and helped to give Mesopotamian armies a decided advantage in battle against outsiders.

URBANIZATION IN OTHER AREAS OF WESTERN ASIA (c. 3300–2300 B.C.E.)

Early Bronze Age Syria and Palestine

The inhabitants of the Syria-Palestine region were probably mostly Semitic from at least 3000 B.C.E. The ancestral tongue for the Semitic language family seems to have originated in southern Syria and developed into subfamilies (West Semitic, East Semitic, South Semitic), each containing one or more different languages (such as Canaanite, Akkadian, and Arabic), as its speakers moved to different parts of western Asia. Akkadian, the language of the Semites who first settled in Mesopotamia, is East Semitic, but the seminomads who lived just west of the Euphrates River (in what is now western Iraq) spoke a West Semitic language. The Akkadians called these people Amurrum (later Amurru). Today the Amurru are commonly referred to as **Amorites**, since that is the name used for them in English translations of the Bible. The people of the Levant around 3000 B.C.E. also seem to have spoken a Semitic language based on a few fragmentary place names mentioned in Egyptian Old Kingdom documents. However, it is not known if this early Semitic tongue was a direct ancestor of the Canaanite language spoken in the Levant in later times.

Palestine and Syria form a natural corridor between northern Egypt and Mesopotamia. Over Levantine roads passed almost all trade and other contacts between the early cultures of the Nile and Tigris-Euphrates valleys. Mesopotamians and Egyptians were also interested in the Levant's natural resources, especially timber from the hills of Lebanon and Syria. Largely due to contacts with the developing river-valley civilizations, the peoples of Syria and Palestine began to develop their own urban culture just before 3000 B.C.E. This initial period of urbanization in the Levant is known as the Early Bronze (EB) Age, and it has three flourishing phases: EB I (c. 3300 to 3000 B.C.E.)°, EB II (c. 3000 to 2700 B.C.E.), and EB III (c. 2700 to 2200 B.C.E.). A fourth phase, EB IV (c. 2200 to 2000 B.C.E.), witnessed the collapse of urban life in Palestine and parts of Syria and will be discussed in Chapter 3.

Some elements of the early EB I or "proto-urban" culture continued from the earlier Neolithic cultures, but many new features (mainly different pottery styles) also emerged. Archaeologists disagree about whether the different regional cultural traditions that developed were created by the native population or introduced by new groups infiltrating into the land. The most important change during this period was in the economy, and this almost certainly was due to outside influences (though not necessarily to the immigration of new people). Previously, the people of the Levant had been seminomadic pastoralists or village-based farmers dependent on rainfall alone. Now they gradually began adopting an urban lifestyle dependent upon more productive irrigation-based agriculture and increased trade. While some earlier sites such as Jericho continued to be occupied, many were abandoned and new, larger towns were created near rivers or streams that provided irrigation and drinking water. Where there were no perennial streams (such as at Arad in the Palestinian Negev), residents constructed large reservoirs to collect and store the run-off from winter rains.

By about 3000 B.C.E., there were many cities throughout the Levant, making the EB II and III Periods a thriving urban era. These cities had various public structures such as temples, administrative buildings, palaces, and granaries in addition to private houses. Strong defensive walls surrounded each city, yet most of the walls and cities were destroyed several times during the EB II and III Periods. Some of these destructions (especially those in southern Palestine) were probably caused by Egyptian invasions mentioned in Old Kingdom texts, but others must have been due to internecine strife. This evidence of conflict indicates that, as in Mesopotamia, the cities of Syria and Palestine probably were independent city-states controlling the land and small villages around them.

Egypt doesn't seem to have wielded political control over Palestine and coastal Syria, but it does seem to have dominated trade and to have had a strong cultural influence over those areas. The main Palestinian trade products were wine and olive oil, while timber was the primary commodity sought from Byblos and other Syrian coastal cities. During the Egyptian Fifth Dynasty, Egyptians began traveling to Byblos almost exclusively by sea, thus bypassing the Palestinian EB III cities and reducing their prosperity.

Palestinian cities were generally smaller than Syrian ones such as Ugarit, Byblos, Alalakh, Emar, Ebla, and Hama (see Map 2.2). These Syrian cities seem to have been more directly influenced by Egypt and/or Mesopotamia than were those in Palestine. Despite this influence and the likelihood that the Early Bronze city-states had urban institutions that required written records, until relatively recently, archaeologists had found little evidence of local writing at Syro-Palestinian EB sites. That situation changed dramatically in 1974 during excavations at Tell Mardikh (ancient Ebla) in Syria. In the ruins of Ebla's royal palace (destroyed around 2250 B.C.E.), excavators found more than 1,700 complete or nearly complete cuneiform clay tablets, almost 5,000 fragmentary ones with substantial amounts of text, and many thousands of small pieces containing only a few lines or less.

We now know that the village that became Ebla was founded around 3500 B.C.E. It developed into a city by about 2700 B.C.E. and into a large, powerful city-state by about 2500 B.C.E. It seems to have controlled a large territory stretching eastward from the Orontes River to the borders of Emar on the Euphrates, and from the foothills of the Amanus and

---

°Some archaeologists previously divided the period we are calling EB I into two periods, Proto-Urban (c. 3300 to 3100 B.C.E.) and EB I (c. 3100 to 3000 B.C.E.).

Taurus Mountains in the north to the territory of Hama on the south. For a time, its influence even extended into northern Mesopotamia, for Ebla conquered Mari around 2400 B.C.E. and developed friendly relations (and probably an alliance) with Hamazi (northeast of Mesopotamia).

The Ebla tablets mention scribes at Kish in south-central Mesopotamia, Mari on the western border of Mesopotamia, and Emar, a Syrian city almost due east of Ebla. Not only was a portion of the population in Ebla and Emar literate, but these city-states also seem to have had scribal schools like those of Mesopotamian cities. Many of the Ebla tablets were written in Sumerian and others in Akkadian, like contemporary Mesopotamian documents. However, a third group of Ebla texts turned out to be written in the city's native language, an archaic Semitic tongue now called Eblaite. These documents used so many Sumerian ideograms for words or ideas (as much as 80 to 90 percent of the signs in economic tablets) that the Semitic nature of the texts was not immediately apparent. However, the syllabic writing of some words and the syntax of sentences showed that the language of the texts was Semitic. There is still much scholarly debate about Eblaite's relationship to other Semitic languages. Some linguists have concluded that Eblaite is a form of Old Canaanite or Amorite (both of which are West Semitic languages), while others argue that it is more closely related to East Semitic Akkadian. This debate will undoubtedly be resolved when more of the syllabic texts from Ebla are published. But in the meantime, the Ebla archive supports the evidence from Egyptian texts that the population of the Levant during the Early Bronze Age spoke a Semitic language. The Ebla tablets also show that the cities of the Levant, or at least the Syrian portion of it, had assimilated the elements of civilization much more thoroughly than was previously believed.

Early Bronze Age Anatolia and Iran

Much of Anatolia seems to have became fairly densely populated during the Early Bronze Age. Many towns and at least a few cities developed during this era,

especially during the flourishing era designated EB II in Anatolia (c. 2600 to 2300/2200 B.C.E.). However, not enough Early Bronze sites and levels have been excavated to determine the full extent of Anatolia's early urbanization. Sites where archaeologists have uncovered important EB deposits include Troy (Hissarlik), Beycesultan, Alaca Hüyük, Alishar, Kanesh (Kültepe), Tarsus, Gedikli, and Zincirli. Most of the excavated sites exhibit strongly fortified citadels, occasional destructions and restorations, and regional cultural variations. These features suggest that, as in contemporary Mesopotamia, Syria and Palestine, Early Bronze Anatolia was a land of small, independent city-state kingdoms. However, these cities were smaller and probably less complex than those of Syria and Mesopotamia. So far, they have revealed no knowledge of writing.

The prosperity of Anatolia's petty states was largely dependent upon exploitation of the region's wealth of metallic ores. Anatolia's mountains contained an abundance of iron (which could not yet be fully utilized), also copper and silver, and some lead. As metallurgical knowledge spread during the Early Bronze Age, Anatolia became one of the principal suppliers of metals and metal products to the rest of the Near East. The objects from several "treasures" uncovered by archaeologists have revealed the EB Anatolians' skill in casting and beating metal. The so-called "Treasure of Priam" and materials from burials at Troy in Anatolia's northwestern corner included bronze axes, daggers, chisels, saws, nails, earrings, pins, rings, and bowls, as well as silver and gold jewelry and vases. The "Dorak Treasure," supposedly from another group of tombs in the Troad, contained similar objects, some of even higher craftsmanship than those found at Troy, but its authenticity is disputed. Thirteen "Royal Tombs" at Alaca Hüyük yielded bronze stags inlaid with silver, elaborate bronze open grillwork ornaments (called "standards" for lack of a better word), weapons (including a dagger with an iron blade), and golden figurines, jugs, cups, and jewelry (pins, bracelets, and a filigree diadem with a ribbon tassel, also of gold).

There was trade and probably some sharing of ideas between western Anatolia (especially Troy) and the developing towns and small cities of Greece and the Aegean islands during the Early Bronze era. Merchants in Anatolia and the Aegean probably traded grain, wine, cloth, and other perishable materials in addition to the metal weapons, jewelry, marble idols or figurines, and pottery vessels that archaeologists can document. The pottery wheel was also introduced into Greece from the Near East during this period. Most of the trade between Greece and Asia Minor seems to have moved along maritime routes through the Aegean Sea, for ships with 20 to 35 oars on a side are frequently depicted on Greek and Cycladic pottery vessels. Unfortunately, the increase in trade and prosperity probably also led to the growth of piracy in the Aegean region. Inland Greek towns were usually not fortified, but coastal sites generally found it necessary to protect themselves with defensive walls. Archaeologists have uncovered Early Bronze fortifications at Poliochni on Lemnos, Thermi on Lesbos, Emporio on Chios, Chalandriani on Syros, Phylakopi on Melos, Aegina in the Saronic Gulf, Askitario on the east coast of Attica, and Lerna on the Bay of Nauplion in the Peloponnesus. Despite their walls, some of these towns were destroyed more than once during the third millennium.

Products and ideas also moved along trade routes through Iran and the Persian Gulf. Elam, of course, had been urbanized as early as Mesopotamia. The Proto-Elamite expansion just before 3000 B.C.E. led to the establishment of several towns or small cities on the Iranian plateau. Some of these sites such as Tepe Yahya, Shahdad, and Shar-i Sokhta continued to grow during the Early Dynastic Period and exhibit ongoing Mesopotamian influences. Much of Iran, though, remained nonurbanized, populated by semi-nomadic peoples.Though small in number, Iranian towns on the plateau became important intermediaries between Mesopotamia and two new civilizations beyond the eastern and northeastern borders of the Near East. The Indus (or Harappan) civilization developed along and near the Indus River and its tributaries in what is now Pakistan and northwestern India. The Central Asian Oxus civilization, unknown until the 1970s, emerged in southeastern Turk-

menistan and Uzbekistan (former Soviet Republics) just north of Afghanistan. These two civilizations seem to have arisen independently c. 2500 to 2300 B.C.E., though their knowledge of agriculture was probably derived indirectly from Mesopotamia. It's possible that these cultures also received other stimuli from Mesopotamia through their contacts with Iranian towns such as Shar-i Sokhta and Tepe Yahya, but they did not borrow or copy Mesopotamian institutions. They developed their own unique patterns of urbanization rooted in their quite different social and economic systems. Both of these civilizations reached their zeniths between c. 2200 and 1700 B.C.E., so they will be discussed in more detail in Chapter 3.

SUGGESTIONS FOR FURTHER READING AND INFORMATION

Internet Sites

Information on Mesopotamia (Sumer, Babylon, Assyria) from the British Museum: http://www.mesopotamia. co.uk/menu.html

Kings of Mesopotamian cities: http://www.mpiwg-berlin. mpg.de/Yearnames/yearnames.html

Books and Articles
General Works on Ancient Mesopotamia and Elam

Black, Jeremy, and Anthony Green. *Gods, Demons and Symbols of Ancient Mesopotamia: An Illustrated Dictionary.* London: British Museum Press, 1992.

Bottéro, Jean. *Mesopotamia: Writing, Reasoning, and the Gods.* Translated by Zainab Bahrani and Marc van de Mieroop. Chicago: University of Chicago Press, 1992.

Carter, Elizabeth, and M. W. Stolper. *Elam, Surveys of Political History and Archaeology.* Berkeley: University of California Press, 1984.

Collon, Dominique. *First Impressions: Cylinder Seals in the Ancient Near East*, 2nd ed. London: British Museum Press, 1993.

Dalley, Stephanie. *Myths from Mesopotamia: Creation, the Flood, Gilgamesh, and Others.* New York: Oxford University Press, 1991.

Foster, Benjamin R. *Before the Muses: An Anthology of Akkadian Literature*. 2nd ed. 2 vols. Bethesda, MD: CDL Press, 1996.

———. *From Distant Days: Myths, Tales, and Poetry of Ancient Mesopotamia*. Bethesda, MD: CDL Press, 1995.

Hinz, Walther. *The Lost World of Elam: Re-creation of a Vanished Civilization*. Translated by Jennifer Barnes. New York: New York University Press, 1973.

Jacobsen, Thorkild. *The Treasures of Darkness: A History of Mesopotamian Religion*. New Haven, CT: Yale University Press, 1976.

Lloyd, Seton. *The Archaeology of Mesopotamia*. Rev. ed. New York: Thames and Hudson, 1984.

McCall, Henrietta. *Mesopotamian Myths*. Austin: University of Texas Press, 1990.

Moortgat, Anton. *The Art of Ancient Mesopotamia: The Classical Art of the Near East*. Translated by Judith Filson. London: Phaidon, 1969.

Oates, Joan. *Babylon*. Rev. ed. London: Thames and Hudson, 1986.

Oppenheim, A. Leo. *Letters from Mesopotamia: Official, Business, and Private Letters on Clay Tablets from Two Millennia*. Chicago: University of Chicago Press, 1967.

Pollock, Susan. *Ancient Mesopotamia*. Cambridge: Cambridge University Press, 1999.

Reade, Julian. *Mesopotamia*. London: British Museum Press and Cambridge, MA: Harvard University Press, 1991.

Roaf, Michael. *Cultural Atlas of Mesopotamia and the Ancient Near East*. New York: Facts on File, 1990.

Roth, Martha T. *Law Collections from Mesopotamia and Asia Minor*. 2nd ed. Atlanta: Scholars Press, 1997.

Roux, Georges. *Ancient Iraq*. 3rd ed. New York: Penguin, 1992.

Saggs, H. W. F. *Babylonians*. Norman: University of Oklahoma Press, 1995.

———. *The Greatness That Was Babylon: A Survey of the Ancient Civilizations of the Tigris-Euphrates Valley*. Rev. ed. London: Sidgwick and Jackson, 1988.

Van De Mieroop, Marc. *The Ancient Mesopotamian City*. London and New York: Oxford University Press, 1999.

Works on Early Western Asia (c. 4000–2300 B.C.E.)

Adams, Robert McC. *Heartland of Cities*. Chicago: Aldine, 1981.

Algaze, Guillermo. *The Uruk World System: The Dynamics of Expansion of Early Mesopotamian Civilization*. Chicago: University of Chicago Press, 1993.

Bermant, Chaim, and Michael Weitzman. *Ebla: A Revelation in Archaeology*. New York: Times Books, 1979.

Crawford, Harriet. *Sumer and the Sumerians*. Cambridge: Cambridge University Press, 1991.

Kramer, Samuel Noah. *History Begins at Sumer: Thirty-nine Firsts in Recorded History*. 3rd ed. Philadelphia: University of Pennsylvania Press, 1998.

———. *Sumerian Mythology: A Study of Spiritual and Literary Achievement in the Third Millennium B.C.* Rev. ed. Philadelphia: University of Pennsylvania Press, 1998.

Matthiae, Paolo. *Ebla: An Empire Rediscovered*. Translated by Christopher Holme. London: Hodder and Stoughton, 1980.

Moorey, P. R. S. *Ur "of the Chaldees": A Revised and Updated Edition of Sir Leonard Woolley's Excavations at Ur*. Ithaca, NY: Cornell University Press, 1982.

Pettinato, Giovanni. *Ebla: A New Look at History*. Translated by C. Faith Richardson. Baltimore: Johns Hopkins University Press, 1991.

Postgate, Nicholas, and J. N. Postgate. *Early Mesopotamia: Society and Economy at the Dawn of History*. London: Routledge, 1994.

Potts, Timothy. *Mesopotamia and the East: An Archaeological and Historical Study of Foreign Relations ca. 3400–2000 B.C.* Oxford: Oxford University Committee for Archaeology, 1994.

Richard, Suzanne. "The Early Bronze Age: The Rise and Collapse of Urbanism." *Biblical Archaeologist*. Vol. 50, No. 1 (March 1987), pp. 22–43.

Schmandt-Besserat, Denise. *How Writing Came About*. Austin: University of Texas Press, 1996.

Walker, C. B. F. *Cuneiform*. London: British Museum Press, 1987.

Woolley, Sir Leonard. *Excavations at Ur*. New York: Apollo Books, 1965.

Yakar, J. *The Later Prehistory of Anatolia: The Late Chalcolithic and Early Bronze Age*. Oxford: Oxford University Press, 1985.

NOTES

1. G. M. Lees and N. L. Falcon, "The Geographical History of the Mesopotamian Plains," *Geographical Journal*, vol. 118 (1952), pp. 24–39.

2. Hans J. Nissen, *The Early History of the Ancient Near East, 9000–2000 B.C.* (Chicago: University of Chicago Press, 1988), pp. 55–56. Nissen's views, accepted here, are based on W. Nützel, "The Climatic Changes of Mesopotamia and Bordering Areas," *Sumer*, vol. 32 (1976), pp. 11–24.

3. Robert McC. Adams and Hans Nissen, *The Uruk Countryside* (Chicago: University of Chicago Press, 1972), p. 18.

4. Nissen (1988)., pp. 83–85.

5. Guillermo Algaze, "The Uruk Expansion: Cross-Cultural Exchange as a Factor in Early Mesopotamian Civilization," *Current Anthropology*, vol. 30, no. 5 (1989), pp. 571–608, and *The Uruk World System: The Dynamics of Expansion of Early Mesopotamian Civilization* (Chicago: University of Chicago Press, 1993), especially pp. 2–5. (However, see pp. 9–10 where he also recognizes formal imperial domination as the reason for at least some of the Uruk colonies).

6. C. C. Lamberg-Karlovsky and Jeremy A. Sabloff, *Ancient Civilizations: The Near East and Mesoamerica*, 2nd ed. (Prospect Heights, IL: Waveland Press, 1995), pp. 150–151.

7. For further information on the development of writing from the Near Eastern token system, see Denise Schmandt-Besserat, "The Earliest Precursor of Writing," *Scientific American*, vol. 238, no. 6 (June, 1978), pp. 50–59, and *Before Writing* (Austin: University of Texas Press, 1992).

8. C. B. F. Walker, "Cuneiform," *Reading the Past: Ancient Writing from Cuneiform to the Alphabet* (New York: Barnes and Noble, 1998), p. 19. Walker's section of this book was originally published as a separate work: *Cuneiform* (London: The British Museum Press, 1987).

9. For a description and criticism of the reasons that have been advanced for changes in the signs' orientation and the direction of writing, see Walker, *Reading the Past*, p. 24.

10. See, for example, Tom B. Jones, ed., *The Sumerian Problem* (New York: Wiley, 1969); Samuel Noah Kramer, *The Sumerians: Their History, Culture and Character* (Chicago: University of Chicago Press, 1963), pp. 40–43; and William W. Hallo and William Kelly Simpson, *The Ancient Near East: A History*, 2nd ed. (Fort Worth: Harcourt Brace College Publishers, 1998), pp. 19–23. William F. Albright disputes the assertion that the early place names are not Sumerian in "The Evidence of Language" in I. E. S. Edwards, et al., eds., *The Cambridge Ancient History*, 3rd ed. (Cambridge: Cambridge University Press, 1971), vol. 1, part 1, pp. 145–152.

11. See, for example, Albright in Edwards, et al., eds., *The Cambridge Ancient History*, 3rd ed., especially p. 151; Joan Oates, *Babylon*, rev. ed. (London: Thames and Hudson, 1986), pp. 20–22; and Georges Roux, *Ancient Iraq*, 3rd ed. (New York: Penguin Books, 1992), pp. 80–84.

12. Jerrold S. Cooper, "Sumer, Sumerians" in David Noel Freedman, editor-in-chief, *The Anchor Bible Dictionary* (New York: Doubleday, 1992), vol. 6, p. 233. See also M. Gibson, "By Stage and Cycle to Sumer" in D. Schmandt-Besserat, ed., *The Legacy of Sumer* (Malibu: Undena Publications 1976), pp. 51–58, and Oates, *Babylon*, pp. 20–22.

13. Daniel C. Snell, *Life in the Ancient Near East, 3100–332 B.C.E.* (New Haven and London: Yale University Press, 1997), p.19. See also K. Kamp and N. Yoffee, "Ethnicity in Ancient Western Asia during the Early Second Millennium B.C.: Archaeological Assessments of Ethnoarchaeological Perspectives," *Bulletin of the American Schools of Oriental Research*, no. 237 (1980), pp. 85–104.

14. Amélie Kuhrt, *The Ancient Near East c. 3000–330 BC.* (London: Routledge, 1995), vol. I, p. 45.

15. H. W. F. Saggs, *Babylonians* (Norman: University of Oklahoma Press, 1995), p. 32.

16. This selection is taken from A. Leo Oppenheim's translation in James B. Pritchard, ed., *Ancient Near Eastern Texts Relating to the Old Testament*, 2nd ed. (Princeton, NJ: Princeton University Press, 1955), pp. 265–266. The material in parentheses and square brackets is part of Oppenheim's translation. However, in the words SHU-PESH, "sh" has been substituted for the linguistic symbol "s" with a small "v" on top which Oppenheim and other Assyriologists use to represent the sign pronounced like English "sh."

17. Kramer (1963), pp. 79–83.

18. Woolley found an inscription of Mesannepadda, first king of Ur's First Dynasty according to the *King List*, in debris above the "Royal Tombs." If the stratigraphy of these deposits was interpreted correctly, it would seem to contradict a suggestion drawn from the Tummal Text that Mesannepadda was a contemporary of Enmebaragesi and an older contemporary of Gilgamesh. Enmebaragesi clearly belongs to the mid-ED II Period. Kramer (1963), p. 50, questions the stratigraphic evidence and maintains the possibility that the First Dynasty of Ur was *earlier* than the "Royal Tombs."

19. This suggestion is made by P. R. S. Moorey, *Ur "of the Chaldees": A Revised and Updated Edition of Sir Leonard Woolley's Excavations at Ur* (Ithaca, NY: Cornell University Press, 1982), pp. 93–94. See also Moorey's "What Do We Know About the People Buried in the Royal Cemetery?" *Expedition*, vol. 20 (1977–1978), pp. 24–40. For information on the later multiple burials at Ur, see Moorey (1982), pp. 131–132.

For a more recent discussion of the nature of the "Royal Tombs" at Ur, see S. Pollock, "Of Priestesses, Princes and Poor Relations: The Dead in the Royal Cemetery of Ur," *Cambridge Archaeological Journal*, vol. 1 (1991), pp. 171–189.

20. Kramer (1963), p. 225.
21. Ibid., p. 225.
22. Ibid., p. 226
23. In the Babylonian account, Marduk, god of Babylon, is called "the Enlil of the gods," suggesting that Enlil was the hero in the original version of the story.
24. In the Bible, as in Canaanite mythology, the evil sea monster is known by a variety of names: Yam ("Sea"), Rahab ("the Raging One?"), Leviathan (or Lothan), Tannin ("the Serpent" or "Dragon"), and Tehom ("the Primeval Sea"). Allusions to the battle between God and this monster can be found in Psalms 74:13–17 and 89:9–12 (10–13 in Hebrew); Isaiah 27:1, and 51:9–10, 12–13; and in Job 3:8; 7:12; 9:13; 26:12–13; and 40:25 in addition to Genesis 1.
25. See, for example, Sir Leonard Woolley, *Excavations at Ur* (New York: Apollo Books, 1965), pp. 27–36.
26. John Bright, "Has Archaeology Found Evidence of the Flood?" *Biblical Archaeologist*, vol. 5, no. 4 (December 1942), pp. 55–62. See also Moorey (1982), pp. 34–35.

27. See William Ryan and Walter Pitman, *Noah's Flood: The New Scientific Discoveries About the Event That Changed History* (New York: Simon & Schuster, 1999).
28. This idea was first developed by Thorkild Jacobsen in "Primitive Democracy in Ancient Mesopotamia," *Journal of Near Eastern Studies*, vol. 11 (1943), pp 159–172. This article and another, "Early Political Developments in Mesopotamia" *Zeitschrift für Assyriologie*, vol. 52 (1957), pp. 91–140, were reprinted in Thorkild Jacobsen, *Toward the Image of Tammuz and Other Essays on Mesopotamian History and Culture*, edited by William L. Moran (Cambridge, MA: Harvard University Press, 1970), pp. 157–170 and 132–156. For recent treatments of this theory, see Piotr Steinkeller, "On Rulers, Priests and Sacred Marriage: Tracing the Evolution of Early Sumerian Kingship," in Kazuko Watanabe, ed., *Priests and Officials in the Ancient Near East: Papers of the Second Colloquium on the Ancient Near East—The City and Its Life* (Heidelberg: C. Winter, 1999), pp. 103–137, and Jacob Klein, "The Birth of Kingship: From Democracy to Monarchy in Sumer," *Archaeology Odyssey*, vol. 4, no. 1 (January/February 2001), pp. 17–25.
29. Oates (1986), p. 28.
30. Kramer (1963), pp. 78, and 250–257. The quote comes from p. 255.

3

The First Mesopotamian Empires

THE AKKADIAN EMPIRE (c. 2334–2193 B.C.E.)

Sargon of Agade (c. 2334–2279 B.C.E.)

A new era for Mesopotamia began with the victories of an Akkadian-speaking king whose birth name is unknown. We know him as Sargon, but he almost certainly was not originally called "the legitimate (or true) king," which is what Sargon (*Sharrum-kên* in Old Akkadian) means. He probably was a commoner who seized the throne, but we know little about his origins or rise to power, even though they became the subject of later folk stories and legends. According to one late account, Sargon's mother was an *entum* (a high cultic functionary, probably a high priestess). He didn't know his father (see Document 3.1). This passage has often been interpreted as insinuating that Sargon was illegitimate. However, its purpose may have been to establish his noble birth, since only a woman from a highly placed family would have been made a high priestess. An *entum* seems to have been the cultic "bride" of the god she served, so possibly this text is implying that Sargon's father was divine (though it states that the father's brothers lived in the mountains). Other traditions from the early part of the second millennium B.C.E. may be closer to the truth. They indicate that Sargon's father was a date grower and make no claim that his mother was a high-born priestess. There is probably some validity also in the claim that Sargon rose to the position of cup-bearer (**vizier**) of Urzababa, King of Kish, but revolted against his master and became king in his place. However, the *Sumerian King List* names five people who supposedly ruled Kish after Urzababa. It's likely though, that those last five members of Urzababa's dynasty were only vassal rulers under either Lugalzagesi of Umma or Sargon. All that is fairly certain is that Urzababa, Lugalzagesi, and Sargon were all contemporaries.

Surviving inscriptions from this time (or Old Babylonian copies of them) show that Lugalzagesi claimed hegemony over all of Mesopotamia, that Sargon defeated Lugalzagesi, and that Sargon had to restore Kish and return it to its population. So, it is likely that Lugalzagesi gained control of Kish for a time, destroying or damaging the city in the process. It is not known, though, whether during Lugalzagesi's ascendency Sargon was master of Kish and/or already ruling Agade. All we know is that Lugalzagesi was the

DOCUMENT 3.1
The Birth Legend of Sargon

The earliest text of this legend about the birth and upbringing of Sargon of Agade was found on an eighth-century Assyrian tablet.[1] It employs the popular folkloric theme of the hero who assumes his proper role of leadership only after being abandoned in a floating basket, saved, and raised by a stranger. Similar stories are told about Moses, Romulus and Remus, and Krishna.

> I am Sargon the great king, king of Agade.
> My mother was a high priestess, I did not know my father.
> My father's brothers dwell in the uplands.
> My city is Azupiranu, which lies on Euphrates bank.
> My mother, the high priestess, conceived me, she bore me in secret.
> She placed me in a reed basket, she sealed my hatch with pitch.
> She left me to the river, whence I could not come up.
> The river carried me off, it brought me to Aqqi, drawer of water.
> Aqqi, drawer of water, brought me up as he dipped his bucket.
> Aqqi, drawer of water, raised me as his adopted son.
> Aqqi, drawer of water, set [me] to his orchard work.
> During my orchard work, Ishtar loved me,
> Fifty-five years I ruled as king.

major power in Mesopotamia, ruling Uruk as well as Umma, Lagash, Ur, and 50 other towns. Sargon opposed and defeated Lugalzagesi, captured him, and marched him in a yoke or neck-stock to Nippur where he presented him as a trophy to Enlil. Sargon then conquered Ur, Lagash, Umma, and the rest of southern Mesopotamia, and "washed his weapons in the sea" (the Persian Gulf). He "restored" Kish and claimed hegemony over Sumer.[2] Was it at this point that he founded his capital city of Agade?° Or had he built this city earlier, before his struggle with Lugalzagesi? Unfortunately, neither the surviving inscriptions nor the later legends indicate exactly when Agade was established. Even its location is unknown, though it probably was in the neighborhood of Kish and Babylon.

Sargon consolidated his dominion over Sumer by replacing most of the rulers who had opposed him with governors who were citizens of Agade and probably Akkadian-speakers like himself. He also demolished the walls of all the southern cities to prevent rebellions. Furthermore, he installed his daughter Enheduanna as *entum* of the moon god Nanna in Ur and of An, the god of heaven, at Uruk. Enheduanna took her religious responsibilities seriously and maintained the Sumerian traditions. In fact, she is credited with composing a beautiful Sumerian hymn to Inanna and producing a collection of temple hymns. Her conscientious dedication to her religious roles may have reconciled some people to her father's rule, while her

---

°Agade was the Sumerian form of the city's name and was the one usually used in texts of this period. Akkadê, an alternate spelling of the name, became Akkad in the Bible which, in turn, is the source the of the term "Akkadian" for the Semitic language spoken by Sargon and his successors and for the era of his empire.

almost constant presence in either Ur or Uruk undoubtedly forced any disgruntled citizens of those cities to think twice before plotting revolt. However, the local priests and leaders of Ur seem to have regarded her appointment as an affront. Sometime after Sargon's death they drove her out of the city.

The chronology for Sargon's campaigns and conquests is not clear. But, it was probably after placing Sumer under his control that Sargon undertook a campaign in Elam. He defeated a coalition army led by the King of Awan and forced the rulers and governors of the area to become his vassals. Moreover, though Sargon selected an Elamite to be governor of the province, he made Akkadian Elam's official language. In addition, he chose Susa, a small city on the plain, rather than Awan, the old capital in the mountains, to be Elam's new administrative center. This change began Susa's rise to prominence.

Sargon also led his army up the Euphrates River, conquering several cities, including the important states of Mari and Ebla. He continued his march northwestward as far as "the Cedar Forest and the Silver Mountain" (probably the Amanus and Taurus ranges) and possibly advanced deeper into Anatolia as later legends claim. However, he doesn't seem to have established permanent control over the areas west of Ebla, nor is it likely that he sailed to Cyprus and Kaptara (Crete), or conquered the coastal areas of the entire Persian Gulf as later stories and **omens** declare. Nevertheless, Sargon secured the trade routes along the upper Euphrates River down which timber, silver, and other metals could move freely into southern Mesopotamia. During his reign, merchant ships from Dilmun, Magan, and Meluhha, cultures of the Persian Gulf and beyond, also unloaded their cargo at Agade's docks.

Many historians have assumed that Sargon also conquered northeastern Mesopotamia, and a magnificent bronze head of an Akkadian ruler found at Nineveh (see Figure 3.1) has often been thought to depict Sargon. However, none of Sargon's surviving inscriptions mention campaigns in this area, and archaeologists have found no direct evidence of his rule at Nineveh or Asshur. It's probable that the Assyrian region was not added to the empire until the time of

FIGURE 3.1   Bronze Head of an Akkadian King
This head possibly represents Sargon of Agade, but is more likely an image of Manishtusu or Naram-Sin. The inlaid eyes were gouged out in antiquity.
Source: Iraq Museum, Bagdad.
Photo: Hirmer Photoarchiv, Munich.

Sargon's son Manishtusu, so it is likely that either he or Sargon's grandson, Naram-Sin, is the king portrayed by the Nineveh bronze.

A late chronicle claims that near the end of Sargon's reign, many areas of his empire revolted against him. Considering the long history of independent city-states in Mesopotamia, such a revolt against a king who was elderly and possibly thought to be getting feeble is not unlikely. However, the old king seems to have been still vigorous enough to defeat the rebels and maintain control over his empire until his death (c. 2279 B.C.E.). He set the standard for later Mesopotamian rulers and certainly deserved the name history has bestowed upon him, Sargon the Great.

Sargon was succeeded by his son Rimush (c. 2278 to 2270 B.C.E.) who had to face new rebellions throughout Mesopotamia and Elam. Nevertheless, he suppressed the revolts and preserved the empire until he was assassinated by some of his own courtiers. His brother Manishtusu (who may have instigated the palace conspiracy responsible for Rimush's death) then became king (see Table 3.1). Manishtusu (c. 2269 to 2255 B.C.E.) probably added Assyria as well as Anshan and Sherihum (areas southeast of Susa) to the Akkadian Empire (see Map 3.1). According to a damaged inscription, he also seems to have taken a fleet down the Persian Gulf where he defeated a coalition of 32 kings and gained control over their country at the southern end of the Gulf and beyond, "up to the silver mines" (probably in what is now the United Arab Emirates and Oman). Despite these successes, problems persisted within the inner circles of the administration, and like his brother, Manishtusu probably was murdered in a palace conspiracy.

Divine Kingship

Manishtusu's son, Naram-Sin ("Beloved of Sin"), then ascended to the throne (see Table 3.1). He had a long and glorious reign (c. 2254 to 2218) which, like that of his grandfather Sargon, would inspire many later folk tales and legends. When he became king, though, he faced many problems. Ebla had become independent again sometime after Sargon's northwestern campaign, and a people known as the Hurrians had begun occupying the mountain regions of southern Anatolia and northern Syria. (This population movement will be discussed more fully later in this chapter.) The fierce Lullubi and Guti peoples in the northern Zagros mountains were also unfriendly. Thus, the trade routes through northern Syria to the Taurus Mountains and through the Zagros Mountains to northern Iran and Afghanistan were no longer safe. Inability to obtain silver, bronze, lapis lazuli, and other products from the northwest and northeast had likely been a major reason for Manishtusu's campaign down the Persian Gulf to the region of Magan (the United Arab Emirates and Oman), an area rich in metals and beautiful black diorite stone. So, Naram-Sin retraced his grandfather's march to the "Cedar Mountain," in the process recapturing Mari, destroying Ebla, and conquering Arman (probably Aleppo). He also campaigned against the Hurrians, marching into eastern Turkey where he erected a **stele** with an image of

TABLE 3.1

Chronology of the Akkadian Period and the Third Dynasty of Ur (all dates are B.C.E.)

Agade	Lagash	Uruk	Ur
Sargon (c. 2334–2279)		Lugalzagesi (c. 2340-2316)	
Rimush (c. 2278–2270)			
Manishtusu (c. 2269–2255)			
Naram-Sin (c. 2254–2218)			
Shar-kali-sharri (c. 2217–2193)			
Anarchy; Destruction by the Guti			
	Ur-Bawa (c. 2155–2142)		
	Gudea (c. 2141–2122)	Utuhegal (c. 2123–2113)	
	4 Rulers (c. 2121–2111)		
			Ur-Nammu (c. 2112–2095)
			Shulgi (c. 2094–2047)
			Amar-Sin (c. 2046–2038)
			Shu-Sin (c. 2037–2029)
			Ibbi-Sin (c. 2028–2004)

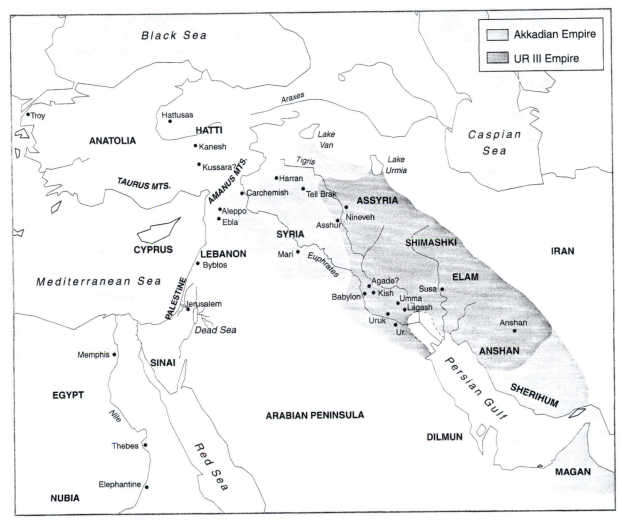

MAP 3.1   The Akkadian Empire at Its Greatest Extent (Under Naram-Sin) and the Empire of the Third Dynasty of Ur

himself near modern Diyarbakir. At Tell Brak on the Habur River, he constructed a fortress and left a garrison to guard the major roads connecting northern Mesopotamia with Anatolia and northern Syria. He then led punishing attacks on the Lullubi, celebrating his victory over them by erecting a sandstone stele that centuries later was carried off to Susa (see Figure 3.2). Finally, when the ruler of Magan revolted,

Naram-Sin rushed southward and captured the rebellious king. His extensive victories led him to adopt a more grandiose title than those used previously—"King of the Four Quarters," that is, ruler of the entire world to its outer limits.

At some point during his reign, Naram-Sin proclaimed himself a god. His inscriptions began writing his name with the determinative sign used to indicate

FIGURE 3.2   The Victory Stele of Naram-Sin

Source: Louvre, Paris.

Photo: Chuzeville/Réunion des Musées Nationaux/Art Resource, New York.

the names of deities, and the seals of his courtiers proclaim him "the god of Agade." The stele he erected to celebrate his victory over the Lullubi shows Naram-Sin wearing a horned helmet, a symbol of divinity in Mesopotamia (see Figure 3.2). However, since his helmet has only one set of horns, he is claiming to be

only a minor god. Major deities wore helmets with four sets of horns. Another new feature of this stele is the size of the king in relation to the other figures. In earlier carvings, kings were rendered on the same scale as their subjects or only slightly larger (see Figures 2.3 and 2.6 in Chapter 2), while gods were depicted much larger than the humans who served them. On Naram-Sin's stele, *he* is the major divine figure, towering over the defeated enemy and his own soldiers alike. The other gods have not been depicted in human form so that the size of Naram-Sin relative to that of the traditional gods is not an issue. The heavenly gods are shown only as two modest-sized stars (or possibly suns, since this stele was erected in the city of Utu, the sun god) shining down upon the king and observing his great victory.

The reason for Naram-Sin's establishment of divine kingship in Mesopotamia is not known. His action almost certainly went against long-standing tradition. If Mesopotamian kings had ever claimed divinity, they had ceased to do so several centuries before Naram-Sin's time. Early Dynastic III Sumerian rulers considered themselves only their city-gods' chosen stewards or viceroys, and not even the great Sargon had elevated himself to the rank of a god. Some scholars have argued that divinity was claimed only by those kings who became the bridegroom of the goddess during the Sacred Marriage ceremony.[3] Thus, the sign for "god" in front of Naram-Sin's name would be an honorary title, a reference to his assimilation with the god during magical religious rites, not an indication that he personally deserved worship. Others assert that Naram-Sin was stressing only his role as the embodiment of the guiding "genius" (or spirit) of his country and as the agent of its good fortune.[4] On the other hand, an inscription on a bronze statue found in northern Mesopotamia credits Naram-Sin's divinity to the citizens of Agade. It states that because of Naram-Sin's victories, the people begged the major gods to make him "the god of their city Agade and they built him a temple in the midst of Agade."[5] A temple and cult seems to imply more than just a role as "bridegroom" of the goddess or "guiding genius" of the land. Maybe by becoming Agade's city god, Naram-Sin was making a claim to all of its possessions, especially its land, since traditionally a city was believed to belong to its divine patron.[6] Perhaps he was trying to provide a common religious focus to unify the various parts of his empire and guarantee the obedience of his subjects.[7] Or, maybe he was justifying or legitimizing his appointment of governors in the old city-states, since city rulers were supposed to be chosen by the local city gods. Whatever Naram-Sin's intent was, however, his idea doesn't seem to have been successful. The institution of divine kingship did not bring unity to the Akkadian Empire, nor did it prevent revolts. Moreover, though the remaining Akkadian kings and most of the rulers of the Third Dynasty of Ur would claim divinity, the concept was not generally accepted by the Mesopotamian people. Most later Mesopotamian rulers reverted to the idea that the king was only a human agent of the gods, not a minor divinity in human form.

Administration of the Empire

Since the Akkadian Empire was the first in Mesopotamia to govern an extensive area for more than just a decade or two, later empires often copied its organization and administrative procedures. One of the precedents established by Sargon was the appointment of his daughter as high priestess of the moon god at Ur. Enheduanna held this position through her father's reign and those of her brothers until she was driven out of the city during a revolt. However, Naram-Sin established his daughter Enmenanna in the post, and in later times, it was regarded as a sinecure for the ruler's daughter. Another daughter of Naram-Sin became high priestess of Enlil at Nippur, a third was a priestess of the sun god at Sippar, and a granddaughter was a lamentation-singer of the moon god. Sargon's successors in the Akkadian Dynasty also followed his lead in appointing Akkadian-speaking family members and supporters as high priests, governors, or military commanders throughout the empire.

Probably the longest lasting and most significant change Sargon and his descendants introduced was the use of Akkadian as the official language of government and commerce. The Sumerian cuneiform script was adapted, possibly for the first time, to write Sargon's Semitic tongue. Scribes continued to use a mixture of **ideograms** and **phonograms** (phonetic signs) as before, but they often added phonetic signs behind ideograms to indicate inflected endings or other grammatical features. These signs show that the ideograms were being read as Akkadian words, not Sumerian ones. Also, by the time of Naram-Sin, scribes were using fewer ideograms, instead preferring to write Akkadian words with phonetic signs. Not only the language, but the clay tablets themselves changed. They became more rectangular and somewhat flatter than their Early Dynastic predecessors. Moreover, the tablets have a much more attractive appearance than in earlier times, for the signs are beautifully formed and placed carefully within ruled lines.

The Sumerian language continued to be used, especially for religious hymns and ceremonies, and scribes continued to study it. However, outside of the extreme southern portion of Mesopotamia, Sumerian probably had been spoken by only a small minority of the population. It was a very difficult language, and its earlier use for almost all written documents had not led others to adopt it as a spoken tongue. On the other hand, the use of Akkadian for governmental decrees and trade during the Akkadian Empire and the presence of Akkadian-speaking governors throughout the realm resulted in Akkadian becoming the common spoken language throughout most of Mesopotamia. Akkadian also became commonly used in Elam; even the Lullubi in the Zagros and the Hurrians in northern Mesopotamia and southeastern Anatolia began producing inscriptions in Akkadian.

Another innovation of the Akkadian Dynasty was the creation of a common system for dating events throughout the empire. Before this time, individual city-states had dated their records by reference to the names of eponymns, local officials chosen yearly for this purpose, or by the regnal years of city-rulers. The unification of Mesopotamia required that a single chronology be used. To this end, Sargon began naming each year after a significant event of the previous year. This system continued to be used by the Third Dynasty of Ur and Hammurabi's dynasty in Babylon.

Sargon and his successors enlarged their imperial armies by recruiting contingents from the tribes in the mountains or the desert fringes of Mesopotamia and by forcing the conquered cities to contribute men. The rulers also had dependents who owed them military service. An inscription mentions that 5,400 of these personal retainers ate daily in Sargon's presence. To provide estates for these and other supporters and to supply rations for the army, the Akkadian kings greatly increased the amount of land belonging to the crown. They acquired some of this land through their military campaigns, but much of it was purchased from the owners. And, since fields usually belonged to families rather than to individuals, land sales normally involved many people. The king paid all those who had any claim to the land and, as custom required, he distributed presents to these individuals at banquets that he provided. However, the price paid to the sellers, though based on computations of the amount of grain the land would yield, was usually little more than the value of one year's crop. Probably most of the sellers were impoverished farmers who had suffered reverses or lost many family members during the wars. They most likely were desperate, willing to take any offer. On the other hand, it's also possible that some, if not many, felt threatened by the king and were too frightened to resist. Like Mario Puzo's fictional "Godfather," the king may have "made them an offer they couldn't refuse." It should be noted, though, that the king usually provided maintenance (probably as soldiers or tenant farmers on the royal estates) for those displaced by his land acquisitions.

Land, of course, was not the only asset that Akkadian kings acquired. In addition to tribute and taxes from conquered states, the rulers of Agade were enriched by their monopoly over foreign trade. Trade routes were opened and secured by military action. The roads and river routes from Asia Minor and Iran and the seaways from Dilmun, Magan, and Meluhha carried precious materials that the Akkadian kings disbursed as lavish gifts to temples, important officials, and dependents. Moreover, state slaves provided the kings with additional wealth for redistribution. Tens of thousands of Mesopotamians and neighboring peo-

ples must have been killed in battles during the Akkadian Period, but many thousands more were captured and enslaved. These slaves were themselves a form of wealth the king could give to supporters or temple establishments. Most, however, were retained by the state and put to work in quarries or mines extracting stone or ores to be used for **stelae** and statues to glorify the king or to make products for later redistribution. The ruler's ability to create and dispose of these various forms of wealth obviously increased his power and enlarged his already paramount status.

The Empire's Collapse

Later accounts such as *The Curse of Agade* and *The Cuthean Legend of Naram-Sin* usually considered Naram-Sin the last king of Sargon's dynasty. They blamed the downfall of the Akkadian Empire on the gods' desire to punish his arrogance and misdeeds. Supposedly Enlil sent the Guti, a savage people from the mountains, to despoil the land and destroy Agade. Possibly Naram-Sin's institution of divine kingship led to these tales of his disdain for the gods. However, there is no archaeological indication that Naram-Sin destroyed Enlil's temple in Nippur as *The Curse of Agade* claimed. In fact, inscriptions show that he repaired Enlil's temple and sponsored other building projects in Nippur, as well. Moreover, the Guti do not seem to have moved into Mesopotamia until sometime during the reign of Naram-Sin's son, Shar-kali-sharri ("King of All Kings"). The empire survived, though at a reduced size, at least to Shar-kali-sharri's death.

Shar-kali-sharri reigned for 25 years (c. 2217 to 2193 B.C.E.). Unlike his predecessors, he was unable to quell all the rebellions and maintain the empire's size. Puzur-Inshushinak, the governor of Elam appointed by Naram-Sin, revolted against the new ruler, established himself as king of Elam, and restored his native Elamite tongue as the state language of Elam. There were revolts in northern Mesopotamia and Syria as well, and many sites in these regions were abandoned around 2200 B.C.E. Many former residents of the northern area seem to have moved to the south, putting increased pressure on the resources of the empire's heartland. There are also indications that the Guti were beginning to filter down into Mesopotamia from their mountain homeland. When Shar-kali-sharri was struck down in a palace revolt like those that had toppled Sargon's sons, the empire collapsed and anarchy reigned. The summation in the *Sumerian King List* ("Who was king? Who was not king?") described the situation succinctly.

As we have seen, later Mesopotamians generally credited the empire's demise to the Guti (aided by the gods), but these tribes had been easily held in check by Sargon and Naram-Sin. While their intrusion into Mesopotamia probably increased the chaos within the land, they seem to have taken advantage of the empire's decline rather than being the primary cause of its death. The Sumerian historiographic poem, *The Curse of Agade*, written a little more than a century after the destruction of the city, claims that famine, caused by the Guti invasion, also ravaged Mesopotamia. Archaeologist Harvey Weiss thinks that this tradition actually reversed the cause and effect. In 1993, during his excavations at Tell Leilan in Syria, Weiss uncovered what he believes is evidence that a century-long drought caused the end of the Akkadian Empire in Mesopotamia and of the contemporaneous Syrian cities.[8] A relatively abrupt change to much drier weather in the eastern Mediterranean, culminating in severe periods of drought from around 2200 to 2000–1900 B.C.E., would have most acutely affected the areas of the Near East where agriculture was dependent on rainfall. Drought might at least partially account for the frequent revolts against the Akkadian Empire. It would also explain the apparent movement of population from the dry farming area of northern Mesopotamia to the south where fields were irrigated by rivers and canals. Weiss thus joined an increasing number of scholars who recognize climatic change as a significant factor in the political and cultural changes that took place in the eastern Mediterranean from 2200 to 2000 B.C.E.

As we have seen in Chapter 2, the climate of the Near East seems to have become somewhat drier around 3700 B.C.E. Though there was less rainfall than during the previous era, evidence indicates that there was still more than at the present time. The urban civilizations of Egypt and Mesopotamia developed during this period of declining moisture, but they depended on irrigation from their rivers. However, as we have seen, urban culture also became widespread in dry farming areas of the Near East during the Early Bronze Age (c. 3100 to 2200 B.C.E.). In Palestine and Syria, large walled cities, often much larger than those of later times, flourished during EB II and III, and settlements even expanded into the Palestinian Negev and Sinai, areas that are now deserts. At the same time, urbanization spread across Asia Minor and Greece.

But all these areas suffered widespread destruction and decline near the end of the Early Bronze Age. Nearly all the Palestinian EB III towns and villages were destroyed around 2200 B.C.E. and lay abandoned for about two centuries. During the following EB IV era, urban civilization disappeared in Palestine, and only a few poor villages continued to exist. The size of the population dropped drastically, largely leaving the land to groups of pastoral seminomads.[9] Most of the towns in Asia Minor and Greece were also destroyed c. 2200 B.C.E., at the end of the period that in Anatolia is called Early Bronze II and in Greece, Early Helladic II. In the period following these destructions, there were only about one-fourth as many settlements in Anatolia as there had been in EB II.[10] The material culture in western and southern Anatolia also declined significantly. Though some areas recovered by c. 2000 B.C.E., others remained without settled population centuries longer. In Greece, the destruction was not universal, for several sites continued to exist without interruption into the Early Helladic III era. Nevertheless, according to M. I. Finley, the change at the end of EH II was "so massive and abrupt, so widely dispersed" that "nothing comparable was to happen until the end of the Bronze Age a thousand years later," while what followed "differed unmistakably in scale and quality."[11] Meanwhile, at the same time as these Near Eastern and Aegean destructions, the level of the Nile floods was extremely low, causing hardship and turmoil in Egypt and contributing to the collapse of the Old Kingdom.[12]

Several scholars suggested recently that impacts made by the remnants of a comet possibly caused climatic change at the end of the Near Eastern Early Bronze Age. Aerial photographs of southern Iraq revealed a two-mile-wide circular depression with the classic hallmarks of a meteor crater, including a ring-like ridge inside its outer edges. Around 2200 B.C.E., the area in question would have been covered by the northern end of the Persian Gulf or by shallow marshes. Since the sediments in that region were all deposited within the past six thousand years, this crater must have been produced within that time span. Moreover, soil samples from three regions of the Near East taken from levels dating from that time contained microscopic spheres of calcite material not found on Earth but commonly found in meteorites. Only one impact of the size indicated by the Iraqi depression probably would have affected only the southern portion of Mesopotamia and would have had no more than a temporary effect on weather patterns. On the other hand, if several large fragments hit other parts of the planet at the same time, their cumulative effect could have produced a climatic change, causing the drought that Weiss and others have postulated.[13] The depression will have to be carefully investigated to see if it is actually an impact crater and if so, whether it can be dated more exactly.

Caused by meteor impact or not, there seems to have been a relatively dry period in much of the Near East during the last phase of the Early Bronze Age and during the Egyptian First Intermediate Period (c. 2200 to 2000 B.C.E.). It is evidence of this dry period that Weiss feels he has uncovered at Tell Leilan. Moreover, segments of sediment cores from the sea bed of the Gulf of Oman radiocarbon-dated to about 2000 B.C.E. (+ 100 years) show two to six times more evidence of wind-borne Mesopotamian silt than segments from earlier or later times. This suggests that dry conditions around the end of the third millennium B.C.E. had turned parts of Mesopotamia into a dust bowl.[14]

Major migrations also probably took place during this time. In the past, many archaeologists argued that the people of EB IV Palestine were pastoral invaders, but today, most see them as remnants of the EB III population.[15] However, other movements are more certain. Hurrians began occupying the mountains of southeastern Anatolia and northern Syria, the Guti and Amorites invaded Mesopotamia, seminomads settled in the Delta area of Egypt, and probably Indo-European-speaking groups from Armenia and the Caucasus moved into Asia Minor and Greece. The revival of urbanism in much of the eastern Mediterranean area occurred only after 2000 to 1900 B.C.E., when moister weather seems to have returned.

Of course, not everyone agrees with the drought hypothesis.[16] Amihai Mazar notes that while urbanization ended in Palestine, it seems to have continued in the Transjordanian highlands east of the Dead Sea, an area that a weather change probably would have affected as much as Palestine. Also, archaeologists have found small Early Bronze IV settlements in the normally dry areas of the Palestinian Negev and northern Sinai.[17] On the other hand, these EB IV towns and settlements were located by perennial streams or springs which may have allowed their populations to survive and adapt to the changing conditions. And, as Arlene Rosen has pointed out, "failure to adapt to changing climatic conditions can be as much a social problem as a technological one."[18] She suggests that most of the Early Bronze Palestinian towns were probably unable to make the change from floodwater farming to canal irrigation farming, while some of the Transjordanian settlements, because of their locations, did manage to adapt and survive.

Even if climatic change was largely responsible for precipitating the end of Early Bronze urbanization in Palestine and parts of Syria and Asia Minor, it probably was not the sole reason for the collapse of the Akkadian Empire. Unlike the Early Dynastic Egyptians, early Mesopotamians never developed a sense of nationhood. They remained committed to their local patron deities and their city-states. Sargon and his successors conquered the entire region and created an empire, but it remained a collection of city-states and foreign provinces rather than a nation. It was held together by force rather than by a sense of cultural unity, national identity, and common destiny. Even though Mesopotamians accepted the concept that the gods intended that there be only *one* king over the entire world, almost every city-state ruler, supported by his citizens, thought *he* was the one the gods had selected! Thus, later Mesopotamian empires would experience the same problems that tore apart the Akkadian Empire: frequent internal revolts and external pressure from peoples living along Mesopotamia's borders. Strong kings could overcome these difficulties for a time, but sooner or later (usually within 100 to 200 years) the forces of destruction and decentralization would become more powerful than the ruler, causing decline and collapse. The Akkadian Empire survived for slightly more than 140 years. So, even without a drought, it is unlikely that it would have been able to endure much longer.

THE THIRD DYNASTY OF UR (c. 2112–2004 B.C.E.)

Ur's Rise to Power

The *Sumerian King List* ascribes dominance over southern Mesopotamia to a Gutian dynasty in the period after the fall of Agade. But in reality, after sacking Agade, the Guti seem to have controlled only Nippur and some of the territory north of it. Within a couple of decades, these "barbarians" and their kings (originally probably only chieftains) began assimilating the local culture and adopting Akkadian names. Meanwhile, Lagash, Uruk, and probably other city-states were governed by their own rulers. So, following a brief period of anarchy and chaos, the old system of local autonomy and independent city-states seems to have reestablished itself for almost a century.

The widely known and recognized Sumerian ruler Gudea (c. 2141 to 2122 B.C.E.) was an *ensi* of Lagash during this period (see Table 3.1). Many of his statues and inscriptions were found during late nineteenth- and early twentieth-century French excavations at Telloh, the site of Girsu, a religious center that was part of the city-state of Lagash (modern Al-Hiba). Gudea restored the temples of Lagash and Girsu and undertook at least one raid into Elam. However, his inscriptions provide little or no information on the political situation in Mesopotamia during the so-

called "Gutian" period. Mesopotamia must have been relatively peaceful, though, for Lagash seems to have been prosperous, and there is no mention of any military threats. In addition, the trade routes were open; Gudea imported materials for his buildings from most of the traditional sources, including Elam, the Gulf states, and Lebanon.

Nevertheless, many people still resented having the Guti living on Mesopotamian soil. About 2120 B.C.E., with the support of a few other Sumerian city-state leaders, Utuhegal, *ensi* of Uruk, attacked the remnants of the Guti. His propagandistic inscription claimed that he rid Mesopotamia of this "stinging serpent of the hills, who was the enemy of the gods" and who "filled Sumer with evil."[19] Utuhegal seems to have established hegemony over several other city-states, including Ur, where he installed a family member, Ur-Nammu, as governor. A few years later, Utuhegal seems to have accidentally drowned while fishing or building a dam, and Ur-Nammu proclaimed himself King of Ur.

Ur-Nammu's reign (c. 2112 to 2095) began the Third Dynasty of Ur, also known as the Ur III Period or the Sumerian Renaissance. He rebuilt the fortification walls and defeated the *ensi* of Lagash and other rulers who refused to acknowledge Ur's supremacy. In his fourth regnal year, he enlarged his title to King of Sumer and Akkad. The rapid growth of his power over southern Mesopotamia was probably due in large part to the foundation already established by Utuhegal. Ur-Nammu then seems to have extended his empire northward without much opposition, for many sites, including Asshur, had been destroyed during the latter part of the Akkadian Dynasty and had to be rebuilt. He made a treaty with Mari, cementing the alliance through a marriage of his son to the daughter of Mari's ruler, and brought southwestern Iran back under Mesopotamian control through campaigns in Anshan and Elam. He is best known, however, not as a military leader (even though Ur-Nammu means "Warrior of the Goddess Nammu"), but as a builder. He constructed temples at several cities, placing those at Ur, Eridu, Uruk, and Nippur upon massive solid brick platforms known as ziggurats (or ziqqurats). As we have seen in Chapter 2, Mesopotamian temples had been built on platforms since Ubaid times, and because of the practice of building new temples over the ruins of previous ones, by the Jemdet Nasr Period, these platforms had become quite high (see Figure 2.1). Under Ur-Nammu, the temple-platform attained its classic form as a ziggurat, a monumental stepped pyramid-like structure with several stages or levels. Ziggurats probably were intended to raise temples as close to heaven as possible so the gods would not have to come down so far to partake of their offerings or to meet their worshipers during major festivals. The base of Ur-Nammu's ziggurat for the temple of the moon god Nanna at Ur (see Figure 3.3) measured about 200 by 140 feet. With its temple on top, it probably stood more than 100 feet high.

Today, it is still about 65 feet high even though its temple, third stage, and about half of its second stage have eroded away.

The era of Gudea and the Third Dynasty of Ur has often been characterized as a Sumerian "renaissance" or revival, during which Sumerian rulers attempted to restore their Sumerian language and cultural heritage. This view, of course, assumes that a uniquely Sumerian culture had almost vanished during the time of the Akkadian Empire. It is true that during the Ur III Period, Sumerian again became the main language for administrative documents and that Sumerian literature flourished, but there is no indication that Sumerian "culture" needed to be revived or that the language became more widely spoken. It has already been stressed that there were no major

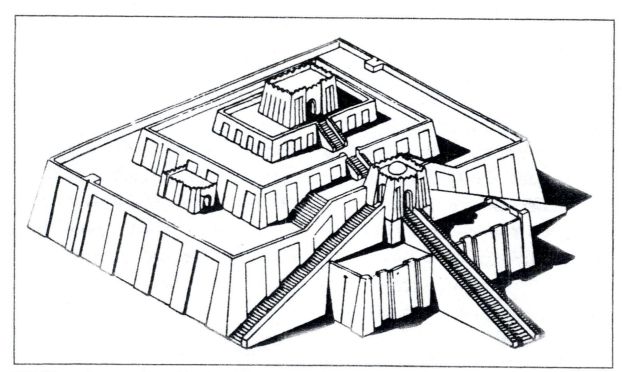

FIGURE 3.3   Reconstruction of the Ziggurat and Temple of Nanna, the Moon God, at Ur
This shows how the temple probably looked during the Third Dynasty of Ur.
Source: Courtesy of the Trustees of the British Museum, London.

cultural differences between Sumerians and Akkadians. There also is no evidence of hostility between Sumerian-speakers and Akkadian-speakers as stated or implied by some earlier historians. In fact, it is clear that the kings of the Third Dynasty of Ur hearkened back to the Akkadian Empire as the foundation and pattern for their own empire and their claims of divinity. Thus, while they established new cults for themselves, they also carefully maintained the worship of the divine Naram-Sin at Nippur. Moreover, except for Ur-Nammu and Shulgi, all of the kings, queens, and children of the "Sumerian" royal family at Ur had Akkadian names! They also gave Akkadian names to new towns they built, such as Puzrish-Dagan near Nippur. So, even the Ur III rulers may not have *spoken* Sumerian, which probably already had become essentially a dead language. The flowering of Sumerian literature during the Ur III era and the following Isin-Larsa period may be due to the schools' emphasis on Sumerian as a formal, exclusively written language used only by the educated class.

Shulgi's Reforms

Ur-Nammu died in battle and was succeeded by his son Shulgi (c. 2094 to 2047 B.C.E.) who completed his father's ziggurat and temple for Nanna at Ur. The first two decades of Shulgi's reign were peaceful, and he spent them building temples throughout Sumer and Akkad. At some point early in his reign he followed the precedent of Naram-Sin, taking the title "Ruler of the Four Quarters (of the earth)" and declaring himself a god. He introduced a new calendar with a month named "Divine Shulgi," and he decreed that throughout the empire priests were to make offerings to his statues twice a month. The priests of Ur and Nippur, at least, readily accepted Shulgi's divinity and eventually produced many hymns in his honor. He became known as a kind of "renaissance man," skilled in many fields from music and scholarship to hunting and warfare. In the second half of his reign, he supported the claims for his ability as a general through many military campaigns by which he extended his rule over the Zagros area of northwestern Iran (see

Map 3.1). To hold this area and keep the trade routes open, Shulgi constructed a string of garrison settlements in the mountains housing between 60,000 and 100,000 men. He also built roads with relay-houses a day's walk apart between the capital and the border districts to expedite the travel of messengers and, if necessary, to hasten the movement of troops to trouble spots. When he died after 48 years on the throne, Shulgi bequeathed a large, well-organized empire to his son and successor, Amar-Sin (see Table 3.1).

At about the same time that he began embarking on his military conquests, Shulgi reorganized the empire. He divided Sumer and Akkad into 23 districts and appointed an *ensi* (governor) for each. These governors were directly responsible to the king. Earlier beliefs that individual city-state rulers were appointed by and responsible to the local patron gods may explain why Shulgi (and his Akkadian predecessors?) claimed divinity and established cults for themselves throughout the land. As a precaution against revolt, governors were given no control over the troops garrisoned within their districts. Instead, each administrative area had one or more military commanders who answered directly to the king or his vizier. If a civil governor and military commander disagreed on policy, the issue would be settled in the courts or by the king himself. The northern and eastern parts of the empire were ruled by appointed military governors. Governors and other civil servants seem to have been transferred to new posts frequently, either because they had special skills that were needed in other problem areas or, more likely, to keep them from building a power base of local support in one place. A large contingent of royal messengers, utilizing the roads and relay-stations Shulgi constructed, kept the king informed about affairs throughout the empire. Royal inspectors periodically checked on the condition and government of the provinces.

Shulgi instituted two different kinds of taxation within the empire. The districts of Sumer and Akkad, the empire's heartland, each paid a monthly *bala* ("rotation") tax for the upkeep of the major temples, especially those of Nippur. This tax was paid with goods, since there was no currency yet. Military personnel in the peripheral areas paid a yearly tax called *gun ma-da* ("tax of the provinces") that usually consisted of animals. In addition to these revenues, tribute and booty were obtained from the conquered areas in the Zagros. Taxes and tribute were sent to regional centers where they were recorded and redistributed. Scholars are gradually learning more about this system from the thousands of economic tablets uncovered at Ur, Nippur, Girsu, Umma, and especially, Puzrish-Dagan. Shulgi built Puzrish-Dagan (modern Drehem) near Nippur to handle livestock accounting and redistribution for the region. Each year, tens of thousands of animals, paid as taxes or voluntarily contributed, came to this town from all parts of the empire. Bureaucrats then distributed them as offerings to various temples, "salary" to officials, or payments to the royal household, carefully recording in cuneiform ledgers every single arrival and departure. There were similar redistribution centers in other areas and for other commodities.

International trade was a royal monopoly, and the central government tightly controlled other aspects of the economy as well. Government-run factories employed thousands of workers (mostly women) producing leather, flour, beer, linseed oil, textiles, and other products. These commodities, along with agricultural surpluses, were traded for metals and other goods from outside the empire. Private property still existed, and there undoubtedly was a private sector of the economy as in earlier times. However, archaeologists have uncovered few private economic documents from this time, and the multitude of royal administrative texts that exist provide little insight into the "other" economy.

Shulgi also produced the earliest law code yet known, but unfortunately, it survives only in a poorly preserved later copy. This collection of laws used to be ascribed to Ur-Nammu, but a recently recognized fragment of the prologue makes it clear that Shulgi was its author. Like later Mesopotamian examples (most notably the *Code of Hammurabi*), this list of laws was not truly a legal "code." It was not an exhaustive compendium of laws, nor did courts refer to it when settling legal cases. In the Mesopotamian system of justice, judges reached their decisions by applying basic legal principles to the individual circumstances of the cases brought before them. Thus, Shulgi's "code" probably was a collection of royal edicts and court decisions that would exemplify the king's justice and illustrate the standards that should be applied throughout the empire.

Like Uruinimgina much earlier, Shulgi claimed that he prevented "grabbers" (bribe- and graft-seeking nobles and officials?) from taking citizens' oxen, sheep, and donkeys. He established a standardized system of weights and measures and protected the weak and powerless: "I did not deliver the orphan to the rich man, the widow to the mighty man, the man with one shekel to the man with one mina [60 shekels]."[20] Among the laws that survive are ones requiring that a divorced woman be compensated by her former husband—one mina of silver if she had been a virgin at the time of the marriage, and half a mina (30 shekels) if she had been previously married. Murder was punished by execution, but those who inflicted other injuries did not receive "an eye for an eye" punishment as in *The Code of Hammurabi* or the Bible. They paid monetary fines that varied with the severity of the offense.

The Fall of Ur

Shulgi's son Amar-Sin seems to have had a relatively uneventful reign of nine years (c. 2046 to 2038 B.C.E.). He died from the "bite" of shoe, probably infection that resulted from a cut or some other injury to his foot. His brother Shu-Sin then became king and also ruled for nine years (c. 2037–2029 B.C.E.). Early in his reign, Shu-Sin had to put down several revolts in the northern and northeastern areas of the empire. The biggest threat seems to have come in his third year, for his fourth year was named "year [when] the wall of Martu [called] *Muriq-Tidnum* ('keeping away Tidnum') was built." Martu was the Sumerian word for the area west of the Euphrates in what is now Syria. It also was used for the tribes of West Semitic seminomads that lived there. Tidnum and, more commonly, Amurru were Akkadian equivalents of Martu. The Amurru (or Amorites, as we call them) had made a serious raid into Mesopotamia, and though they were driven back, Shu-Sin was obviously shaken. So, he erected a fortified wall some 170 miles long, stretching from the Euphrates to the Tigris just north of Baghdad, to keep the Amorites out of southern Mesopotamia.

Shu-Sin's effort proved to be futile, for early in the reign of his son, Ibbi-Sin (c. 2028 to 2004 B.C.E.), groups of Amorites again attacked areas south of the wall. They were joined by the Elamites, who declared their independence and began raiding into Sumer. Ibbi-Sin fortified Ur and Nippur, but he couldn't prevent the raids, nor could he stop the slow disintegration of his empire. The conquered territories revolted and, one by one, the city-states of Sumer and Akkad decided to abandon the empire that could not protect them.

Just as with the end of the Akkadian Empire, several scholars have suggested that the invasions were only part of a much larger problem. After all, some Amorites had entered Mesopotamia earlier, settled, and become an important component of the Ur III state. Why then did large numbers of the seminomadic Amorites from the desert fringes invade Mesopotamia at the end of the second millennium, and why was the Ur III state unable to defeat them? One theory is that instead of causing the demise of the empire, the invaders merely "took advantage of the collapsing imperial structure" and just "made an already critical situation worse."[21] Moreover, the imperial structure was collapsing, some contend, because of continuing problems due to low water levels in the rivers. Studies of Persian Gulf sediments indicate that the stream flow of the Tigris and Euphrates was very low around 2100–2000 B.C.E. The drought that is thought to have contributed to the end of the Akkadian Empire probably had not abated by the beginning of the Third Dynasty of Ur. Even if rainfall had improved somewhat by then, the rivers still seem to have been low. Hans Nissen believes that the many Ur III irrigation works built in already-settled areas were necessary because the low water levels in the rivers reduced or negated the usefulness of earlier facilities.[22] If he is correct, it must have

required more effort and more careful bureaucratic oversight to produce the high agricultural yields of the Ur III era than would have been necessary in earlier times. Any damage to the agricultural system by enemy raids, bureaucratic mismanagement, or an inattentive ruler would result in food shortages. So, in addition to invasion, there may have been other causes for the skyrocketing increase in the price of grain to 60 times its normal rate during Ibbi-Sin's seventh and eighth years. The severe decline in grain production indicated by this inflation soon led to famine and economic collapse.

By the last years of Ibbi-Sin's reign, his kingdom consisted of no more than the city of Ur. Then the city itself fell to an onslaught by the Elamites and tribesmen from the region of Shimashki in the Zagros Mountains. The enemy plundered and destroyed the city (see Document 3.2). and carried Ibbi-Sin away to Elam, where he died in captivity.[23]

PERSIAN GULF AND CENTRAL ASIAN CIVILIZATIONS

Dilmun, Magan, and Meluhha

During the latter half of the third millennium B.C.E., Mesopotamia engaged in trade with three foreign countries—Dilmun, Magan, and Meluhha—reached via the Persian Gulf. They were often mentioned in texts of the Akkadian and Ur III Periods, so for a long time, scholars have known of their existence. Moreover, the consistent order in which the names were written indicated that Dilmun was closest to Mesopotamia and Meluhha the furthest away. It is only in the past few decades, though, that archaeology has been able to reveal the probable locations of these lands.

Dilmun almost certainly comprised the present day islands of Bahrain and Failaka, though it probably also included part of the eastern Arabian coast and all or part of Qatar (see Map 3.1). Excavations have revealed that this area came under strong Mesopotamian influence during the latter part of the Ubaid

DOCUMENT 3.2

A Lamentation Over the Destruction of Ur

This Sumerian poem was composed during the Old Babylonian Period, probably within a century or two after the destruction of Ur at the end of the Ur III era. In the first selection, Ningal, goddess of Ur, tells how she pleaded with the leading gods Anu and Enlil not to destroy her city. However, their decision has already been made and they will not change their minds. The second passage, from the next section of the poem, vividly describes the carnage after the Elamites sacked the city.[24]

I dragged my feet and I stretched out my arms.
In truth, I shed my tears in front of Anu.
In truth, myself I mourned in front of Enlil:
"May not my city be destroyed!" I said indeed to them.
"May Ur not be destroyed!" I said indeed to them.
"And may its people not be killed!" I said indeed to them.
But Anu never bent towards those words,
and Enlil never with an, "It is pleasing, let it be,"
did soothe my heart
(Behold), they gave instruction that the city be destroyed,
(behold), they gave instruction that Ur be destroyed,
and as its destiny decreed that its inhabitants be killed. . . .
(Dead) men, not potsherds,
Covered the approaches.
The walls were gaping,
The high gates, the roads,
Were piled with dead.
In the wide streets, where feasting crowds would gather,
Scattered they lay.
In all the streets and roadways bodies lay.
In open fields that used to fill with dancers,
They lay in heaps.
The country's blood now filled its holes, like metal in a mold;
Bodies dissolved—like fat left in the sun.

Period (c. 4700 to 3700 B.C.E.) and reached the height of its prosperity in the late third and early second millennia B.C.E.. Archaeologists have uncovered large temples on raised platforms (but not multistory ones) at several sites, and at Qal'at Bahrain they found an enclosed area containing a storeroom, houses, and a workshop for manufacturing stamp seals. The people of Dilmun used the cuneiform script and the Akkadian language for writing purposes, and probably Akkadian was the spoken language as well.

Despite these connections with Mesopotamia, few post-Ubaid Mesopotamian imports have been found in the area. On the other hand, several sites in what was probably Dilmun's territory have revealed pieces of Indus pottery, and Dilmun's system of weights and measures was identical to that of the Indus civilization. This evidence agrees with textual indications that Dilmun was an intermediary in the trade between Mesopotamia and the Indus Valley. Dilmun probably imported copper and precious stones from Magan and the Indus region and shipped much of it on to Mesopotamia. Dilmun also supplied pearls from its own waters. Mesopotamian texts indicate that, in exchange, large amounts of barley were shipped to Dilmun, most of which this kingdom retained to feed its own population. Other Mesopotamian goods such as textiles and manufactured products, as well as Dilmun's Gulf pearls, were sent on to Magan and the Indus Valley in trade for their metal, ivory, and other goods.

Most scholars now agree that Magan, once thought to be in southern Iran, encompassed the southeastern area of the Arabian Peninsula at the end of the Persian Gulf, just south of the Strait of Hormuz and Gulf of Oman (see Map 3.1). This region is now occupied by the eastern portion of the United Arab Emirates and the northern part of Oman. This area was rich in metals and fine stone, materials prized in Mesopotamia. At Maysar in Oman, archaeologists have found installations for copper mining, crushing, and smelting and many finished copper ingots. Magan shipped copper ingots and ore to Mesopotamia, sometimes by way of Dilmun, in exchange for manufactured bronze objects and other finished products, some of which turned up at sites in Oman. Magan was also a source for ivory and other materials from the Indus area. As we have seen, for a brief time during the Akkadian Empire, Magan was probably conquered by Agade and at least made a subject ally to assure the continued flow of its products to Mesopotamia.

The many Indus stamp seals, etched carnelian beads, and other products uncovered at sites along the Persian Gulf and in Mesopotamia proved that Mesopotamia, Dilmun, and Magan were actively involved in trade with the Indus civilization between c. 2400 and 1900 B.C.E. These finds suggested that the Indus area was Meluhha. But, while some of the

trade between Mesopotamia and Meluhha undoubtedly came through Magan and Dilmun, as well as by land routes through Iran, textual references showed that much of it arrived directly by sea. An Akkadian inscription claims that ships from Meluhha docked at Agade, and an Ur III text refers to a "Meluhha village," probably a merchant settlement or trade depot, within Lagash's territory. A cylinder seal of a "Meluhha translator" also indicated direct contact between Mesopotamians and representatives of Meluhha. It is only since the 1950s, when archaeologists discovered Lothal and other Indus civilization ports, that evidence has indicated that this culture was directly involved with maritime trade. Thus, it is now generally agreed that the Indus Valley must have been the distant place known to the Mesopotamians as Meluhha.

The Indus civilization is also known as the Harappan civilization after Harappa, one of its largest sites and one of the first to be excavated. As we have seen, this civilization developed in Pakistan and northwest India around 2600 to 2500 B.C.E., probably from earlier cultures in the area. By the time it came into direct contact with Mesopotamia c. 2400 B.C.E., the Indus civilization had spread to cover an area from the banks of the Oxus River in the north to the Narmada River south of New Delhi, and from Iran on the west to the Ganges plain on the east. So far, archaeologists have found over 700 Indus settlements in this immense expanse that is more than 750 miles long and equally as wide, an area far larger than that occupied by either Egypt or Mesopotamia. Most Indus settlements were small, but three were huge: Harappa in the highlands of the Punjab, Ganweriwala on a now dried-up river almost 190 miles southwest of Harappa, and Mohenjo-Daro in the Indus lowlands almost 200 miles further to the southwest (see Map 2.2 in Chapter 2). Some archaeologists argue that these three cities, which despite their distance from one another, display exactly the same culture, were regional capitals in a tripartite political organization. Others think that there was a unified Indus empire with Mohenjo-Daro as its capital and the other two cities as secondary capitals. On the other hand, since the greatest cluster of sites is around Ganweriwala, the civilization may have begun in that region and then spread north and south, with Harappa and Mohenjo-Daro becoming capitals of the "provincial" or "colonial" regions. More excavation, especially of early strata, is needed to clarify the origins, growth, and organization of this civilization.

All the Indus settlements, whether large or small, display careful town planning. They are laid out in a grid pattern with streets crisscrossing at right angles. They had well-planned drainage systems with private indoor latrines that emptied into covered drains. The larger drains had manholes for clearing out waste. The major cities had large public buildings, the biggest of which were probably communal granaries. This evidence suggests that Indus cities were much more cen-

trally controlled than the Mesopotamian city-states, which exhibited a fairly random growth pattern.

Unfortunately, our knowledge of the Indus society and its political, economic, religious, and social structures is very sketchy and hypothetical, for we have no readable texts. The Indus culture did develop a writing system, probably inspired by ideas from Mesopotamia and Iran. The script probably consists primarily of phonograms (signs for sounds or syllables), for it has almost 400 signs—too many for an alphabet and too few for every sign to be a word. Most inscriptions are on seals (see Figure 3.4) and are short (usually only four to six signs long), with few containing more than ten signs. None has more than 17 signs. Recent computer analysis of the script has led Finnish

FIGURE 3.4   Indus Seals with Brief Inscriptions in the Undeciphered Indus Script
Source: National Museum of Pakistan, Karachi.
Photo: Borromeo/Art Resource, New York.

and Russian scholars to suggest that the structure of the Indus language is similar to that of the Dravidian languages of India. Nevertheless, they still have not been able to read the script. Walter Fairservis agrees that the language is related to Dravidian and argues that the inscriptions on seals indicate names, titles, and/or occupations, while the animals depicted are totems indicating kin relationships, possibly clans.[25] However, nothing resembling economic, literary, or historical documents have turned up, so there will still be large gaps in our knowledge of the Indus culture even if, or when, the script is deciphered.

It is surprising that though archaeologists have found many Harappan or Meluhhan artifacts at Mesopotamian sites, they have not uncovered a single Mesopotamian artifact in the Indus Valley. The Indus civilization must have imported only perishable commodities or raw materials. This fact, plus the formal layout of the cities, standardization of products, emphasis on sanitation, lack of evidence of wealth-based social stratification, among other features of the archaeological record, suggest to some scholars that the Indus society was caste- rather than class-structured. In a caste system, individuals belong to exclusive groups, usually defined by their functions or occupational duties. Status is dependent on caste identity rather than wealth. Individuals must marry within their own caste, and social contact with those outside the caste results in pollution that must be ritually cleansed. Even contact with the material culture of someone outside of the caste is sometimes thought to cause pollution. Thus, if such a system existed in the ancient Indus civilization, the rigid planning and standardization, lack of emphasis on accumulation of wealth, and disdain for finished products from other cultures would be understandable.[26]

The Indus civilization's contacts with Mesopotamia end around 1900 B.C.E. Not long afterward, around 1800 to 1700 B.C.E., the Indus cities were abandoned and the civilization crumbled. What caused this collapse is unknown. The *Rig-Veda*, an ancient Hindu sacred epic, claims that **Indo-European** invaders called **Aryans**, armed with bronze weapons and riding light horse-drawn chariots, destroyed the cities

they found in India. Several modern scholars argue that this tradition is based on fact. Some cities, especially in the central region, were burned, and at Mohenjo-Daro, archaeologists found the skeletal remains of as many as 30 unburied bodies in the streets, some showing signs of violence. However, most of the cities seem to have been abandoned rather than destroyed by military action. In fact, it's possible that the collapse was not sudden, but took place in stages. The settlements in northwest India east of the Indus River seem to be later and may have been built by refugees from the earlier Indus centers that were in decline. The decline itself, though, remains to be explained.

A few modern scholars have argued that an outbreak of a deadly disease such as malaria might have caused such a great loss of life that the civilization could not survive. An epidemic, though, would probably have resulted in many large cemeteries containing burials primarily from the last phase of the civilization. Archaeologists have not found evidence of extremely large numbers of late burials. Another possibility is that environmental changes, due to nature and/or human activity, may have caused the civilization's demise. It is clear from the Indus seals that rhinoceroses, elephants, crocodiles, tigers, and other animals that no longer inhabit the Indus Valley were once indigenous there. This evidence suggests that environmental conditions in the region have changed since the third millennium B.C.E. The changes could have been due to overgrazing, deforestation, salt build-up in the soil due to extensive irrigation, soil depletion from excessive cultivation, or other human activities. Or, nature may have changed the environment. There seems to be some evidence of extensive flooding and the formation of large lakes around Mohenjo-Daro shortly before its end. Some hydrologists argue that floods might have been produced by gradual geological uplift of the coast near the river's mouth. Presumably, this would have prevented the river from draining properly into the sea, causing it to form large lakes and swamps upstream. According to this theory, the cities were overwhelmed by the constant effort to raise the level of their streets and buildings and to create retaining walls to hold back the water. However, while chronic flooding might explain why southern Indus cities such as Mohenjo-Daro and Chanhu-Daro were abandoned, it is hard to imagine that such floods would have reached all the way to Harappa or that they could have caused the collapse of a civilization that spread over such a large area. The solution to the problem of the Indus civilization's fall, of course, is likely to include several factors and probably a combination of both natural and human causes. Archaeologists and historians are not yet in a position to determine what that solution is likely to be.

The Oxus Civilization

As mentioned in Chapter 2, in recent years, archaeologists from the former Soviet Union have discovered a previously unknown Central Asian civilization along lower reaches of the Murghab River and the upper portions of the Oxus River, now known as Amu Darya (see Map 2.2). These regions were known to the later Greeks as Margiana and Bactria. The Oxus civilization developed from Neolithic and Early Bronze Age settlements such as Jeitun, Anau, and Altyn Tepe east of the Caspian Sea. These Central Asian Bronze Age cities were smaller than the major Mesopotamian and Indus cities, though comparable in size to those in other parts of the Near East. They display all of the main elements of early civilization with one major exception—they seem to lack writing. However, at Anau, archaeologists recently uncovered a small piece of stone (possibly a stamp seal) engraved with four or five red symbols. The excavator, Fredrik Hiebert, believes that the symbols or signs on this object (dated c. 2300 B.C.E.) probably represent a form of writing.[27] The function and meaning of these symbols are not certain, for they do not seem to be directly derived from the signs used in early Mesopotamian, Iranian, or Indus civilization writing.

Around 2300 to 2200 B.C.E., the time of the suggested drought in the Near East, Altyn Tepe and the other sites in western Turkmenistan were abandoned. The population seems to have shifted eastward to the area around the Murghab and Oxus Rivers. The creation of new cities in these regions of Margiana and Bactria c. 2200 B.C.E. marks the real advent of the Oxus civilization (see Map 2.2). This civilization's settlements arose in oases or along the riverbanks where there was sufficient water for irrigation of their fields. They were hemmed in by mountains to the south and uninhabitable deserts to the north. Nevertheless, they developed wonderful bronze, gold, and silver artifacts, stone statues, and monumental architecture. The cities were protected by fortification walls, and each was dominated by a single monumental building that was also fortified. These impressive structures usually contain dozens of rooms, in a couple of cases, probably more than a hundred. Clearly, they were the most important buildings in the cities, but their nature and function is debated. They could have served as citadels during wartime, and archaeological evidence indicates that they also were storage sites for agricultural produce and workplaces for craftsmen.

Some archaeologists have interpreted the large structures as temples or palaces and argued that, like Mesopotamian cities, the Oxus civilization's settlements were ruled by religious establishments or mighty kings. Others, drawing upon Central Asian ethnographic parallels from the Iron Age and later, more persuasively see the buildings as the dwellings of rulers in a lineage-based society. Later Central Asian societies organized themselves around powerful clans or lineages, each of which had its own *khan* or ruler. One distinguished lineage always supplied the society's hereditary ruling *khan* who governed the other lineage *khans* as a first among equals. The ruling *khan*, his family, and retainers lived in a structure called the *qala*. The Oxus civilization's monumental buildings resemble the Iron Age *qalas*. So, perhaps they were the residences of ruling *khans*, their extended families, servants and retainers, as well as a place for food storage and craft production.[28] Since each Oxus city had a *qala*-type building, each probably had its own principal ruler. However, we can't determine their relationships to one another. Possibly all of the city-rulers were independent, but some might have been subordinate to others, or there might have been one preeminent leader to whom all the rest were vassals.

Archaeologists discovered a number of elaborate statues and figurines of women with different parts made of stone, alabaster, ivory, and lapis lazuli. They also noted that burials of women contain greater wealth than those of males. These finds suggest that women probably had a high status in Oxus society. Possibly, like some later Central Asian lineage-structured societies, the Oxus culture was matrilineal, that is they traced descent exclusively through the female line.

Though they made their own square and round stamp seals, Oxus artisans also borrowed the idea of the cylinder seal from Mesopotamia. However, they carved their own animal motifs and geometric designs on them. The Oxus people do not seem to have used these seals as Mesopotamians did as signatures on documents or to secure containers, for archaeologists have found few seal impressions. Possibly they were personal ornaments signifying rank, status, or lineage. Another commonly found type of artifact, a never-used decorated bronze axe, also may have served as a symbol identifying its owner as having a specific rank or function.

Around 1900 B.C.E., people from the Oxus civilization began to move into other areas, with individuals or small groups settling in towns in southeastern Iran (Khurab, Khinaman, and Shadad) and Pakistan (Sibri and Quetta). They have been identified by their burials in which 100 percent of the grave goods were Oxus artifacts. Excavators have also uncovered Oxus artifacts at Susa, Tepe Hissar, and Tepe Yahya in Iran, and from the last level of the Indus site of Nousharo, though there is no firm evidence of Oxus settlers at those sites. The expansionist phase of the Oxus civilization lasted only about a hundred years, for Oxus objects are not found in Iran after c. 1800 B.C.E. About a century later, all of the Oxus cities were abandoned and the civilization disappeared.

The Oxus civilization ended about the same time as that of the Indus Valley, c. 1700 B.C.E. Settlements in eastern Iran were also abandoned around this time. It is likely that there is some connection between these events, but so far, scholars don't know what it is. Some have suggested that a climatic change caused a reversion to nomadism in the area, but no evidence has been found to support this idea. Another possibility is that the Oxus expansion might have produced an extensive "clash of cultures" between incompatible social and military systems. There is some evidence that the Oxus people had horses and chariots, so maybe their use of this new, seemingly invincible weapon caused internal problems within the Iranian and Indus cultures.[29] But why, then, did the Oxus civilization itself collapse? Maybe attacks by seminomads or the movements of the Aryans (Indo-Iranians) into the area caused the collapse of all three cultures, but there are no signs of warfare and destruction in the Oxus cities, just as there are few in the Indus Valley. Hopefully, further excavation and research will suggest reasons for the mid-second millennium B.C.E. cultural collapse in eastern Iran, Central Asia, and the Indus Valley.

THE OLD BABYLONIAN PERIOD (c. 2000–1595 B.C.E.)

The "Interregnum" After the Fall of Ur

During the century after the collapse of the Ur III Empire, the newly-independent city-state of Asshur established several merchant colonies at Anatolian cities. The most important of these colonies was located at Kanesh (modern Kültepe, see Map 3.1) where archaeologists have found some 15,000 tablets recording the merchants' activities over more than a century and a half (c. 1920 to 1750 B.C.E.). Each large merchant community (like the one at Kanesh) was controlled by an organization called a *karum*, a kind of board of trade, which handled the internal affairs of the colony and served as a liaison with local authorities. Assyrian merchants at smaller towns were under the jurisdiction of the nearest *karum*. Donkey caravans transported goods back and forth between Asshur and the colonies along protected routes and were taxed several times by local kingdoms along the way. Such caravans took as long as three months to cover the approximately 950-mile round trip between Asshur and Kanesh. Their cargo from Asshur to Anatolia was primarily tin (from points further east) and woven textiles, while on the return trip it was mostly copper, silver, and gold.

While this trade was flourishing in the north, Amorites continued to move into Mesopotamia, gaining control of many Mesopotamian city-states. In fact, during the period covered by the Kanesh tablets, Amorites poured into Assyria and shortly before 1800 B.C.E., a chieftain named Shamshi-Adad seized Asshur. This change of leadership doesn't seem to have affected the commerce with Anatolia. In southern Mesopotamia, many of the Amorites had arrived before the end of the Third Dynasty of Ur. As usual, though, within a generation or two, the newcomers became thoroughly "Mesopotamianized," worshiping Mesopotamian deities, adopting local customs, and speaking and writing Akkadian.

Two cities ruled by Amorite dynasties, Isin and Larsa, emerged as Mesopotamia's most powerful political and cultural centers between c. 2000 and 1800 B.C.E. Thus, the first part of the Old Babylonian Period, the time between the fall of Ur and the rise of Hammurabi, is often called the Isin-Larsa Period. Ishbi-Erra (c. 2017 to 1985 B.C.E.), the founder of Isin's Amorite dynasty, came from Mari. For a few years after becoming ruler of Isin, he was a vassal of Ur, but he soon declared his independence and established his control over Nippur, Uruk, and Eridu as well. Ishbi-Erra even became master of Ur late in his reign by defeating the Elamite force garrisoned in the city. His son and successor, Shu-Ilushu (c. 1984 to 1975 B.C.E.), carried the fight to Elam and recovered the stolen cult statue of Nanna, Ur's patron god. Before succumbing to the power of Larsa around 1924 B.C.E., Isin's kings ruled the entire lower Euphrates Valley from Sippar to the Gulf. Despite their Amorite origins, these monarchs considered themselves the heirs of the Ur III dynasty. They used Sumerian for their official inscriptions, copied the Ur III administrative system and, like Shulgi and his successors, had themselves worshipped as gods. Their ardent adoption of Sumerian culture also led them to order copies of

Sumerian literary works, and fortunately, many of these copies have survived.

The Amorite dynasty of Larsa was founded at about the same time as that of Isin, but for much of the twentieth century B.C.E. it remained politically negligible. However, King Gungunum (c. 1932 to 1906 B.C.E.) changed Larsa's fortunes. In his eighth year (c. 1925 B.C.E.), he seized Ur from Lipit-Ishtar of Isin, who died soon afterward. Isin's power waned over the next decade while usurpers battled to gain control of its throne. Meanwhile, Larsa grew stronger, conquering Lagash, Susa, and probably Uruk. However, water shortages caused Larsa to decline, and its dynasty fell to an usurper around 1865 B.C.E. After this, the fortunes of Isin and Larsa seesawed back and forth until a new enemy, Babylon, rose to threaten both.

During this time of conflict and crisis, there occurred an instance of a custom that some think explains the unusual burials in the "Royal Tombs" of Ur—the "substitute king" ceremony. Because of bad omens and disasters, Isin's king Irra-imitti (c. 1868 to 1861 B.C.E.) tried to placate the gods by placing a commoner on the throne. Later examples of this rite indicate that the "substitute king" would have a brief "reign" during the performance of various propitiation rituals. Then, as a climax of the ritual, the "king" would be killed to appease the gods, whereupon the real king would assume the throne again. This time, though, according to a Babylonian chronicle, things did not turn out as planned:

> That the dynasty might not end, King Irra-imitti made the gardener Enlil-bani take his place upon his throne and put the royal crown upon his head. Irra-imitti died in his palace because he had swallowed boiling broth. Enlil-bani who was upon the throne did not relinquish it and was installed as king.[30]

Enlil-bani reigned for 24 years (c. 1860 to 1837), but though the former gardener seems to have governed well, he was unable to restore Isin's power.

Larsa had one last period of glory when Kudur-Mabuk took over the city around 1834 B.C.E. He seems to have been an Amorite chieftain with an

Elamite name whose tribe had served the Elamites as mercenaries. He was more interested in fighting than in administration, so he put his son, Warad-Sin, on the throne (c. 1834 to 1823 B.C.E.). However, Warad-Sin died prematurely, and his younger brother, Rim-Sin, succeeded him (c. 1822 to 1763 B.C.E.). In a series of military campaigns, Rim-Sin gained control of all of Sumer, even conquering Isin around 1804 B.C.E. But, to the north, other foes were blocking further growth of Rim-Sin's kingdom—the growing empire of Shamshi-Adad and, closer to home, the upstart kingdom of Babylon.

Hammurabi and His Rivals

Shamshi-Adad was the ruler of Ekallatum, a town somewhere on the middle Tigris conquered earlier by his father. The young king had not been on the throne for long before the king of Eshnunna overpowered Ekallatum and other towns in the area, forcing Shamshi-Adad to flee to Babylon. He spent a few years building an army, then moved northward and recaptured his old city. Around 1809 B.C.E. he seized Asshur and became Shamshi-Adad I (c. 1809 to 1776 B.C.E.), Assyria's first true king (*sharrum*), for formerly its rulers had called themselves only "prince" (*ruba'um*), "lord" (*belum*) or, in inscriptions, "viceroy of the god Asshur." Shamshi-Adad appointed his heir, Ishme-Dagan, to rule his old capital, Ekallatum, as his viceroy. Then, when the king of Mari was murdered around 1796 B.C.E., Shamshi-Adad took advantage of the ensuing confusion to capture the city and install his younger son, Yasmah-Adad, as vassal king of the city and its extensive territory. Shamshi-Adad's kingdom then embraced virtually all of northern Mesopotamia. Later in his reign, he built a new, centrally located capital called Shubat-Enlil (modern Tell Leilan) and allowed Ishme-Dagan to become vassal ruler of Asshur.

Archaeological excavations at Mari have uncovered more than 20,000 letters belonging to the time of Shamshi-Adad and Hammurabi, many of them exchanges between Shamshi-Adad and his son, Yasmah-Adad. These not only provide valuable information on government, diplomacy, society, and religion (see the following section on Old Babylonian Cultural Developments), but also give us insight into the personal relationships between Shamshi-Adad and his sons.[31] Shamshi-Adad frequently criticized his younger son, Yasmah-Adad, who seems to have been a poor administrator, often berating him in humiliating fashion. The old king also worsened the natural sibling rivalry between his two sons by boasting about Ishme-Dagan and comparing Yasmah-Adad to him. Obviously these letters irritated (and undoubtedly hurt) Yasmah-Adad. On one occasion, he angrily repeated his father's frequent harangue:

> I have received and read the letter that you sent me. It reads as follows: "How long will it be necessary for us continually to guide you? Are you a child and not a man? Don't you have a beard on your chin? How much longer will you be incapable of administering your own household? Don't you see your brother commanding far-flung armies? Now, [let's see] you govern your palace and your household!" *That* is what you wrote to me![32]

Ishme-Dagan also occasionally criticized his younger brother, and even when he offers to help Yasmah-Adad, it is not clear that his motives are altogether altruistic. For example, he advises Yasmah-Adad:

> Do not write to the king [Shamshi-Adad, our father]. The country where I reside is nearer the capital city. The things you want to write to the king, write to me, so that I can advise you.[33]

If Yasmah-Adad followed that advice, then Ishme-Dagan effectively enlarged his own authority and the scope of his administration.

Meanwhile, Hammurabi° had become king of Babylon (see Table 3.2). Babylon was a small town mentioned for the first time during the reign of Shar-kalli-sharri (c. 2217 to 2193 B.C.E.). Originally it probably was called Babil or Babila, a non-Semitic name whose

---

°The name should be spelled Hammurapi (which probably meant "the god Hammu is a healer"), but the spelling Hammurabi has become so familiar that it has been retained here.

TABLE 3.2
The Chronology of Hammurabi's Dynasty

(All dates are B.C.E. and are only approximate.)

Babylon	Assyria	Mari	Others
Sumu-abum (1894–1881)			
Sumu-la-El (1880–1845)			
Sabium (1844–1831)			
Apil-Sin (1830–1813)			
Sin-muballit (1812–1793)	**Shamshi-Adad** (1809–1776)	**Yashmah-Adad** (1796–1776)	**Rim-Sin** of Larsa (1822–1763)
Hammurabi (1792–1750)	**Ishme-Dagan** (1775–1736)	**Zimri-Lim** (1776–1758)	**Ibal-pi-El II** of Eshnunna (1741–17??)
	Hammurabi conquers Asshur?	Hammurabi destroys Mari (1758)	Hammurabi conquers Larsa (1763) and destroys Eshnunna (1755)
Samsu-iluna (1749–1712)			
Abi-eshuh (1711–1684)		Kassites rule Mari (1700?)	
Ammiditana (1683–1647)			
Ammisaduqa (1646–1626)			**Hattusilis** I of Hatti (1650–1620)
Samsuditana (1625–1595)			**Mursilis** I of Hatti (1620–1590)
Hittites conquer Babylon (1595)			

meaning is unknown. But Akkadian-speakers called it *Bab-ilim* ("gateway of god") and much later *Bab-ilani* ("gateway of the gods"), which became the basis of the Greek *Babulon* and our Babylon. An Amorite sheikh, Sumu-abum, became its ruler around 1894 B.C.E., but it remained a small, relatively insignificant city-state until the time of Hammurabi (c. 1792 to 1750 B.C.E.).

Early in his reign, Hammurabi seems to have made an alliance with Shamshi-Adad, probably becoming his vassal. The protection this treaty afforded allowed him to extend his kingdom considerably. In his fifth and sixth years, he took Isin and Uruk from Rim-Sin of Larsa, then probably signed a treaty with Rim-Sin to stabilize Babylonian relations with Larsa. In his tenth year, he occupied a key city in the territory between the Tigris and the Zagros, and in his eleventh year he captured Rapiqum, a city north of Sippar. He then seems to have concentrated on Babylon's internal affairs, waiting for his opportunity to further extend his borders.

When Shamshi-Adad and Yasmah-Adad both died (probably in a battle) around 1776 B.C.E., the situation changed dramatically. Zimri-Lim, son of a former king of Mari, easily regained control of his father's city. Hammurabi then formed an alliance with Zimri-Lim to keep Mari from falling to the kings of Eshnunna and Elam who were casting covetous eyes in that direction. A frequently quoted report sent to Zimri-Lim by one of his officials summed up the situation at that time:

> There is no king who by himself is strongest. Ten or fifteen kings follow Hammurabi of Babylon, as many follow Rim-Sin of Larsa, Ibal-pi-El of Eshnunna and Amut-pi-El of Qatna, while twenty kings follow Yarim-Lim of Yamhad [Aleppo].[34]

The Mari letters provide evidence not only about the diplomacy these kings practiced, but also about their intelligence services. Even while allies, Zimri-Lim of Mari and Hammurabi of Babylon had intelligence agents (spies) in each other's cities keeping them abreast of important developments. These agents describe troop movements, pending alliances, and other interesting information, some of it presumably secret. For example, one of Zimri-Lim's agents was able to detail to his king the contents of an exchange of letters between Rim-Sin and Hammurabi. Another seems to have become a confidant of Hammurabi, for he informs Zimri-Lim that:

> Whenever Hammurabi is perturbed by some matter, he always sends for me, and I go to him wherever he is. He tells me whatever is troubling him, and all of the important information which he tells me I continually report to my lord.[35]

In Hammurabi's twenty-ninth year (c. 1764 B.C.E.), a coalition army led by Elam and Eshnunna invaded Babylonian territory, but he defeated these troops. This victory may have convinced him he was now strong enough to move to the offensive. The following year, he attacked Rim-Sin, conquered Larsa, and added all southern Mesopotamia to his kingdom. Then, when Eshnunna and the Elamites attacked again (c. 1762 B.C.E.), he not only defeated them once more, but afterward, thrust northward and conquered Eshnunna. Because his ally, Zimri-Lim, didn't aid him in the conflict with Eshnunna, Hammurabi attacked Mari and forced Zimri-Lim to become his vassal. When Mari rebelled two years later, Hammurabi's armies returned and destroyed the city (c. 1758 B.C.E.). Finally, in his thirty-sixth and thirty-eighth years of reign (c. 1757 and 1755 B.C.E.), Hammurabi defeated Assyria and seems to have made Ishme-Dagan into a vassal. Between these two campaigns, he also destroyed Eshnunna, diverting water over its ruins. These conquests created an empire that rivaled the size of the Ur III domain.

Hammurabi proved to be as good an administrator as he was a general. His kingdom, it seems, was governed efficiently and fairly. As witness to this fact, toward the end of his reign, Hammurabi had his well-known "law code" carved on stelae (see Figure 3.5) and placed in several temples. He raised Babylon to such prominence that, from his time onward, all of southern Mesopotamia was usually known as Babylo-

FIGURE 3.5 Hammurabi's Law Stele

The top of the stele depicts Hammurabi before Shamash, god of justice.

Source: Louvre, Paris.

Photo: Ch. Larrieu/Réunion des Musées Nationaux/Art Resource, New York.

nia rather than Sumer and Akkad. But the empire he created proved to be as fragile as earlier ones in Mesopotamia. His dynasty lasted another 155 years, but the extensive empire barely outlived his son.

Old Babylonian Cultural Developments

The Old Babylonian Period (or the "Age of Hammurabi," as it is often called) is one of the best documented in Mesopotamian history. We have already mentioned the extensive collection of trade documents found at Kanesh in Anatolia and the thousands of letters from Mari. In addition, there are many surviving building inscriptions, lists of year names, a chronicle, fragments of Lipit-Ishtar's "law code" and the laws of Eshnunna, Hammurabi's virtually intact "law code," hundreds of Hammurabi's letters, and various collections of documents from several other sites. To these must be added recently discovered tablets from Shamshi-Adad's capital, Shubat-Enlil. Later copies and translations of writings from this time are also very valuable.

This era was the classical period for the Akkadian language and grammar and for the development of Akkadian literature. Though Sumerian, by then a dead language, continued to be studied in schools, Sumerian myths and epics were translated into Akkadian or rewritten as Akkadian compositions based upon Sumerian originals. The most important of these new compositions was the *Epic of Gilgamesh,* which was based on five earlier Sumerian poems. The Old Babylonian author of this epic wove the older stories into a unified work dealing with basic human concerns, especially the quest to escape the curse of aging and death. It gives eloquent expression to the age-old Mesopotamian fatalism—"when the gods created humans, they decreed death for mankind; life they retained in their own hands" (Tablet X, col. iii). Even a hero who is two-thirds god and one-third human must die. Though Gilgamesh struggles heroically to avoid this fate, he eventually realizes its inevitability. Near the end of the poem he is given a small ray of hope, a plant from the bottom of the sea that confers not immortality, as many interpreters claim, but rejuvenation.[36] Instead of eating the plant immediately, Gilgamesh decided to take it home and share it with his people. However, humanity lost even this limited blessing of remaining youthful until the moment of death, for while Gilgamesh was bathing in a pond, a snake gobbled up the plant.

There were also several significant developments in Mesopotamian religion during the Old Babylonian Period. The most important was Hammurabi's elevation of Marduk, patron god of Babylon, to supremacy over the Mesopotamian pantheon. To make this change acceptable to Mesopotamians outside of Babylon, Hammurabi claimed that Anu and Enlil, the old supreme gods, raised Marduk above the other great gods and gave him Enlil's functions. When Sumerian myths, especially the *Epic of Creation,* were rewritten in Akkadian during this time, Marduk was simply substituted for Enlil. Marduk also assumed the title *Bel* ("lord") adopted for Enlil during the Akkadian Period, and this appellation frequently came to be used in place of Marduk's name.

Mesopotamian temples and their staffs had gradually grown larger since Early Dynastic times, and many categories of cultic personnel are listed in Hammurabi's Code and other documents from this era. An interesting class of women attached to some temples was called *naditum.* These women lived in a "cloister" within the temple compound, and could marry, but were not allowed to bear children. They were of high social status, often held royal land, and usually engaged in various business operations such as lending wheat or silver to individuals, financing trading ventures, or buying and renting out houses and land. Two other groups of temple functionaries mentioned for the first time in this era were male and female cultic prostitutes. The males seem to have been passive homosexuals, probably **eunuchs** (castrates). In the temples of Ishtar, goddess of carnal love, and possibly in other temples as well, these consecrated men and women performed sexual acts with male worshipers as part of the sacred rites. The money obtained from these cultic sexual acts went into the temple treasury. Such cultic prostitution seems to have been practiced in other parts of the Near East as well, including early Israel, where it probably wasn't prohibited until late in the period of the Divided Monarchy (2 Kings 23:7; Deuteronomy 23:18–19, verses 17–18 in English).

Also interesting are references at Mari to divine messages delivered through ordinary citizens. Of course, Mesopotamia had professional diviners, soothsayers, seers, and other religious officials who provided information from the gods through omens and other means. However, the Mari letters indicate that the gods sometimes chose to give their messages (usually in dreams) to individuals who were not part of the religious establishment. In one instance, a governor tells King Zimri-Lim that a man reported a dream in which Dagan spoke to him in Dagan's temple in Terqa. The god complained that Zimri-Lim had not sent messengers to report to Dagan and, that because of that inattention, Zimri-Lim was still having trouble with a band of seminomads. Dagan then demanded that the man go to Zimri-Lim and tell him to send messengers to place the matter before the god in his temple. The governor not only informed the king of this dream, but, in addition, urged him to obey the god's demands. In another case, Dagan gives a young man a message warning the ruler and citizens of Terqa not to rebuild a particular temple. Many scholars see in these texts parallels with pre-exilic Israelite and Judean prophets who delivered messages from God to their society, often chastising religious leaders and kings. The Aramaeans and Phoenicians also had similar beliefs about prophets, suggesting that these ideas were native to West Semitic peoples and were introduced into Mesopotamia by the Amorites.

Our greatest single source of information about Old Babylonian society, of course, is Hammurabi's Law Stele (see Document 3.3). Like earlier "law codes," it probably was compiled from examples of customary law, royal legal edicts, past court cases, extrapolations from earlier legal decisions, and amendments to former laws. It was not meant to be comprehensive, but rather demonstrated to the gods and the people that the king was performing his duty to uphold justice. It could provide guidance for citizens who wished to know their rights, and in at least one instance, it seems to have been cited in a contract from Ur:[37]

> The [amount of] wages for a hired worker is written on the stele, [therefore] in accordance with what they told you, do not withhold their wages, be it barley or silver.

The stele indicates that Mesopotamian society was stratified into three classes at Hammurabi's time: *awêlum*, *mushkênum*, and *wardum*. *Wardum* means "slave," obviously the lowest level on the social scale, but the meaning of the other two words is not certain. The words related to *mushkênum* in other Semitic languages mean "pauper" or "commoner," and members of this class are clearly inferior to those of the *awêlum* class. They probably were dependents of the palace or of nobles, working as tenant farmers on their lands. *Awêlum* literally means "man" and sometimes can refer to a man of any class, even a slave. On other occasions, it can mean any *free* man, and as a class designation, it seems to refer to a landowner or noble. Some laws on Hammurabi's stele distinguish between *awêlum* and "son of an *awêlum*," so it is likely that in most instances the word *awêlum* means "free man," including members of the *mushkênum* class. "Son of an *awêlum*" probably means "member of the *awêlum* class" ("landowner" or "noble"). So, laws 196 to 198 (in Document 3.3) probably mean:

> If a free man has put out the eye of a landowner (or noble?), they shall put out his eye. If a free man has broken the bone of a landowner, they shall break his bone. If a free man has destroyed the eye of a *mushkênum* (dependent?) or broken a *mushkênum's* bone, he shall pay one mina of silver.

Individuals had to prove any accusations they made or suffer the consequences (Document 3.3, Law 1), unless the charge was sorcery (Law 2). In that case, the river ordeal was used, allowing the gods to decide guilt or innocence by drowning the accused or allowing him to swim to the other side. Crimes against persons were punished differently, depending upon the class of the victims, as Laws 196 through 199 show. Injuries to members of the upper class were punished by direct retribution ("an eye for an eye, a tooth for a tooth") to guarantee that the punishment fit the crime. On the other hand, crimes committed against those of lesser status were punished only by fines.

There seems to have been a deliberate effort to protect women and children from the arbitrary treatment and abuse possible in a patriarchal society. For example, a woman who had to take refuge with

DOCUMENT 3.3
Selected Laws from Hammurabi's Stele

Since the word *awêlum* is used in all three of its senses in the "code" and since we cannot really be sure what a *mushkênum* was, the words have been left untranslated here to allow the reader to note the distinctions and ambiguities for himself or herself.[38] The laws have been numbered by modern scholars; the numbers are not found in the original text.

1: If an *awêlum* has accused another *awêlum* of a capital offense and has not proved him guilty, the accuser shall be put to death.

2: If an *awêlum* has accused another *awêlum* of sorcery, but has not proved him guilty, the person accused of sorcery shall go to the river and plunge into it. If the river overcomes him, his accuser shall take his estate. If the river proves that *awêlum* innocent and he returns unharmed, the one who brought the charge of sorcery against him shall be put to death and the one who threw himself into the river shall take the estate of his accuser.

9: If an *awêlum* who has lost some property has seized that lost property in another *awêlum*'s possession, and the *awêlum* in whose possession the lost property was found has stated, "a seller sold it to me; I bought it before witnesses," and the owner of the lost property has said, "I will produce witnesses who know my lost property," (and then) the buyer has produced the seller who sold (the property) to him and the witnesses before whom he bought it and the owner of the lost property (also) has produced witnesses who know the lost property, the judges shall examine their statements and the witnesses before whom the property was bought and the witnesses who know the lost property shall state what they know before the god. Then, the seller is a thief; he shall be put to death. The owner of the lost property shall take his lost property. The buyer shall take the money he has paid from the estate of the seller.

129: If an *awêlum*'s wife has been caught lying (in bed) with another man, they shall bind them and throw them into the water. If the husband of the woman wishes to spare his wife, then the king may also spare his subject.

131: If an *awêlum*'s wife was accused by her husband, but she was not caught lying with another man, she shall swear (her innocence) by the life of a god and return to her house.

132: If a finger has been pointed at an *awêlum*'s wife because of another man, but she was not caught lying with the other man, she shall leap into the river (and undergo the water ordeal) for the sake of her husband.

134: If an *awêlum* has been made prisoner and there is nothing to eat in his house, his wife may enter another man's house; that woman shall suffer no punishment.

142: If a woman so hates her husband that she states "you may not have (sex with) me," her record shall be investigated in her district, and if she has kept herself chaste and was not at fault, while her husband has been going out and has greatly maligned her, that woman shall suffer no punishment; she may take her dowry and return to her father's house.

DOCUMENT 3.3, CONTINUED

Selected Laws from Hammurabi's Stele

196–197: If an *awêlum* has put out the eye of a son of an *awêlum*, they shall put out his eye. If an *awêlum* has broken the bone of an *awêlum*, they shall break his bone.

198: If an *awêlum* has destroyed the eye of a *mushkênum* or broken a *mushkênum*'s bone, he shall pay one mina of silver.

199: If an *awêlum* has destroyed the eye of an *awêlum*'s slave or broken the bone of an *awêlum*'s slave, he shall pay one half the slave's value.

202–203: If an *awêlum* has struck the cheek of an *awêlum* who is superior (in rank) to himself [or, possibly, "older than himself"], he shall be beaten sixty times with an oxtail whip in the assembly. If an *awêlum* has struck the cheek of an *awêlum* equal (in rank) [or, perhaps, "in age"] to himself, he shall pay one mina of silver.

204: If a *mushkênum* has struck the cheek of a *mushkênum*, he shall pay ten shekels of silver.

215: If a surgeon has performed a major operation on an *awêlum* with a bronze scalpel and has saved the *awêlum*'s life, or he opened an eye infection of an *awêlum* with a bronze scalpel and has saved the *awêlum*'s eye, he shall receive ten shekels of silver.

218: If a surgeon has performed a major operation on an *awêlum* with a bronze scalpel and has caused the *awêlum*'s death, or he opened an eye infection of an *awêlum* and has destroyed the *awêlum*'s eye, they shall cut off his hand.

229–230: If a builder has constructed a house for an *awêlum* but has not made his work strong, with the result that the house that he built collapsed and caused the death of the house's owner, that builder shall be put to death. If it has caused the death of the owner's son, they shall put to death the builder's son.

another man in her husband's absence (due to imprisonment or captivity) because he had left her with nothing to eat did not incur a penalty (Law 134). A husband who divorced his wife because she did not bear him sons not only had to return the dowry she brought into the marriage from her family, but also give her the amount of money he had given her parents as her bridal price (Law 138). If there was no bridal price, a member of the upper class must give the wife a mina of silver (Law 139) and a *mushkênum* one-third of a mina of silver (Law 140). Moreover, though a husband of a diseased woman was permitted to take another wife, he had to keep the diseased wife in his house and provide for her as long as she lived (Law 148). Also, the faithful wife of a husband who had been disparaging her outside of the house, had the right to refuse him sex and even to end the marriage (Law 142). Children inherited their mother's dowry as well as property from their father (Laws 162 and 167), and a father could not disinherit a son who had not committed at least two serious offences (Laws 168 and 169).

An interesting feature of Mesopotamia's economic system is that prices that could be charged for some goods and services were fixed by law, but at the same time, the work carried a warranty. If a person had a boat caulked, and the boat leaked within a year, the boatman who did the caulking had to redo it at his own expense (Law 235). If a house collapsed because of poor workmanship, the builder had to pay for repairs and for any of the owner's property that was damaged (Law 232), and if someone was injured, the builder or a member of his family was injured in the same way or, in the worse case scenario, killed (see Law 229). Unfortunately, Mesopotamians treated medicine as a craft, so surgeons were responsible if an operation didn't succeed or if the patient died (Law 218). This approach undoubtedly hindered the development of surgery in Mesopotamia and encouraged doctors to rely more on magical incantations and internal medicine to cure illness.

The End of Hammurabi's Dynasty and the Rise of the Hittites

Hammurabi's successor, Samsu-iluna (c. 1749 to 1712 B.C.E.) had to face challenges from an invading army of Kassites from the Zagros mountains, Rim-Sin II of Larsa, nephew of Hammurabi's foe, and the emerging power of the Sealand, a new kingdom that had arisen in the marshes where the Tigris and Euphrates flow into the Persian Gulf. The Babylonian king defeated the Kassites and after a few years, crushed the rebellion of Rim-Sin II, killing him in the process. Although he did lose some territory in the far south to the ruler of the Sealand, Samsu-iluna managed to hold on to most of the empire Hammurabi had bequeathed him. But soon after his death, Babylon lost Mari and the middle Euphrates region to the Kassite rulers of the new kingdom of Hana. The slow but steady decline continued under the dynasty's last four kings (see Table 3.2), until Samsu-ditana (c. 1625 to 1595 B.C.E.) controlled little more than the central part of Mesopotamia, the area around Babylon itself. Then disaster struck in the form of a Hittite raid. The Hittites conquered and looted Babylon around 1595 B.C.E. and brought the dynasty of Hammurabi to an end. Soon afterward, the Kassites occupied Babylon.

Who were the Hittites who had burst into prominence so suddenly? When, early in the twentieth cen-

tury B.C.E., the Hittite language was first discovered written in cuneiform signs on tablets from **Amarna** in Egypt and Boghazkoy (Hattusas) in Turkey, it could not be read. However, in 1915, Bedrich Hrozny demonstrated that it was an early member of the Indo-European language family. Scholars designated this language and the people who spoke it "Hittite," because their land was called **Hatti**, and other ancient nations used "Hatti" to designate the inhabitants, as well. However, we now know that these so-called "Hittites" retained an older name, "Hatti," for their kingdom, but they didn't call themselves Hittites. They termed their own language "Nesite" or "Nesian" (*neshili*, "in the language of Nesa") after the city of Nesa or Nesha (Kanesh), one of their early capitals in Anatolia. They used the designation "Hittite" (or *hattili*, "in the language of Hatti") for the non-Indo-European tongue of the previous population of the area (the people we now call Hattians or "Proto-Hittites").

We actually know little about the emergence of Hittite power. It is clear that these Indo-European immigrants had slowly blended with the Hattians and adopted much of their culture, especially in the areas of religion and art. The Hittite rulers who dominated central Anatolia around 1650 to 1590 B.C.E. claimed that their dynasty originated in a city named Kussara. They also memorialized the conquests of Pithanas, a king of Kussara, and his son Anittas, including Anittas' utter destruction of Hattusas and his placing a curse on anyone who resettled it. Though much of the Anittas text is apocryphal, Anittas was a real person, for a spearhead inscribed with his name was found at Nesa/Kanesh. Possibly these kings were ancestors of the later Hittite rulers, though the Hittites never explicitly made that claim. Moreover, the Hittite rulers rebuilt Hattusas, the city Anittas had cursed, and made it their capital.

The collapse of Anittas' Nesa-based kingdom and the destruction of Nesa/Kanesh and the Assyrian merchant colony there c. 1750 B.C.E. ended written records in Anatolia for about a century. The darkness lifted during the reign of Hattusilis I (c. 1650 to 1620 B.C.E.), the first clearly attested king of the Hittite Old Kingdom (c. 1650 to 1420 B.C.E.). Probably he was not the founder of his dynasty, for he claims to have succeeded someone named Labarnas and mentions a rebellion against his grandfather (Labarnas' father). However, there are no writings from the reigns of these kings (who, like Hattusilis, presumably were from Kussara), and some scholars doubt that they ever existed. At some point in his reign, Hattusilis occupied Hattusas and made it his capital. He gained control of most of eastern Anatolia, even crossing the Taurus Mountains and extending his kingdom's borders to the Mediterranean. He also campaigned against the Luwian area of Arzawa in western Asia Minor, but this was little more than a raid. He probably died on a campaign against the kingdom of Yamhad (Aleppo) in northern Syria.

During his reign, Hattusilis' greatest challenge had been choosing a successor who would be able to preserve the unity of the kingdom. His sons had rebelled against him and had been removed from the succession. He then adopted his nephew and named him as his successor, but that choice seems to have been unpopular with many members of the landholding aristocracy and threatened more civil war. Since his nephew took no steps to placate and win over his opponents, Hattusilis repudiated his adoption. Shortly before his death, Hattusilis named his teenaged grandson Mursilis as his successor and adopted him. The nobles seem to have accepted this choice and when Hattusilis died, Mursilis I (c. 1620 to 1590 B.C.E.) succeeded peacefully to the throne.

Mursilis (or possibly his regent at first) moved to consolidate his hold over the areas of southern Anatolia conquered by Hattusilis. Then he avenged his grandfather's defeat and death by conquering Aleppo and destroying the kingdom of Yamhad. Now the way was open for the greatest display of Hittite power in Old Kingdom times, the attack on Babylon. Why Mursilis undertook an expedition so far from the Hittite homeland is unknown. Perhaps he was just seeking booty or possibly fame to rival that of Sargon of Agade who was said to have marched from Babylonia deep into Anatolia. Others have suggested that his attack was part of an alliance with the Kassites to put them in power in Babylon so they could act as a check on the growing strength of the Hurrians in Syria. In any case, as we have seen, his campaign was successful.

This long campaign, though, put too much strain on the fragile peace Mursilis had created within the Hittite realm. Plots were hatched in his absence, and soon after his return, he was assassinated by his brother-in-law. This began a period of anarchy, palace murders, and civil war that lasted for several generations. The new kingdom of Mitanni seized the opportunity to conduct several destructive raids into Hittite territory. Also, many former Hittite vassals in Asia Minor revolted. The territory Hittite kings could control effectively contracted to the Hittite homeland surrounding Hattusas, the capital. Conditions improved somewhat when Telepinus (c. 1525 to 1500 B.C.E.) seized the throne and instituted a law clearly defining the rules of succession. However, though he restored some order at home, Telepinus was unable to reconquer Hatti's former territories. So, it remained only a modest-sized Anatolian kingdom until the advent of the Hittite New Kingdom almost a century later.

THE EMERGENCE OF NEW PEOPLES

Indo-Europeans

Our earliest evidence for Indo-European-speakers in the Near East comes from the tablets of Assyrian merchants who lived at Kanesh in Anatolia around 2000 to 1900 B.C.E. Many Indo-European personal names appear in these records, so Indo-European groups must have been present in central Anatolia by the beginning of the second millennium, at the latest. Scholars once thought that the original Indo-European homeland was on the steppes of southern Russia or in the Ukraine, and a few still hold this view. But in recent decades, studies have shown that all the Indo-European languages and dialects share words concerning agriculture and the domestication of animals. So the earliest Indo-European speakers were agriculturalists, not seminomadic herders, and their language must have originated in an area that experienced the Neolithic Revolution. Thus, the view currently favored is that Proto-Indo-European, the common tongue from which the various Indo-European languages descended, developed c. 5500 to 4500 B.C.E. in the area between the Black and Caspian Seas and between the Caucasus Mountains and northern Mesopotamia.[40] This is essentially the area of ancient Armenia (which is now northeastern Turkey, the Republics of Armenia, Georgia, and Azerbaijan, and the northwestern tip of Iran).

The Indo-European languages spoken in ancient Asia Minor—Hittite (i.e., Nesite, in the central area), Luwian (in the south and west) and Palaic (in the north)—are very closely related, but they are quite different from other Indo-European tongues. For example, Sanskrit, the classical language of India, is closer in structure and vocabulary to Greek and Latin than it is to Hittite. Probably by the mid-third millennium B.C.E., Proto-Indo-European had developed into two different branches or subfamilies. Speakers of one branch, Proto-Anatolian, moved into Asia Minor where the separate Hittite, Luwian, and Palaic languages developed. Groups speaking the other branch moved north and then west, becoming the ancestors of the European language families (Celtic, Italic, Germanic, Baltic, and Slavic). Other groups from the second branch became the speakers of Proto-Armenian, Proto-Greek, and Indo-Iranian (which diverged into Median, Persian, Sanskrit, and other languages). The Proto-Greek speakers moved west while the Indo-Iranians moved east and south. As we shall see, some Indo-Iranians likely became a ruling class among the Hurrians and possibly also among the Kassites in the mountains north and northeast of Mesopotamia.

At present, we cannot date these early Indo-European movements with certainty. Most scholars agree, though, that the initial Indo-European migrations which brought the Proto-Greek speakers into Greece and the Proto-Anatolian speakers into Asia Minor *probably* occurred as part of the turmoil and destruction that swept over the eastern Mediterranean area around 2200 B.C.E.[41] The migrating Indo-European groups apparently destroyed some of the Greek and Anatolian settlements that were sacked and abandoned at this time. But they did not cause all of the destruction. As we have seen, this was probably a time of weather change and drought. The dete-

riorating environment that likely forced many Indo-Europeans to move also must have caused much local conflict and devastation in the areas they would eventually settle. By about 2000 to 1900 B.C.E., the bands of Proto-Greek-speakers seem to have occupied most of Greece, and the Proto-Anatolian-speakers had spread throughout Asia Minor. Moreover, the speech of these groups had probably begun to develop into Greek on the one hand and the Hittite, Luwian, and Palaic languages on the other.

It is also possible that around 1700 B.C.E., chariot-using Indo-Iranian speakers migrated into eastern Iran and India, causing the mysterious cultural collapse in Central Asia, eastern Iran, and the Indus Valley. However, as we have seen, there is little direct evidence to support that theory except for Vedic tradition and the fact that by c. 1000 B.C.E., related Indo-European languages were spoken in India and in much of Iran. So, while it is very probable that an Indo-Iranian migration into Iran and India did occur sometime during the Bronze Age, we can't pinpoint its route or its chronology.

Recently, Robert Drews revived an old theory linking the Indo-European migrations and conquests with the use of horse-drawn light chariots.[42] We have noted that heavy, solid-wheeled chariots pulled by small donkeys were used in Mesopotamia during the Early Dynastic Period. However, these vehicles were little better than wagons or carts—they were slow, cumbersome, and difficult to steer. In contrast, the agile horse-drawn light chariot with spoked wheels changed the nature of warfare. It seems to have been developed early in the second millennium B.C.E. by horse-breeding Indo-Iranian speakers in eastern Anatolia.[43] Domesticated horses had been known in the Near East much earlier, but their usefulness in warfare could not be exploited without use of the bit. The horse bit is a metallic mouthpiece attached to the bridle and reins. When pulled, it presses against the tender rear parts of the horse's mouth, forcing the animal to accept direction by means of the reins. It seems to have been introduced into the Near East shortly before 1800 B.C.E., though it probably had been used on the Russian steppes at an earlier time. Horse bits allowed chariot drivers to control steeds galloping at top speed, something that was impossible with the nose rings used earlier.

At first, the chariot was just a luxury item used by kings and the very rich for rapid transportation or as a status symbol. During the eighteenth century B.C.E., it also probably began to be used for hunting. However, by the early part of the seventeenth century B.C.E., horse-drawn chariots began to be used in warfare. Chariot warfare is first attested in Asia Minor and Syria, but the new tactics quickly spread throughout the Near East and into other areas. Drews connects the spread of chariot warfare with the movement of Indo-European conquerors, arguing that the Greeks only entered Greece c. 1600 B.C.E., bringing the war chariot with them, and that around the same time, Aryan chariot warriors conquered India, as the *Rig Veda* claims.[44] However, if there were earlier Indo-European movements into Asia Minor and Greece c. 2200 B.C.E. as most scholars contend, then the spread of the light war chariot likely was due more to cultural diffusion and the need to match the military innovations of opponents than to Indo-European conquests.[45]

Hurrians and the Mitanni

Like the Indo-Europeans, the Hurrians seem to have originated somewhere within the south Caucasus and Armenia, possibly in the mountains north and northwest of Lake Van. Their language is only imperfectly understood, but it is a non-Semitic and non-Indo-European tongue of the Asianic (possibly Caucasian) type. Its only close relative is Urartian, the language of a first millennium B.C.E. kingdom that developed around Lake Van. Urartian and Hurrian probably descended from a common linguistic ancestor, though some would argue that Urartian was just a late form of Hurrian. The Hurrians may be the people referred to in the Bible as Horites.

As early as the latter part of the Early Dynastic Period, some Hurrians seem to have begun moving southward; during the Akkadian Period they were ruling some small city-states in northern and northeastern Mesopotamia. The most important of their early city-states was Urkesh, which Hurrian myth identified as the residence of the primordial god Kumarbi. Hurrian migrations southward and westward seem to have increased during the Akkadian and Ur III periods, probably as part of the widespread disturbances occurring from about 2200 to 2000 B.C.E. As we have seen, Akkadian and Ur III rulers campaigned against the Hurrians in northern Mesopotamia and Syria, possibly in an attempt to stop or slow their influx into those areas.

By the early part of the second millennium B.C.E., a significant portion of the population of Syria and southeastern Anatolia was Hurrian, though they were still in the minority there. There were Hurrian colonies or enclaves at Mari, Ebla, and Alalakh, and individuals with Hurrian names lived in Chagar-Bazar, Carchemish, Aleppo, and Ugarit. Hurrian month names were used in seventeenth-century B.C.E. Yamhad (Aleppo) and Alalakh, and about half the names in the texts from Alalakh Level VII were Hurrian when the city was destroyed by the Hittite king Hattusilis I (c. 1650–1620 B.C.E.).

The Hittite destruction of Yamhad and Babylon around 1600 B.C.E. and the subsequent Hittite internal problems left a power vacuum that the Hurrians rushed to fill. They settled in large numbers at Tepe Gawra, Nuzi, and Arrapha in Northern Mesopotamia; Qatna, Tunip, Ugarit, Alalakh, and Emar in Syria; and Kizzuwatna in southeastern Anatolia. At about this same time (soon after c. 1600 B.C.E.), an Indo-Iranian group seems to have joined the Hurrians and unified the various Hurrian city-states into a single kingdom or confederation of kingdoms. This new kingdom, centered between the Habur and Balikh Rivers where its capital Wasshukanni (Tell el-Fekheriyeh?) was probably located, was known by several names. The Hittites called it the Land of Hurri after the main component of its population. The Assyrians called it Hanigalbat, which originally was the name of an important area or a kingdom within the confederation. The Egyptians knew it as Naharina, derived from a Semitic term ("the rivers") for northern Mesopotamia, especially the area around the upper Euphrates, Balikh, and Habur rivers. However, the people of this new kingdom called it Mitanni (or Maittani in its earliest form). The rulers and aristocracy of Mitanni had Indo-Iranian (Aryan) names such as Tushratta (which probably means "owner of terrible chariots") and Biridashwa ("possessing great horses"). In addition to Hurrian gods, the upper classes worshipped the Indo-Iranian or Proto-Vedic deities Mitrasil (Mithra), Indar (Indra), Arunasil (Varuna), and Nasattyana (the Nasatyas). Some personal names also probably contain the names of Indar/Indra (the war god) and other Indo-Iranian divine elements such as Soma (a plant whose juice gives immortality), Vaya (the wind god), the Devas (a group of deities), Svar (heaven), and Rta (the divine law). Texts also contain Indo-Iranian numerals and technical words pertaining to horses and chariots. Moreover, members of the chariot-using military elite were called *maryannu*, a term which probably was formed from the Indo-European word *marya* ("young man" or "warrior") with a Hurrian ending. This Indo-European (or more specifically Indo-Iranian) elite is often designated "the Mitanni" (after the name of the kingdom) to distinguish them from their Hurrian subjects. However, the Mitanni probably were absorbed into the Hurrian population relatively quickly, though Indo-Iranian names remained traditional for kings and members of the upper classes. Hurrian seems to have been the kingdom's spoken language, used even by its ruling class, though Akkadian was used for most written records and correspondence.

By about 1500 B.C.E., Mitanni had expanded to become the most powerful kingdom in western Asia. It controlled virtually all of Syria, northern Mesopotamia (including Assyria), southeastern Anatolia, and the Levantine coast down to a point about midway between Qadesh and Gubal (Greek Byblos). Meanwhile, the Egyptians were extending their control over Palestine and Lebanon, leading to clashes between these two great powers (see Chapter 6). The Hittite kingdom also was threatened by the growth of Mitanni, losing territory in northern Syria and southeastern Anatolia. By the late fifteenth century B.C.E. when a new dynasty began the restoration of Hittite power, Hurrians were a significant part of the population in several former Hittite lands, and Hittite culture had come under strong Hurrian cultural influence (see Chapter 7).

Kassites

The Kassites probably originated in the central Zagros mountains (the area of modern Luristan), south of the homeland of the earlier Guti and Lullubi. So far, linguists have not been able to determine the family relationship of the Kassite language, which is known only from personal names and a few Assyrian word lists. It may have been distantly related to Elamite. However, once the Kassites gained control of Babylon, they adopted Babylonian Akkadian for both speech and writing. Some scholars have suggested that an Indo-Iranian group joined the Kassites or influenced them, for the names of a few Kassite gods such as Shuriash and Maruttash seem to be Indo-European (Surya and Marut). Furthermore, many of the surviving Kassite words relate to horses or parts of chariots, and the light war chariot probably was first developed in Armenia by Indo-Europeans. However, the evidence for Indo-European connections with the Kassites is not as persuasive as that for an Indo-European aristocracy among the Hurrians.

As we have seen, a Kassite army entered Mesopotamia during the reign of Samsu-iluna (c. 1749 to 1712 B.C.E.). However, others continued filtering in peacefully for some time after that, for documents list Kassites working as herdsmen and harvesters. By around 1700 B.C.E., the Kassite name of a king of Hana on the middle Euphrates indicates that Kassites probably had gained control of that city-state. Around the same time they took Mari. Their hold on the middle Euphrates (through their occupation of Mari and the kingdom of Hana centered on Terqa) may have facilitated the Hittite army's movement down the Euphrates to attack Babylon in 1595 B.C.E. Whether by prior agreement or happenstance, after the Hittites left, the Kassites moved into Babylon and established themselves in power. The Kassite Dynasty ruled Babylonia (or Karduniash as they called it) for slightly more than four centuries, longer than any other dynasty in Mesopotamian history.

Little is known about the early Kassite kings of Babylon, for no documents from this period have been found. Like earlier conquerors of Mesopotamia, the Kassites seem to have quickly adopted the local language, religion, and customs, their origins being recognizable only by their names. By the middle-to-late sixteenth century B.C.E. they conquered the Sealand, giving them control over all of Babylonia. But they abandoned hope of regaining the north and agreed to a boundary treaty with Assyria, effectively dividing Mesopotamia into two lands: Babylonia and Assyria. Kassite rule does not seem to have been oppressive, for the old southern Mesopotamian city-states, often rebellious in the past, became docile and enjoyed a long period of peace and prosperity.

Among the accomplishments of the Kassite Period, three innovations are particularly noteworthy. They abandoned the use of year names and instead counted years from the first New Year following a king's coronation. Thus, events and documents would be dated, for example, "first year of king X" or "fifth year of king Y." The Kassites also introduced the use of the *kudurru*, a small decorated and inscribed stele recording an official land grant from the king or a high official. Such stones were probably erected in the fields they described while archival copies on clay tablets were deposited in temples. The Kassites also developed a new type of adornment for southern Mesopotamia's mud-brick buildings. Since stone for decorative sculpture had to be imported and was expensive, the Kassites molded bricks so that when they were assembled properly, they formed images in relief. This type of decoration continued into Neo-Babylonian and Persian times, perhaps the best-known examples being the figures on the sixth century B.C.E. Ishtar Gate.

SUGGESTIONS FOR FURTHER READING AND INFORMATION

Internet Sites

Mesopotamian history: http://www.history.evansville.net/meso.html

The city of Ur reproduced with computer graphics: http://www.taisei.co.jp/cg_e/ancient_world/ur/aur.html

Information on Meteorite Impacts and Climate Change at the End of the Early Bronze Age: http://abob.libs.uga.edu/bobk/ccc/cc110501.html

Books and Articles

Mesopotamia, Syria and Elam

Bermant, Chaim, and Michael Weitzman. *Ebla: A Revelation in Archaeology*. New York: Times Books, 1979.

Bucccellati, Giorgio G. *The Amorites of the Ur III Period*. Naples, Italy, 1966.

Carter, E., and M. W. Stolper. *Elam: Surveys of Political History and Archaeology*. Berkeley: University of California Press, 1984.

Dalfes, H. Nüzhet, George Kukla, and Harvey Weiss, eds. *Third Millennium BC Climate Change and Old World Collapse*. New York: Springer, 1997.

Dalley, Stephanie. *Mari and Karana: Two Old Babylonian Cities*. London and New York: Longman, 1984.

Foster, Benjamin R., et al. *The Epic of Gilgamesh: A New Translation, Analogues, Criticism*. New York: Norton, 2000.

Foster, Benjamin R. *Umma in the Sargonic Period*. Memoirs of the Connecticut Academy of Arts and Sciences, 20. Hamden, CT: Published for the Academy by Archon Books, 1982.

Frayne, Douglas R. *Sargonic and Gutian Periods, 2334–2113 BC*. Toronto: University of Toronto Press, 1993.

———. *Ur III Period, 2112-2004 BC*. Toronto: University of Toronto Press, 1997.

Kraus, Fritz R. *The Role of Temples from the Third Dynasty of Ur to the First Dynasty of Babylon*. Translated by Benjamin Foster. Malibu: Undena Publications, 1990.

Liverani, Mario, ed. *Akkad, the First World Empire: Structure, Ideology, Traditions*. Padua: Sargon SRL, 1993.

Matthiae, Paolo. *Ebla: An Empire Rediscovered*. Garden City, NY: Doubleday, 1981.

Orlin, Louis. *Assyrian Colonies in Cappadocia*. The Hague: Mouton and Company, 1970.

Pettinato, Giovanni. *The Archives of Ebla*. Garden City, NY: Doubleday, 1981.

———. *Ebla: A New Look at History*. Baltimore: Johns Hopkins Press, 1991.

Richard, Suzanne. "The Early Bronze Age: The Rise and Collapse of Urbanism," *Biblical Archaeologist*, vol. 50, no. 1 (1987), pp. 22–43.

Roth, Martha T. *Law Collections from Mesopotamia and Asia Minor*. Atlanta: Scholars Press, 1995).

Vallat, François. "Elam," in David Noel Freedman, editor-in-chief, *The Anchor Bible Dictionary*, vol. 2, pp. 424–429.

Young, Gordon D., ed. *Mari in Retrospect: Fifty Years of Mari and Mari Studies*. Winona Lake, IN: Eisenbrauns, 1992.

The Emergence of New Peoples

Drews, Robert. *The Coming of the Greeks: Indo-European Conquests in the Aegean and the Near East*. Princeton, NJ: Princeton University Press, 1988.

Gamkrelidze, T. V., and V. V. Ivanov. *Indo-European and the Indo-Europeans: A Reconstruction and Historical Analysis of a Proto-Language and a Proto-Culture*. Berlin: 1995.

Mallory, J. P., and D. Q. Adams, eds. *Encyclopedia of Indo-European Culture*. Chicago: Fitzroy Dearborn, 1997.

Mallory, J. P. *In Search of the Indo-Europeans: Language, Archaeology and Myth*. London and New York: Thames and Hudson, 1989.

Renfrew, Colin. *Archaeology and Language: The Puzzle of Indo-European Origins*. New York: Cambridge University Press, 1988.

Wilhelm, G. *The Hurrians*. Translated by J. Branes, with a chapter by D. L. Stein. Warminster: Aris and Phillips, 1989.

The Arabian Gulf and Indus Valley Cultures

Bryant, Edwin. *The Quest for the Origins of Vedic Culture: The Indo-Aryan Migration Debate*. New York: Oxford University Press, 2001.

Chakrabarti, Dilip K. *The Archaeology of Ancient Indian Cities*. New York: Oxford University Press, 1995.

Chakrabarti, Dilip K. *India—An Archaeological History: Paleolithic Beginnings to Early Historic Foundations*. London and New York: Oxford University Press, 2000.

Crawford, H. *Dilmun and Its Gulf Neighbors*. Cambridge: Cambridge University Press, 1998.

Fairservis, Walter A. Jr. *The Harappan Civilization and Its Writing*. New Delhi: Oxford and IBH Publishing, 1992.

Khalifa, Haya Ali Al, and Michael Rice, eds. *Bahrain Through the Ages: The Archaeology*. London: KPI, 1986.

Potts, D. T. *The Arabian Gulf in Antiquity*. Oxford: Oxford University Press, 1990.

Ratnagar, S. *Encounters: The Westerly Trade of the Harappan Civilization*. Delhi and Oxford: 1981.

Reade, Julien, ed. *The Indian Ocean in Antiquity*. London: Kegan Paul International, 1996.

NOTES

1. See the translations of the Old Babylonian copy of Sargon's inscription by Amélie Kuhrt, *The Ancient Near East c. 3000–330 BC* (London: Routledge, 1995), vol. I, p. 49, and A. Leo Oppenheim in J. B. Pritchard, ed., *Ancient Near Eastern Texts Relating to the Old Testament*, 2nd ed. (Princeton, NJ: Princeton University Press, 1955), p. 267.

2. The translation is from Benjamin R. Foster, *Before the Muses: An Anthology of Akkadian Literature* (Bethesda, MD: CDL Press, 1993), vol. II, p. 819.

3. See, for example, Henri Frankfort, *Kinship and the Gods* (Chicago: University of Chicago Press, 1948), pp. 295–301, and Georges Roux, *Ancient Iraq*, 3rd ed. (London and New York: Penguin Books, 1992), p. 156.

4. Thorkild Jacobsen, "Early Political Development in Mesopotamia," *Toward the Image of Tammuz and Other Essays on Mesopotamian History and Culture*, William L. Moran, ed. (Cambridge, MA: Harvard University Press, 1970), p. 395, note 108.

5. Kuhrt (1995), vol. I, p. 51.

6. Hans J. Nissen, *The Early History of the Ancient Near East, 9000–2000 B.C.* (Chicago: University of Chicago Press, 1988), pp. 172–173.

7. See Joan Oates, *Babylon*, rev. ed. (London and New York: Thames and Hudson, 1986), p. 41, though she herself prefers Thorkild Jacobsen's suggestion that Naram-Sin was just a guiding national "genius."

8. Harvey Weiss, M. A. Courty, W. Wetterstrom, F. Guichard, L. Senior, R. Meadow, and A. Curnow, "The Genesis and Collapse of Third Millennium North Mesopotamian Civilization," *Science*, vol. 261, no. 5124 (August 20, 1993), pp. 995–1003; Marie-Agnès Courty and Harvey Weiss, "The Scenario of Environmental Degradation in the Tell Leilan Region, NE Syria, During the Late Third Millennium Abrupt Climate Change," pp. 107–147 and Harvey Weiss, "Late Third Millennium Abrupt Climate Change and Social Collapse in West Asia and Egypt," pp. 711–723 in H. Nüzhet Dalfes, George Kukla and Harvey Weiss, eds., *Third Millennium BC Climate Change and Old World Collapse* (New York: Springer, 1997).

9. See Suzanne Richard, "The Early Bronze Age: The Rise and Collapse of Urbanism," *Biblical Archaeologist*, vol. 50, no. 1 (1987), pp. 22–43. For evidence that the col-

lapse of the Palestinian EB III cities was triggered by a climate change, see Arlene M. Rosen, "Environmental Change and Human Adaptational Failure at the End of the Early Bronze Age in the Southern Levant," in Dalfes, Kukla, and Weiss, eds. (1997), pp. 25–38.

10. There were 421 (probably c. 450) sites in EB II and only 108 (probably c. 125) in EB III. James Mellaart, "Anatolia c. 4000–2300 B.C." in I. E. S. Edwards, et al., eds., *The Cambridge Ancient History*, 3rd ed., vol. I, part 2 (Cambridge: Cambridge University Press, 1971), p. 406.

11. M. I. Finley, *Early Greece: The Bronze and Archaic Ages*, 2nd ed. (New York: Norton, 1981), p. 13. At the place cited in note 10, J. Mellaart used almost the same words, describing what happened in Anatolia as "a catastrophe of such magnitude as to remain unparalleled until the very end of the Bronze Age."

12. Fekri A. Hassan, "Nile Floods and Political Disorder in Early Egypt," in Dalfes, Kukla, and Weiss, eds. (1997), pp. 1–23.

13. See Nigel Hawkes, "Bronze Age Cities May Have Been Destroyed by Comet," *The Times* (London), March 8, 1997; Sharad Master, "A Possible Holocene Impact Structure in the Al 'Amrah Marshes, Near the Tigris-Euphrates Confluence, Southern Iraq," *Meteoritics and Planetary Science*, vol. 36 (September 2001), Supplement, p. A124; Robert Matthews, "Meteor Clue to End of Middle East Civilisations," *The Sunday Telegraph* (London), November 4, 2001.

14. Richard A. Kerr, "Sea-Floor Dust Shows Drought Felled Akkadian Empire," *Science*, vol. 279, no. 5349, January 6, 1998, pp. 325–326.

15. See, for example, the article by Suzanne Richard cited in note 9 and Amihai Mazar, *Archaeology of the Land of the Bible, 10,000–586 B.C.E.* (New York: Doubleday, 1990), pp. 169–171.

16. See, for example, Karl W. Butzer, "Sociopolitical Discontinuity in the Near East c. 2200 B.C.E.: Scenarios from Palestine and Egypt," in Dalfes, Kukla, and Weiss, eds. (1997), pp. 245–296.

17. Mazar (1990), pp. 154–158.

18. Rosen in Dalfes, Kukla, and Weiss, eds. (1997), p. 25. (Entire article is pp. 25–38.)

19. C. J. Gadd, "The Dynasty of Agade and the Gutian Invasion," in *CAH*, 3rd ed. *(1971)*, vol. 1, part 2, p. 462.

20. H. W. F. Saggs, *Babylonians* (Norman: University of Oklahoma Press, 1995), p. 88. The information in brackets was added by W. Stiebing for clarification.

21. Kuhrt (1995), vol. 1, p. 71.

22. Nissen (1988), p. 194.

23. The translation used here is by Thorkild Jacobson with the aid of Mrs. H. A. G. Frankfort in H. and H. A. Frankfort et al., *The Intellectual Adventure of Ancient Man* (Chicago: University of Chicago Press, 1946), pp. 142 and 197. For the complete poem, see Samuel N. Kramer's translation in J. B. Pritchard, ed., *Ancient Near Eastern Texts*, pp. 455–463.

24. See, for example, the work edited by Dalfes et al. cited in note 8.

25. Walter A. Fairservis, Jr., *The Harappan Civilization and Its Writing* (New Delhi: Oxford and IBH Publishing, 1992).

26. C. C. Lamberg-Karlovsky and Jeremy A. Sabloff, *Ancient Civilizations: The Near East and Mesoamerica*, 2nd ed. (Prospect Heights, IL: Waveland Press, 1995), pp. 211–213.

27. Diego Ibarguen, "Early Writing Found on Artifact," *The Times-Picayune* (New Orleans), May 14, 2001, p. A-4. The article is taken from an Associated Press report.

28. Lamberg-Karlovsky and Sabloff (1995), p. 219.

29. Ibid., p. 227.

30. Roux (1992), p. 183.

31. For an English translation of several of the Mari letters dealing with administration, war and peace, and the court, see A. Leo Oppenheim, *Letters from Mesopotamia* (Chicago: The University of Chicago Press, 1967), pp. 96–110.

32. Georges Dossin, *Archives Royales de Mari, I: Correspondance de Samsi-Addu et de Ses Fils* (Paris: Imprimerie Nationale, 1950), letter 108, pp. 182–183, translation by W. Stiebing. The material in brackets was added to clarify the meaning. For letters to Yasmah-Adad in this vein, see *Dossin (1950)*, I, letters 61 and 69. The relevant portions of these letters are translated by Georges Roux in Roux (1992), p. 192.

33. Roux (1992), p. 192 from *Archives Royales de Mari*, IV, letter 70. The material in brackets was added by W. Stiebing to clarify the meaning.

34. Georges Dossin, "Les archives épistolaires du Palais de Mari," *Syria*, vol. 19 (1938), p. 117, translation by W. Stiebing.

35. Dossin (1950), II, letter 31, translation by W. Stiebing.

36. Ephraim A. Speiser pointed this out long ago. See his translation and notes in Pritchard, ed. (1955), p. 96. The plant's name is "Man Becomes Young in Old Age" and

after eating it, the snake sheds its old skin, becoming shiny and "new" again. This clearly indicates that the plant confers renewed youthfulness, not immortality. Snakes continue to shed their skins and remain "youthful," but experience surely must have taught the ancient Mesopotamians that despite that fact, snakes do die!

37. Kuhrt (1995), vol. I, p. 112.

38. The translation is by W. Stiebing. For the entire "law code," see Theophile Meek's translation in Pritchard, ed. (1955), pp. 163–180.

39. See, for example, H. B. Huffmon, "Prophecy in the Mari Letters," *Biblical Archaeology Review*, vol. 3 (1970), pp. 199–224, and Abraham Malamat, "A Forerunner of Biblical Prophecy: The Mari Documents" in P. D. Miller, P. D. Hanson, and S. D. McBride, eds., *Ancient Israelite Religion: Essays in Honor of Frank Moore Cross* (Philadelphia: 1987), pp. 33–52.

40. See, for example, Robert Drews, *The Coming of the Greeks: Indo-European Conquests in the Aegean and the Near East* (Princeton, New Jersey: Princeton University Press, 1988), pp. 32–35; and T. V. Gamkrelidze and V. V. Ivanov. *Indo-European and the Indo-Europeans: A Reconstruction and Historical Analysis of a Proto-Language and a Proto-Culture* (Berlin: 1995).

41. For dissenting views, see the following works: Colin Renfrew, *Archaeology and Language: The Puzzle of Indo-European Origins* (New York: Cambridge University Press, 1988), pp. 145–175 and 263–277 places the Proto-Anatolian speakers in Asia Minor much earlier, before the beginning of the Bronze Age (c. 3000 B.C.E.). Drews (1988), pp. 158–201 supports the view of Leonard R. Palmer, *Mycenaeans and Minoans: Aegean Prehistory in the Light of the Linear B Tablets*, 2nd ed. (New York: Knopf, 1961), pp. 321–353 that the Greeks (or Proto-Greeks) did not arrive in Greece until the beginning of the Late Bronze Age around 1600 B.C.E.

42. Drews (1988), especially pp. 136–157.

43. Drews (1988) provides an excellent discussion of the beginnings of chariot warfare, pp. 102–105. See also Mary Aiken Littauer and J. H. Crouwel, "Chariots" in David N. Freedman, editor-in-chief, *The Anchor Bible Dictionary* (New York: Doubleday, 1992), vol. 1, pp. 888–892.

44. Drews (1988), pp. 158–201.

45. A few scholars such as Annelies Kammenhuber, *Die Arier im vordern Orient* (Heidelberg: Carl Winter Universitätsverlag, 1968), and I. M. Diakonoff, "Die Arier im Verderen Orient: Ende eines Mythos," *Orientalia*, vol. 41 (1972), pp. 91–120, have challenged all attempts to connect the introduction of light war-chariots with Indo-Europeans. However, their attempt to date the use of horse-drawn chariots for warfare earlier than the second millennium is almost certainly incorrect as Robert Drews has shown (see note 43).

4

Egypt to the End of the Old Kingdom

THE LATE PREDYNASTIC ERA (c. 3500–3000 B.C.E.)

The Geography of Egypt and Nubia

The Nile River alone makes life in Egypt possible. The ancient Greek historian Herodotus recognized this fact long ago when he made his famous statement that "Egypt is the gift of the Nile." The Delta area gets only four to eight inches of rain a year, and the rest of the Nile Valley gets far less. Thus, the river creates a long narrow oasis through terrain that otherwise would be just the eastern end of the great Sahara Desert. The Nile rises far to the south in Uganda and Ethiopia from lakes and tributaries fed by summer monsoon rains. Two main streams, the Blue Nile and the White Nile, join at Khartoum in southern Sudan to form the Nile proper. Another large tributary, the Atbara, feeds into the Nile a little further north. While the White Nile supplies most of the Nile's flow during the winter and spring, the Blue Nile and Atbara provide most of the extra water and silt carried downstream during the flood season in summer and early fall.

Through the ages, the Nile has cut a narrow valley through the largely sandstone rock of Sudan, leaving cataracts (small waterfalls or rapids) across its path wherever it encountered more resistant types of stone. These cataracts constantly stirred up the Nile's waters, preventing most of the silt it carried from being deposited before it reached Egypt. North of the second cataract (now under the waters of Lake Nasser), the Nile Valley widens considerably. The rock layers from this area northward are largely limestone, which is less resistant to erosion. So, at various times in the past, the river was able to cut new channels and more easily shift its position in this northern segment. In antiquity, it was the 700-mile-long northernmost section of the Nile Valley from the first cataract in the south (at Aswan) to the Mediterranean coast in the north that comprised Egypt. As mentioned in Chapter 1, Egypt, in turn, was divided into two parts: Upper Egypt (the long thin portion of the Nile Valley from the first cataract to the beginning of the Delta) and Lower Egypt (the Delta area north of Cairo). The portion of the valley south of the first cataract was known as Nubia or **Kush**.

Flanking the Nile within Egypt there are two bands of fertile soil (called *kemet*, "the black land," by the Egyptians) averaging in antiquity about one quarter mile in width on either side of the river. In Nubia, the fertile strips are much narrower. Beyond the "black land" on both sides of the Nile stretches desert, known as *deshret*, "the red land." Within Egypt south of the Delta, the "red land" rises on either side of the river until it meets a range of mountains or hills (see Figure 4.1). Beyond these hills is more desert. On the west is the vast Sahara Desert (called the Western or Libyan Desert by the Egyptians) punctuated by only a few nearby oases. On the east, another desert (called the Eastern Desert) continues to the Red Sea and then across Sinai and Arabia.

Today the Nile's flow is regulated by a series of dams. However, until recent times it had regular, very predictable floods (inundations). It would begin to rise about the same time every year (July). Then, at the beginning of August, the river surged through overflow channels and covered most of the valley up to the desert plateau. The waters remained at this high level from mid-August through September. Finally, in October, the water slowly began to subside

and return to its banks, leaving behind a rich new layer of black silt. This constant renewal of the soil's fertility made Egyptian agricultural yields the highest in the ancient Near East. The Nile's cycle also led the Egyptians to divide the year into three seasons: "Inundation" (July through October), "Going Down of the Inundation" (sowing and cultivation of crops, November through February) and "Drought" (harvest and lowest levels of the Nile, March through June). Because the Egyptian civil calendar had only 365 days while the solar year is actually 365¼ days long, the official seasons often did not correctly correspond to the natural ones.

Over time, the Nile's silt deposits raised the ground level near the river higher than the areas closer to the desert plateau. So most settlements were built on these higher ridges near the river or on the edge of the desert beyond the limits of the flood. Some very low-lying basins behind the riverbanks and in parts of the Delta retained water, creating marshes and swamps. These areas supported abundant wildlife, especially waterfowl, crocodiles, and hippopotami. They also contained thickets of papyrus plants whose stalks were invaluable for making boats,

FIGURE 4.1   The West Bank of the Nile at Luxor in Upper Egypt
The "black land," desert plateau, and hills are clearly visible.
Source: Courtesy of the author.

mats, and other useful objects, including a paper-like writing material. The somewhat drier parts of these marshes, while still too wet for agriculture, made excellent grazing areas for cattle.

The People of the Nile Valley

In recent years, there has been much popular interest in the racial identity of the ancient Egyptians.[1] Archaeologists, anthropologists, and historians usually try to avoid such discussions, because the concept of race is a cultural construct rather than a legitimate biological category. People ask whether the Egyptians were "white" or "black." However, such questions usually assume two incorrect premises. First, they imply the existence of biologically distinct "pure races" that developed in isolation from one another over long periods of time. Second, the questioners generally believe that there is a link between what they regard as racial distinctions and cultural achievement. The answer to the question about the racial identity of the ancient Egyptians is important to many because they want to claim early Egypt's accomplishments for themselves.

Today, social scientists agree that the evidence does not support either of these premises. Most human populations do not seem to have developed in almost total isolation from one another. Thus, separate biological races probably never existed, leading present-day biologists and anthropologists to oppose the use of the term "race" as a biological category. Modern genetic studies have shown that only 16 percent of the variations between individual humans exist *between* the major so-called "races," while 94 percent of the differences occur *within* specific population groups.[2] Differences in easily observable physical traits usually provide the basis upon which cultures distinguish "races" from one another. However, often-used racial characteristics such as skin color, hair texture, the shape of eyelids, noses, lips, or other features often vary independently through space and over time. For example, as anthropologist Robert Wenke noted, "southern Indians, West Africans, some Pacific Islanders, and others share a relatively dark skin pigmentation but differ greatly in nose and lip shape, hair texture, and other features."[3] Furthermore, there is no demonstrable relationship between such physical features and cultural achievement.

Egypt provides a good example of the mixture of groups that often occurred in antiquity. After 10,000 B.C.E., the Nile Valley became a magnet for immigrants from North Africa, Sinai, Palestine, and the southern reaches of the Nile. In the Nile Valley, physical types varied so gradually that differences were perceptible only between places widely separated geographically. Skin color, for example, gradually changed from light olive brown in the Delta to an almost blue-black near the Nile's sources. Other physical features varied bit-by-bit along the same continuum. But such physical changes were not as important to the ancient Egyptians as to modern Westerners. The Egyptians *did* distinguish themselves as a group from Libyans, Nubians, "Asiatics," and others in artistic representations by emphasizing differences in facial features and skin tone between these groups and the "average" Egyptian. However, the main criteria Egyptians used to define themselves relative to others were *cultural* in nature. Anyone who lived in Egypt, spoke the Egyptian language, and shared the Egyptian culture was an Egyptian. Outsiders spoke differently, dressed differently, wore different hairstyles, and had different customs. To the ancient Egyptians, there was a world of difference between an Egyptian who lived in the Delta and his Libyan and Palestinian neighbors, even though they all might resemble one another physically. In the same way, a darker-skinned Egyptian resident of Elephantine was a "person,"° while his physically similar Nubian neighbors just to the south were only "wretched foreigners."

Prelude to Civilization: The Naqada II Period

The final phase of the Egyptian Predynastic Era is usually known as the Naqada II (or Gerzean) Period. However, some scholars prefer to call the last century or so of this era, the time just before the unification,

---

°In the ancient Egyptian language, the same word meant "Egyptian" and "person." Non-Egyptians were not truly people to the Egyptians.

Naqada III (or the Protodynastic Period or Dynasty 0). As we saw in Chapter 1, several different cultures existed in different parts of Egypt during the prehistoric period. By about 4000 B.C.E., two cultures prevailed: Omari A in Lower Egypt and Naqada I in Upper Egypt. This situation continued into the era after c. 3500 B.C.E. when the Naqada II culture developed out of Naqada I. It was best represented in southern Egypt where Naqada and Gerza, the sites after which the period is named, are located. The first part of Naqada II was contemporary with the Omari B and Maadi cultures of the north (named after sites just south of Cairo). However, the characteristic features of Naqada II gradually spread into the Nile Delta, bringing a degree of cultural uniformity to Egypt during the latter part of this era (see Table 4.1).

The skills needed to produce the beautiful flint knives, drilled and polished stone bowls, painted well-fired pottery, and other characteristic artifacts of this period indicate that experts were involved. Thus, differentiation of labor, including craft specialization, had become widespread. There is also evidence of social stratification and growing disparities in wealth. Elite members of society were able to afford stone bowls, ivory-handled flint knives, carved slate cos-

metic palettes, and other luxury artifacts, while building large houses and tombs for themselves.

Fortified settlements with rectangular mud-brick houses developed at Hierakonpolis, Naqada, Abydos, and at other places along the Nile. Gradually, these settlements seem to have been consolidated into several small principalities or kingdoms, perhaps corresponding to some of the **nomes** or administrative districts of later Egypt. According to later tradition, by the end of the Predynastic Era rulers had forged these principalities into two realms—the kingdoms of Upper and Lower Egypt. Many archaeologists doubt whether there was ever a unified kingdom embracing all of Lower Egypt in Predynastic times. Also, though there does seem to have been a kingdom in Upper Egypt centered on Hierakonpolis, it probably did not control the entire Nile Valley from the Delta to the first cataract. Though the later tradition may be oversimplified, several major kingdoms do seem to have emerged by the latter part of Naqada II. Furthermore, archaeological evidence seems to support the tradition of warfare between the rulers of Hierakonpolis and groups in the Delta.

The rapid cultural and political development that occurred during the Naqada II Period may have been

TABLE 4.1
Chronology of the Egyptian Predynastic and Early Dynastic Periods

(All dates are B.C.E. Not all rulers of the First and Second Dynasties are listed.)

Badarian (in the South), **Merimde and Faiyum A** (in the North)	5000–4000
Naqada I (= Amratian; Omari A in the North)	4000–3500
Naqada II (= Gerzian; Omari B, Maadi in the North)	3500–3000
The Protodynastic Era or Dynasty "0"	3050–3000
"Scorpion"	
Narmer	
The Early Dynastic (or Archaic) Period (Dynasties 1 and 2)	3000–2686
First Dynasty	3000–2890
Aha	3000–?
Second Dynasty	2890–2686
Peribsen (originally Sekhemib)	
Khasekhemwy (originally Khasekhem)	?–2686

spurred at least in part by outside influences. Today, few scholars would support the old idea that foreign invaders brought civilization to Egypt and established the First Dynasty. There seems to have been continuity and development from Egypt's earliest cultures into those of late Predynastic and Early Dynastic times. Though some new cultural features certainly appear in the Nile Valley during the Naqada II Period, they probably resulted from trade rather than invasion.

There is archaeological evidence of extensive Egyptian trade with Palestine and Nubia. Palestinian pottery, especially jars with wavy ledge handles, became widespread in Egypt. Archaeologists also have uncovered Egyptian objects from this era at Palestinian sites. Though few Nubian objects have been found in Egypt, Egyptian pottery vessels are commonplace in Nubia. The trade goods coming from Nubia must have been primarily raw materials, as in later times—ivory, gold, copper, animal skins, precious stones, ebony, and other fine woods.

However, it was trade with Mesopotamia that seems to have had the greatest cultural impact on Egypt at this time. Archaeologists have not found Egyptian artifacts from this era in Mesopotamia, but they have uncovered Mesopotamian Late Uruk and Jemdet Nasr cylinder seals and pottery vessels in

Egypt. This suggests that either, like Nubia, the Egyptians were trading raw materials or, more likely, that the Mesopotamian goods were coming to Egypt through intermediaries in Syria or Palestine. As noted in Chapter 2, archaeologists have found both Egyptian Naqada II and Mesopotamian Late Uruk objects at Habuba Kabira in Syria. So, it was probably at this site and at similar ones in Syria and Palestine that the two cultures were meeting. By whatever means they came to the Nile Valley, the Mesopotamian wares and ideas seem to have strongly influenced Egyptian culture. Many Egyptian building facades from this time and the following Early Dynastic Period have numerous niches or inset panels like those of Mesopotamian structures (see Figure 4.2). Egyptians began copying the Mesopotamian practice of using cylinder seals to make impressions in clay to indicate ownership. Also, several Mesopotamian-like artistic motifs appear on Egyptian artifacts. These include a bearded "hero" holding animals at bay on either side, a lion attacking the hindquarters of its prey, a Mesopotamian-style boat, entwined snakes, and creatures with long wavy or intertwined necks. Some think that Mesopotamians may have taught the Egyptians more advanced techniques for carving stone vessels and working copper.

FIGURE 4.2 Part of the Enclosure Wall of Djoser's Step Pyramid
The wall's inset niches copy those used on earlier *mastabas*.
Source: Courtesy of the author.

More significant, though, is the probability that contact between Mesopotamia and Egypt contributed to the development of writing in both areas.

THE FORMATION OF THE EGYPTIAN STATE (c. 3050–2686 B.C.E.)

The Process of Unification

Around 3100 or 3050 B.C.E., a ruler of Upper Egypt supposedly conquered Lower Egypt and unified the Two Lands. Later Egyptian tradition as preserved by an Egyptian priest named Manetho and various Greek writers credited this unification to a king called Menes. Supposedly, Menes not only made himself ruler of Upper and Lower Egypt, but also founded Memphis. Nineteenth Dynasty king lists also name the first king of Egypt Meni. However, scholars do not agree on which historical figure known from artifacts or texts might be this Menes.

The Palermo Stone, a Fifth Dynasty list of early Egyptian rulers, does not mention Menes or Meni. Instead, it lists someone named Aha (or Hor-Aha) as the first king of the First Dynasty. However, Aha follows Meni (Menes) on the Turin Canon, a king list written around 1200 B.C.E. Moreover, the Turin Canon lists Meni twice in succession, once designated as a human ruler and once designated as a god. To complicate matters, archaeologists have found objects that suggest two other candidates for the title of "first king" or "unifier" of Egypt.

One of these artifacts is known as the Scorpion Macehead. It is the carved stone head of a ceremonial or votive mace found at Hierakonpolis. The scene depicted on it shows a ruler wearing the "White Crown," the traditional crown of Upper Egypt (see Figure 4.3), performing some ceremonial act with a hoe. Possibly he is opening an irrigation canal or beginning temple construction. He is identified by two symbols in front of his face, a rosette and a scorpion. We do not know how these signs are to be read, so he is conventionally called King Scorpion (or Rosette-Scorpion). Clumps of papyrus plants seem to indicate that this action is taking place in the Delta. Around the top of the macehead, lapwing birds are hanging from standards bearing symbols of some of Upper Egypt's later nomes or provinces. The lapwing in later writing was the hieroglyph for "common peo-

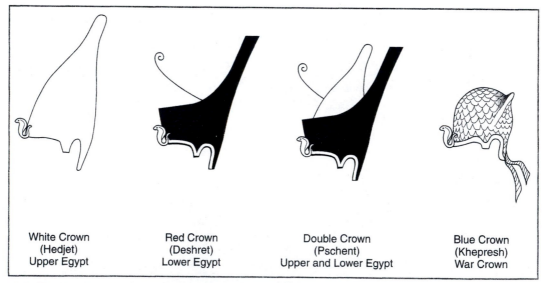

| White Crown (Hedjet) Upper Egypt | Red Crown (Deshret) Lower Egypt | Double Crown (Pschent) Upper and Lower Egypt | Blue Crown (Khepresh) War Crown |

FIGURE 4.3   The Most Common Ancient Egyptian Crowns

Source: Courtesy of the author.

ple." This would seem to indicate that Scorpion, a king of Upper Egypt, had conquered at least part of Lower Egypt and was performing acts of kingship and administration there.

A slightly later cosmetic palette from Hierakonpolis also seems to depict a king of Upper Egypt conquering Lower Egypt. However, on this object, the king is named Narmer, his name written with signs that remained part of the hieroglyphic writing system of later times. On one side of the palette, Narmer, wearing the "White Crown" of Upper Egypt, is brandishing a mace to give the death blow to a kneeling captive (see Figure 4.4, View A). Above the prisoner's head, a falcon is holding captive a human-headed papyrus clump. This symbol seems to represent the king, the human incarnation of Hierakonpolis's falcongod Horus, as conqueror of the Delta region (represented by the papyrus plants). The other side of the palette shows Narmer wearing the "Red Crown" traditionally associated with Lower Egypt (see Figure 4.4, View B). He is surveying the battlefield where the enemy dead are laid out in rows. Two beasts with their necks entwined seem to symbolize the unification of the Two Lands. Narmer also wears the "Red Crown"

FIGURE 4.4   The Narmer Palette
Left: view of front; right: view of back.
Source: Egyptian Museum, Cairo.
Photo: Erich Lessing/Art Resource, New York.

on a carved ceremonial macehead from Hierakonpo-lis. Thus, Narmer seems to have been a king of Upper Egypt who defeated the occupants of the Delta and became king of Lower Egypt as well.

Unfortunately, this interpretation of the palette is not as certain as it seems. A Naqada I jar (c. 4000 to 3500 B.C.E.) from Upper Egypt seems to depict the "Red Crown." So, this crown may not always have been associated only with Lower Egypt. It may have been designated as the symbolic crown of the North only at a later date. Thus, Narmer's use of the "Red Crown" does not necessarily show that he claimed to be King of Lower Egypt. We cannot even be sure he won a victory in the Delta. One scholar has argued that the palette depicts a ritual re-enactment of an earlier victory over a Libyan group rather than an historical battle from Narmer's reign.[4] However, a recently discovered label from Narmer's reign mentions the "smiting" of a land symbolized by papyrus plants. This label supports the traditional interpretation of the palette as celebrating Narmer's conquest of Lower Egypt.

Aha, the first king of the First Dynasty according to Old Kingdom sources, also may have conducted military campaigns in the Delta. His name means "warrior." Also, Aha is the earliest king attested at Memphis, a city that he seems to have established. Since the founding of Memphis was later ascribed to Menes, Aha and Menes may be the same person. Moreover, an ivory label depicts Aha before a structure inscribed "Two Ladies *Men.*" In later times, rulers' royal titles consisted of five names, the first called the **Horus name** and the second called the *nebty* **name** (the "Two Ladies" name, referring to the patron goddesses of Upper and Lower Egypt). Thus, the label may indicate that Men or Meni (Menes in Greek) was the *nebty* name of the king whose Horus name was Aha.

Unfortunately, this interpretation of the label's meaning is not certain. Some scholars think the building depicted is a funerary shrine that Aha is dedicating to his predecessor, Menes (probably Narmer). The Egyptian word *men* means "to endure" or "the enduring one." So, it is also possible that the shrine was dedicated to worship of the two patron goddesses and named "The Two Ladies Endure."

So who was Menes? Scorpion? Narmer? Aha? Or perhaps Menes was another king even earlier than these three. Scholars disagree. Some have argued that two or more of these kings are the same person known by different names.[5] Another suggests that Menes is a later historical construct possibly based on an erroneous reading of an early text, since Egyptian *men-i* can mean "So-and-so who once came."[6] Most think it likely that the Menes known to later tradition was either Narmer or Aha. Obviously, though, the tradition of a single conquest and unification by one king is greatly oversimplified.

Some scholars argue that Upper and Lower Egypt had gradually achieved a cultural and political unity during the Naqada II Period and that there was no need for a conquest.[7] However, the Scorpion Macehead and Narmer Palette seem to commemorate two different Upper Egyptian campaigns or "conquests" in the Delta, though this area was probably not a unified kingdom. Furthermore, there may have been other military campaigns against areas of the Delta before those of Scorpion and Narmer. The process of unification must have taken generations before it became an accepted fact of life. Perhaps the later tradition telescoped the complex developments that led to the establishment of a unified Egyptian state, crediting the accomplishments of three or more kings to Menes alone.

However complicated the unification process may have been, it seems to have been completed by the reign of Aha. The various parts of Egypt had been welded into a single nation-state—the first known to history. Fictional or not, the idea of two kingdoms, Upper and Lower Egypt, united by and through one king became a basic element of Egyptian civilization. It was constantly depicted in artistic motifs, religious rituals, and royal titles. Egypt, unified in the person of its ruler, was ready to begin its 3,000 years of pharaonic civilization.

The Development of Egyptian Writing

The primary writing system developed by the ancient Egyptians is known as **hieroglyphic** writing. This name comes from the ancient Greeks who called it *hieroglyphikà grámmata*, "sacred carved letters." Since they saw hieroglyphs primarily on temple walls, tombs, stelae, and other religious objects, Greek travelers may have gotten the false impression that Egyptians used them only for religious purposes. However, it is also possible that the Greek term reflected the native Egyptian expression for writing: *medu netjer*, "divine words."

The fully developed hieroglyphic writing system first appeared at about the same time as the unification. However, crude pictographs (ideograms) representing concepts, objects, or actions had been used somewhat earlier. Recently, at Abydos, German archaeologists unearthed bone and ivory labels, pottery, and clay seal impressions bearing hieroglyphs. These artifacts, dated by the excavators between 3400 and 3200 B.C.E., bore written signs indicating the quantity and place of origin of various trade commodities. However, these glyphs were not ideograms. They were phonetic signs that utilized the principle of rebus writing.[8] Rebus puzzles consist of words or phrases written with letters, numerals, or pictures whose names have the same sounds as the words to be read. For example, in English we might write "belief" with drawings of a bee and a leaf. The Abydos hieroglyphs may represent the earliest phonetic writing found so far and seem to be precursors of the

more complex system of the Dynastic Age. However, some Egyptologists question the early dates given to the Abydos labels.[9]

Around the time of Narmer and Aha scribes began using a mixture of ideograms, phonetic signs and determinatives to clarify the meaning of inscriptions. Some words with the same sound had different meanings, and there were many signs that sometimes could be used to represent complete words and at other times, only a sound (see Figure 4.5). Therefore, scribes began adding determinatives to many words. These signs were symbols or ideograms designed to remove any possible ambiguity in the meaning of the written signs. For example, a straight vertical line under a sign indicated that it was to be read as an ideogram for a word, not just as a sound. Or, a drawing of a seated man could be placed behind a sign such as *neb* ("lord") to show that the masculine form of the word was intended. On the other hand, the sign for *neb* followed by the phonetic sign for "t" and a seated woman would be read *nebet* ("lady; mistress"). Small running legs would be written behind verbs that describe motion, and so forth (see Figure 4.5).

Unfortunately, as in later Hebrew and Arabic, only consonants were written. Thus, since vowels were not represented, we have only a vague idea of how ancient Egyptian words were actually pronounced. This is why scholars spell Egyptian words and names

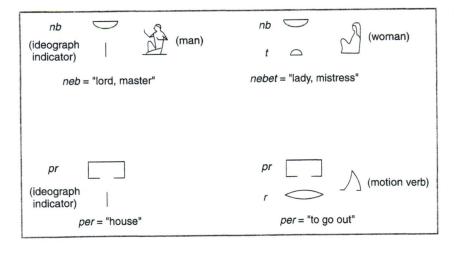

FIGURE 4.5 Examples of Egyptian Hieroglyphic Writing

in diverse ways. Also, although Egyptian hieroglyphic writing contained 24 signs that represented only one consonant each, they never developed these signs into a true alphabet. They continued to use a mixture of ideograms, biconsonantal and triconsonantal phonetic signs, determinatives, and single-consonant "alphabetic" signs. Eventually, Egyptian scribes created a cursive version of the hieroglyphic signs known as hieratic and a still-later version known as demotic for everyday use on papyrus. Nevertheless, they continued to use elaborate hieroglyphs for important inscriptions until the end of the fourth century C.E.

As mentioned above, archaeological evidence indicates that about the time Egyptian hieroglyphic writing first appeared, there was some Mesopotamian influence on Egyptian culture. Thus, in the past, many scholars argued that writing was another Mesopotamian gift to Egypt. However, though Mesopotamians had used symbolic tokens and ideographic inscriptions much earlier than the Egyptians, Sumerian phonetic writing may be slightly later than the Egyptian examples from Abydos. On the other hand, as previously stated, the dates for the Abydos labels are not certain. Thus, Mesopotamian syllabic writing may be earlier. Whichever way this argument is resolved, it appears that contact between these two areas led to "cross-fertilization" and to the appearance of complex writing systems in both regions at about the same time. It is clear, though, that only *ideas* about writing were being exchanged. The Egyptians created their own hieroglyphic symbols, which were quite different from the cuneiform signs developed by the Mesopotamians.

The Early Dynastic Period (Dynasties 1 and 2)

The era of the first two Egyptian Dynasties is usually called the Early Dynastic or Archaic Period. It is also sometimes called the Thinite Period since, according to Manetho, the capital of Egypt during the first two dynasties was at This (or Thinis), a town very close to Abydos (see Map 4.1). The movement of the capital from Hierakonpolis to This may reflect the new prominence of Abydos's chief god, Khentiamentiu

("Foremost of the Westerners"). This god, the ruler of the blessed dead, was later identified with Osiris, and his name became one of Osiris's titles. The merging of deities and blending of myths, a feature of later Egyptian religion, was probably already underway in the Early Dynastic Period.

During this era, rulers strengthened and consolidated the union created by Aha and his predecessors. They began developing the administrative system that would become so effective during the Old Kingdom. They divided Egypt into administrative districts called nomes, 22 in Upper Egypt and 20 in Lower Egypt. Each was governed by an official called a **nomarch**. While the capital remained in the south, Memphis became the center from which powerful officials controlled the newly incorporated Delta region. The regional differences apparent during the Predynastic era disappeared, and Egyptian culture became homogeneous once Egypt had only one king and one ruling class. On the other hand, the Egyptian and Nubian cultures, which had been at comparable levels during the Predynastic Period, began to diverge considerably after Egypt's unification. As the Egyptians developed their own identity, all outsiders, including the Nubians, became foreigners and enemies.

Our earliest reference to an Egyptian military campaign outside of Egypt comes from the First Dynasty. One of the regnal years of King Djer, successor to Aha, is named "The Year of Smiting the Land of Setjet" (Syria-Palestine). Despite (or perhaps because of) such raids, trade with Palestine continued, and even increased somewhat from its earlier levels. Djer also conducted campaigns in Nubia and against the Libyans to the west. In addition, the kings of the first two dynasties sent expeditions into Sinai where they began acquiring turquoise and copper from the natives.

Another interesting development during the First Dynasty was the reign of a woman, Meritneith. She does not seem to have claimed the titles and prerogatives of kings, for an early list of rulers on a clay seal impression designates her only as "King's Mother." After the death of her husband, she probably acted as regent for her infant son (probably King Den). However, she did exercise royal power for sev-

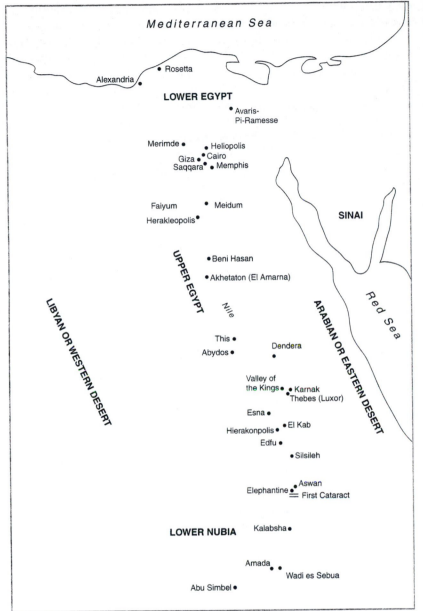

MAP 4.1   Ancient Egypt

Source: Adapted from Peter Clayton, *The Rediscovery of Ancient Egypt* (London: Thames and Hudson, 1982), p. 56.

eral years and was buried in a tomb indistinguishable from those of Early Dynastic kings.

Just before the end of the Second Dynasty there may have been some conflict, possibly even civil war, between different areas of Egypt or worshipers of

competing deities. Early Dynastic rulers customarily inscribed their names within rectangles depicting the royal palace surmounted by the image of a falcon (almost certainly the god Horus). In this way, they were probably claiming to be the incarnation of

Horus. However, the Horus Sekhemib ("Powerful in Heart") seems to have changed his name during his reign to honor Seth rather than Horus. He put the Seth animal (possibly a dog) over his name in place of the falcon and became the Seth Peribsen ("Hope of all Hearts"). Seth was later regarded as the mortal enemy of Horus, so some scholars argue that this name change suggests disputes between followers of Horus and Seth or between parts of Egypt represented by Horus and Seth.[10] If there was conflict or war at this time, Peribsen's successor seems to have ended it. Originally named the Horus Khasekhem ("The Powerful One [= Horus] Appears"), he changed this Horus name to Khasekhemwy ("The Two Powerful Ones Appear") and placed both the Horus falcon and Seth animal above it. In addition, he added a second name, "The Two Lords Are at Peace in Him."

The Early Dynastic era was a period of experimentation and amazing creativity. It saw the emergence or standardization of most of the basic political and cultural elements that would remain characteristic of ancient Egyptian civilization throughout its history. Many Old Kingdom developments (such as the construction of the pyramids) cannot be understood adequately without reference to these fundamental concepts. So, we will briefly examine some of them before proceeding to a discussion of the Old Kingdom.

MAJOR ELEMENTS OF EGYPTIAN CULTURE

Ma'at

The concept of **ma'at** is basic to ancient Egyptian thought. This term cannot really be translated by a single English word, though its meaning is often given as "truth." However, it meant much more. *Ma'at* was also order, stability, balance, harmony, wisdom, and justice. It was the state in which everything was in its right place, everything was in order, just as the gods had made it. *Ma'at* was personified as a goddess, the daughter of the sun god Re. She was represented either by the image of a woman with a feather in her headband or just by the feather, her special symbol. One of the basic duties of the great divinities and their divine representative on earth, the king, was to maintain *ma'at* in nature and in society.

The Egyptian belief in *ma'at* probably was prompted and encouraged in part by Egypt's physical environment. The Nile Valley had an order, harmony, and stability not found in other areas of the Near East. As indicated earlier, there is balance and symmetry in much of the Egyptian landscape. The Nile flows down the center of the country with bands of fertile soil, desert, hills, and desert on either side. One side of the valley often seems to reflect the other.

The "black land" on either side of the river and throughout much of the Delta provided the Egyptians with their food. Yet the hills and dry desert plateaus were also useful. The hills provided semiprecious stones and some gold. Their main contribution, however, was the building stone that the Egyptians eventually used for stelae, statues, tombs, and temples. The desert areas just beyond the reach of the Nile's inundations were where Egyptians often built their villages. They also buried their dead in the desert, at first in graves and tombs near the villages and towns, and later in tombs cut into the hillsides a bit further away. So, the Egyptians recognized a harmonious relationship between the "black land" and "red land" similar to the beneficial union created between the other Two Lands, Upper and Lower Egypt.

The Nile also contributed to the Egyptians' sense of order and stability. Its inundations began about the same time each year. Since houses were located on the desert plateaus or on other pieces of high land, the Nile's floods did not usually endanger them. Thus, Egyptians saw this pattern of flooding as useful and created by the gods for Egypt's benefit. Furthermore, once one king ruled the entire valley, the floods were made even more constructive. Rulers had canals cut to better direct the water's flow. They also set up Nilometers at various places in Egypt. These were measuring instruments, usually steps carved out of rock surfaces by the river with measuring marks cut into the side walls. The Egyptians used them to determine exactly when each inundation began as well as to estimate how high it would be and when it would reach various points in Egypt. Thus, people came to view the inundations as even more regular and predictable.

The daily movements of the sun probably also reinforced ideas of symmetry and stability. Every day the sun rose from behind the hills in the east, crossed the sky, and set behind the hills in the west. During the night, it was presumably circling under the earth until it rose above the eastern horizon again the next morning. This unchanging orderly cycle formed the basis for some of Egypt's most important myths and theological concepts.

Furthermore, nature gave Egypt a large measure of protection from external invasion. The large deserts beyond the eastern and western hills were too vast and harsh to harbor inhabitants or allow the passage of enemies. So, despite the length of its eastern and western borders, Egypt did not have to fear invasions from either side. Outsiders could enter Egypt only at limited points in the south or north. From the south, people could move into Egypt along the banks of the Nile or by boat down the Nile until they reached the cataracts. From the north, groups could enter by one of the mouths of the Nile or by coastal roads from Libya or Palestine. But when Egypt was unified and strong, it could build forts at these entry places and keep out any unwanted foreigners.

Thus, unlike Mesopotamians, Egyptians did not see their world as subject to the whims of capricious gods. Egyptian deities were mostly helpful and good. Floods were not punishments sent by the gods; they were life-sustaining gifts. Invaders were not always moving in to take over the land. Occasionally, Nile floods were too low or too high, storms came in from the Mediterranean or the deserts, or political disruptions occurred. However, such disturbances of the natural and social harmony were infrequent. Damage was usually quickly repaired and forgotten. Egyptians believed that *ma'at*, the order and stability established by the gods, prevailed in this world. And, with the support and maintenance of the gods and the king, it would continue to prevail. So the Egyptians were usually a happy, optimistic people who thought they were living in the best of all possible worlds. As we shall see

later, this made it much harder for Egyptians to adjust to times of political collapse and social chaos when these eventually occurred.

Divine Kingship

As we have seen, Mesopotamians believed that their rulers were intermediaries between the gods and humans. Mesopotamian kings, however, were usually not divine; they were only the viceroys or earthly representatives of the gods. In Egypt, though, the king was himself a god, ruling the country for his fellow deities. He was the real owner of all its land, people, and resources.

The belief that the king was divine seems to go back to the very beginning of kingship in Egypt. Predynastic depictions of rulers such as "Scorpion" and Narmer (see Figure 4.4) already show them much larger than the ordinary people around them. Similar illustrations from this time found in Nubia indicate that rulers there probably also were considered divine. It is now impossible to determine how and where this idea originated. Many scholars now regard it as a fairly universal concept that appeared independently in slightly different forms in many different areas. However and wherever it arose, belief that the king was in some way divine remained a dominant concept in Egypt throughout antiquity.

The ancient Egyptians didn't actually have a word that directly corresponds to our term "king." For example, the title *nisut bity*, which we, for convenience, translate as "King of Upper and Lower Egypt" is literally "The One Belonging to the Sedge Plant and the Bee." (The sedge was a symbol of Upper Egypt and the bee represented Lower Egypt.) The word "pharaoh," which we commonly use for Egyptian rulers, is derived from the Hebrew Bible. The Hebrew term was an attempt to reproduce the Egyptian word *per'o* (or *per'aa*), which meant "great house." This word was originally one of many terms for the royal palace, but from the Eighteenth Dynasty on, it came to be used to refer to the king himself. Modern historians follow the biblical usage, applying it to all kings of Egypt, even though this term is anachronistic for pre-Eighteenth Dynasty rulers.

From the Old Kingdom onward, Egyptians commonly called the king "the good god," and myths indicated his divine status. According to one story, Osiris had once been ruler of Egypt. However, his wicked brother Seth killed and then dismembered him. Osiris's wife (and sister) Isis carefully collected the scattered pieces of his body and formed them into a mummy. She then used her magic to restore Osiris to life, but he now became ruler of the afterlife rather than this world. Isis bore Osiris a son named Horus who avenged his father by defeating Seth and becoming the new king of Egypt. Thus, every king of Egypt was the earthly embodiment of Horus. He overcame Seth (evil, disorder, and chaos) and preserved *ma'at*. When he died, he became Osiris and his son ruled as the new Horus.

We cannot be certain that during the Early Dynastic Period this myth was already known in its later classic form. However, the Narmer Palette seems to depict the king in the form of a falcon, the symbolic representation of Horus. Also, Early Dynastic rulers placed the image of a falcon above their names, suggesting that they were claiming to be Horus incarnate. Furthermore, as mentioned above, a Second Dynasty king changed the falcon above his name to a Seth symbol. This suggests not only that both gods were worshiped at this time, but also that the whole Osiris-Seth-Horus conflict myth was already known. Probably as early as the late Predynastic Era, Egyptians believed the ruler to be the earthly embodiment of Horus, as they did in later times.

The Narmer Palette also shows a bull demolishing a walled city. This is probably a symbolic representation of Narmer as the "Mighty Bull," another of the later royal titles. In addition, "Scorpion" and Narmer, like later kings, wear a bull's tail hanging from the back of their belts, a further indication of their role as embodiment of the divine bull. These rulers also wear a special beard worn only by gods, and their crowns bear the **uraeus**, a protective image of a rearing cobra thought to spit fire at enemies of the king. Thus, many of the images and titles associated with the divinity of the king in later times were already present at the beginning of Egypt's dynastic history.

Egyptian rulers came to have a royal titulary of five different names which signified their divine status. The first name was the Horus name indicating that the ruler was the current incarnation of Horus. This was the only name used in most Early Dynastic inscriptions. However, the differences between the names on inscriptions and those known from later king lists and Manetho probably indicates that these rulers had other names that were still known in later times. The second royal name was the *nebty* or "Two Ladies" name. This name designated the king as the favorite of Nekhbet, the vulture goddess of Upper Egypt, and Wadjet, the cobra goddess of Lower Egypt. The third name was the **Golden Horus name** whose significance is unclear. Scholars call the fourth and fifth names the **praenomen** (or throne name) and **nomen** (or personal name). These two names were each enclosed in an oval labeled a **cartouche**. The praenomen was preceded by the title *nisut bity*, "King of Upper and Lower Egypt." The *nisut bity* name or praenomen appeared for the first time near the end of the First Dynasty. If in later times a text or inscription referred to a pharaoh by only one name, it was usually the praenomen that was used. The nomen, generally the name the ruler had been given at birth, was preceded from Fourth Dynasty on by the designation "Son of Re" (the sun god). It didn't seem to bother the Egyptians that the pharaoh was designated as the son of Re and also as Horus, the son of Osiris.

Because of belief in the divine nature of kingship, the Egyptians do not seem to have created law codes like those of the Mesopotamians, Hittites, and Israelites. As a god, pharaoh's word was law. However, he would not have felt able to do anything he pleased. He was expected to uphold *ma'at*. His legal decisions and those of his officials seem to have followed traditional concepts of personal rights, fairness, and justice designed to maintain the status quo. This created a sort of common law system for Egypt.

Despite their constant references to the king's divinity, Egyptians knew that his knowledge was limited, that he could not perform miracles, and that he aged and died. There were later stories and wisdom compositions that even stressed the king's weaknesses. So how could people believe he was a god? The Egyptians, at least those in the upper classes, seem to have distinguished between the human being who was ruler at any given time and the eternal office of kingship that he exercised. This distinction was expressed by the concept of the divine **ka** possessed by every Egyptian king. Every person was thought to have a *ka*, a vital force that animated his or her body. The *ka* of the king, however, was divine. In fact, artistic representations of the upraised arms (symbolizing the *ka*) with the Horus name of the king between them seem to indicate that Horus himself was the *ka* of the king. Furthermore, Isis, the mother of Horus, seems originally to have been the deified throne of Egypt.[11] During the coronation ceremony for a new king, the mortal taking the throne received the divine *ka* of kingship and became Horus, the divine son of Isis and Osiris, by virtue of his office. In the words of Thomas Schneider, "the individual, temporal person of the ruler and the transcending, idealized being from the ideology were united within him."[12]

To the Egyptians, the divine king was "a bond between nature and man."[13] Since the occupant of Egypt's throne embodied the divine *ka*, he naturally would rule in accordance with *ma'at*. He would also conduct the religious rites necessary to maintain *ma'at* and keep the forces of chaos at bay (see Figure 4.6). As Stephen Quirke has pointed out, "all cult in Egypt was royal cult; it was part of a cosmic pact in which the king offered up to heaven the fruits of the earth, in exchange channelling down to earth the blessings of heaven."[14] Thus, the divine king assured the continued well-being of the land and its people. He was the necessary link between society and nature, and between the people and their other gods.

Burial and the Afterlife

Egyptian beliefs about the afterlife seem to have been developed by the Naqada II Period, if not earlier. In the Naqada I Era (c. 4000 to 3500 B.C.E.) the peoples of both Upper and Lower Egypt buried their dead in simple graves, each containing only a few pots or other small objects in addition to a body. Most of the bodies had been placed on their sides in a fetal position as if they were sleeping (or perhaps as if they were in the womb awaiting a second birth). Generally, their faces were turned to the west, the later Egyptian land of the dead, but no attempts had been made to preserve the bodies. Nevertheless, since the cemeteries in Upper Egypt were in the desert, the hot dry sand often desiccated the tissues, producing natural mummies. However, we can't determine whether

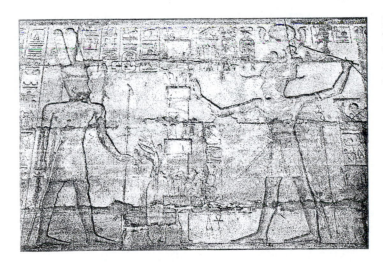

FIGURE 4.6   Pharaoh Making Offerings to a God

This image from the Luxor Temple shows Amenhotep III making offerings to Amun.
Source: Courtesy of the author.

these Predynastic Egyptians held beliefs about the afterlife similar to those of later times.

During the Naqada II Period (c. 3500 to 3000 B.C.E.), members of the growing elite began to bury their dead with large numbers of grave offerings reflecting their wealth and social position. The articles buried with the dead are mostly objects that would have been used in everyday life. The mud-brick tombs were much larger than before, and the walls were sometimes decorated with paintings. The bodies were usually carefully placed on or wrapped in reed mats and surrounded by their possessions. The similarities between these tombs and those of later times suggest that the Egyptians already believed in an afterlife that would be principally like this one.

This era also saw the beginning of intentional mummification. Perhaps accidental discoveries of well-preserved earlier remains led to the first deliberate attempts to preserve the bodies of the dead. Later Egyptians believed that a person's spiritual elements needed the body to survive. Maybe in the Naqada II Era people began to reason that if they could make the body last forever, they could assure the survival of other aspects of a person. For a long time Egyptologists believed that mummification had not been attempted before the Early Dynastic Period.[15] However, since 1997, excavators have been uncovering a Naqada II cemetery at Hierakonpolis filled with mummies. It is not yet known whether natron, a natural salt found near Cairo, had been used to dry out the bodies. There is also no evidence of attempts to remove the internal organs as was done in later times. However, the embalmers had inserted linen pads in places to flesh out the bodies and make them look more lifelike. Then they applied resin to the bodies, wrapped them in linen bandages, and applied more resin before encasing them in linen shrouds.[16]

Gradually, the mummification process became more complex. By the Old Kingdom period at the latest, the Egyptians had discovered that natron absorbed moisture. Thus, it could dry out bodies in the way the hot desert sands had in early times. Natron is also mildly antiseptic, a quality that helped

it ward off putrefaction. From the late Old Kingdom on, embalmers would wash a corpse with a natron solution then remove its internal organs. However, they left the heart, to Egyptians the seat of reason, will, and emotion, in place. They rinsed the abdomen and chest cavity with spices and palm wine and packed them with rags, straw, or other temporary stuffing. They then covered the body and internal organs for 40 days with heaps of dry natron. At the end of this period, the internal organs were dressed with scented oil and resin, wrapped in linen, and placed in special jars for burial with the body. The embalmers washed and dried the body itself, stuffed it again with resin-soaked linen or sawdust, rubbed it with a lotion containing oils, beeswax, spices, and natron, then covered it with a thin layer of molten resin. This process toughened the skin and made it waterproof. They then wrapped the body, concealing many amulets and bits of jewelry between the layers of bandages. Finally, they covered the whole body with one or more shrouds bound in place by linen strips, placed it in a coffin, and returned it to relatives for burial. This entire mummification process usually took 70 days.

Ancient Egyptians thought that a person consisted of many elements, including a name and a shadow, in addition to a body. The most important spiritual element was the *ka*. The word is often translated as "spirit" or "soul," but "life-force" would probably be better. The *ka* was a person's spiritual double, created by the gods at the same time as his or her body. It provided animation and vitality to the body. The *ka* needed its body to survive; it also needed food. Thus, the Egyptians tried to preserve the body so it could continue to serve as an abode for the *ka*. They also provided food offerings (both real and representational) so the *ka* could be sustained in the afterlife.

Other spiritual entities known from the Old Kingdom onward are the **ba** and the **akh**. We can't be sure that Early Dynastic Egyptians believed in these two spiritual beings, for we have few texts from this time. However, the *ba* and *akh* are mentioned in the later Pyramid Texts, a series of very old hymns, rituals, magical incantations, and fragments of myths that probably go back to Early Dynastic, if not Predynastic, times. As in Old Kingdom times, Early Dynastic Egyptians probably believed that only the king and other gods possessed a *ba* and became an *akh*.

The *ba* (often translated "soul") was that element within kings and gods that allowed them to express their personalities, presence, and power within the world. The *ba* could move about the world freely and invisibly, visiting its favorite places. It did, however, have to return to the tomb at night, and like the *ka*, it could not survive if the body did not survive. In later times it was represented as a human-headed bird, symbolizing both the *ba*'s connection with human personality and its freedom of motion.

Since the king was a god, when he died, he naturally would join the other gods to live and rule eternally. However, first his earthly being had to be transformed into an *akh*, a "glorified being of light." Every day, the sun god entered the western **akhet** (usually rendered "horizon"). However, the *akhet* was not just the place where the sky seems to meet the earth. It was the home of light, the region between this world and the underworld, and the place where the sun god was transfigured into an *akh*. As a glorified and effective spirit he traversed the underworld until he reached the eastern *akhet*. There he was transformed once again for his journey across the daytime sky. So, too, the dead king would become an *akh*, joining the gods and participating in their eternal activities.

The mud-brick tombs constructed for Early Dynastic kings, queens, and their high officials were even larger and more elaborate than those of the Naqada II Era. These rectangular tombs, called *mastabas*,° usually had paneled (offset-inset) facades like the structures (thought to represent royal palaces) depicted beneath Early Dynastic kings' names. In addition to a shaft leading down to a burial chamber under it, each *mastaba* also had several rooms for storing burial objects. Thus, the *mastaba* was likely conceived as a "house for eternity," as were later tombs.

Like their Predynastic predecessors, Early Dynastic Egyptians placed within tombs many objects used in everyday life as well as some having only religious or ritual significance. Presumably,

through magic, these objects could be used by the dead in an afterlife that was to be much like this one. This practice of burying objects with the dead, including jewelry and articles made of gold and other precious materials, led some individuals to engage in tomb robbing. There is evidence that even during Predynastic times, thieves had looted many graves and tombs. Despite all attempts to prevent it, this nefarious activity continued throughout Egyptian history, especially flourishing during times of internal strife and chaos.

First and Second Dynasty rulers not only tried to take much of their wealth with them to the other world, but also their servants. Around the royal tombs of this era at Abydos there are rows of subsidiary graves for attendants who were sacrificed and buried with the monarch they had served. During this time, even some of the powerful officials buried at Saqqara near Memphis had servant burials associated with their tombs. This custom reached its height during the First Dynasty when more than 300 retainers were killed and buried with King Djer. In succeeding reigns, the number of servant burials gradually diminished, and this practice of human sacrifice ceased at the end of the Second Dynasty.

Religion and Ritual

Ancient Egyptian religion is usually more difficult for modern Westerners to understand than other ancient Near Eastern religions. Mesopotamians, Hittites, Canaanites, and other Near Eastern people generally worshiped anthropomorphic gods. However, the Egyptians usually depicted their deities with human bodies and animal heads or totally in animal form. Horus was a falcon, Hathor a cow, Thoth an ibis, Sobek a crocodile, Sekhmet a lioness, and so forth. Westerners are also confounded by the Egyptians' ability to affirm two or more concepts that to us seem

---

°*Mastaba* is the Arabic word for bench. It was applied to these rectangular tombs because, to the Arabs, they resembled the solid mud-brick benches erected in front of traditional village houses.

totally contradictory. One myth credits the creation of all that is to Atum, while another ascribes it to Ptah. The sun was sometimes thought of as Re, while at other times it was Horus, or Khepri. It sailed across the sky on a boat or was pushed by a dung beetle. All these different ideas were simultaneously believed to be true by the Egyptians.

The ancient Egyptians seem to have believed that there was divine power all around them, immanent within nature. The world was not just a physical object, an "it"—it was a being in its own right, a "thou."[17] Sometimes Egyptians perceived this divine force in what we would call natural phenomena, such as the sun going through its daily cycle or the Nile's silt bringing forth vegetation. At other times, the Egyptians recognized aspects of the divine in animals—for example, the power exhibited by lions or bulls, the cleverness displayed by baboons, or the motherly nature of a cow suckling her calf. From very early prehistoric times, Egyptians seem to have believed that to access the power experienced in nature, they had to name and thus particularize divine beings.[18] On the one hand, this view led to a multiplicity of deities. On the other hand, beneath the many gods was a unity that allowed the Egyptians to identify gods with one another in order to combine their functions or powers. Re-Horakhty, Amun-Re and other conjoined deities presented no problems for Egyptians. In the same way, when pharaoh died, he became identified with Osiris, god of the dead, and Re, the sun god, and Atum, the creator god, and any other deity through whom he could live and reign forever.

As in Mesopotamia, each Egyptian deity had a special cult center, a place where he or she was considered the primary or patron deity. The cult of Horus was originally centered on Hierakonpolis and later Edfu, while Seth's was at Ombos. Ptah's main sanctuary was located at Memphis. Atum was god of Heliopolis, and so forth. This situation may derive from prehistoric times when the various areas of Egypt possibly had different gods. However, if there ever was such diversity of religion in Egypt, it had ended by the time of the unification or soon afterward. From the Early Dynastic Period onward a sin-

gle pantheon of major gods seems to have been accepted throughout Egypt. Nevertheless, minor local deities continued to exist and the importance of various deities rose and fell depending upon the prestige and power of the cities containing their cult centers.

Also, as in Mesopotamia, the most basic Egyptian myths concerned cosmology, beliefs about how the universe came into being and how it was structured. Both cultures agreed that before creation, there was only a watery chaos. Order was brought out of chaos and had to be constantly maintained by the gods. However, the Egyptian conceptions about how that happened were somewhat different from those of the Mesopotamians. Egyptians were much more confident than Mesopotamians that the gods could and would maintain the order (*ma'at*) they had established.

What is probably the earliest of the official Egyptian cosmologies seems to have originated at Heliopolis, center for the worship of Atum, a solar deity.° According to this myth, originally there was nothing but Nun, a chaotic sea. Then a mound of earth appeared above the waters (just as such life-giving mounds appeared every year when the inundation began to wane). From that primeval island came Atum ("All"), who from himself created everything. In some graphic versions of the story, Atum produced the first two deities, Shu ("dry air") and Tefnut ("moisture"), by masturbation. Another rendition states that Atum sneezed out Shu and spat out Tefnut. This male and female then mated and brought forth Geb ("earth") and Nut ("sky"). This couple in turn produced all the other elements of creation. A less physical version of the myth has Atum create specific gods by naming (that is, differentiating and particularizing) parts of his body.

A different creation story regarded Ptah, patron god of Memphis, as the primary creator god. This so-

---

°The Egyptian name for Heliopolis ("City of the Sun" in Greek) was Iunu, which was rendered On in Ezekiel 30:17. During the Old Kingdom, Re became another name for the sun god. So, Re was identified with Atum, and Heliopolis became Re's holy city as well.

called Memphite Theology claimed that Ptah was the heart and tongue (mind and speech) of the gods. The heart generated thoughts that were spoken by the tongue, bringing Atum, Re, Horus, and the other gods (the physical world) into being. This more abstract view of creation has often been compared to the Israelite account in Genesis 1 where God creates by merely speaking words. It has also been likened to the concept expressed in the first words of the Gospel of John: "In the beginning was the Word, and the Word was with God, and the Word was God." Though it seems to have gotten some official support when Memphis became Egypt's capital during the Old Kingdom, this myth never really replaced the Heliopolitan tradition.

Other creation accounts featured Min, a fertility god of Coptos; Amun, a creator god from the area around Thebes; and other deities. However, they remained primarily local stories in early times. The Heliopolitan myth attributing creation to Atum (or later Re-Atum and still later Amun-Re) continued to be the most widely recognized account throughout pharaonic history. It was reflected in the architecture of almost every Egyptian temple. A typical temple's floor level gradually rose from its entrance to its holy of holies. This high spot represented (or, in Egyptian thought, magically became) the mound of creation that first rose above the waters of Nun. The papyrus, palm, and lotus columns of the hall in front of the holy of holies are plants of the primeval marsh. They support a roof that was decorated to represent the sky. Most temples had the following features: one or more fortress-like gateways (**pylons**), an open court, a roofed **hypostyle** ("many columned") **hall**, then rooms leading to the holy of holies (see Figure 4.7). As one moved from the open court into the hypostyle hall, then to the holy of holies, the rooms became increasingly darker, leaving the shrine of the deity in primordial darkness. Thus, each temple was a microcosm, a powerful structure refashioning the world and reestablishing *ma'at*. In the words of Egyptologist Stephen Quirke, "an Egyptian temple is a machine for the preservation of the universe," and its closest parallels are not with churches, synagogues, or mosques, but rather with power stations producing the energy society needs to function.[19]

It is important to remember that the Egyptians, like most ancient peoples, believed in sympathetic magic. This is the conviction that through spells or ritual one can make a representation actually become the object it represents. So, as mentioned, the high ground beneath a temple did not symbolize the creation mound from which the universe came. It *was* that creation mound with all of the power and energy of the original. In the same way, images of everyday life in tombs were not just "remembrances" of the dead person. They became real again in the afterlife, assuring the tomb owner that he or she would continue to enjoy the depicted possessions, activities, and family relationships forever.

In the temples, the gods, present in tangible form in their cult statues, were housed, clothed, and fed. Pharaoh, himself a god, was the official celebrant of all religious rites. Every morning in every temple in Egypt, pharaoh took his fellow deities' images from their shrines, dressed them in fresh clothes, fed them, and offered them prayers and incense. Every evening he offered them food again, then returned them to their shrines, and closed and bolted the doors. Obviously the king could not be physically present in every temple in Egypt at dawn and sunset. He delegated priests to represent him. But in theory, only the king could properly approach his fellow gods and conduct their rites. This action is repeatedly illustrated in every Egyptian temple that has survived, and these images made what they showed true (see Figure 4.6). It was pharaoh who performed the ritual duties through the priests and other temple personnel. Temple reliefs seldom show priests (and almost never common people) worshiping the gods. If priests do appear, it is only in secondary roles such as carrying the boat bearing a god's cult statue. Temples constantly depicted the king, the necessary link between humans and the divine, attending to the gods' needs.

The creation of the universe was not only reflected in temples, but also in the coronation rites of each new king and in New Year rituals. The beginning of each reign was a new creation, a renewal of

FIGURE 4.7   The Temple of Isis at Philae

This is a well-preserved Egyptian temple. The main entrance is on the right.
Source: Courtesy of the author.

ma'at by a new incarnation of Horus, and a reunification of the Two Lands. Also, as in Mesopotamia and other areas, the start of each new year was a time of crisis requiring rituals to maintain the establishment of this orderly universe. Creation also was renewed during the **heb-sed** or jubilee festival, usually celebrated when a king had been on the throne for 30 years. It was then repeated at varying intervals thereafter. This rite goes back to Predynastic times. Originally it was a ritual to renew the king's vitality, probably replacing a much earlier custom of killing a chieftain or ruler when his strength began to wane. It became, however, not only a rite of rejuvenation, but also an enthronement ceremony. On the first day of the festival, a statue of the old king was buried. Then, the "new" pharaoh was again crowned king of Upper and Lower Egypt, uniting the Two Lands once more. And, just as at the original coronation, so during the *heb-sed* the world was ritually generated anew.

Except for priests and other temple personnel, commoners, especially the peasants, had little or no part to play in the official rites of the major state deities except as observers at various festivals. For example, during the *Opet*-festival celebrated at Thebes in New Kingdom times, representatives of the common people and the nobility were allowed into the Luxor Temple's court to witness the rites. When the king and cult statues processed from one place to another, cheering crowds lined the routes and gathered at the way stations where the procession rested. They got to see the barques, or portable shrines, if not the cult statues of their gods and offer them adoration, hymns, and perhaps petitions. Commoners could also offer prayers and petitions to *ka* statues of kings that were usually in front of temples. These images of the divine *ka* embodied in the king would pass the petitions on to the other gods.

Usually, though, ordinary citizens' direct worship was concentrated on minor divinities who watched over individuals and households. Commoners prayed primarily to Bes, a dwarf who warded off sickness and evil and promoted fertility, and to Tauret, the pregnant hippopotamus goddess who protected women during pregnancy and childbirth. For the rest, they were confident that pharaoh would preserve *ma'at*, assuring that the Nile floods would be adequate, crops would flourish, and all would be well. Finally, when death came, they hoped for rebirth into another world where they would eternally enjoy a life much like the one they had lived here.

THE OLD KINGDOM (DYNASTIES 3–6, c. 2686–2180 B.C.E.)

Djoser and the First Pyramid

The Third Dynasty begins a new period known as the Old Kingdom (see Table 4.1). Building upon the foundations laid during the Early Dynastic era, this 500-year-long period would see Egypt attain unprecedented affluence, stability, and power. This era is also known as the "Pyramid Age" after its most characteristic constructions. This is fitting, for as we shall see, changes in pyramid size and construction methods parallel the growth, apogee, and decline of royal power, centralization, and general prosperity.

We know little about Sanakhte, the first king of the Third Dynasty, except that he reigned about 18 years and seems to have begun Egyptian mining of Sinai's turquoise (and possibly copper) deposits. He also seems to have been the first king to use a cartouche for his personal name (Nebka). He was succeeded by Djoser (or Zoser), who was probably his brother.

When Djoser (c. 2668 to 2649 B.C.E.) ascended to the throne, he began building his tomb at Saqqara, near Memphis, which he seems to have made his capital. He put his vizier or chief minister, Imhotep, in charge of the work. This choice was either excellent planning or tremendously good luck, for Imhotep was a genius who erected for Djoser the first monumental stone building in the world. Imhotep's abilities were so great that later generations considered him a

god, and today Djoser is remembered primarily because of the Step Pyramid Imhotep created. Officials of the Early Dynastic Period had built their mud-brick *mastaba* tombs on the edge of the desert plateau just northwest of Memphis. Imhotep chose a site for Djoser's tomb a little further south and slightly higher on the plateau than the earlier *mastabas*. Thus, the large *mastaba* he was intending to build could have been seen easily from Memphis. His first departure from tradition was the use of stone rather than brick for the *mastaba*, though he had the stones cut to the size of large mud-bricks. Stone had been used for statues and for portions of buildings before this time, but palaces, *mastabas*, temples, and other structures had continued to be made primarily of brick.

After completing this *mastaba*, Imhotep enlarged it twice. Then he decided on a completely different plan. He enlarged the basic *mastaba* a bit more, then erected a series of three other *mastaba*-like structures on top if it, each a little smaller than its predecessor. This produced a four-stage stepped pyramid, the first pyramid ever built. Djoser must have been in very good health, because Imhotep decided he had time to make the pyramid even larger. He increased the size of the base to 411 by 358 feet (125 by 109 meters) and added two more steps, making a six-stepped pyramid 204 feet (62 meters) high. Around this massive structure Imhotep constructed many dummy buildings with false doors that cannot actually be entered. They were not meant to be used by the living. There is evidence that these fake structures were buried almost immediately after their construction. Among them is a *heb-sed* court and series of stone shrines for celebrating the king's jubilee festivals through eternity (see Figure 4.8). Imhotep surrounded the entire complex (which was more than 1,700 feet long and 900 feet wide) with a huge paneled enclosure wall 34 feet high (see Figure 4.2). The manpower and resources needed to construct these monuments testify to Egypt's growing human and economic wealth and to Djoser's absolute control over both.

The burial complex constructed by Imhotep is a large version of the earlier royal *mastaba* tomb translated into stone. The *mastaba* had been the palace in

FIGURE 4.8   The Step Pyramid of Djoser at Saqqara
The dummy *heb-sed* court and shrines can be seen in the foreground.
Source: Courtesy of the author.

which the dead king's *ka* would live for eternity, while his *ba* occasionally visited places he had loved within this world and his *akh* joined the gods in the other world. Over the shaft leading to a *mastaba*'s burial chamber was an earthen or mud-brick mound, a magical version of the mound of creation that first rose from the waters of Nun. Just as all life had come from that original creation mound, so this mound had the power to guarantee the eternal life of the king whose body was beneath it. Djoser's Step Pyramid, built over his burial chamber, is a monumental creation mound, and the fake buildings around it are the king's palace and official buildings that his spirit can magically use forever.

Perhaps Imhotep's use of a stepped pyramid over the burial chamber was intended just to make the structure higher and thus more mound-like. However, it may also have been intended to represent a gigantic magical staircase to heaven. The later Pyramid Texts, many of which preserve burial rituals probably in use at Djoser's time (if not earlier), include the dead king's statement that "a stairway to the sky is set up for me that I might ascend on it to the sky" (Document 4.1, Spell 267).[20] It would not have bothered Egyptians for the pyramid to be both the creation mound and a magical staircase. For them, embracing one magical identification did not mean rejecting others. In fact, they believed that the more such identifications there were, the better.

The next two successors of Djoser followed his lead and constructed stepped pyramids for themselves. However, these structures were never completed. Only the lowest layers survive, suggesting that these kings died only a few years after work on their burial monuments had begun. The last king of the dynasty, Huni, seems to have constructed three small step pyramids in southern Egypt, but the location of his main structure and burial is unknown.

DOCUMENT 4.1

Examples of the Pyramid Texts

The Pyramid Texts were found inscribed on the walls of pyramids belonging to the latter part of the Old Kingdom. They generally consist of short spells or potent formulas designed to magically insure that the deceased king will live forever in the other world. The examples below[21] are meant to guarantee that the king will join the other great gods in the sky. Most of these texts seem to have been already ancient when written down in the Fifth and Sixth dynasties, and most of the ideas they contain probably go back to the Early Dynastic Period or earlier. The titles and the explanatory material in square brackets have been added to the translations by W. Stiebing.

Spell 217: The King Joins the Sun God

O Re'-Atum, this King comes to you, an imperishable spirit [*akh*], lord of the affairs(?) of the place of the four pillars; your son comes to you, this King comes to you. May [both of] you traverse the sky, being united in the darkness; may you rise in the horizon [*akhet*], in the place where it is well with you. . . .

O Re'-Atum, your son comes to you, the King comes to you; raise him up, enclose him in your embrace, for he is the son of your body for ever.

Spell 219: The King is Identified with Osiris

O Atum, this one here [the King] is your son Osiris whom you have caused to be restored that he may live. If he [Osiris] lives, this King will live; if he does not die, this King will not die; if he is not destroyed, this King will not be destroyed; if he does not mourn, this King will not mourn; if he mourns, this King will mourn. . . .

Spell 267: The King Joins Re in his Solar Boat

. . . A stairway to the sky is set up for me that I may ascend on it to the sky, and I ascend on the smoke of the great censing.

I fly up as a bird and alight as a beetle; I fly up as a bird and alight as a beetle on the empty throne which is in your bark, O Re'. Stand up, remove yourself, O you who do not know the Thicket of Reeds, that I may sit in your place and row over the sky in your bark, O Re', that I may push off from the land in your bark, O Re'. When you ascend from the horizon [*akhet*], my sceptre will be in my hand as one who rows your bark, O Re'. . . .

Spell 508: The King Ascends on the Sun's Rays

. . . I have laid down for myself this sunshine of yours as a stairway [or ramp] under my feet on which I will ascend to that mother of mine, the living uraeus [protective snake goddess] which should be upon me, O Re'. She will have compassion on me and will give me her breast that I may suck it; "My son," says she, "take this breast of mine and suck it," says she; "turn about, O you who have not yet come to the number of your days."

The Zenith of Royal Power: The Fourth Dynasty (c. 2613–2498 B.C.E.)

Snefru (c. 2613 to 2589 B.C.E.), first king of the Fourth Dynasty, constructed the first true pyramid (one with smooth sides) and was the greatest pyramid builder in Egyptian history. He built three large pyramids (one at Meidum and two at Dahshur) and a smaller step pyramid at Seila. The total volume of these structures is slightly larger than that of the Great Pyramid of Giza built by his son Khufu.

The earliest of Snefru's pyramids was the pyramid at Meidum (possibly begun by his predecessor Huni). It started out as a step pyramid. Today this pyramid consists of a three-step tower (the core of the original pyramid) surrounded by a mound of collapsed rubble. However, when and why the outer layers of the pyramid collapsed is a mystery. The evidence suggests that the collapse did not take place until long after Snefru's time. The Meidum pyramid was completed as a step pyramid with eight steps. At that time, however, Snefru seems to have abandoned the site and started a new pyramid at Dahshur, just south of Saqqara.

The Dahshur pyramid was the first true or smooth-sided pyramid, a design probably influenced by the *benben* at Heliopolis. This cult object, sacred to the sun god, was probably a cone-shaped stone. However, a smooth-sided pyramid would look the same from the side and was the closest the Egyptians could come to constructing a tomb with a similar shape. Each side of Snefru's first Dahshur pyramid was 617 feet (188 meters) long, and its sides sloped at just under 55°. However, about the time that the pyramid was halfway done, the angle of the sides' slope was changed to 43° 22′, creating a very visible "bend" in the sides. Probably some instability had been detected, causing the engineers to lessen the slope to reduce the pyramid's height and volume. It still wound up being 345 feet (105 meters) high.

Snefru must not have been satisfied, for he immediately began another true pyramid at Dahshur, about a mile north of the Bent Pyramid. This pyramid is known as the North or Red Pyramid (because of the pinkish color of its weathered limestone). The North Pyramid of Dahshur has a 722-foot (220-meter)-square base and is 345 feet (105 meters) high. Its sides slope at the same 43° 22′ used for the top of the Bent Pyramid. While this pyramid was being built, Snefru had the Meidum pyramid made into a true pyramid. However, this work does not seem to have been completed by the time he died, possibly contributing to the later robbing of the pyramid's shell and its collapse.

The smooth sides of these pyramids probably represented the sun's rays as ramps upon which the king could mount to heaven (see Document 4.1, Spell 508). However, each true pyramid had a step pyramid within it, so it could still also serve as a staircase to heaven. In addition, it was still a mound of creation. All these magical relationships were true simultaneously for Egyptians, making each pyramid a source of great spiritual power.

Snefru was succeeded by his son, Khufu (c. 2589 to 2566 B.C.E.),[22] later known to the Greeks as Cheops. Under Khufu, the centralization of power into pharaoh's hands, the size and efficiency of the bureaucracy needed to exercise his authority, and Egypt's human and other resources seem to have reached their peak. Thus, he was able to construct the Great Pyramid, the largest Egyptian pyramid and the most impressive of the wonders of the ancient world.

Khufu erected his pyramid, called *Akhet Khufu* ("The Place of Khufu's Transfiguration"), at Giza, a few miles north of Saqqara. Its sheer size inspires awe. It was 756 feet (230.33 meters) long on each side and originally 481 feet (146.59 meters) high. That means that its base would cover more than four square city blocks, and it would have been about 18 feet higher than the top of the dome of Saint Peter's Basilica in Rome and more than 170 feet higher than the Statue of Liberty's torch. Until the construction of the Eiffel Tower in 1889, the Great Pyramid was the tallest structure on earth. The Great Pyramid contains about 2.3 million stone blocks, averaging about 2.5 tons each (see Figure 4.9). The largest of its stones weighs about 50 tons.

FIGURE 4.9   The Sides of the Great Pyramid Today
This view shows the immense size of the stones. The outer casing stones that would have made the sides smooth were robbed long ago.
Source: Courtesy of the author.

The accuracy of the builders is also amazing. The perimeter of the base sits on an almost perfectly level plane with the southeast corner only a little more than one-half inch higher than the northwest corner. The sides are aligned almost exactly to true north-south and east-west, the average error being only 3′ 6″ (less than ⅕ of a degree). Furthermore, all of this was done with only the relatively primitive technology available to the ancient Egyptians.

When Herodotus visited Egypt in the fifth century B.C.E., he was told that 400,000 men (working in three-month shifts of 100,000 men each) labored for 20 years to build the Great Pyramid. However, study of the pyramid-builders' town and tombs recently found at Giza suggests that about 20,000 people (men and women) were used at a time, 15,000 laborers and 5,000 craftsmen, overseers, bakers, cooks, and other specialists. There may have been a few thousand others serving in distant quarries or on boats to carry food supplies or stones to Giza in addition to the workers who lived at the pyramid site. Evidence from bones found in the workers' tombs at Giza proves that the pyramid builders were native Egyptians, not foreign slaves. This corvée labor force was gathered from all parts of Egypt, and at least the unskilled laborers would have been periodically replaced with a new group of recruits, but probably only once a year. Using yearly shifts of 15,000 or 20,000 at a time, the Egyptians should have been able to complete the Great Pyramid in the 20 years mentioned by Herodotus.[*]

Most of the limestone for the core of the pyramid was quarried near the pyramid site. However, the fine limestone for the outer casing stones came from Tura, on the east bank of the Nile. The builders obtained the granite for columns, door jambs, lintels, and other special features from Aswan, in the south. The flood waters facilitated movement of these fine stones down the Nile and allowed them to be brought right up to the desert plateau. There, work gangs probably placed them on sleds (made with wood imported from Lebanon) and dragged them up a causeway to the pyramid. At the pyramid, the workmen would have dragged the stone-laden sleds up ramps made from mud-brick, earth, and rubble. However, we don't know how the ramps were arranged. There are several plausible theories, but we'll probably never know which is correct unless a partially finished pyramid is discovered with its construction ramps still in place.

---

[*]It should be noted that archaeologists found a stone block near the mid-level of Snefru's North Pyramid at Dahshur with a painted date only four years later than that on a similar stone at the pyramid's base.

The most amazing aspect of pyramid construction is not the movement of the stones (which only took a great amount of brute force), but the planning and organization that was necessary. Someone had to decide how many people were needed for each task. Others had to be ready to secure these workers and take them to their new occupations. Still others had to store food to feed the multitude of workers at the various sites (quarries, docks, boats, and pyramid). Someone also had to calculate the time needed for each job and work out a timetable so that the activities of the various work gangs were synchronized for maximum efficiency. The skill of the bureaucrats who did all this planning was equal, if not superior, to that of the architects and engineers who designed the pyramids.

Originally, Khufu planned to be buried in a chamber cut into the rock beneath the Great Pyramid. However, he changed his plans (possibly twice) while the pyramid was being built. He eventually was buried within the pyramid in a chamber reached by a majestic 28-foot-high corridor (now called the "Grand Gallery"). Relieving compartments above this chamber prevented the weight of the pyramid above it from cracking its ceiling stones. Khufu's sarcophagus remains in this burial chamber, but his body and any objects buried with him were removed long ago.

When finished, the Great Pyramid was surrounded by an enclosure wall 26 feet (8 meters) high. On the eastern side, there were four smaller pyramids (three for queens and one possibly dedicated to Khufu's *ka*), a mortuary temple, a causeway, and a valley temple. Archaeologists have also found seven boat pits. Five are boat-shaped excavations in the rock, which were probably intended to magically become boats on which the king could travel with Re across the heavens. However, two of the pits were rectangular and contained dismantled full-size wooden boats. It is likely that these boats were the ones used to take Khufu's body and other funerary objects across the Nile at the time of burial. One of these boats has been restored and is on display in a museum next to the Great Pyramid.

When Khufu died, his son Djedefre became pharaoh (c. 2566 to 2558 B.C.E.) and began building a pyramid at Abu Rawash, north of Giza. He died after a short reign, leaving his tomb unfinished. His son or brother Khafre (Chephren to the Greeks) then became king, reigning c. 2558 to 2532 B.C.E. His architects and engineers designed a pyramid just slightly smaller than Khufu's (708 feet to a side, 471 feet high), and Khafre decided to erect it at Giza. However, he didn't want his pyramid overshadowed by Khufu's. So, his builders placed it on higher ground, creating the illusion that it is larger than its illustrious neighbor.

Like all of the Fourth Dynasty pyramids, Khafre's pyramid had a mortuary temple at the pyramid site connected by a long causeway to a valley temple at the edge of the desert plateau. Just north of the causeway near the valley temple, a depression had been created by quarrying stone for the valley temple's construction. However, a large spur of stone was left in the center, because it was of poor quality and had fissures running through it. Despite its faults, Khafre's sculptors carved it into a huge hybrid creature with the body of a recumbent lion and the head of the king (see Figure 4.10). This Great Sphinx was over 240 feet (73 meters) long and 66 feet (20 meters) high. It was regarded as an embodiment of Horus and Atum and a symbol of divine kingship.[23]

In recent years, there have been several theories claiming that the Great Sphinx is much older than the time of Khafre. Some would date it as early as 10,500 B.C.E., when at the vernal equinox, the sun would have arisen at dawn in the constellation Leo (seen as a lion like the Sphinx) at exactly the place toward which the Great Sphinx is staring. Supporters of this view also claim that the pyramids of Giza, Abu Rawash, and Zawiyet el-Aryan were meant to represent on the ground the positions of the stars in the constellation Orion. Actually, as Paul Jordan has pointed out, "there is nothing to suggest that the Egyptians entertained any of the signs of the zodiac, including Leo... before the last few centuries B.C.E."[24] Furthermore, the positions of the pyramids of Giza, Abu Rawash, and Zawiyet el-Aryan do not correctly

FIGURE 4.10   The Great Sphinx and the Great Pyramid
The Great Pyramid can be seen behind the Sphinx. Note how the limestone of the Sphinx's body is badly eroded.
Source: Courtesy of the author.

correspond to the positions of stars in Orion. There are also several stars of Orion that have no matching pyramids at all.[25] Finally, there is no archaeological evidence of any advanced civilization or culture in Egypt around 10,500 B.C.E. that could have created the Sphinx.

A more serious challenge to the conventional dating of the Great Sphinx has been raised by geologist Robert Schoch. Study of the Great Sphinx convinced Dr. Schoch that it had been eroded by rainwater (see Figure 4.10). The last time when there would have been sufficient rainfall in the area to create such erosion, he argued, was the wet period between c. 7000 and 5000 B.C.E. Thus, he believes that the Sphinx was carved at least 2,500 years before the time of Khafre.[26]

However, further geological study of the Sphinx has shown that Schoch's chronological conclusions are unwarranted. The erosion of the Sphinx and its enclosure was probably not caused primarily by running water (though there was more rainfall in the area in Old Kingdom times than at present). Much of the erosion probably resulted from accelerated weathering due to a covering of wet sand. The Sphinx often has been covered with sand in both ancient and modern times. The sand trapped and held the rain run-off coming from the area around the pyramids. Also, at times the Nile floods either reached the enclosure around the Sphinx or came close enough for water to be drawn into the sand by capillary action.[27] It has also been shown that porous limestone like that of the body of the Sphinx often disintegrates in a desert climate due to condensation produced by temperature extremes. As moisture condenses, seeps into the stone, then evaporates, the expansion of salt crystals within the stone causes pieces of the surface to flake off.[28] So the geological evidence does not force us to adopt a date for the Sphinx earlier than the Old Kingdom. On the other hand, the archaeological evidence strongly supports a date in Khafre's reign.[29] Therefore, Egyptologists have rejected the pre-Fourth Dynasty dates for the Sphinx.

The power of Fourth Dynasty pharaohs seems to have decreased dramatically after the reign of Khafre. The third pyramid at Giza, built by Khafre's successor Menkaure (Mycerinus to the Greeks), is only half the size of the other two. And the following king, Shepseskaf, built only a large stone *mastaba* at Saqqara instead of a pyramid. Shepseskaf did not have any sons. So the throne passed to his cousin and brother-in-law, Userkaf, whose reign marks the official beginning of Dynasty 5.

However, there may have been another brief reign by a female pharaoh named Khentkaues between those of Shepseskaf and Userkaf. Later legend claimed that the first three kings of the Fifth Dynasty were the direct offspring of Re and a priestess of Re. This story may not only recall the importance Re came to have in Dynasty 5, but also possibly the important role that a woman played in the change of dynasties. Khentkawes seems to have been the mother of Userkaf and his successor Sahure. A title on the door of her tomb may be read "The Mother of Two Kings of Upper and Lower Egypt." However, it could also be translated "The King of Upper and Lower Egypt and Mother of the King of Upper and Lower Egypt." Furthermore, on the same granite door there is an incised drawing of the "queen" wearing the uraeus and a false beard, both symbols of kingship.[30] So, although she was not included in the later king lists, Khentkawes may have ruled for a brief time as pharaoh before passing power on to her son, Userkaf.

The Latter Part of the Old Kingdom: Dynasties 5 and 6 (c. 2498–2180 B.C.E.)

Though the Old Kingdom lasted for another 300 years after the end of the Fourth Dynasty, there seems to have been a gradual decline in royal authority. This decline, however, was very slow and for most of the fifth and sixth dynasties, had little effect on ordinary Egyptians. The almost imperceptible deterioration of royal power resulted mainly from actions of the pharaohs themselves abetted by forces beyond their control. One of the problems pharaohs brought upon themselves was the growing power of the sun god Re and his priests at Heliopolis. Before the time of Khafre, the king was the primary national deity for Egypt. Most of the wealth and labor of the country was dedicated to constructing the king's tomb, which would protect his body forever and guarantee him an afterlife. In the other world, he would reign eternally with his fellow gods and continue to look after Egypt. The Fourth Dynasty kings, however, began emphasizing Re, a new name for the sun god of Heliopolis. *Re* had been used as a word for the sun as a physical object earlier, but it seems to have become a divine name at the end of the Third Dynasty. The Fourth Dynasty rulers' use of true pyramids and boat-pits for solar barges and Khafre's adoption of the title "Son of Re" illustrate their growing allegiance to this god. They made Re into a national deity and elevated him to supremacy within the pantheon. Fifth Dynasty kings built sun temples containing large obelisks (symbols of Re) near their own poorly constructed pyramids. The kings also began to give land donations to these temples and to others throughout Egypt, making them financially independent and their priests more self-reliant. The land grants also reduced the resources available to the crown. Even Horus, the god believed to be incarnate in the pharaoh, became identified with Re. The compound deity was known as Re-Horakhty, "Re, the Horus of the Horizon" (or "Re, the Horus [arising] from the *akhet* [the place of transformation]").

The nobles also became more independent and self-reliant during the Fifth and Sixth dynasties. In the early part of the Old Kingdom, the most important officials and governors usually had been loyal members of the royal family. However, as the royal power and control grew, so too did the bureaucracy, reducing the ruler's effective oversight of it. Also, fewer of its leaders were relatives of the king and many bureaucratic positions became hereditary, further reducing the king's control. Moreover, officials often had to serve at great distances from pharaoh, leading them to become more autonomous. The great Egyptologist John Wilson has pointed out that this "decentralization showed itself in a clear geographic way."[31] In the Fourth Dynasty, nobles had clustered their *mastabas* around the pyramid of pharaoh in the hope that being near his awesome power would assure them an afterlife. During the Fifth Dynasty, many nobles chose to be buried in the districts where they had lived and worked. By the Sixth Dynasty, burial in the provincial areas had become the norm. Clearly the nobles no longer believed that their immortality depended on proximity to the king.

Finally, nature itself was working to weaken Egypt's kings. As mentioned in Chapter 3, the Near East seems to have experienced a period of drought around 2200 B.C.E. There is evidence that the Nile flood levels had been gradually declining during the Old Kingdom, and that they were seriously low between c. 2200 and 2100 B.C.E.[32] The consequent reduction in agricultural production not only would have had an economic impact, but also psychological, religious, and political effects. If pharaoh could not assure adequate Nile floods and food production, he was not maintaining *ma'at*. How, then, could he be a god? Loss of confidence in the king's ability to intercede with his fellow deities, when combined with the other factors weakening royal authority, proved to be disastrous.

The last moderately strong king of the Sixth Dynasty was Pepi II who had the longest recorded reign in Egyptian history. He came to the throne as a young child and ruled for more than 90 years according to both the Turin Canon and Manetho. Such a long reign, with its almost inevitable consequence—reduction of the king's vigor for a time at its end—very probably contributed to the collapse of central authority. Pepi's successor seems to have died after a reign of only a year or two. However, this successor's wife, Nitiqret (called Nitocris by Manetho and the Turin Canon), probably continued ruling for another two or three years. Once again, a woman ruler closed out a dynasty, and soon after her death, the Old Kingdom's more than 500 years of stability and order came to an end.

Early Egyptian Society and Culture

The nature of the surviving sources makes our knowledge of early Egyptian society very incomplete. However, the basic social structure that would prevail through most of Egyptian history seems to have been in place at the beginning of the Old Kingdom. At the top of the social hierarchy, of course, was the royal family. Though in theory, the king, as a god, had absolute authority and owned everything in Egypt, he and his close relatives were hemmed in by obligations of ritual and duty. The mores or conventions that applied to the king and his family were sometimes quite different from those of the rest of the population. For example, while most Egyptians were monogamous (though nobles often had several concubines in addition to a wife), pharaohs usually had several wives. In addition, kings often married their sisters (as the gods did in Egyptian myths) and sometimes their daughters, while other Egyptians almost always married outside of their immediate families. The multiple roles that some women of the royal family held as sisters, daughters, wives, and mothers of pharaohs gave them power that ordinary women did not have. As we have seen, occasionally a queen could rule the country as regent for her son or possibly even as king in the cases of Khentkaues and Nitiqret (Nitocris). However, it is clear that these examples of female rule were exceptional cases in times of crisis. Egyptian ideology normally did not allow for the possibility of a female king.

Below the royal family were the families of the viziers, provincial governors, priests of major deities, and other high-ranking members of pharaoh's bureaucracy. Minor officials and priests of local gods were a bit lower in the social order. Nevertheless, they were all nobles, and the scenes in their tombs show the lives of luxury they generally led. Most of these nobles probably derived from wealthy landowning families of Predynastic times. However, there seems to have been some social mobility within the noble class, for pharaoh could advance capable individuals of modest means to high positions and grant them estates and other rewards. He also could remove persons from office and seize their lands. As we have seen, though, kings tended to make many offices hereditary and the lands granted to these families essentially became their private property. Thus, toward the latter part of the Old Kingdom, many of these nobles were powerful in their own right and largely independent of royal oversight.

Craftsmen and artisans (e.g., goldsmiths, sculptors, painters, jewelers, carpenters, etc.) as well as other specialized workers (including bakers, millers, potters, stone masons, vintners, sailors, and merchants) formed a very small "middle class" between the nobles and peasants. It is not known how such individuals were recruited, other than sons following in the occupations of their fathers. Unlike craftsmen in the largely free-enterprise system of Mesopotamia, most Egyptian artisans and skilled workers performed specialized tasks in large workshops owned by nobles or pharaoh. The best artisans, of course, were in pharaoh's employ, making objects for the king's burial or foreign trade (which was largely a royal monopoly).

The vast majority of the Egyptian people were semifree peasants. They were like the serfs of the western European Middle Ages. They farmed land that belonged to pharaoh, nobles, or temples. They were not allowed to leave the estates on which they worked, and if the land changed hands, the peasants went with it. Because resident peasants could not be evicted, though, profits for landowners were not as high they might have been if the land had been

unoccupied. Thus, prices for land were very low in Old Kingdom Egypt (about two acres for a cow or its equivalent). The peasants not only supplied the food Egypt needed, they also provided the labor that built Egypt's great monuments. Bright and talented individuals from the peasant class occasionally might have been able to advance into the artisan class. And, in theory at least, a peasant might rise even higher. A Middle Kingdom story called *The Protests of the Eloquent Peasant* tells of a peasant whose eloquence in trying to right an injustice earns him great rewards. However, this work is set during the troubled First Intermediate Period; during the stable Old Kingdom such a dramatic change in status must have been extremely unusual. Most peasants continued to live as their fathers and grandfathers had lived—in small houses in villages just beyond the limits of the inundation. They continued to bury their dead in the sand as in Predynastic times. While they may have hoped for an afterlife, because they did not have the money for tombs, mummification, and elaborate magical burial rites, they probably had little confidence that their hopes would be fulfilled.

In many ancient societies, free women ranked near the bottom of the social ladder, just slightly higher than slaves. However, though Egypt was a patriarchal society, women had many rights. They could own property and dispose of it as they saw fit. They could enter into contracts with individuals other than their husbands and sue in court. They were entitled to generous compensation if they were divorced without being at fault. And in their marriages, they were the virtual equals of their husbands. They even seem to have earned equal pay for equal work. Certain occupations such as spinning and weaving probably were reserved for women. However, texts also mention women as overseers of restaurants, wig shops, and other businesses. There are even references to women doctors and a female overseer of doctors.[33]

At the bottom of the social pyramid were the slaves. They worked as servants in temples, royal palaces, and the houses of the nobility. They were also used for brutal labor such as quarrying stone. However, they were drawn from war captives and their numbers were never very high. The bulk of the labor in ancient Egypt, whether in agriculture or monument construction, was done by the Egyptians themselves.

Because of their belief in *ma'at*, most Egyptians, even the peasants, seem to have been content with their lives. This fact explains why Egyptian society and culture were so conservative and seemingly unchanging over hundreds of years. The Egyptians were living in the best of all possible worlds, ruled by a god in human form. What more could anyone want?

We have already noted that the essentials of the ancient Egyptian world view and religion were in place by the end of the Early Dynastic Age. The basics of Egyptian art and science also go back to Old Kingdom times or earlier. Almost all Egyptian art was created for religious purposes—to glorify the king or other gods or for magical applications within tombs. For example, the walls of the nobles' *mastabas* were covered with reliefs and paintings depicting the everyday events of this world that they hoped to enjoy forever in the afterlife. Old Kingdom sculpture and painting were regarded as "classic" by later Egyptians. At various times, especially after periods of disorder and confusion, later Egyptians turned to the Old Kingdom for inspiration. In such periods, artists revived and copied the Old Kingdom's canons of style and proportion.

Early Egyptian discoveries in mathematics, astronomy, and medicine also established the standards for later times. Egyptian mathematicians used a decimal numerical system and were very adept at calculating areas of triangles and quadrilaterals. Though they did not use a constant such as *pi*, they were able to estimate the area of a circle by measuring the diameter, subtracting ⅑ of it and squaring the result. It is likely that they also knew the principle of the Pythagorean Theorem. The Egyptians also became adept at calculating the volumes of various objects such as pyramids, cylinders, and truncated pyramids. However, they did not try to understand the abstract principles behind such calculations. Like the Mesopotamians, Egyptians confined their mathematical thought to solving practical problems such as determining the amount of men and material necessary to build a ramp or pyramid of a certain size or calculating the amount of food necessary to feed the workers engaged in such tasks.

Egyptian astronomy was also essentially practical. Early observation of the stars led to the realization that after a period of invisibility, the star Sirius (*Sepdet* or Sothis to the Egyptians) reappears at about the time the Nile's inundation begins. Thus, Egyptians made the day when Sirius reappears the first day of the civil new year. They also had a natural calendar of 12 lunar months (29½ days each) that was used for determining dates for various religious celebrations.

TABLE 4.2

Chronology of the Egyptian Old Kingdom

(All dates are B.C.E. and may vary from the true date by as much as 75–125 years. Only the Third and Fourth Dynasties have all rulers listed. Since some scholars use the Greek forms of various royal names, these are given in parentheses.)

Third Dynasty	**2686–2613**
Sanakhte Nebka	2686–2668
Netjerikhet Djoser	2668–2649
Sekhemkhet	2649–2643
Khaba	2643–2637
Huni	2637–2613
Fourth Dynasty	**2613–2498**
Snefru	2613–2589
Khufu (Cheops)	2589–2566
Djedefre or Redjedef	2566–2558
Khafre (Chephren)	2558–2532
Menkaure (Mycerinus)	2532–2504
Shepseskaf	2504–2500
Fifth Dynasty	**2498–2345**
Sixth Dynasty	**2345–2180**
Pepi II	2278–2184

DOCUMENT 4.2
The Diagnosis and Treatment of Two Injuries

The following examples of an Egyptian doctor's diagnosis and recommended treatment for two injuries are from the Edwin Smith Surgical Papyrus. This composition has generally been thought to be the work of an Old Kingdom army surgeon, but some scholars think it might have come from a doctor who treated construction-related injuries (such as those incurred while building a pyramid). The text indicates which injuries can be cured ("an injury I will deal with") and which ones are hopeless ("an injury not treated").[34] The question marks in square brackets are in the original translation, but the sentence in parentheses at the end of the second selection is by W. Stiebing.

A Bone-Deep Wound Above the Eyebrow

"You probe his wound, and you bring together his gash for him with a stitch [?], and you say about him: '… An injury I will deal with.' After you stitch [?] it, you bandage it up with fresh meat the first day. If you find that this wound is loose with its stitches [?], then you bind it together with bandages, and anoint it with oil and honey every day until it gets better."

Symptoms Resulting from a Fractured Skull

"If … you find that swellings protrude behind the break in his skull, and his eye is squinting under it, on the side that has the blow to his skull, and he walks shuffling with the sole of his foot on the side that has the blow to his skull, you diagnose him as one struck by what enters from outside…. An injury not treated." (A note in the text explains that "what enters from outside" refers to "the breath of god, or death.")

Their observations of the fixed northern stars allowed them to bisect the rising and setting points of these stars and thus determine true north. We have already mentioned how precisely this was done in orienting the sides of the Great Pyramid to true north, south, east, and west.

The Edwin Smith Surgical Papyrus, a late copy of what seems to have been an Old Kingdom composition, indicates the state of early Egyptian medicine (see Document 4.2). It shows that Egyptian doctors knew that the heart "speaks" in several parts of the body and that they estimated a patient's general condition by observing whether his pulse was too fast or too slow. It also provides descriptions of how to treat various kinds of broken bones, recommending rest, medications, and certain foods in addition to physically setting the bones. For its time, it is remarkably scientific, generally omitting references to demons and magic. However, like Mesopotamian doctors, Egyptian physicians often used magic as part of their treatments. Nevertheless, because of the practice of mummification, Egyptian doctors seem to have developed a better understanding of anatomy and far greater surgical skills than their Mesopotamian counterparts. In medicine, as in other areas, later Egyptian knowledge was firmly based on the accomplishments of the Early Dynastic and Old Kingdom eras.

SUGGESTIONS FOR FURTHER READING AND INFORMATION

Internet Sites

Ancient Egypt: The Eternal Voice: http://mcclungmuseum. utk.edu/permex/ egypt.html

The British Museum, Department of Egyptian Antiquities: http://www. thebritishmuseum.ac.uk/egyptian/EA

The Egyptian Museum in Cairo: http://www.egyptianmuseum.gov.eg/ frame_bar.html

A tour of Giza, Luxor and other major Egyptian sites: http://www.memphis.edu/egypt/egypt.html

Nova interview with Egyptologist and pyramid expert, Mark Lehner: http://www.pbs.org/wgbh/pages/nova/pyramid/excavation/lehner.html

Rigby's World of Egypt—information and pictures of Egyptian sites: http://www.powerup.com.au/~ancient/index.html)

Secrets of the Pharaohs: http://www.pbs.org/wnet/pharaohs

Books and Articles

General Works on Ancient Egypt and/or Nubia

Adams, W. Y. *Nubia, Corridor to Africa*. London: Allen Lane, 1977.

Aldred, Cyril. *The Egyptians*. Revised and updated by Aidan Dodson. New York and London: Thames and Hudson, 1998.

Assmann, Jan. *The Search for God in Ancient Egypt* Translated by David Lorton. Ithaca, NY: Cornell University Press, 2001.

Baines, John, and Jaromir Malek. *Atlas of Ancient Egypt*, rev. ed. New York: Checkmark Books, 2000.

Butzer, Karl W. *Early Hydraulic Civilization in Egypt: A Study in Cultural Ecology*. Chicago: University of Chicago Press, 1976.

Capel, Anne K., and Glenn E. Markoe, eds. *Mistress of the House, Mistress of Heaven: Women in Ancient Egypt*. New York: Hudson Hills Press, 1997.

Casson, Lionel. *Everyday Life in Ancient Egypt*. Revised and expanded ed. Baltimore: Johns Hopkins University Press, 2001.

Clayton, Peter A. *Chronicle of the Pharaohs*. New York and London: Thames and Hudson, 1994.

David, Rosalie. *Handbook to Life in Ancient Egypt*. New York and London: Oxford University Press, 1999.

Davies, Vivian, and Renée Friedman. *Egypt*. London: British Museum Press, 1998.

Davies, W. D. *Egyptian Hieroglyphs*. Reading the Past. London: British Museum Press, 1987.

Dodson, Aidan. *Monarchs of the Nile*. London: The Rubicon Press, 1995.

Estes, J. Worth. *The Medical Skills of Ancient Egypt*. Canton, MA.: Watson Publishing, 1993.

Foster, John L., translator. *Hymns, Prayers and Songs: An Anthology of Ancient Egyptian Lyric Poetry*. Atlanta: Scholars Press, 1995.

Ghalioungui, Paul. *Magic and Medical Science in Ancient Egypt*. Amsterdam: B. M. Israël, 1973.

Grimal, Nicolas. *A History of Ancient Egypt*. New York: Barnes and Noble, 1988.

Hawass, Zahi. *Silent Images: Women in Pharaonic Egypt*. New York: Harry N. Abrams, 2000.

Haynes, Joyce L. *Nubia: Ancient Kingdoms of Africa*. Boston: Museum of Fine Arts, 1992.

Hornung, Erik, *History of Ancient Egypt: An Introduction*. Translated by David Lorton. Ithaca, NY: Cornell University Press, 1999.

Kemp, Barry J. *Ancient Egypt: Anatomy of a Civilization*. London: Routledge, 1989.

Lefkowitz, Mary R., and Guy MacLean Rogers, eds. *Black Athena Revisited*. Chapel Hill: University of North Carolina Press, 1996.

Lefkowitz, Mary R. *Not Out of Africa: How Afrocentrism Became an Excuse to Teach Myth as History*. San Francisco: HarperCollins, 1997.

Lesko, Barbara S. *The Remarkable Women of Ancient Egypt*. Berkeley: B. C. Scribe Publications, 1978.

Lichtheim, Miriam. *Ancient Egyptian Literature: A Book of Readings*. 3 vols. Berkeley: University of California Press, 1975–1980.

O'Connor, David. *Ancient Nubia: Egypt's Rival in Africa*. Philadelphia: University Museum Publications, 1994.

Quirke, Stephen, ed. *The Temple in Ancient Egypt: New Discoveries and Recent Research*. London: The British Museum Press, 1997.

Redford, Donald B., editor-in-chief. *The Oxford Encyclopedia of Ancient Egypt*. 3 vols. New York: Oxford University Press, 2001.

Robins, Gay. *The Art of Ancient Egypt*. Cambridge, MA.: Harvard University Press, 1997.

————. *Women in Ancient Egypt*. London: British Museum Press, 1993.

Schulz, Regine, and Matthias Seidel, eds. *Egypt: The World of the Pharaohs*. Cologne: Könemann, 1998.

Shafer, Byron E., ed. *Temples of Ancient Egypt*. Ithaca, NY: Cornell University Press, 1997.

————. *Religion in Ancient Egypt*. Ithaca, NY: Cornell University Press, 1991.

Shaw, Ian, ed. *The Oxford History of Ancient Egypt*. Oxford and New York: Oxford University Press, 2000.

———— and Paul Nicholson. *The British Museum Dictionary of Ancient Egypt*. London: British Museum Press, 1995.

Shinnie, P. L. *Ancient Nubia*. London and New York: Kegan Paul, 1996.

Silverman, David P., ed. *Ancient Egypt*. New York: Oxford University Press, 1997.

Simpson, William Kelly, ed. *The Literature of Ancient Egypt: An Anthology of Stories, Instructions, and Poetry*, new ed. New Haven: Yale University Press, 1973.

Strouhal, Eugen. *Life of the Ancient Egyptians*. Norman, OK: University of Oklahoma Press, 1992.

Trigger, Bruce G. *Early Civilizations: Ancient Egypt in Context*. Cairo: American University in Cairo Press, 1993.

Tyldesley, Joyce A. *Daughters of Isis: Women of Ancient Egypt*. New York: Penguin Books, 1994.

Watterson, Barbara. *The Egyptians*. Cambridge: Blackwell Publishers, 1997.

————. *The Gods of Ancient Egypt*. London: B. T. Batsford, 1984.

Wente, Edward. *Letters from Ancient Egypt*. Atlanta: Scholars Press, 1990.

Early Egypt Through the Old Kingdom

Andreu, Guillemette. *Egypt in the Age of the Pyramids*. Translated by David Lorton. Ithaca, NY: Cornell University Press, 1997.

Edwards, I. E. S. *The Pyramids of Egypt*, rev. ed. New York: Penguin, 1993.

Faulkner, Raymond O. *The Ancient Egyptian Pyramid Texts*. London: Oxford University Press, 1969.

Goedicke, Hans. *The Report about the Dispute of a Man with His Ba*. Baltimore: The Johns Hopkins University Press, 1970.

Hart, George. *Pharaohs and Pyramids: A Guide through Old Kingdom Egypt*. London: Herbert Press, 1991.

Hoffmann, Michael A. *Egypt Before the Pharaohs: The Prehistoric Foundations of Egyptian Civilization*. New York: Alfred Knopf, 1979.

Jordan, Paul. *Riddles of the Sphinx*. New York: New York University Press, 1998.

Lehner, Mark. *The Complete Pyramids*. London and New York: Thames and Hudson, 1997.

Malek, Jaromir, and Werner Forman. *In the Shadow of the Pyramids: Egypt during the Old Kingdom*. Norman, OK: University of Oklahoma Press, 1986.

Rice, Michael. *Egypt's Making: The Origins of Ancient Egypt 5000–2000 BC*. London and New York: Routledge, 1990.

Spencer, A. J. *Early Egypt: The Rise of Civilisation in the Nile Valley*. London: British Museum Publications, 1993.

Strudwick, N. *The Administration of the Old Kingdom*. London: Kegan Paul International, 1985.

NOTES

1. Stuart Tyson Smith, "People: Race of the Ancient Egyptians," in Donald B. Redford, Editor-in-Chief, *The Oxford Encyclopedia of Ancient Egypt* (Oxford: Oxford University Press, 2001), vol. 3, p. 27. See also Stuart Tyson Smith's article on "Race" in the same volume, pp. 111–116.

2. See, for example, Frank J. Yurco, "Were the Ancient Egyptians Black or White," *Biblical Archaeology Review*, vol. 15, no. 5 (September/October, 1989), pp. 24–29, 58 and the letters under "Queries and Comments" in the same issue. The racial issue has been emphasized particularly in Afrocentric works such as Molefi Kete Asante, *The Afrocentric Idea*, rev. ed. (Philadelphia: Temple University Press, 1998) and Ivan Van Sertima, ed., *Egypt Revisited: Journal of African Civilizations*, 2nd ed. New Brunswick: Transaction Publications, 1990). For a response, see Mary Lefkowitz, *Not Out of Africa: How Afrocentrism Became an Excuse to Teach Myth as History* (San Francisco: HarperCollins, 1997). Martin Bernal's *Black Athena*, 2 vols. (New Brunswick: Rutgers University Press, 1987 and 1991), though not truly an Afrocentric work, brought scholarly attention to the subject. See also Peter A. Young, "Was Nefertiti Black?" and the articles by John Coleman and Martin Bernal on Bernal's *Black Athena* in *Archaeology*, vol. 45, no. 5 (September/October, 1992), pp. 2; 48–52, 77–81; 53–55, 82, 86.

3. Robert J. Wenke, *Patterns in Prehistory: Humankind's First Three Million Years,* 4th ed. (New York: Oxford

University Press, 1999), p. 470. The same point is made by Bruce G. Trigger during his excellent discussion of the Nile Valley's continuum of physical types, "Nubian, Negro, Black, Nilotic?," in *Africa in Antiquity: The Arts of Ancient Nubia and the Sudan, I: The Essays* (New York: The Brooklyn Museum, 1978), pp. 26–35. For a recent analysis of the ancient Egyptians' physical and genetic relationship to other groups based on study of hundreds of ancient bodies, see C. L. Brace, D. P. Tracer, L. A. Yaroch, J. Robb, K. Brandt, and A. R. Nelson, "Clines and Clusters Versus 'Race': A Test in Ancient Egypt and the Case of a Death on the Nile," *Yearbook of Physical Anthropology*, vol. 36 (1993), pp. 1–31.

4. Alan R. Schulman, "Narmer and the Unification: A Revisionist View," *Bulletin of the Egyptological Seminar*, vol. 11 (1991–1992), pp. 79–105. See also A. J. Spencer, *Early Egypt: The Rise of Civilisation in the Nile Valley* (London: British Museum Press, 1993), pp. 55–57.

5. For example, Jaromir Malek argues for the common identity of "Scorpion" and Narmer in *In the Shadow of the Pyramids: Egypt during the Old Kingdom* (Norman, OK: University of Oklahoma Press, 1986), p. 29.

6. See William J. Murnane, "Three Kingdoms and Thirty-four Dynasties: The First Nation State" in David P. Silverman, ed., *Ancient Egypt* (New York: Oxford University Press, 1997), p. 23, and Malek (1986), p. 29.

7. See, for example, Amélie Kuhrt, *The Ancient Near East, c. 3000–330 BC* (London and New York: Routledge, 1995), vol. I, pp. 132–134.

8. Larkin Mitchell, "Earliest Egyptian Glyphs," *Archaeology* 52/2 (March/April 1999), pp. 28–29, and John Noble Wilford, "When No One Read, Who Started to Write?," *The New York Times*, April 6, 1999, pp. D1–D2.

9. For example, Egyptologist John Baines quoted in John Noble Wilford, *The New York Times*, April 6, 1999, p. D2.

10. For example, Peter A. Clayton, *Chronicle of the Pharaohs* (London: Thames and Hudson, 1994), pp. 27–28.

11. Henri Frankfort, *Kingship and the Gods* (Chicago: University of Chicago Press, 1948), p. 43.

12. Thomas Schneider, "Sacred Kingship" in R. Schulz and M. Seidel, eds., *Egypt: The World of the Pharaohs* (Cologne: Könemann Verlagsgesellschaft, 1998), p. 323. See other discussions of Egyptian kingship in David O'Connor and David P. Silverman, eds., *Ancient Egyptian Kingship* (Leiden: E. J. Brill, 1995). More concise treatments can be found in the rest of Schneider's chapter, pp. 323–329, and in Lanny Bell, "Divine Kingship and the Royal *Ka*" in B. E. Shafer, ed., *Temples of Ancient Egypt* (Ithaca, NY: Cornell University Press, 1997), pp. 137–144, Frankfort (1948), pp. 36–47, and David P. Silverman, chap. 8, "Lord of the Two Lands," in Silverman, ed. (1997), pp. 106–113, especially pp. 112–113.

13. Frankfort (1948), p. 47.

14. Stephen Quirke, *Ancient Egyptian Religion* (London: British Museum Press, 1992), p. 81.

15. See, for example, James Hamilton-Paterson and Carol Andrews, *Mummies: Death and Life in Ancient Egypt* (New York: Penguin Books, 1979), pp. 35–36.

16. Salima Ikram and Aidan Dodson, *The Mummy in Ancient Egypt: Equipping the Dead for Eternity* (London: Thames and Hudson, 1998), p. 109.

17. H. and H. A. Frankfort in H. Frankfort, et al., *The Intellectual Adventure of Ancient Man* (Chicago: University of Chicago Press, 1946), pp. 4–6.

18. Ulrich Luft, "A Different World—Religious Conceptions," in Schulz and Seidel, eds. (1998), p. 417.

19. Quirke (1992), p. 70.

20. See also I. E. S. Edwards, *The Pyramids of Egypt* (New York: Penguin Books, rev. ed., 1993), p. 280.

21. The selections are from R. O. Faulkner, *The Ancient Egyptian Pyramid Texts* (London: Oxford University Press, 1969), pp. 44–46, 76, and 183.

22. Egyptologist Kate Spence of Cambridge University recently argued that the ancient Egyptians used an alignment of stars in the Big and Little Dipper constellations to orient the pyramids to the north. If this argument is valid, comparison of the stars' past alignments with the orientation of the Great Pyramid indicates that construction of the pyramid began in 2467 B.C.E. plus or minus 10 years. This date, if correct, would mean that the dates for the Old Kingdom pharaohs given here are about 124 years too old.

23. Paul Jordan, *Riddles of the Sphinx* (New York: New York University Press, 1998), pp. 181–182.

24. Ibid., p. 138.

25. Ibid., pp. 139–143. See also Robert Chadwick, "A Rebuttal to the So-called Orion Mystery," *KMT: A Modern Journal of Ancient Egypt*, Vol. 7, No. 3 (Fall 1996), pp. 74–83.

26. Robert Schoch, "A Modern Riddle of the Sphinx," *Omni*, vol. 14 (August 1992), pp. 46–51. See also Jordan (1998), pp. 147–153.

27. James Harrell, *KMT* (Summer 1994, Fall 1994, Fall 1996), and Jordan (1998), pp. 153–156.

28. K. L. Gauri, et al., "Geological Weathering and Its Implications on the Age of the Sphinx," *Geoarchaeology*, vol. 10, no. 2 (April 1995), pp. 119–133, and Jordan (1998), pp. 160–161.

29. Zahi Hawass and Mark Lehner, "The Sphinx—Who Built it and Why?," *Archaeology*, vol. 47, no. 5 (September/October 1994), pp. 30–47, and Jordan (1998), pp. 159–161.

30. Mark Lehner, *The Complete Pyramids: Solving the Ancient Mysteries* (London: Thames and Hudson, 1997), p. 138.

31. John A. Wilson, *The Burden of Egypt* (Chicago: University of Chicago Press, 1951), p. 95.

32. Barbara Bell, "The Dark Ages in Ancient History: I. The First Dark Age in Egypt," *American Journal of Archaeology*, vol. 75 (1971), pp. 1–26. Bell's conclusions, based on analysis of textual evidence, have been supported by studies of past levels of the lakes that serve as sources of the Nile. See Karl Butzer, *Early Hydraulic Civilization in Egypt* (Chicago: University of Chicago Press, 1976), pp. 28–33. See also Brian Fagan, *Floods, Famines and Emperors: El Niño and the Fate of Civilizations* (New York: Basic Books, 1999), pp. 99–117.

33. Gay Robins, *Women in Ancient Egypt* (London: British Museum Press, 1993), especially pp. 111–141; Eugen Strouhal, *Life of the Ancient Egyptians* (Norman, OK: University of Oklahoma Press, 1992), p. 59.

34. The translation is from Christopher Eyre, "The Boundaries of Knowledge," in Silverman, ed. (1997), p. 97.

5

The Rise and Fall
of the Egyptian Middle Kingdom

THE FIRST INTERMEDIATE PERIOD: DYNASTIES 7–11A (c. 2180–2040 B.C.E.)

Where is *Ma'at*?

Scholars disagree about exactly when the Egyptian Old Kingdom ended and the First Intermediate Period began. Rulers of the Seventh and Eighth dynasties ruled from Memphis and claimed sovereignty over the entire country. So, some would place the end of the Old Kingdom at the end of the Eighth Dynasty (c. 2160 B.C.E.). However, the individual kings of these two dynasties had very short reigns. From the Abydos King List, it is likely that a total of 15 to 17 rulers have to be fit into a span of only about 20 years, c. 2180 to 2160 B.C.E. This estimate is better, though, than the version of Manetho quoted by Africanus. According to this account, the Seventh Dynasty consisted of 70 kings who reigned for only 70 days! Actually, the kings comprising what were later designated the Seventh and Eighth Dynasties do not seem to have been able to control most parts of Egypt, and the centralized administration of the state seems to have largely collapsed at the end of the Sixth Dynasty. Thus, many scholars regard the Seventh and

Eighth dynasties (if the Seventh is not mythical) as the initial phase of the First Intermediate Period when division and disorder characterized Egypt. This is the view taken in this work (see Table 5.1).

By about 2160 B.C.E., the weakness of the Seventh and Eighth Dynasty pharaohs and the strength of some noble families led to a partitioning of the state. The nomarchs of Herakleopolis, a city some 70 miles south of Memphis, declared themselves kings. Manetho designated these Herakleopolitan kings as Dynasties Nine and Ten. Their kingdom included the Faiyum basin, which was part of their own nome, and extended northward to the apex of the Delta, just past Memphis, and southward to around Asyut. However, as texts from Beni Hasan show, these kings had little real control over the local rulers in central Egypt. The nomarch of Thebes also declared himself king at about the same time, establishing Manetho's Eleventh Dynasty. These two sets of kings contended for control of the central Egyptian area, fighting several battles in the area just north of Abydos.

Meanwhile, large portions of Egypt, especially the Delta and parts of Central Egypt, remained outside the effective control of these dynasties and often experienced disorder, turmoil, and strife. As mentioned in

TABLE 5.1
Chronology of the First Intermediate Period, Middle Kingdom, and Hyksos Era

(All dates are B.C.E. Only the Twelfth Dynasty has all its rulers listed. Since some scholars use the Greek forms of various royal names, these are given in parentheses.)

The First Intermediate Period (Dynasties 7–11a)	**2180–2040**
Middle Kingdom (Dynasties 11b–13a)	**2040–1720**
Postconquest Eleventh Dynasty	**2040–1991**
Nebhepetre Mentuhotep II	2060–2010
Sankhkare Mentuhotep III	2010–1998
Nebtowyre Mentuhotep IV	1998–1991
Twelfth Dynasty	**1991–1782**
Amenemhet (Ammenemes) I	1991–1962
Senusret (Sesostris) I	1971–1926
Amenemhet (Ammenemes) II	1929–1895
Senusret (Sesostris) II	1897–1878
Senusret (Sesostris) III	1878–1841
Amenemhet (Ammenemes) III	1842–1797
Amenemhet (Ammenemes) IV	1798–1786
Sobekneferu	1785–1782
The Early Thirteenth Dynasty	**1782–1720**
The Second Intermediate Period (Dynasties 13b–17)	**1720–1540**
The Latter Part of the Thirteenth Dynasty	**1720–1650**
The Fourteenth Dynasty (Miscellaneous Rulers of Parts of the Eastern Delta?)	**1720–1650**
The Fifteenth Dynasty (The Hyksos)	**1650–1540**
Sheshi (Salitis?)	
Khyan	
Auserre Apopi (Apophis)	1591–1550
Khamudi	1550–1540
The Sixteenth Dynasty (Hyksos Vassals in Middle Egypt?)	**1650–1540**
The Seventeenth Dynasty (at Thebes)	**1650–1550**
Sanakhtenre Tao I	?–1559
Seqenenre Tao II	1559–1554
Kamose	1554–1550

Chapter 4, the level of the Nile's floods also had been declining since the latter part of the Old Kingdom. Obviously, years of very low floods would have added to the people's hardship. Under these unsettled conditions, tomb robbing became rampant, foreign trade came to an end, the Egyptians' standard of living declined dramatically, and famine and disease seem to have been widespread. An Egyptian inscription claims that during years of famine, "the entire south died of hunger, every man devouring his own children."[1] This text clearly exaggerates for rhetorical effect. However, the widespread political and social chaos must have compounded the effects of low Nile floods, causing severe food shortages and even starvation in parts of Egypt. At the same time, some Syro-Palestinian groups, driven from their own lands by drought, took advantage of Egypt's weakness by moving in and settling in the eastern Delta.

The Intermediate Period's Effects

This era of discord and chaos shattered Egyptian confidence in the ability of pharaohs and the gods to maintain *ma'at* in this world. How could a thinking person believe in order, stability, or the divine "rightness" of nature and the state when in every aspect of life there was evidence that these qualities of *ma'at* no longer prevailed? In response, the disillusioned scribes and intellectuals produced some extraordinary literary works and new religious ideas.

Pessimism, an attitude almost completely unknown in Old Kingdom texts, pervades First Intermediate Period compositions. Several writings even question some of the cornerstones of Egyptian belief. One of these works, the *Song of the Harper from the Tomb of King Intef* (an early Eleventh Dynasty ruler), describes the uncertainties surrounding death and burial. Tombs have been destroyed and looted, and the afterlife is uncertain. So, it concludes, we should enjoy this life while we have it:

> Make holiday, and weary not therein!
> Behold, it is not given to a man to take his property with him.
> Behold, there is not one who departs who comes back again![2]

Another composition from this era is known as the *Dispute of a Man with His Ba* or *A Dispute over Suicide*. It records a debate between a man and his *ba* (the spiritual and personal element of his being) over the man's desire to end his life. The depression and despair expressed in this work are foreign to the optimistic life-affirming attitude of Old Kingdom times. The protagonist of this piece argues that death will be a beneficial release from this deplorable life. In the other world, he can plead his case before the gods and he will surely be happier than he is here. However, his *ba* cautions that, even with a proper burial, a person cannot be certain his body will survive and that he will attain the afterlife. Rather than suicide, the *ba* recommends the Mesopotamian-like ideas found in the *Song of the Harper from the Tomb of King Intef*— since life after death is uncertain, pursue pleasure now. However, the man answers his soul with four poems that graphically portray the misery of living in a world without *ma'at* and restate his faith in a better afterlife (see Document 5.1). In the end, the *ba* urges the man to choose life and to accept death only when it comes naturally so that the *ba* can abide with him after death.

A novel feature in the genre of Egyptian literature known as "Instructions" also appeared during this time. These wisdom texts supposedly present the instructions a pharaoh handed down to his son and successor. They usually consist of wise sayings, proverbs, and practical advice about life and kingship. However, in the *Instruction for King Merikare*, composed during the First Intermediate Period, a king of Herakleopolis (the supposed author) expresses regrets and admits he made mistakes:

> Lo, a shameful deed occurred in my time:
> The nome of This [the border area near
>   Abydos] was ravaged;
> Though it happened through my doing,
> I learned it after it was done.[3]

This open acknowledgment of the king's fallibility and humanity is something new, but it would continue to occur in similar Middle Kingdom compositions.

The *Instruction for King Merikare* emphasizes the need for everyone, king and commoner alike, to act in accordance with *ma'at*. It stresses social justice and mercy—for example, providing comfort for those who weep, compassion for widows, respect for property rights, and fairness in legal judgments. Furthermore, it declares that the character of an upright person is more acceptable to god than the religious sacrifices of the unjust. These ideas are similar to the much later Israelite prophetic teachings. However, perhaps this work's most significant new feature is that it declares that good actions are not just practical or beneficial in this world, but also in the world to come. It contains the earliest known reference to a final judgment in the afterlife: "As for the tribunal which judges the needy, you know that they will not be lenient on that day of judging the poor. . . . Do not put your trust in length of years, for they regard a lifetime as an hour; a man survives after death, and his deeds are laid before him in a heap."[4]

While the *Dispute of a Man with His Ba* questions how a person can live in a chaotic world devoid of *ma'at*, the *Instruction for King Merikare* provides an answer that some Egyptian thinker(s) had developed: Evil, injustice, and social and political anarchy may flourish at times in this world, but in the afterlife, *ma'at* will prevail. The gods will judge each person's deeds, and those who have not acted in accordance with *ma'at* will not enjoy an afterlife. However, the person who passes the judgment and attains the afterlife "will be like a god yonder, striding forward like the lords of eternity."[5]

At this time, Re was thought to head the council that judged the dead. However, by the New Kingdom, Egyptians had come to believe that Osiris, god of the dead, would preside over the final judgment. Before Osiris, an individual's heart—the source of thought and will—was weighed against *ma'at*, often symbolized by her feather (see Figure 5.1). A crocodile-headed creature known as the "Devourer" waited anxiously to consume those who failed the test. Those who passed were described as "true of voice" (or "justified"). Thus, by linking people's everyday actions in this world with a final judgment, Egyptian religion anticipated by some 1,500 years a concept that became basic within Judaism, Christianity, and Islam.

DOCUMENT 5.1
Despair over Life in a World without *Ma'at*

This selection comes from *A Dispute of a Man with His Ba*, probably composed during the First Intermediate Period (c. 2180–2040 B.C.E.).[6] In this work, a man and his *ba* (a spiritual element of a person that expressed his or her personality and power) argue about whether the man should commit suicide. This text reflects the despondency caused by a world devoid of *ma'at* (justice, truth, order). It also affirms the new ideas that commoners as well as kings have *ba*-spirits and will become like gods in the afterlife. (The explanatory material in square brackets has been added by W. Stiebing to the original translation.)

To whom can I speak today?
Brothers are evil
And the friends of today unlovable.
To whom can I speak today?
Hearts are rapacious
And everyone takes his neighbor's goods. . . .
To whom can I speak today?
There are no just persons
And the land is left over to the doers of wrong. . . .
To whom can I speak today?
The wrong which roams the earth,
There is no end to it.
Death is in my sight today
[As when] a sick man becomes well,
Like going out-of-doors after detention.
Death is in my sight today
Like the smell of myrrh,
Like sitting under an awning on a windy day. . . .
Death is in my sight today
As when a man desires to see home
When he has spent many years in captivity.
Verily, he who is yonder [i.e., in the realm of the dead] will be a living god,
Averting the ill of him who does it.
Verily, he who is yonder will be one who stands in the Bark of the Sun, [i.e., sails with Re in
     his solar boat]
Causing choice things to be given therefrom for the temples.
Verily, he who is yonder will be a sage
Who will not be prevented from appealing to Re when he speaks.

FIGURE 5.1   Weighing the Heart Against *Ma'at*

Source: British Museum, London.

Photo: The Art Archive/British Museum/Jacqueline Hyde.

A final point to be noted is that in the afterlife, the righteous dead will exist *like gods*. As we have seen, during the Old Kingdom, only a king or a god had a *ba*, and the king was the only earthly creature who in the afterlife was transformed into an *akh*, a being of light, like the other gods. An ordinary person's *ka* might enjoy some kind of afterlife within its tomb, magically consuming food offerings and experiencing the everyday activities depicted on the tomb's walls, but it did not become like a god. During the era of chaos after the collapse of the Old Kingdom, it seems that nobles not only usurped pharaoh's power and titles, but also his unique *ba* and afterlife. They began to claim that every person had a *ba*, as the *Dispute of a Man with His Ba* shows. Furthermore, they believed that every individual could become an *akh* after death. To guarantee this result, on the interiors of their wooden coffins, nobles inscribed versions of the once-exclusive magical texts designed to assure the king eternal life with the gods. These First Intermediate Period and Middle Kingdom versions of the Old Kingdom Pyramid Texts are therefore called the Coffin Texts. Their descendants, written on papyrus in New Kingdom times, have come to be known as the *Book of the Dead*.

Scholars have termed these revolutionary changes in mortuary beliefs and practices "the democratization of the afterlife." From this time on, anyone who could afford mummification, a tomb and its furnishings, proper burial rites, and who also passed the final judgment would become like a god in the other world. Like the king, he or she would become an Osiris and would join Re and the other gods in their eternal activities (see the last section of Document 5.1). However, lest the word "democratization" be taken too seriously, it should be noted that all these mortuary requirements were very expensive. Only a small portion of the Egyptian population had the wealth needed to guarantee themselves a blissful afterlife.

THE MIDDLE KINGDOM: DYNASTIES 11B–13A (c. 2040–1720 B.C.E.)

The Establishment of the Middle Kingdom

The early kings of Dynasty 11, ruling from Thebes, had fought the Herakleopolitan kings for control of the territory around Abydos. By about 2065 B.C.E., the Theban monarchs had managed to extend their rule almost to Asyut. Nebhetepre Mentuhotep II° (c. 2060 to 2010 B.C.E.) continued his predecessors' drive northward, and finally, near the middle of his long reign, reunified Egypt. This reestablishment of peace, unity, and centralized control around 2040 B.C.E. constitutes the beginning of the Middle Kingdom.

Mentuhotep II changed his Horus name to "Unifier of the Two Lands" to celebrate the restoration of Egyptian unity. He also undertook campaigns to the south, regaining control of most of Lower Nubia, the area between the first and second cataracts. Once again, Nubian raw materials and trade goods began flowing into Egypt. The most important of these products was gold. The pharaohs' demand for gold continually increased while Egypt's own gold deposits were decreasing, so from the Middle Kingdom onward, Nubia became Egypt's primary source for this precious metal. Almost as important as Nubia's gold were the skilled archers the Egyptians began recruiting there. Mercenary Nubian bowmen became an important component of Middle Kingdom Egyptian armies (see Figure 5.2).

Chief among Mentuhotep II's many building projects is his mortuary temple and tomb on the West Bank at Thebes. He chose a location at the southern end of a semicircular bay in the cliffs almost directly across the river from the Temple of Amun at Karnak. This area is today known as Deir el-Bahri. There, Mentuhotep II erected a series of terraces in front of a hall and shrine cut into the cliffs. The base was a large square platform with a colonnade of square pillars across its front. Atop the platform was a second colonnade surrounding a square structure that might have been capped by a small pyramid or, more likely, a *mastaba* or "primeval mound" (see Figure 5.3). Mentuhotep II's tomb chamber was reached by a shaft that entered the cliffs from the rear of this temple complex, but there was another chamber directly beneath the platform. This cenotaph, or memorial chamber, held an empty sarcophagus, a statue of the king in *heb-sed* (Jubilee Festival) ritual garb, and

---

°Some scholars refer to this king as Mentuhotep I, while others (the present author included) believe that there was an earlier Mentuhotep near the beginning of the Eleventh Dynasty. No matter what number they give him, all scholars agree that the Mentuhotep whose praenomen was Nebhetepre reunified Egypt.

FIGURE 5.2 Middle Kingdom Model of a Contingent of Nubian Archers

This model is on display at the Nubian Museum, Aswan.
Source: Courtesy of the author.

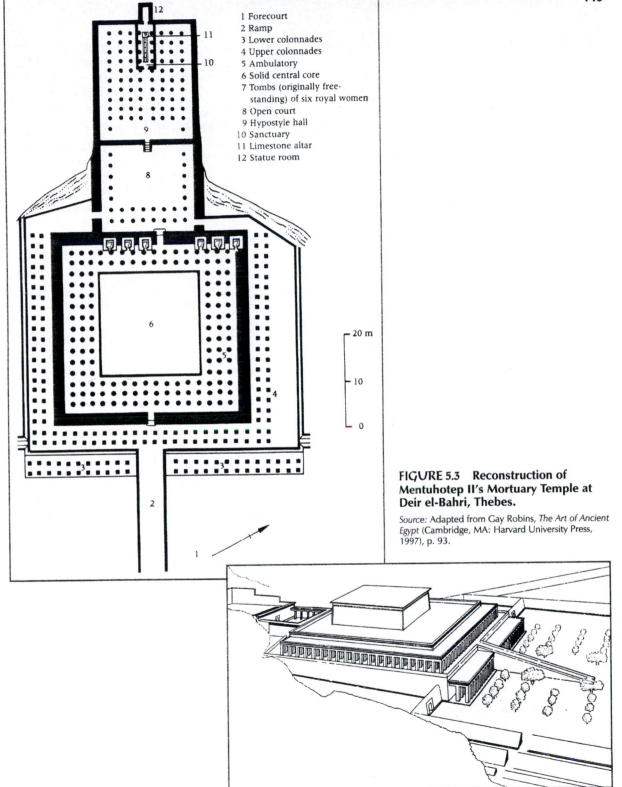

1 Forecourt
2 Ramp
3 Lower colonnades
4 Upper colonnades
5 Ambulatory
6 Solid central core
7 Tombs (originally free-
   standing) of six royal women
8 Open court
9 Hypostyle hall
10 Sanctuary
11 Limestone altar
12 Statue room

**FIGURE 5.3   Reconstruction of
Mentuhotep II's Mortuary Temple at
Deir el-Bahri, Thebes.**

Source: Adapted from Gay Robins, *The Art of Ancient
Egypt* (Cambridge, MA: Harvard University Press,
1997), p. 93.

other objects associated with the king's jubilee, probably celebrated in his thirtieth year of rule.

As might be expected, several of Mentuhotep II's high officials were buried in nearby tombs. However, also near Mentuhotep's temple, there was a remarkable tomb containing the bodies of 60 of his soldiers. Their wounds show that they were killed in combat, and the condition of the bodies indicates that they were buried after being brought back from some distant battlefield. Mentuhotep II must have chosen to honor the fallen heroes of one of his major victories (either his conquest of the north or his conquest of Lower Nubia) by giving them a mass burial near his own resting place.

After the reign of Mentuhotep II's son and successor, Mentuhotep III (c. 2010 to 1998 B.C.E.), internal conflict seems to have broken out again. Mentuhotep IV's relatively short reign (c. 1998 to 1991 B.C.E.) was not recognized by the Turin Canon or the Abydos and Saqqara king lists. They move directly from Mentuhotep III to Amenemhet I. However, inscriptions show that Amenemhet was first the vizier and then successor of Mentuhotep IV. He may have overthrown his master and seized the throne, or he may have been designated by Mentuhotep IV as his heir. In any case, Amenemhet I (c. 1991 to 1962 B.C.E.) was a commoner of Upper Egyptian origin who began the Twelfth Dynasty.

The Impressive Twelfth Dynasty

Perhaps some support for the theory that Amenemhet I usurped the throne may be drawn from *The Prophecy of Neferti*. This propagandistic literary composition was probably produced during Amenemhet I's reign or soon afterward and seeks to justify his (and his successors') right to the throne. It is set in Old Kingdom times and claims to be a prophecy made to King Snefru by a priest named Neferti. This priest "predicts" the famine, bloodshed, and chaos of the First Intermediate Period. However, he claims that a king named Ameny (a shortened form of Amenemhet), a commoner from the area around the first cataract, will reunite the country, defeat its enemies

and restore Egypt's peace and well-being. Thus, supposedly the gods had long ago chosen Amenemhet I to be Egypt's savior and through Neferti had foretold his rule. It is doubtful that Amenemhet would have needed such a fictitious defense if he had been the legitimate successor of Mentuhotep IV.

Clearly, though, Amenemhet I was a man of great ability. He not only restored order within Egypt, but also in Lower Nubia. Moreover, according to *The Prophecy of Neferti*, he constructed fortifications in the north (probably in the Wadi Tumilat) to stop the Asiatics' influx into Egypt. Though he came from the far southern part of Egypt, he decided to move the capital from Thebes, where his Eleventh Dynasty predecessors had ruled, to a site in the north. There, he constructed a new administrative center named Itjtawy-Amenemhet ("Amenemhet is Seizer of the Two Lands"). The site of Itjtawy, as it was usually called, has not yet been found. However, it probably was located near modern Lisht (about 20 miles south of Memphis) where the early Twelfth Dynasty kings were buried.

Amenemhet I seems to have brought almost all of the nomarchs and other strong nobles under his royal authority. However, he was unable to completely destroy their power and attain the almost unlimited dominion enjoyed by early Old Kingdom pharaohs. So, in his twentieth year of rule, Amenemhet I made his son Senusret I (c. 1971 to 1926 B.C.E.) king and co-ruler. This move ensured that his son would succeed him. It also guaranteed that there would be a strong young pharaoh to keep the nobles under control as Amenemhet aged. Such a period of joint rule is called a **co-regency**, and this one lasted for ten years. It established a precedent followed by almost all of the succeeding Twelfth Dynasty rulers, though their co-regencies proved to be much shorter (only one to three years long).

Despite Senusret I's co-regency with his father, a harem conspiracy seems to have been hatched when it was learned that Amenemhet was planning to yield his power totally to Senusret. While the young king was away fighting Libyans and before the planned abdication had been publicly announced, the plotters succeeded in assassinating Amenemhet I. This event is described in *The Instruction of King Amenemhet I for His Son Senusret I*, which claims to be the words of the dead king as revealed to his son in a dream. This document probably was written by a court scribe during the reign of Senusret I and likely reflects what was known about the old king's death. Amenemhet I had dozed off after supper and awoke suddenly to the sound of fighting by his guard. He is depicted as admitting his fallibility, fear and weakness:

> If I had made haste with weapons in my hand, I would have made the cowards retreat [in confusion], but no one is brave at night, and no one can fight alone; no happy outcome can result without a protector.[7]

Who was behind this conspiracy? The texts do not say, though Manetho claims that the king was murdered by his eunuchs. Probably Senusret I was also supposed to be killed and replaced by a younger prince. However, if we can trust the account in *The Story of Sinuhe*, a Middle Kingdom equivalent of a historical novel, Senusret was secretly informed about what had happened and quickly returned to the capital, foiling the plot. After such an experience, it is likely that Senusret I subsequently followed the advice given in *The Instruction of King Amenemhet I*: "Be on your guard against all who are subordinate to you. . . , trust no brother, know no friend, make no intimates, for there is no profit in it."[8]

The rest of Senusret I's reign and the reigns of his successors Amenemhet II (c. 1929 to 1895 B.C.E.) and Senusret II (c. 1897 to 1878 B.C.E.) were largely peaceful and prosperous. The Faiyum area began to be utilized more for hunting, fishing, and cultivation, so the channel from the Nile to the Faiyum's lake was enlarged. Senusret II even had his tomb, a small mud-brick pyramid, constructed at Lahun in the Faiyum. Egypt resumed its trade with Levantine centers such as Gubal (known to the Greeks as Byblos) and with the southern Red Sea area called Punt. It also established contacts with the Minoan civilization on Crete. Probably also during these reigns, the Egyptians began to build fortresses at the second cataract and

within Lower Nubia to regulate the movement of native Nubian groups. By the end of the Twelfth Dynasty, seven bastions standing on islands as well as at strategic points along the riverbank guarded the 40-mile stretch of the second cataract. Another six watched over the conquered territory between the second cataract and Elephantine.

Commerce also resumed between Egypt and Palestine. It is clear that by the beginning or early part of the Twelfth Dynasty, Palestine had recovered from its seminomadic interlude (the Early Bronze IV/Middle Bronze I Period) and was again becoming urbanized. Around 2000 to 1900 B.C.E., ideas, artifacts, and probably population groups moved southward into Palestine from eastern Syria, initiating the true Palestinian Middle Bronze Age (MB II A). As cities and towns developed once again, so did trade with Egypt. This commerce is evidenced not only by Egyptian artifacts found at Canaanite sites and Canaanite objects found in Egypt, but by a tomb painting at Beni Hasan from the reign of Senusret II. This painting depicts a group of Canaanites (called 'Amu by the Egyptians) seeking permission to enter Egypt. They were delivering cosmetics, but their donkeys carry what seem to be bellows. This suggests that they were also itinerant metal smiths who sought to ply their trade in Egypt. Other groups of Canaanite merchants, artisans, and mercenaries also seem to have been allowed to live and work in Egypt during the Twelfth Dynasty.

The Middle Kingdom reached its zenith during the reigns of Senusret III (c. 1878 to 1841 B.C.E.) and Amenemhet III (c. 1842 to 1797 B.C.E.). Senusret III (see Figure 5.4) repaired and enlarged an Old Kingdom bypass channel around the rapids of the first cataract so military forces could be deployed in Nubia more quickly. He also conducted at least one military campaign in Palestine to demonstrate Egyptian power and keep the trade routes open. Because of Senusret III's military prowess, later New Kingdom pharaohs built temples for his worship in Nubia, and he became the model for the world-conquering Sesostris described by Herodotus and other Greek writers. Senusret III also instituted internal administrative

FIGURE 5.4 Portrait of Senusret III

Source: British Museum, London.
Photo: Hirmer Fotoarchiv; Munich.

reforms, ending the autonomy of the nomarchs and dividing Egypt into three departments, the North (Lower Egypt), the South (Upper Egypt) and the Head of the South (Elephantine and Lower Nubia). Each of these departments was administered by a senior official assisted by a council, lower ranking officials, and their staffs of scribes. In addition to the three geographical departments, there were departments of agriculture, justice, labor, and the treasury. All were under the overall direction of Egypt's vizier or chief minister.

The peaceful 45-year-long reign of Senusret III's son Amenemhet III saw Egypt's economy reach new heights. Expeditions obtained alabaster and hard black graywacke stone from quarries within Egypt and diorite, amethyst, and large quantities of gold from Nubia. The turquoise mines at Serabit el-Khadim and other sites in the Sinai were also exploited as never before. Meanwhile, agricultural production in the Faiyum and foreign trade continued to increase.

To help preserve Egypt's internal security as well as its control over Lower Nubia and the trade routes through the Levant, Middle Kingdom pharaohs utilized magical inscriptions called Execration Texts. Similar ritual documents had been used during the late Old Kingdom and First Intermediate Period. However, the two most important collections of Exe-

cration Texts come from the reigns of Senusret III and Amenemhet III. These documents consist of lists of real or potential enemies written on bowls or on clay figurines depicting bound captives that were ceremonially cursed, then broken and buried. This ritual action magically destroyed the ability of the named groups or individuals to harm Egypt or the king. Many of the names belonged to dead Egyptians whose spirits, it was feared, might still cause harm. More interesting for modern scholars, though, are the lists of Nubian peoples and the many references to various tribes, cities, and individuals in Syria and Palestine. Gubal (Byblos), Tyre, Acre, Hazor, Shechem, Jerusalem, Beth Shemesh, Ashkelon, and Aphek and are among the identifiable places mentioned in these texts.

Unfortunately, the Twelfth Dynasty's ascendancy ended with Amenemhet III. His successor, Amenemhet IV (c. 1798 to 1786), had a brief co-regency with his father and perhaps a decade or so of independent rule. However, little is known about him. Soon after his death, a queen, Sobekneferu, assumed the throne (c. 1785 to 1782). Possibly she had been regent for a minor child who died soon after his father. In any case, like at least Nitiqret in the Old Kingdom, she seems to have ruled in her own right for a short time, using pharaonic titles. The Twelfth Dynasty ended with Sobekneferu, and though the transition to its successor seems to have been peaceful, we don't know the relationship, if any, between the founder of the Thirteenth Dynasty and his Twelfth Dynasty predecessors. The rulers later tradition grouped together as the Thirteenth Dynasty were much weaker than those of the Twelfth Dynasty. They generally had short reigns and did not all belong to the same family. Soon Egypt descended again into a period of internal division and chaos.

Cultural Developments During the Middle Kingdom

The Middle Kingdom in Egypt is often described as a feudal period. This characterization reflects the fact that during much of this era, the great nobles retained considerable power and some independence. However, the terminology is also due to the Middle Kingdom's changed perception of the ruler. Instead of the all-powerful, aloof divinity of Old Kingdom times, Middle Kingdom literature and art depict the king as a lonely, conscientious protector and "good shepherd" of his people. As the examples quoted earlier in this chapter show, in the literature, kings admit to lack of knowledge, to being unprepared, and even to fear. Also, the texts stress the awesome responsibility and personal loneliness of the king who must ensure *ma'at* for his people while being unable to trust anyone around him. This changed perception of kingship is further reflected in the world-weary, lined faces of Middle Kingdom royal portraits (see Figure 5.4).

The Middle Kingdom was also the classical period for Egyptian secular literature. The elegant compositions of this era became literary models in the later scribal schools. They were copied over and over again, allowing many of these works to survive to the present. Continuing a trend from the First Intermediate Period, didactic moral essays, reflections on times of anarchy and distress, and pseudo-prophecies remained popular. *The Instruction of King Amenemhet I for His Son Senusret I*, *The Prophecy of Neferti*, and *The Eloquent Peasant* have already been mentioned. Other Middle Kingdom works belonging to these categories are *The Complaints of Khakheperre-sonbe*, *The Satire of the Trades*, *The Instruction of a Man for His Son*, and possibly *The Admonitions of Ipuwer* (which more likely belongs to the Second Intermediate Period). This era also saw the rise of romantic prose stories with historical settings such as *Tales of King Khufu and the Magicians*, *The Shipwrecked Sailor*, *The Story of King Neferkare and General Sisenet*, and the famous *Story of Sinuhe*.

Middle Kingdom burial practices also continued to evolve from those of Old Kingdom times. Toward the end of the Old Kingdom, noble burials in chambers cut directly into the cliff sides of central and southern Egyptian hills had become common (see Figure 5.5). This type of tomb remained popular during the First Intermediate Period, and a modified form of it with a larger court in front was utilized by the Eleventh Dynasty kings. However, Amenemhet I and his Twelfth Dynasty descendants tried to emulate Old Kingdom precedent by resuming the practice of building pyramids. Their structures, erected at Lisht and later at Lahun and Dahshur, were comparable in size and construction to those of Fifth and Sixth dynasty rulers. However, only Amenemhet I's pyramid was built entirely of stone. The other Twelfth Dynasty pyramids, like their late Old Kingdom models, had rubble or mud-brick cores with only outer casings of

FIGURE 5.5   Late Old Kingdom (Dynasty 6) and Middle Kingdom Nobles' Shaft Tombs at Aswan

Source: Courtesy of the author.

limestone blocks. These pyramids are poorly preserved, for their stone exteriors were robbed for reuse in later times, allowing their cores to deteriorate.

Nobles continued to be buried in chamber tombs cut into the stone of the hills (see Figure 5.5). It is interesting, though, that these commoners did not totally abandon their old ideas when they adopted the new belief that at death they would become like gods. They still depicted scenes of daily life in their tombs so that they could continue to experience them in the afterlife. In addition to wall paintings (and less frequently bas-relief sculptures), wooden models of everyday activities were placed in Middle Kingdom tombs. As in Old Kingdom times, Egyptians believed that after death they would journey to the "Beautiful West." This land of the dead seems to have been located beneath the earth. There, they would live lives similar to those they lived in this world. Yet, at the same time, they became *akhu* ("transfigured beings") and joined the circumpolar stars in the north. They also traveled with Re in his solar boat and joined the other gods in their activities. The Egyptians never tried to reconcile these various conceptions of the afterlife that to us seem so contradictory. They steadfastly continued to affirm all of them.

They did make a few concessions to change, however. To prevent themselves from having to actually row Re's boat or perform any other labor in the afterlife, Egyptians began placing figurines called **shabtis** or *ushabtis* ("answerers") in the tombs (see Figure 5.6). Inscriptions on these statuettes magically empowered them to work in place of a dead person in the afterworld. If the deceased was called upon to perform any labor, the *shabti* would volunteer to do it (see Document 5.2, Section A). Thus, the tomb owner would enjoy uninterrupted rest and bliss in the hereafter.

The idea of a final judgment had appealed to scribes and intellectuals as a way of preserving *ma'at*, if not in this world, then at least in the next. However, as soon as order and stability were restored within Egypt, the elite began seeking ways to circumvent this judgment. Instead of a welcome assurance that *ma'at* prevailed in the afterlife, the judgment became another obstacle that had to be overcome if the dead were to enjoy a blessed hereafter. To successfully pass

FIGURE 5.6   Examples of *Shabti* Figurines
These are on display at the Nubian Museum in Aswan.
Source: Courtesy of the author.

the judgment, Egyptians began to rely more on the magical potency of spells and funerary inscriptions than upon truly moral lives and clear consciences. They created large, elaborately carved stone **scarabs** (images of dung beetles) with human faces in place of the beetles' heads. Because of the inscriptions on their flat undersides, these objects are called heart scarabs. The texts on them are designed to magically prevent a person's heart from testifying against him or her when the heart is weighed against *ma'at* (see Document 5.2, Section B). Other spells to control the heart's testimony and attain vindication at the judgment were later incorporated into the *Book of the Dead*. They include the declaration of innocence, or "negative confession," as it is usually known, (see Document 5.2, Section C), and the following:

> This my heart shall not rise against me.
> Obey me, my heart,
> I am your owner. . . .

DOCUMENT 5.2
Some Magical Funerary Texts

These magical texts were placed in tombs to guarantee individuals a blessed afterlife. The inscription on a *shabti* figurine made it capable of volunteering to perform work for the deceased in the other world. The heart scarab inscription and declaration of innocence guaranteed that when the hearts of the deceased individuals were weighed against *ma'at*, they would be judged righteous and the individuals would be admitted into the afterlife. The explanatory material in square brackets has been added by W. Stiebing; the material in regular parentheses is part of the original translation.

A. Inscription on a *Shabti* [9]

O figure of (name of deceased), if I am summoned, if I am registered to do any work that is wont to be done in the underworld, then the task will be transposed to you there, as a person to his duty. Apply yourself in my place at any moment to cultivate the fields, irrigate the banks, transport sand from east to west. "Here I am!" you shall say.

B. Inscription on a Heart Scarab[10]

The high steward Nebankh. He says:
Heart of my mother, heart of my mother!
Do not stand up against me, do not witness against me,
do not oppose me in the tribunal,
do not incline against me in the presence of the keeper of the scales.
You are my *ka*, the one within my body,
the Khnum [a ram-headed creator god who shaped humans' bodies on a potter's wheel]
who makes my body whole.
You come to happiness with me.

C. The Declaration of Innocence (*Book of the Dead*, Spell 125)[11]

I have not done falsehood against men, I have not impoverished my associates, I have done no wrong in the Place of Truth. . . . I have done no evil, I have not daily made labour in excess of what was due to be done for me, my name has not reached the offices of those who control slaves, I have not deprived the orphan of his property, I have not done what the gods detest, I have not calumniated a servant to his master, I have not caused pain, I have not made hungry, I have not made to weep, I have not killed, I have not commanded to kill, I have not made suffering for anyone. . . .

Rise not as a witness,
Accuse me not before the Lord of All.[12]

The ascent of the gods Sobek and Amun to national importance is another religious development of Middle Kingdom times. The crocodile god Sobek was a water and vegetation deity from the Faiyum. However, as one of the patrons of the Twelfth and Thirteenth Dynasty kings, his worship spread to other parts of Egypt, especially to the Delta and Ombos (near Naqada) in Upper Egypt. Amun, whose name means "the Hidden One," was a previously obscure deity worshiped at Thebes. He had not even been the principal god of Thebes before the Middle Kingdom. That honor had gone to Montu, a hawk-headed war deity whose cult seems to have originated at nearby Hermonthis (modern Armant). Montu was the favorite deity of the Theban Mentuhoteps ("Montu is Content") of Dynasty 11. However, Amenemhet I began to emphasize the worship of Amun. Amenemhet means "Amun is in Front" or "Amun is at the Head (of the Divine Forces)." Amenemhet I and his Twelfth Dynasty successors not only displayed their devotion to Amun in their names, but through the monuments they erected to him at Thebes. Montu's temple at Karnak on the northern edge of Thebes became a subsidiary of the larger temple of Amun that developed there. In addition, Amun absorbed the nature and identity of Min, a fertility god worshiped at nearby Coptos. Sobek and Amun remained prominent in later times; Amun even became the head of the Egyptian pantheon.

THE SECOND INTERMEDIATE PERIOD: DYNASTIES 13B–17 (c. 1720–1540 B.C.E.)

The Onset of the Second Intermediate Period

Just as with the First Intermediate Period, it is difficult to determine exactly when the Second Intermediate Period began. Some scholars, following the example of the Abydos King List, end the Middle Kingdom at the end of Dynasty 12. Others argue that the early rulers of the Thirteenth Dynasty maintained their sovereignty over all of Egypt. Only after c. 1720 to 1715 B.C.E. does centralized control seem to have broken down, signaling the start of another intermediate period.

Whether or not one places the first part of the Thirteenth Dynasty in the Middle Kingdom or Second Intermediate Period, it is clear that during that

era, large numbers of Canaanite immigrants had filtered into the eastern Delta, settling at Tell ed-Dab'a (Avaris), Tell el-Maskhuta (Pithom), and other sites. These Semitic newcomers quickly began to adopt aspects of Egyptian culture and blend them with their own. For example, they identified several of their deities with Egyptian gods. They equated their storm god Ba'al with the Egyptian god Seth, and the fertility goddess Asherah with Hathor. Even the Egyptians in the area eventually came to worship these composite deities. In New Kingdom times, for example, there was a popular Delta cult dedicated to Asherah/Hathor under her epithet, Qudshu ("The Holy One").

When royal authority over the Delta and central Egypt deteriorated around 1720 B.C.E., several local leaders were able to establish their hegemony over their own areas. Manetho seems to have grouped these largely contemporaneous rulers into his Fourteenth Dynasty. Some of these local rulers from the Delta area probably constitute the non-Fifteenth Dynasty Hyksos kings whose scarabs have been found at Palestinian and Syrian sites.[13] Meanwhile, the last members of the Thirteenth Dynasty continued ruling at Thebes. However, the area they controlled was very limited—their monuments and inscriptions have been found only from Abydos southward.

The chaos and confusion that followed the collapse of the Middle Kingdom lasted almost a century and seems to have been as bad as that of the First Intermediate Period, if not worse. A text that probably belongs to the end of this era, the *Admonitions of Ipuwer*,[14] describes conditions in Egypt during the late eighteenth and early seventeenth centuries B.C.E.:

> Foreigners have become people [i.e., Egyptians] everywhere. . . .
>
> Lo, poor men have become men of wealth,
>
> He who could not afford sandals owns riches. . . .
>
> What the pyramid hid [i.e., the king's sarcophagus] is empty.
>
> See now, the land is deprived of kingship
>
> By a few men who ignore custom.[15]

The Kingdom of Kush (Upper Nubia)

During the Egyptian Middle Kingdom, the flow of trade northward along the Nile from the far south to Egypt brought prosperity to those in the Nile Valley south of the second cataract. In this area, a powerful Upper Nubian state developed with its center at Kerma, just south of the third cataract. From the beginning of the Twelfth Dynasty onward, the Egyptians called this kingdom "Kush." The many Twelfth Dynasty fortresses constructed in Lower Nubia and especially along the second cataract (the least treacherous of the Nile's rapids) were largely a reaction to the growth of this state.

During the early Thirteenth Dynasty, the Egyptians stopped rotating the garrisons of the Lower Nubian fortresses, and they became permanent settled communities. When the Middle Kingdom collapsed around 1720 B.C.E., what little support these communities had gotten from the central government ceased. The Egyptian and Egyptianized Nubian settlers of Lower Nubia had to fend for themselves. So, during the early part of the Second Intermediate Period, the fortress communities of Lower Nubia became independent entities. Furthermore, like their counterparts elsewhere in Egypt, some of Lower Nubia's local rulers claimed pharaonic status. However, without hope of help from Egypt, these "kings" realized that they would not be able to hold out for long against the forces of Kush. Thus, by c. 1650 B.C.E. the people of Lower Nubia seem to have peacefully accepted an Upper Nubian takeover of the fortresses and thus became part of the Kingdom of Kush (see Map 5.1).[16]

The kings of Kush recognized that their best interests lay in keeping the native Egyptian dynasty at Thebes weak. So, they formed an alliance with the Hyksos rulers in the north. This alliance allowed Kush continued access not only to Egyptian objects, but also to trade goods from other parts of the eastern Mediterranean world. As we shall see, there is evidence of contact between the Hyksos and Crete. Thus, it was undoubtedly through Lower Egypt by way of the trade routes connecting the oases west of the Nile that a few Minoan objects reached Kush (like a Middle Minoan bowl with incised decoration found at Kerma).

The rulers of Kush were buried at Kerma on beds placed in open pits covered by large earthen mounds. Animal and human sacrifice accompanied the burial rites. Like other aspects of Kushite culture, these burials were typically Nubian and derived from earlier practices in the area. However, after gaining control of Lower Nubia and the Egyptians living there, the Kushites began merging Egyptian technology and artistic elements into their culture. Egyptian artifacts became increasingly common in Kerma and elsewhere in Kush. Some of these objects were imports or booty from raids into southern Egypt, but others were the products of Egyptians living within Kush. These Egyptian artisans included not only individuals from Lower Nubia, but also immigrants from Egypt who moved southward to work for the Kushite rulers. Thus, new types of buildings, paintings, and other artifacts developed—Kushite at heart, but utilizing Egyptian styles and techniques.

Hyksos Rule and the Dynasty at Thebes: Dynasties 15 and 17 (c. 1650–1540 B.C.E.)

Around 1650 B.C.E., the Fifteenth Dynasty, a dynasty of foreigners, arose in the eastern Delta and gained control of Lower Egypt. The Egyptians called these rulers *hekau khasut* ("chieftains of foreign lands"), a designation previously used for leaders of seminomadic groups in Syria and Palestine. This appellation was later corrupted into the Greek term Hyksos and applied to the entire people, rather than just the kings. Manetho (as quoted by Josephus) preserved New Kingdom and later Egyptian traditions about the ruthless Hyksos, claiming that:

> incredibly out of the parts of the east men of despicable ethnicity marched boldly against the land, and seized it easily by overwhelming force without fighting a battle. And having taken prisoner those who were the leaders here, they thereafter savagely burned the cities and demolished the gods' shrines. They treated all the inhabitants most hatefully, slaughtering some, and leading into slavery the children and wives of others.[17]

MAP 5.1   Egypt During the Latter Part of the Second Intermediate Period

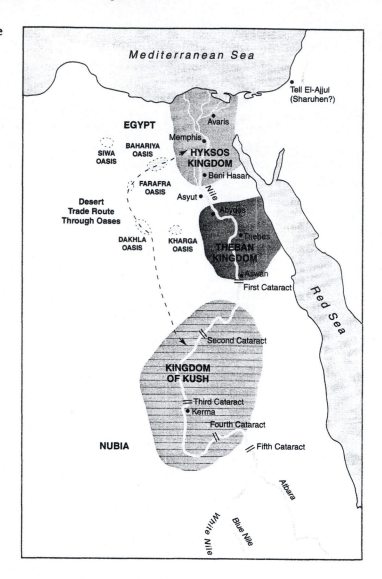

Josephus' quote from Manetho goes on to say that the first Hyksos king was named Salitis, that he ruled from Memphis, but that his fortified stronghold was located at Avaris, a city in the eastern Delta.

Over the past 50 years, intensive textual research and archaeological finds (especially those from Tell ed-Dab'a, the site of ancient Avaris) have shown that the rise of the Hyksos was a far more complex event than one might suspect from Manetho's account. As

we have seen, large numbers of Semitic-speaking Canaanite immigrants settled in the eastern Egyptian Delta during the late Middle Kingdom, and some of their chieftains gained control over their local areas after c. 1720 B.C.E. The complete collapse of the Egyptian central government led to an even larger influx of immigrants from Canaan after that date. Then, c. 1650 B.C.E., one group of these newcomers took control of the entire Delta and defeated the petty Egyptian princes who ruled areas of Middle Egypt, making them vassals (see Map 5.1). They even seem to have forced the native rulers at Thebes to pay tribute to them for a time, though the distance between Thebes and the Delta allowed the southerners to maintain a fair amount of freedom and local sovereignty. Though some of the earlier Canaanite rulers of small areas of the eastern Delta had accepted the Egyptian term *hekau khasut* (Hyksos) for themselves, it is the line of six powerful kings who controlled much of Egypt from c. 1650 to 1540 B.C.E. that constitutes Manetho's Hyksos dynasty (Dynasty 15).

Like the other Canaanite immigrants who preceded them, the Hyksos embraced Egyptian culture. They utilized the titles and symbols of Egyptian kingship, adopted Egyptian names, and used hieroglyphs to write inscriptions in the Egyptian language. They worshiped and built temples to Egyptian gods, especially Seth, who was considered the Egyptian form of their god, Ba'al. They also supported the traditional Egyptian arts and sciences and employed native Egyptians in their bureaucracy and as vassal rulers of some parts of Egypt. Therefore, Manetho's claim that the Hyksos destroyed Egyptian cities and temples and treated the population cruelly seems to have little or no basis in fact. That tradition almost certainly derives from later nationalistic New Kingdom propaganda.

Actually, Egypt clearly benefited from the innovations in technology and warfare introduced during the Second Intermediate Period. Palestinian immigrants brought with them the technique for blending copper and tin to produce bronze. Bronze tools and weapons were much harder and more durable than the copper ones Egyptians had used previously. In addition, during this era, the Egyptians probably learned to use horse-drawn war chariots with spoked wheels, composite bows, bronze helmets, and protective armor made of bronze scales attached to leather shirts.

The most significant of these new military items was the horse-drawn light chariot. Horses were known in Egypt during the early part of the Second Intermediate Period, c. 1700 to 1650 B.C.E. Archaeologists have uncovered horse remains from that time

at Buhen in Nubia and Tell ed-Dab'a and Tell el-Maskhuta in the eastern Delta. Whether or not horses were first brought into the country by Asiatics is still undetermined. It is likely, though, that Canaanite immigrants introduced the chariot into Egypt some time during the Hyksos Period. There are no Egyptian references to or illustrations of horses or chariots before Kamose's war against the Hyksos, c. 1554 to 1550 B.C.E. Nevertheless, contrary to the earlier popular view, chariots seem to have played little, if any, role in the Hyksos' rise to power or in their expulsion.[18] However, afterward, chariots became a major component of Egypt's New Kingdom armies.

Complementing the introduction of chariots was the composite bow. Like the chariot, the composite bow had been used in other parts of the Near East long before its introduction into Egypt. A composite bow was made of fine wood strengthened by bands of sinew and horn. Thus, it was far more powerful and accurate than the simple bow. This bow could be used by infantry forces or defenders of fortified cities, but it was most effective in the hands of chariot warriors. After c. 1550 B.C.E., the chariot warriors of all the great powers, including Egypt, generally were armed with composite bows.

Shortly after the time that the Hyksos took control of most of Egypt, the Thirteenth Dynasty seems to have died out at Thebes. It was replaced by a new dynasty of Theban origin (later designated the Seventeenth Dynasty) that controlled only the territory between Abydos and Elephantine. As has been mentioned, for a time, these southern kings seem to have paid tribute to the Hyksos in order to avoid a direct confrontation. There may even have been some marriage ties between the two royal families. However, Hyksos control of Lower Egypt cut off Theban access to the Levant and the rest of the Near East. Moreover, the Hyksos alliance with Nubia threatened to strangle and destroy the native dynasty at Thebes. So, after slowly building up their military forces, the Theban rulers decided to strike first. A later popular story, *The Quarrel of Apopi and Seqenenre*, claims that the Hyksos king Auserre Apopi taunted the Theban king, goading him into attacking. Whatever the reason for the war, Seqenenre Tao II (c. 1559 to 1554 B.C.E.) began the attempt to expel the Hyksos by invading Middle Egypt. However, the Egyptian vassals of the Hyksos remained loyal to their overlords and resisted the advance of the Theban forces. Though Seqenenre Tao II conquered all of the territory northward to Cusae (just south of Hermopolis in central Egypt), he did not succeed in destroying the Hyksos. His mummy was found in 1881, and the terrible wounds to its head show that the king died in battle.

His son Kamose then became king c. 1554 B.C.E. After some preliminary attacks on Lower Nubia to secure his southern frontier, Kamose invaded Hyksos territory (see Document 5.3). He gained control of Middle Egypt and ravaged the countryside around Avaris. However, as he was preparing an assault on Avaris itself, his forces captured a Hyksos courier carrying a message urging the Nubian King of Kush to attack the Egyptians from the south. This captured letter is our main evidence that there was an alliance between the Hyksos and Kush. So Kamose had to break off his northern campaign, return home, and shore up his southern defenses. He was given an enthusiastic welcome by the Theban people, and erected two stelae commemorating his victories. Unfortunately, he died soon afterward (c. 1550 B.C.E.). He had seriously reduced the size of the Hyksos realm, but he had been unable to dislodge the Hyksos from Avaris. That feat was left for his successor, his younger brother, Ahmose.

Hyksos Relations with the Levant

As one might suspect, relations between the Semitic Hyksos rulers of Lower Egypt and the Canaanites of Palestine and eastern Syria were especially close. Kamose's inscription states that hundreds of ships filled with products from the Levant were moored at Avaris. And archaeological excavations there have uncovered thousands of Canaanite storage jars and other vessels that came from Canaan, the vast majority deriving from southern Palestine. This fact has been demonstrated by scientific analysis of their clays.[19] However, scholars disagree about the nature of the relationship between the two peoples.

The once-popular idea of a Hyksos Empire stretching over all of Palestine and Syria (and according to a few scholars, even including Crete) has now been almost universally abandoned. The main evidence thought to support this hypothesis (other than Manetho's account of an invasion from the Northeast) was the appearance of new defense systems at Palestinian and Syrian Middle Bronze Age cities. Scholars also noted that a few objects inscribed with Hyksos names had been found in Syria and Crete. The new fortifications involved surrounding cities with high steeply sloping beaten-earth or plaster-faced ramparts. The cities' inhabitants then usually built their defensive walls atop these ramparts. They also commonly made it even more difficult for attackers by digging deep ditches in front of the ramparts. However, it is now clear that this type of fortification developed within the Near East from earlier traditions, probably to protect city walls from assault by battering rams, ladders, and tunneling.[20] It was not introduced from the outside by an invading horde of newcomers. Also, the Hyksos objects found as far away as Crete do not prove Hyksos rule over the areas involved. Since archaeologists have found no Hyksos monuments within the presumed "Empire" or textual references to Hyksos control of areas outside of Egypt, almost all Near Eastern specialists now credit the spread of Hyksos artifacts to trade.

However, it is possible that the Hyksos rulers controlled at least the city-states of southern coastal Palestine. There were demonstrably close connections between those cities and the Hyksos Fifteenth Dynasty. Also, immediately after destroying Avaris, the Hyksos capital, the Eighteenth Dynasty pharaoh Ahmose attacked Sharuhen, a fortified city in southern Palestine.[21] This fact suggests to some scholars that the Hyksos controlled Sharuhen. Others argue that the fortified cities of southern Palestine were part of a "kingdom of Sharuhen."[22] In fact, Manfred Bietak, excavator of Tell ed-Dab'a (Avaris), has suggested that the Sixteenth Dynasty, a sub-dynasty of the Hyksos, ruled from Sharuhen rather than in Egypt.[23] Thus, the "kingdom of Sharuhen" would have been a truly unified kingdom controlling southern Canaan and an ally of the Egyptian Hyksos. However, it is more likely that if a "kingdom of Sharuhen"

DOCUMENT 5.3
The War Between Kamose and the Hyksos

Kamose erected two stelae in Thebes celebrating his victories over the Hyksos. They are unique in that the second inscription seems to take up the story where the first ended (unfortunately, the end of the first stele is missing). This account of the campaign seems to be historically reliable and based on historical sources, probably including the actual captured letter "quoted" on Stele 2. The following translation contains only portions of these two important texts. The material in parentheses was added by the translator,[24] but the explanatory material in square brackets has been added to the translation by W. Stiebing.

His majesty [Kamose] spoke in his palace to his council of magistrates who were in his train: "To what end do I know my (own) strength? One chief is in Avaris, another in Kush, and I sit (here) associated with an Asiatic and a Nubian! Each man has his slice in this Egypt and so the land is partitioned with me! None can pass through it as far as Memphis (although it is) Egyptian water! See he [the Hyksos king] (even) has Hermopolis! No one can be at ease when they are milked by the taxes of the Asiatics (*Sttyw*). I shall grapple with him that I might crush his belly, (for) my desire is to rescue Egypt which the Asiatics (*'3mw*) have destroyed."

The king's counselors advise against war, but Kamose rejects their advice. The rest of the surviving portion of the stele records the king's victories in Middle Egypt. The lost portion of the text presumably described the Egyptian advance toward Avaris. The second stele opens with Kamose taunting the Hyksos king in Avaris, telling him of the destruction he has wrought within the Hyksos territory. Then follows the narrative given below.

"I captured his messenger in the oasis upland, as he was going south to Kush with a written dispatch, and I found on it the following in writing by the hand of the Ruler of Avaris:

"*3wsr-r'* [Auserre], son of Re, Apophis greets my son the ruler of Kush. Why have you arisen as ruler without letting me know? Do you see what Egypt has done to me? The Ruler which is in her midst—Kamose-the-Mighty, given life!—is pushing me off my (own) land! I have not attacked him in any way comparable to all that he has done to you; he has chopped up the Two Lands to their grief, my land and yours, and he has hacked them up. Come north! Do not hold back! See, he is here with me: There is none who will stand up to you in Egypt. See, I will not give him a way out until you arrive! Then we shall divide the towns of Egypt. . . .

He [the Hyksos king] feared me [Kamose] even when I was sailing north, before we had fought, before I reached him! When he saw my flame he beat a path as far as Kush to seek his deliverer. (But) I seized it [the Hyksos letter] en route and did not let it arrive. . . . So I fared south confident and happy, destroying all the enemy who were in my way!"

(other than the single city of that name) really existed, it was only "a loose confederation of city-states under the hegemony of Sharuhen."[25]

In fact, all these speculations go beyond the actual evidence. All that can be said with certainty is that many Palestinian products, mostly from far southern

Palestine, have been found in Egyptian Delta cities, especially Avaris. Possibly these objects were sent as tribute. Possibly there was Hyksos control over southern Palestine, or possibly the Hyksos were allied with a coalition of southern Palestinian cities. However, it is also possible that the southern Palestinian objects in Egypt resulted from trade between the Hyksos Delta kingdom and individual Palestinian city-states that were independent and self-governing. In the absence of written evidence to the contrary, that last possibility seems the most likely to be correct.

Egyptian and Levantine Contacts with the Minoan Culture of Crete

As we saw in Chapter 3, like much of the Near East, Greece experienced major disruptions at the end of the Early Bronze Age (c. 2300 to 2200 B.C.E.). New people, probably speaking Greek or Proto-Greek, seem to have become the dominant population group there. Crete, however, does not seem to have been affected during this time. The Minoan culture continued to develop without interruption, and around 2000 B.C.E. major palace complexes arose in five different areas of Crete. The largest palace was at Knos-

sos, near Crete's north-central coast. However, similar structures appeared at Mallia (on the north coast, east of Knossos), Zakros (on the east coast), Phaistos (near the south-central coast), and Khania (on the northwest coast). These palaces served as redistribution hubs for agricultural goods and production centers for trade commodities.

Prior to the beginning of the Middle Minoan Period (see Table 5.2) there seems to have been little or no Minoan trade with the Near East, other than with the western coast of Asia Minor. Only a few Egyptian, Mesopotamian, and other Near Eastern objects had made their way to Crete before that time, probably through intermediaries in Asia Minor. However, with the rise of the Minoan palaces, Cretan ships began sailing further afield, at least to Cyprus and probably occasionally to Egypt as well.

By the Late Minoan I A Period (see Table 5.2), Minoan civilization was reaching its zenith. Crete dominated the Aegean, bringing the Greek mainland under strong Minoan cultural influence. In addition, Minoan settlements were established on Thera (Santorini), Rhodes, and other Aegean islands. However, during this era, Minoan trade with Egypt and the Levant does not seem to have been extensive. Archaeolo-

TABLE 5.2

Chronologies of the Middle Minoan and Late Minoan I Periods in Crete

(All dates are B.C.E. MM = Middle Minoan and LM = Late Minoan.)

The Traditional Chronology			The "High Chronology"	
MM I A	2200–2000		MM I A	2200–2000
MM I B	2000–1900	Palaces arise on Crete	MM I B	2000–1900
MM II A	1900–1800		MM II A	1900–1850
MM II B	1800–1700	Palaces destroyed (by earthquake?) at the end of MM II B, but rebuilt	MM II B	1850–1800
MM III A	1700–1650		MM III A	1800–1750
MM III B	1650–1550		MM III B	1750–1700
LM I A	1550–1500	Thera explodes near the end of LM I A; palaces damaged but repaired	LM I A	1700–1620
LM I B	1500–1450	Minoan Palaced Destroyed at the end of LM I B; only Knossos was rebuilt	LM I B	1620–1500

gists have found few Late Minoan I objects at Near Eastern sites. Nevertheless, there was probably at least some commerce in raw materials from time to time. Most of the gold, copper, silver, ivory, and ostrich eggs found in Crete probably came from the Near East. In exchange, the Minoans might have traded cloth, spices, agricultural products, or other items that would not have been preserved in the archaeological record.

In recent years, archaeologists have uncovered a different kind of evidence for Minoan contacts with Egypt and the Levant during the Late Minoan I Period. Instead of pottery and other trade goods, they found Late Minoan I A style paintings at various Near Eastern sites. The finds at Tell Kabri in northern Palestine included a painted stucco floor and bits of a fresco depicting rocks, a river, buildings, and other motifs reflecting Aegean themes and style.[26] At Avaris (Tell ed-Dab'a) in the Egyptian Delta, archaeologists excavated fragmentary paintings of griffins, bulls, bull leapers, and other clearly Minoan designs.[27] These recent finds complement the earlier discovery of similar Aegean-style paintings at Alalakh in Syria.[28] These paintings seem to have been executed by Minoan artists. They may indicate the presence of Minoan merchants, ambassadors, or even royal brides in Egypt and some Levantine cities.

The Aegean frescoes at Tell Kabri and Alalakh were roughly contemporaneous with the early part of the Hyksos era in Egypt (c. 1650 to 1540 B.C.E.). The paintings from Avaris were at first also dated to the Hyksos era. However, now their excavator argues that they belong to a structure built just after Ahmose's conquest of Avaris.[29] As a result, these art works have become points of contention in ongoing arguments about the chronology of the Late Minoan (LM) I A Period.

This era was brought to an end by a great volcanic explosion on the Cycladic island of Thera (also called Santorini). That explosion destroyed much of the island and buried Akrotiri, the site of the Minoan LM I A settlement on Thera. It also damaged the palaces in Crete, but they were quickly repaired and continued to flourish in the following LM I B Period. The traditional archaeological chronology for Crete dated the eruption and the end of LM I A at about 1500 B.C.E. (see Table 5.2). However, various scientific dating methods placed the eruption more than a century earlier, between 1645 and 1625 B.C.E., with 1627 as the most likely date.[30] That date was earlier than the traditional date for the *beginning* of LM I A (c. 1550 B.C.E.). If the scientific dates are correct, LM I A must have begun and ended much earlier than previously thought. The finds at Tell Kabri and Alalakh fit into this higher chronology. They indicate that the LM I A Period was largely contemporaneous with the Egyptian Second Intermediate Period and the Syro-Palestinian Middle Bronze II B era.[31] On the other hand, LM I A style frescoes in an early New Kingdom building at Avaris support the traditional Minoan chronology.[32]

At present, the evidence seems to favor the early date for the eruption of Thera and the end of LM I A, but a consensus has not been reached on this issue. Whatever the final decision about Aegean chronology, it is clear that there was contact. There may even have been intimate connections between Crete and the Near East during all or part of the Hyksos era.

SUGGESTIONS FOR FURTHER READING AND INFORMATION

Internet Sites

Accounts of the war against the Hyksos and the reigns of Ahmose and Amenhotep I: http://emuseum.mankato.msus.edu/prehistory/egypt/history/dynasties/dynasty15.html

The site of Akrotiri on Thera: http://www.perseus.tufts.edu/cgi-bin/siteindex?lookup=Akrotir

Books and Articles

Egypt

Badawy, Alexander. *A History of Egyptian Architecture: The First Intermediate Period, the Middle Kingdom, and the Second Intermediate Period.* Berkeley and Los Angeles: University of California Press, 1966.

Bourriau, J. D. *Pharaohs and Mortals: Egyptian Art in the Middle Kingdom.* London: Cambridge University Press, 1988.

Bietak, Manfred. *Avaris, The Capital of the Hyksos: Recent Excavations at Tell el-Deba'a. New Excavation Reports.* London: The British Museum Press, 1996.

Oren, Eliezer D., ed. *The Hyksos: New Historical and Archaeological Perspectives*. Philadelphia: University Museum Publications, 1997.

Parkinson, Richard B. *Voices from Ancient Egypt: An Anthology of Middle Kingdom Writings*. London: British Museum Press, 1991.

Parkinson, Richard B. *The Tale of Sinuhe and Other Ancient Egyptian Poems, 1940–1640 B.C.* Oxford and New York: Oxford University Press, 1997.

Quirke, Stephen, ed. *Middle Kingdom Studies*. Sia Publications, 1991.

Robins, Gay, ed. *Beyond the Pyramids: Egyptian Regional Art from the Museo Egizio, Turin*. Atlanta: Emory University Museum of Art and Archaeology, 1990.

Ryholt, K.S.B. *The Political Situation in Egypt during the Second Intermediate Period c.1800–1550 B.C.* Carsten Niebuhr Institute Publications vol. 20. Copenhagen: The Carsten Niebuhr Institute of Near Eastern Studies, University of Copenhagen, and Museum Tusculanum Press, 1997.

Van Seters, John. *The Hyksos: A New Investigation*. New Haven: Yale University Press, 1966.

Ward, William A. *Egypt and the East Mediterranean World, 2200–1900 B.C.* Beirut: American University in Beirut, 1971.

Wegner, Josef. "The Nature and Chronology of the Senwosret III-Amenemhat III Regnal Succession: Some Considerations Based on New Evidence from the Mortuary Temple of Senwosret III at Abydos," *Journal of Near Eastern Studies*, vol. 55 (1996), pp. 249–279.

The Minoan Culture

Doumas, Christos G. *Thera: Pompeii of the Ancient Aegean*. London and New York: Thames and Hudson, 1983.

Hood, Sinclair. *The Minoans: The Story of Bronze Age Crete*. New York: Praeger, 1971.

Manning, Sturt W. *A Test of Time: The Volcano of Thera and the Chronology and History of the Aegean and East Mediterranean in the Mid Second Millennium B.C.* Oxford: Oxbow Books, 1999.

NOTES

1. Alan Gardiner, *Egypt of the Pharaohs* (London: Oxford University Press, 1961), p. 111. The inscription belongs to Ankhtify, a nomarch of Nekhen (Hierakonpolis), the third nome of Upper Egypt. See also Barbara Bell, "The Dark Ages in Ancient History: I. The First Dark Age in Egypt," *American Journal of Archaeology*, vol. 75 (1971), pp. 1–26.

2. John A. Wilson, "A Song of the Harper" in J. B. Pritchard, ed., *Ancient Near Eastern Texts Relating to the Old Testament*, 2nd ed. (Princeton, NJ: Princeton University Press, 1955), p. 467.

3. Miriam Lichtheim, *Ancient Egyptian Literature, Vol. I: The Old and Middle Kingdoms* (Berkeley: University of California Press, paperback ed., 1975), p. 105.

4. The translation is by R. O. Faulkner in William Kelly Simpson, ed., *The Literature of Ancient Egypt: An Anthology of Stories, Instructions, and Poetry*, new ed. (New Haven: Yale University Press, 1973), pp. 183–184.

5. Ibid., p. 184.

6. Ibid., pp. 206–209.

7. Ibid., p. 195. The bracketed words are in the original and represent what the translator thinks is the thrust of a word in the text whose meaning is not certain.

8. Ibid., p. 194.

9. Stephen Quirke, *Ancient Egyptian Religion* (London: The British Museum Press, 1992), p. 160.

10. Werner Forman and Stephen Quirke, *Hieroglyphs and the Afterlife in Ancient Egypt* (Norman, OK: University of Oklahoma Press, 1996), p. 104.

11. Raymond O. Faulkner, translator, *The Ancient Egyptian Book of the Dead*, Carol Andrews, ed. (Austin: University of Texas Press, 1990), pp. 29–31.

12. Erik Hornung, *The Valley of the Kings: Horizon of Eternity*, translated by David Warburton (New York: Timken Publishers, 1990), p. 136.

13. David O'Connor, "The Hyksos Period in Egypt" in Eliezer D. Oren, ed., *The Hyksos: New Historical and Archaeological Perspectives* (Philadelphia: The University Museum, 1997), pp. 48–52.

14. It was once generally accepted that the *Admonitions of Ipuwer* belonged to the First Intermediate Period. However, many Egyptologists now agree with John Van Seters, *The Hyksos in Egypt* (New Haven: Yale University Press, 1966), pp. 103–120 that it dates to the Second Intermediate Period or the beginning of the New Kingdom. Some, though, still prefer the earlier date. Its claims about the chaos of the Intermediate Period are somewhat exaggerated in order to contrast them with the restoration of order. Nevertheless, its descriptions probably reflect some memories and traditions about life just after the collapse of the Middle Kingdom.

15. Lichtheim (1975), pp. 150–151, 156. The explanatory material in square brackets was added by W. Stiebing and is not in Lichtheim's translation.

16. O'Connor in Oren, ed.(1997), p. 63.

17. Donald B. Redford, "Textual Sources for the Hyksos Period," in Oren, ed. (1997), p. 19.

18. Alan F. Schulman, "Chariots, Chariotry, and the Hyksos," *The SSEA Journal*, vol. 10, no. 2 (1980), pp. 105–153.

19. Patrick E. McGovern and Garman Harbottle, "'Hyksos' Trade Connections Between Tell el-Dab'a (Avaris) and the Levant: A Neutron Activation Study of the Canaanite Jar," in Oren, ed. (1997), pp. 141–157.

20. Van Seters, (1966), pp. 27–37; Peter Parr, "The Origin of the Rampart Fortifications of Middle Bronze Age Palestine and Syria," *Zeitschrift des Deutschen Palästina-Vereins*, vol. 84 (1968), pp. 18–45; Amihai Mazar, *Archaeology of the Land of the Bible, 10,000–586 B.C.E.* (New York: Doubleday, 1990), pp. 180–181, 198–208.

21. The exact location of Sharuhen is unknown. Some scholars have identified it with Tell el- Far'ah (S), while others place it at Tell el-'Ajjul or Tell Abu Hurere (Tel Haror). See Aharon Kempinski, "Tell el-'Ajjul—Beth-Aglayim or Sharuhen?," *Israel Exploration Journal*, vol. 24 (1974), pp. 145–152; Anson F. Rainey, "Sharhan/Sharuhen—The Problem of Identification, *Eretz Israel*, vol. 24 (1993), pp. 178–187; and Rüdiger Liwak, "Sharuhen," in David Noel Freedman, editor-in-chief, *The Anchor Bible Dictionary* (New York: Doubleday, 1992), vol. 5, p. 1164.

22. Eliezer D. Oren, "The 'Kingdom of Sharuhen' and the Hyksos Kingdom," in Oren, ed. (1997), pp. 253–283.

23. Manfred Bietak, "Avaris, Capital of the Hyksos Kingdom: New Results of Excavations," in Oren, ed. (1997), p. 113.

24. The translation is by Redford in Oren, ed. (1997), pp. 13–15.

25. Oren in Oren, ed. (1997), p. 256.

26. Aharon Kempinski and W.-D. Niemeier, "Kabri 1989–1990," "Notes and News," *Israel Exploration Journal*, vol. 41 (1991), pp. 188–194; B. Niemeier and W.-D. Niemeier, "The Fragments of Minoan Wall Painting from Loc. 723" in A. Kempinski and W.-D. Niemeier, eds., *Excavations at Kabri*6: Preliminary Report of the 1991 Season* (Tel Aviv: Tel Aviv University, 1992).

27. Manfred Bietak, "The Center of Hyksos Rule: Avaris (Tell el-Dab'a)" in Oren, ed. (1997), pp. 117–124.

28. Leonard Woolley, *Alalakh: An Account of the Excavations at Tell Atchana in the Hatay, 1937–1949* (London: Oxford University Press, 1955), pp. 128–129, 233–234.

29. Bietak, "The Center of Hyksos Rule: Avaris (Tell el-Dab'a)" in Oren, ed. (1997), p. 117.

30. These methods included study of frost damage to tree rings caused by volcanic ash in the atmosphere, discovery of high acid levels (due to major volcanic eruptions) in Greenland ice cores, and radiocarbon dating of grain from the Minoan settlement on Thera. See M. G. L. Bailie and M. A. R. Munro, "Irish Tree Rings, Santorini and Volcanic Dust Veils, *Nature*, no. 332 (1988), pp. 344–346; C. U. Hammer, H. B. Clausen, W. L. Friedrich and H. Tauber, "The Minoan Eruption of Santorini in Greece Dated to 1645 B.C.?," *Nature*, no. 328 (1987), pp. 517–519; and S. W. Manning, "The Eruption of Thera: Date and Implications," *Thera and the Aegean World III* (London: Thera and the Aegean World, 1990) vol. 3, pp. 29–40.

31. Support for the early date for the eruption of Thera and the end of LM I A can be found in H. N. Michael and P. P. Betancourt, "The Thera Eruption II: Further Arguments for an Early Date," *Archaeometry*, vol. 30 (1988), pp. 169–175; P. I. Kuniholm, et al., "Anatolian Tree-rings and the Absolute Chronology of the East Mediterranean 2220–718 BC," *Nature*, no. 381 (1996), pp. 780–783, especially p. 782; P. P. Betancourt, "Relations between the Aegean and the Hyksos at the End of the Middle Bronze Age" in Oren, ed. (1997), pp. 429–432; and especially, Sturt W. Manning, *A Test of Time: The Volcano of Thera and the Chronology and History of the Aegean and East Mediterranean in the Mid Second Millennium BC* (Oxford: Oxbow Books, 1999).

32. In addition to the work by Manfred Bietak cited in Note 29, see the following articles by P. M. Warren for support for the traditional date for the end of LM I A: "Absolute Dating of the Aegean Late Bronze Age," *Archaeometry*, vol. 29 (1987), pp. 205–211; "The Minoan Civilisation of Crete and the Volcano of Thera," *Journal of the Ancient Chronology Forum*, vol. 4 (1990–1991), pp. 29–39 and "Aspects of Minoan Chronology" in P.P. Betancourt, V. Karageorghis, R. Laffineur and W.-D. Niemeier, eds., *Meletemata: Studies in Aegean Archaeology Presented to Malcolm H. Wiener as He Enters His 65th Year*. Aegaeum 20. (Université de Liège: Service d'Histoire de l'art et archéologie de la Grèce antique, and Austin: Program in Aegean Scripts and Prehistory, The University of Texas at Austin, 1999), vol. III, pp. 893–903.

6

The Era of Egyptian Greatness

THE BEGINNING OF THE EGYPTIAN NEW KINGDOM (c. 1550–1479 B.C.E.)

The Early Eighteenth Dynasty

Ahmose, who reigned c. 1550 to 1525 B.C.E., was only a child when he became king, so his mother Ahhotep served as regent during the early years of his reign. She not only exercised power during his minority, but she remained an important figure even after Ahmose assumed control. A stele that Ahmose erected at Karnak credits her with military exploits—looking after the soldiers, bringing back fugitives, pacifying Upper Egypt, and expelling rebels. However, we don't know whether this activity occurred while she was regent or later while Ahmose was engaged in military activity elsewhere.

When he came of age, Ahmose resumed his father's and brother's war against the Hyksos. He laid siege to Avaris, but the assault seems to have been interrupted by the need to suppress a revolt in the previously captured territory. However, Ahmose renewed his attack on the Hyksos stronghold, which finally fell around his eleventh regnal year. With the Hyksos rulers in the Delta defeated, Ahmose began reasserting Egyptian power in Palestine and Nubia. He attacked

the fortress of Sharuhen in southern Palestine and captured it after a three-year siege. He then conducted a campaign in Nubia and at some later time seems to have raided the coastal areas of Phoenicia and northern Palestine. By the time he died, Ahmose had reunified Egypt internally and restored her power and prestige abroad. The ancient Egyptians themselves thought these accomplishments so important that they made Ahmose the first king of a new dynasty, the Eighteenth, even though his father and brother were counted as members of the Seventeenth Dynasty. Present-day historians also see Ahmose's reign as the beginning of a new era, the period we call The New Kingdom.

Ahmose's Chief Wife was his sister, Ahmose Nefertari, and she seems to have been no less powerful than their mother, Ahhotep. Ahmose named her "God's Wife of Amun," a title and office in the cult of Amun that usually had been held by commoners. Now the king would have even more influence over a cult that was steadily growing in religious authority, and through its oracle could also wield some political power. The office of God's Wife would continue to be a source of power and authority for a female from the royal family through the time of Hatshepsut. In fact, Ahmose Nefertari's power in religious affairs became so great that she and her son

Amenhotep I were later jointly worshiped as patron deities by the Theban necropolis workers.

Amenhotep I, the oldest surviving son of Ahmose and Ahmose Nefertari, succeeded his father reigning c. 1525 to 1504 B.C.E. (see Table 6.1). Like his father and grandfather before him, Amenhotep I married one of his sisters, Meritamun, and made her his Chief Wife and God's Wife of Amun. However, Meritamun does not seem to have been as prominent or as powerful as her mother or grandmother had been. This may have been due to the fact that Ahmose Nefertari remained alive throughout her son's reign. Aside from a campaign in Nubia and possibly one in Libya, Amenhotep I's reign seems to have been peaceful. He continued his father's work of political consolidation and temple building, especially at the Temple of Amun at Karnak in Thebes.

The early Eighteenth Dynasty kings considered Amun their patron and protector, and they repaid him with lavish building projects and massive gifts of

TABLE 6.1
Chronology of the Eighteenth Dynasty

(All dates are B.C.E. and approximately correct, within about ±25 years. Since some scholars use the Greek forms of various royal names, these are given in parentheses.)

The New Kingdom	1550–1070
The Eighteenth Dynasty	**1550–1293**
Ahmose	1550–1525
Amenhotep (Amenophis) I	1525–1504
Thutmose (Tuthmosis) I	1504–1491
Thutmose (Tuthmosis) II	1491–1479
Hatshepsut	1479–1458
Thutmose (Tuthmosis) III	1479–1425
Amenhotep (Amenophis) II	1428–1397
Thutmose (Tuthmosis) IV	1397–1388
Amenhotep (Amenophis) III	1388–1350
Amenhotep IV/Akhenaton	1350–1334
Smenkhkare	1336–1334
Tutankhamun	1334–1325
Ay	1325–1321
Horemheb	1321–1293

land and wealth. Amenhotep I and his successors not only built temples to Amun, they emphasized Amun's cult to the extent of elevating him to supremacy within the Egyptian pantheon. Egypt's Twelfth Dynasty had begun the rise of this once relatively obscure Theban god. However, early in the Eighteenth Dynasty, he was assimilated with Re, the earlier divine patron of the monarchy, and became known as Amun-Re, King of the Gods.

During the early New Kingdom era, Memphis remained the site of the principal royal residence and, thus, Egypt's political capital. However, Thebes became the nation's religious capital and the royal family periodically resided there in palaces near Karnak. The West Bank at Thebes also became the royal burial place. Following the lead of his Seventeenth Dynasty predecessors, Ahmose chose to be buried there. His tomb has not yet been identified, but it was located at Thebes, for his mummy was part of a cache of royal mummies found at Deir el-Bahri (see Map 6.1) in the late nineteenth century. Amenhotep I's mummy was also found in the cache, and a recently discovered tomb at Dra Abu el-Naga probably belonged to him. He was the first king to build his mortuary temple in a different location from his tomb. Amenhotep I's successors followed his example, trying to make it more difficult for tomb robbers to find and despoil the royal burials. New Kingdom pharaohs had their tombs cut into the hills across the river from Thebes, first at Dra Abu el-Naga, then in the Valley of the Kings. Their mortuary temples were constructed at the edge of Thebes' western flood plain (see Map 6.1).

Amenhotep I seems to have been childless, and he was succeeded by Thutmose I, a general whose background is not known. It was once thought that Thutmose I, who reigned c. 1504 to1491 B.C.E., gained his right to the throne by marrying one of Amenhotep I's daughters. However, Thutmose I's Chief Wife, Ahmose, never used the title "King's Daughter," so she probably wasn't a child of Amenhotep I. Perhaps Thutmose I was from a junior branch of the royal family, possibly a grandson of Pharaoh Ahmose and a nephew of Amenhotep I. Whatever his claim to the throne, this warrior pharaoh proved to be an extremely

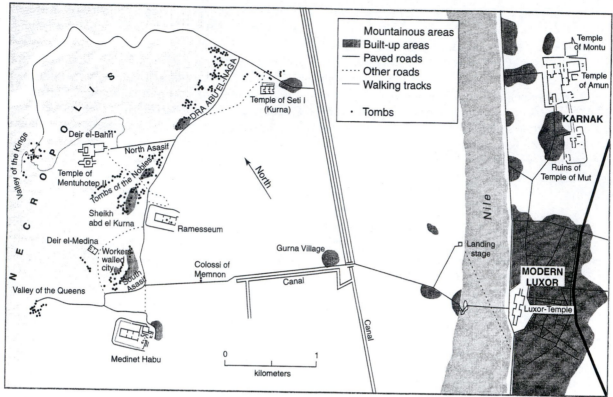

MAP 6.1   Remains of Ancient Thebes

Source: Adapted from Jill Kamil, *Luxor: A Guide to Ancient Thebes*, 2nd ed. (New York: Longman, 1976), inside cover and facing page.

able ruler. He conducted a series of military campaigns in Nubia and Syria-Palestine, extending the frontier in both areas. In Asia, he marched all the way to the Euphrates in Syria. Probably he was trying to forestall the growing kingdom of Mitanni from moving into western Syria. In addition to his successful military activities, Thutmose I also extensively remodeled and enlarged the Temple of Amun at Karnak.

Thutmose I's two oldest sons predeceased him, so Thutmose II, a younger son by a secondary wife, became king. He married his half-sister Hatshepsut, the oldest daughter of Thutmose I and his Chief Wife Ahmose, and made her his Chief Wife and God's Wife of Amun. Like his father, Thutmose II campaigned in Nubia and Syria. However, he does not seem to have accomplished as much as Thutmose I even though his approximately 12-year reign (c. 1491

to 1479 B.C.E.) was probably only a year shorter than that of his father. Thutmose II and Hatshepsut seem to have had only one child, a daughter named Neferure. So, Thutmose II's son by a minor wife succeeded him as Thutmose III.

The "Royal Heiress" Theory

There was a series of very powerful women during the late Seventeenth and early Eighteenth dynasties, including Tetisheri, Ahhotep, Ahmose Nefertari, and Hatshepsut. In addition, most of the women designated "King's Chief Wife" during this era also had the title "God's Wife of Amun" and were sisters of their respective husbands. Some scholars suggest that this matriarchal tendency may have been due to some Nubian ancestry in the Seventeenth-Eighteenth Dynasty line.

It also led many Egyptologists to adopt what is called the "royal heiress theory." This hypothesis claims that Egyptian society was matrilineal—that is, descent was traced through an individual's mother rather than father. In the royal family, the theory goes, the right to the throne was transmitted through a line of "royal heiresses." These women could not actually rule, but the men they married would. Thus, even a son of the king and his Chief Wife would have to marry his heiress sister in order to become pharaoh. This idea made the New Kingdom's royal incestuous marriages more acceptable both to scholars and the general public.

Despite the popularity of this theory over the past century, it needs to be abandoned. As Gay Robins has shown, the hypothesized line of royal heiresses did not exist.[1] While Eighteenth Dynasty kings often married their sisters (as did the gods in Egyptian myths), they did not *always* do so. Furthermore, Ahmose (Chief Wife of Thutmose I), Satioh, and Meritre Hatshepsut (successive Chief Wives of Thutmose III), Tiy (Chief Wife of Amenhotep III), and Nefertiti (Chief Wife of Akhenaton) were not daughters of the previous rulers. The evidence seems to indicate that the succession normally went to the oldest son of the king and his Chief Wife. If the king's Chief Wife did not have a son, then the throne passed to the king's oldest son by any of his other wives. Only if there were no sons might the throne pass to the husband of the oldest daughter of the king and his Chief Wife (as happened in the cases of Ay and Horemheb). However, as the successions of Thutmose I and Ramesses I show, even this last scenario did not always prevail.

The title "God's Wife of Amun" once was thought to belong to the royal heiress as well. It supposedly referred to the myth that Amun himself impregnated the heiress to produce the next pharaoh. However, for the royal heiress theory to be consistent, the next *heiress*, not the next king, should have been the product of this union. Moreover, the mother of Hatshepsut and the mother of Amenhotep III, two queens who, their children claimed, were impregnated by Amun, did not have the title of God's Wife. Also, before the time of Ahmose, the God's Wives were usually not from the royal family at all. Finally, the position of God's Wife was de-emphasized after the death

of Hatshepsut, and after the reign of Thutmose IV, it disappeared for most of the rest of the Eighteenth Dynasty. It is now clear that this priestly cult position had nothing to do with succession to the throne.[2]

HATSHEPSUT AND THUTMOSE III (c. 1479–1425 B.C.E.)

Hatshepsut's Seizure of Power

Thutmose III's aunt and stepmother, Queen Hatshepsut, was named regent for the child-king when his father died (c. 1479 B.C.E.). The monuments show that for at least two years, she kept her old titles of God's Wife and King's Chief Wife and was depicted dutifully standing behind the new pharaoh. However, soon afterward, she is depicted as king, co-regent with her nephew, with all the typical pharaonic titles except "Mighty Bull." On at least four earlier occasions, women probably had ruled Egypt: Meritneith, Khentkawes, and Nitiqret during the Old Kingdom, and Sobekneferu at the end of the Twelfth Dynasty. However, only two of them, Nitiqret and Sobekneferu, were included in the king lists. Even so, it is not certain that they considered themselves pharaohs and were regarded as such rather than regents. With Hatshepsut, though, there is no question. She became *king*! She was usually depicted as a male in the traditional garb and poses of past pharaohs (see Figure 6.1). On most of her statues, she wore the royal beard, and in many inscriptions, scribes applied masculine titles and pronouns to her.

Despite these appearances to the contrary, Hatshepsut was not trying to deny that she was a woman. The traditional symbolic representations of pharaoh were male. Also, the titles and terms used for rulers were all masculine. Nonetheless, the scribes were aware that this "king" was female. So, sometimes they used feminine titles for her such as "Daughter of Re" (rather than "Son of Re") or "the female Horus" as well as referring to her with feminine pronouns. Furthermore, a few statues do show her as a female.

It is not clear what precipitated Hatshepsut's assumption of power. Some have seen it as the result of a power struggle between two factions within the

FIGURE 6.1 Amun Confirming Hatshepsut as King

This is from the top of a fallen granite obelisk at Karnak. Note that Hatshepsut is depicted as a male.
Source: Egyptian Museum, Cairo.
Photo: Courtesy of the author.

Egyptian bureaucracy. According to this view, Thutmose III and his supporters had to suffer in silence until the end of Hatshepsut's reign. Then Thutmose took his revenge, destroying Hatshepsut's statues, hacking her name out of inscriptions and eliminating all references to her reign.[3] However, in recent years, evidence has surfaced that shows that Thutmose III's attack on Hatshepsut's monuments and memory didn't take place until very late in his reign, year 42 or later. There is no evidence of conflict between the two while Hatshepsut was still alive, nor did he seem to display much resentment in the years immediately following her death. Why wait at least 20 years to take his revenge? Thus, one of the main supports for the factional conflict hypothesis has been undermined. Joyce Tyldesley now argues that possibly "a sudden threat to the security of the immediate royal family, such as an insurrection in the royal harem, might well have prompted Hatchepsut [sic] to take drastic action to safeguard her stepson's position."[4] Some support for this view can be found in the fact that Hatshepsut did not eliminate Thutmose III

after she became pharaoh. An "accident" or "fatal illness" would probably have been relatively easy to arrange. But she was content simply to serve as senior co-regent, even allowing Thutmose III to receive military training with the army. She doesn't seem to have feared that he might try to turn the officer corps against her and lead a military rebellion.[5]

Soon after claiming the throne, Hatshepsut began building her mortuary temple at Deir el-Bahri in western Thebes. Construction of this beautiful temple was supervised by an official named Senenmut. A man of humble origins, Senenmut became one of Hatshepsut's favorite administrators and the steward and tutor of her daughter, Neferure. Some modern scholars have suspected, though without evidence, that he was also Hatshepsut's lover. Hatshepsut's temple, called *Djeser-Djeseru* ("Holy of Holies" or "The Most Sacred Place"), was located directly opposite the temple of Amun at Karnak on the other side of the Nile. It was also right next to, and partially inspired by, the Middle Kingdom mortuary temple of Mentuhotep II. Its three colonnaded terraces harmonize perfectly with the hills behind it, leading many people to consider it the most beautiful structure in Egypt (see Figure 6.2). Its primary purpose was to house a mortuary chapel for Hatshepsut. However, she also added a smaller mortuary chapel for her father Thutmose I, and chapels for Hathor, Anubis, Re-Horakhty and, most importantly, Amun. It became the location for the meeting of the cult statues of Amun and Hathor during one of the principal Egyptian religious festivals, "The Beautiful Feast of the Valley."

To justify her rule, Hatshepsut had a political/mythical account of her birth carved on the walls of the northern half of the middle terrace of her mortuary temple. According to this story, Amun had disguised himself as Hatshepsut's father Thutmose I and impregnated her mother Ahmose. Thus, Hatshepsut was the direct offspring of Amun and was destined to be pharaoh even before her birth. Furthermore, she states that her father Thutmose I made her his co-regent and publicly designated her as his successor. Her claim, then, was that she had been pharaoh and co-regent throughout the reigns of her brother/husband Thutmose II and of her stepson Thutmose III. Obviously, this is fiction, as Hatshepsut's lesser titles

in inscriptions from the reign of Thutmose II and the beginning of the reign of Thutmose III show. Nonetheless, the ancient Egyptian belief in the magical potency of images and inscriptions suggests that just by placing this account within her temple, Hatshepsut was magically making it true.

Egyptian pharaohs had always claimed to be incarnations of the god Horus. Each king had also adopted the title "Son of Re," indicating his relationship to the sun god. A Middle Kingdom story even claims that the first three kings of the Fifth Dynasty were triplet sons of Re through his union with their earthly mother. However, Hatshepsut was the first living ruler to display an account of her own conception and birth or claim to be the direct physical offspring of one of the major gods (in this case, Amun). Her birth narrative represents a more literalistic understanding of the ancient doctrine of the divine ruler in Egypt. Her concept would be followed later by pharaohs Amenhotep III, Akhenaton, and Ramesses II.

Hatshepsut also seems to have reshaped, if not created, the *Opet* Festival in Thebes. This festival featured a procession of the cult statues of Amun, Mut, and their son Khons from their temples at Karnak to a shrine at Luxor, known as the "Southern *Opet*"

FIGURE 6.2 The Mortuary Temple of Hatshepsut at Deir el-Bahri, Thebes.

The ruins of Mentuhotep's temple can be seen next to Hatshepsut's temple.

Source: Hirmer Fotoarchiv, Munich.

("domicile" or "harem") of Amun. The earliest depictions of this festival come from Hatshepsut's time. A major part of the celebration centered on rituals at the Luxor shrine renewing the divine *ka* of the ruler and reemphasizing the king as the human embodiment of Amun-Re.

Hatshepsut ruled Egypt for 21 years (c. 1479–1458) while her younger co-regent acquired and sharpened his military skills. She did conduct at least one major military campaign against Nubia and probably another in southern Palestine. However, these early military actions seem to have been sufficient to maintain Egypt's interests in both areas. Thus, Hatshepsut was able to concentrate her attention on maintaining prosperity within Egypt and on the construction of monuments. One of the most important events of her reign was the success of a trade expedition to Punt. This mysterious land was probably located near the southern end of the Red Sea along the East African coast between southern Sudan and northern Somalia. Hatshepsut's fleet returned with a cargo of potted myrrh trees, spices, ivory, gold, electrum, ebony, exotic animal skins, apes, dogs, and some natives of Punt. The spice trees were planted on the middle terrace of Hatshepsut's mortuary temple, and the story of the expedition was depicted on the walls of the southern half of that terrace.

As king, Hatshepsut could not perform her former duties as God's Wife of Amun. So, she bestowed the position of God's Wife on her daughter, Neferure. Her daughter also appears in scenes where the king's Great Wife would have been depicted in earlier times. It is possible that Hatshepsut was grooming Neferure to follow in her footsteps and become Thutmose III's co-regent. However, Neferure died before her mother did, ending any possible plans for a line of female pharaohs.

The Sole Rule of Thutmose III

Hatshepsut died around 1458 B.C.E., probably of natural causes. Thutmose III, now about 30 years old, was finally pharaoh in his own right. About this time, a crisis developed in Syria-Palestine. The Mitanni Kingdom had begun expanding its power into western Syria, and its growing strength led the rulers of several Syrian and Palestinian cities to abandon their allegiance to Egypt.

The Hittite empire had also been expanding southward along the Syrian coast. Thutmose III reacted swiftly to these events, leading an army into Canaan in the second year of his independent rule. At Megiddo, a fortress in northern Palestine guarding the main road into Syria, a coalition of Canaanite rulers awaited him. Thutmose III led his troops through a narrow pass over the hills rather than along the wider roads around them, catching his opponents by surprise. The Canaanite forces were decisively defeated, though it took a seven-month siege before Megiddo itself fell.

During the next 30 years Thutmose conducted 16 more campaigns in Palestine and Syria, culminating with the capture of Qadesh. The strength of the Kingdom of Mitanni seems to have been perceived as the major threat to Egypt. So, the warrior pharaoh led raids across the Euphrates River into Mitanni's territory, blunting Mitanni's westward expansion. Southwestern Syria and Palestine were placed firmly under Egyptian control with garrisons stationed at key cities. To keep Canaanite subject kings loyal, Thutmose III took their sons as hostages to Egypt. There they were educated and immersed into Egyptian culture so that they became reliable vassals when they returned home to rule their city-states.

Thutmose III also conducted campaigns in Nubia, pushing Egyptian control southward to Napata and the fourth cataract. His brilliant military tactics and his ability to organize subject territories into a stable Egyptian Empire (see Map 6.2) caused the great American Egyptologist James Breasted to consider him the "Napoleon" of ancient Egypt. Clearly, such a comparison was well deserved.

Late in his reign, Thutmose began systematically destroying all traces of the reign of Hatshepsut. Her name was chiseled off monuments, her statues were destroyed, and references to her reign were deleted from documents and king lists. Since he waited so long to begin this attack, it is likely that something other than spite and personal hatred were involved. As he aged and began looking toward the reign of his son, Thutmose may have considered the era of Hatshepsut's dominance an affront against *ma'at*. Moreover, since his son was still a child who might need a female regent if Thutmose died in the near future, Hatshepsut's assumption of kingship might become a dangerous precedent. The elimination of all trace of the female king's reign probably seemed the best way to assure Amenhotep II and future male rulers a smooth succession.[6] However, Thutmose III lived to see his son reach adulthood, and late in his reign, he made Amenhotep II his co-regent (c. 1428 B.C.E.). A little over two years later, the old king died. Amenhotep II became sole pharaoh with no signs of opposition. It is not known if any of the precautions Thutmose III had previously taken played a part in this peaceful succession.

THE EGYPTIAN EMPIRE AT ITS HEIGHT (c. 1425–1350 B.C.E.)

The Reigns of Amenhotep II and Thutmose IV

Amenhotep II (c. 1428 to 1397 B.C.E.) followed in the footsteps of his illustrious father. He was a warrior whose strength and skill with a bow became legendary. Reliefs show him piercing thick copper targets with his

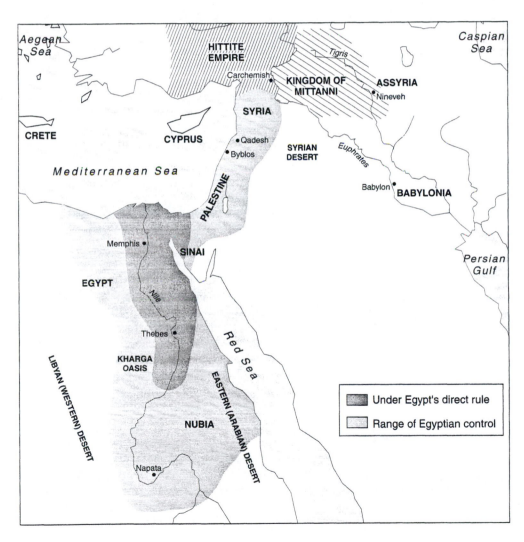

MAP 6.2 The Egyptian Empire c. 1425 B.C.E.

Source: Adapted from William Dunstan, *The Ancient Near East* (New York: Harcourt Brace and Co., 1998), p. 137.

arrows while charging in his chariot. Mitannian and Hittite subversion were still threats, so early in his reign, Amenhotep II undertook a military campaign across the Orontes River in Syria. He brought back the bodies of seven Syrian rulers he had slain. A stele he erected at Amada in Nubia claims that "six of these enemies were hanged on the face of the enclosure wall of Thebes, the hands likewise, and the other enemy was shipped up to Nubia and hanged upon the enclosure wall of Napata in order to cause to be seen the victorious might of His Majesty for ever and ever."[7] Amenhotep II also conducted several military actions against wavering vassals in Palestine. After one of these campaigns, he returned to Egypt with more than 2,200 prisoners, 820 horses, 730 chariots and their equipment, as well as many precious objects of silver and gold.

Among the various groups of people mentioned in the lists of captives from Amenhotep II's campaigns in Syria and Palestine are *maryannu* and Hurrians. *Maryannu* originally was an Indo-European term applied to the warrior aristocracy who fought in chariots, and by Amenhotep II's time, this term was also being applied to the highest rank of Canaanite warriors. The presence of probably some Indo-Europeans as well as many Hurrians in coastal Syria and Palestine demonstrates how widespread the movements of these groups had been c. 1600 to 1550 B.C.E. Once the Kingdom of Mitanni began growing, still more Indo-European and Hurrian speakers probably entered the Levant. Egypt viewed these population movements and continuing attempts by Mitanni to expand westward as dangerous threats to Egyptian interests. Almost certainly, Mitannian power and aggrandizement provided the main impetus for the Asiatic campaigns of Thutmose I, Thutmose III, and Amenhotep II.

Amenhotep II was succeeded by Thutmose IV, who probably had not always been the crown prince. This conclusion is suggested (but not proved) by a propagandistic stele he erected between the paws of the Great Sphinx at Giza. Many scholars have seen this stele as an attempt to explain an unlikely accession or to justify a usurpation of the throne. The text claims that once, while on a hunting trip, Thutmose fell asleep in the Sphinx's shadow. In a dream, the sun god embodied in the Sphinx told the young prince that he would become pharaoh if he cleared away the sand covering the Sphinx's body. Thutmose complied, and the god kept his promise. Thus, a likely, though not necessary, conclusion is that Thutmose IV was a younger son of Amenhotep II who succeeded to the throne only after the premature death of one or more older brothers.

The reign of Thutmose IV (c. 1397 to 1388 B.C.E.) was essentially a peaceful one. Mitanni, stung by the earlier Egyptian attacks and now facing the growing power of the Hittites and Assyria, decided to make peace with Egypt. After a series of negotiations, the two former enemies agreed to become allies. The new relationship was sealed by the marriage of a daughter of Artatama, King of Mitanni, to Thutmose IV. The Egyptian-Mitannian alliance protected both powers against the threat of Hittite aggression and brought almost 50 years of peace to the Egyptian Empire in the Levant.

Amenhotep III, "The Magnificent"

Egypt now entered into one of the most tranquil and prosperous periods in its history. Amenhotep III (reigned c. 1388 to 1350 B.C.E.), son of Thutmose IV and his Chief Wife, Mutemwiya, was probably only about 10 to 12 years old when he became pharaoh. Despite his youth, in his first or second year of rule, Amenhotep III married Tiy, an even younger girl of nonroyal ancestry. Though she was a commoner, her father, Yuya, was an important noble who held a high military position. Tiy eventually bore her husband at least four daughters and two sons, including the future pharaoh, Amenhotep IV. Two of her daughters, Sitamun and Isis, married their father during the last decade of his reign and, like their mother, each received the title "Chief Royal Wife." However, Tiy not only became Amenhotep III's Chief Wife, she attained more preeminence and authority than any preceding queen. Major inscriptions almost always linked her name with that of her husband, and she was portrayed as a sphinx trampling enemies, an image hitherto reserved for pharaohs.

There seem to have been only two insignificant campaigns in Nubia during Amenhotep III's reign of slightly more than 38 years. He was able to live a life of luxury and ease, enjoying the fruits of the empire his predecessors had created. He continued the alliance with Mitanni, sealed by his marriage to Gilukhepa, daughter of King Shuttarna II. Later, shortly before his death, Amenhotep III also married Tadukhepa, daughter of Tushratta, the new Mitannian ruler. Likewise, he maintained good relations with Babylon, adding a sister and a daughter of the Babylonian king Kadashman-Enlil to his harem.

With Egyptian strength and diplomacy preserving the peace in Asia and Nubia, Amenhotep III turned his attention to building monuments, surpassing even the volume of construction undertaken by Hatshepsut and Thutmose III. He erected more statues of himself throughout Egypt than any other pharaoh. Many of them were usurped and modified by later rulers, especially Ramesses II. Amenhotep III built the Serapeum at Saqqara for the Apis bulls sacred to Ptah, and temples for other gods at Heliopolis, Athribis, Bubastis, El-Kab, Abydos, Hermopolis, and other sites. He also constructed many sanctuaries in Nubia. His most important building projects, however, were at Thebes. There, at Malqata on the west bank, Amenhotep III built a large palace for

himself named "Mansion of Nebma'atre-is-the-Dazzling-Aton (the Solar Orb)." (Nebma'atre, translated as "Re is Lord of Truth," was the *praenomen*, throne name, of Amenhotep III.) Though built largely of mud-brick, like all Egyptian dwellings, it was elaborately decorated with beautiful paintings on its walls and plastered floors. It became his permanent residence during the last decade of his reign. Moored at a harbor in front of this palace was the royal barge named *The Dazzling Aton* or *Aton Gleams* on which the king and queen sailed during religious and state festivals. Nearby, Amenhotep III also constructed his luxurious mortuary temple, parts of which were covered with gold, silver and electrum (an alloy made of gold and silver). In keeping with Amenhotep III's increasing emphasis on solar worship, the sanctuary in this mortuary establishment was a large open solar court like the Fifth Dynasty solar temples. On either side of the temple's main entrance pylon stood two 64-foot-high seated statues of the king. Unfortunately, Merneptah later used Amenhotep III's mortuary temple as a quarry to obtain stone for his own constructions. Today, the huge statues, called the Colossi of Memnon (see Figure 6.3), are almost the only elements that remain.

FIGURE 6.3 The Colossi of Memnon (Amenhotep III) at Thebes

Source: Courtesy of the author.

On the east bank at Thebes, Amenhotep III raised a new monumental gateway (the Third Pylon) for the Temple of Amun at Karnak. He also erected new temples nearby for Mut, Amun's consort, and Montu, a war god. At the southern end of Thebes (now called Luxor), he replaced Hatshepsut's small shrine for Amun with a magnificent new temple. His beautiful papyriform-columned open court (see Figure 6.4) and the seven pairs of huge columns that originally formed the temple's entrance colonnade are still the most impressive parts of this monument. He also connected the Luxor temple with that of Karnak by an avenue of sphinxes so that Amun, Mut, and Khons could travel majestically between their two homes, especially during the *Opet* Festival, the most important yearly religious festival at Thebes.

The Luxor temple was dedicated both to Amun (in the form of the fertility god Min) and to the divine royal *ka*. This made it the perfect spot for Amenhotep III to emphasize his own divinity. In a room within the sanctuary, he depicted his conception as the result of a sexual liaison between Amun and Queen Mutemwiya, a story copied from Hatshepsut's temple at Deir el-Bahri. Amenhotep III also declared his divinity in other ways. Statues of the gods that he

erected had Amenhotep's own features. The temple he built at Soleb in Nubia was dedicated to the worship of Amun and to a deified form of himself as Lord of Nubia. Furthermore, he claimed divinity for Queen Tiy as well. In Egypt, artists often made her representation the same size as that of her divine husband, and portrayed her as the personification of the goddess Ma'at. And at a temple at Sedeinga in Nubia, Tiy was worshiped as a form of the goddess Hathor, the wife of Horus and a female principle of creation.

Amenhotep III increasingly emphasized the sun god during his reign, especially under the name of Aton, whose name was included in the names of his palace and royal barge. He also named a division of the army "Nebma'atre is the Dazzling Aton" and his youngest daughter was named Beketaton ("Handmaiden of the Aton"). The word *aton* originally referred to the physical shining ball that we see in the sky. It is usually translated "sun disk," but "solar orb" would be better, for bas-relief sculptures make it clear that the Egyptians thought of the sun as a sphere. However, during the Middle and New kingdoms, *aton* came to be used also as another name for Re, the sun as a deity. By the time of Amenhotep III, there was a temple to Aton in Heliopolis, for inscriptions from his

FIGURE 6.4
Amenhotep III's Papyriform-Columned Court at the Luxor Temple, Thebes

Source: Courtesy of the author.

reign mention a "Steward in the Temple of Aton" and a "Scribe of the Treasury of the Temple of Aton."

Amenhotep III celebrated a *heb-sed* (Jubilee Festival) in his thirtieth year and then two others in years 34 and 37. At the first of these rites designed to restore the vitality of the king, Amenhotep III seems to have elevated himself to full godhood. He had already been worshiped as a god in Nubia, but now he is depicted worshiping himself as a god in Egypt as well. During the festival he proclaimed himself the earthly embodiment of the Aton, and choirs sang hymns to Tiy as the incarnation of Hathor. For the rest of Amenhotep III's reign, his courtiers greeted him every morning as the image and personification of the sun god. The stage was set for his son to stretch the doctrine of the divine king to its farthest limits.

The New Egyptian Army

The New Kingdom Egyptian military forces which defeated the Hyksos and conquered Nubia and Syria-Palestine were quite different from Egyptian armies of earlier times. New weapons, especially the chariot, brought to Egypt during the Second Intermediate Period were adopted by the Egyptians, changing the structure and tactics of their military. Horse-drawn chariots provided fast mobile platforms from which archers could fire volleys of arrows at their enemies. At the same time, the chariots' speed made it difficult for opposing archers to hit the charioteers. Chariots usually carried two warriors, a driver and an archer, though Hittite chariots are shown carrying three—a driver, shield carrier, and archer (see Figure 6.5). Chariot divisions could outmaneuver infantry forces, getting around them to attack from the flank or the rear. They could cross back and forth across the enemy's front, firing arrows into the massed troops to weaken them before a charge by their own infantry. Or, the chariots themselves could charge through the enemy's infantry ranks, scattering them and making them easy prey for the troops following the chariots. In close-quarter fighting, the chariot warrior might use javelins or a sword instead of his bow. If both sides in a battle had chariot forces, as they generally did, the chariot divisions usually attacked one another. The enemy's chariots had to be neutralized or destroyed before the infantry could be attacked. The skill of the drivers and the accuracy of the archers as well as the numbers of chariots involved became decisive in such encounters. The Egyptians soon proved to be exceptionally skilled in making fast, durable light chariots, and the training and skill of their drivers and archers usually gave them the advantage in battle.

As mentioned in Chapter 5, the powerful composite bow was the weapon of choice for chariot warriors during the Late Bronze Age (c. 1550 to 1150 B.C.E.). However, composite bows were expensive and difficult to make, so few of the soldiers or chariot warriors of small kingdoms or tribal groups possessed them. Only the larger kingdoms could produce them in ample numbers. This fact gave the armies of Egypt, Hatti, Mitanni, and other great powers an important advantage against the forces of smaller states. Other weapons generally used by military forces during this time include long thrusting spears, javelins, curved sickle swords, narrow axes designed to pierce rather than cut, and toward the end of the era, long slashing swords.

As in the Middle Kingdom, New Kingdom Egypt had a standing army. Royal recruiting officers toured the villages, forcing one man in ten into compulsory military service. Some men, of course, volunteered for duty, especially in the chariot corps. The young male members of the nobility used chariots for hunting and racing, and they were expected to follow their king into battle. Some of these nobles became professional soldiers, forming the Egyptian officer corps. Hired groups of Libyans, "Sea Peoples" from the Aegean area, and other mercenaries supplemented the native Egyptian forces. In addition, auxiliary troops from the conquered areas—charioteers and infantry from Syria-Palestine and archers from Nubia—fought alongside the Egyptian divisions.

During the early part of the New Kingdom, the Egyptian army consisted of two infantry divisions, each containing 5,000 men (probably at least half of them mercenaries). Each division had almost 2,000 bowmen, while most of the remaining soldiers were armed with spears, axes, or sickle swords and leather-covered

FIGURE 6.5   The Battle of Qadesh

This image is depicted in Ramesses II's temple at Abu Simbel. It shows Egyptian chariots (left) attacking Hittite chariots (right) during the battle.

Source: Courtesy of the author.

wooden shields. The contingents from the Sea Peoples were usually armed with long slashing swords and round shields. The basic unit of the army was the platoon of 50 men. Five platoons made up a 250-man company, and there were 20 companies in each division. During the reign of Seti I, the number of army divisions was increased to three, and under Ramesses II, to four.

The basic unit of the chariot forces was a squadron of 50 chariots. At the beginning of the New Kingdom, the entire Egyptian chariot division contained only about 100 to 150 chariots. However, by the time of Thutmose III, the Egyptians deployed about 1,000 chariots, and when Ramesses II met the Hittites at the battle of Qadesh, there seem to have been about 3,500 chariots on each side.

Late Bronze Age Canaan (Palestine and Coastal Syria)

Egyptian control over Palestine and coastal Syria, attained largely through the efforts of Thutmose I, Thutmose III, and Amenhotep II, continued until almost 1100 B.C.E. The pharaohs' destructive attacks,

especially those of Thutmose I (c. 1504 to 1490 B.C.E.), seem to have marked the archaeological transition from Canaan's Middle Bronze II C (or Middle Bronze III) era to its Late Bronze Period. Archaeological excavations and surveys show that there were fewer towns and cities in Late Bronze Canaan (c. 1500 to 1150 B.C.E.) than there had been in the Middle Bronze Age, and those settlements that remained were often smaller than before. This suggests that the Canaanite population seriously declined during the early period of Egyptian control. Egyptian military campaigns and the tribute exacted by the pharaohs were probably major reasons for this decline, though other factors such as climatic conditions and plague likely contributed to it as well.

Despite the population decline, this era was characterized by widespread trade and internationalism. Canaanite cities exchanged products with Egypt, naturally, but also with other regions of the eastern Mediterranean, especially Cyprus, Crete, and Greece. Akkadian, the Semitic language of Mesopotamia, became the common language of diplomacy throughout the Near East. The rulers of Egypt, Mitanni, Hatti, Arzawa (a state in western Asia Minor), Alasiya

(Cyprus), and the vassal city-states of Canaan as well as the kings of Babylonia and Assyria, communicated with one another on clay tablets inscribed with Akkadian cuneiform.

In 1887, a peasant woman digging at **El-Amarna**, Egypt for decomposed stone and brick to use as fertilizer found a cache containing more than 370 cuneiform tablets. These documents represented diplomatic correspondence from the last years of Amenhotep III through the beginning of the reign of Tutankhamun. Because of the location where they were found, they are usually called the El-Amarna Tablets or the **Amarna Letters**. They include 42 letters from kings of major states, while the rest are from Egyptian vassals in Canaan. These documents show that the Egyptian empire at its height was maintained by gold in addition to military might. The pharaoh sent expensive gifts to allies such as the kings of Mitanni and Babylon, though they sometimes complained that what they received was not as much as they had been promised. Even Egypt's Asiatic vassals constantly asked pharaoh to send them gold. In most instances, however, it is clear that the "gifts" exchanged between rulers of great powers were in reality trade in disguise.

The vassal rulers of Amurru, Gubal (Byblos), Tyre, Sidon, Jerusalem, Gezer, and some other Canaanite city-states seem to have been in almost constant conflict with one another. They competed for territory, power, and wealth either by defeating (or even murdering) rival princes or by denouncing them as enemies of Egypt. Each petty king accused his neighbors of treason, proclaimed himself Egypt's only loyal vassal, and asked pharaoh to support him against his enemies. Furthermore, the Hittites seem to have tried to use these rivalries to bring some of Egypt's subject cities into the Hittite sphere (see Chapter 7).

It is tempting to see these letters as evidence that Amenhotep III and his successor, Akhenaton, had little interest in the empire and were letting it fall apart. However, such conflict between rival vassals seems to have been the normal state of affairs in Canaan, even during the height of Egyptian power. We must remember that we don't have the messages that must have gone back and forth between the Egyptian commissioners stationed in Canaan and their pharaoh.

These communications between Egyptians would have been written in hieroglyphic signs on papyrus, and none of them has survived. They possibly would give us a very different perspective on these conflicts within Egypt's Asian possessions. Despite all the accusations and conflict between their various vassals, the Egyptians maintained their hegemony over most of the Levant until late in the reign of Akhenaton.

In the Amarna Letters, one of the charges various Canaanite rulers level against their rivals is that they are aiding or becoming *Habiru* (or better, *Hapiru*). These people are almost certainly the same as the *'Apiru* mentioned in various Egyptian texts from the time of Amenhotep II onward. The Egyptian form of the word is probably closer to the actual West Semitic term. Obviously the word *Habiru* (as it was originally transcribed) is very similar to "Hebrew" (*'bri* in Hebrew), and many scholars have argued for a connection between them. Some scholars have even contended that the Amarna Letters were describing the Israelite conquest of Canaan under Joshua.[8] However, study of cuneiform literature has shown that the *Hapiru* were known for too long a time and were active over too wide an area for us to equate them with the biblical Hebrews. It is also clear that *Hapiru* is not an ethnic term—the people so designated come from many different ethnic groups. This point is illustrated in the Amarna Letters by the fact that various groups or individuals, even city-state rulers, might *become Hapiru*. The term seems to have signified people from varying ethnic backgrounds who shared an inferior social status. It was a term of contempt for dissident individuals or groups who separated themselves from their society and, depending upon circumstances, became renegades, mercenaries, bandits, refugees, hired laborers, or settled retainers.[9] Thus, it is now generally recognized that while the biblical Hebrews may have come from the *Hapiru* class, not all (or even most) *Hapiru* were Hebrews. Furthermore, the people and events described in the Amarna Letters are very different from those found in the biblical conquest stories. The proposed identification of the Amarna Letters' *Hapiru* with the conquering Israelites must be abandoned.

An archive of cuneiform texts found at Ugarit on the coast of northern Syria also throws great light on fourteenth- and thirteenth-century B.C.E. Canaan. In addition to valuable historical and linguistic information, the Ugaritic texts provide examples of the epic literature and religious mythology prevalent in this area. The texts concerning El (creator god and head of the pantheon), Asherah (fertility goddess and El's consort), Ba'al (the storm god), Yamm (the chaotic Sea), Mot (Death) and other Canaanite deities find many parallels in the Bible. They indicate how much Canaanite concepts and cult practices influenced those of the early Israelites.

Many of the tablets found at Ugarit were written in Akkadian, some in Sumerian and Hurrian, and a few in Hittite, Egyptian, and an undeciphered script called "Cypro-Minoan." However, most were written in the local language (now called Ugaritic), a dialect of the West Semitic Canaanite tongue. These documents in the Ugaritic language help us understand the grammar, vocabulary, word usage, and additional linguistic details of other West Semitic texts, including the Hebrew Bible. Scribes at Ugarit used the Mesopotamian syllabic cuneiform script for almost all of the texts in the non-Ugaritic languages. However, to write their own Ugaritic language they used an alphabetic cuneiform script in which each sign represented a single consonant. Vowels were not written.

Alphabetic writing was probably developed by Canaanite mercenaries or merchants in Egypt around 2000 B.C.E. Archaeologists have found an early alphabetic inscription from about 1800 B.C.E. in Egypt's western desert between Abydos and Thebes.[10] However, the Proto-Canaanite signs in this inscription seem to be derived from forms of hieroglyphs used only in the early Middle Kingdom (c. 2000 to 1900 B.C.E.), indicating the alphabet's earlier origin. By about 1700 to 1650 B.C.E., similar alphabetic signs were used on a late Middle Kingdom sphinx and in other inscriptions at the Egyptian mines at Serabit el-Khadim in the Sinai.[11] So, in Egypt during the Middle Kingdom, Canaanites familiar with Egyptian hieroglyphic writing seem to have come up with the brilliant idea of simplifying this complex system. The alphabet eliminated ideograms, multiconsonant phonetic signs, and determinatives and kept only signs representing single consonants. The head of

an ox would be used for the consonant at the beginning of the word 'aleph ("ox"). A sketch plan of a house would be used for the consonant at the beginning of the word beth ("house"), and so forth (see Figure 6.6).

Inscriptions in the Proto-Canaanite alphabet became a bit more frequent in the early New Kingdom era. They continued to be used for inscriptions at mines in Sinai and have been found on Late Bronze Age objects in Palestine. These semipictorial signs developed into the letters of the later Phoenician and Hebrew alphabets (see Figure 6.6). Furthermore, those later alphabets continued to have their letters in the same sequence as that used for the Proto-Canaanite signs.

The Ugaritic alphabetic signs also follow the same order as those letters it shares with the Proto-Canaanite alphabet. This shows that these two alphabets were not independently invented. There was once some debate about which version of the alphabet, the Proto-Canaanite or the Ugaritic, came first. However, it is now clear that Proto-Canaanite alphabetic inscriptions precede the earliest attested Ugaritic ones by hundreds of years. Furthermore, the Ugaritic alphabet has three signs not found in the Proto-Canaanite list of signs. The fact that these signs are placed together at the end of the Ugaritic alphabet suggests that they were added to an alphabet whose order was already fixed. Therefore, it is virtually certain that the Proto-Canaanite alphabet was the first one. The Phoenicians later passed a descendent of the Proto-Canaanite alphabet on to the Greeks, and the Greek modification of it lies behind all Western alphabets. Thus, other than the Israelite religion (which also developed in Canaan), the alphabet is the Canaanites' greatest contribution to Western civilization.

Relations with the Aegean Kingdoms

Despite the damage to Cretan palaces and cities caused by the explosion of Thera c. 1627 B.C.E., Minoan civilization had continued to flourish. During the era archaeologists call the Late Minoan I B Period (c. 1620 to 1500 B.C.E.), Minoan trade with the Near East increased. The Egyptians seem to have called Crete (and its people) Keftiu (which is equivalent to

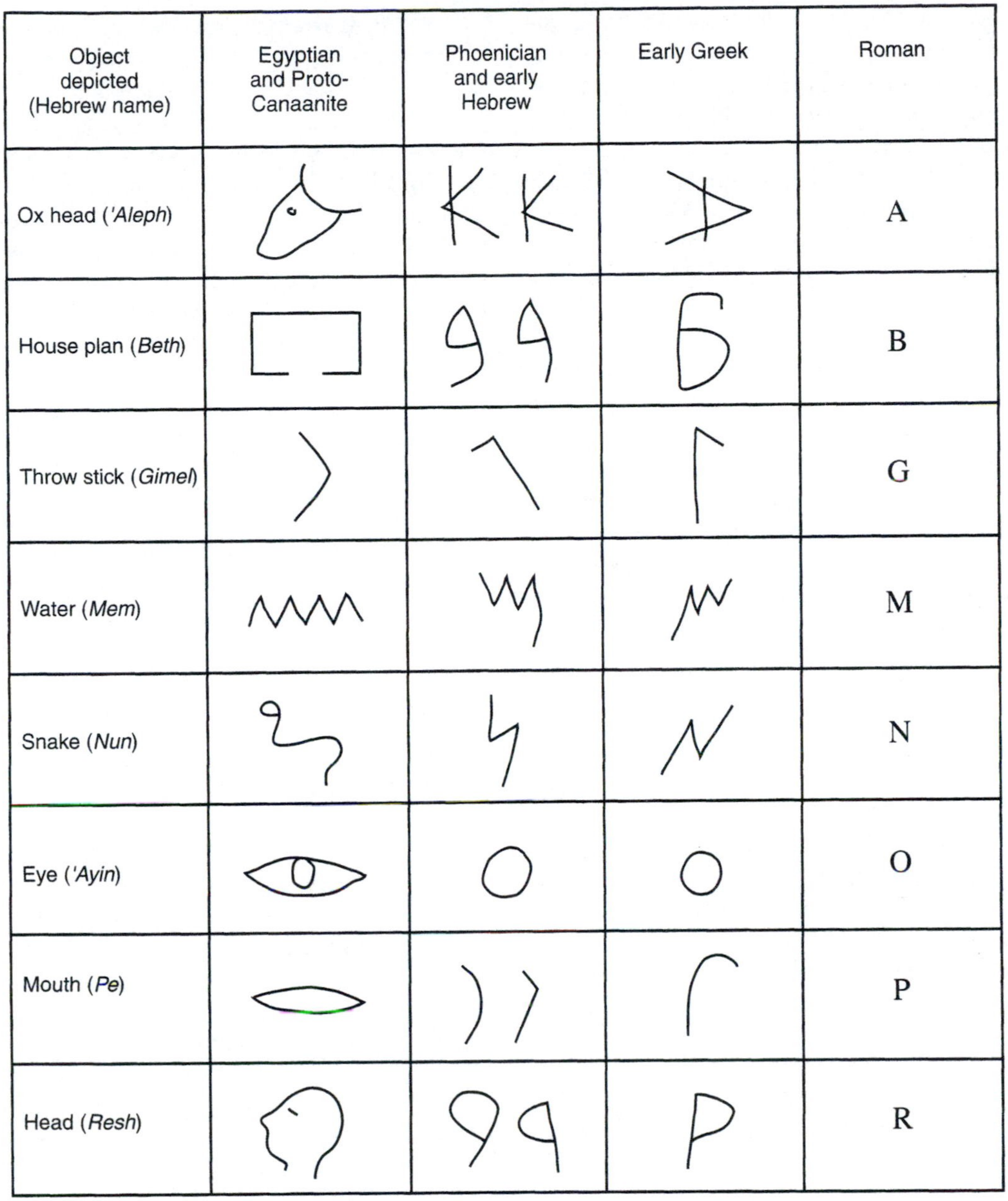

Object depicted (Hebrew name)	Egyptian and Proto-Canaanite	Phoenician and early Hebrew	Early Greek	Roman
Ox head ('Aleph)				A
House plan (Beth)				B
Throw stick (Gimel)				G
Water (Mem)				M
Snake (Nun)				N
Eye ('Ayin)				O
Mouth (Pe)				P
Head (Resh)				R

FIGURE 6.6   The Development of the Alphabet

Source: Courtesy of the author.

the biblical name Kaphtor and Akkadian Kaptara). Not only are Minoan objects found at Near Eastern sites, but Egyptian tomb paintings depict Keftiu in typical Minoan dress bringing such objects to Egypt.

However, shortly before (or possibly during the early part of) the reign of Thutmose III (c. 1479 to 1425 B.C.E.), disaster overwhelmed Minoan Crete. All of the palaces were burned, and only Knossos was rebuilt and reoccupied. Some scholars have blamed this destruction on natural causes such as earthquakes (or the eruption of Thera, before the weight of evidence made that connection impossible). However, most authorities agree that the widespread burning must have been due to some human agency, and that the likely culprits were invaders from mainland Greece.

The Greek-speaking population of the southern part of Greece had been under Minoan cultural influence for centuries. They had developed a palace-centered economy like that of Crete, borrowed some aspects of Minoan religion, and copied Minoan artistic motifs. However, these people, whom we call Mycenaeans (after their most important site, Mycenae) or Achaeans (using a name from Homer's poems), seem to have been more aggressive than the Minoans. Their palaces were usually protected within strongly fortified citadels, and depictions of hunting and warfare are more common than in Crete. Probably each palace had its own king and was an independent entity controlling the territory around it. Though some kings were stronger than others, it is not likely that one ruler controlled all of southern Greece.

Around 1500 to 1470 B.C.E., a group of Mycenaean warriors probably invaded Crete, destroyed the Minoan palaces, then ruled the island from the rebuilt palace at Knossos. They adapted the Minoan writing system (known as Linear A) to write the early form of Greek that they spoke. Their modified script is called Linear B, and it was used on the mainland as well as in Crete. The Mycenaean culture was similar enough to that of the Minoans that the Egyptians do not seem to have distinguished them. They continued to call all Aegean people "Keftiu" long after the Mycenaean conquest of Crete.

Mycenaean adventurers gradually spread throughout the eastern Mediterranean. They conquered and ruled some places, such as Rhodes, or settled peacefully as merchants in other places, such as Miletus (on the western coast of Asia Minor), Cyprus, and Alalakh (in Syria). They continued the Minoan trade relationships with Near Eastern cultures, and Mycenaean products became common throughout the area. Judging from the pottery vessels archaeologists have uncovered, perfumed oils or salves seem to have been the Near East's favorite import from Mycenaean lands. Near Eastern merchants probably paid for these Aegean commodities primarily with precious metals or raw materials such as ivory and timber.

AKHENATON AND THE AMARNA PERIOD (c. 1350–1334 B.C.E.)

Controversies of the Amarna Age

Amenhotep III seems to have groomed his oldest son, Thutmose, to be his successor. However, Thutmose predeceased his father. So the succession passed to a younger son, Amenhotep IV (c. 1350 to 1334 B.C.E.), better known by the name he later adopted, Akhenaton. We call this pharaoh's era the "Amarna Period" because the capital city he built was located in the area of Egypt called El-Amarna by the Arabs. It is the most written about and controversial period in Egyptian history. There is debate about whether Akhenaton's reign overlapped that of his father, and argument about the nature of his religious ideas. James Breasted claimed that Akhenaton was "the most remarkable of all the Pharaohs, and the first *individual* in human history."[12] Some have seen him as a religious visionary who anticipated the monotheism of Judaism by a century or more.[13] Several scholars also have argued that Akhenaton's monotheism influenced that of Moses. On the other hand, one scholar has noted that Akhenaton's elimination of mythology—his emphasis on the sun as a natural force rather than a personal one—might better be designated atheism than monotheism.[14] Still others have claimed that Akhenaton had a disease that left him mentally retarded or deranged.[15] These individuals usually credit the many changes introduced during his reign to his mother or wife ruling behind the scenes.

A major reason for the wide disparity of views about this historical period is that later Egyptians regarded its revolutionary changes as heresies. They smashed monuments and objects associated with the hated era. They erased the names of Akhenaton and his immediate successors from inscriptions and eliminated them from king lists, suppressing almost all memory of the period. Even though modern archaeology has been able to rescue some of the buildings, art, and inscriptions from this time, those remnants are usually in very fragmentary condition. Thus, virtually any interpretation of the evidence must be tenuous and can be contested.

Did Akhenaton Have a Co-Regency With His Father?

Over the years, many scholars have proposed a period of joint rule between Amenhotep IV/Akhenaton and his father, Amenhotep III. This view stems primarily from the fact that Tutankhamun (the famous "King Tut"), Akhenaton's successor, calls Amenhotep III his father in several inscriptions. Tutankhamun was only about nine or ten years old when he became king, while Akhenaton reigned into his seventeenth year. Thus, for Amenhotep III to be Tutankhamun's father, there would have to have been a considerable overlap (at least seven years) in the reigns of Amenhotep III and Akhenaton.

The existence of a long co-regency naturally would affect the interpretation of Akhenaton's religious revolution. However, during the Eighteenth Dynasty, Egyptians sometimes used the word "father" to mean "ancestor" as well. And when the inscriptions were made, Tutankhamun may have wished to stress his relationship to Amenhotep III and minimize his connections with Akhenaton. Thus, the inscriptions do not prove that Amenhotep III was Tutankhamun's father rather than his grandfather. Other evidence for a co-regency comes from tomb reliefs and paintings that various scholars interpret in very different ways. So, it too is not very convincing.

Furthermore, there is evidence indicating that a lengthy co-regency between Amenhotep III and Akhenaton is very unlikely. Tushratta, ruler of Mitanni, wrote a letter to Akhenaton soon after Amenhotep III's death. In this letter Tushratta says he was devastated when he learned that Amenhotep III had died, but his optimism revived when he learned that Amenhotep IV was now king in his father's place.[16] This statement suggests that Akhenaton became king only after the death of his father. Moreover, Tushratta expresses hope for continued good relations with Egypt and suggests that Akhenaton ask his mother, Queen Tiy, about the former friendly relationship between the two nations.[17] It is very unlikely that Tushratta would have written such a thing to a person who had been on the throne as co-regent with his father (even as minor partner) for many years. There is also another letter from Tushratta that was probably written not long after the death of Amenhotep III.[18] Unfortunately, the clay tablet on which the letter was inscribed is damaged where the Egyptian scribe wrote the date when the letter was received. A "2" is clear, but there is room for a "10" as well in the broken place. Thus, we cannot determine for certain whether this letter arrived in Egypt in Akhenaton's second or twelfth year of reign. It can, then, be used to support arguments for no co-regency or for a long co-regency. However, fairly long intervals of time elapsed between many of the letters to pharaoh from other Great Kings and from Egypt's vassals in Syria and Palestine. It is difficult to fit these letters into the five years of sole rule Akhenaton would have had if his reign had overlapped that of his father by 12 years.

Moreover, Akhenaton's attack on the old Egyptian religion seems to have begun around his sixth year on the throne. At about that time, revenues from Amun's temples were diverted to the Aton temples in Akhetaton, and the Amun temples in Thebes were not mentioned after year 6. Then, probably in or before Akhenaton's ninth regnal year, Amun's name began to be hacked off monuments, and even removed from the cartouches of Amenhotep III's name. But until the time he died, Amenhotep III continued to worship Amun. Furthermore, through at least Amenhotep III's thirty-seventh year, work continued on his temple for Amun at Luxor. It should also be noted that there seems to have been no attempt to attack the references to Amun in Amenhotep III's tomb, even though Akhenaton would have officiated at his father's burial rites. So, Amenhotep III probably was dead and buried before Akhenaton's sixth year or by his ninth year, at the latest. Thus, an 11- or 12-year co-regency would be excluded. However, the previously mentioned letter from Tushratta probably allows for *only* an 11- or 12-year co-regency, a very short co-regency (less than two years), or no co-regency at all. Consequently, many (if not most) Egyptologists have rejected the idea of a co-regency between Akhenaton and Amenhotep III. Nevertheless, a brief co-regency less than two years long remains possible.

The Beginning of Amenhotep IV's Reign

Amenhotep IV probably became pharaoh only when his father died (c. 1350 B.C.E.). The woman he chose as his Chief Wife was probably his first cousin. She seems to have been the daughter of Ay, who in turn, was probably a brother of Queen Tiy. Her name was Nefertiti ("The Beautiful Woman has Come"), and except for Cleopatra, she is the best known of all ancient Egyptian queens.

Like his grandfather and even more so his father, Amenhotep IV emphasized the worship of the Aton (the Solar Orb), erecting two temples to this god in Thebes. As we have seen, there was already a temple to Aton at Heliopolis during the time of Amenhotep III. So, dedicating temples to this Solar Orb was not a revolutionary act. However, the new temples' form and decoration were quite different from that of most Egyptian temples. Like his father's mortuary temple, Amenhotep IV's temples were basically open courts into which the sun could shine, somewhat like the sun temples of the Old Kingdom. Within the main temple, Amenhotep IV erected grotesque statues of himself (see Figure 6.7). Artists had depicted previous pharaohs as perfectly proportioned, godlike rulers. But these early statues of Amenhotep IV show an ugly, thin-faced king with fleshy lips and an oversized jaw. He also has a long skinny neck, narrow sloping shoulders, effeminate breasts, protruding abdomen, fleshy hips and thighs, and spindly lower legs. The temples' decoration also

FIGURE 6.7   Statue of Akhenaton from the Aton Temple, Thebes
This colossal statue is made of sandstone.
Source: Egyptian Museum, Cairo.
Photo: Courtesy of the author.

emphasized the role of the king's Chief Wife. In some reliefs, Nefertiti was shown dutifully standing behind the king as he made offerings to Aton. But in others, she was shown making offerings to the Solar Orb by herself. This was something only pharaohs had been shown doing in the past. Thus, like Queen Tiy, she was being presented as almost the equal of her divine husband.

The king's physique as portrayed in the Aton temple is so abnormal that, as has been mentioned, several scholars believe that he suffered from some terrible disease.[19] Some of the diseases that have been suggested, though, would have left Akhenaton mentally retarded. If he had one of these diseases, someone else must have actually been responsible for "Akhenaton's" religious reforms. The latest medical affliction suggested for Akhenaton is lipodystrophy. This disease affects fat metabolism, causing loss of fat in the upper portions of the body and often increased fat deposits in the hips and buttocks. Sometimes the disorder also causes psychological disturbances, which, it is claimed, might have led to Akhenaton's religious extremism.[20]

However, later statues of the king do not emphasize his deformities as much as the early ones do. So, it is possible that he may not have had any disfiguring disease. It is more likely that the artists, unused to producing nonidealized works, at first created "expressionistic" caricatures of the nonathletic king, rather than realistic portraits. Some scholars have also suggested theological reasons for the distorted portraits.[21]

Nevertheless, if Amenhotep IV did have some ailment, it had to be something that would not have affected his mind or his ability to produce children.[22] If he had been only a figurehead with Tiy or Nefertiti making the decisions, it is safe to say that there would have been no Amarna revolution. Surely the person behind the scenes would have taken care to present an appearance of normality in the royal family. It would have been important that no one realize that the king was mentally defective. Neither Tiy nor Nefertiti would have allowed people to suspect the king's true state by placing grotesque portraits of Amenhotep IV in the Aton temple. Only the king himself would have ordered artists to violate the traditional way pharaoh was portrayed. While his mother and his wife may have supported his efforts, Amenhotep IV must have provided the primary impetus for the artistic and other changes of the Amarna Period.

Akhenaton's Religion

For the first few years of his reign, Amenhotep IV made only mild breaks with the past. On the third anniversary of his accession, he celebrated a joint *heb-sed* or Jubilee Festival with the Aton. Jubilees were usually held only after a pharaoh had been on the throne for 30 years. Some scholars who support the long co-regency hypothesis claim that this jubilee is the same one Amenhotep III celebrated in the thirtieth year of his reign. The Aton mentioned in Amenhotep IV's *heb-sed* inscriptions, they argue, is really Amenhotep III who had become assimilated with the Solar Orb.[23] However, Amenhotep III reigned into his thirty-eighth year at least. If the third year of Amenhotep IV was also the thirtieth year of his father, there had to be a ten-year co-regency between the kings. Thus, we would have to accept the idea that Amenhotep III continued building operations at the temples of Amun at Thebes after his son had taken away all of those temples' revenues and made the name of Amun anathema. As we have seen, this is very dubious. It is more likely that the festival commemorated Amenhotep IV's thirtieth birthday. He seems to have thought that he and the Aton had really begun their rule at the same time—the moment Amenhotep IV was born. This interpretation is also supported by the fact that Akhenaton had the Aton's name written in two cartouches like the name of a king and had the sun globe depicted wearing an uraeus cobra like that worn by every pharaoh.

In his fourth year of rule, the king began building a new city for his god. He chose a location about halfway between Memphis and Thebes, at present-day El-Amarna. He named this city Akhetaton (usually rendered "Horizon of the Sun Disk," but better is "The Place Where the Solar Orb is Transformed"). A year later, he changed his personal name from Amenhotep ("Amun is content") to Akhenaton ("The Transfigured Spirit of the Solar Orb," or less likely, "He Who is Effective for [or Serviceable to] the Solar Orb"). The following year (his sixth year of reign) he moved his family and the court to the new capital. There they could devote themselves to the worship of the Aton.

As previously mentioned, some time after moving from Thebes, probably between his sixth and ninth regnal years, Akhenaton closed the temples of the major traditional Egyptian gods. His conception of the Aton had grown more and more abstract. About his eighth or ninth year, he changed the official name of the Aton to remove from it hieroglyphs symbolizing the sun as a falcon. At the same time, words like *ma'at* ("truth; order") and *mut* ("mother") began to be spelled out phonetically instead of being expressed ideographically by hieroglyphs that could also be read as divine names.

Even the plural word for "gods" was erased from some inscriptions. Also about this time, the king's agents began hacking the names of the proscribed deities off monuments and destroying their sacred images. Akhenaton especially hated the name of Amun, which he ordered erased wherever it occurred, even in the name of his father, Amenhotep III.

At Akhetaton, the royal family worshiped the Aton as the sole god, the creator of all things (see Document 6.1). Many have seen this new religion as a monotheistic faith on the order of later Judaism, Christianity, and Islam. However, those who hold such ideas usually neglect an important aspect of the Amarna religion—the position of the royal family. Akhenaton's new religion continued a trend emphasizing the divinity of the monarch begun during earlier reigns. To support her right to the throne, Hatshepsut had claimed to be the direct offspring of Amun who had impregnated her mother while disguised as Thutmose I. Amenhotep III made the same claim about his conception, thus emphasizing that he was personally divine, not just a god in his role as king. And, like his father, Akhenaton asserted his divinity as the bodily offspring and earthly embodiment of the sun god. His capital city was Akhetaton, usually rendered "the Horizon of the Aton." However, as we have seen, for Egyptians, *akhet* ("horizon") was not just the place where the sky seems to meet the earth. It was the home of light, and the place where a dead person was changed into an *akh* ("a glorified spirit") and where the sun was transformed daily. So the meaning of Akhetaton was "the place where the Aton is transfigured into a glorified being." And the king's name, Akhenaton, proclaimed that *he* was the transfigured earthly form of the Solar Orb—"the *akh* (glorified spirit) of the Aton."[24] The Aton hymn also makes it clear that the god-king was the intermediary between humans and the Aton: "No one knows you [Aton] except your son Neferkheperure Waenre [Akhenaton]" (see Document 6.1).

Akhenaton also seems to have had Nefertiti treated as a divine or semidivine being. He had her depicted in ways normally reserved only for kings. The Aton temple in Thebes showed her making offerings to the Aton by herself. In some later scenes, she also wears royal crowns. She is even shown smiting kneeling captives, a favorite pose of pharaohs from the time of the unification onward.

The new religion taught that the well-ordered world that Aton created provided for the general needs of all humanity. But special favors or individual blessings came through the divine couple on earth. Tomb inscriptions show that courtiers at Akhetaton addressed prayers to the Aton's earthly embodiment, Akhenaton (see Document 6.2), and occasionally to his wife, Nefertiti. When individuals prayed directly to the Solar Globe, it was usually to ask for continued blessings on the royal family whose welfare was deemed so necessary for the well-being of Egypt.

Akhenaton's religion did not just eliminate devotion to Amun and other state deities. Probably for most Egyptians, this revolution hit closest to home when it ended veneration of household deities and suppressed traditional beliefs about the afterlife. People could no longer worship Osiris or perform the old burial rites. At Akhetaton, individuals could attain the afterlife only as a gracious gift of the divine king (see Document 6.2). Even the images covering the walls of Amarna's private tombs depict the activities of Akhenaton, Nefertiti, and other members of the royal family rather than those of the tomb-owners, as in the past. All attention is focused on the god-king through whom the Aton's blessings must be mediated.

Moreover, scenes of the royal couple playing with their daughters and displaying their love for one another (see Figure 6.8) probably were not just "homey" vignettes. Such relief carvings are found on altars and in shrines in private houses. They seem to have been objects of veneration. These scenes likely served as replacements for images of the old forbidden fertility deities. The divine couple's love and fecundity became the assurance of fertility and prosperity for individuals and for the land itself. There was now a new divine triad in place of the old creator god Atum, his son Shu, and Shu's sister/consort Tefnut. The new trinity consisted of Aton, Akhenaton (Aton's son and earthly image), and Nefertiti (Akhenaton's female counterpart, soul mate, and wife).

These religious changes may have been intended, in part, to reduce the power of the priesthood of

FIGURE 6.8   The Aton Blessing Akhenaton and Nefertiti While They Play with Their Daughters

This image is part of an altar panel.
Source: Egyptian Museum, Cairo.
Photo: AKG London.

Amun as many have argued. But the pharaoh probably had the means to control the priests without transforming the entire religion. Akhenaton was continuing his father's trends of emphasizing the king's divinity and the worship of the sun god. He seems to have been attempting to revive the early Old Kingdom conception of the king as the primary national deity. Once again pharaoh—not Amun or Ptah or even Re or Aton—would be the god who was responsible for everything that happened within Egypt. And once again, like Old Kingdom rulers, only Akhenaton would have a true afterlife by becoming one with Aton. Others would have only a limited existence in and around their tombs and the Aton temples, praising the sun's light and warmth during the day and sleeping during the night. Furthermore, even that meager future life would exist only if the king willed it.

Seen in this light, it is not surprising that Akhenaton's religion failed to take root in the hearts of most Egyptians. It took away the local and household gods from whom ordinary people could ask favors or to whom they could turn for solace. For these ever-present divinities, it substituted a distant impersonal Solar Orb whose grace had to be mediated by an almost as distant pharaoh. Moreover, it stressed that life after death was a gift from the king. Thus, it denied an afterlife to anyone who did not know the pharaoh personally. Only those with direct and constant access to the royal family could have drawn much comfort from such a religion.

DOCUMENT 6.1
The Hymn to the Aton

This great Hymn to the Aton was found inscribed on a wall in the tomb of Ay, a high official under Akhenaton who was probably Nefertiti's father and who later became pharaoh. Variations of it also were found in other tombs at El-Amarna. The Aton Hymn, presumably composed by Akhenaton himself, has often been compared to Psalm 104. It is usually cited by those who consider Akhenaton's religion monotheistic, since it hails the Aton as "sole god" and the source of all life. The author's translation below is based on those listed in the notes.[25]

Your beauty is apparent as you rise from the *akhet* [the place of transformation],
O living Aton, the source of life!
When you rise in the east,
You fill every land with your beauty.
You are beautiful and great, gleaming high above every land;
Your rays shine upon all of the lands you have created. . . .
When you set in the west,
The land is dark, like the darkness of death. . . .
Darkness covers the earth, and all is still,
For he who created them is resting in the *akhet*.
At daybreak, when you rise from the *akhet*,
shining as the Solar Orb by day,
You pour forth your rays, driving away the darkness,
and the Two Lands engage in festal celebration! . . .
How manifold are your works,
But they are unperceived by humans.
O sole god, like whom there is no other,
You created the world according to your plan—
You, and you alone,
(Made) all people, domestic animals and wild creatures. . . .
You assign every person a place,
And you supply their necessities.
Everyone is fed, and the length of each lifetime allotted. . . .
No one knows you except your son Neferkheperure Waenre [Akhenaton],
To whom you have revealed your plans and your power. . . .

The many differences in detail, as well as in basic concepts, between Akhenaton's religion and that of early Israel make it highly unlikely that there could have been a direct relationship between the two. There is a definite similarity between parts of the Aton Hymn and Psalm 104. But phrases used in the Aton Hymn were applied to other Egyptian gods before Akhenaton's reign and again after his death. It was probably some of those later hymns, perhaps mediated by Canaanite sources, which

DOCUMENT 6.2

Prayers to Akhenaton

The monotheism many see in the Hymn to the Aton must be tempered by other considerations. Akhenaton continued to be considered a god, and his wife Nefertiti also may have been thought to be divine. The following are samples of prayers addressed to the divine king by the sycophants of the royal court. These prayers refer to Akhenaton by his praenomen, Neferkheperure Waenre ("Perfect are the Manifestations of Re, The Sole One of Re") or just the short form, Waenre. The material in brackets is part of the original translation.[26]

> May you grant me the good funeral which is your Ka's to give, in the tomb in which you decreed for me to rest—the mountain of Akhet-Aten, the place of the favored ones. O my millions of Niles flooding daily, NEFERKHEPRURE-WAENRE, my god who made me, by whose Ka one lives, cause me to be sated with following you without cease. O one whom the Aton fashioned: you are continual!

> Adoration to your Ka, O one who lives on Maat, Lord of the Two Lands, [NEFERKHEP-RURE-WAENRE]—O Nile, upon whose command one becomes rich, my Ka of every day! The one who heeds your designs and causes it [sic] to be repeated in his heart does not grow poor. How fortunate is the one who stands in your presence and turns his heart to <your> instructions—for you then grant him the old age that is yours to give, and a goodly period by means of your governance.

> Adoration to you, O Waenre! I give adoration to the height of heaven and I propitiate the one who lives on Maat, the Lord of Crowns AKHENATEN, long in his lifetime. O Nile, at whose command one grows rich, food and provisions for Egypt; O good ruler, my builder, who made me, brought me up and caused me to mingle with officialdom; O Light (*Shu*), at the seeing of whom I live; my Ka of every day! . . . I give you adoration, I adore your beauty, [I] extol your good regulations. O my lord, may <you> give me old age not far from [you], [without] my eyes having to search for your beauty, until the state of reveredness occurs in peace in the august highland of Akhet-Aten.

influenced the psalmist long after the end of the Amarna Age.

The Revolution's Denouement

Our knowledge of the last five years of Akhenaton's reign is even more confused and uncertain than it is for the rest of the Amarna Period. Nefertiti disappears from the record a year or two after year 12. Reliefs showing the royal couple mourning the death of their daughter Meketaton about this time are the last to depict Nefertiti. In the past, some historians surmised that Nefertiti and Akhenaton had quarreled over the king's religious policy. Supposedly, Akhenaton removed Nefertiti from her position as Chief Wife and banished her to the northern part of the city.[27] However, few scholars support this view any longer. Nefertiti's name and image were not regularly removed from all earlier monuments. That probably would have occurred if she had fallen from the king's favor. A more recent theory to explain her disappearance is that Nefertiti assumed a new name and, like Hatshepsut, became king, co-regent with Akhenaton.[28]

However, a fragmentary *shabti* made for Nefertiti and found in the royal tomb at Amarna contains her traditional titles as Chief Wife of Akhenaton.[29] Such figurines were usually made only at the time of death, and this *shabti's* presence in the royal tomb suggests it was actually used during Nefertiti's burial. "King's Chief Wife" is also the only title used for her in later texts describing her children's filiation. Thus, it is likely that when she died, Nefertiti had not become king under a different name, nor had she fallen into disgrace. It is probable that Nefertiti disappeared from the monuments because she died soon after the burial of Meketaton.

Another of Akhenaton's wives, Kiya, disappeared from the record shortly before this time, while his mother, Queen Tiy, and his three youngest daughters, Neferneferuaton the younger, Neferure, and Setepenre, all seem to have died around Akhenaton's fourteenth year. Akhenaton then probably elevated his oldest daughter, Meritaton, to her mother's former position (though he may have married her earlier). On some monuments, the name of Kiya (not that of Nefertiti as originally thought) was replaced by that of Meritaton.

Hittite texts and some of the Amarna Letters indicate that a plague was spreading in Near Eastern lands about this time. This fact probably explains the rapid succession of deaths in the royal family. Perhaps the loss of Meketaton, followed swiftly by the deaths of his Chief Wife, mother, younger daughters, and possibly others in his court caused Akhenaton to consider his own mortality and take steps to provide for the succession. He seems to have chosen a young man named Smenkhkare as co-regent. Smenkhkare took the praenomen Ankhkheperure ("Kheperure [a shortened form of Akhenaton's praenomen] Lives," or possibly "Living are the Manifestations of Re"). He assumed Nefertiti's place as the third deity in the Amarna religion and eventually seems to have adopted the name Neferneferuaton ("Incomparably Beautiful [or Perfect] is the Aton") that Nefertiti had

used earlier. Furthermore, he incorporated into his name the epithet "Beloved of Waenre (Akhenaton)." It is Smenkhkare's use of these names that has led some scholars to regard this king as Nefertiti in disguise.

At one time, the assumption made in the last paragraph that Ankhkheperure Smenkhkare and Ankhkheperure Neferneferuaton were the same person was almost universal. However, several Egyptologists now argue that they are different kings, the first being Smenkhkare and the second Nefertiti. Support for this view is found in the fact that in some instances, Ankhkheperure Neferneferuaton is written with a feminine element in the first part of the name— Ankh*et*kheperure Neferneferuaton. "Beloved" in the epithet "Beloved of Waenre" is also sometimes given a feminine ending. However, as stated above, it is unlikely that Nefertiti was ever king. Her title at death still seems to have been only "King's Chief Wife." So, most scholars still believe that there was only one king whose praenomen was Ankhkheperure— Smenkhkare—and that he was male.[30] Why the scribes sometimes used feminine forms for parts of Smenkhkare's name is unknown, but possibly it is related to the fact that he seems to have taken on (at least in part) the role in the Amarna trinity of deities that formerly belonged to Nefertiti.

There are no texts detailing Smenkhkare's parentage, but he probably was Akhenaton's son. Akhenaton and Nefertiti had only daughters, but Akhenaton had other wives who were seldom mentioned in inscriptions. He had at least *two* sons by one or more of these minor wives. We know this because letters to Akhenaton from his fellow great kings refer to his sons several times. These foreign rulers must have had some knowledge of the Egyptian court and would not have been solicitous about the well-being of nonexistent princes. So the frequent assertion that Akhenaton fathered only daughters should be quietly buried and forgotten.

Soon after naming Smenkhkare as co-regent, Akhenaton seems to have given his current Chief Wife, Meritaton, to him so she could serve as Smenkhkare's Chief Wife. He then probably married his next oldest daughter, Ankhesenpaaton. Akhenaton's new queen was probably only about ten years old. Nevertheless, sometime during the two or two-and-a-half years of marriage to her father, it is likely that Ankhesenpaaton bore him a daughter (named Ankhesenpaaton, the younger).

Akhenaton died in his seventeenth year on the throne. Smenkhkare must have immediately decided to make his peace with the old religion and reopen the temples of Amun. A Theban tomb graffito makes it certain that by the third year of Ankhkheperure Neferneferuaton (who, as we have seen, was probably Smenkhkare), Amun's worship had resumed at Thebes. But Smenkhkare's third year of rule (probably the same calendar year as Akhenaton's seventeenth year) was to be his last. Less than a year after Akhenaton's death, the young co-regent followed him to the grave. A mummy discovered in 1907 in a small tomb in the Valley of the Kings (KV 55) is probably that of Smenkhkare. It indicates that the king was only about 20 to 24 years old when he died.[31]

THE END OF THE EIGHTEENTH DYNASTY (c. 1334–1293 B.C.E.)

Tutankhamun and the Restoration of Amun

The throne now passed to Tutankhaton (who ruled c. 1334 to 1325 B.C.E.). This nine- or ten-year-old pharaoh was probably also a son of Akhenaton. A damaged inscription on a stone found at Hermopolis (but originally from Akhetaton) refers to Tutankhaton as "the bodily son of the king." This phrase was used to designate a pharaoh's natural son and was not used for a son-in-law, nephew, or grandson. Unfortunately, though, the king in question is not named. X-ray studies and blood tests have revealed a close genetic relationship between Tutankhaton's mummy and the one believed to be Smenkhkare's. These two young kings were probably full brothers, both sons of Akhenaton and one of his minor wives (probably Kiya who was designated "Great Beloved Wife").

The child-king took as his Chief Wife his 12- to 13-year-old half-sister, Ankhesenpaaton. Of course,

Tutankhaton was too young to actually rule the country. The government was in the hands of Ay, probably Nefertiti's father and Ankhesenpaaton's grandfather. Ay had been Master of the Horse (commander of chariotry) under Akhenaton, and now served as vizier and regent for Tutankhaton.

Tutankhaton continued Smenkhkare's policy of reconciliation with the old faith, but for a couple of years, the new pharaoh and his court remained at Akhetaton. It was not enough, though, for the royal family merely to acquiesce to the people's worship of the old gods. A more positive step was needed to bridge the chasm that Akhenaton's rule had created between the king and his subjects. So the young pharaoh and his queen changed their names to Tutankhamun and Ankhesenamun respectively. They abandoned Akhetaton and made Memphis the capital once more. Without the pharaoh and royal court to sustain it, Akhenaton's city quickly became a ghost town.

Under Ay's direction, Tutankhamun instituted a widespread building program to repair the temples damaged by Akhenaton. He appointed new priests and prophets from the nobility. He also gave the refurbished temples many of the singers, dancers, and slaves who had been attached to the palace or were the king's own property. The temples of local gods once more received revenues that Akhenaton had diverted to the temples of Aton or to the royal treasury. The royal administration made an attempt to make everything seem to be the way it had been before the Amarna revolution.

While the old religion was reinstated and Amun resumed his position of primacy in the pantheon, the Aton continued to be worshiped. Akhenaton's Aton temples remained open, and objects displaying the image or name of the Aton continued to be used. But now the Aton was once again only one god among many, and he was no longer the pharaoh's favorite.

The Egyptian empire also had to be restored. Akhenaton was not a pacifist as sometimes claimed. His army had conducted a military campaign in Nubia, and Egyptian garrisons had remained in Canaan. Also, like previous pharaohs, he had himself depicted killing foreign prisoners kneeling before him. So, his religious beliefs would not have precluded his sending out troops to crush rebellion. Nevertheless, as the Amarna Letters indicate, there had been some internecine fighting among Egypt's Asiatic vassals during his reign and he doesn't seem to have taken any action. More troubling, though, had been the Hittite conquest of Qadesh and other cities in northern Syria towards the end of Akhenaton's life. Also, revolts had broken out in Nubia once again. So, early in Tutankhamun's reign, his generals seem to have begun a series of military campaigns to reestablish Egyptian power.

A painted wooden box from his tomb shows Tutankhamun triumphing over Nubians and Asiatics. Did the king personally lead military expeditions into Nubia and Syria-Palestine when he reached adulthood at age 16? Scholars have usually regarded these paintings as copies of traditional scenes of pharaoh defeating his enemies rather than as illustrations of actual events in Tutankhamun's reign. However, recent study of the young king's mummy has necessitated a reevaluation of this view. X-rays have suggested to some pathologists that Tutankhamun died from a blow to the base of his skull that caused a cerebral hemorrhage. The location of the injury makes it unlikely that it was accidental, so some argue for murder.[32] (Ay is the principal suspect.) On the other hand, other pathologists do not see strong evidence for skull damage and hemorrhage in the X-rays. Moreover, if there was such an injury, it could have been the result of battle rather than murder. Tutankhamun was 18 or 19 when he died, certainly old enough to assume personal leadership of Egypt's armies. There is no compelling reason, then, to doubt the essential historicity of the paintings on a box in his tomb showing Tutankhamun in battle. The boy pharaoh who had reestablished Egypt's traditional religion may have lost his life trying to restore her traditional empire as well.

Tutankhamun and Ankhesenamun seem to have had two stillborn children. But there was no living heir. Tutankhamun was the last male member of the line of pharaohs who had ruled Egypt since the expulsion of the Hyksos some two and a quarter centuries earlier. Ay seems to have considered himself Tutankhamun's rightful successor and he undoubtedly planned to marry his granddaughter Ankhesenamun to strengthen his claim to the throne. It is also possible that various people were pressuring the queen to marry one of her vigorous and competent high officials such as the general Horemheb to make him king. Ankhesenamun, though, had other ideas. The Hittites were at that time campaigning in Syria. So, she wrote to the Hittite king Suppiluliumas who, like Egyptian rulers, claimed descent from the sun god:

> My husband died and I have no son. People say you have many sons. If you were to send me one of your sons, he might become my husband. I am loath to take a servant of mine and make him my husband.[33]

Suppiluliumas could not believe this offer was genuine. So he sent his chamberlain to Egypt to secure reliable information. When he discovered that Ankhesenamun was in earnest, he complied with her request. However, it was too late. Someone, probably Ay or Horemheb, had learned of the plan. The Hittite prince was murdered during his journey to Egypt, prompting war between the two powers.

The Reigns of Ay and Horemheb (c. 1325–1293 B.C.E.)

Ay assumed the throne and married Ankhesenamun. He officiated at the burial rites as the body of Tutankhamun was laid to rest in the Valley of the Kings. However, he seems to have taken for himself Tutankhamun's unfinished tomb and interred the boy king in a small, hastily decorated tomb not originally intended for a king.

Howard Carter's discovery of this tomb in 1922 caused a sensation. Tomb robbers had entered it on two different occasions in antiquity. However, in both instances, the robberies were discovered quickly and the tomb resealed. The thieves made off with some jewelry and other small objects, but thousands of burial gifts remained. Fortunately, the robbers barely penetrated the door into the burial chamber. There the pharaoh's mummy reposed in three nested coffins within a quartzite sarcophagus surrounded by four shrines. The innermost coffin (see Figure 6.9) was solid 22-karat gold and weighed almost 250 pounds! Though the objects in the tomb had been hastily assembled and were not all of the best quality, they still astound visitors to the Egyptian Museum in

FIGURE 6.9   The Solid Gold Inner Coffin of Tutankhamun

Source: Egyptian Museum, Cairo.

Photo: Araldo De Luca Archive, Rome.

Cairo. They are a unique testimony to the wealth and glory of pharaonic Egypt. We can only wonder what the burial goods of great pharaohs such as Thutmose III or Ramesses II must have been like.

Ay continued implementing the policies of restoration and reconciliation he had initiated as Tutankhamun's regent. But he was already an old man when he became pharaoh, and he had no sons. He died after a brief reign of only four or five years (c. 1325 to 1321), leaving Egypt's throne to General Horemheb who may also have been his co-regent during the last months of his life.

Horemheb (c. 1321 to 1293 B.C.E.) legitimized his rule by marrying Ay's daughter and Nefertiti's sis-

ter, Mutnedjmet. Perhaps to win popular support and to strengthen his somewhat tenuous hold on the throne, the new king began a campaign of vengeance against the Aton. He destroyed the Aton temples, razed Akhetaton to the ground, and obliterated inscriptions mentioning Aton or Akhenaton. Horemheb's agents probably even entered the tombs of Akhenaton, Smenkhkare, and Ay, hacking out images and names of the Aton and the heretical kings. He dated his reign from the death of Amenhotep III, eliminating all official references to the Amarna pharaohs. On the rare occasions when a text had to mention Akhenaton, it referred to him simply as "the enemy from Akhetaton."

Horemheb usurped monuments and statues built by Tutankhamun and Ay, removing their names and substituting his own. But he did not violate Tutankhamun's burial. In fact, it was probably during Horemheb's reign that thieves were caught robbing Tutankhamun's tomb. The tomb was resealed and not entered again until 1922. Perhaps Tutankhamun's restoration of the worship of Amun saved his burial from suffering the fate that befell those of Akhenaton, Smenkhkare, and Ay.

In addition to appropriating earlier monuments, Horemheb undertook extensive building operations of his own, especially at Thebes. He also instituted many reforms during his reign, suppressing corruption and illegal acts by members of the bureaucracy. Akhenaton had centralized Egypt's administration and its army, which had led to many abuses. Horemheb reversed this policy, establishing law courts in all the major towns with temple priests and town mayors as judges. Furthermore, he personally rewarded those who performed their duties well. While he continued the restoration of the old religion, he did not just turn power over to the old priests. He appointed many new priests from army leaders who were fiercely loyal to him. He split legal power between viziers at Memphis and Thebes and divided the army into northern and southern branches.

After more than 25 years on the throne, Horemheb died childless. His successor, a military commander and vizier named Ramesses I, inaugurated a new era, the Ramesside Period (Dynasties 19 and 20). The kings of this era would first try to restore, and then desperately to maintain, Egyptian power in Syria and Palestine. However, the sun was setting on the period of Egyptian greatness.

SUGGESTIONS FOR FURTHER READING AND INFORMATION

Internet Sites

Text of a lecture on Akhenaton given at Western New England College: http:// mars.acnet.wnec.edu/~grempel/courses/wc1/lectures/03akehnaton.html

Akhenaton and Nefertiti in the Louvre Museum: http://www.as.wvu.edu/history/Faculty/warnett/102/indy14

Books and Articles

The Egyptian New Kingdom through the Reign of Amenhotep III

Benson, Douglas S., *Ancient Egypt's Warfare: A Survey of Armed Conflict in the Chronology of Ancient Egypt, 1600 BC–30 BC*. Chicago: D. S. Benson, 1995.

Bryan, Betsy M., *The Reign of Thutmose IV*. Baltimore: Johns Hopkins University Press, 1991.

Dorman, P. F. *The Monuments of Senenmut*. London: Kegan Paul International, 1988.

Fletcher, Joann. *Chronicle of a Pharaoh: The Intimate Life of Amenhotep III*. New York and London: Oxford University Press, 2000.

Harris, James E., and Edward F. Wente, eds. *An X-Ray Atlas of the Royal Mummies*. Chicago: University of Chicago Press, 1980.

Hornung, Erik. *The Valley of the Kings: Horizon of Eternity*. Translated by David Warburton. New York: Timken, 1990.

Kozloff, Arielle P., and Betsy M. Bryan. *Egypt's Dazzling Sun: Amenhotep III and His World*. Cleveland: Cleveland Museum of Art, 1992.

Murnane, William L., *Ancient Egyptian Coregencies*. Chicago: The Oriental Institute, 1977.

O'Connor, David, and Eric H. Cline, eds. *Amenhotep III: Perspectives on His Reign*. Ann Arbor, MI: University of Michigan Press, 1998.

Romer, John. *The Valley of the Kings*. New York: Henry Holt, 1981.

Strudwick, Nigel and Helen. *Thebes in Egypt: A Guide to the Tombs and Temples of Ancient Luxor*. Ithaca, NY: Cornell University Press, 1999.

Tyldesley, Joyce. *Hatchepsut, the Female Pharaoh*. New York: Viking, 1996.

Akhenaton and the Amarna Period

Aldred, Cyril. *Akhenaton, King of Egypt*. London: Thames and Hudson, 1988.

Brier, Bob. *The Murder of Tutankhamen: A True Story*. New York: Putnam, 1998.

Campbell, Edward F. Jr. *The Chronology of the Amarna Letters*. Baltimore: The Johns Hopkins Press, 1964.

Cohen, Raymond, and Raymond Westbrook, eds. *Amarna Diplomacy: The Beginnings of International Relations*. Baltimore: The Johns Hopkins Press, 1999.

Hornung, Erik. *Akhenaton and the Religion of Light*. Translated by David Lorton. Ithaca, NY: Cornell University Press, 1999.

Mahdy, Christine El. *Tutankhamen: The Life and Death of the Boy King*. New York: St. Martin's Press, 1999.

Martin, Geoffrey T. *The Hidden Tombs of Memphis: New Discoveries from the Time of Tutankhamun and Ramesses the Great*. London: Thames and Hudson, 1991.

Moran, William L. *The Tell el-Amarna Tablets*. Baltimore: Johns Hopkins University Press, 1992.

Murnane, William J. *Texts from the Amarna Period in Egypt*. Atlanta: Scholars Press, 1995.

Redford, Donald B. *Akhenaton, the Heretic King*. Princeton, NJ: Princeton University Press, 1984.

Reeves, Nicholas. *Akhenaten: Egypt's False Prophet*. London: Thames and Hudson, 2001.

———. *The Complete Tutankhamun*. London: Thames and Hudson, 1990.

Samson, Julia. *Amarna, City of Akhenaten and Nefertiti: Nefertiti as Pharaoh*. London: Warminster, 1978.

———. *Nefertiti and Cleopatra: Queen-monarchs of Ancient Egypt*. Rev. ed. London: Rubicon Press, 1990.

Tyldesley, Joyce. *Nefertiti: Egypt's Sun Queen*. New York: Viking, 1999.

Watterson, Barbara. *Amarna: Egypt's Age of Revolution*. Stroud, Gloucestershire, UK: Tempus Publishing, 1999.

The Levant and Eastern Mediterranean Area

Chadwick, John. *The Mycenaean World*. Cambridge: Cambridge University Press, 1976.

Cline, Eric H. *Sailing the Wine-Dark Sea: International Trade and the Late Bronze Age Aegean*. Oxford: Oxford University Press, 1994.

Healey, John F. *The Early Alphabet*. Reading the Past, no. 9. London: British Museum Press, 1990.

Parker, Simon B., ed. *Ugaritic Narrative Poetry*. Atlanta: Scholars Press, 1997.

Redford, Donald B. *Egypt, Canaan, and Israel in Ancient Times*. Princeton: Princeton University Press, 1992.

Taylour, Lord William. *The Mycenaeans*. Rev. ed. New York and London: Thames and Hudson, 1983.

Tubb, Jonathan N. *Canaanites*. Norman, OK: University of Oklahoma Press, 1998.

NOTES

1. Gay Robins, "A Critical Examination of the Theory that the Right to the Throne of Ancient Egypt Passed through the Female Line in the 18th Dynasty," *Gottinger Miszellen*, vol. 62 (1983), pp. 67–77. See also Robins, *Women in Ancient Egypt* (London: British Museum Press, 1993), pp. 26–27, and "The Enigma of Hatshepsut: Egypt's Female Pharaoh," *Archaeology Odyssey*, vol. 2, no. 1 (Winter 1999), p. 40.

2. Robins (1993), pp. 150–151 and "The Enigma of Hatshepsut," *Archaeology Odyssey*, vol. 2, no. 1 (Winter 1999), p. 40.

3. See, for example, Alan H. Gardiner, *Egypt of the Pharaohs* (London: Oxford University Press, 1961), pp. 181–184 and Peter A. Clayton, *Chronicle of the Pharaohs* (London: Thames and Hudson, 1994), pp. 102, 104.

4. Joyce Tyldesley, *Hatchepsut, the Female Pharaoh* (New York: Viking, 1996), p. 113. See also Amélie Kuhrt, *The Ancient Near East, c. 3000–330 B.C.* (London: Routledge, 1995), vol. 1, p. 193.

5. Tyldesley (1996) pp. 113–114.

6. Ibid., pp. 216–226, especially 225–226. See also Robins (1993), pp. 51–52, and "The Enigma of Hatshepsut," *Archaeology Odyssey*, vol. 2, no. 1 (Winter 1999), p. 41.

7. Gardiner (1961), p. 200.

8. See, for example, Theophile Meek, *Hebrew Origins* (New York: Harper Torchbooks, 1960), pp. 21–23, and John J. Bimson, *Redating the Exodus and Conquest* 2nd ed. (Sheffield, UK: The Almond Press, 1981), p. 227.

9. Moshe Greenberg, *The Hab/piru* (New Haven, CT: The American Oriental Society, 1955), pp. 86–96; John M. Halligan, "The Role of the Peasant in the Amarna Period" in David Noel Freedman and David Frank Graf, eds., *Palestine in Transition: The Emergence of Ancient Israel* (Sheffield, UK: The Almond Press, 1983), pp.21–22.

10. Elizabeth J. Himelfarb, "First Alphabet Found in Egypt," *Archaeology*, vol. 53, no. 1 (January/February 2000), p. 21; Steven Feldman, "Not as Simple as A-B-C: Earliest Use of Alphabet Found in Egypt," *Biblical Archaeology Review*, vol. 26, no. 1 (January/February 2000), p. 12.

11. John F. Healy, *The Early Alphabet,* Reading the Past, no. 9 (London: The British Museum Press, 1990), pp. 16–17.

12. James H. Breasted, *A History of Egypt* (New York: Charles Scribner's Sons, 2nd ed., 1909), p. 356 (italics in the original).

13. For recent arguments that Akhenaton was the first true monotheist, see Bob Brier, *The Murder of Tutankhamen: A True Story* (New York: G. P. Putnam's Sons, 1998), pp. 61–76, and James P. Allen, "Monotheism—the Egyptian Roots," *Archaeology Odyssey*, vol. 2, no. 3 (July/August 1999), pp. 44–45, 59. Erik Hornung's *Akhenaton and the Religion of Light*, translated by David Lorton (Ithaca: Cornell University Press, 1999), pp. 52–60, 87–104 provides a more nuanced interpretation of Akhenaton's supposed monotheism than either Brier or Allen.

14. Donald B. Redford, *Akhenaten, the Heretic King* (Princeton, NJ: Princeton University Press, 1984), pp. 233–234.

15. The most extreme and consistent presentation of this view is that of F. J. Giles, *Ikhnaton, Legend and History* (Rutherford, NJ: Fairleigh Dickinson University Press, 1970).

16. Letter EA (an abbreviation for El-Amarna) 29, lines 55–64. See William L. Moran, *The El-Amarna Tablets* (Baltimore: Johns Hopkins University Press, 1992), p. 94.

17. Ibid., p. 92 (also see p. 94).

18. EA 27, Moran (1992), pp. 86–90.

19. For an argument that Akhenaton had Froelich's Syndrome, a disease that would have made him severely mentally retarded, see Cyril Aldred, *Akhenaten, Pharaoh of Egypt—A New Study* (New York: McGraw-Hill, 1968), pp. 134–135. Aldred later abandoned this view. Brier (1998), pp. 53–56 argues that Akhenaton suffered from Marfan's Syndrome. Giles (1970), p. 92 claims that Akhenaton became mentally incompetent or deranged and that Akhetaton was his "asylum" where he could play at being king (until Amenhotep III died and he became king for real).

20. Barbara Watterson, *Amarna: Ancient Egypt's Age of Revolution* (Stroud, Gloucestershire: Tempus Publishing, 1999), p. 76. Since lipodystrophy affects females 80 percent of the time, Watterson suggests that Nefertiti might have been the one to develop the disease. Then, because Nefertiti had been his ideal of beauty, Akhenaton had himself depicted with the same deformities as his once shapely wife. Watterson admits, though, that this is all speculative and "based on an over-interpretation of the data."

21. Cyril Aldred, *Akhenaton, King of Egypt* (London: Thames and Hudson, 1988), pp. 235–236.

22. One such disease that has been suggested is Marfan's Syndrome (see Note 19). This illness causes elongated bones, especially fingers and toes, similar to those depicted in Amarna art. It also causes a lowering of lifespan, but doesn't affect the mind or reproductive system. Abraham Lincoln probably suffered from Marfan's Syndrome.

23. See, for example, Kent R. Weeks, *The Lost Tomb* (New York: Morrow, 1998), pp. 230–232.

24. Hornung (1999) has objected that *akh*, meaning "glorified spirit," applies "only to the soul of a deceased person," p. 50, so he prefers to translate Akhenaton's name "He who is useful to Aton." However, Akhenaton's religion did away with the old conception of the afterlife. The spirits of the dead slept at night and during the day visited the temples of Aton in Akhetaton. This world and the world to come were blended into one and Akhetaton is the home of the blessed dead as well as of the living. So, Akhenaton could have considered himself the "otherworldly" glorified spirit of the Aton here on earth.

25. Compare this translation with the following translations of the entire hymn: Alan H. Gardiner, *Egypt of the Pharaohs*, pp. 224–227; John A. Wilson in J. B. Pritchard, ed., *Ancient Near Eastern Texts* (Princeton, NJ: Princeton University Press, 2nd ed., 1955), pp. 369–371; Miriam Lichtheim, *Ancient Egyptian Literature: A Book of Readings*, vol. 2: *The New Kingdom* (Berkeley: University of California Press, 1976), pp. 96–100; William J. Murnane, *Texts from the Amarna Period in Egypt* (Atlanta: Scholars Press, 1995), pp. 113–116; Joyce Tyldesley, *Nefertiti: Egypt's Sun Queen* (New York: Viking, 1998), pp. 86–87; James P. Allen, "Monotheism—the Egyptian Roots," *Archaeology Odyssey* 2/3 (July/August 1999), p. 48.

26. The translations are by William J. Murnane, *Texts from the Amarna Period in Egypt*, Atlanta: Scholars Press, 1995, pp. 144, 155, 159.

27. For example, see J. D. S. Pendlebury, *Tell el-Amarna* (London: L. Dickson and Thompson, 1935), pp. 28–29; John A. Wilson, *The Burden of Egypt* (Chicago: University of Chicago Press, 1951), p. 232; Donald B. Redford, *History and Chronology of the Eighteenth Dynasty of Egypt: Seven Studies* (Toronto: University of Toronto Press, 1967), pp. 173–174.

28. J. R. Harris, "Nefertiti Rediviva," *Acta Orientalia*, vol. 35 (1974), pp. 5–13, and "Nefernefruaten Regnans," *Acta Orientalia*, vol. 36 (1975), pp. 11–21; Julia Samson, "Nefertiti's Regality," *Journal of Egyptian Archaeology*, vol. 63 (1977), pp. 88–97, and *Amarna, City of Akhenaten and Nefertiti: Nefertiti as Pharaoh* (London: Warminster, 1978); Nicholas Reeves, *Akhenaten: Egypt's False Prophet* (London: Thames and Hudson, 2001), pp. 162–173.

29. Aldred (1988), pp. 229–230; Tyldesley, *Nefertiti: Egypt's Sun Queen*, pp. 151, 176. On the other hand, Nicholas Reeves claims that the statuette was not really a *shabti* used at Nefertiti's burial, but a votive image of the queen presented during an earlier burial (2001, p. 170). If his interpretation is correct, the idea of Nefertiti's co-regency could still be maintained.

30. In 1980, John Baines and Jaromir Malek accepted the theory that Smenkhkare and Nefertiti were the same person. However, in the revised edition of *Cultural Atlas of Ancient Egypt* (New York: Checkmark Books, 2000), they changed their minds, listing Smenkhkare as a separate ruler who is male. They still say, though, that at Akhenaton's death "a woman may have succeeded him briefly, perhaps his eldest daughter Meritaten" (p. 46). This theory is also unlikely. Meritaton became Smenkhkare's wife, and is not treated as his co-regent. It is difficult to believe that she reigned briefly as king (as Ankhetkheperure Neferneferuaton) after his death.

31. This was the opinion of anatomists Grafton Elliot Smith in 1912, Douglas Derry in the late 1920s, and R. G. Harrison in 1966 (see Brier [1998], pp. 163–164). After a new examination of the body in 1988, Fawzia Hussein and James E. Harris claimed the individual's age at death was about 35 or slightly older. If this estimate is correct, then the body could possibly be that of Akhenaton, and Ankhkheperure Smenkhkare/Neferneferuaton could be Nefertiti (see Reeves [2001], pp. 80–84). The most recent study of the body, though, by Egyptologist and physical anthropologist Joyce M. Filer supports the earlier views that the body belonged to a male who was probably between 18 and 20 years old, and almost certainly not older than 25 years. See Joyce M. Filer, "Anatomy of a Mummy," *Archaeology*, vol. 55, no. 2 (March/April 2002), pp. 26–29 and Mark Rose, "Who's in Tomb 55?," *Archaeology*, vol. 55, no. 2 (March/April 2002), pp. 22–27.

32. Brier (1998), pp. 165–174.

33. A. Goetze, "Suppiluliumas and the Egyptian Queen," in Pritchard, ed. (1955), p. 319.

7

The End of the Bronze Age

THE ZENITH OF HITTITE POWER (c. 1344–1180 B.C.E.)

Revival and Extension of the Hittite Empire

As we have seen in Chapter 3, following Mursilis I's conquest of Babylon (c. 1595 B.C.E.), infighting within the Hittite royal family produced civil wars that greatly weakened the kingdom. The new kingdom of Mitanni seized the opportunity and conducted several destructive raids into Hittite territory. Also, many former Hittite vassals in Asia Minor revolted. The territory Hittite kings could effectively control contracted to the Hittite homeland surrounding Hattusas, the capital. Thus, Hatti again became only a modest-sized Anatolian kingdom and remained so for almost 200 years.

However, around 1420 B.C.E., Tudhaliyas I seized power and founded a vigorous new dynasty. He inaugurated a new era known as the Hittite New Kingdom or Empire (see Table 7.1). He and his three (or possibly four) immediate successors began to rebuild Hittite power in Asia Minor and once more challenged Mitannian control of northern Syria. They

TABLE 7.1

Probable Chronology of the Hittite New Kingdom or Empire

(Not all kings are listed. All dates are B.C.E.)

Tudhaliyas I (and three or four successors)	1420–1344
Suppiluliumas I	1344–1322
Arnuwandas II	1322–1321
Mursilis II	1321–1295
Muwatallis II	1295–1272
Urhi–Teshub (= Mursilis III)	1272–1267
Hattusilis III	1267–1237
Tudhaliyas IV	1237–1209
Arnuwandas III	1209–1207
Suppiluliumas II	1207–1180?

paved the way for the greatest of the Hittite kings, Suppiluliumas I (c. 1344 to 1322 B.C.E.), to make Hatti the most powerful empire in the Near East.

Suppiluliumas became king only after overthrowing and killing his older brother who had briefly succeeded their father on the throne. It must have seemed to many that Hatti was about to resume its debilitating civil wars. However, Suppiluliumas, a former general who had the respect of the Hittite nobles, quickly gained complete control of Hatti. He rebuilt the fortifications of Hattusas to protect it against possible attacks. Then he began using his considerable abilities as a diplomat and military strategist to expand Hittite dominion.

Suppiluliumas sought to isolate Mitanni, Hatti's principal foe. He cultivated good relations with Akhenaton in Egypt and married the daughter of Burnaburias II, the Kassite king of Babylon. He also signed a treaty recognizing the legitimacy of a Mitannian prince who was challenging King Tushratta's claim to the Mitannian throne. Thus, Suppiluliumas hoped to divide Mitanni internally. He then made alliances with Isuwa to the northeast and Nuhasse to the southwest of Mitanni (see Map 7.1). So, Tushratta could

expect no help from those quarters. The alliance with Nuhasse would even block the route Egyptian troops would normally take to reach Mitanni.

Tushratta could feel the Hittite vise tightening around his kingdom. He tried to break it by encouraging an anti-Hittite revolt in Isuwa and sending an army to attack Nuhasse. But Suppiluliumas was prepared. He immediately launched a massive invasion of Mitanni. He moved much more quickly than Tushratta expected, capturing and looting Wassukanni, the Mitannian capital, before Tushratta could gather his troops. The Mitannian king was forced to flee to avoid capture by the Hittite army.

Suppiluliumas then moved westward, conquering Aleppo and other Mitannian subjects in the region and installing Hittite rulers in the key cities. While he was engaged in these activities, the king of Qadesh,

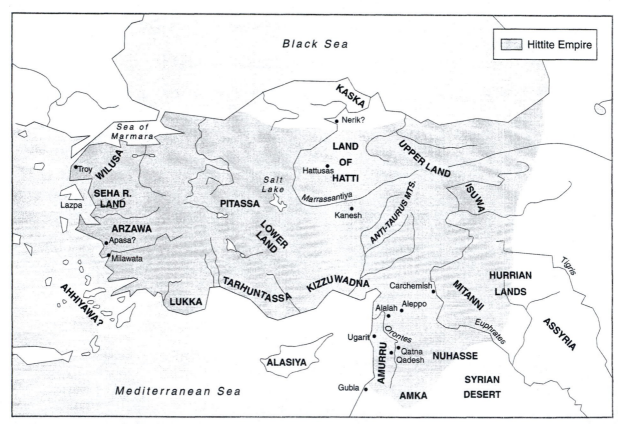

MAP 7.1   The Hittite Empire at Its Greatest Extent (c. 1322–1220 B.C.E.)

an Egyptian vassal, attacked the Hittite forces. Suppiluliumas defeated the attacking army, captured Qadesh, and deported its king and leading citizens to Hatti. Qadesh now became a Hittite vassal, and Amurru, Qatna, and Egypt's other north Syrian vassals soon came under Hittite control. Thus, shortly before Akhenaton's death, Egypt lost the northernmost section of its Asiatic empire.

A little more than ten years later, Egypt sent an army to regain control of Qadesh. This attack and the threat of a Mitannian revival caused Suppiluliumas to lead a large army into Syria once again. He laid siege to Carchemish, the last Mitannian ally in the region, and sent a force to invade the Land of Amka, an Egyptian vassal. It was while Suppiluliumas was involved in these activities that Tutankhamun died and his wife wrote to the Hittite king asking for a marriage to one of his sons (see Chapter 6). Suppiluliumas completed his conquest of Carchemish and eventually sent a son to Egypt. However, as noted, the Hittite prince was killed and the union of the two great empires never took place.

Meanwhile, Mitanni's days as a great power came to an end. A group of conspirators assassinated Tushratta and Assyria took advantage of the situation by seizing the northern and eastern portions of Mitannian territory. Suppiluliumas took much of the rest. Tushratta's son was forced to become a Hittite vassal, retaining only a small portion of the former kingdom. A few years later, Suppululiumas I died, a victim of plague brought to Hatti from the captured Egyptian territories in Syria. However, by the end of his reign (c. 1322), the Hittite Empire stretched from far western Asia Minor to northern Mesopotamia and from the Black Sea to the area just south of Qadesh (see Map 7.1).

Hatti's Showdown With Egypt

Suppululiumas' successor also contracted the plague and died within a year, leaving the throne to a younger brother, Mursilis II (c. 1321 to 1295 B.C.E.). Despite his inexperience in military affairs, Mursilis suppressed revolts in the west, totally destroying the troublesome kingdom of Arzawa, and bringing the entire

western coast of Asia Minor back under Hittite control. He also crushed revolts in Syria and kept the growing power of Assyria in check. To prevent future revolts, he transported large numbers of conquered people from their homelands to Hatti. This policy was later adopted by the rulers of the Neo-Assyrian Empire. Despite the losses the plague inflicted on the Hittite population, Mursilis maintained his empire's strength throughout his reign.

However, a major threat to Hittite power confronted Mursilis' son, Muwatallis II (c. 1295 to 1272 B.C.E.). A new dynasty intent on restoring the Egyptian empire had arisen in Egypt. In his first regnal year (c.1291 B.C.E.), Seti I won a skirmish with Hittite troops during a military expedition into Syria to restore Egyptian power in the area. Seti conducted several more campaigns in Lebanon and Syria during his first six years, eventually recapturing Qadesh and Amurru, important Hittite vassals in Syria. However, Muwatallis, busy with problems within Anatolia, did not immediately respond. It's possible that he even signed a treaty with Egypt recognizing the new boundaries in order to keep Egypt from trying to proceed further northward.[1]

Muwatallis had to deal with revolts in the west, incited by a troublesome kingdom called Ahhiyawa (see the following section "Achaeans and Trojans in Hittite Texts?"). Muwatallis rushed to the support of a loyal ally, Wilusa, and eventually suppressed the uprisings. He was not able to turn his attention to Syria until the last years of Seti I, from about 1280 to 1279 B.C.E. Probably aware that Seti was old and sick, Muwatallis sent his forces into Syria, recapturing the city of Qadesh. He also succeeded in stirring up revolt among some of Egypt's other Syrian vassals.

Seti's successor, Ramesses II, began gathering a 20,000-man force to crush the Syrian revolts and regain control of Qadesh. In the spring of his fifth year (c. 1274 B.C.E.), he led this large army north against the Hittites. As he approached Qadesh, the four divisions of his army were strung out over many miles. Captured Hittite spies misled Ramesses into believing that the Hittites were still far to the north, when in fact Muwatallis and a huge army were hidden just to the east of Qadesh. As Ramesses II and the Division of Amun began setting up camp west of Qadesh, and the Division of Re was approaching from the south, the Hittite chariot force launched a surprise attack across a ford in the Orontes River. The Division of Re was shattered and its disorganized remnants fled toward the Egyptian camp followed by the Hittite chariots. The Egyptians finally succeeded in beating the truth out of a couple of captured Hittite scouts. Ramesses had barely begun calling his division to arms when the Hittite juggernaut burst upon them.

Much of the Division of Amun panicked and was scattered. However, the pharaoh showed great personal bravery, leading the few chariots that were ready in a charge to blunt the Hittite attack. Just when everything seemed lost, Ramesses and his army were saved by two fortuitous events. First, some of the Hittite charioteers began looting the Egyptian camp instead of continuing the attacks on Ramesses and his small contingent of chariots. Second, an Egyptian force made up primarily of allied Canaanite troops arrived from the coast. The Canaanite chariots attacked the Hittites' left flank, catching them totally by surprise. (This attack is depicted in Figure 6.4 in Chapter 6). As the Hittite chariot force briefly fell back to regroup, Ramesses was able to organize his forces enough to launch several counterattacks. The sudden change in fortune seems to have destroyed Hittite morale, and their chariots were soon in full retreat. Finding themselves surrounded and backed against the river, the confused Hittite forces abandoned their chariots and swam to the safety of the east bank.

Though almost all of Muwatallis' chariots had been destroyed, his infantry (which outnumbered the entire Egyptian army) was able to hold its own against Ramesses' subsequent attacks. Recognizing that he could not destroy the Hittite army and recapture Qadesh, Ramesses marched the remnants of his army home. Once back in Egypt, he celebrated the campaign as a great triumph. However, as Ramesses II retreated southward, Muwatallis regrouped his forces and followed, regaining control of Amurru and seizing Syrian territory as far south as Damascus. Though the outcome of the Battle of Qadesh is often called a draw, it was really a Hittite victory because it kept the Egyptians from regaining Qadesh and, in its aftermath, the Hittites actually extended their territory.

A few years after the Battle of Qadesh, Muwatallis died. His son Urhi-Teshub (who renamed himself Mursilis III) reigned for only a few years (c. 1272 to 1267 B.C.E.). He seems to have aroused much opposition by several controversial actions and also because he was the son of a concubine, not the queen. Thus, when his powerful and ambitious uncle Hattusilis decided to depose Urhi-Teshub and assume the throne, there was little opposition.

Hattusilis III (c. 1267 to 1237 B.C.E.) inherited an uneasy truce with Egypt. Ramesses II still controlled Palestine and the Phoenician cities, and had not relinquished the dream of regaining the lost Syrian territories. He had led two more abortive Egyptian incursions into Syria early in the reign of Urhi-Teshub. However, it became evident that the warfare was exhausting both powers. Neither the Hittites nor the Egyptians had the strength to prevail absolutely, so they settled for an undeclared armistice. Eventually, Hattusilis and Ramesses discerned that their conflict was aiding only Assyria. Adad-Nirari I of Assyria (c. 1296 to 1264 B.C.E.) and his successor, Shalmaneser I (c. 1263 to 1234 B.C.E.), had first conquered and then destroyed Hanigalbat, a small remnant of the old Mitannian kingdom. Assyrian power had been growing rapidly, and Assyrian expansion was a threat to both Hatti and Egypt. So, in 1258 B.C.E., 16 years after the battle of Qadesh, Ramesses II and Hattusilis III made peace.

Fortunately, both Egyptian and Hittite copies of the treaty have survived. It declared an end to the fighting between Egypt and Hatti, but it didn't discuss the territories in Syria that had been in dispute. Thus, it implicitly recognized the then-current border between Egyptian and Hittite holdings. Qadesh and most of western Syria would remain Hittite. However, Egyptian control over the Phoenician ports was accepted, and Egypt was granted access to Ugarit, which had been closed to her for almost a century. Moreover, this treaty not only ended the warfare, it made the former enemies allies (see Document 7.1). It also included extradition clauses, as was common in Hittite treaties. However, it stressed that extradited individuals were to be treated leniently once they were returned. The version of the treaty sent from Egypt to

DOCUMENT 7.1

The Treaty Between Hattusilis III and Ramesses II

The terms of the following peace treaty between Hatti and Egypt were worked out in negotiations. Then the Egyptians translated their version of the agreement into Akkadian, inscribed it on a silver tablet, and sent it to Hattusas. Hattusilis III sent his version, also in Akkadian on a silver tablet, to Pi-Ramesse, the Egyptian capital. Ramesses II had the Hittite version translated into Egyptian and inscribed in hieroglyphs on temple walls at Karnak and the Ramesseum. Hattusilis III had the Egyptian version copied on clay tablets for the Hittite archives. These copies of both versions survive, and they do not differ significantly. The following is a translation of the Karnak inscription in which Hattusilis III (or Hattusil III as K. A. Kitchen writes his name) addresses Ramesses II. Material in parentheses or square brackets is part of Kitchen's translation. Boldface printing has been used here to indicate Kitchen's summaries of untranslated portions of the treaty.

"Behold, Hattusil III . . . binds himself by treaty to Ramesses II . . . beginning from today, in order to create peace and good brotherhood between us forever—he being friendly and at peace with me, and I being friendly and at peace with him, forever . . . .

The Great Ruler of Hatti shall never trespass against the land of Egypt, to take anything from it. Ramesses II . . . shall never trespass against the land of Hatti, to take anything from it . . . .

If some other foe should come against the territories of Ramesses II . . . , and he sends word to the Great Ruler of Hatti, saying, 'Come with me as ally against him!',—then the Great Ruler of Hatti shall act [with him, and] shall slay his foes. But if the Great Ruler of Hatti is not disposed to go (personally), then he shall send his troops and chariotry and they shall slay his foes . . . ."

And so reciprocally, Ramesses II for Hattusil.

"If an Egyptian, or two, or three, shall flee, and they come to the Great Ruler of Hatti, then the Great Ruler of Hatti shall seize them and have them brought back to Ramesses II, Great Ruler of Egypt. As for the person handed back to Ramesses II, Great Ruler of Egypt, let not his error be charged against him, let not his house, his wives or his children be destroyed, and let him not be killed . . . ."

And similarly in the other direction, in the paragraph that followed . . . .

"As for these terms, a thousand gods of the deities male and female who belong to Hatti, together with a thousand gods of the deities male and female who belong to Egypt—they are with me as witnesses, and they have heard these terms . . . .

As for him who does not keep them, the thousand gods of Hatti together with the thousand gods of Egypt shall destroy his house, his land and his servants.

As for him who shall keep these terms (written) on this silver tablet, Hittites or Egyptians, . . . the thousand gods of Hatti and the thousand gods of Egypt will cause him to flourish, will make him to live, together with his household, his land and his servants."[2]

Hatti also explicitly recognized the right of Hattusilis' son to succeed him. Thus, Egypt abandoned its previous support for Urhi-Teshub's right to the throne. At the end of the treaty, Egyptian and Hittite deities were invoked as witnesses and guarantors of the pact.

Hattusilis was succeeded by his son, Tudhaliyas IV (c. 1237 to 1209 B.C.E.). However, Hittitologists have uncovered few written sources for his reign or those of his two successors. His early years seem to have been peaceful, allowing him to concentrate on religious reforms and the creation of relief carvings of divine processions at Yazilikaya, near Hattusas. However, Assyrian power continued to grow, causing the defection of several of Hatti's easternmost vassals. At some time during Tudhaliyas' reign, there also may have been a coup that briefly put Kurunta, a son of Muwatallis, in power in Hattusas. If so, Tudhaliyas regained his throne and eventually passed it on to his son and grandson. However, Hatti's power was waning. Around 1180 B.C.E., the empire collapsed due to causes that, as we shall see, are still being debated.

Achaeans and Trojans in Hittite Texts?

Since ancient times, scholars have been arguing about the historicity of the Trojan War described in legends and immortalized in the Greek poet Homer's epic poem, *The Iliad* (composed c. 800 to 750 B.C.E.). Heinrich Schliemann's late–nineteenth-century excavations at Hissarlik in Turkey uncovered a Bronze Age city where Troy was supposedly located. Today, most scholars agree that Troy was a real place and that Hissarlik represents its remains. But what of the events that supposedly took place there? When the Hittite archives were discovered and deciphered, many scholars hoped that these texts would provide the final answers about Troy. However, they have simply furnished more fuel to keep the fiery arguments raging.

Early New Kingdom Hittite sources mention two places, one called Wilusiya (Wilusa in later texts) and the other, Taruisa. These places seem to have been near one another or related in some way. Several scholars have argued that these names were the Hittite versions of Ilios (Wilios in early Greek) and Troia, Homeric terms for Troy. Though these parallels are

disputed by some, their likelihood has been strengthened by recently recognized evidence that Wilusa was located north of the Seha River Land.[3] This information locates Wilusa in the general area of the Troad, the peninsula where Greek tradition placed Troy. Perhaps it is also noteworthy that Egyptian lists of the Hittite allies at the Battle of Qadesh include the Dardany. These might be the *Dardanoi* (Dardanians), a Homeric name for inhabitants of the Troad.

There are other possible connections between the Hittite texts and Greek tradition. The Hittite king Muwatallis II (c. 1295 to 1272 B.C.E.) made a treaty with a king of Wilusa named Alaksandus. This name is clearly similar to Alexandros (Alexander Paris), Homer's Trojan prince. Furthermore, over a span of about two centuries, the Hittites were in contact with a kingdom called Ahhiyawa (or Ahhiya in the earliest texts). This kingdom was sometimes a Hittite friend and at other times a foe, but it was never under Hittite control. An early text mentions conflicts with Attarsiyas or Attarissiyas, "the man of Ahhiya," that take place within western Anatolia and Alasiya (Cyprus). Later texts state that Ahhiyawa had at least nominal control of Milawata (also known as Millawanda) and was harboring a fugitive who had stirred up trouble in western Asia Minor. The evidence indicates that Ahhiyawa was a sea power, but its location is unknown. Most scholars now agree that the people of Ahhiya or Ahhiyawa are Mycenaean Greeks, the Homeric *Achaioi* (originally *Achaiwoi*) or Achaeans.[4] Some go further and claim that Attarsiyas represents Atreus, the name of an early king of Mycenae.[5] Those who strongly believe in the historical accuracy of the early Greek traditions argue that Ahhiyawa was southern Greece with its capital at Mycenae.[6] Others place it in Cyprus or western Asia Minor. Still others, the present author included, think Ahhiyawa probably was a Mycenaean kingdom based on Rhodes or another Aegean island with control over most of the eastern Aegean islands. Occasionally, it also dominated parts of Asia Minor's western coast, particularly Milawata (which probably was the city of Miletus, where Mycenaean remains have been found).

So, is the Trojan War historical or not? Clearly, some parts of Homer's poems accurately reflect the

Late Bronze Age during which the Trojan War supposedly occurred. However, other parts do not. Evidence from archaeology and the Mycenaean Linear B texts show that the epics mix material from early and late parts of the Late Bronze Age and the "Dark Age" that followed.[7] As Trevor Bryce pointed out, "These inconsistencies support the notion of a dynamic oral tradition, in which details can readily be adapted to accord with contemporary fashions, practices, and beliefs."[8] Generations of poets not only passed on early traditions, they also modified, blended, embellished, and romanticized them. Through this process, early ballads about the conflicts between groups of Achaeans, Hittites, and Trojans described in the Hittite texts may have developed into the Trojan War tradition. The final results of this development, the Homeric epics, are wonderful poetic literature, but they are not history.

HITTITE CULTURE

Economy, Society, and Government

From the time they settled in Anatolia through the height of their New Kingdom period, the Hittites remained essentially rural, village-dwelling folk. Their land contained a few moderate-sized towns, but large cities like Hattusas were extremely rare. Most people lived in small, self-sufficient agricultural communities surrounded by arable land from which they eked out a living. Only a few individuals, presumably craftsmen, leased private holdings from the village. Most of the village land was held in common.

The Hittites' principal crops were barley and emmer wheat supplemented by peas, beans, and various fruits, especially apples, figs, and apricots. Vineyards on the hills produced an abundance of grapes that were used primarily to make wine. The villagers had beehives for honey, and obtained dairy products and, occasionally, meat from herds of sheep, goats, and cattle. They also raised horses for warfare, and utilized a Mitannian manual on training them. In the Anatolian mountains, the Hittites found deposits of silver, copper, lead, tin, and iron. However, despite

an earlier generation's emphasis on the Hittite use of iron, it was not the reason for Hittite military dominance.[9] They had not yet perfected the techniques for smelting iron and working it properly. Therefore, the Hittites primarily worked with meteoric iron and used it mostly for ornaments and statues. The few iron weapons they made were no stronger than the bronze ones of the time. Iron remained rare and more precious than gold throughout the second millennium B.C.E.

Like other ancient peoples, the Hittites owned slaves. In early times when slaves probably were few in number, they could own property and had certain legal rights. However, during the New Kingdom Period (c. 1420 to 1180 B.C.E.), the expansion of the Hittite empire greatly increased the number of slaves. They became mere chattel, the property of owners to do with as they pleased. Most New Kingdom slaves were war captives or individuals deported from their homelands after a rebellion. Such slaves were the property of the king. He gave many of them to his nobles, but most he settled on land within Hatti. They remained state property, providing increased agricultural productivity while freeing Hittite citizens for military service.

Hittite society was patriarchal and patrilineal, with the male elders of the local households forming each village's primary governing body. However, free women retained some rights. In certain (though rare) situations, a mother could disown her son. Also, while the father "gave" his daughter in marriage, his wife seems to have had some say in choosing the prospective husband. Hittite law prohibited marriage or sexual intercourse between close relatives, even relatives by marriage. However, there was an exception to this ban. If a man died, his widow would be married first to his brother, then (if the brother died) to his father, then if the father died, to his nephew. This custom is similar the levirate marriage of early Israel (Deuteronomy 25:5–6), which was designed to perpetuate the family of a man who died childless. But since the Hittite law doesn't mention children, it was probably meant to provide for widows who had no one to look after them and to keep them within the extended family.

The example just cited is one of many that suggest that Hittite society was regulated both by written laws and by traditional customs. As in Mesopotamia, there were written law codes expressed in conditional terms—"if a person does such and such, then. . . ." Again, like Mesopotamian codes, the Hittite written laws probably derive from judgments in court cases. Many of their details suggest individual cases, and in one instance, the law even summarizes a case brought before the king. The written laws were probably meant to clarify problem areas in the customary rules of behavior that had caused disputes. It is also clear that the law code was revised on at least one occasion to make it conform to then-current standards. In many places it mentions a punishment used formerly, but states that "now" the king has decreed another (usually milder) penalty.

Localized village self-government coexisted with the higher administration of the kingdom. Provincial governors, garrison commanders, members of palace departments, and other royal officials were drawn from a small number of families or clans that comprised the Hittite aristocracy. The most important of the noble families, of course, was the "Great Family" of the king. Most Hittite kings reserved the highest positions in the state for members of their own family. The wealthy and powerful nobles, "the fighting men and servants of the king," had a kind of feudal relationship to the ruler. They swore to give him loyal service (military and otherwise), and he assigned them estates from his vast land holdings. The aristocratic state officials were expected to cooperate with the local councils of elders to administer justice, perform religious rites, and ensure the common people's safety and welfare.

The Hittite king was the highest authority in the state. He was commander of the armies, chief priest, highest judge, and chief administrator, ultimately responsible for all domestic and foreign affairs. He was a "Great King" controlling many subject states that had their own vassal kings. During the era of the Empire, his power became virtually absolute. New Kingdom kings assumed the titles "My Sun" and "Hero, beloved of the god (or goddess) X." However,

during their lifetimes, they were not believed to be divine. They were the favorites and agents of the Sun Goddess of Arinna, the Weather God of Hatti, and the other deities. Only at death did a king become a god and receive cult offerings at the place where his remains were deposited.

An unusual feature of the Hittite monarchy was the position of the queen. She bore the title *Tawanannas*, and if she outlived her husband, she retained her position. A new king's consort could be only "the king's wife" until the previous *Tawanannas* (usually the king's mother) died. The duties of the *Tawanannas* were essentially religious, but in addition, she often participated in affairs of state. For example, Paduhepa, wife and *Tawanannas* of Hattusilis III, carried on independent correspondence with the Egyptian royal family as well as with several vassal rulers. She also usually was associated with her husband in proclamations and other state documents.

The powerful New Kingdom Hittite rulers maintained their empire as much by diplomacy as by military might. As we have seen, they often used alliances to isolate real or potential enemies. They also bound vassal kings to Hatti by treaties that clearly defined the vassals' relationship with the Great King. Fortunately, a large number of these vassal treaties have survived. They always began with a historical preamble stressing the gracious and beneficial actions Hittite kings had performed for the vassal ruler or state in the past. They then usually defined the vassal's territory and listed his obligations. The primary obligations were exclusive loyalty to the Great King, agreement to support his designated successor, obedience to his demand for soldiers in time of war, turning over to him any of his foes who sought refuge in the vassal state, and annual payment of tribute. For his part, the Hittite king usually promised to protect the vassal against all enemies. The treaties then ended with a list of gods who would punish whoever violated the agreement. Some scholars have compared these vassal treaties to the covenant that the Bible claims God made with the Israelites at Mt. Sinai. Treaties also regulated the relationships between the Hittite king and the rulers of the other great powers. However, since these agreements were between equals, the clauses were reciprocal, imposing equal obligations on both parties (see Document 7.1).

Religion

Many different divinities were worshiped in the various parts of Anatolia. Though the Hittites eventually brought these areas into their empire, they did not impose Hittite religion on them. They allowed local religions and cults to continue and even supported them. They also did not try to integrate these local gods and their own deities into a common hierarchical or mythological system. Nor did they give the names of their own gods to local deities with similar attributes or functions. The local gods usually continued to be worshiped under their own names.

The Hittites' own religion contained a mixture of deities, myths, and rites drawn from many sources, including the pre-Hittite Hattians, Mesopotamians, and especially the Hurrians. Because of these borrowed features, many of the surviving Hittite myths concern deities who were not featured in the official state religion. The two most important deities in the state religion were the Sun Goddess of Arinna and her consort, the Weather God of Hatti (occasionally called the Weather God of Heaven). Arinna was a holy city within a day's journey of Hattusas, though its exact location is unknown. Its cult centered on the sun goddess who was also the principal goddess of fertility. She was hailed as "Queen of the Land of Hatti, Queen of Heaven and Earth, mistress of the kings and queens of the Land of Hatti, directing the government of the King and Queen of Hatti."[10] There was also a sun god who was king of the gods according to some Hittite myths. He is placed first in the lists of gods in some treaties, and hymns and prayers hail him as the lord of justice. However, he is not usually connected with the Sun Goddess of Arinna. Since he is said to arise from the sea, this sun god was possibly introduced into Hatti from an area that had water to its east.

It is the Weather God of Hatti, rather than the sun god, who is emphasized in most Hittite texts. His life-giving rains caused his wife, the Sun Goddess of Arinna, to conceive. He was also a war god (see Figure 7.1; he may be the warrior god depicted in this relief). His power was displayed in thunder, lightning, and the ferocity of storms. As in Syria and Palestine, the Weather God's sacred animal was the bull, which at times could symbolically represent him. Similar

FIGURE 7.1   Bas-Relief of a Hittite Warrior God
This is from the King's Gate at Hattusas (Boghazkoy).
Source: Archaeological Museum, Ankara.
Photo: Hirmer Fotoarchiv, Munich.

weather gods were worshiped throughout Asia Minor, but, as mentioned, these other gods retained their local names. So, when writing the names of most gods, the Hittites used cuneiform ideograms that could be read as different names in different parts of the Empire.

Telepinus, the god of agriculture and fertility, was the child of the Weather God and Sun Goddess. A myth recounted his temporary disappearance, the hardship it produced, and the life and well-being that returned when he was found and brought home. This story embodied the Hittite understanding of nature's yearly cycle of seasons. It also occasionally could be used to explain longer periods of drought, famine, or plague. However the Hittites usually blamed such irregular disasters on the anger of some deity, either Hittite or foreign.

During the New Kingdom, as the Hittites expanded into Syria and eventually conquered Mitanni, Hurrian religion became increasingly influential in Anatolia. Teshub, the Hurrian name for the Weather God, began to be used in Hatti as well as in

Hurrian-speaking areas. Hittite worship of Teshub's consort, the fertility goddess Hepat, also spread widely. Hepat's popularity was especially due to the devotion given her by Hattusilis III's queen, Paduhepa. The Hurrians themselves had borrowed many Mesopotamian gods, often equating them with native Hurrian deities. These they also passed on to the Hittites, especially Ishtar (Shaushka in Hurrian), whom Hattusilis III regarded as his patron goddess. The Hittite Ishtar, however, was more a goddess of war than of love. The great sculptured processions of deities at Yazilikaya near Hattusas depict the essentially Hurrian pantheon worshiped in the latter part of the New Kingdom (see Figure 7.2).

To keep the gods satisfied or to win back their favor when they were angry, the Hittites performed many types of religious rituals. At each cult center, the gods were fed daily by offerings of food and drink (usually beer). The deities also received animal sacrifices, particularly at the great festivals. Even human sacrifice, though rare, was not unknown. A ritual to purify the army after a defeat directs that

FIGURE 7.2   Central Group of Deities in Chamber A at Yazilikaya
Shown: Teshub, The Weather God (standing on the backs of two mountain deities), facing his consort Hepat (standing on a lion).
Source: From John Garstang *The Hitite Empire*. (London: Constable).

they 'cut through' a man, a goat, a puppy, and a little pig; they place half on this side and half on that side, . . . light fires on this side and on that, and the troops walk right through, and when they come to the river they sprinkle water over them.[11]

The text doesn't indicate whether the sacrificial victim was a member of the Hittite army or a prisoner of war. However, he was probably a war captive since another broken text has "a prisoner" listed with other creatures to be sacrificed.

The king, who was the High Priest of all the gods, played the paramount role in most of the major rites and festivals. The most important religious festival, or actually group of festivals, took place in the spring. It consisted of a series of rites at several different cult centers over a period of 38 days. This festival was connected with the reawakening of the earth at springtime. It may also have been the Hittite New Year festival during which the gods fixed the fates for the coming year. Whatever its purpose, it was important enough that Mursilis II once had to leave a military campaign in order to return to Hattusas to celebrate it.

Like most other ancient peoples, the Hittites used various means to determine the will of the gods. Deities could take the initiative in communicating with humans by sending unusual signs or portents or delivering messages through dreams or ecstatic seizures. Usually, though, mortals had to discover the divine will through the process of divination. Hittites generally took omens before military campaigns or other important actions. They also used them to learn the reasons for plagues or other disasters. The three major Hittite methods of divination were essentially derived from Mesopotamia. Priests could sacrifice an animal and study the pattern of folds on its liver or other entrails. They could observe the activities of birds (some actions were considered favorable and others unfavorable). Or, female soothsayers could pose questions to the gods, then cast lots to learn the answers.

In addition to the major rituals, Hittite religion contained many folk rites to purify individuals, ward off evil, reconcile brothers, and otherwise deal with personal problems. One of these rites, designed to alleviate sickness or trouble, is similar to the Israelite scapegoat ritual (Leviticus 16:8–10). A priestess went through elaborate ceremonies that ended with her magically transferring the problems to a captive mouse. She then released the mouse, beseeching it to carry the troubles far away.

Languages and Literature

Many different languages were spoken within the Hittite Empire, and phrases or brief passages from several of them are found in Hittite texts. However, the overwhelming majority of the documents in the Hittite archives were written in either Akkadian or Hittite. As noted in Chapter 6, Akkadian, the Semitic language of Mesopotamia, had become the international language of diplomacy in the Near East during the Late Bronze Age. Thus, most Hittite diplomatic letters and treaties were written in Akkadian (see Document 7.1). Since the Sumerians originally created the cuneiform script borrowed to write Hittite as well as Akkadian, there were also a few Sumerian-Hittite word lists at Hattusas. These were used to teach scribes the Hittite meanings of common Sumerian (and Akkadian) ideograms.

Naturally, many of the tablets excavated at Boghazkoy (Hattusas) were written in Hittite (which, as we have seen, its speakers actually called Nesite), the Indo-European language of the rulers of the Hittite Empire. In addition to documents in Akkadian and Hittite, the Hittite tablets contained many passages and a few complete works in Hurrian. The Hurrian sections of Hittite texts are generally religious songs or ritual utterances. A fragmentary Hurrian translation of the Babylonian *Epic of Gilgamesh* was also found at Hattusas. However, the most important Hurrian document in the Hittite archives is a treatise on horse training by a Mitannian named Kikkuli. Though most of the text is in Hurrian, many of its technical terms are in an Indo-Iranian language similar to Sanskrit. As we saw in Chapter 3, this Indo-Iranian tongue may have been spoken by the people who first introduced the horse-drawn war chariot into the Near East. It may also have been the language originally spoken by the rulers of Mitanni.

Other languages are found in Hittite texts only in isolated passages, phrases, or words within longer documents. A number of religious incantations and prayers in Hattian, the pre-Hittite language of the area, occur in ritual texts. Also, there are more extensive passages in a language called Luwian. This Indo-European language, closely related to Hittite, was spoken in parts of western, southwestern, and southern Asia Minor, including Arzawa. Around the middle of the second millennium B.C.E., Luwian speakers seem to have created a hieroglyphic script to write their language. The Hittites used this hieroglyphic writing on a few monuments and to write Hittite royal names on seals during the New Kingdom era (see Figure 7.3). It survived the collapse of the Hittite Empire and became the main script of the later Neo-Hittite kingdoms (see Chapter 8).

In addition to legal texts, diplomatic documents, ritual texts, and "scientific" works on omens, horoscopes, and medicine, the Hittite archives also contained compositions of a more literary nature. These

FIGURE 7.3 A Hittite Royal Seal Impression
The King's name, Muwatallis, appears in the Hittite (Luwian) hieroglyphic script and cuneiform.
Source: From O.R. Gurney, *The Hittites.* (London: Penguin Books).

include epics, myths, legends, royal testaments, and annals. The inspiration and models for most of these works came from Mesopotamia by way of the Hurrians. The *Epic of Gilgamesh* seems to have been a Hittite favorite. In addition to a Hurrian version, at Hattusas, archaeologists uncovered fragmentary copies of the original Akkadian epic and a Hittite translation of it. They also found Hittite versions of legends about Sargon of Agade and Naram-Sin.

Many of the Hittite myths were Hurrian in origin. One of the most complete myths described how the god Kumarbi overthrew Anu, the divine King of Heaven. In the process, he bit off and swallowed Anu's genitals. However, Anu's seed impregnated Kumarbi with several gods, including the Weather God, Teshub. When Teshub emerged, he vanquished Kumarbi, thus becoming the new King of Heaven. This story seems to have inspired the Greek myth recorded in Hesiod's *Theogony*. According to Hesiod, after overthrowing and emasculating his father Ouranos, Kronos swallowed each of his newborn sons (except Zeus, for whom his mother substituted a wrapped-up stone) to prevent any of them from challenging him. When Zeus grew up, he defeated and replaced his father as ruler of the heavens. Many scholars are also convinced that the *Epic of Gilgamesh* influenced the development of parts of the Heracles (Hercules) legend. These Near Eastern stories (in addition to Mesopotamian mathematics and time-reckoning systems) probably reached Greece from Phoenicia via the Hurrians and/or western Asia Minor via the Hittites.

The most fascinating elements of Hittite literature are their historical writings: preambles to official proclamations and treaties, royal testaments, and annals. It has already been mentioned that the Hittites used introductory recitations of past events to provide the context and/or vindication for specific decrees or pacts. Like the Mesopotamians, Hittites believed that the past was not just a meaningless series of accidental events. It had a pattern from which humans could draw lessons. Mursilis II (c. 1321 to 1295 B.C.E.) took the step of using historical narrative not just to explain particular proclamations or treaties, but to clarify and justify the events of his entire reign. Furthermore, he not only produced annals for his own reign, but also for that of his father, Suppiluliumas. Thus, James G. Macqueen goes so far as to argue that "in thus examining the past, stressing its value and interpreting its patterns in terms of human behaviour" the Hittites can claim to have anticipated Herodotus as Father of History.[12]

Later kings followed Mursilis II's example, though often only fragments of their annals have survived. The Hittite historical writings are similar to those of Mesopotamia and Egypt in that their main purpose was to glorify the gods and explain the actions of kings. Success and victory were seen as the result of divine favor and obedience to the gods' will. Calamity could occur because someone offended the deities. However, the Hittites believed that disasters could also be due to human errors or incompetence. They were willing to acknowledge that even their kings made mistakes. For example, Mursilis II conceded in his *Comprehensive Annals* that his father's preoccupation with Syria allowed the Kaskans to devastate and occupy portions of Hatti. Furthermore, sometimes the Hittites went so far as to admit royal sins. Perhaps such admissions were inspired by the Mesopotamian story that the god Enlil had destroyed the Akkadian Empire because Naram-Sin had looted Enlil's temple in Nippur. Similarly, in his plague prayers, Mursilis II confesses that the plague that ravaged Hittite lands from the last years of Suppiluliumas into his own reign was due to Suppiluliumas's transgressions. The Hittite king had failed to perform a sacrifice for the River Euphrates. He had also broken two oaths, first by rebelling against and killing his brother, and later, by violating a treaty with Egypt when he invaded Amka. These and similar acknowledgments are like a breath of fresh air after one has been reading Egyptian New Kingdom accounts in which the king can do no wrong and every misfortune is blamed on his advisors, his cowardly army, or some other scapegoat.

The Hittites produced animated narratives about the past with vividly drawn characters and clearly described, realistic events. They also recognized that the present had developed out of the past in ways that inquiring rational minds could comprehend. Thus, we may legitimately debate whether they should be credited with creating the concept of history and, therefore, be designated the first true historians. At the least, the Hittites are probably the only people who have the right to contend for that honor with the ancient Israelites and Greeks.

THE TWILIGHT OF THE EGYPTIAN EMPIRE (C. 1293–1150 B.C.E.)

The Empire's Final Flash of Greatness

Ramesses I, the general who succeeded Horemheb, had a very short reign (c. 1293 to 1291 B.C.E.). However, he passed the throne to his son, Seti I (c. 1291–1279 B.C.E.), thus initiating the Nineteenth Dynasty (see Table 7.2). Seti served as general and vizier under his father, and he seems to have become co-regent during Ramesses I's last two or three months on the throne. As we have seen, he conducted several campaigns in Lebanon and Syria, trying to regain Egyptian territory. Seti I also conducted campaigns against the Libyans and Nubians, securing Egypt's western and southern borders.

TABLE 7.2

Chronology of the Nineteenth and Twentieth Dynasties

(Not all rulers of the Twentieth Dynasty are listed. All dates are B.C.E.)

The Nineteenth Dynasty	**1293–1185**
Ramesses I	1293–1291
Seti I	1291–1279
Ramesses II	1279–1212
Merneptah	1212–1202
Amenmose, Seti II, Siptah and Tawosret	1202–1185
The Twentieth Dynasty	**1185–1070**
Sethnakhte	1185–1182
Ramesses III	1182–1151
Ramesses IV through Ramesses XI	1151–1070

Seti's reign is most remembered, though, for his building projects and the quality of their decoration. During the reigns of Horemheb and Ramesses I, plans had been made for a large new **Hypostyle Hall** in the Temple of Amun at Karnak. However, the work had barely begun by the time Seti I came to the throne. Seti completed at least half of this massive structure, leaving the rest to be finished by his son and successor, Ramesses II. The Great Hypostyle Hall, considered by many the most breathtaking sight in Egypt, is 335 feet wide and 174 feet long. The huge Paris landmark, the Notre Dame Cathedral, could fit within the walls of this single hall! It contains 134 gigantic columns—a dozen 75-foot-high central columns with open papyrus flower capitals that measure 50 feet in circumference. Along the sides, there are 122 slightly shorter columns with closed bud capitals (see Figure 7.4). The reliefs decorating this and other monuments of Seti's reign are considered among the best ever produced in ancient Egypt.

Seti undertook many other construction projects, including a temple for Osiris at Abydos. A noteworthy feature of this temple was the so-called "Hall of Records" or "Abydos King List," where Seti I and his young son Ramesses are depicted standing before rows of cartouches of earlier kings stretching back to the beginnings of Egyptian history. Another extraordinary work was his tomb in the Valley of the Kings. It is not only the longest and deepest in the valley, it is also generally acknowledged to be the most exquisitely decorated, as well.

Ramesses II (c. 1279 to 1212 B.C.E.) became co-regent with his father for a year or two at the end of Seti's reign. However, he dated his reign only from the time of Seti's death. At that time, the Hittites were again flexing their muscles in Syria. Recognizing the need for a marshaling point closer to Canaan than Memphis, Ramesses began building a new Delta capital, Pi-Ramesse (or Per-Ramesses, "House [or Domain] of Ramesses"), partly on the site of ancient Avaris. It was here that he mobilized the armies for his Asiatic campaigns.

Ramesses' attempts to regain control over Syria were unsuccessful, as we have seen. Nevertheless, he claimed to have won a great victory at Qadesh and

FIGURE 7.4   The Great Hypostyle Hall of the Temple of Amun at Karnak

This view, looking across the Great Hall, shows side columns in the foreground. Two of the taller central columns are visible beyond them.
Source: Courtesy of the author.

had scenes of his "triumph" carved on his major monuments. Though not as great a conqueror as he wanted people to believe, Ramesses II truly was a great builder. He erected a palace, temples, and other structures at Pi-Ramesse, which became a large and beautiful city. At Thebes, he finished the Great Hypostyle Hall at Karnak, added a court and pylon to the Luxor Temple, and constructed a grand mortuary temple (the Ramesseum) and a tomb for himself. At Memphis, he enlarged the Temple of Ptah and had his son Khaemwaset construct a new shrine and underground burial place for future Apis Bulls (the Serapeum). He also had several other temples built in Egypt and Nubia. In addition, he laid claim to many of the monuments of his predecessors, placing his name on earlier temples and royal statues.

However, these other works pale in comparison with his greatest construction project, the temples at Abu Simbel in Nubia. These two temples were carved directly out of the sandstone mountains. The facade of the Great Temple is like a large recessed pylon with four gigantic (65-feet-high) seated images of Ramesses II in front of it (see Figure 7.5). Its chambers extend some 200 feet into the mountain, ending in a sanctuary with statues of four deities cut out of the rock. Twice a year, on February 21 and October 21, the rising sun came directly through the entrance and bathed three of the statues in light—the deified Ramesses II flanked by Amun and Re-Horakhty. The fourth god, Ptah, a god of darkness and the underworld, remained in shadow. The smaller temple nearby had four standing statues of Ramesses II and two of his favorite wife, Nefertari, carved into its facade. This temple was dedicated to the goddess Hathor and her living personification, Nefertari. The creation of Lake Nasser by the construction of the High Dam at Aswan in the 1960s would have permanently flooded these monuments. So, through an international effort, the temples were cut into blocks and removed from the mountainside. They were reassembled on the mountaintop, beyond the reach of the lake's waters (see Figure 7.6).

By the time Ramesses II became king, he already had two major wives, Nefertari and Isisnofret, and at least five sons and two daughters. During his more than 66-year reign, he would take many more wives, including his younger sister, three of his daughters, and several Hittite, Syrian, and Babylonian princesses. Before his death, he would boast of having sired more than 100 children. However, he lived so long that many of his children died before he did. It is thought that many of his sons, at least those who predeceased

FIGURE 7.5   The Facade of the Great Temple of Ramesses II at Abu Simbel

Source: Courtesy of the author.

FIGURE 7.6 **The Abu Simbel Temples on the Shore of Lake Nasser**
Source: Courtesy of the author.

him, were buried in a single gigantic tomb recently uncovered in the Valley of the Kings.[13] Merneptah, Ramesses II's thirteenth son, was already 60 years old when he finally succeeded his father on the throne.

Invasions of the Sea Peoples

Merneptah (c. 1212 to 1202 B.C.E.) immediately had to deal with a series of major problems. Egypt's Hittite allies appealed for help because of famine in their land. So, the Egyptian pharaoh responded by dispatching shiploads of grain to Hatti. Then, in his third year, whether prompted by similar agricultural problems or other causes, revolts broke out in Palestine and Syria. Merneptah quickly moved northward and crushed the opposition, according to his famous Victory Stele (see Document 7.2). However, he was not able to savor his triumph very long. During his fifth year (c. 1208 B.C.E.), Libyan tribes, supplemented by five other groups (Shardana, Shekelesh, Akawasha, Lukka, and Tursha), invaded the Egyptian Delta. Merneptah's inscription on a wall of the Karnak temple suggests that these marauders also were experiencing famine:[14]

> They spend their time going about the land, fighting, to fill their bodies daily. They come to the land of Egypt, to seek the necessities of their mouths.

The Libyans' allies are described as "northerners" or "of the Countries of the Sea," so scholars have come to call them "Sea Peoples." Some of these Sea Peoples had been known in the eastern Mediterranean area for more than a century. One of the mid-fourteenth-century B.C.E. Amarna Letters (EA 38) refers to piratical raids on coastal towns in Cyprus and Syria by the Lukka people. The Shardana also had launched surprise attacks by sea, occasionally pillaging coastal areas of Egypt from the time of Amenhotep III on. Ramesses II complained about these pirates "whose renown crossed the sea" and who "came boldly [sailing] in their warships from the midst of the sea, none being able to withstand them."[15] Because of the Shardana's reputation as warriors, Nineteenth Dynasty pharaohs hired contingents of them as mercenary troops. They were even members of Ramesses II's royal bodyguard.

While the Libyans and Sea Peoples were attacking the Delta, Nubia also revolted. However, Merneptah was able to defeat the northern raiders quickly, killing about 6,000 and capturing 9,000. He then rushed southward and crushed Nubia before the revolt had become widespread. Egypt and its Empire were saved for the moment. The Nineteenth Dynasty ended with four brief conflict-filled reigns, the last being that of a queen,

DOCUMENT 7.2
Merneptah's Victory Stele

This series of hymns primarily commemorates Merneptah's victory over the Libyans and their allies in his fifth regnal year. The inscription uses the terms Rebu and Tehenu (as well as Temeh and Meshwesh) for the Libyans. These words once denoted separate tribes in Libya, but by Merneptah's time, they had become largely interchangeable. Rebu likely was pronounced "Lebu" or "Libu" (the Egyptians used the sign for "r" to also write "l" which wasn't used in their language). This tribal name is probably the source of "Libya," the classical and present name for the area. The closing poem celebrates the pharaoh's triumphs over all of Egypt's enemies, including the Asiatics he defeated in his third year. It not only mentions cites in southern Canaan (Ashkelon and Gezer) and northern Canaan (Yanoam), but also a people or tribe named *Ysyry'r*. Almost all scholars agree that this term should be read "Israel" (*Yishra'el* in Hebrew), which at that time was probably a small group located in Palestine's central hills. This is the earliest known reference to Israel in a nonbiblical source. Thus, the monument has also become known as "the Israel Stele." In the following rendition of the inscription, W. Stiebing has added the explanatory material in square brackets to John A. Wilson's translation.[16]

> Woe to Rebu [Lebu, i.e., the Libyans]! They have ceased to live (in) the pleasant fashion of one who goes about in the field. Their going *is checked* in a single day. The Tehenu *are consumed* in a single year, for Seth has turned his back upon their chief; their settlements are abandoned *on his account* . . . .

Great joy has arisen in Egypt;
Jubilation has gone forth in the towns of Egypt.
They talk about the victories
Which Mer-ne-Ptah Hotep-hir-Maat made in Tehenu:
"How amiable is he, the victorious ruler!
How exalted is the king among the gods! . . ."
The princes are prostrate, saying: "Mercy!" [literally, *Shalom*]
Not one raises his head among the Nine Bows [traditional enemies of Egypt].
Desolation is for Tehenu; Hatti is pacified;
Plundered is the Canaan with every evil;
Carried off is Ashkelon; seized upon is Gezer;
Yanoam is made as that which does not exist;
Israel is laid waste, his seed is not;
Hurru [Syria and Palestine] is become a widow for Egypt!
All lands together, they are pacified;
Everyone who was restless, he has been bound
by the King of Upper and Lower Egypt: Ba-en-Re Meri-Amon; the Son of Re: Mer-ne-Ptah
    Hotep-hir-Maat, given life like Re every day.

Tawosret, who had declared herself pharaoh. Ramesses III (c. 1182 to 1151 B.C.E.), the second king of the Twentieth Dynasty, largely restored Egypt's internal stability. However, the turbulence outside the Nile Valley continued unabated. Libyan warriors as well as "clans, wives, children, and cattle"[17] again invaded the Delta in Ramesses III's fifth and eleventh years (c. 1178 and 1172 B.C.E.). Between these two incursions, Ramesses III had to repel a massive migration that had already progressed through Asia Minor and Syria. Inscriptions and reliefs on Ramesses III's mortuary temple at Medinet Habu record the turmoil:

> The foreign countries made a conspiracy in their islands. All at once the lands were removed and scattered in the fray. No land could stand before their arms, from Hatti, Qode [Cilicia], Carchemish, Arzawa, and Alashiya [Cyprus] on, being cut off at (one time). A camp was set up in one place in Amor [Amurru, coastal Syria]. They desolated its people, and its land was like that which has never come into being. They were coming forward toward Egypt, while the flame was prepared before them. Their confederation was the Philistines [actually Peleset], Tjeker, Shekelesh, Denyen, and Weshesh, lands united. They laid their hands upon the land as far as the circuit of the earth, their hearts confident and trusting: "Our plans will succeed!"[18]

The invading Sea Peoples moved in a two-pronged attack. One group occupied a fleet of ships that sailed along the coast while the other traveled overland. However, in addition to infantry and chariot warriors, the land force included ox-drawn carts containing women, children, and family possessions (see Figure 7.7). Thus, the Egyptian reliefs seem to depict entire tribes of people on the move. Moreover, the texts also indicate that the force included clans, not just warriors.[19]

Ramesses III defeated the Sea Peoples' army in a battle fought somewhere in Canaan or near the borders of Egypt. However, the attacking fleet sailed on to Egypt itself. There, in one of the eastern branches of the Nile, the Egyptian navy, supported by archers firing arrows from the river banks, decimated the enemy force. Egypt was saved, but she had been severely weakened. The *Harris Papyrus*, a long

record of the piety and benefactions of Ramesses III, states that the king settled the Sea Peoples as mercenaries in garrison towns of Palestine and Syria. But soon after his death, Egypt lost control over Canaan. The garrisons of Sea Peoples, perhaps supplemented by more recent arrivals, gained control of Dor and other coastal sites.

Who were these mysterious Sea Peoples and where did they come from? Of the many groups mentioned in Egyptian texts—Akawasha, Denyen, Lukka, Peleset, Shardana, Shekelesh, Tjeker, Tursha, and Weshesh—only two can be identified with a high degree of probability. It is generally agreed that the Peleset almost certainly were the Philistines (Hebrew *Pelishtim*, or in the singular, *Peleshet*) mentioned frequently in the Bible, and that the Lukka were the Classical Lycians. Both of these groups have connections with the Aegean area.

Biblical tradition claimed that the Philistines came to Canaan from Caphtor (actually, Kaphtor),[20] the place called Kaptara in Akkadian texts and Keftiu in Egyptian ones. Other biblical texts refer to Philistines as "Cretans" ("Cherethites") and to the southern part of the Philistine coast as "the Cretan Negev."[21] The Egyptians described Keftiu as a place "in the midst of the Great Green" (the Mediterranean Sea) and depicted its people wearing Minoan-Mycenaean style costumes and carrying Minoan-Mycenaean types of objects. So, Keftiu/Kaphtor probably was the ancient Near Eastern name for Crete or the Minoan-Mycenaean culture area in general (the Aegean region). The non-Semitic names of two out of five local kings in a recently discovered inscription from Ekron and the few Philistine words preserved in the Bible also support the biblical tradition that the Philistines came from outside of Palestine and specifically, from the Aegean area.

Moreover, archaeologists have traced much of the Philistine material culture to the Aegean. They have shown that many of the characteristic types of pottery found in twelfth-century strata of Philistine cities in Palestine developed from Mycenaean prototypes (the style known as Mycenaean or Late Helladic IIIC:1b). Moreover, it is important to note that Philistine pottery of Aegean type was not imported

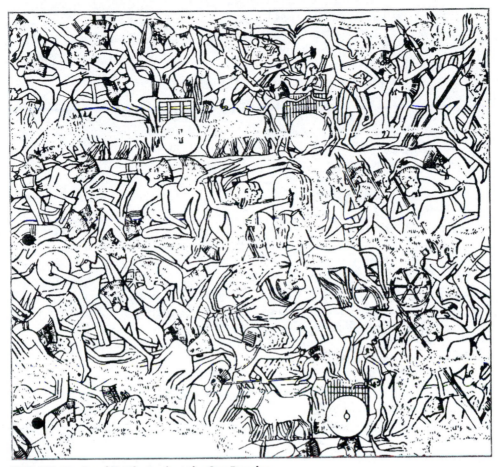

FIGURE 7.7   Land Battle Against the Sea Peoples

This is a detail from a line drawing of a relief on Ramesses III's mortuary temple at Medinet Habu. Note the oxcarts carrying women and children.

Source: Courtesy of the Oriental Institute of the University of Chicago.

or copied from imported wares. Archaeologists have found very little imported Mycenaean IIIC pottery in Palestine. Thus, the Philistine pottery must have been produced in Palestine by potters with Aegean traditions.[22] While the Mycenaean influence is predominant, some Philistine pottery types reflect Cypriot styles, suggesting a connection with that island as well.[23] We know that many Mycenaeans settled in Cyprus during the thirteenth century B.C.E. There was an additional influx of Aegean groups during the early twelfth century B.C.E. So the evidence

seems to support Trude Dothan's conclusion that Philistine pottery "was not the product of a people coming directly from their country of origin with a homogeneous tradition but rather reflects the cultural influences picked up along the way in the long, slow, meandering migration from their Aegean homeland."[24]

The Lukka were also from the Aegean area, but they were not Mycenaeans. We have seen that some of them were known as seafaring pirates at the time of Akhenaton. They also were Hittite subjects who were part of the Hittite army that fought Ramesses II at Qadesh (c. 1274 B.C.E.). Hittite and Ugaritic sources indicate that the Lukka lands probably were located in southwestern or southern Asia Minor (see Map 7.1). The south-southwestern corner of Asia Minor was still called Lycia (*Lukia* in Greek) in Classical times. Furthermore, the language spoken in Classical Lycia was related to the Luwian tongue spoken in the area during the Bronze Age.

It is likely that the other Sea Peoples mentioned in the Egyptian accounts also came largely from the eastern Aegean region and coastal Asia Minor, for their apparel and ships are of Aegean type.[25] Some scholars have suggested that the Akawasha are equivalent to the Hittite Ahhiyawans and should be identified with Homer's Achaeans (*Achaiwoi*). The Denyen (or Danuna) have often been equated with the Danaans (*Danaoi*), a synonym for "Achaeans" in the *Iliad*. However, others connect them with Cilicia in southern Asia Minor and derive their name from the city of Adana. The Tursha may be from the place the Hittites called Taruisa (or Taruisha) located in western Asia Minor. As we have seen, some think that Taruisa was equivalent to Troia (Troy). On the other hand, other scholars have equated the Tursha with the Tyrrhenians (*Tursenoi* in Greek). The Greek name refers to the Etruscans who, according to Herodotus, moved from Asia Minor to Italy. The Shardana and Shekelesh have often been identified as Sardinians and Sicilians (*Sikeloi*). However, supporters of this identification disagree about whether these tribes were arriving in the Near East from Sardinia and Sicily or whether the names belonged to groups who later settled in Sardinia and Sicily and gave their names to those islands. The Tjeker may be the Teucrians (*Teukroi*), based on Greek tradition that says the hero Teukros moved to Cyprus after the Trojan War. However, some scholars argue that Tjeker should be read Tjekel and regard it and Shekelesh as alternate renderings of *Sikeloi*. Finally, it is possible that the Weshesh had some connection with Wilusa in northeast Asia Minor. All of these possible identifications, however, are questionable. None is as probable as the equation of the Peleset with the Philistines and the Lukka with the Lycians.[26]

THE COLLAPSE OF BRONZE AGE SOCIETIES IN THE EASTERN MEDITERRANEAN

The Mycenaean Kingdoms

During the thirteenth century B.C.E., Greek-speaking Mycenaeans, primarily settled in southern Greece, dominated the Aegean world. As mentioned in Chapter 6, around 1500 B.C.E. or shortly thereafter, mainland groups invaded Crete, destroyed the Minoan palaces, and took control of the island. The descendants of these invaders continued to rule Crete from Knossos into the thirteenth century B.C.E. We have noted that there were also Mycenaean settlements on Rhodes and at Miletus in Asia Minor, perhaps ruled by the king of Ahhiyawa referred to in Hittite texts.

Trade flourished during the thirteenth century B.C.E., and Mycenaean products were in great demand throughout the eastern Mediterranean. However, peace did not always accompany prosperity in the Aegean region. A few palaces, like the ones at Pylos and Knossos, were defended only by geography or by outlying forts, but most royal dwellings and administrative centers were enclosed within strongly fortified citadels. The rulers of Gla, Athens, Tiryns, and Mycenae found it necessary to enlarge or strengthen their fortification walls during the thirteenth century, and around the middle of the century, the palace at Thebes in Boeotia was burned. The Mycenaean palace at Knossos in Crete probably was destroyed about the same time.[27]

Then came the widespread disasters of the early twelfth century B.C.E. Around 1200 B.C.E., Pylos was destroyed. At about the same time, Thebes was burned again, along with Gla, Iolkos, and Tiryns. Portions of Mycenae were burned at least once and possibly twice during the early twelfth century B.C.E., but this great citadel survived. Then, around 1150 B.C.E., Mycenae, too, was razed and abandoned. Population shifts were immense, with refugees settling in Attica, Achaea, the Ionian Islands (especially the island of Kephallenia) off the west coast of Greece, and the far-off island of Cyprus. Meanwhile, areas of Thessaly,

Boeotia, and parts of the Peloponnese, which formerly had contained many settlements, became seriously depopulated for about a century. The total population of Greece declined by as much as 75 percent. The areas that continued to be settled experienced a marked decline in material culture, and the cultural unity of the Mycenaean Age came to an end. The highly centralized Mycenaean palaces with their elaborate bureaucracies disappeared, and small, poor agricultural villages took their place.

The situation was much the same in Crete, where there was a great decline in population, and the material culture became much poorer. People abandoned the previously well-populated coastal areas (especially in South Crete) and built new villages in the hills or in other easily defensible positions. Without the palace bureaucracies to maintain it, knowledge of writing was lost here and in Greece. A "Dark Age" descended over the entire Aegean region.

The Demise of the Hittite Empire

The Hittite Empire, the dominant power in the Near East during most of the thirteenth century B.C.E., suddenly collapsed just after 1200 B.C.E. Only a few texts survive from the reign of Suppiluliumas II, the last Hittite king. However, they make several general references to discontent among the Hittite people. Possibly the population's displeasure was due to food shortages that probably afflicted the Hittites around this time. Merneptah had sent them several shiploads of grain around 1212 B.C.E. Then, about a generation later, among the last letters received by the king of Ugarit before his city's destruction were three mentioning famine in Hatti. One demanded that Ugarit furnish a ship to transport two thousand measures of grain to Cilicia immediately. It is, the letter says, a matter of life or death![28]

Meanwhile, Hittite vassals in western Anatolia and elsewhere rebelled. As we have seen, Egyptian records claim that the Sea Peoples also moved through Asia Minor at this time. The Hittites raised an army and navy from their citizens and faithful vassals and deployed them to meet these threats. However, this move left vassals like the kings of Alasiya

(Cyprus) and Ugarit virtually defenseless. Ammurapi, the last king of Ugarit, answered an appeal for help from the king of Alasiya:

> "My father," writes Ammurapi, "behold, the enemy's ships came (here); my cities(?) were burned, and they did evil things in my country. Does not my father know that all my troops and chariots(?) are in the Hittite country, and all my ships are in the land of Lycia [Lukka]?... Thus, the country is abandoned to itself. May my father know it: the seven ships of the enemy that came here inflicted much damage upon us." He asks the king of Alashia to inform him if other ships of the enemy were noticed.[29]

Whether the ships attacking Cyprus and coastal Syria were opportunistic local pirates or contingents of the Sea Peoples is unknown. Early in the twelfth century B.C.E., the Hittite and Ugaritic records became silent. So we also have no information about what happened to the Hittite army and navy to which Ugarit had committed its troops and ships. It is highly probable that the Hittite forces were defeated, for a wave of destruction swept over the Hittite Empire. Hattusas was violently sacked and burned along with Troy, Miletus, Alaca Hüyük, Alisar, Tarsus, Alalakh, Ugarit, Qatna, Qadesh, and most other cities of the empire. Many were never occupied again. The Egyptians claimed that Carchemish was also destroyed, but it seems to have been one of the few cities that managed to survive the crisis relatively intact.

The Hittite Empire was gone, but Hittite culture did not totally disappear. In Syria during the twelfth century B.C.E., several small kingdoms arose (one of which was Carchemish) whose rulers bore Hittite royal names and whose religious, artistic, and epigraphic traditions derived from those of the Hittite Empire. The Assyrians called these kingdoms "Hatti," the old name for the Hittite Empire. However, the language of these "Neo-Hittites" was not the Hittite of the former rulers of Hattusas. It was a dialect of Luwian, the related Indo-European language that had been spoken by groups in western and southern Asia Minor during the Bronze Age. Obviously, people from Cilicia and/or areas further west migrated to Syria during the upheavals of the early twelfth century B.C.E.

Probably led by descendants of various branches of the old Hittite royal line, these migrants established several small kingdoms and tried to maintain many of the Hittite traditions under which their ancestors had lived. Other Luwian-speaking groups preserved some elements of Hittite civilization in eastern Cilicia and in south-central Anatolia, the area the Hittites had called the Lower Land.

Meanwhile, migrations were taking place elsewhere within Asia Minor (see Map 7.2). The Kaska people who had long lived on the southern shore of the Black Sea north of Hatti probably moved southward into the old Hittite heartland. Later Luwian

inscriptions from Tabal, the former Hittite Lower Land, indicate that people called the Kasku (almost certainly descendants of the Kaska) were settled in what previously had been Hatti. A Kaska army even penetrated into northern Syria during the reign of the Assyrian king Tiglath-pileser I (c. 1115 to 1077 B.C.E.). Many scholars think it likely that the Kaska, not the Sea Peoples, destroyed Hattusas (as they had at times in the past) and then occupied the surrounding territory.

Another group, known as the Muski, also migrated through Anatolia in the twelfth century. Like the Kaska, the Muski got as far as northern Syria

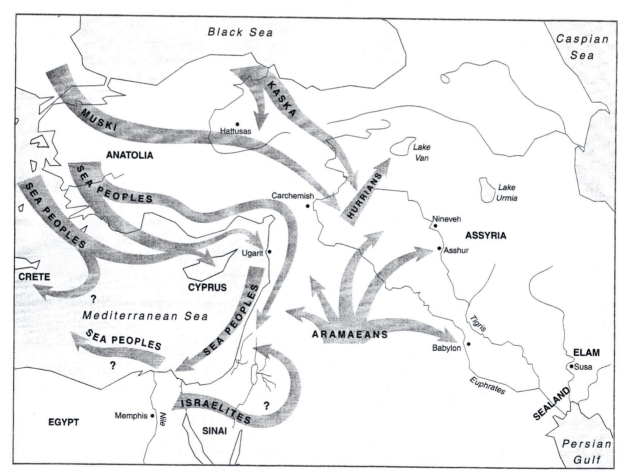

MAP 7.2   Migrations at the End of the Bronze Age (c. 1200–1100 B.C.E.)

before the Assyrians drove them back. Some think they allied themselves with the Kaska and participated in the destruction of Hattusas and Hatti. Possibly the Muski were the people the Greeks called Mysians, who legend says entered Asia Minor from Thrace with another group known as the Phrygians. The Muski seem to have settled eventually in west-central Anatolia, where they probably amalgamated with the Phrygians by the eighth century B.C.E.

The End of Egyptian Power

The Egyptian vassal states in Syria and Palestine also experienced devastation and destruction, probably due mostly to the Sea Peoples' invasion. However, Egypt itself weathered the twelfth-century-B.C.E. tumult better than most other areas of the eastern Mediterranean. The fabric of Egyptian society and civilization remained essentially intact, in contrast to the almost total collapse that occurred in Mycenaean and Hittite lands. Egypt also successfully prevented groups of Libyans and Sea Peoples from occupying the Nile Delta. However, not even Egypt could maintain her former strength and grandeur in the face of the widespread calamities. Egyptian control over Canaan came to an end around the middle of the twelfth century B.C.E., and there are indications of hardship and trouble within the Nile Valley itself during this era.

From the time of Ramesses III (c. 1182 to 1151 B.C.E.) through that of Ramesses VII (c. 1133 to 1127 B.C.E.), the price of emmer wheat in Egypt gradually rose to a level eight (and for at time, 24) times higher than its earlier rate. It remained at a high level for the rest of the century.[30] Only in the time of Ramesses X (c. 1108 to 1098 B.C.E.) did the price drop, but even then it remained twice what it was at the beginning of the twelfth century B.C.E. During this period, the government also sometimes failed to pay the generous grain and other food rations owed to the elite artisans who cut and decorated the royal tombs. The craftsmen staged strikes at least six times between Ramesses III's twenty-ninth regnal year (c. 1154 B.C.E.) and the third year of Ramesses X (c. 1106 B.C.E.) because their grain allotments were months in arrears.

Grain shortages and inflation also encouraged other evils. Corruption among public officials was rampant. Royal tombs were robbed, often by the very craftsmen who had worked on them. During the reign of Ramesses IX (c. 1126 to 1108 B.C.E.), eight of these tomb robbers were caught and forced to confess. Obviously, they had many accomplices—necropolis police, priests, boatmen, merchants, various officials, and perhaps even the mayor of Western Thebes himself. However, no high officials were ever brought to justice. It is interesting that the item the thieves most often purchased with their loot was food. Another large share went as bribes to granary guards and officials so that the thieves could obtain grain in the future.[31]

Banditry and civil war also destabilized society. Several times during the latter half of the twelfth century B.C.E., marauding groups of Egyptians and Libyan mercenaries terrorized the area around Thebes, looting and killing. On one occasion they destroyed an entire town. Anarchy broke out in Thebes, and looters stripped the gold and copper from the walls, doors, and statues of the city's temples. By the time Ramesses XI died (c. 1070 B.C.E.) and the Twentieth Dynasty ended, Upper Egypt was being ruled by an army commander of Libyan descent. The era of Egyptian greatness was over.

The Decline of Assyria and Babylonia

During the late fourteenth and early thirteenth centuries B.C.E., Assyria had grown into a major power. Asshur-Uballit I (c. 1353 to 1313) established Assyria's independence from Kassite Babylonia, claimed the status of a "Great King," and initiated correspondence with Egypt. Then under Adad-Nirari I (c. 1295 to 1264) and Shalmaneser I (c. 1263 to 1234), Assyria had advanced her power into eastern Syria. Shalmaneser's successor, Tukulti-Ninurta I (c. 1233 to 1197), not only extended Assyrian territory northward at the expense of the Hittites, but he finally succeeded in conquering Babylon and making it an Assyrian vassal. By the time he died, Assyria controlled all of Mesopotamia, including the portion of Syria east of the Euphrates River.

After Tukulti-Ninurta was murdered by one of his sons, the Assyrian empire went into decline. Babylon reestablished its independence, and Assyria seems to have lost much of her Syrian territory. Emar, a city on the Euphrates River, suffered "staggering grain prices" before being destroyed around 1185 B.C.E. by unknown raiders probably "driven by the general famine."[32] Seminomadic Aramaean tribes began occupying parts of Syria and occasionally launched raids into Mesopotamia, as well (see Map 7.2). Muski and Kaska groups from Asia Minor also invaded Assyrian territory. Tiglath-pileser I (c. 1115 to 1077 B.C.E.) arrested the decline for a time, marching all the way to the Mediterranean on one expedition and north of Lake Van on another. However, most of his campaigns seem to have been essentially defensive in nature. Twenty-eight times during his reign he had to defeat invading Aramaeans or launch preemptive strikes into their territory. Some of the Aramaean attacks reached far into the Assyrian heartland, destroying small towns and villages and adding to hardships produced by nature. An Assyrian letter from this time complains about "rains which have been so scanty this year that no harvests were reaped."[33] Just a few years later, an Assyrian chronicle records that "a famine (so severe) occurred (that) [peop]le ate one another's flesh."[34]

Despite the heroic efforts of Tiglath-pileser I and Asshurnasirpal I (c. 1049 to 1031 B.C.E.), Assyrian territory continued to contract. By the end of the eleventh century B.C.E., Assyrian rulers were able to control only the territory from Asshur in the south to Nineveh in the north and from just west of the Tigris River to Arbil in the east. Other problems also continued into the tenth century B.C.E. Drought, famine, and hunger are mentioned at least 14 times in texts dating from the eleventh and first half of the tenth centuries B.C.E. At the end of the eleventh century, the situation was so bad that food and drink offerings for many of the gods had to be canceled. Considering the importance that ancient Near Eastern peoples placed on maintaining the rites of their gods, especially when divine help was needed, this act could only have been prompted by an extreme emergency.

Rival Babylon was unable to take advantage of this period of Assyrian weakness, for she, too, was beset with problems. Elam, the kingdom just to the east, began sending her armies into Babylonia after Tukulti-Ninurta I of Assyria put his puppet king on Babylon's throne. The Elamites fought to prevent Assyrian domination of lower Mesopotamia, often destroying Babylonian towns in the process. As a result of one of these invasions, the Elamites sacked Babylon, carrying Naram-Sin's victory stele and Hammurabi's law stele off to Susa, capital of Elam. There, French archaeologists found them in the mid-nineteenth century. The Elamite attacks destroyed the Kassite Dynasty in Babylon around the middle of the twelfth century B.C.E., bringing to a close more than 400 years of Kassite rule.

From about 1100 B.C.E. on, Aramaean groups also raided into Mesopotamia (and possibly Elam), increasing the devastation and turmoil. The political chaos was accompanied by severe food shortages. The normal price of barley in Mesopotamia had been about one silver shekel for 30 *seahs* (approximately two bushels). However, in the eleventh and early tenth centuries B.C.E., grain usually fetched two to four times that normal price. The inflationary peak seems to have been reached in the mid-tenth century B.C.E., when an inscription records that in Babylon, a gold shekel purchased only two *seahs* of barley.[35] One gold shekel was usually worth ten silver ones. So, this text indicates that grain was selling for 150 times its normal price! Obviously, the food shortages in Mesopotamia were even worse than those in Egypt.

As one might expect, the area's population seriously declined during this period. Many Elamite towns were abandoned around 1100 B.C.E. or soon afterward, and those still occupied decreased in size. In Mesopotamia, archaeological surveys indicate that in the old Sumerian heartland just north of the Persian Gulf, the population declined by about 25 percent during this era. However, in central Mesopotamia, the area surrounding Babylon proper, the population loss seems to have been about 75 per cent.[36]

Babylonia's turmoil and calamities from the twelfth through tenth centuries B.C.E. probably are reflected in the *Epic of Erra* written to celebrate the later return to normalcy. In this poetic composition, Marduk abandons Babylon and Erra, the god of pestilence, war, and the underworld, gains control. He proceeds to destroy the people—just and unjust, strong and weak alike—through fighting, plague, famine, lack of water, and natural disasters. Pleased with the devastation he has wrought, Erra reflects how his actions have eliminated all national and social cohesion and bred a "dog eat dog" sense of desperation:

> Sealand [the area at the head of the Persian Gulf] shall not spare Sealand, . . . nor Assyrian Assyrian,
>
> Nor shall Elamite spare Elamite, nor Kassite Kassite, . . .
>
> Nor country country, nor city city,
>
> Nor shall tribe spare tribe, nor man man, nor brother brother, and they shall slay one another.[37]

What Caused the Collapse?

What could have brought about such widespread devastation and chaos throughout the eastern Mediterranean area? Why, after a long period of stability, did Bronze Age civilization collapse? It used to be common to blame destructive invasions by less-civilized outsiders—Dorians in Greece, the Sea Peoples in Asia Minor and Syria, and Philistines and Israelites in Canaan. However, archaeology and linguistics have provided evidence that invading Dorians did *not* destroy Mycenaean civilization.[38] They didn't settle in the Peloponnese and Crete until a few generations *after* the Mycenaean collapse. There are also serious doubts about the Sea Peoples' role in the destruction of the Hittite Empire and about an Israelite invasion of Canaan (as we shall see in Chapter 8). Furthermore, the established kingdoms had fortified citadels and experienced defenders. They were used to fighting well-trained armies. So why did they now fall so easily to less-organized groups of invaders? The various invasions and population movements seem to have been *symptoms* of the widespread political, economic, and cultural collapse, rather than its cause.

Robert Drews proposed an interesting variation of the invasion explanation that sees changes in warfare as the reason for the end of the Bronze Age. According to this view, barbarians like the Sea Peoples who had long been employed as mercenaries by the Great Powers, abruptly turned on their masters. They had recognized that massed infantry soldiers armed with long slashing swords and javelins were superior to the chariot forces upon which the major empires relied.[39] However, Drews underestimates the role of the infantry in the Bronze Age as well as the continued effectiveness of chariots in the early part of the Iron Age. Infantry represented the bulk of both the Egyptian and Hittite forces that fought at Qadesh. The major empires had infantry of their own that they could have used against that of the raiders if tactics had been the only issue. Furthermore, the demise of chariotry in the Near East was probably due more to the later development of more effective mounted cavalry than to the infantry tactics Drews describes.

Drews's theory also eliminates ethnic migrations in connection with the catastrophe. He argues, for example, that the Sea Peoples were only looting gangs of warriors, not whole tribes or populations on the move. He rejects the view that the Peleset/Philistines are migrants from the Aegean. Instead, he interprets the Peleset as "Palestinians," Canaanite privateers who joined with Tjekel (Sicilian) and Denyen (Greek) groups in raiding Egypt. He also argues that there was no land battle against the Sea Peoples. The conflict depicted at Medinet Habu (see Figure 7.7) supposedly reflects a minor Egyptian campaign into the Levant. The families shown in oxcarts belong to seminomadic bedouin groups fleeing from Ramesses III's army or were refugees from local Palestinian villages.[40] While this position is well-argued, the evidence does not seem to support it. In the relief showing oxcarts, the Egyptians' enemies wear the garb of the Sea Peoples, not that of Canaanites.[41] The Egyptian account also describes the Peleset and other Sea Peoples as coming from afar, from "islands," not from next-door Palestine.[42] Moreover, there is no evidence of the use of "Palestine" as a place name (by the Egyptians or anyone else) at this time, so Egyptians would not have called Canaanites "Peleset" meaning "Palestinians." The term "Philistia" (*Palastu*) as a place name for the coastal area of Canaan occurs in Assyrian texts for the first time during the reign of Adad-nirari III (810 to 783 B.C.E.), and "Palestine" was not used as a term for all of Canaan before the time of Herodotus. These place names almost certainly derived from the ethnic term "Philistine," not the other way around as Drews would have it. Also, despite Drews's denials, archaeology clearly indicates the presence of new population groups along the coastal plain of Canaan just after 1200 B.C.E. Finally, Drews's arguments notwithstanding, there almost certainly *were* significant eastern Mediterranean migrations of various groups of people (though not "nations" in the later sense of the word) at the end of the Bronze Age (see Map 7.2). These population movements or displacements almost certainly were not due to changes in military organization or tactics.

Others have argued that the Bronze Age civilizations experienced a systems collapse. Their economies were too narrowly based and their trade networks depended on relatively peaceful conditions. Also, there were major social problems (such as debt slavery, alienation of land, abuse of peasants by the ruling aristocracy) that caused internal discontent. Then, at the end of the thirteenth century, piracy and military conflicts disrupted trade. The substantial decline of trade, in turn, led to economic collapse, revolts, and a general breakdown of the economic, political, and social systems.[43] This theory helps to explain why the Bronze Age societies could not recover after the catastrophes of the twelfth century B.C.E. However, once more, it seems to confuse symptoms of the collapse with causes. Why did piracy increase and trade decline at the end of the Bronze Age? What made the conflicts around 1200 B.C.E. different from those that had frequently taken place earlier? Why did social inequities that had existed throughout the Bronze Age suddenly lead to revolutions?

Still other scholars have argued that only natural forces can explain the extensive Bronze Age social and political collapse. Earthquakes have been the choice of some to explain at least a few of the destructions (usually Knossos, Mycenae, Tiryns, Midea, Troy, Hattusas, Alalakh, and Ugarit).[44] However, since earthquakes are usually very localized phenomena and the destructions were widespread in Greece, Anatolia,

Syria, and Palestine, most scholars have dismissed earthquakes as a cause of the disasters.[45] It has also been argued that in antiquity, earthquake fires did not usually consume entire sites and that "there is little or no demonstrable archaeological evidence of earthquake activity, at least on such a scale as to have caused the total destruction and abandonment of a site."[46] However, Amos Nur and Eric Cline have argued for what they call "earthquake storms," a series of successive earthquakes along several connected geological faults over a period of 50 years. Such an "earthquake storm" might account for many of the destroyed cities in Greece and Asia Minor, but not all of the devastation around the eastern Mediterranean. Their claim, though, is that the earthquakes triggered other problems such as population movements, economic disruptions, and systems collapse.[47]

There has been much wider support for the idea that a severe drought provoked the crisis.[48] Much of the agricultural land in the eastern Mediterranean is marginal at best. Even a small change in rainfall amounts can have a major impact, even in the volume of water carried by the rivers. Thus, the soaring prices for grain in Egypt and Mesopotamia and the Hittite appeals for grain have been used to support the drought hypothesis. Also, studies of paleoenvironmental data for the Nile, the Tigris, and the Euphrates indicate that they were at very low levels during the twelfth century B.C.E.[49] Moreover, studies of tree-ring sequences show that there was a climatic change in the northern hemisphere between 1300 and 1000 B.C.E. A series of very narrow rings on a log unearthed at Gordion in Asia Minor indicate a period of very dry weather there c. 1200 to 1150 B.C.E.[50] That was about the time the Hittites appealed to Egypt for grain to alleviate famine.

Obviously, food shortages due to an extended drought or sequences of several dry years occurring at close intervals could have led to discontent, increased piracy, revolts, conflicts, and population movements like those of the twelfth century B.C.E. Such conflicts and movements, once begun, would have had a multiplier or "domino" effect on other areas. However, it has been objected that there simply is no evidence of a drought long enough and intense enough to cause the collapse. The texts at Pylos in Greece produced just before its destruction give no indication of drought, food shortages, or famine. The food shortages mentioned in Near Eastern texts and the inflationary prices for grain could have been *due to* disorder and social collapse rather than being their cause. Also, some of the Greek palaces still had stores of wheat, barley, and other foodstuffs in their storerooms when they were burned. So their attackers do not seem to have been seeking food.[51] (It should be noted, though, that there is no way to determine how the fires at these sites started. If defeat seemed inevitable, defenders could have set them to keep the enemy from being able to benefit from his victory.)

Thus, there is as yet no consensus on what caused the catastrophes at the end of the Bronze Age. Most scholars opt for a mixture of the systems collapse hypothesis with raiders, ethnic movements, revolts, or temporary drought as the triggering mechanism to begin the collapse. Scholars, especially geologists, now will have to also evaluate "earthquake storms" as possible "triggers." The following statement by Trevor Bryce concerning the end of the Hittite kingdom is characteristic:

> If the kingdom of Hatti in particular was becoming increasingly dependent on importation of grain supplies, even temporary shortfalls in local grain production caused by drought would have given an increased urgency to ensuring that regular shipments from abroad were not disrupted. And if other factors intervened which seriously affected the Hittites' ability to maintain political stability throughout their kingdom, then food shortages caused by drought or the disruption of supply routes might well have led to a crisis of major proportions.[52]

Some such statement is about the best we can do at present. *Something* disturbed the fragile economic, social, and political systems of Bronze Age states and set off a series of chain reactions. It could have been a series of devastating earthquakes in Greece and Anatolia, and there *is* tree ring evidence for deterioration in the climate during the twelfth century and fairly reliable evidence for low water levels in the

Nile, Tigris, and Euphrates rivers at the same time. So, in some (but not necessarily all) areas it may have been earthquakes that upset the balance and, in many others, drought. Or earthquakes may have added to the problems caused by drought. Whatever started the process, inflation, piracy, loss of trade, internal strife, warfare, population movements, destruction of cities, plague, population decline, and systems collapse weakened or destroyed the eastern Mediterranean Bronze Age civilizations. When relative calm returned to the region after 1100 B.C.E., a new world had dawned. The old empires were gone or reduced to impotence. In their place there developed new nations and new societies ready to make their mark on the pages of history.

SUGGESTIONS FOR FURTHER READING AND INFORMATION

Internet Sites

Hatti, Land of the Hittites—reliefs, articles, and related links: http://www. multimedia.com/hatti/en/frame.html

Information on Ramesses II and his temples at Abu Simbel: http://www.abusimbelegypt.com

Abu Simbel: http://www.ccer.ggl.ruu.nl/abu_simbel/abu_simbel1.html

Books and Articles

The Hittites

Akurgal, Ekrem. *The Art of the Hittites*. New York: H. N. Abrams, 1962.

Beckman, G. *Hittite Diplomatic Texts*. Atlanta: Scholars Press, 1996.

Bittel, Kurt. *Hattusha, the Capital of the Hittites*. Oxford: Oxford University Press, 1970.

Bryce, Trevor. *The Kingdom of the Hittites*. Oxford: Oxford University Press, 1998.

Gurney, O. R. *The Hittites*, rev. 2nd ed. New York: Penguin Books, 1990.

Hoffner, Harry A. Jr. *Hittite Myths*, 2nd edition. Atlanta: Scholars Press, 1998.

Lehmann, Johannes. *The Hittites: People of a Thousand Gods*. Translated by J. Maxwell Brownjohn. New York: Viking, 1977.

Macqueen, J. G. *The Hittites and Their Contemporaries in Asia Minor*, rev. ed. New York and London: Thames and Hudson, 1986.

Mikasa, Prince Takahito, ed. *Essays on Ancient Anatolia and Its Surrounding Civilizations*. Wiesbaden: Harrassowitz Verlag, 1995.

The Egyptian Nineteenth and Twentieth Dynasties

Černy, Jaroslav. *A Community of Workmen at Thebes in the Ramesside Period*. Cairo: Institut Français d'Archéologie Orientale, 1973.

Kitchen, Kenneth A. *Pharaoh Triumphant: The Life and Times of Ramesses II, King of Egypt*. Warminster, UK: Aris and Phillips, 1982.

Montet, Pierre. *Everyday Life in Egypt in the Days of Ramesses the Great*. Translated by A. R. Maxwell-Hyslop and Margaret S. Drower. Philadelphia: University of Pennsylvania Press, 1981.

Murnane, William J. *The Road to Kadesh*. Chicago: Oriental Institute of the University of Chicago, 1990.

Peet, Thomas E. *The Great Tomb-Robberies of the Twentieth Egyptian Dynasty*. Hildesheim: Georg Olms Verlag, 1977.

Redford, Susan. *The Harem Conspiracy: The Murder of Ramesses III*. DeKalb, IL: Northern Illinois University Press, 2002.

Schmidt, Heike C., and Joachim Willeitner. *Nefertari*. Mainz: Verlag Philipp von Zabern, 1994.

Schmidt, John D. *Ramesses II: A Chronological Structure for His Reign*. Baltimore: Johns Hopkins University Press, 1973.

Tyldesley, Joyce. *Ramesses, Egypt's Greatest Pharaoh*. New York: Viking, 2000.

Weeks, Kent R. *The Lost Tomb*. New York: William Morrow, 1998.

The End of the Late Bronze Age

Crossland, R. A., and Ann Birchall, eds. *Bronze Age Migrations in the Aegean: Archaeological and Linguistic Problems in Greek Prehistory*. Park Ridge, NJ: Noyes Press, 1974.

Dothan, Trude, and Moshe Dothan. *People of the Sea: The Search for the Philistines*. New York: Macmillan, 1992.

Drews, Robert. *The End of the Bronze Age: Changes in Warfare and the Catastrophe Ca. 1200 B.C.* Princeton: Princeton University Press, 1993.

Foxhall, L., and J. K. Davies, eds. *The Trojan War: Its Historicity and Context*. Bristol: Bristol Classical Press, 1984.

Gitin, S., A. Mazar, and E. Stern, eds. *Mediterranean Peoples in Transition: Thirteenth to Early Tenth Centuries B.C.E.* Jerusalem: Israel Exploration Society, 1998.

Karageorghis, V., and J. D. Muhly, eds. *Cyprus at the Close of the Bronze Age*. Nicosia: A. G. Leventis Foundation, 1984.

Sandars, Nancy K. *The Sea Peoples: Warriors of the Ancient Mediterranean*, rev. ed. New York and London: Thames and Hudson, 1985.

Ward, William A., and Martha S. Joukowsky, eds. *The Crisis Years: The Twelfth Century B.C.—From Beyond the Danube to the Tigris*. Dubuque, IA: Kendall/Hunt, 1992.

NOTES

1. Trevor Bryce, *The Kingdom of the Hittites* (Oxford: Oxford University Press, 1998), p. 251. See also William Murnane, *The Road to Kadesh*, rev. 2nd ed. (Chicago: University of Chicago Press, 1990), pp. 37–38.
2. Kenneth A. Kitchen, *Pharaoh Triumphant: The Life and Times of Ramesses II* (Warminster, UK: Aris and Phillips, 1982), pp. 78–79.
3. Bryce (1998), p. 395.
4. Bryce (1998), pp. 59–63; O. R. Gurney, *The Hittites*, rev. 2nd ed. (New York: Penguin Books, 1990), pp. 38–45.
5. However, Hans Güterbock opposes this view in "Hittites and Akhaeans: A New Look," *Proceedings of the American Philosophical Society*, vol. 128 (1984), p. 119.
6. For example, see Michael Wood, *In Search of the Trojan War* (New York and London: Facts on File, 1985), pp. 178–185.
7. For example, see John Chadwick, *The Mycenaean World* (Cambridge: Cambridge University Press, 1976), pp. 180–186, and Carol G. Thomas, "Searching for the Historical Homer," *Archaeology Odyssey*, vol. 1, no. 1 (1998), pp. 26–33.
8. Bryce (1998), p. 402.
9. See James D. Muhly, et al., "Iron in Anatolia and the Nature of the Hittite Iron Industry," *Anatolian Studies*, vol. 35 (1985), pp. 67–84.
10. Gurney (1990), p. 115.
11. Ibid., p. 126.
12. J. G. Macqueen, *The Hittites and Their Contemporaries in Asia Minor*, rev. ed. (London: Thames and Hudson, 1986), p. 152.
13. More than 65 chambers have been found, and archaeologists think that a lower level with many more corridors

and chambers remains to be found. See Kent R. Weeks, *The Lost Tomb* (New York: William Morrow, 1998).

14. James H. Breasted, *Ancient Records of Egypt: The Historical Documents* (Chicago: University of Chicago Press, 1905), vol. 3, *The Nineteenth Dynasty*, § 580, p. 244.

15. Kitchen (1982), pp. 40–41.

16. John A Wilson, "Hymn of Victory of Mer-ne-Ptah (The 'Israel Stele') in James B. Pritchard, ed. *Ancient Near Eastern Texts Relating to the Old Testament*, 2nd ed. (Princeton, NJ: Princeton University Press, 1955), pp. 376–378.

17. Donald B. Redford, "Egypt and Western Asia in the Late New Kingdom: An Overview" in Eliezer Stern, ed., *The Sea Peoples and Their World: A Reassessment* (Philadelphia: The University Museum of the University of Pennsylvania, 2000), p. 12.

18. Wilson, "The War Against the Peoples of the Sea," in Pritchard, ed. (1955), p. 262. Bracketed material added by W. Stiebing.

19. Redford in Stern, ed. (2000), p. 12.

20. Deuteronomy 2:23; Jeremiah 47:4; and Amos 9:7. For a discussion of the biblical traditions about Philistine origins, see Peter Machinist, "Biblical Traditions: The Philistines and Israelite History" in Stern, ed. (2000), pp. 53–55.

21. 2 Samuel 8:18 and 20:23; Ezekiel 25:16; Zephaniah 2:5; and 1 Samuel 30:14.

22. Trude Dothan, *The Philistines and Their Material Culture* (New Haven, CT: Yale University Press, 1982), pp. 94–160, 198–215; Trude Dothan and Moshe Dothan, *People of the Sea: The Search for the Philistines* (New York: Macmillan Publishing Company, 1992), pp. 89–92; Ann E. Killebrew, "Aegean-Style Early Philistine Pottery in Canaan During the Iron I Age: A Stylistic Analysis of Mycenaean IIIC:1b and Its Associated Wares" in Stern, ed. (2000), pp. 233–253.

23. Trude Dothan (1982), pp. 160–198.

24. Ibid., p. 217.

25. The Egyptians' depiction of the Sea Peoples' attire are similar to those of the Keftiu, and both are similar to the clothing worn by males shown in Mycenaean frescoes. For the Aegean origin of the Sea Peoples' bird-headed ships, see Shelley Wachsmann, "To the Sea of the Philistines" in Stern, ed. (2000), pp. 103–143.

26. For more on the attempts to identify the Sea Peoples, see R. D. Barnett, "The Sea Peoples" in I. E. S. Edwards, et al., eds., *The Cambridge Ancient History*, 3rd ed. (Cambridge: Cambridge University Press, 1975), vol. II, part 2, p. 367; Nancy K. Sandars, *The Sea Peoples: Warriors*

of the Ancient Mediterranean, rev. ed. (New York and London: Thames and Hudson, 1985), pp. 106–113, 158, 161–165, 170, 199–201; Itamar Singer, "The Origins of the Sea Peoples and Their Settlement on the Coast of Canaan" in M. Heltzer and E. Lipinski, eds., *Society and Economy in the Eastern Mediterranean (c. 1500–1000 B.C.)* (Louvain: Uitgeverij Peeters, 1988), pp. 239–250 and "Sea Peoples" in David N. Freedman, editor-in-chief, *The Anchor Bible Dictionary* (New York: Doubleday, 1992), vol. 5, pp. 1059–1061; Bryce (1998), pp. 367–374; and Robert Drews, "Medinet Habu: Oxcarts, Ships, and Migration Theories," *Journal of Near Eastern Studies*, vol. 59 (2000), pp. 177–182.

27. The final destruction of Knossos traditionally has been dated c. 1400–1380 B.C.E., the date given by Sir Arthur Evans. However, a review of the evidence has indicated that the palace probably continued to exist well into the thirteenth century B.C.E. Exactly when in the thirteenth century the palace was destroyed is uncertain. See Erik Hallager, *The Mycenaean Palace at Knossos: Evidence for the Final Destruction in the III B Period* (Stockholm: Medelhavsmuseet, 1977).

28. Michael C. Astour, "New Evidence on the Last Days of Ugarit," *American Journal of Archaeology*, vol. 69 (1965), p. 255. For a different interpretation of this letter, see Harry A. Hoffner, "The Last Days of Khattusha" in William A. Ward and Martha S. Joukowski, eds., *The Crisis Years: The Twelfth Century B.C.* (Dubuque, IA: Kendall/Hunt, 1992), p. 49.

29. Astour, *AJA* 69, p. 255.

30. See Jaroslav Černy, "Fluctuations in Grain Prices during the Twentieth Egyptian Dynasty," *Archiv Orientální*, vol. 6 (1933–1934), pp. 173–178 and J. J. Janssen, *Commodity Prices from the Ramesside Period* (Leiden: E. J. Brill, 1975), pp. 551–552.

31. T. Eric Peet, *The Great Tomb Robberies of the Twentieth Egyptian Dynasty*, 2 vols. (Oxford: Oxford University Press,1930). See also John Romer, *Ancient Lives: Daily Life in Egypt of the Pharaohs* (New York: Holt, Rinehart and Winston, 1984), pp. 145–162.

32. Itamar Singer, "New Evidence on the End of the Hittite Empire" in Stern (2000), pp. 24–25.

33. J. Neumann and Simo Parpola, "Climatic Change and the Eleventh-Tenth-Century Eclipse of Assyria and Babylonia," *Journal of Near Eastern Studies*, vol. 46, no. 3 (July1987), p. 178. See also D. J. Wiseman, "Assyria and Babylonia c. 1200–1000 B.C." in Edwards, et al., eds. (1975), vol. II, part 2, p. 465.

34. Neumann and Parpola, JNES 46/3 p.178.

35. Ibid., p. 181.

36. J. A. Brinkman, "Settlement Surveys and Documentary Evidence: Regional Variation and Secular Trends in Mesopotamian Demography," *Journal of Near Eastern Studies*, vol. 43, no. 3 (July 1984), pp. 172–175.

37. Amélie Kuhrt, *The Ancient Near East* (London and New York: Routledge, 1995), vol. I, p.380. For the entire epic, see Benjamin R. Foster, *Before the Muses: An Anthology of Akkadian Literature* (Bethesda, MD: CDL Press, 1993), vol. 2, pp. 771–801.

38. See, for example, J. T. Hooker, *Mycenaean Greece* (London: Routledge and Kegan Paul, 1977), pp. 144–147, 170–173; William H. Stiebing, Jr., "The End of the Mycenaean Age," *Biblical Archeologist*, vol. 43, no. 1 (Winter 1980), pp. 7–21.

39. Robert Drews, *The End of the Bronze Age: Changes in Warfare and the Catastrophe Ca. 1200 B.C.* (Princeton, NJ: Princeton University Press, 1993), pp. 97, 209–225.

40. See Ibid., especially pp. 48–72, 97 and 209–225, and *JNES* 59, pp. 161–190.

41. Drews's attempt to explain away this fact in *JNES* 59, p. 187 is very lame. The scene he mentions on the interior of the temple (Figure 9, p. 188) depicts captive Hittites as well as Canaanites and Sea Peoples. It probably summarizes *all* of Ramesses's victories rather than representing the result of one campaign.

42. See Redford in Stern, ed. (2000), p. 12.

43. See, for example, Philip P. Betancourt, "The End of the Greek Bronze Age," *Antiquity*, vol. 50 (1976), pp. 40–47; Sandars (1985), pp. 47–49, 77–79, 197; Carlo Zaccagnini, "The Transition from Bronze to Iron in the Near East and in the Levant: Marginal Notes," *Journal of the American Oriental Society*, vol. 110 (1990), pp. 493–502; and Oliver Dickinson, *The Aegean Bronze Age* (Cambridge and New York: Cambridge University Press, 1994), pp. 307–309.

44. See the summary in Drews (1993), pp. 33–37. See also Eberhard Zangger, *The Flood from Heaven: Deciphering the Atlantis Legend* (New York: William Morrow, 1992), pp. 82–85.

45. See Drews (1993), pp. 33–47.

46. Bryce (1998), p. 374. See also Drews (1993), pp. 37–47.

47. Amos Nur and Eric H. Cline, "Poseidon's Horses: Plate Tectonics and Earthquake Storms in the Late Bronze Age Aegean and Eastern Mediterranean," *Journal of Archaeological Science*, vol. 27 (2000), pp. 43–63 and "What Triggered the Collapse? Earthquake Storms," *Archaeology Odyssey*, vol. 4, no. 5 (September/October 2001), pp. 31–36, 62–63.

48. See, for example, Rhys Carpenter, *Discontinuity in Greek Civilization* (New York: W. W. Norton, 1966); R. A. Bryson, H. H. Lamb, and D. L. Donley, "Drought and the Decline of Mycenae," *Antiquity*, vol. 48 (1974), pp. 46–50; B. Weiss, "The Decline of Late Bronze Age Civilizations as a Possible Response to Climatic Change," *Climatic Change*, vol. 4 (1982), pp. 172–198; Neumann and Parpola, op. cit. (Note 33); R. L. Gorny, "Environment, Archaeology, and History in Hittite Anatolia," *Biblical Archaeologist*, vol. 52, nos. 2 and 3 (June and September 1989); William H. Stiebing, Jr., *Out of the Desert?: Archaeology and the Exodus/Conquest Narratives* (Buffalo, NY: Prometheus Books, 1989), pp. 182–187 and "Climate and Collapse—Did the Weather Make Israel's Emergence Possible?," *Bible Review*, vol. 10, no. 4 (August 1994), pp. 19–27, 54; and Philip Betancourt, "The Aegean and the Origin of the Sea Peoples" in Stern, ed. (2000), pp. 300–301.

49. Karl W. Butzer, *Early Hydraulic Civilization in Egypt* (Chicago: University of Chicago Press, 1976), pp. 30–33; P. A. Kay and D. L. Johnson, "Estimation of Tigris-Euphrates Streamflow from Regional Paleoenvironmental Proxy Data," *Climatic Change*, vol. 3 (1981), pp. 251–263.

50. H. H. Lamb, "Reconstruction of the Course of Postglacial Climate Over the World," in A. P. Harding, ed., *Climatic Change in Later Prehistory* (Edinburgh: Edinburgh University Press, 1982), pp. 147–148; M. G. L. Baillie, "Irish Oaks Record Volcanic Dust Veils Drama!," *Archaeology Ireland*, vol. 2, no. 2 (1988), pp. 71–74 and "Marker Dates—Turning Prehistory into History," *Archaeology Ireland*, vol. 2, no. 4 (1988), pp. 154–155 for the general tree ring sequences and P. I. Kuniholm, "Archaeological Evidence and Non-Evidence for Climatic Change," *Philosophical Transactions of the Royal Society of London*, Annual 330 (1990), pp. 645–655 for the Gordion evidence.

51. See Drews (1993), pp. 82–84.

52. Bryce (1998), p. 375.

8
Recovery and Transformation
(c. 1100–745 B.C.E.

MESOPOTAMIA AND EGYPT

Assyria and Babylonia

The effects of invasions, famine, and population decline continued to be felt throughout Mesopotamia until the end of the tenth century B.C.E. Other than their names, little is known about most of the Mesopotamian kings of the eleventh and tenth centuries B.C.E. Babylon experienced several dynastic changes during this time, and its rulers had a difficult time regaining control over the lower Tigris and Euphrates valleys. Their task was complicated by the presence of the Chaldeans, a group of people who seem to have settled in the extreme southern part of Mesopotamia between 1100 and 900 B.C.E. Their origin is unknown, but they probably spoke a Semitic language, for most of their names found in ninth and eighth century B.C.E. sources are Akkadian, while a few are Aramaic. Some scholars think the Chaldeans were originally Aramaeans, while others suggest that they came from eastern Arabia, and still others believe they were related to earlier groups like the Kassites. All of these theories are possible, but there is no direct evidence to indicate that one is more probable than another. Like other immigrants into

Mesopotamia, the Chaldeans quickly assimilated the local Mesopotamian culture, though they retained their tribal organization, being divided into four tribes, each with its own sheikh or "king."

Unlike Babylon, Assyria managed to keep its royal line intact during the time of turmoil. Finally, around 900 B.C.E., Assyria began to stir again, driving the Aramaeans out of the Tigris Valley and reestablishing Assyrian authority over most of northern Mesopotamia. A treaty with Babylon in 891 B.C.E. secured peace on the southern front, allowing the Assyrian rulers to concentrate on expanding their territory to the north and west.

The conquests of Asshurnasirpal II ("Asshur is Guardian of the Heir," 883 to 859 B.C.E.) are generally accepted as the real beginning of a Neo-Assyrian Empire (see Table 8.1). This king undertook several military campaigns against small states in the mountains north of Assyria, forcing them to become vassals. He also extended Assyrian power to the east, placing most of the western foothills of the Zagros Mountains under his control. Fearing the growing Assyrian might, the Aramaean state of Bit-Adini on the middle Euphrates west of the Balikh River encouraged some Assyrian vassals in the lower Habur region to revolt.

TABLE 8.1

Chronology of Assyrian Kings from 911 to 745 B.C.E.

(All dates are B.C.E. The most significant rulers are printed in boldface.)

Adad-nirari II	911–891
Tukulti-Ninurta II	890–884
Asshurnasirpal II	**883–859**
Shalmaneser III	**858–824**
Shamshi-Adad V	823–811
Adad-nirari III	**810–783**
Shalmaneser IV	782–773
Asshur-dan III	772–755
Asshur-nirari V	754–745

Asshurnasirpal quickly crushed the revolts, savagely impaling, flaying alive, dismembering, or walling up alive many of the princes and nobles who had led the rebellion. He then invaded Bit-Adini to punish its ruler for inciting revolt. He captured one of its main cities and forced Bit-Adini's king to pay a large amount of tribute and to provide hostages to Assyria. The news of Asshurnasirpal's victories spread, and when he crossed the Euphrates, he was able to march unopposed from Carchemish westward across the Orontes River and southward through Lebanon to the sea. The Neo-Hittite king of Carchemish and the rulers of many Phoenician cities, including Tyre, Sidon, and Byblos, decided not to risk Assyria's wrath and voluntarily paid tribute. To guard against future revolt, Asshurnasirpal established several Assyrian garrison towns in the territories he had conquered. These included Tushhan on the upper Tigris and two fortresses on opposite sides of the middle Euphrates. He also seems to have been the first Assyrian king to follow the earlier Hittite practice of mass deportations of defeated peoples. Some of the captives became slave labor, while others were settled in sparsely populated areas of Assyria.

The results of Asshurnasirpal's campaigns provided a strong motive for later Assyrian expansion. The vast amount of booty and captive labor he brought back to Assyria allowed him to construct a new capital city, Kalhu (called Calah in the Bible and Nimrud today),

near the intersection of the Tigris and Zab rivers north of Asshur. The city was largely settled with prisoners brought back to Assyria following his campaigns and with groups of soldiers voluntarily contributed by Carchemish and other subject-allies. The walls of Asshurnasirpal's new royal palace were decorated with frescoes and carved stone slabs exhibiting beautiful bas-relief scenes of *genii* (protective demigods), hunting, warfare (see Figure 8.1), and ritual activities, as well as bands of cuneiform inscriptions. There were also sculptures of winged human-headed bulls and lions flanking the major doorways, a practice derived from earlier Hittite and Neo-Hittite examples. These sculptures were among the first objects excavated in Mesopotamia in the 1840s, and they now constitute some of the greatest treasures of the British Museum.[1]

Asshurnasirpal's victories had established only nominal Assyrian authority over Syria west of the Balikh River. So, his son and successor, Shalmaneser III ("The god Shulmanu is Greatest," 858 to 824 B.C.E.), attempted to convert this ascendancy into permanent control. However, this time the Syrian kingdoms were better prepared for the Assyrian invasion. Bit-Adini, supported by Carchemish and other north Syrian states, held out for three years before its capital, Til-Barsip (modern Tell Ahmar) was captured and turned into an Assyrian fortress. Shalmaneser eliminated the kingdom of Bit-Adini and made the area into an Assyrian province. In the meantime, the small states of Phoenicia, southern Syria, and Palestine also had formed coalitions to oppose Shalmaneser, and he was able to win only partial victories over them. In 853 B.C.E., for example, at the battle of Qarqar in Syria, a coalition army of about 70,000 men led by the king of Damascus supported Irhuleni of Hamath against the Assyrian advance (see Document 8.1). Shalmaneser claimed victory, but he did not capture any of the major cities of the region. The ruler of Damascus maintained his leadership of the anti-Assyrian coalition, keeping the Levant free of Assyrian control for several more years. However, the alliance broke down when usurpers seized the thrones of Damascus and Israel between c. 845 and 841 B.C.E. The Phoenician cities of Tyre and Sidon as well as Jehu, the new king of Israel, paid tribute and become Assyrian vassals in

FIGURE 8.1   A Relief from Kalhu Depicting Asshurnasirpal II and His Forces Attacking a City

Source: Courtesy of the Trustees of the British Museum, London.

841 B.C.E., leaving the kingdom of Damascus alone to withstand Shalmaneser's attacks. Damascus, though, remained free, as did several other Syrian cities.

Near the end of Shalmaneser III's reign, the Assyrian dominion over the Levant that he had struggled so hard to establish crumbled. Shalmaneser's oldest son led a rebellion against his aging father, and the revolt took root in Nineveh, Asshur, and many other Assyrian cities. Shalmaneser designated a younger son, his eventual successor, Shamshi-Adad V (823 to 811 B.C.E.), to quell the uprising, but it was only with Babylonian aid that Shamshi-Adad finally extinguished the revolt two years after Shalmaneser III died. All areas west of the Euphrates were lost, and Assyria's power declined even in parts of western Mesopotamia.

Shamshi-Adad V was succeeded by his son, Adad-nirari III (810 to 783 B.C.E.). It was once thought that Adad-nirari was still a minor when his father died and that his mother, Sammuramat, ruled as regent for a few years. That view has now been rejected, but Sammuramat does seem to have had more influence than normal for a queen-mother during her son's reign. She was powerful enough to inspire later legends about a beautiful, but cruel, Oriental queen named Semiramis. Adad-nirari III restored Assyrian preeminence within Mesopotamia for a time and briefly forced Syria, including Damascus, into tributary status. However, internal revolts, plague, and pressure from the new and growing kingdom of Urartu in the north combined to keep Assyria dormant throughout most of the first half of the eighth century B.C.E. Power struggles for the throne of Babylon kept it weak also, allowing the Chaldeans to assume more power in the south. Meanwhile, Mesopotamian power east of the Tigris was also at a low ebb. The Medes, a still largely seminomadic Indo-European people, seem to have been gradually settling southeast of Lake Urmia without much interference. South of the Medes, the kingdom of Ellipi (modern Luristan), a center for bronze casting, also flourished during this time.

The Third Intermediate Period in Egypt

In Egypt, the chaos and confusion of the last years of the twelfth century continued through the era of the Twenty-first Dynasty (1075 to 945 B.C.E.). A new line

DOCUMENT 8.1

The Assyrian Account of the Battle of Qarqar

The following account is taken from the annals of Shalmaneser III's sixth year (853 B.C.E.) according to the so-called "Monolith Inscription" engraved on a stele found at Kurkh, Iraq.[2] Other less detailed accounts of the campaign were found inscribed on bull statues and on Shalmaneser III's famous Black Obelisk at Kalhu (the biblical Calah, modern Nimrud).

I departed from the banks of the Euphrates and approached Aleppo (*Hal-man*). They (i.e., the inhabitants of A.) were afraid to fight and seized my feet (in submission). I received silver and gold as their tribute and offered sacrifices before the Adad of Aleppo. I departed from Aleppo and approached the two towns of Irhuleni from Hamath (*Amat*). I captured the towns Adennu, Barga (and) Argana his royal residence. I removed from them his booty (as well as) his personal (lit: of his palaces) possessions. I set his palaces afire. I departed from Argana and approached Karkara {Qarqar}. I destroyed, tore down and burned down Karkara, his (text: my) royal residence. He brought along to help him 1,200 chariots, 1,200 cavalrymen, 20,000 foot soldiers of Adad-'idri (i.e. Hadadezer) of Damascus (*Imerishu*), 700 chariots, 700 cavalrymen, 10,000 foot soldiers of Irhuleni from Hamath, 2,000 chariots, 10,000 foot soldiers of Ahab, the Israelite (*A-ha-ab-bu Sir-'i-la-a-a*), 500 soldiers from Que, 1,000 soldiers from Musri, 10 chariots, 10,000 soldiers from Irqanata, 200 soldiers of Matinu-ba'lu from Arvad, 200 soldiers from Usanata, 30 chariots, 1[0?],000 soldiers of Adunu-ba'lu from Shian, 1,000 camel-(rider)s of Gindibu', from Arabia, [. . .],000 soldiers of Ba'sa, son of Ruhubi, from Ammon—(all together) these were twelve kings. They rose against me [for a] decisive battle. I fought with them with (the support of) the mighty forces of Ashur {Asshur}, which Ashur, my lord, has given to me, and the strong weapons which Nergal, my leader, has presented to me, (and) I did inflict a defeat upon them between the towns Karkara and Gilzau. I slew 14,000 of their soldiers with the sword, descending upon them like Adad when he makes a rainstorm pour down. I spread their corpses (everywhere), filling the entire plain with their widely scattered (fleeing) soldiers. . . . With their (text: his) corpses I spanned the Orontes before there was a bridge. Even during the battle I took from them their chariots, their horses broken to the yoke.

of kings established themselves at Tanis in the Delta, but they had to share power with a line of army generals based at Thebes. These generals successively assumed the office of high priest of Amun and set up a theocracy in which oracles of the gods Amun, Mut, and Khons validated priestly appointments and major policy decisions. While they nominally recognized the authority of the Tanite kings, the Theban warrior-priests effectively controlled Upper Egypt to the region of el-Hiba, just south of the Faiyum.

Internally divided and decentralized, Egypt could not exercise much influence abroad, either. A literary work called *The Report of Wenamun*, probably based on an actual travel diary from the early part of Dynasty 21, indicates the depths to which Egyptian power and prestige had sunk just after 1100 B.C.E. Wenamun, an envoy sent to Gubal (Byblos to the Greeks) to buy cedar for a new processional barge for Amun-Re, was robbed by one of his own crewmen, ignored by the ruler of Dor, refused timber by the king of Gubal until more gold and silver arrived from Egypt, forced to leave the harbor while several ships of the Tjekker (one of the Sea Peoples) were waiting to attack him, and assaulted by the people of Alasiya (Cyprus) when winds forced him to land there. Though eventually he must have gotten the timber to Thebes (the end of the story is lost), it is clear that an emissary from Egypt no longer commanded the respect and deference that would have been accorded him a few generations earlier.

Though Ramesses III had turned back Libyan invasions during his reign (see Chapter 7), his successors had allowed many Libyans to settle peacefully in the western Delta and the Faiyum. Much of the army during the Twentieth and Twenty-first dynasties consisted of Libyan mercenaries, and many of the leading figures were doubtless of Libyan descent. In 945 B.C.E., Sheshonq I, a Libyan general and the son-in-law of the last king of Dynasty 21, inaugurated the Twenty-second Dynasty. For the next 200 years, Egypt was ruled by Egyptianized Libyan pharaohs (Dynasties 22 and 23, 945 to 712 B.C.E.). Sheshonq (945 to 924 B.C.E.) reunified Egypt and, near the end of his reign, tried to restore Egyptian power in Palestine and Syria. Called Shishak in the Bible, he attacked the newly created kingdoms of Judah and Israel, forcing Rehoboam of Judah to buy him off with "the treasures of the house of the Lord and the treasures of the king's house" (I Kings 14: 25–26; 2 Chronicles 12: 2–9). This brief resurgence of Egyptian power, however, could not be maintained by Sheshonq's successors. Provincial rulers within Egypt became increasingly powerful, and key offices, especially that of high priest of Amun, once more became hereditary. In 818 B.C.E., the royal authority splintered again with a new dynasty (the Twenty-third) ruling from Lentopolis in the central Delta while the Twenty-second Dynasty continued at Tanis in the northeastern Delta. Egypt then suffered through another century of anarchy, fragmentation, and sporadic civil war.

ANATOLIA

The Kingdom of Urartu

Urartu seems to have coalesced as a kingdom in the mountainous area around Lake Van sometime between 1100 and 850 B.C.E. In this region (called Ararat in the Bible, the locale where Noah's Ark supposedly landed), three mountain ranges—the Pontic, Zagros, and Caucasus—come together. Many small independent city-states had occupied the area in earlier times, but Hittite attacks from the west and Assyria's expansion to the north in the thirteenth and twelfth centuries B.C.E. may have precipitated the formation of a unified Urartian state. The Urartians called their kingdom Bia or Biainili (the name Urartu comes from Assyrian texts), and adapted the Assyrian cuneiform system to write their language, which was related to Hurrian. They also may have used a hieroglyphic writing system influenced by Hittite hieroglyphs, but so far, only a small number of these signs have been found, incised on jars and other containers. It is possible that the hieroglyphs were only symbols for capacity and were not used for other kinds of writing. Unfortunately, the number of known Urartian texts of any kind is small, and they provide us with little historically useful information. Thus, historians must derive their understanding of Urartian history and society primarily from the accounts of Urartu's enemy, Assyria.

The kingdom of Urartu eventually occupied most of the territory of later Armenia, with its heartland in the triangular region bounded by Lake Van, Lake Urmia, and Lake Sevan. This area is rich in copper, silver, and iron. Urartian artisans were noted for their metalwork, especially in bronze and iron. Their products were very popular and were exported widely, even to places as far away as northern Italy. Urartian use of griffins, lions, bulls, and other decorative motifs on metal objects (see Figure 8.2) exerted a strong influence on Phrygian metalwork and helped to inspire the Orientalizing phase of Greek art.

There are fertile plains in Armenia protected by high mountains and watered by many mountain springs and streams. Here the Urartians maintained extensive herds of horses, cattle, sheep, and goats, and with the help of irrigation canals, grew grain, grapes, and fruit trees. They stored the produce from the plains in heavily garrisoned and fortified royal citadels usually built atop steep rocky ridges. For withstanding sieges, these almost impregnable strongholds generally had stockpiles of weapons, enormous cisterns cut into the rock, and many large storage jars filled with grain and other agricultural products. They guarded approaches to the heart of the kingdom and served as refuges for the residents of lower-lying areas during invasions.

Urartu's principal deity was Haldi, probably a war god, whose main temple was eventually located at Musasir, a strong fortress on the southeastern border of the kingdom, between Assyria and Lake Urmia. Haldi also had important temples in Tushpa, the religious and political capital of Urartu, though Tushpa's city god was Shiwini, the sun god. Another major deity was Teisheba, the Urartian equivalent of Teshup, the Hurrian weather god. The temples of these gods, as revealed by archaeological excavations, were usually square (about 50 feet per side) with very thick walls. These walls could have supported upper stories, and the Urartian temples may have been tower-like buildings similar to those of the later Persians.

The kingdom was divided into several districts, each with its own governor. On the edges of Urartu, particularly in the west, were small states governed by local rulers who were subject allies or vassals of the Urartian king. Urartu's royal court seems to have been similar to that of Assyria, with the highest officials and generals drawn from the royal family. At the head of the governmental and military elite or noble class was the king, whose position was hereditary. He controlled large royal estates worked by military retainers, slaves, and prisoners of war. The crown prince also had a considerable amount of power, for inscriptions show that he normally participated in the king's military campaigns and is usually named with the king as the donor of offerings to the gods.

Around the beginning of the eighth century B.C.E., an Urartian king named Menua protected his kingdom's southeastern flank by destroying the town

FIGURE 8.2   Urartian Bronze Cauldron

This cauldron was found in an Etruscan tomb in Italy. Note the cast heads of lions and griffins around the top.
Source: Museo Nationale di Villa Giula, Rome.
Photo: Scala/Art Resource, New York.

of Hasanlu on the southern shore of Urmia and building a heavily fortified bastion on its ruins. He also conquered Musasir on the border of Assyria and made it one of the god Haldi's principal centers. Menua also probably erected the large fortress of Bastam between Lake Urmia and Lake Sevan. On the west, his successors established an outpost at Altin Tepe and probably formed an alliance with Phrygia.

This gradual Urartian expansion threatened to block Assyria's access to the east via trade routes through the upper Zagros Mountains and to central Anatolia through the Taurus Range. Thus, when it became strong again after 744 B.C.E., Assyria launched attack after attack on Urartu. However, though Urartu is relatively close to Assyria, the high mountains between them made a direct approach from the south almost impossible. For much of the year, the mountain passes were covered with deep snow, and even in the summer, the rugged terrain made it extremely difficult to move horses, siege equipment, and baggage carts through them. Therefore, the Assyrian armies usually had to circle around and attack along less-precipitous routes from the east or west. Moreover, even when the Assyrians succeeded in besieging and destroying some Urartian cities, others remained protected by the mountain ranges dividing the country. So most of the Assyrian victories proved to be ephemeral, and Urartu remained a thorn in Assyria's side until both collapsed at the end of the seventh century B.C.E.

The Phrygian and Neo-Hittite Kingdoms

As we have seen, the Phrygians probably entered Asia Minor during the turmoil of the twelfth century B.C.E. (see Chapter 7). However, little is really known about these people or their origins. The Phrygian language is probably Indo-European, but it is not closely related to the Anatolian languages (Hittite, Luwian, and Palaic) spoken elsewhere in Asia Minor. Some scholars believe Phrygian is related to Thracian, and if this connection can be demonstrated, it will support the ancient Greek tradition that the Phrygians were originally from Thrace. The earliest known Phrygian inscriptions come from the eighth century B.C.E. and are written with an alphabet borrowed either from Greece or from Phoenicia (probably through inscriptions of Neo-Hittite states in southeastern Anatolia who began using the Phoenician alphabet in addition to Hittite hieroglyphs).

The Phrygian kingdom, probably created during the "dark age" between c. 1100 and 850 B.C.E., was located in west-central Anatolia. Its capital, Gordion, was probably named for Gordias, an early king or possibly one of several early kings of that name, for some

historians think that Gordias was a dynastic name, alternating with Mita (Midas). During the ninth century B.C.E., Phrygia seems to have expanded its power eastward, absorbing the territory of the Muski. These people, possibly allies of the Phrygians when they first moved into Anatolia, had settled in the heartland of the old Hittite Empire, the area around the ancient sites of Alaca Hüyük, Hattusas, and Alisar. When the Phrygians absorbed the Muski into their kingdom, the Assyrians began using the name Muski for the entire Phrygian realm and for the Phrygians themselves.

The Phrygians' main deity was a fertility goddess called Matar Kubileya, the same goddess later worshipped in Lydia and on the western coast of Asia Minor as Kybele (or Cybele). She was the life-giving goddess of mountains and nature. On monuments in the Phrygian highlands, sculptors usually depicted her standing in the doorway of a building, possibly her temple. Unlike the later depictions of Kybele from Ephesus, the Phrygian goddess wears a long belted dress, a tall cylindrical hat and a veil covering her entire body. Midas City was a principal religious center for the worship of Kybele and other Phrygian deities, and many tombs of kings and nobles were cut into the hillsides there.

As in Urartu, much of Phrygia's prosperity stemmed from exploitation of Anatolia's metal deposits. The kingdom became known for its fabulous wealth, so much so that in Greek legend, King Midas of Phrygia turned anything he touched into gold. Phrygian metal smiths, modeling their work in part on that of Urartu, produced many beautiful objects, some of which were traded to Greece and points further west. A huge eighth century B.C.E. intact burial mound at Gordion (traditionally credited to Midas) has yielded hundreds of bronze vessels, fibulae (large, decorated safety pins), and other objects, as well as some of the earliest known brass vessels, but no gold or other precious materials.[3] Some scholars have suggested that the Phrygian discovery of brass, a bright yellow alloy of copper and zinc, might have been behind the Greek belief in Midas's golden touch.

Phrygia became an ally of Urartu, but it also had political links with Carchemish and other Neo-Hittite states. These small descendants of the Hittite empire developed along and across principal trade routes in south-central Anatolia, Cilicia, and northern Syria. They usually centered around one or more heavily fortified cities like Carchemish or Samal and taxed all trade passing through their territories. The Neo-Hittite (or "Syro-Hittite") kings of Carchemish traced their ancestry to the Hittite viceroys of that city who were descendants of Suppiluliumas I (c. 1344 to 1322 B.C.E.), and the rulers of other Neo-Hittite states probably also came from branches of the old Hittite royal family. The citizens of these states, however, were a mixture of remnants of the previous local peoples, Hurrians, Luwian-speaking Anatolian refugees, and, increasingly in Syria and Cilicia, Aramaeans. Though they were not united or even always allied with one another, these kingdoms continued to reflect many aspects of Hittite culture. They maintained the old Hittite beliefs in the king's responsibility for security, prosperity, and justice and the need for vassals to be absolutely loyal to their overlords. Their principal deities derive from those of the Hittite Empire, and their art continues Hittite conventions and style. Initially, they also used the earlier Hittite hieroglyphs to write their language, which, as we have seen in Chapter 7, was a dialect of Luwian. However, in Samal (modern Zinjirli), a Neo-Hittite state on the border between Syria and Anatolia, most inscriptions eventually were written in Aramaic and some of the kings had Aramaean names.

One of the most important Neo-Hittite kingdoms in the eighth century B.C.E. was Tabal (biblical Tubal), located south of the Halys River in the area the Hittites had called the Lower Land. In the mid-ninth century B.C.E., there were many small independent kingdoms in this area, but early in the eighth century they merged into a single state or confederacy. In Tabal, a dynasty descended from someone named Burutas ruled a mixed Luwian and Hurrian population. The main deity of the kingdom was the goddess Kubaba, a later form of the Hurrian/Hittite goddess Hepat. Like Carchemish, Tabal was a major partner in eighth century B.C.E. alliances to block Assyrian expansion into northern Syria and Anatolia.

SYRIA

The Aramaeans

The Aramaeans, speakers of a West-Semitic language closely related to Canaanite (Phoenician and Hebrew), probably developed in southern Syria in the latter part of the Bronze Age. As we have seen, during the population movements accompanying the disasters of the late thirteenth through the twelfth centuries B.C.E., groups of Aramaeans repeatedly invaded Babylonia, Elam, Assyria, northern Syria, and eastern Anatolia. By the time they erupted onto the scene, they were divided into many different tribes and clans (at least 40 Aramaean tribes are known from Babylonian sources alone). In most of the areas they invaded, especially in Assyria, eastern Babylonia and southeastern Anatolia, the Aramaeans settled and became a part of the population. In much of Syria and western Mesopotamia, they became the dominant portion of the population and the rulers of several small kingdoms. In Mesopotamia west of the Habur River, the region known in the Bible as Aram-Naharaim ("Aram of the Rivers"), the Aramaean kingdoms of Bit-Adini, Bit-Bahyani (whose capital, Guzana, was called Gozan in the Bible and is now Tell Halaf), Bit-Zamani, and Bit-Halupe became powerful. Several of these kingdoms remained intact and continued to flourish until the seventh century B.C.E., despite being brought under Assyrian control by Shalmaneser III (858 to 824 B.C.E.).

The most important of the Aramaean states, though, was centered on Damascus, an ancient city in south-central Syria. This kingdom is called Aram-Damascus in the Bible. The exact antiquity of Damascus is unknown, for its earliest remains are buried under the present-day Old City and have not been excavated. However, third millennium B.C.E. pottery sherds have been found in the Old City, and the city's original name, Dimaska, is not Semitic, suggesting that the city was founded in prehistoric times. Moreover, Damascus was first mentioned in an inscription of Thutmose III from c. 1457 B.C.E., so clearly it had been occupied long before the Aramaeans began ruling it. Many think it is the oldest continuously inhabited city in the world.

No Aramaean royal annals and few royal inscriptions have survived, so historians have to reconstruct Aramaean history largely from biblical references and Assyrian texts. According to the Bible, in the tenth century B.C.E., Damascus was an ally or vassal of the Aramaean kingdom of Zobah. This kingdom, centered around the region of Beth Rehob in Lebanon's Beqaa Valley, came into existence at about the same time as the Israelite state and attained dominion over most of southern Syria. David supposedly defeated Zobah's king Hadadezer and an Aramaean army from Damascus that came to his aid, thus gaining control of Zobah's territory (2 Samuel 8 = I Chronicles 17). The Bible further states that during Solomon's reign, an Aramaean leader (there "named" Rezon which means "prince") made himself king of Damascus and established its independence, creating the foundation for its later political power in Syria (I Kings 11:23–25).

As previously mentioned, in the ninth century, Damascus led several coalitions seeking to prevent Assyrian expansion beyond the Euphrates River. Assyrian texts from the reign of Shalmaneser III indicate that the king of Damascus during the 850s B.C.E. was named Adad-idri (Hadad-idhr in Aramaic and Hadadezer in Hebrew). The Assyrian accounts also attest that one of Hadadezer's most powerful allies was king Ahab of Israel (see Document 8.1). However, the Bible (1 Kings 20 and 22; 2 Kings 5–8) states that Ben-Hadad (Bir-Hadad or Bar-Hadad in Aramaic) was the ruler of Aram-Damascus at the time of Ahab and his sons. This king is usually called Ben-Hadad II, since another Ben-Hadad is supposed to have reigned earlier in the ninth century during the reigns of Baasha of Israel and Asa of Judah (1 Kings 15:16–22). Some historians identify the Adad-idri mentioned in the Assyrian sources with Ben-Hadad (II) of the Bible.[4] Others, however, argue that originally, 1 Kings 20–22 and Kings 8 did not name the Israelite king who opposed Ben-Hadad. They theorize that a later editor wrongly assumed that these passages belonged to the time of Ahab (c. 873 to 852 B.C.E.) when they really referred to the reign of Jehoahaz (c. 813–797 B.C.E.). These scholars agree with the Assyrian evidence that the king of Aram-Damascus at the time of Ahab was Hadadezer.[5]

Hadadezer seems to have been assassinated around 845 B.C.E. by Hazael, a usurper (called "the son of a nobody" by the Assyrians), who seized the throne and reigned c. 845 to 800 B.C.E. Upon Hadadezer's death, the successful anti-Assyrian alliance he had led for many years collapsed. Jehoram (also called Joram), a son of Ahab and king of Israel (c. 851 to 841 B.C.E.), attacked Hazael, presumably to restore the old dynasty to the throne of Damascus. However, Jehoram was seriously wounded in a battle with the Aramaeans at Ramoth-Gilead in Transjordan. Hazael captured some of Israel's territory, erecting a victory stele at Dan (see Figure 8.3).[6] With the Israelite army tied down by the confrontations with Damascus, Moab, which probably had revolted against Israelite control around the time of Ahab's death (c. 852 B.C.E.), attained its freedom under the leadership of Mesha of Dibon. Meanwhile, Edom also successfully freed itself from Israel's ally, Judah. These losses, as well as local opposition to some of the religious policies of Omri's dynasty (see the following section "The Kingdoms of Israel and Judah"), fueled a military *coup d'etat* in Israel led by an officer named Jehu. The Bible claims that Jehu killed the wounded king Jehoram of Israel and his visiting ally, the king of Judah (2 Kings 9:14–27). However, the inscription on Hazael's monument at Dan (see Figure 8.3), if restored correctly, claims that Hazael killed the two kings (though he may have considered Jehu his instrument). In any case, Jehu became king of Israel (c. 841 to 813 B.C.E.) and, along with the Phoenician cities of Tyre and Sidon, hastened to make peace with Assyria, paying tribute and possibly encouraging Shalmaneser III to attack Damascus.

Damascus had to stand alone against Shalmaneser's attacks in 841 B.C.E., but though Hazael was defeated in battle, he retreated to his capital city, which withstood the Assyrian assault. Shalmaneser made a final unsuccessful attempt to conquer Damascus in 838 B.C.E. before abandoning his efforts to control all of Syria. Hazael was then able to raise Damascus to the height of its power. He took his revenge on Jehu, conquering most of Israel's territory east of the Jordan (2 Kings 10:32–33) and virtually reducing Israel to a state of vassalage. He also overpowered Philistia and forced Judah to become a tributary ally (2 Kings 12:17–18). Thus, by

FIGURE 8.3   Fragments of an Aramaic Stele at Dan

This stele celebrates a victory by a king of Damascus (almost certainly Hazael) over Israel and Judah (called the "House of David" on the stele).

Source: Courtesy of Tel Dan Excavations, Hebrew Union College, Nelson Glueck School of Archaeology, Jerusalem. *Photo:* Zev Radovan

the end of his reign, Hazael had made Damascus into the strongest state in the Levant.

Around 800 B.C.E., Hazael was succeeded by his son Ben-Hadad (Bir-Hadad), probably the second king of Damascus to have that name (or the third if one accepts the theory that a Ben-Hadad briefly succeeded Hadadezer and was the king killed by Hazael, as the Bible claims). Ben-Hadad inherited a thriving kingdom, but he was unable to maintain the dominion his father had achieved. Adad-nirari III of Assyria attacked Damascus in 796 B.C.E. and forced Ben-Hadad to pay tribute and become a vassal. Israel was able to reestablish its independence from Damascus, inflicting several defeats on Ben-Hadad's forces, and the hapless king also suffered a reverse while attacking the Aramaean kingdom of Hamath. Aram-Damascus then continued to decline until Assyria ended its status as an independent state in the mid-eighth century B.C.E.

The Aramaeans assimilated much of the culture that already existed in places that they settled. Their chief deity was the Amorite and Canaanite storm god Hadad (known as Adad in Mesopotamia) or Ramman (Rimmon in the Bible). Hadad was the proper name of the deity called Ba'al ("Lord") in the Ugaritic texts and the Bible. Ramman was one of his epithets, probably meaning "the Thunderer" or "the Roaring One." Hadad was also known as Ba'al-shamayn ("Lord of the Heavens") and was responsible for life-giving rain, and thus, was a god of fertility. But he also caused destructive storms (lightning was his weapon and thunder his voice), so he was seen as a warrior and god of battle, as well. Like the Hittite weather god, Teshub, Hadad's sacred animal was the bull, and he was sometimes depicted standing on the back of a bull while launching his thunderbolts. The Aramaeans' principal goddess was Atar'ate (later known as Atargatis), Hadad's consort. She was an amalgam of the Canaanite goddesses Ashtart (Astarte in Greek, Ashtoreth in the Bible, and *'atar* in Aramaic) and Anat (*'at* in Aramaic), and like her male partner, she was both a fertility and a war deity.

Like the neighboring Phoenicians and Israelites, the Aramaeans believed that the gods could communicate with humans by means of ordinary people as well as through professional prophets and seers attached to specific cult places. The eighth century B.C.E. inscription of King Zakkur of Hamath provides an example of the acceptance of such messages:

> I lifted my hands to Baal-shamayn, and Baalshamayn answered me, and Baalshamayn [sic] spoke to me through prophets and messengers; and Baalshamayn said to me: 'Fear not! It was I who made you king, [and I shall stand] with you, and I shall deliver you from all these kings who have forced a siege upon you.'[7]

This text sounds very much like biblical passages in which Israel's god, Yahweh ("the LORD" in English translations), delivers similar messages through prophets.

The prosperity of the major Aramaean cities came primarily from their positions on major trade routes. Damascus became especially wealthy because of its position on both the north-south and east-west camel caravan routes through Syria. Though camels had been domesticated much earlier, their usefulness as mounts and beasts of burden does not seem to have been widely exploited until around 1100 B.C.E. when they start to be mentioned in Near Eastern texts and depicted in art.[8] Once they began to be used for more than food, they revolutionized Near Eastern trade. Camels could eat a wide variety of plants, including desert shrubs and thorn bushes, and could go without water for much longer than donkeys, the primary beasts of burden in earlier times. Thus, camel caravans could take shorter, more direct paths between distant cities rather than following the meandering courses of rivers or circuitous routes with many water sources along the way, as had been customary earlier. They also allowed merchants to transport spices, incense, and other materials from southern and coastal Arabia overland along Arabia's western coast through Trans-jordan or Palestine to Damascus and Phoenicia.

The significant role of Damascus as a center for caravan trade, as well as the widespread settlements of Aramaeans between the Zagros Mountains and eastern Anatolia, resulted in Aramaic becoming a second language for most individuals involved in long-distance overland trade. Moreover, around 1100 B.C.E., some Aramaeans had adopted the Canaanite (Phoenician) alphabet to write their language, and by the mid-eighth century B.C.E., they had developed a cursive script from it. Aramaic thus became much easier to read and write than Akkadian cuneiform, and after Assyria's conquest of the Aramaean states in the eighth century B.C.E., the Assyrians began to use Aramaic to communicate with their western provinces. Due to the forced resettlement of many Aramaeans in Assyria and various conquered territories, Aramaean eventually became a second official language of the Assyrian Empire (see Figure 8.4). By Persian times, Aramaic had become the *lingua franca* of the entire Near East. It eventually replaced Hebrew as the common spoken language of Palestine, and the Aramaic script not only was adopted to write Hebrew, but also became the ancestor of the later scripts used to write Arabic and Syriac.

The Phoenicians

The classical Greeks called the people who lived in the Levantine coastal cities north of Palestine "Phoenicians" (*Phoinikes*), and later historians have followed their lead. Most scholars think that the name was derived from *phoinix*, the Greek word for the Mediterranean murex (a shellfish) and the dark red or red-purple color of the dye made from it. Thus, to the Greeks, the Phoenicians would have been the "people of the dark red-purple dye," since this was their most famous product. Some experts argue, though, that the name Phoenician came from *Fenkhu*, one of the Egyptian appellations for northern Canaan. In any case, the designation was a foreign one. The Phoenicians called themselves Canaanites (as had their Bronze Age ancestors), or more specifically identified themselves by the names of their city-states (e.g., Sidonians or Tyrians). Their language and culture continued to be closely related to those of the southern Canaanites of Palestine.

During the Late Bronze Age, the Phoenician cities, especially Gubal (Byblos), had been important subjects of the Egyptian Empire, and most of their trade had been monopolized by Egypt. However, when the major empires were shattered during the general eastern Mediterranean political and cultural collapse in the early part of the twelfth century B.C.E., the Phoenician cities became free to pursue their own destinies. Moreover, Ugarit, the most important Late Bronze Age maritime outlet for trade from inland Syria and eastern Anatolia, had been totally destroyed, leaving a vacuum for other coastal cities to fill. The Phoenicians rushed into the void, becoming the main maritime traders of the Mediterranean world until the seventh century B.C.E. when they had to start sharing that distinction with the Greeks.

The mountains of Lebanon often come down almost to the sea, with spurs and gorges dividing the coastal area into many small districts. So, as in ancient Greece, there was no unified Phoenician nation or realm. Though occasionally a large city like Sidon would dominate a smaller neighbor like Sarepta, most

FIGURE 8.4   Eighth-Century B.C.E. Assyrian Relief
This relief shows scribes making records in Akkadian cuneiform (scribe on the left with clay tablet) and in Aramaic (scribe on the right with papyrus or parchment).
Source: Courtesy of the Trustees of the British Museum, London.

Phoenician cities were independent self-governing states. They developed on small offshore islands or on promontories with protected anchorages and some space between the sea and the hills. Arvad (modern Ruad, Syria), Sidon (modern Saida, Lebanon), and Tyre (modern Sur, Lebanon), located at points where roads from the interior reached the coast by means of passes through or around the Lebanon mountains, became Phoenicia's major cities. Other ports such as Berytus (Beirut), Sarepta, and even Gubal (Byblos) were relegated to secondary status.

Archaeology shows that during the late twelfth and early eleventh centuries B.C.E., trade resumed between Phoenicia, Cyprus, and the Philistine towns along the coast of Palestine, restoring prosperity to these areas. Phoenician cultural influence spread into parts of Cyprus, Cilicia, Syria, northern Palestine, Philistia and the Nile Delta. In the case of northern Palestinian sites such as Dan, Tell Keisan, and Dor, it is possible that the Phoenician elements were imposed after military conquest (by Tyre?).[9] Within Phoenicia itself, towns began expanding, improving their layouts, and rebuilding their defensive walls. By the tenth century B.C.E., there is evidence that Phoenician ships were not only sailing frequently to Cyprus, but also further west to Crete and the Greek island of Euboea. In fact, it is likely that they were already sailing as far as the island of Sardinia. Such long-distance trade paved the way for subsequent Phoenician colonization.

Though Sidon initially had the advantage of having a larger territory to support its population as well as access through the mountains to the rich Beqaa Valley and Damascus, by the tenth century B.C.E., Tyre surpassed it in wealth and power. The Bible claims that King Hiram I of Tyre (c. 971 to 939 B.C.E.) formed an alliance with Solomon that included joint commercial expeditions to Ophir from Ezion-geber (perhaps modern Jezirat Far'oun), a port on the Gulf of Aqaba near modern Elat. The fabled land of Ophir was noted for its choice, high-quality gold, precious stones, fine hardwoods, and exotic animals. Its location is unknown, though some scholars have placed it in Arabia and others as far as India. However, Ophir likely was located on the lower part of the Red Sea in southwestern Arabia, opposite the African land the Egyptians called Punt. The treaty with Israel also gave Tyre access through Israelite territory to Damascus and Syria. Solomon later sold Hiram 20 cities in the agriculturally productive Acco plain and Galilee, allowing Tyre to feed its population without having to rely on agricultural imports.

Even if the biblical accounts of Solomon's reign are disregarded as late and fanciful (see below), archaeological evidence testifies to strong Phoenician connections with Dan, Hazor, Tel Amal (just west of Beth-shean) in the north, and Tel Masos in the Negev, the dry southern part of Palestine. The locations of these sites suggest Phoenician (almost certainly Tyrian) trade routes across northern Israel to the main north-south overland route ("the King's Highway") from Arabia through Transjordan as well as to the route that ran through Palestine, the Negev, and **Arabah** to the Gulf of Aqaba and thence by sea to Africa or southern Arabia. Moreover, Tyre had usually been allied with Egypt, and the reassertion of Egyptian power by Sheshonq (945 to 924 B.C.E.) must have strengthened Tyre's position in relation to Israel, Judah, and the Philistines. In fact, Tyre became so powerful by the first half of the ninth century B.C.E. that even Sidon seems to have become its vassal. King Ithoba'al I of Tyre (c. 887 to 856 B.C.E.) claimed to be also "king of the Sidonians," and his successors continued to use that title until the end of the eighth century B.C.E.[10]

During this time of prosperity, Tyre, Sidon, and Gubal (Byblos) voluntarily offered gifts (which the Assyrians called "tribute") to the Assyrian kings Asshurnasirpal II (around 870 B.C.E.) and Shalmaneser III (858 and 841 B.C.E.). The Assyrian campaigns, though, were aimed at the Neo-Hittite and Aramaean states of western Mesopotamia and Syria, and, as we have seen, were only partly successful. So, probably the southern Phoenician "tribute" was paid not so much to avoid attack as to secure continued trading rights in the areas the Assyrians had conquered. Considering the affluence Tyre, Sidon, and to a lesser extent, Gubal enjoyed during the ninth century B.C.E., their payments to Assyria seem to have been wise investments. Moreover, despite their failure to join the Aramaean military coalition against the Assyrians, the southern Phoenician states continued to have a strong commercial relationship with Damascus as well as political and economic ties to Israel. Damascus and Israel supplied Tyre and Sidon with wines and access to the incense trade from Arabia as well as most of the wool the Phoenicians wove into textiles and dyed their expensive red-purple color.

Their widespread Mediterranean trade led the Phoenicians to begin establishing overseas trading posts, which usually became self-governing colonies. The earliest known Phoenician colony (mid-ninth century B.C.E.) was at Kition (modern Larnaka) in Cyprus, though there is some disagreement about whether it was founded by Tyre or Sidon.[11] There is also disagreement about whether it was Kition or a slightly later settlement near modern Limassol that became known as Cypriot Qart-hadasht ("New City" in Phoenician, which became "Carthage" in western languages). From Cyprus, Phoenician merchants (mostly from Sidon, Arvad, and the Cypriot colonies) proceeded westward by way of Rhodes, Crete, and Greece to the northern Aegean as well as to Sicily, Italy, and Sardinia. The Phoenicians possibly settled Nora in Sardinia as early as the late ninth century B.C.E., and other colonies in Sardinia, Sicily, and Malta were established during the eighth century B.C.E. (see Map 8.1).

Meanwhile, Tyrian sailors were proceeding to Egypt and thence, since the current along the coast of Libya usually runs from west to east, across open sea to Tunisia, where at the site of modern Tunis they established another Qart-hadasht (Carthage). This "New City," probably founded around 750 B.C.E., became, of course, not only the most important Phoenician colony, but eventually a state far richer and more powerful than even its mother city, Tyre. The Tyrian merchants continued from Carthage along the coast of North Africa to Spain. They even sailed outside of the Straits of Gibraltar into the Atlantic Ocean, planting their first Spanish colony, Gadir ("Fortified Citadel"), on a small island in a sheltered bay. This settlement would develop into later Cadiz (see Map 8.1). In the seventh century B.C.E., the Phoenicians also

established several colonies on the Atlantic coast of Morocco. They probably sailed to the Canary Islands and possibly as far as the Azores, Brittany, and England. In the employ of the Egyptian pharaoh Necho II (610 to 595 B.C.E.), a contingent of Phoenicians circumnavigated Africa.

There was a common thread connecting most of these areas of Phoenician exploration, trade, and colonization—the metals trade. Cyprus was an important source of copper, and Crete produced iron ore. Thasos and nearby Thrace in the northern Aegean region had rich deposits of gold and silver. The Etruscan area of northern Italy yielded copper, lead, iron, and especially, silver ores. Sardinia also was rich in copper, iron, and silver-bearing lead ores. Morocco's mountains contained gold, copper, iron, and lead, while Spain was one of the Mediterranean's most important metal-producing areas, blessed with deposits of gold, silver, copper, tin, and iron. In some of these places, especially Spain, archaeologists have uncovered evidence of eighth through seventh century B.C.E. mines and/or metalworking tools such as smelting furnaces, bellows, and crucibles.[12]

As one might expect, the seafaring Phoenicians, endowed with large amounts of native timber, were excellent shipbuilders. They constructed several types of merchant vessels from small galleys for coastal and river traffic to large, wide seafaring ships that could carry large cargoes. They also probably first developed the bireme, a ship with two sets of oars on each side, which gave it double the rowing power without adding much to its length. Cargo vessels often had oars to use in calm weather or when coming into port, but the extra oars of a bireme were most effective on warships, providing additional speed and power behind the rams affixed to their bows (see Figure 8.5). The trireme, an improved version of this concept with three banks of oars to a side, was the main warship used by both the Greek and Persian (largely Phoenician) fleets during the Greek-Persian Wars of the fifth century B.C.E.

For the raw metals and other native goods they desired, the Phoenicians traded timber, their celebrated dyed cloth, and manufactured products (including finished metallic goods) created by their craftsmen. Skilled Phoenician metal workers pro-

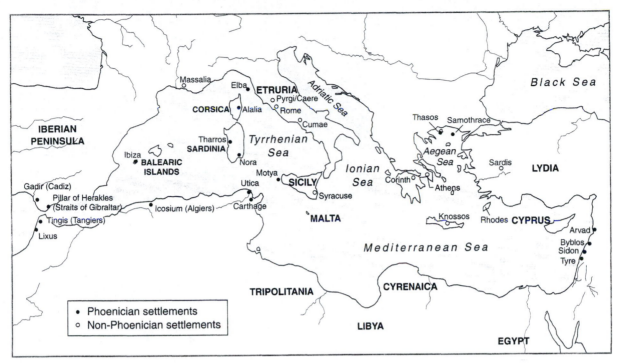

MAP 8.1   Major Phoenician Colonies of the Ninth Through Seventh Centuries B.C.E.

duced bronze incense stands, cast figurines, and jugs as well as beautiful decorated bronze, gold, and silver bowls and various kinds of jewelry (such as bracelets, pendants, rings, and earrings). The biblical descriptions of the bronze objects in Solomon's Temple suggest that they were made by Phoenician artisans, just as the temple building itself supposedly was designed and constructed by Phoenicians. In addition to shipbuilding, the Phoenicians were noted for their other woodworking skills. They used their native cedar and cypress trees to produce fine paneling, cabinets, coffins, chests, stools, couches, tables, and chairs. The wooden furniture often had wonderful carved ivory or bone inlays, also created by Phoenician artists who blended Egyptian and Asiatic styles in their work. In addition to inlays, ivory was used to make many small objects such as carved statuettes, boxes, fly-whisk handles, cosmetic spoons, amulets, combs, and hairpins. Stone cutting and carving, seal making, and glass making were other fields in which Phoenicians excelled.

In addition to their own products, the Phoenicians traded goods from other Near Eastern areas. For example, Gubal (called Byblos by the Greeks) provided Greece with sheets of papyrus made from plants grown in Egypt. Thus, for the Greeks the name Byblos became associated with paper and writing and eventually its diminutive form (*biblion*) became the word for "book" and the source of our word "Bible."

Phoenician cities in the homeland for which we have information were governed by kings who seem to have had a large amount of administrative and religious authority and power. As in many other Near Eastern societies, Phoenician kings were also the chief priests who presided over major religious ceremonies. However, the king's power and authority was not absolute. According to the eleventh-century Egyptian *Report of Wenamun*, Zakarba'al, the king of Gubal (Byblos), convened an "assembly" to help handle the problem of the Tjekker who wanted to seize Wenamun. The assembly seems to have given weight to the king's decision by

FIGURE 8.5   An Assyrian Depiction of Phoenician Biremes

This drawing, based on an original relief, shows Phoenician bireme cargo vessels and war galleys (the ships with masts and rams) at sea.
Source: Courtesy of the Trustees of the British Museum, London.

demonstrating community support. A seventh-century B.C.E. treaty between Tyre and Assyria mentions a similar advisory body, a Council of Elders, that helped the king govern. In other areas of the Near East with a similar institution (such as Mesopotamia), members of the Council of Elders seem to have been drawn from the heads of the major landowning aristocratic families. In Phoenicia, though, based on later evidence from Carthage, historians have generally assumed that the members of the council were drawn from a "merchant

aristocracy" whose wealth and power stemmed from commerce rather than land. Ancient texts also refer to a "People's Assembly," probably consisting of all of a city's free male citizens, but its functions and powers are unknown.

Little is known about the administration of the early Phoenician colonies. Initially, they probably were closely tied to their mother-cities politically, economically, and religiously. Each colony had a temple to the founding city's patron deity, which helped maintain the relationship between mother and daughter cities. When Phoenicia fell under the control of the Babylonians and Persians, the colonies became self-governing, and some even established colonies of their own. In Carthage and other western colonies, the position of "governor" or suffete° became an elective office. Two suffetes who seem to have had most of the powers of the mother-cities' kings were elected each year by the Carthaginian citizen assembly. The formerly advisory oligarchic Council of Elders (or Senate), guided by a smaller inner council, gained the power to declare war and oversee foreign affairs.

Phoenician culture had gradually evolved from that of the Bronze Age Canaanites, so there was much continuity with earlier customs. This is particularly true in regard to the religious pantheon and cultic practices. Most of the Canaanite deities mentioned in Bronze Age Egyptian sources and in the Ugaritic texts were still worshipped in Phoenicia and Palestine during the first millennium. However, Phoenician/Canaanite religion was not static. Some new deities were also introduced and some of the major gods assimilated the names and characteristics of originally separate deities. Unfortunately, the lack of direct Phoenician documentation makes it impossible to be certain about the details of their religious beliefs and rituals.

Each Phoenician city seems to have had its own divine couple as primary patrons. At Gubal (Byblos), the chief god was Ba'al Shamem ("Lord of the Heavens") whose name probably represents the local title by which Hadad (Ba'al), the weather god, was known. His consort was called Ba'alat Gubal ("Lady of Byblos"), which probably is a title for Ashtart (Astarte), goddess of fertility and the principal Phoenician goddess elsewhere. Sidon's chief deities were Eshmun (originally an underworld deity who, nevertheless, promoted health and healing) and Ashtart, while Tyre's were Melqart ("Ruler of the City") and Ashtart (also called Tanit, particularly in the western colonies). Melqart is a title, so this god may have been

known by a different name elsewhere. Some think Melqart was originally a solar deity[13] possibly related to Resheph, a god of fire with solar connections who also was an underworld deity responsible for plague. In the Phoenician colonies on Cyprus, Resheph was identified with Apollo and became the patron god of metalworking. However, at Carthage, there was a temple to Resheph (Apollo) distinct from the temple of Melqart. It is more likely that Melqart was the Tyrian title for Ba'al,[14] since at Carthage he was sometimes called Ba'al Melqart. In any case, he became the patron god of seafarers and was the principle god of Carthage and Gadir (Cadiz) as well as Tyre.

All of these chief male deities were probably just localized variants of Ba'al-Hadad, while their consorts are versions of the fertility goddess Ashtart. Whatever their origins, the male patron deities of the major Phoenician cities seem to have been dying and rising fertility deities. Later classical authors describe an annual celebration of Melqart's resurrection at Tyre and similar rites at Byblos for Adonis (a name derived from the Semitic 'adon, "lord" or 'adonai, "my lord"), almost certainly the Byblian Ba'al. Eshmun also seems to have been associated with death and rebirth. These ideas probably were derived originally from Mesopotamian rituals associated with Ishtar (the Akkadian equivalent of Ashtart) and Tammuz. However, the Canaanites had borrowed them in the second millennium B.C.E. or earlier. A Ugaritic myth describes a conflict between Mot ("Death") and Ba'al in which Mot kills Ba'al and takes him into the underworld, producing a period of totally dry weather on earth. Ba'al's consort (Anat in the Ugaritic story) challenges Mot to battle, kills him, and subjects his body to ritual agricultural acts: "with a sickle she cut him, with a winnowing tool she winnowed him, with fire she burned him, with millstones she ground him, in a field she scattered him."[15] These actions bring about Ba'al's rebirth and a restoration of rain and fertility. Judging from the later references, the Phoenicians continued to accept a version of this myth about the yearly agricultural cycle and to perform rituals associated with it throughout the first millennium B.C.E.

Though Phoenicians sometimes made figurines or statuettes of their deities or depicted them (often

---

°"Suffete" is derived from the Latin *sufes* and is used in Western languages to represent the Phoenician title *shuphet* (*shophet* in Hebrew). This word had the more general meaning of "executive, leader, ruler" and in the colonies, more specifically, "governor."

in stylized form) on pendants, amulets, and stelae, they don't seem to have erected cult statues in their temples. Instead, the gods' presence was indicated by empty thrones or standing stones known as betyls (from the Semitic word for "home of the god") that could be roughly cut stone slabs or carefully dressed pillars. Such stones were called *masseboth* ("dressed stones") in the Bible and were often associated with open air "high places" (*bamot*) as forms of Canaanite worship. Instead of a stone pillar, the fertility goddess Asherah was represented by a wooden post or stylized tree that itself was called an *asherah*. Like most aspects of Phoenician religion, the use of such non-figural objects as signs of the presence of the divine was very ancient. Archaeologists have uncovered several Middle and Late Bronze Age Canaanite sanctuaries in Phoenicia and Palestine containing obelisks or standing stones. The Phoenician use of betyls continued into Roman times.

Also like their Bronze Age predecessors, the Iron Age Canaanites and Phoenicians practiced cultic prostitution, especially in connection with the worship of Ashtart. Later inscriptions testify to the presence of both male and female prostitutes at Ashtart's temple at Kition, Cyprus. Documentation is lacking in the Phoenician homeland, but biblical attacks on this Canaanite custom indicate that it was native to the Levant. As in earlier Mesopotamia, individuals seem to have offered themselves as prostitutes for a time to fulfill a vow to the gods or as a sign of their devotion. In Phoenicia, this practice continued into Roman times.

One Phoenician/Canaanite religious rite that has been hotly debated is their supposed practice of sacrificing children, burning them and presenting them to their gods. Classical authors made this claim about the Carthaginians, and Jeremiah, the biblical prophet, castigates his fellow Judeans for following Canaanite practices, including burning their sons and daughters at Tophet ("Place of Burning"?), a ceremonial site near Jerusalem (Jeremiah 7:30–32; see also 2 Kings 23:10). At Carthage, Motya, Tharros, and several other sites in Tunisia, Algeria, Sicily, and Sardinia, archaeologists have found sacred burial places which, adopting the biblical term, they call Tophets. Buried beneath stelae in these Tophets were tens of thou-

sands of urns containing cremated remains, some of animals but most of small children, seemingly supporting the classical and biblical authors' claims. But some dissenters deny that these cremated remains are those of sacrificial victims.[16] These scholars question the reliability of the classical and biblical accounts, noting that they were highly polemical in nature. Moreover, they point out that there was an extremely high infant mortality rate in antiquity, and that a high percentage of the remains in the Tophets belong to newborn or premature infants. On the other hand, few infant burials have been found in the regular adult cemeteries at sites containing Tophets. So, these scholars claim, the Tophet remains likely are those of stillborn babies or infants who died from natural causes. The gods had "recalled" these individuals to the divine realm, so the grieving parents gave the children's bodies back to the gods, incinerating them and burying them in the sacred precinct. "In return, the parents hoped that Ba'al Hammon and Tanit would provide a replacement for the retroceded child—and this request was inscribed on a funeral stela."[17]

However, there are serious problems with this argument.[18] Most of the stelae placed above the jars containing cremated remains refer to vows made to the gods rather than requests for future offspring. They suggest that the cremated offerings, animal or human, were given in fulfillment of those vows. Moreover, the presence of animal remains (mostly sheep and goats) is difficult to explain if the Tophets are burial places for infants who died naturally. "The animals were sacrificed to the gods, presumably in place of children. It is highly likely that the children unlucky enough not to have substitutes were also sacrificed and then buried in the Tophet."[19] Moreover, in an eighth century B.C.E. Phoenician inscription recently discovered in Cilicia, a Tyrian priest advises the local ruler to sacrifice his son or grandson as well as a lamb to alleviate a plague ravaging the area.[20] So, most historians and archaeologists have continued to see the cremated remains in the Tophets as evidence that the Phoenicians sacrificed infants as votive offerings to their deities. While some infants may have been offered to the gods to prevent or atone for disasters or catastrophes, others were probably unwanted children given back to the gods, just as ancient Greeks exposed unwanted babies.[21]

So far, all of the examples of Tophets have been found in the western colonies. However, the Tophet at Carthage goes back to the late eighth century B.C.E., not long after the founding of the city. This early appearance suggests that infant sacrifice was a practice brought with the colonists from their homeland rather than a new custom developed in the colonies. In addition, the biblical references to the burning of children are largely contemporary descriptions of eighth-through seventh-century Canaanite (and Judean) practices within the Levant, indicating that the custom was at home there. Finally, the recently discovered Cilician inscription shows that infant sacrifice was practiced in Tyre during the eighth century B.C.E. Clearly, we do not yet fully understand many aspects of this rite, including its purpose, processes, timetable, and the socioeconomic groups that participated in it. But it was an aspect, probably a very ancient one, of Phoenician/Canaanite worship of Ba'al and Ashtart (Tanit).

Biblical writers, especially the prophets, usually had a profoundly negative reaction to Phoenician/Canaanite religious beliefs and customs such as *asherahs*, "high places," cultic prostitution, and infant sacrifice. However, prophecy itself seems to be an element of Phoenician/Canaanite religion that the Israelites borrowed. Like other Near Eastern peoples, the Phoenicians used many different types of signs and omens to understand supernatural phenomena and to determine the will of the gods. Cultic prophets interpreted such portents. Phoenician cultic prophets were closely associated with priests, and in the biblical Elijah narrative, the prophets of Ba'al perform sacrifices (1 Kings 18:23), normally a priestly function. Together the priests and professional prophets maintained and passed on the Phoenician religious tradition. However, the Phoenicians seem to have recognized nonprofessional prophets as well, believing that ordinary citizens could be given messages by the gods. In the *Report of Wenamun*, when the king of Gubal (Byblos) was trying to send Wenamun away, a boy (possibly a court page) became prophetically possessed, experiencing a seizure or convulsion caused by a god. A divine revelation assured him that Wenamun was indeed sent by the god

Amun, and he conveyed this message to the king. Similar beliefs are attested in the Mari Letters from the time of Hammurabi, and likely had been held by Bronze Age Canaanites, as well. Thus, like other elements of Bronze Age religion, acceptance of both professional and nonprofessional prophets passed naturally into Phoenician religion and into that of early Israel.

The most important contribution of the Phoenicians to other cultures, though, was the alphabet. The Phoenicians used the Canaanite alphabet, a direct descendent of the Proto-Canaanite alphabet developed in the early part of the second millennium B.C.E. (see Chapter 6). The Phoenicians introduced the alphabet into Cilicia, from whence it may have spread into central Anatolia. Around 1100 B.C.E., contact with the Phoenicians led the Arameans to create a modified form of the alphabet to write their own language. Through the visits of Phoenician merchants to Greece in the tenth and ninth centuries B.C.E., Greeks learned of the alphabet and adapted it to write Greek (see Figure 6.6 in Chapter 6). They used some of the signs for Semitic consonants that didn't exist in Greek for vowels, but they kept the signs in the same order and even continued to use the Canaanite names of the letters, after a fashion. Thus Canaanite *aleph*, *beth*, *gimel*, and *daleth* became Greek *alpha*, *beta*, *gamma* and *delta*. All western alphabets derive from this modified Greek alphabet either directly (as in the case of Russian and other Slavic scripts) or indirectly (by way of the Etruscans who passed it on to the Romans who spread it through the West).

EARLY ISRAEL

The Emergence of Israel

Because its religion and Scriptures became basic components of Western civilization, ancient Israelite history generally has merited greater attention than would be expected from the nation's size, political influence, or military power. It is one of the few ancient states to preserve an account of its origins, and most Westerners are acquainted with the biblical stories of patriarchal wanderings, Exodus from Egypt, conquest of

Canaan, and creation of a monarchy. Orthodox Jews and fundamentalist Christians believe that this biblical account is correct in every detail. But mainstream Western scholarship has come to realize that these narratives were written long after the times they describe and contain inaccuracies and legendary material. Scholars also recognize that writers of biblical "history," like the authors of other ancient Near Eastern annals and inscriptions, did not approach their subject with the objectivity and detachment attempted by modern historians. The biblical "historians" had a religious purpose: to teach Israelites about the covenant between God and his people; to show how he had chosen the Israelites as part of his plan of salvation and how he had been consistently faithful to his promises to them; and thus, to lead them to more faithful devotion to him. Using the methods of literary criticism developed for the study of other literature, nineteenth- and early twentieth-century biblical scholars delineated several "documents" or written works that eventually had been compiled into the Pentateuch (Torah) and other "historical" prose books of the Bible. They generally dated the earliest of these writings, a Pentateuchal source called *J* (for the "Yahwist" or "Jahwist" work) and another composition called "The Court History of David" (2 Samuel 9 through 1 Kings 2), to the time of Solomon or just afterward.[22] So, through the 1960s, most biblical scholars, historians, and archaeologists thought that the stories concerning early Israel were based on authentic oral traditions that were written down relatively early, and thus, were essentially (though not totally) historical.

However, over the past generation, the work of several biblical scholars and archaeologists has undermined this consensus. Today, the origin and early history of the Israelite state is probably the most fiercely debated topic in Israelite history. Some scholars now claim that *J*, the Court History, and the other biblical prose narratives were not written until after the Babylonian Exile, during the Persian and Hellenistic Periods, and present an idealized, largely fictional account of Israel's early history.[23] A few scholars, basing their contentions mainly on archaeological evidence, also deny the existence of the United Monarchy. They assert that Judah and Israel were always separate states and did not emerge as small kingdoms (really chieftainships) until the ninth or eighth centuries B.C.E., after the supposed era of David and Solomon (rulers these scholars consider legendary). On the other hand, most specialists in biblical history and Syro-Palestinian archaeology continue to accept somewhat more traditional views of Israelite history.[24] What follows (and what was covered previously in discussions of the Aramaeans and Phoenicians) will generally reflect a moderate historical-critical view of the Bible, while at least mentioning some leading alternatives.

Today, there is much skepticism about whether we can know anything about Israel's history before the time of the Judges (twelfth through eleventh centuries B.C.E.) or the beginning of the monarchy (tenth century B.C.E.), and some think we know nothing before the ninth century B.C.E. Many scholars still believe that the patriarchal traditions may have been based on a dim memory that some of Israel's ancestors participated in Amorite movements of the late third and early second millennia B.C.E. However, the confidence of the previous generation that we could clearly place the patriarchs within their Near Eastern context and provide firm dates for their era has dissipated. While the stories possibly contain some ancient elements passed down by oral tradition, their final version (including the family relationships of the various figures) probably reflects the interests and ideology of Judah from the ninth through seventh centuries B.C.E. or later.[25]

Some scholars also question the historicity of the Exodus, but most agree that at least a portion of the later population of Israel was in Egypt for a time.[26] The majority generally consider it unlikely that any nation would invent a tradition that its founders had suffered shameful slavery in a foreign land. However, the various accounts (later woven into one narrative) of how Moses led the Israelites out of Egypt and to the borders of Canaan contain many discrepancies and elements of folklore.[27] The number of people involved was almost certainly much smaller than the 600,000 adult males (indicating a total population of about two million) given in Numbers 1 and 26. Nevertheless, there probably was a real Moses, for his name is Egyptian (from the word for "begotten" or "child of," as in Egyptian names such as Ahmose and Thutmose).° The Bible provides an inaccurate Hebrew folk etymology for this name (Exodus 2:10), suggesting that the later Israelites did not understand its origin and meaning, and thus, probably did not fabricate it or the person who bears it. Other Egyptian names such as Phinehas, Hophni, and Merari also occur among the Levites, Moses' tribe, probably further supporting the tradition of an Egyptian background for at least a portion of the Israelites. Moreover, many scholars are still convinced that the references in the oppression and Exodus narratives to Raamses (Egyptian Pi-Ramesse or Per-Ramesses), a city named after and largely built by Ramesses II (c. 1279 to 1213 B.C.E.) and abandoned around 1000 B.C.E., date the Exodus to the thirteenth century B.C.E. A date in the thirteenth century B.C.E. or earlier for the Exodus is also suggested by the fact that Ramesses II's successor, Merneptah, claims to have destroyed a people called "Israel" in Palestine c. 1208 B.C.E. (see Document 7.2 in Chapter 7). Since 1 Kings 6:1 indicates that the Exodus occurred in the 1440s B.C.E., some scholars argue that two or more groups ancestral to later Israel may have left Egypt at different times and traveled to Canaan by different routes.

The religious idea associated with the Exodus in the Bible—acceptance of a covenant demanding sole worship of a god named **Yahweh** and obedience to his laws—is also problematic. Biblical and archaeological evidence both indicate that Israelite acceptance of monotheism was a gradual process that wasn't completed until the sixth century B.C.E., and most of the "Mosaic" laws belong to the era of the Divided Monarchy or later.[28] Furthermore, archaeology has turned up no artifacts from the time of the Exodus (which must have been sometime in the Late Bronze Age) anywhere in Sinai except at the Egyptian mines at Serabit el-Khadim and the Egyptian way stations along the Mediterranean coastal road. There

are also no signs of Late Bronze Age occupation at Kadesh Barnea, Arad, Heshbon, Dibon, and other sites mentioned in the Exodus-Numbers accounts.[29]

In recent decades, support for the biblical tradition of an Israelite military acquisition of Canaan has also faded due to the fact that much of the archaeological evidence from Israel and Jordan is very difficult to reconcile with the biblical conquest narratives. Several cities that play an important role in the narratives, especially Jericho, Ai, and Gibeon, were not occupied during the fifteenth or thirteenth centuries B.C.E., the two most probable times for the Exodus. Moreover, the pottery styles and other aspects of material culture of the presumed "Israelite" villages that appear in the Palestinian hills in the Iron Age I are closely related to the previous Canaanite culture of the Late Bronze Age. Many leading archaeologists and biblical scholars have abandoned the traditional views of an Israelite conquest (as described in the Book of Joshua) or of a gradual and largely peaceful influx of nomads from outside of Canaan (consistent with Judges 1). Instead, they have adopted theories that indicate that during the era that the Bible later claimed was the time of the Judges, Israel was created in the Palestinian hill country primarily out of groups of people who were already native to Canaan.[30]

How and why did groups of Canaanites move to the hills, organize themselves into tribes, and join together into an entity called Israel? The answers are not known, though several hypotheses or models have been offered. Many scholars accept the "Internal Nomadic Settlement" model of Israel Finkelstein.[31] This theory is a variation of the old "Peaceful Infiltration" hypothesis. It traces Israel's origins to the Shasu seminomads of Palestine and Transjordan mentioned in Late Bronze Age Egyptian texts. These native pastoralists began settling in the hill country at the beginning of the Iron Age and eventually became the Tribes of Israel.

This theory, though, requires the existence of far more Palestinian seminomads during the Late Bronze Age than the evidence seems to indicate. If there were as many seminomads as Finkelstein and his supporters claim, and the climate then was much the same as now (which Finkelstein believes), surely some of them would have pastured their flocks in the

---

°There should have been an Egyptian god's name before "Mose(s)" originally, but obviously this divine element (such as Ptah, Thoth, Re or Amun) was dropped when Moses came to worship a different god.

Negev for part of the year, and traces of their presence would have remained. Seminomads of other periods, including today, have utilized this area when plants spring up after the rainy season, and archaeologists have noted the evidence of their encampments. But no Late Bronze Age remains have been found in the Negev.[32] This fact suggests that the Negev was drier in Late Bronze times than at present and/or there were far fewer Palestinian seminomads in that period than Finkelstein thinks, too few to occupy all the Iron I villages that have been found in the hills.

Other scholars, arguing that the Iron Age I villagers in the hills have an agrarian rather than pastoralist background, favor the "Peasants' Revolt" theory first proposed by George Mendenhall and modified by Norman Gottwald.[33] This model proposes that Israel originated from dissident peasants who, inspired by teachings about a liberating god named Yahweh or impoverished by noble landowners and Egyptian tribute demands, revolted against their masters, attacked their city-states, and then fled to the sparsely occupied Palestinian hill country. Some adherents of this model modify it by emphasizing that the fleeing peasants were more refugees than revolutionaries. They argue that it was the effects of drought or military conflict in the plains rather than revolutionary religious ideology or longstanding economic discontent that forced many individuals to seek refuge in the hills.[34] Whatever their reasons for fleeing, in the hill country, the survivors joined with other dispossessed people to create small agrarian villages, which in turn bonded with one another to form relatively unstratified social units and tribes. "Their sense of kinship with each other and separateness from other groups resulted from living in proximity with each other and from patterns of marriages and mutual support over time."[35] Probably taking the name of one of their component groups that had lived in the central hill country for some time, this collection of tribes became Israel.

The Proto-Israelites also came to worship a god called Yahweh, a deity probably introduced into Palestine by a small group of former Egyptian slaves who had learned of him in Midian. It should be noted, though, that since the vast majority of the Proto-Israelites probably were once Canaanite peasants, they seem to have continued their old religious practices, even after adopting the worship of Yahweh. Probably most would have seen Yahweh as another name for a familiar Canaanite god such as El or Ba'al. In fact, Yahweh's identification with El even seems to have been officially promoted during the time of the monarchy. Local Canaanite forms of El such as El Berith, El Bethel, El Olam and El Shaddai worshipped at shrines at Shechem, Bethel, and other Palestinian sites were claimed to be earlier manifestations of the god Yahweh who had revealed himself to Moses. There is also evidence that down to the time of Josiah's reforms in the seventh century B.C.E., Yahweh, like El or Ba'al, was thought to have the fertility goddess Asherah as his consort.[36] Thus, the Canaanite features present in later Israelite religion were probably not the result of "backsliding" from an early pure monotheism. They likely had been present from the time that Israel itself came into being during the Iron Age I (c. 1150 to 900 B.C.E.).

The Formation of the Israelite State (The United Monarchy)

The Bible claims that after initially functioning as independent units that only sporadically participated in joint military actions, the Israelite tribes were welded together into a monarchy. In recent years, though, some scholars have questioned the reality of Israel's United Monarchy. They suggest that "there were *always* two distinct highland entities, of which the southern was always the poorer, weaker, more rural, and less influential—until it rose to sudden, spectacular prominence *after* the fall of the northern kingdom of Israel."[37] They support this view by arguing that Stratum VA-IVB (to be read as 5a-4b) at Megiddo, usually dated to the tenth century B.C.E., actually belongs to the time of Ahab, the mid-ninth century B.C.E. Thus, the similar pottery and remains at various sites such as Jerusalem, Megiddo, Gezer, and Hazor usually claimed to be from the time of David and Solomon actually belong to the following century. There would then be no monumental architecture or other signs of a new state within Palestine that could correspond to the Bible's description of the United Monarchy.[38]

Most archaeologists and biblical historians have rejected these views.[39] The preponderance of evidence indicates that Stratum VA-IVB at Megiddo did belong to the tenth century B.C.E. and therefore, that the related material at Jerusalem and other sites did also. Moreover, as B. S. J. Isserlin has pointed out, if Israel and Judah developed as independent kingdoms and were never united, certain features of the biblical tradition, put into its final form by Judeans, are difficult to understand.[40] Why would Judeans at the time of the Exile or later have called themselves Israelites when the northern kingdom had often been Judah's enemy and, in Judean traditions, is castigated for its sinful religious practices? Even more significant is the "striking fact that the deity worshipped in the temple at Jerusalem is referred to (especially by Isaiah) as 'the God of Israel,' but never as the god of Judah."[41] These features are best explained by the biblical assumption that there was an early unified Israel from which the later kingdoms of Israel and Judah derived.

Just as Assyrian expeditions into the Lake Van area probably forced the small kingdoms of that region to unite into a single kingdom (Urartu), pressure from the expanding Philistine cities likely drove the newly formed Israelite tribes to unite more completely. Limited alliances of a few tribes at a time led by charismatic commanders (*shophetim*)° had sufficed during Israel's formative period when the enemies were also small and relatively disorganized. But larger, better-supplied and more efficiently organized armies were needed to withstand the Philistine forces. Saul (c. 1027 to 1005 B.C.E.), a member of the small tribe of Benjamin, was chosen to solve the problem.

We know relatively little about Saul, though it seems clear that he served as a transition figure between leadership by "Judges" and a true monarchy. The biblical narratives usually designate him as *nasi'* ("prince") or *nagid* ("commander; crown prince")

rather than *melekh* ("king"), and several different accounts of his selection, both favorable (1 Samuel 9:1–10:16 and 11:1–11;) and unfavorable (1 Samuel 8; 10:17–27; 12), have survived. Despite the generally hostile depiction of Saul in the Bible (especially in 1 Samuel 16–27 which supports the claims of his rival, David), he seems to have been a brave and skillful military leader who had some success against Israel's enemies (1 Samuel 14:47–48). However, he seems to have been unable to convert Israel from a tribal confederation into a centralized kingdom, and if the Bible is correct, he became increasingly prone to severe bouts of depression. He also failed to eliminate the Philistine threat, dying at the conclusion of an unsuccessful battle with them. (Compare the divergent traditions about Saul's death in 1 Samuel 31:3–5 and 2 Samuel 1:6–10.) Despite these failures, Saul had managed to stabilize Israelite control over its core territory of the central hill country and the hill country of Transjordan (the probable extent of his "kingdom"). Moreover, he inspired such devotion among most of his subjects that they wanted his son Eshba'al to succeed him and accepted David only when there was no viable alternative.

David (c. 1005 to 970 B.C.E.), the ideal king during a "golden age" according to later legend, seems to have been the first true ruler of a united Israel. As we have seen, some deny that we can derive any genuine historical information about David from the biblical legends and propagandistic stories about him. However, it is difficult to explain why later writers would have invented the unflattering information about David found in 1 and 2 Samuel and then have worked so hard to explain it away. This material likely stems from well-known accounts that could not simply be ignored or suppressed. David, a Judean from Bethlehem, began his career as an officer in Saul's army (compare 1 Samuel 16:14–23 with the more legendary account in 1 Samuel 17). Eventually he broke with Saul and became an outlaw hiding out in the Judean hill country where he gathered together a band of fellow brigands and rebels against Saul. Then David and his army of malcontents joined the forces of Achish, the Philistine king of Gath, who gave him command over a small town on the border of Judah. There, David built up his power, hiring Philistine mercenaries (Cheretites,

---

°The Hebrew noun *shophet/shophetim* is usually translated "Judge/Judges" in English versions of the Bible. However, comparisons of its cognates in Phoenician and Akkadian and study of its contexts in the Bible show that the word had the more general meaning of "executive, leader, or ruler" who might also function as a judge, deliverer, or arbitrator.

Peletites, and Gittites) to supplement his band of former outlaws who were now also professional warriors, loyal to David alone. He used his position to endear himself to the leaders of Judah by defeating their local enemies. These maneuvers resulted in his eventually being anointed as "king" of Judah when Saul and his three oldest sons died at the battle of Mt. Gilboa. On the other hand, Israel chose Saul's surviving son, Eshba'al, as king. But after a couple of years of warfare with David and the death of Israel's leading general, two of Eshba'al's own officers (possibly in collusion with David) assassinated him. The northern tribes then accepted David as king, bringing about an incorporation of Israel and Judah into one kingdom called Israel.

Though at times David could be ruthless in obtaining his objectives and proved to be incapable of handling the rivalries and intrigues within his own family, he seems to have been a gifted and charismatic military leader. His professional troops formed the core of his army, and with them, he was able to compel obedience from the Israelite tribes in ways that Saul could not. David augmented this mercenary force with Israelite tribal levies and led it to a series of stunning victories. He captured the previously independent city of Jerusalem and made it his capital. At the time, Jerusalem seems to have been only a small, possibly unwalled town (though the Middle Bronze Age wall may still have been in use), but it was ideally located on the border between the rival areas of Israel and Judah. David established a shrine for Yahweh there, and the city soon became the religious as well as the political capital of the new state. David went on to defeat the Philistines, his former overlords, and drive them back into their coastal enclave. He also defeated the nearby lands of Edom, Moab, and Ammon as well as the Aramaean state of Zobah, but how much control he exercised over these areas is debated. If David did conquer part of Syria, it is unlikely that he dominated it for more than a very brief period. Despite his many victories, David was not universally loved by his people. He weathered two rebellions against his rule mainly because of the loyalty of his mercenary troops. Though his power and empire were probably not nearly as extensive as the Bible claims, he does seem to have built Israel into a state

rather than just a chieftainship. His fame was lasting; a hundred years after his death, the Aramaean ruler of Damascus called the southern Hebrew kingdom not Judah, but "the House of David" (see Figure 8.3).

David's successor, Solomon (c. 970 to 931 B.C.E.), consolidated and developed the state that David had created. He better organized the central administration and divided the country into 12 administrative districts, each of which would support the court for one month a year. He also engaged in a major construction program during his reign. The Bible claims that he fortified Hazor, Megiddo, and Gezer, important cities guarding major trade routes or possible invasion routes into the kingdom. At these sites (as well as at Ashdod and Lachish), archaeologists have found very similar tenth century B.C.E. six-chambered monumental gateways (see Figure 8.6). A few archaeologists date these gates to the following century, but most have rejected the arguments for this proposal and continue to see the gates as evidence of Solomon's building activities. He may also have constructed a series of forts in the Negev to guard oases and the kingdom's southern approaches, but the dates of these structures are difficult to determine. Solomon's most famous building activity, of course, occurred in Jerusalem. He increased Jerusalem's size, erecting a temple for Yahweh on a previously unoccupied hill just north of the city and a palace for himself just south of the temple. He also seems to have utilized a massive thirteenth- through twelfth-century B.C.E. stone mantle or retaining wall on the city's steep eastern side to support some of his public buildings at the top of the mound and terraces and houses along its sides.[42]

In foreign affairs, Solomon maintained good relations with Egypt and entered into an alliance with King Hiram I of Tyre. Hiram provided craftsmen to design and construct the Temple of Yahweh in Jerusalem, which seems to have had the three-room Canaanite temple plan that had been common since the Middle Bronze Age. The Tyrians also built a fleet of ships for Israel on the Gulf of Aqaba and participated with Solomon in joint trading expeditions to Ophir and Africa. In exchange, Tyre received access to trade routes that passed through Israelite territory, half the profits from the joint trade missions, and 20

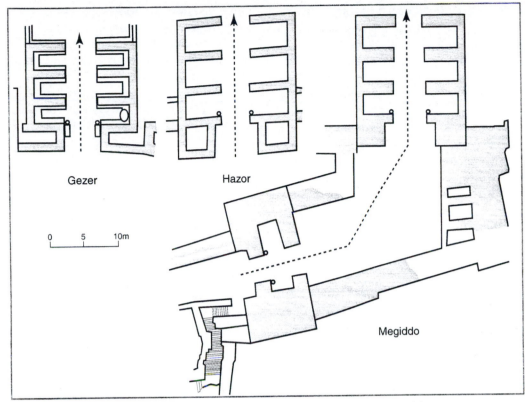

Gezer

Hazor

0   5   10m

Megiddo

FIGURE 8.6   Plans of Tenth-Century B.C.E. Gates at Gezer, Hazor, and Megiddo
The outer gate at Megiddo was probably added later.
Source: Adapted from Amihai Mazar, *Archaelogy of the Land of the Bible, 10,000–586 B.C.E.* (New York: Doubleday, 1990), p. 384.

cities in the rich agricultural area of the Acco Plain and the northwestern end of the Jezreel Valley.

To pay for his construction projects and his luxurious lifestyle, the Bible says that Solomon collected tribute from the subject nations David had conquered and taxed trade that passed through the territory he controlled. Israel's importance to the Arabian spice trade is suggested by the later folkloric biblical account of a visit to Solomon by the Queen of Sheba (a kingdom in southern Arabia). Solomon also received income from his commercial ventures. He acted as a middleman in the arms trade, buying chariots in Egypt and horses in Que (Cilicia) and selling them to Aramaean and Neo-Hittite rulers. In addition, the joint Israelite-Tyrian trading ventures down the Gulf of Aqaba were probably very profitable. Nevertheless, the considerable income

from these sources was not enough, so Solomon also had to tax his own people heavily. Moreover, he secured manpower for his building enterprises by subjecting his citizens to corvée (forced) labor.

In addition to the high taxes and corvée labor, the social changes caused by creation of a bureaucracy were very unpopular, especially with some members of the northern tribes. The Bible says that there was also some discontent with Solomon's religious policies, which allowed his foreign wives, brought into his harem as a result of diplomatic marriages, to worship their own gods in the Jerusalem temple. Despite his increasing unpopularity that led to at least one revolt, Solomon managed to maintain his throne until he died. Soon after his death, though, the United Monarchy came to an end.

The Kingdoms of Israel and Judah

When Solomon died (c. 931 B.C.E.), representatives of the northern tribes demanded that his son Rehoboam promise to make changes. He balked, so the ten northern tribes refused to accept him as their ruler. They kept the name Israel (which probably had originated in the central hill country) and chose Jeroboam, a former rebel against Solomon, as king. Only Judah and the small tribe of Benjamin remained loyal to David's line, becoming the kingdom of Judah (see Table 8.2). Soon after the split, Pharaoh Sheshonq of Egypt tried to reassert Egyptian control over all of Palestine, causing widespread destruction in both kingdoms. Though this resurgence by Egypt was fleeting (Sheshonq died soon after his Palestinian campaign), it weakened both Israel and Judah, ensuring that the break between them would remain permanent.

Jerusalem remained the capital of Judah, and Solomon's temple remained the focal point for its worship. On the other hand, Jeroboam I (c. 931 to 910 B.C.E.) not only had to choose a capital for Israel, but also had to make provisions for the national religious cult. He established centers for the worship of Yahweh at Bethel and Dan, cities near the southern and northern borders of his kingdom, respectively. The later biblical editors considered him an idolater because he placed golden statues of young bulls within these temples. However, these statues were probably considered sacred to Israel's traditional god, Yahweh. In Jerusalem, Yahweh was thought to be invisibly enthroned above the Ark of the Covenant between two large statues of cherubim,° while at Bethel and Dan, Yahweh was probably believed to be invisibly standing on the back of a bull in the way that Ba'al was often depicted.

Throughout the era of the Divided Monarchy, Judah had a relatively stable government under descendants of David. These southern monarchs generally ruled with strong religious backing, for they had

persuaded religious leaders and the people that Yahweh had formed a covenant with David, promising that his dynasty would rule the nation forever. It was the smaller, weaker, less populous and poorer of the two states, but that fact made it less attractive to possible invaders. Israel, on the other hand, experienced several revolutions and changes of dynasties, all accomplished by military leaders. Prophetic denunciations of various kings helped produce this instability, for many people in the northern kingdom seem to have continued to accept the old tradition of charismatic leadership that had existed during the time of the "Judges." A valid king should show signs that he

TABLE 8.2

Chronology of the Rulers of Israel and Judah, c. 1027–750 B.C.E.

(All dates are B.C.E. and are probably correct to within about ±10 years. The names of the most important rulers are printed in boldface.)

The United Monarchy of Israel
Saul (c. 1027–1006)
David (c. 1005–970)
Solomon (c. 970–931)

The Divided Monarchy

The Kingdom of Israel	The Kingdom of Judah
Jeroboam I (c. 931–910)	Rehoboam (c. 931–914)
Nadab (c. 909)	Abijam (Abijah, c. 914–911)
Baasha (c. 909–886)	Asa (c. 911–871)
Elah (c. 885)	
Zimri (c. 885)	
Omri (c. 885–874)	
Ahab (c. 873–852)	**Jehoshaphat** (c. 871–848)
Ahaziah (c. 852–851)	
Jehoram (Joram, c. 851–841)	Jehoram (c. 848–841)
Jehu (c. 841–813)	Ahaziah (c. 841)
	Athaliah (c. 841–835)
Jehoahaz (c. 813–797)	Jehoash (c. 835–796)
Jehoash (c. 797–782)	Amaziah (c. 796–767)
Jeroboam II (c. 782–747)	**Uzziah** (Azariah, c. 767–739)

_____

°Cherubim were winged sphinx-like semidivine figures with human heads and the bodies of bulls or lions. In Canaanite mythology, they were thought to guard divinities and kings and were often depicted on the sides of royal thrones.

was Yahweh's chosen one, these people thought. Thus, if a king lost a war or his policies were denounced by religious leaders or prophets, he was likely to face a military revolt led by one of his ambitious officers. Moreover, Israel's relative wealth, nearness to Phoenicia and Damascus, position astride important trade routes, and lack of natural barriers to invasion all made it more attractive to Aramaeans, Assyrians, and other would-be conquerors (see Map 8.2).

Israel entered its greatest era of power and prosperity almost 50 years after its creation when Omri, an army commander, seized power. Omri (c. 885 to 874 B.C.E.) crushed his opposition and restored a semblance of stability after a series of military defeats, coups, civil wars, and assassinations following the death of Jeroboam I (c. 910 B.C.E.). He built a new, strongly fortified capital city in the center of the country at Samaria. He also seems to have regained control over areas of Israel previously captured by the king of Damascus and rebuilt cities like Dan and Hazor that the Aramaeans had destroyed. To strengthen his hand against Damascus, Omri entered into a pact with King Ithoba'al I of Tyre (c. 887 to 856 B.C.E.), marrying his son Ahab to Ithoba'al's daughter Jezebel to cement the bond. He also ended the long conflict with Judah, creating an alliance between the two kingdoms in which Israel was the dominant partner. This alliance was eventually strengthened by the marriage of Omri's daughter (or, less likely, granddaughter) Athaliah to Jehoram, son and heir of Judah's king, Jehoshaphat. Omri also once again conquered most of Moab, regaining control over "the King's Highway," the major trade route through Transjordan. These actions seem to have been effective, for not only did the conflict with Damascus cease, but during the reign of Omri's son, Israel and Aram-Damascus became allies against Assyria. Though he reigned for only 12 years, he so impressed the Assyrians that long after his dynasty had been overthrown and replaced, they continued to call Israel "the House of Omri."

Omri's successor, Ahab (c. 873 to 852), continued the developments his father had started, building Israel into one of the strongest states in the region. As we have seen, Ahab contributed the second largest contingent of troops (and the largest number of chariots) to the coalition army that met Shalmaneser III at Qarqar in 853 B.C.E. His reign also seems to have increased the prosperity begun during Omri's time. He completed the building projects his father had started, with key buildings constructed in Phoenician style out of carefully cut and smoothed stones (ashlars) with rectangular stone columns surmounted by carved Proto-Aeolic capitals. These buildings and the houses of the Israelite aristocracy contained furniture inlaid with beautifully carved pieces of ivory, much of it probably imported from Tyre.

The Bible remembers Ahab as a very wicked king, claiming he was despotic and unscrupulous. His main sin in the eyes of the biblical authors, though, was allowing his wife Jezebel to build temples to Tyrian Ba'al (Melqart) in Israel. Despite the later biblical condemnation of his religious policies, it is clear that Ahab still worshiped Yahweh as Israel's national deity, for he gave his children Yahwistic names.[43] Yahweh had already assimilated the characteristics of the local manifestations of El and Ba'al in Israel and Judah, including having Asherah as his consort. But the introduction of a foreign cult with its own temples, priests, and prophets seems to have provoked a nationalistic response on the part of many Israelite worshipers of Yahweh. The prophet Elijah led the opposition to the royal policies, galvanizing and creating support for the "Yahweh alone" movement that would insist on exclusive worship of the national god. As P. Kyle McCarter, Jr. has noted, this was not really a conflict between the worshipers of Ba'al and the worshipers of Yahweh. Rather, the struggle was between supporters of an inclusive Yahwism that did not forbid the worship of other gods (a view accepted by the ruling class and probably most of the people) and those who accepted an exclusive Yahwism (the party of the prophets).[44]

From this clash grew the classical prophetic movement that would be instrumental in shaping the central concepts of the biblical tradition. The Israelites and Judeans, like the Mesopotamians and Canaanites, believed that the divine will could be revealed not only through professional prophets attached to the cult, but also through ordinary individuals. There were no necessary qualifications for a

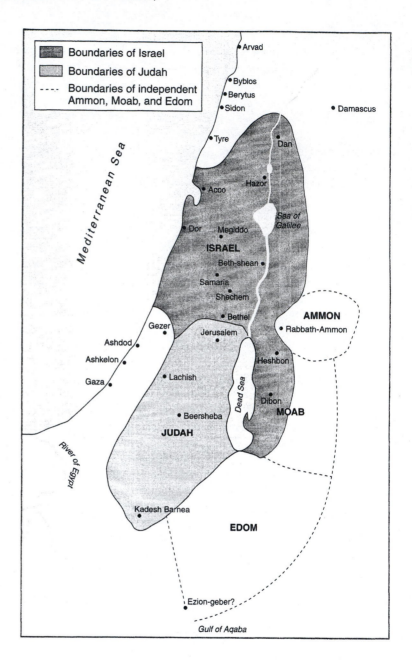

MAP 8.2   The Kingdoms of Israel at the Time of Omri (c. 885–874 B.C.E.)

person to become a prophet other than that person's conviction that God had inspired him or her and provided a message to be delivered to the king and/or people. The classical biblical prophets normally presented this message as the direct speech of God, introduced by "thus says Yahweh" (usually rendered "the LORD" in English translations). Starting with Elijah, a series of such nonprofessional prophets would arise to denounce the worship of deities other than Yahweh and attack many of the Canaanite practices that had long been part of both popular religion and the national cult.

Following Ahab's death, Queen Jezebel remained influential during the reigns of her sons, Ahaziah (c. 852 to 851 B.C.E.) and Jehoram (also written Joram, c. 851 to 841 B.C.E.). However, they were not able to continue the Israelite ascendancy that their grandfather and father had established. Moab revolted against Israelite control, and under the leadership of Mesha, a native of the city of Dibon, secured its freedom and even conquered some Transjordanian portions of Israel. Also, Aram-Damascus became an enemy once again when Hazael usurped that kingdom's throne around 845 B.C.E. Around 842–841 B.C.E., the Aramaean army moved southward and inflicted stinging defeats on the Israelite forces and their Judean allies. As we have noted, Hazael's victory stele (see Figure 8.3) claims that he killed the kings of both Israel and Judah. However, the Bible says that Jehoram, badly wounded in a battle near the Transjordanian border town of Ramoth-Gilead, retired to the royal residence at Jezreel to recuperate, accompanied by his nephew Ahaziah, the new king of Judah. There Jehu, an army commander who had been proclaimed king of Israel by his fellow officers, killed both kings and ordered the queen-mother Jezebel thrown out of one of the palace's upper windows. The new king, Jehu (c. 841 to 813 B.C.E.), then slaughtered the remaining descendants of Omri as well as several members of the Judean royal family who had accompanied their king on his visit to Israel.

When news of Jehu's usurpation and the death of Jehoram and Ahaziah reached Jerusalem, Ahaziah's mother, Queen Athaliah, the only surviving member of Omri's line, decided to seize power in Judah. Possibly backed by an Israelite royal guard that had accompanied her to Jerusalem during the days when Israel had dominated Judah, she killed all of her former husband's other sons except an infant, Jehoash, who was hidden by his sister and the temple's priests. Athaliah reigned into her seventh year (c. 841 to 835 B.C.E.), becoming the first female ruler of Judah and the last until Hellenistic times. She was also the only pre-exilic Judean monarch other than Saul who was not from the line of David. Her reign came to an end when the palace guard, now presumably composed mostly of Judeans once again, secretly assembled in the temple to protect the seven-year-old Jehoash who was brought out of hiding and crowned king. When Athaliah tried to stop the proceedings, she was apprehended and killed. Thus, the Line of David was restored on the throne of Judah. It is possible that this restoration inspired an exceptional writer to produce the account of Israel's early history (now much of Genesis, Exodus, Numbers, and possibly parts of Joshua, Judges, 1 and 2 Samuel, and 1 Kings) that biblical scholars call "the Yahwist Narrative" or *J*.[45] Some consider it the first prose masterpiece in world literature.

The final decades of the ninth century saw Aramaean domination of Israel and Judah, though a degree of peace and affluence returned to both kingdoms after Assyria defeated Ben-Hadad II of Damascus in 796 B.C.E. During the long reign of Jeroboam II (c. 782 to 747 B.C.E.), Israel not only recaptured the territory east of the Jordan that Hazael had conquered, but probably even subjugated parts of Syria itself. In Judah, the reign of Uzziah (Azariah, c. 767 to 739 B.C.E.) was also generally one of stability and well-being, though Judah was once again virtually a vassal of Israel. However, during this time, the gulf between rich and poor became greater than ever before. Moreover, the prosperity of the estate-owning aristocracy, especially in Israel, was often at the expense of formerly independent farmers who lost their land and were forced to become tenant farmers. Such social inequities were denounced by Amos, Hosea, and other prophets whose teachings culminated in the emergence of monotheism and other aspects of the biblical tradition (see Chapter 9).

OTHER SMALL STATES OF THE SOUTHERN LEVANT

The Philistines

The Philistines arrived in the Levant as part of the movement of the Sea Peoples, and as we have seen, their original homeland was probably in the Aegean area (see Chapter 7). After Ramesses III defeated the

Sea Peoples around 1175 B.C.E., he settled groups of them as Egyptian mercenaries in coastal Palestinian sites. The *Onomasticon of Amenope*, an Egyptian work of the late twelfth or early eleventh century B.C.E., reveals that Philistines as well as Shardana and Tjeker were settled in Gaza, Ashkelon, and Ashdod. The eleventh century B.C.E. *Report of Wenamun* also indicates that the Tjeker controlled Dor at that time. In addition, some scholars have suggested that groups of the Danuna became the Israelite tribe of Dan, which, according to the Bible, was originally settled in the central coastal region before moving to the extreme northern portion of Israel. The various groups of Sea Peoples who remained settled along the coast of Canaan seem to have merged and become known as Philistines, possibly taking the name of their most numerous or dominant contingent.

Around 1150 B.C.E., the Philistines, possibly supplemented by the arrival of a new wave of Sea Peoples, overthrew their Egyptian masters and took control of the cities in which they had been settled. At the head of each city-state was a ruler called a *Seren* ("lord"?). Some linguists think this word is Indo-European and possibly related to *tyrannos* ("tyrant"), a word the Greeks borrowed from the Lydians of Asia Minor. The Philistines were excellent warriors, and a *Seren* may have been primarily a warlord, leading his city's well-trained, well-armed (and possibly professional) troops into battle. The city-states of Gaza, Ashkelon, Ashdod, Ekron, and Gath organized into a confederation that became the major power in Canaan until the time of David c. 1000 B.C.E. The area controlled by this confederation gradually expanded northward to the Jezreel Valley and eastward to Beth-shean and the Jordan Valley. The Philistines also gained dominance over much of the Shephelah (the western foothills of Palestine), an area largely settled by Proto-Israelites. It was this Philistine expansion into the Palestinian hills and the Jordan Valley that forced the newly formed Israelite tribes to recognize their need for the unity and leadership provided by a monarchy.

The Philistines were excellent craftsmen and merchants. Their smiths made products of bronze and iron and, according to the Bible (1 Samuel 13:19),

maintained a monopoly over the craft within Palestine. Archaeologists have uncovered twelfth-century B.C.E. furnaces, slag, various bronze and iron artifacts, and other evidence of metalworking at Ekron, Ashdod, Tell Qasile, and other Philistine sites. They have also identified buildings where yarn was spun and textiles woven and dyed. In addition, the Philistines were also excellent farmers and horticulturists, producing choice varieties of wine and olive oil for trade. Based on the foreign pottery found at twelfth- and eleventh-century B.C.E. Philistine sites, most of their early trade in these products was with Cyprus and Phoenicia.

Philistine culture was a blend of elements they brought with them from the Aegean and Cyprus and components they borrowed from the Egyptians and Canaanites among whom they settled. For example, their locally made Mycenaean IIIC:1b pottery developed into the characteristic Philistine bichrome (two-colored) ware. This bichrome pottery was still usually Mycenaean in shape and decoration, but Cypriot, Egyptian, and Canaanite elements appeared as well. Some upper-class Philistines copied the Egyptian practice of placing the dead in coffins with human portraits on the lids, though the human depictions on Philistine clay coffins were much cruder than Egyptian ones. But at some sites, these anthropoid clay coffins were placed in hillside chamber tombs of a local Canaanite type that were similar to the tombs used by the Mycenaeans. Moreover, many Philistines were buried Canaanite-style in plain pits dug into the ground or in makeshift coffins (made by putting together the lower portions of two large storage jars). Philistine religion displayed the mixture of cultural elements, as well. A Philistine temple found at Tell Qasile resembled small sanctuaries uncovered at Mycenae, Melos, and Cyprus, and it contained a bronze double axe of Aegean type. Initially, the Philistines' worship seems to have been centered on a mother goddess of Aegean type, for twelfth-century Aegean-style figurines were found at Ashdod, Ekron, and Tell Qasile. However, by the eleventh century, the main deity in the Philistine pantheon seems to have been Dagon, a male Canaanite god. The Canaanite deities Ba'al-zebub (Ba'al-zebul) and Ashtart were also worshipped by the Philistines.

The Philistine language and writing system are known only from several twelfth-century B.C.E. stamp seals, one cylinder seal from Ashdod, and a few words and names preserved in the Bible and Assyrian texts. The writing on the seals is of Aegean type, similar to the Linear A and Linear B scripts of Crete and Greece and the Cypro-Minoan syllabic script of Cyprus. However, there are too few signs represented for it to be deciphered. The Philistine language originally may have been Indo-European, possibly related to Greek, Illyrian, or Lydian, but too little evidence has survived to allow any firm conclusions.

What is known is that by the early part of the tenth century B.C.E., the originally distinctive Aegean cultural elements had disappeared. Philistine speech, material culture, and religion all had become essentially Canaanite in character. However, the Philistine city-states continued to flourish, even after being defeated by David. They maintained their hold on the coastal region of Palestine south of Joppa (modern Tel Aviv) and remained a major foe of Judah throughout the period of the Divided Monarchy. They also continued to control trade along the coastal road (called "the Way of the Land of the Philistines" in the Bible) that ran from Egypt to Megiddo and points further north. The major Philistine city-states managed to maintain their independence until they were conquered by the Assyrians in the latter part of the eighth century B.C.E.

Ammon, Moab, and Edom

The three small Transjordanian kingdoms of Ammon, Moab, and Edom arose to the east of Israel and Judah (see Map 8.2) between the twelfth and eighth centuries B.C.E. Their populations all spoke languages closely related to Phoenician and Hebrew. In fact, Phoenician, Hebrew, Ammonite, Moabite, and Edomite should all be considered dialects of Canaanite, a West Semitic language. The material culture of the Transjordanian peoples was also closely related to that of the societies west of the Jordan River.

Ammon occupied the western edge of the Syrian desert between the Jabbok River (the Wadi Zerqa) and the northern border of Moab (near the northern end of the Dead Sea). At times, Ammon expanded southward and gained control of northern Moab down to the Arnon River (the Wadi Mujib) near the middle of the eastern side of the Dead Sea. Rabbath-Ammon, its capital, had been occupied since the Early Bronze Age and had become a large city in Middle Bronze times. Although it declined in size during the Late Bronze Period, there was no break in its occupation or culture at the end of the Bronze Age. In fact, Ammon as a whole seems to have passed rather peacefully from the Bronze to the Iron Age. During the Late Bronze Period, most of the inhabitants of Ammon had been pastoralists, and sedentary occupation had been confined to the Baq'ah Valley and the region around Rabbath-Ammon (present-day Amman, Jordan). During the twelfth century B.C.E., though, many small agricultural villages sprang up in Ammon as they did in the hills west of the Jordan River. In addition, towns or cities existed at sites such as Tell Sahab, Tell Umeiri, and the Amman Citadel, indicating a degree of economic, social, and political complexity. Most of Ammon's villages and towns were destroyed during the latter part of the Iron I Period (c. 1100 to 1000 B.C.E.), and a large portion of the population reverted to seminomadic pastoralism for a time. The cause of these destructions remains unknown.

Several Ammonite sites were settled again during the tenth and ninth centuries B.C.E. (the Iron II A and B Periods), and Rabbath-Ammon probably had a rampart built around it. It definitely seems to have been the capital city of at least a tribal kingdom, if not a state, for archaeologists have found ninth-century B.C.E. limestone portrait heads of kings wearing Egyptian-style crowns (see Figure 8.7). Some archaeologists consider Ammon essentially a large city-state—Rabbath-Ammon with its surrounding towns, villages, and fields.

The main deity of Ammon was a god named Milkom (from the Semitic root *mlk*, "to rule, to be king"). Milkom was probably the Ammonite form of the West Semitic weather god, Ba'al Hadad. He seems to have been related to the Phoenician Melqart and possibly to Molech (or Malik), the deity to whom Judeans sacrificed children near Jerusalem.[46]

Moab was to the south of Ammon, occupying the entire eastern side of the Dead Sea. Its core territory was in the south, between the rivers Arnon (Wadi Mujib) and Zered (Wadi Hasa). Most of its cities and population, though, were in northern Moab from Aroer and Dibon just north of the Arnon River to around Medeba or Heshbon. Northern Moab was disputed territory, fought over and ruled at various times by Israelites, Ammonites, and Moabites. This area was important not only because of its agricultural potential and settlements, but also because the famous "King's Highway" ran through it. This road was the main trade route from the northern end of the Gulf of Aqaba to Rabbath-Ammon and northward to Damascus. The major Moabite cities—Kir (also called Kir-hareseth or Kir-Moab), Aroer, Dibon, Medeba, and Heshbon—all lay along this important route.

Israel controlled northern Moab under David and Solomon (c. 1005 to 931 B.C.E.) and again during the reigns of Omri and Ahab (c. 885 to 852 B.C.E.). Mesha, a vassal ruler of Moab who came to the throne around the middle of Ahab's reign, ceased his annual tribute payments and seized northern Moab as soon as Ahab died (c. 852 B.C.E.). A few years later, Jehoram of Israel (c. 851 to 841 B.C.E.), supported by Judah and Edom, undertook a campaign to recapture Moab, marching around the southern end of the Dead Sea and attacking Moab from the south. However, Mesha took refuge in Kir (modern Kerak), a strongly fortified city that Jehoram could not conquer. Although he ravaged the countryside around Kir, Jehoram eventually had to retreat, and Moab maintained its independence. Mesha celebrated this and other victories by erecting a stele in Qarhoh, probably the sacred precinct or royal quarter of Dibon (modern Dhiban, Jordan). This black basalt monument, discovered at Dhiban in 1868 and now in the Louvre, is usually called the Mesha Stele or the Moabite Stone (see Document 8.2).

Mesha credits his victories to Kemosh (usually written Chemosh in English Bibles), Moab's national deity. Kemosh had been worshipped in the Near East for a long time before the appearance of the kingdom of Moab. The Ebla tablets from around 2300 B.C.E. mention a god named Kamish, almost certainly an earlier form of the name Kemosh. The name of this

FIGURE 8.7 Ninth-Century B.C.E. Life-Size Limestone Head of an Ammonite King

Source: Collection of the Israel Museum, Jerusalem.
Photo: © Israel Museum.

deity is also found in the name of the city of Carchemish (*Kar-Kamish*, "Citadel of the god Kamish"), indicating that he was worshipped there, as well. Kemosh was probably a god of the underworld, for in an Assyrian list of gods he is equated with the Mesopotamian deity Nergal. He may have had a female counterpart and consort, a fertility goddess named Ashtar-Kemosh who is also named in Mesha's Stele. However, it is not clear from context whether this is a goddess (possibly related to Ishtar and Ashtart) or another name for Kemosh himself. At a small wayside

DOCUMENT 8.2

The Victory Stele of Mesha, King of Moab

Moabite beliefs about Kemosh as indicated in Mesha's inscription are very close to early Israelite ideas about Yahweh. Notice, also, that the Moabites, like the Israelites (and probably other peoples in the area), on occasion practiced the *herem* or "ban." This custom consisted of dedicating captured goods and prisoners to a deity by destroying them in his or her honor.[47]

I am Mesha, son of Kemosh-[yat], King of Moab, the Dibonite. My father reigned over Moab for thirty years, and I reigned after my father. I made this high place for Kemosh in Qarhoh, [a high place of] salvation, because he delivered me from all the kings, and allowed me to have my way with all my adversaries. Omri, King of Israel, had oppressed Moab for years [lit, many days] because Kemosh was angry with his land. When Omri's son succeeded him, he too said, "I will humble Moab." In my days he said this, but I triumphed over him and his house, and Israel has totally perished for ever. Omri had occupied the land of Medeba and [Israel] dwelt there in his time and half the time of his son, forty years; but Kemosh dwells there in my time. I built the city Ba'al-meon and made a reservoir in it, and I built the city Qaryaten.

Now the men of Gad had always dwelt in the land of Ataroth, for the king of Israel had built Ataroth for them. But I fought against the town and took it and slew all the people of the town as a satisfying offering for Kemosh and Moab. I brought back from there the *arel david* (the royal altar or altar of David?) and I dragged it before Kemosh in Kerioth and settled there (in Ataroth) the men of Sharon and of Maharith.

Then Kemosh said to me, "Go, take Nebo from Israel!" So I went by night and fought against it from daybreak until noon, and took it. I slew all in it—seven thousand men, boys, women, girls and female slaves—for I had devoted them to Ashtar-Kemosh. I took from there the [cult vessels?] of Yahweh and dragged them before Kemosh. Now, the king of Israel had fortified Jahaz, and he occupied it while fighting against me, but Kemosh drove him out before me. Then I took two hundred men from Moab, all of them noblemen, and established them in Jahaz. Thus, I took possession of it and annexed it to (the district of) Dibon.

I built Qarhoh, the wall of the parkland and the wall of the citadel; I built its gates and I built its towers, and I built the royal palace and made both of the reservoirs for water inside the town. . . . I cut beams for Qarhoh with captives from Israel. I built Aroer, made the highway in the Arnon (Valley) and rebuilt the city of Beth-bamoth, for it had been destroyed. . . .

Moabite shrine near Khirbet al-Mudayna in Jordan, archaeologists also recently uncovered several female figurines holding flat circular objects (tambourines or sacrificial loaves of bread?). These may be representations of a goddess or goddesses, but they may also depict female cult participants.[48]

Edom (also called Se'ir) occupied the territory south of the Zered River (Wadi Hasa) from the Arabian Desert to the northern tip of the Gulf of Aqaba. On the west, its border usually ran on an angle from the Gulf of Aqaba to the southeastern border of Judah somewhere in the vicinity of Kadesh-barnea (see Map 8.2).

The primary god of the Edomites was Qaus (later Qos) who seems to have been a weather god. Sedentary occupation did not occur in Edom as early as it did in Moab and Ammon. A few small farms or agricultural villages seem to have been created in northern Edom during the eleventh century B.C.E. However, the Edomites remained primarily seminomadic pastoralists until the eighth century B.C.E. when Bozrah (modern Buseirah), Punon (modern Feinan), Tell el-Kheleifeh, and a few other towns were founded. So probably Edom was not a "nation" or state before the eighth century B.C.E., and even then, it seems to have become only a chieftainship or tribal kingdom.

Edom was important to Israel and Judah (and later, to Assyria and Babylon) because of its copper mines in the Wadi Feinan region about halfway between the Dead Sea and the Gulf of Aqaba. In addition, "the King's Highway," an important route along which passed much of the overland trade from western Arabia, ran through eastern Edom. David and Solomon are supposed to have conquered Edom, but this probably just means that they secured the area of the mines and the main trade routes through the region. Solomon's port, Ezion-geber, was built in Edomite territory somewhere along the northern part of the Gulf of Aqaba (possibly at Jezirat Far'oun). After Solomon's death (c. 931 B.C.E.), Edom gained its independence from Judah, but Jehoshaphat (c. 871 to 848 B.C.E.) is supposed to have defeated an army of Edomites and Moabites and recaptured Ezion-geber. He built a fleet of ships there as Solomon had earlier, but before they could sail down the Gulf of Aqaba, they were wrecked in a storm. Following the failure of this expedition, Edom seems to have been able to maintain its freedom from Judah.

Small Kingdoms and Confederations in Arabia

The earlier kingdoms of Dilmun and Magan along the eastern coast of the Arabian Peninsula had probably collapsed at the end of the third or during the second millennium B.C.E. They continued to be mentioned in later Mesopotamian texts, but as legendary rather than real places. After hundreds of years in which the population seems to have reverted to a nomadic existence, towns reappeared in the northeastern area of modern Oman around 1000 B.C.E. A small kingdom in the area became known to the Mesopotamians as Qade. Several small kingdoms and confederations of nomadic tribes also flourished in southwestern, western, and northern Arabia during the late second and early first millennia B.C.E. and became significant participants in Near Eastern trade. From the mid-ninth century B.C.E. onward, Mesopotamian and other texts refer to Arabian groups as "Arabs." However, rather than representing an ethnic or linguistic designation, this term seems to have been used originally to mean "nomads" or "seminomads."[49]

Ophir, the land with which Solomon and the Phoenicians are supposed to have traded, was probably located along the Red Sea coast of southwestern Arabia. The land of Saba (called Sheba in the Bible) probably was just to the south of Ophir in the southwestern corner of the Arabian Peninsula (in present-day Yemen, see Map 8.3). Other political entities in the area were Ma'in, Qataban, and Hadramawt. These areas may have been organized as small agricultural kingdoms, though it is also possible that they were originally only confederations of local farming and seminomadic tribes such as those described below. But by at least the tenth century B.C.E., Saba was a settled kingdom with extensive irrigation, monumental architecture, and its own alphabetic writing system.[50] In fact, based on the extensive inscriptions that have been found, citizens of the western Arabian states were almost universally literate, a situation that did not exist anywhere else in the ancient Near East.

Saba and the other southwestern Arabian kingdoms became prosperous largely through trade in extremely fine gold, spices, gems, and other precious commodities (Job 28:16; Psalm 72:15; Isaiah 60:6; Jeremiah 6:20; and Ezekiel 27:22), some probably obtained from across the Red Sea in the area of Africa the Egyptians called Punt. The most important spices from this region were frankincense and myrrh, aromatic resins derived from trees that only grow in the southern and southwestern portion of the Arabian Peninsula and in northern Somalia on the east coast of Africa. Frankincense was usually burned to produce a sweet fragrance during religious rites, funerals, and special celebrations in the dwellings of wealthy individuals. Myrrh was a primary ingredient in oils and ointments used in perfumes, medicinal preparations and, especially, for embalming the dead. These products, which commanded extremely high prices in Near Eastern markets, were usually carried by camel caravans up the western coast of Arabia and thence to Egypt, the Levant, Syria, and Mesopotamia. From these areas, they were transported both east and west, becoming known and desired throughout the ancient world.

As in the southwestern coastal lands, there were settled agricultural communities at the major oases in western and northern Arabia. These oasis settlements, especially those at Yathrib (modern Medina), Dedan, Teima, Tabuk, Qurayya, and Duma (see Map 8.3), were important way stations on the incense routes from the south and shared in the wealth produced by that trade. They seem to have been the centers for confederations of nearby seminomadic tribes that

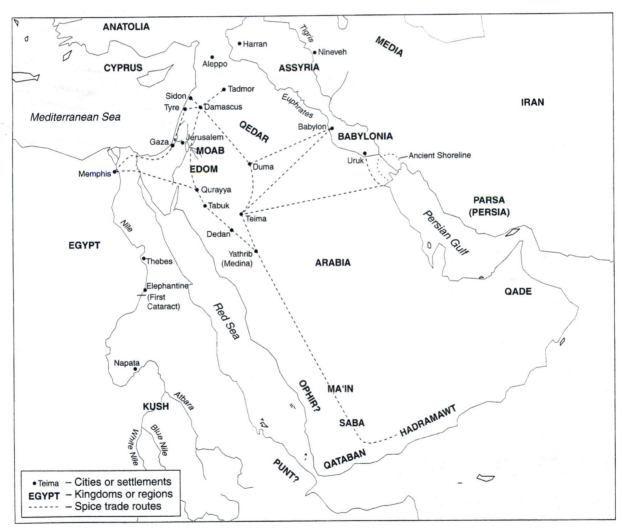

MAP 8.3   Kingdoms and Confederations in First Millennium B.C.E. Arabia

provided camels and guides for caravans passing through the oases. These confederations also probably collected tolls or "protection money" from the caravans, raiding and looting those that refused to pay. The oases were also regional religious centers, housing local deities' shrines that probably were places of pilgrimage during religious festivals. Though not based on an oasis, a similar confederation of related pastoral tribes known as Qedar seems to have controlled the trade routes between Duma and Syria.

Mesopotamian and biblical texts refer to the leaders of the Arabian groups they encountered as "kings" or "queens," but individual tribes were probably led by sheikhs with limited powers, as in later times. "Queens" played an especially prominent role among these "Arabs," but they (including possibly the "Queen" of Sheba who supposedly visited Solomon in the tenth century B.C.E.) were probably priestesses of major Arabian deities.[51] In the eighth century B.C.E. and earlier, these priestesses alone seem to have had the prestige and authority to unify tribes and their competing sheikhs around common shrines, creating the confederations that dominated the oases. The Arab "queens" not only ruled their confederations, but on occasion, even led them into battle. Frequent warfare with the Assyrians in the eighth and seventh centuries B.C.E., though, probably led male leadership to become predominant among the Arabian confederations from the time of Esarhaddon (680 to 669 B.C.E.) onward. Nevertheless, the priestesses continued to exercise important unifying functions alongside the "kings" in later times.

SUGGESTIONS FOR FURTHER READING AND INFORMATION

Internet Sites

Assyria—See the British Museum and Oriental Institute of the University of Chicago web sites listed at the end of Chapter 1.

Phoenicia—Articles on history, religion, archaeology, etc.: http://www.phoenicia.org

Phrygia—Articles, chronology, photos and more about ancient Phrygia:http://www.phrygians.com

http://www.exploreturkey.com/frig.html

Funerary monuments from Phrygia:www.csad.ox.ac.uk/MAMA/l/o/10/l/VolXImages.html

Books and Articles

Mesopotamia, Egypt, Urartu, and Asia Minor

Frankel, D. *The Ancient Kingdom of Urartu*. London: British Museum Press, 1979.

Grayson, A. Kirk. *Assyrian Rulers of the Early First Millennium BC, I: (1114–859 BC)*. Toronto: University of Toronto Press, 1991.

———. *Assyrian Rulers of the Early First Millennium BC, II: 858–745 BC*. Toronto: University of Toronto Press, 1996.

Hanfmann, George M. A. *Sardis from Prehistoric to Roman Times*. Cambridge, MA: Harvard University Press, 1983.

Kitchen, Kenneth. *The Third Intermediate Period in Egypt (1100–650 BC)*. Warminster, UK: Aris and Phillips, 1973.

Kroll, Stephan. "Excavations at Bastam, Iran: The First Urartian Site Uncovered in Iran." *Archaeology*, vol. 25 (October 1972), pp. 292–297.

Merhav, Rivka, ed. *Urartu: A Metalworking Centre in the First Millennium BCE*. Jerusalem: Israel Museum, 1991.

Sams, G. Kenneth. "King Midas: From Myth to Reality," *Archaeology Odyssey*, vol. 4, no. 6 (November/December 2001), pp. 14–26.

Voigt, Mary M., and Robert C. Hendrickson. "The Formation of the Phrygian State: The Early Iron Age at Gordion," *Anatolian Studies*, vol. 50 (2000), pp. 1–18.

Zimansky, Paul E. *Ecology and Empire: The Structure of the Urartian State*. Studies in Ancient Oriental Civilization, 41. Chicago: University of Chicago Press, 1985.

Early Israel

Binger, Tilde. *Asherah: Goddesses in Ugarit, Israel and the Old Testament*. Sheffield: Sheffield Academic Press, 1997.

Bright, John. *A History of Israel*, 4th ed. Philadelphia: Westminster, 2001.

Dever, William G. *What Did the Biblical Writers Know and When Did They Know It?: What Archaeology Can Tell Us About the Reality of Ancient Israel*. Grand Rapids, MI: Wm. B. Eerdman's Publishing Co., 2001.

Finkelstein, Israel. *The Archaeology of the Israelite Settlement*. Jerusalem: Israel Exploration Society, 1988.

———— and Neil Asher Silberman. *The Bible Unearthed: Archaeology's New Vision of Ancient Israel and the Origin of its Sacred Text*. New York: The Free Press, 2001.

Halpern, Baruch. *David's Secret Demons: Messiah, Murderer, Traitor, King*. Grand Rapids, MI: Wm. B. Eerdman's Publishing Co., 2001

Hoffmeier, James K. *Israel in Egypt: The Evidence for the Authenticity of the Exodus Tradition*. London and New York: Oxford University Press, 1998.

Isserlin, B. S. J. *The Israelites*. London and New York: Thames and Hudson, 1998.

Kamm, Anthony. *The Israelites: An Introduction*. London and New York: Routledge, 1999.

Lemche, Niels Peter. *Prelude to Israel's Past: Background and Beginnings of Israelite History and Identity*. Translated by F. F. Maniscalo. Peabody, MA: Hendrickson, 1998.

Lindenberger, James M. *Ancient Aramaic and Hebrew Letters*. Atlanta: Scholars Press, 1994.

McDermott, John J. *What Are They Saying About the Formation of Israel*. Mahwah, NJ: Paulist Press, 1999.

McKenzie, Steven L. *King David: A Biography*. London and New York: Oxford University Press, 2000.

Rogerson, John. *Chronicle of the Old Testament Kings*. London and New York: Thames and Hudson, 1999.

Shanks, Hershel, ed. *Ancient Israel: From Abraham to the Roman Destruction of the Temple*, rev. ed. Washington, D.C. and Upper Saddle River, NJ: Biblical Archaeology Society and Prentice Hall, 1999.

Soggin, J. Alberto. *A History of Ancient Israel from the Beginnings to the Bar Kochba Revolt, A.D. 135*. Philadelphia: Westminster, 1984.

Stiebing, William H. Jr. *Out of the Desert: Archaeology and the Exodus/Conquest Narratives*. Buffalo, NY: Prometheus Books, 1989.

Phoenicia, Syria, Transjordan, and Arabia

Breton, J. F. *Arabia Felix From the Time of the Queen of Sheba*. South Bend, IN: Notre Dame University Press, 1999.

Clapp, Nicholas. *Sheba: Through the Desert in Search of the Legendary Queen*. New York: Houghton Mifflin, 2001.

Dearman, Andrew, ed. *Studies in the Mesha Inscription and Moab*. Atlanta: Scholars Press, 1989.

Dornemann, Rudolph H. *The Archaeology of the Transjordan in the Bronze and Iron Ages*. Milwaukee: Milwaukee Public Museum, 1983.

Eph'al, Israel. *The Ancient Arabs: Nomads on the Borders of the Fertile Crescent, 9th–5th Centuries B.C.* Jerusalem: Magnes Press; Leiden: E. J. Brill, 1982.

Groom, Nigel. *Frankincense and Myrrh: A Study of the Arabian Incense Trade*. London and New York: Longman, 1981.

Harden, Donald. *The Phoenicians*, rev. ed. London: Harmondsworth, 1971.

Harrison, Timothy P. "Rabbath of the Ammonites," *Archaeology Odyssey*, vol. 5, no. 2 (March/April 2002), pp. 13–19.

Herm, Gerhard. *The Phoenicians: The Purple Empire of the Ancient World*. New York: William Morrow and Co., 1975.

Herr, Larry G. "The Iron Age II Period: Emerging Nations." *Biblical Archaeologist*, vol. 60, no. 3 (September 1997), pp. 114–183.

Kitchen, Kenneth. *Documentation for Ancient Arabia, Part I*. Liverpool: Liverpool University Press, 1994.

MacDonald, Burton. *Ammon, Moab and Edom: Early States/Nations of Jordan in the Biblical Period (End of the 2nd and During the 1st Millennium B.C.)*. Amman, Jordan: Al Kutba, 1994.

Markoe, Glenn E. *Phoenicians*. London and Berkeley: British Museum Press and University of California Press, 2000.

Miller, J. Maxwell, ed. "The Archaeology of Moab" (an entire issue dedicated to the archaeology of Moab with articles by leading scholars in the field). *Biblical Archaeologist*, vol. 60, no. 4 (December 1997).

Moscati, Sabatino, ed. *The Phoenicians*. Palazzo Grassi: Rizzoli International Publications, 1999.

Van Beek, G. W. "The Land of Sheba," pp. 40–63 in James B. Pritchard, ed., *Solomon and Sheba*. London: Phaidon, 1974.

Wilkinson, T. J. "Excavating the Land of Sheba: Archaeology Reveals the Kingdoms of Ancient Yemen," *Archaeology Odyssey*, vol. 4, no. 6 (November/December 2001), pp. 44–51, 57–58.

NOTES

1. For accounts of the early archaeologists' discovery and excavation of Kalhu and other Mesopotamian sites see Brian M. Fagan, *Return to Babylon: Travelers, Archeologists and Monuments in Mesopotamia* (Boston and Toronto: Little, Brown and Company, 1979), and Seton Lloyd, *Foundations in the Dust: The*

Story of Mesopotamian Exploration, rev. ed. (London: Thames and Hudson, 1980).

2. The translation is by A. Leo Oppenheim, "Babylonian and Assyrian Historical Texts" in James B. Pritchard, ed., *Ancient Near Eastern Texts Relating to the Old Testament*, 2nd ed. (Princeton, NJ: Princeton University Press, 1955), pp. 278–279. The material enclosed in parentheses and square brackets is part of the original translation by Oppenheim; material in curved brackets—{ }—has been added by W. Stiebing. Normal alphabetic characters have been substituted for the special linguistic signs used in Oppenheim's transliterations of Akkadian words.

3. For photographs of the tumulus and some of the objects it contained, see G. Kenneth Sams, "King Midas: From Myth to Reality," *Archaeology Odyssey*, vol. 4, no. 6 (November/December 2001), pp. 14–26.

4. See, for example, Alan R. Millard, "Arameans" in David N. Freedman, editor-in-chief, *The Anchor Bible Dictionary* (New York: Doubleday, 1992), vol. 1, p.346, and William W. Hallo and William Kelly Simpson, *The Ancient Near East: A History*, 2nd ed. (Fort Worth: Harcourt Brace, 1998), p. 124 where Ben-Hadad II is named as the Aramaean king who fought at Qarqar without any question.

5. Wayne T. Pitard, *Ancient Damascus* (Winona Lake, IN: 1987), pp. 115–125 as well as "Aram (Place)" and "Ben-Hadad" in Freedman, editor-in-chief, (1992), vol. 1, pp. 339–340 and 663–665. Also see Siegfried Horn, "The Divided Monarchy: The Kingdoms of Judah and Israel" (revised by P. Kyle McCarter, Jr.) in Hershel Shanks, ed., *Ancient Israel: From Abraham to the Roman Destruction of the Temple*, rev. ed. (Washington, D.C. and Upper Saddle River, NJ: Biblical Archaeology Society and Prentice Hall, 1999), pp. 145–147,155, and John Rogerson, *Chronicle of the Old Testament Kings* (London and New York: Thames and Hudson, 1999), pp. 104–105. It is also possible that Hadadezer was *briefly* succeeded by a son named Ben-Hadad at the time of Ahab. That would make the Ben-Hadad of Jehoahaz's time Ben-Hadad III. However, this scenario is not very likely.

6. Fragments of this stele were found by Avraham Biran in 1993 and 1994 during his excavations at Dan. It contains the earliest known reference outside of the Bible to the "House of David."

7. Amélie Kuhrt, *The Ancient Near East, c. 3000–330 BC* (London and New York: Routledge, 1995), pp. 459–460.

8. Bactrian (two-humped) camels seem to have been domesticated as early as the third millennium B.C.E. in central Asia while the dromedary (with only one-hump) probably was domesticated during the second millennium in Oman or southeastern Arabia. See Juris Zarins, "Camel" in Freedman, editor-in-chief, (1992), vol. 1, pp. 824–826.

9. Glenn E. Markoe, *Phoenicians* (London and Berkeley: The British Museum Press and The University of California Press, 2000), p. 30.

10. Ibid., p. 39.

11. Ibid., p. 170 claims Kition was a Tyrian colony, while Brian Peckham, "Phoenicia, History of " in Freedman, editor-in-chief (1992), vol. 5, p. 352 claims it was Sidonian.

12. See Donald Harden, *The Phoenicians* (New York: Frederick A. Praeger, 1962), pp. 147–148 and Markoe (2000), pp. 172, 177, 179, 184, 187.

13. Harden (1962), p. 85; Gwendolyn Leick, "Melqart" in Piotr Bienkowski and Alan Millard, eds., *Dictionary of the Ancient Near East* (Philadelphia: University of Pennsylvania Press, 2000), p. 194.

14. Markoe (2000), p. 118.

15. Translation by the author. For a complete translation of what remains of this myth, see H. L. Ginsberg, "Ugaritic Myths, Epics, and Legends" in Pritchard, ed. (1955), pp. 138–141. The lines quoted can be found on p. 140.

16. See, for example, M'hamed Hassine Fantar, "Were Living Children Sacrificed to the Gods?—No," *Archaeology Odyssey*, vol. 3, no. 6 (November/December 2000), pp. 28, 30.

17. Ibid., p. 30.

18. See, for example, Lawrence E. Stager and Joseph A. Greene, "Were Living Children Sacrificed to the Gods?—Yes," *Archaeology Odyssey*, vol. 3, no. 6 (November/December 2000), pp. 29, 31; Markoe (2000), pp. 134–136.

19. Lawrence E. Stager and Joseph A. Greene, op. cit., p. 31.

20. Markoe (2000), p. 135.

21. Lawrence E. Stager and Samuel R. Wolff, "Child Sacrifice at Carthage—Religious Rite or Population Control?" *Biblical Archaeology Review*, vol. 10, no. 1 (January/February 1984), pp. 30–51.

22. See, for example, Bernhard Anderson, *Understanding the Old Testament,* 4th ed. (Englewood Cliffs, NJ: Prentice Hall, 1986), pp. 151–180; Richard Elliott Friedman, *Who Wrote the Bible?* (New York: Summit Books, 1987); and "Torah (Pentateuch)" in Freedman, editor-in-chief (1992), vol. 6, pp. 605–622. In a recent work, *The Hidden Book in the Bible* (San Francisco: Harper-SanFrancisco, 1998), Richard Elliott Friedman argues that the Court History of David was actually part of *J* rather than a separate work written at about the same

time. He dates this enlarged *J* to the latter part of the ninth century B.C.E., rather than to the time of Solomon or soon afterward (mid- or late tenth century B.C.E.).

23. See, for example, Rolf Rendtorff, *The Problem of the Process of Transmission in the Pentateuch*, translated by J. Scullion (Sheffield: Journal for the Study of the Old Testament, 1990), and John Van Seters' works: *Abraham in History and Tradition* (New Haven, CT: Yale University Press, 1975), *In Search of History* (New Haven, CT: Yale University Press, 1983), *Prologue to History: The Yahwist as Historian in Genesis* (Louisville, KY: Westminster/John Knox Press, 1992), and *The Life of Moses: The Yahwist as Historian in Exodus-Numbers* (Louisville, KY: Westminster/John Knox Press, 1994).

24. See the discussion of many of the issues by four leading archaeologists and biblical scholars in "Face to Face, but Not Eye to Eye: Biblical Minimalists Meet Their Challengers," *Biblical Archaeology Review*, vol. 23, no. 4 (July/August 1997), pp. 26–42, 66.

25. For good summaries of the evidence and modern scholarly views of the patriarchal narratives see the work on Abraham by Van Seters mentioned in Note 23; Thomas L. Thompson, *The Historicity of the Patriarchal Narratives* (Berlin: de Gruyter, 1974); P. Kyle McCarter, Jr., "The Patriarchal Age: Abraham, Isaac and Jacob" (revised by Ronald S. Hendel) in Shanks, ed. (1999), pp. 1–31; Rogerson (1999), pp. 14–31; and Israel Finkelstein and Neil Asher Silberman. *The Bible Unearthed: Archaeology's New Vision of Ancient Israel and the Origin of its Sacred Text* (New York: The Free Press, 2001), pp. 27–47, 319–325.

26. For support of the biblical version of the Exodus, see James K. Hoffmeier, *Israel in Egypt: The Evidence for the Authenticity of the Exodus Tradition* (London and New York: Oxford University Press, 1998) and Alan Millard, "How Reliable is Exodus?" *Biblical Archaeology Review*, vol. 26, no. 4 (July/August 2000), pp. 51–57.

27. For a summary of the many problems connected with the Exodus narratives (including dating the event) and an analysis of some of the suggested solutions, see William H. Stiebing, Jr., *Out of the Desert?: Archaeology and the Exodus/Conquest Narratives* (Buffalo, NY: Prometheus Books, 1989). See also Nahum M. Sarna, "Israel in Egypt: The Egyptian Sojourn and the Exodus" (revised by Hershel Shanks) in Shanks (1999), pp. 33–54.

28. See Robert K. Gnuse, *No Other Gods: Emergent Monotheism in Israel* (Journal for the Study of the Old Testament Supplements 241. Sheffield: Sheffield Academic Press, 1997).

29. See Stiebing (1989), pp. 66–78.

30. See, for example, Israel Finkelstein, *Archaeology of the Israelite Settlement* (Jerusalem: Israel Exploration Society, 1988); William G. Dever, "Israel, History of (Archaeology and the Israelite "Conquest")" in Freedman, editor-in-chief (1992), vol 3, pp. 545–558; Finkelstein and Silberman (2001), pp. 72–122, 329–339. Attempts to find alternative dates for the Exodus that would better fit the archaeological evidence have not met with success. See Stiebing (1989), pp. 79–148.

31. Finkelstein (1988), especially pp. 336–356; Finkelstein and Silberman (2001), pp. 97–122.

32. See Steven Rosen, "Finding Evidence of Ancient Nomads," *Biblical Archaeology Review*, vol. 14, no. 5 (September/October 1988), pp. 46–53.

33. See George E. Mendenhall, "The Hebrew Conquest of Palestine," *Biblical Archaeologist*, vol. 25 (1961), pp. 66–87, and Norman K. Gottwald, *The Tribes of Yahweh* (Maryknoll, NY: Orbis Books, 1979. For a more recent defense of the theory, see William G. Dever, "Israel, History of (Archaeology and the 'Conquest')," in Freedman, editor-in-chief (1992), vol. 3, pp. 552–553.

34. See, for example, Joseph Callaway, "A New Perspective on the Hill Country Settlement of Canaan in Iron Age I" in J. N. Tubb, ed., *Palestine in the Bronze and Iron Ages: Papers in Honour of Olga Tufnell* (London: Institute of Archaeology, 1985), pp. 31–49, and "Response" in *Biblical Archaeology Today: Proceedings of the International Congress on Biblical Archaeology, Jerusalem, April 1984* (Jerusalem: Israel Exploration Society, 1985), pp. 72–77; Stiebing (1989), pp. 189–202.

35. Joseph A. Callaway, "The Settlement in Canaan: The Period of the Judges" (revised by J. Maxwell Miller) in Shanks, ed. (1999), p. 82.

36. See Ze'ev Meshel, "Did Yahweh Have a Consort?," *Biblical Archaeology Review*, vol. 5, no. 2 (March/April 1979), pp. 24–35; David Noel Freedman, "Yahweh of Samaria and His Asherah," *Biblical Archaeologist*, vol. 50, no. 4 (December 1987), pp. 241–249; Saul M. Olyan, *Asherah and the Cult of Yahweh in Israel* (Atlanta: Scholars Press, 1988); Judith M. Hadley, *The Cult of the Goddess in Ancient Israel and Judah: The Evidence for Asherah* (New York and Cambridge: Cambridge University Press, 1999).

37. Finkelstein and Silberman (2001), p. 150.

38. The arguments are summarized in Hershel Shanks, "Where is the Tenth Century?," *Biblical Archaeology Review*, vol. 24, no. 2 (March/April 1998), pp. 56–60. For more detailed presentations, see Philip R. Davies,

"In Search of Ancient Israel," *Journal for the Study of the Old Testament Supplement* 148 (Sheffield: Sheffield Academic Press, 1992); Israel Finkelstein, "The Archaeology of the United Monarchy: An Alternative View," *Levant*, vol. 28 (1996), pp. 177–187; Margreet Steiner, "David's Jerusalem, Fiction or Reality? It's Not There: Archaeology Proves a Negative," *Biblical Archaeology Review*, vol. 24, no. 4 (July/August 1998), pp. 26–33, 62; and Finkelstein and Silberman (2001), pp. 123–168, 340–344.

39. See, especially, Daniel Master, "State Formation Theory and the Kingdom of Israel," *Journal of Near Eastern Studies*, vol. 60 (2001), pp. 117–131. See also, for example, the article by Hershel Shanks cited in Note 38 and the works by Richard Elliott Friedman cited in Note 22; William G. Dever, *Recent Archaeological Discoveries and Biblical Research* (Seattle: University of Washington Press, 1990); Amihai Mazar, "Iron Age Chronology: A Reply to I. Finkelstein," *Levant*, vol. 29 (1997), pp. 155–165; Nadav Na'aman, "Cow Town or Royal Capital?: Evidence for Iron Age Jerusalem," *Biblical Archaeology Review*, vol. 23, no. 4 (July/August1997); and Jane Cahill, "David's Jerusalem, Fiction or Reality? The Archaeological Evidence Proves It," *Biblical Archaeology Review*, vol. 24, no. 4 (July/August 1998), pp. 34–41.

40. B. S. J. Isserlin, *The Israelites* (London: Thames and Hudson, 1998), pp. 7–8.

41. Ibid., p. 8.

42. For arguments about the dating of this stone structure, see the previously noted articles by Margreet Steiner and Jane Cahill in vol. 24 of *Biblical Archaeology Review*.

43. Ahaziah means "Yahweh has seized [him]" and Jehoram means "Yahweh has exalted [him]."

44. P. Kyle McCarter makes this observation in his revision of Sigfried Horn's "The Divided Monarchy: The Kingdoms of Judah and Israel" in Shanks, ed. (1999), p. 142.

45. As mentioned in Note 22, Richard Elliott Friedman argues that the *J* work continues through Joshua, Judges, 1 and 2 Samuel into 1 Kings. See Friedman (1998).

46. Traditionally, Molech has been regarded as a deity. But some scholars argue that the word is related to Phoenician *molk,* which seems to be a term for a cultic child sacrifice rather than the god to whom the child was sacrificed. See George C. Heider, "Molech" in Freedman, editor-in-chief (1992), pp. 895–898.

47. This translation is based on those of William Foxwell Albright in Pritchard, ed. (1955), p. 320–321; J. Maxwell Miller and John H. Hayes, *A History of Ancient Israel and Judah* (Philadelphia: The Westminster Press, 1986), p. 283; and Kuhrt (1995), vol. II, pp. 469–471.

48. P. M. Michèle Daviau and Paul-Eugène Dion, "Moab Comes to Life," *Biblical Archaeology Review*, vol. 28, no. 1 (January/February 2002), pp. 48–49, 63.

49. See M. C. A. MacDonald, "Arabia" and "Arabs" in Bienkowski and Millard, eds. (2000), pp. 24–26.

50. See T. J. Wilkinson, "Excavating the Land of Sheba: Archaeology Reveals the Kingdoms of Ancient Yemen," *Archaeology Odyssey*, vol. 4, no. 6 (November/ December 2001), pp. 44–51, 57–58; J. F. Breton, *Arabia Felix From the Time of the Queen of Sheba* (South Bend, IN: Notre Dame University Press, 1999); and Kenneth Kitchen, *Documentation for Ancient Arabia,* Part I (Liverpool: Liverpool University Press, 1994).

51. See M. C. A. MacDonald, "North Arabia in the First Millennium B.C.E." in Jack M. Sasson, ed. in chief, *Civilizations of the Ancient Near East* (New York: Charles Scribner's Sons, 1995), vol. 2, pp. 1355–1369, especially p. 1364.

9

Mesopotamian Supremacy

THE HEIGHT OF ASSYRIAN DOMINION (744–627 B.C.E.)

Reestablishment and Expansion of Assyrian Power (744–681 B.C.E.)

Assyria experienced famines, epidemics, semi-independent provincial governors and, finally, an insurrection during the 40 years before Tiglath-pileser III (744 to 727 B.C.E.) became king. In addition, Urartu had extended its power and made alliances with a people called the Mannaeans (or Mannai) in the Zagros Mountains and with various Aramaean kingdoms in Syria. In southern Mesopotamia, the Chaldeans, with Elamite help, were trying to gain control of Babylon. Thus, Assyrian supremacy was threatened on all sides. A revolt put Tiglath-pileser on the throne, so possibly he was a usurper, but he proved to be a resourceful king and gifted military commander. He reorganized the army, defeated Assyria's enemies in the Zagros and Syria, and attacked Urartu directly, penetrating all the way to the capital city, Tushpa, on Lake Van. Though he failed to take Tushpa, he weakened Urartu and conquered many of her allies. He forced Tyre and Sidon

to continue paying tribute to Assyria, and crushed a coalition of Philistine, Judean, Ammonite, Moabite, and Edomite forces. He also annexed Damascus and rebellious Israel's Galilean and Transjordanian territory as Assyrian provinces. When a Chaldean chieftain briefly took possession of Babylon, Tiglath-pileser III invaded southern Mesopotamia and regained control of the area. Instead of placing a vassal on Babylon's throne, he made himself king of Babylon under the name Pulu (which is written Pul in 2 Kings 15:19 and 1 Chronicles 5:26). He also resumed and enlarged the practice of deporting subject populations, moving vast numbers of people from one part of the empire to another. This program of forcible resettlement, especially of Aramaeans, became standard Assyrian policy under his successors. (See the following section "Administration of the Empire on p. 276) His victories and administrative reforms inaugurated the era of Assyrian dominance in the Near East.

Little is known about the brief reign of Tiglath-pileser III's son and successor, Shalmaneser V (726 to 722 B.C.E. see Table 9.1), except for his destruction of Israel. When Hoshea, Israel's king, revolted, Shalmaneser ravaged the remaining Israelite territory and

TABLE 9.1
Chronology of the Neo-Assyrian and Neo-Babylonian Kings

(All dates are B.C.E. The most important rulers' names are printed in boldface.)

Assyria:
Tiglath-pileser III (744–727)

Shalmaneser V (726–722)
Sargon II (721–705)

Sennacherib (704–681)

Esarhaddon (680–669)
Asshurbanipal (668–c. 627)

4 Kings (c. 626–609)

Conquest of Assyria by Medes and
Babylonians (614–609)

Babylon:
Nabonassar (Nabu-nasir, 747–734)
Pulu (= Tiglath-pileser III, 732–727)
Ululaua (= Shalmaneser V, 726–722)
Merodach-baladan II (Marduk-apal-iddina II,
721–710)
Sargon as Viceroy (709–710)
3 Kings (703–700)
Asshur-nadin-shumi (699–694)
2 Kings (693–689)
Esarhaddon as Viceroy (688–681)
Esarhaddon as King (680–669)
Shamash-shum–ukin (668–648)
Kandalanu (647–627)

Chaldean Dynasty
Babylon X
Nabopolassar (Nabu-apla-usur,
626–605)
Nebuchadnezzar II (Nabu-kudurri-usur II,
604–562)
Evil-Merodach (Amel-Marduk, 561–560)
Neriglissar (Nergal-shar-usur, 559–556)
Nabonidus (Nabu-na'id, 555–539)

besieged Samaria, the capital city, for three years. He probably captured the city as the Bible (2 Kings 17:4–6; 18:9–10) and the Babylonian Chronicle claim, but died (possibly by assassination) soon after its fall. His successor, Sargon II (721 to 705 B.C.E.), who probably usurped the throne, claimed the conquest of Samaria for himself. He may have been the general who was directing the siege on behalf of Shalmaneser. In any case, Sargon seems to have carried out the deportation of a large portion of the population and the division of the country into four Assyrian provinces: Dor, Megiddo, Gilead, and Samaria.

Upon his accession, Sargon II faced problems at home as well as in the provinces. The citizens of the city of Asshur had been protesting some of Shalmaneser's

policies, and their disturbances possibly helped cause his replacement by Sargon. To calm the unrest, Sargon reinstated the traditional exemptions from forced labor and certain taxes for residents of Asshur. While he was occupied by these internal affairs, rebellion broke out in Syria and Gaza, encouraged by promises of Egyptian support. Sargon crushed the Aramaeans at Qarqar then marched southward against Gaza. The Egyptian forces fled, leaving the ruler of Gaza to suffer torture and death at Sargon's hands. Meanwhile, a Chaldean chieftain named Marduk-apal-iddina II (better known as Merodach-baladan from biblical references) had seized the throne of Babylon with Elamite support. In 720 B.C.E., Sargon led an army down the east side of the Tigris to restore Assyrian control over southern Mesopotamia, but an Elamite army met him in battle and forced him to turn back. It would be ten years before he was able to concern himself again with the situation in Babylonia.

In the meantime, he had to deal with continued unrest in northern Syria and Anatolia, generally stirred up by Urartu and Phrygia. Sargon conquered Carchemish in 717 B.C.E. and made it into an Assyrian province. Over the next few years, he destroyed the Neo-Hittite kingdoms of Que (Cilicia), Gurgum, Milid, and Kummuhu and annexed their territories. He seized about half of Tabal's land, as well. Moreover, Urartu and its allies, the Medes, had engineered the overthrow of a pro-Assyrian king in Mannaea, a region southeast of Lake Urmia. Sargon invaded Mannaea, killed the pro-Urartian ruler and installed as king the former monarch's brother. Undaunted, in subsequent years, Rusa I, King of Urartu, continued to raid into Mannaea and cause other problems along Assyria's northeastern frontier. So, in the summer of 714 B.C.E., Sargon launched a major attack on Urartu. The Urartians expected him, so their forces were guarding the mountain passes between Assyria and Urartu. However, Sargon marched east through the Zagros, received tribute from the Medes, then advanced northward through Mannaea to the southwestern shore of Lake Urmia. Somewhere in that region, he met and decimated a Urartian army trying to block his entry into Urartu. As news of the Assyrian victory spread through the country, King Rusa fled into the mountains, leaving Sargon unopposed as he marched through Urartu looting and destroying. Before returning home, Sargon stormed the border fortress of Musasir, sacked the city, and carried off a massive hoard of precious metals and bronze objects in addition to the statue of Urartu's national god Haldi.

Finally, by 710 B.C.E., Sargon was able to turn his attention to Babylon once again. The time was ripe, for internal problems were afflicting Elam, preventing it from aiding Merodach-baladan. Also, many of the old cities of the south were begging for Assyrian intervention, for various Chaldean tribes, allies of Merodach-baladan, had been extorting money from them and interfering with the free flow

of trade in the area. At Sargon's approach at the head of a strong army, the Chaldean ruler of Babylon retreated to the refuge of his homeland, Bit-Yakin, on the shores of the Persian Gulf. There, with the aid of the other Chaldean tribes, he held out for two years, and when his principal city, Dur-Yakin fell, he eluded capture and took refuge in Elam. In the midst of this campaign, Sargon had received the submission of the cities of northern Babylonia including Babylon itself. At the New Year's Festival, he "took the hands of Bel (Marduk)," becoming the ruler of Babylon as Tiglath-pileser III and Shalmaneser V had been. However, rather than call himself "king," Sargon chose to use the ancient Assyrian title "Viceroy (of the God)" in Babylonia. He crowned his conquest of Babylonia by deporting a large number of its Aramaean and Chaldean inhabitants (108,000 according to his annals).

In 717 B.C.E., while beginning campaigns against Carchemish and the north Syrian states, Sargon had launched another project, the construction of a new capital city at a previously unoccupied site. He named this city, located about 14 miles northeast of Nineveh, Dur-Sharrukin, "Sargon's Fortress" (modern Khorsabad). Thousands of deportees, craftsmen, and artisans worked on this city, completing it in only ten years (see Figure 9.1). The statues of the gods were moved into their temples in 707 B.C.E. and Sargon took up residence, though he didn't officially dedicate the city until the following year.

Sargon was not able to enjoy Dur-Sharrukin's beautiful sanctuaries and palaces for long. In 705 B.C.E., while campaigning in Tabal, he died in battle. The agents of his death were the Cimmerians, warlike invaders from southern Russia or the Ukraine, who had crossed the Caucasus Mountains and invaded Urartu. One group of Cimmerians went eastward and raided for a time in northwestern Iran before settling among the Mannaeans and becoming allies of the Medes. Others moved westward into Anatolia, attacking Tabal. Even though Sargon perished, his army prevented the Cimmerians from turning back toward Syria or Assyria. They eventually established themselves in Asia Minor along the southeastern shore of the Black Sea.

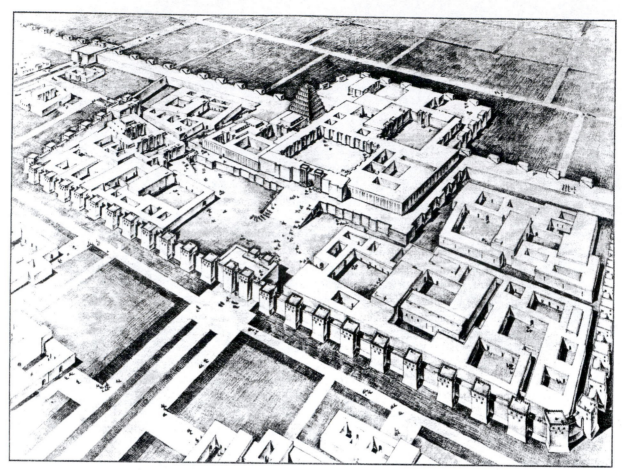

FIGURE 9.1   Reconstruction of the Citadel of Dur-Sharrukin

Source: Courtesy of the Oriental Institute of the University of Chicago.

Mesopotamians generally interpreted disasters as divine punishments. Thus, Sennacherib° (704 to 681 B.C.E.), Sargon's son and successor, felt that his father's death in battle showed that he must have angered the gods. So the new king shifted the capital from Dur-Sharrukin to the ancient city of Nineveh, which he almost totally rebuilt. He constructed a magnificent palace for himself atop the old city mound (Tell Kuyunjik) which now became

the new capital's citadel. He constructed an arsenal and other public buildings nearby (Tell Nebi Yunus). He more than doubled the city's area and surrounded it with a double fortification wall and moat. In order to enlarge Nineveh, Sennacherib had to change the course of a small tributary of the Tigris that formerly ran next to the city. He built a dam on this stream and diverted it so that it emptied into the Tigris north of his new walls. He also constructed a 30-mile-long canal complete with an aqueduct over a valley to bring fresh mountain water to the city from the northern hills. Some of the dams and weirs he built to irrigate the fields and orchards around

---

°Like "Sargon," the name "Sennacherib" is derived from the Bible. In Akkadian, this king's name was Sin-ahhe-eriba, "(the God) Sin has redressed (the death of) the brothers."

Nineveh have been repaired and are still in use. More-over, north of Nineveh, Sennacherib created a large royal botanical park containing many types of exotic plants and trees, including the cotton plant, which he introduced into the Near East.°For some unknown reason, perhaps because he was preoccupied with building his new capital, Sennacherib failed to install himself as king or viceroy of Marduk in Babylon. For two years, Babylon had no official ruler, and Sargon's old enemy, Merodach-baladan, seized this opportunity to again proclaim himself king of Babylon. As earlier, he was supported by Elam, the Aramaean tribes living east of the Tigris, and the Chaldean tribes. Sen-nacherib led his armies southward in 703 B.C.E. and overwhelmed the forces of Merodach-baladan, but once again, the Chaldean leader escaped. Though he could not catch the ringleader, Sennacherib rounded up many of the rebels and claimed to have deported 208,000 of them to Assyria.

Soon after Sargon's death, revolts also broke out in the west, encouraged by Merodach-baladan and Shabako, the second pharaoh of the new Nubian dynasty in Egypt. Hezekiah, king of Judah, against the advice of the prophet Isaiah, joined Sidon, Tyre, Ashkelon, Ekron, and possibly Ammon, Moab, and Edom in refusing to pay tribute. By the time Sen-nacherib realized the seriousness of the situation in the west, he was also being challenged by Merodach-baladan's seizure of Babylon. In 701 B.C.E., though, Sennacherib was free to launch a major assault against the Levantine rebels. He first crushed Sidon and Tyre (at that time under one rule), forcing its king to flee to Cyprus, and the news of the defeat of these great cities led to the rapid submission of Byblos, Arvad, Ashdod, Ammon, Moab, and Edom. Tyre's mainland territory was taken away and given to Sidon, whose throne was given to a pro-Assyrian ruler. Sennacherib then moved down the coast, con-quering the rebellious Philistine towns as he went. At Eltekeh, he routed an Egyptian army sent to aid the rebels, then retook the nearby city of Ekron. He

executed some of the rebellious leaders of the cap-tured cities, deported others, and replaced them with rulers friendly toward Assyria. Then, with Philistia under control, Sennacherib invaded Judah from the west. First, he had to capture the heavily fortified city of Lachish (see Figure 9.2) that con-trolled the approach to Jerusalem. Then Sen-nacherib besieged Jerusalem, later boasting that he made Hezekiah "a prisoner in Jerusalem, his royal residence, like a bird in a cage" (see Document 9.1). But Jerusalem did not fall. Hezekiah had strength-ened its fortifications and improved its water system in anticipation of a siege. But in the end, the Judean king realized the futility of continuing his resistance and offered to surrender and pledge his future loy-alty. Sennacherib accepted Hezekiah's capitulation and marched home, but only after giving some of Judah's territory to the new Philistine kings and mak-ing Judah pay a huge indemnity.[1]

On the other hand, Judean legends about this event credited Jerusalem's escape from destruction to a dramatic miraculous act of God (2 Kings 18:17–19:37 = Isaiah 36–37). There are problems with the biblical account, though, especially the ref-erence to Taharqa (Tirhaka in the Bible) as the Egyptian pharaoh who came to the aid of Hezekiah. Taharqa (ruled 690 to 664 B.C.E.) became pharaoh more than a decade *after* Sennacherib's attack on Jerusalem. Moreover, even if the title "king" in 2 Kings 19 is regarded as an anachronism, he may have been too young in 701 B.C.E. to lead a military campaign against Assyria for his brother, the pharaoh Shebitqu. Thus, some historians have claimed that 2 Kings has combined descriptions of two separate Assyrian attacks, the first in 701 B.C.E. and the sec-ond later in Sennacherib's reign, around 688 B.C.E. (a period for which we have no Assyrian annals).[2] How-ever, while it is likely that two different accounts have been combined in 2 Kings (2 Kings 18:13–16 repre-sents one, and 2 Kings 18:17–19:35 the other), most Near Eastern historians think these are variant tra-ditions about the 701 B.C.E. campaign, the only one mentioned in Assyrian records.[3]

Sennacherib may have been willing to retain Hezekiah as a vassal rather than commit to a

---

°The cotton plant was domesticated in India in the third millen-nium B.C.E., but as far as we know, this was the first time it was grown in the Near East.

FIGURE 9.2   Sennacherib's Assault of the Judean City of Lachish

Source: Courtesy of the Trustees of the British Museum, London.

lengthy siege of Jerusalem because of disturbing news about southern Mesopotamia. The person he had appointed as vassal king of Babylon was having difficulty controling his territory, and Merodach-baladan seems to have been stirring up the Chaldeans in Bit-Yakin again. So, in 700 B.C.E., Sennacherib again invaded Babylonia, imposed order, and placed one of his own sons, Asshur-nadin-shumi, on the throne (699 to 694 B.C.E.). However, even though Merodach-baladan died in Elam soon afterward, the south was not pacified. Sennacherib had to mount campaigns in 694 B.C.E. and again from 690 to 689 B.C.E. against Elamites (who carried off Asshur-nadin-shumi), the Sealand, Bit-Yakin, and assorted Chaldean tribes. Finally, frustrated by the constant rebellions in which Babylon was implicated, Sennacherib sacked Babylon, burned it, dumped its rubble into one of its canals and diverted water over the ruins. He then named

the Assyrian crown prince, his youngest son Esarhaddon (Asshur-aha-iddina in Akkadian), viceroy for Babylonia. Even though his destruction of Babylon may not have been as complete as he claims, its object lesson worked. Sennacherib had no further problems with the south.

The Empire at Its Zenith (680–627 B.C.E.)

In 681 B.C.E., while he was praying in a temple, Sennacherib was stabbed to death by some of his sons who seem to have been angry because of the choice of their younger brother as crown prince. The designated heir, Esarhaddon (680 to 669 B.C.E.), quickly returned and led his army against his brothers. Deserted by most of their own forces, the parricides fled to Urartu, and Esarhaddon received the support of the army and the people of Assyria. The new king had come to love

DOCUMENT 9.1
Sennacherib's Siege of Jerusalem

This account of Sennacherib's siege of Jerusalem is part of the description of his campaign of 701 B.C.E. from his annals recorded on both the Taylor Prism and the Oriental Institute Prism from Nineveh.[4] For the biblical version of these events, see 2 Kings 18:13–19:36.

As for Hezekiah, the Jew [*Ha-za-qi-(i)a-ú* ^amel^*Ia-ú-da-ai*], who did not submit to my yoke, I laid siege to forty-six of his strong walled cities and to countless small villages in their vicinity, and conquered them by means of beaten-earth ramps which allowed me to bring battering-rams near the walls combined with assault by infantry and breeches, tunneling and sapper operations. I drove out of them 200,150 people, young and old, male and female, as well as innumerable horses, mules, donkeys, camels, large and small cattle, and considered them spoils of war. [Hezekiah] himself I made a prisoner in Jerusalem, his royal residence, like a bird in a cage. I erected earthworks around the city to prevent the escape of any who tried to leave by the city gate. I terminated his jurisdiction over his towns which I had plundered and gave them to Mitinti, king of Ashdod, Padi, king of Ekron, and Sillibel, king of Gaza, and so reduced his territory. Nevertheless, in addition to his former annual tribute, I increased the amount of tribute to be given as *katru*-presents due to me as his overlord. Hezekiah himself, overwhelmed by the terror-inspiring splendor of my lordship and deserted by the irregular and elite troops which he had brought in to strengthen Jerusalem, his royal city, later sent me in Nineveh, my lordly city, 30 talents of gold, 800 talents of silver, precious stones, antimony, large blocks of red stone [carnelian?], beds and chairs inlaid with ivory, elephant hides, ivory tusks, ebony-wood, boxwood, all kinds of valuable treasures, as well as his daughters, concubines, male and female musicians. He sent a personal messenger to deliver the tribute and render homage as a slave.

Babylonian culture during his term as his father's viceroy in Babylonia, and his wife was Babylonian. So, one of his first acts was to order the rebuilding and enlargement of the city of Babylon. He allowed what was left of the old population to return and restored their lands and privileges. The reconstruction of the city took Esarhaddon's entire reign. However, when it was complete, just after Esarhaddon's death, the statues of Babylon's gods that had been carried off to Assyria were returned to their temples. Esarhaddon's pro-Babylonian policies won him considerable support in the south, so much so that he was able to use the area as a base for his expedition into Iran in 676 B.C.E.

Early in his reign, Esarhaddon was confronted with another invasion from southern Russia. The Scythians, a people from north of the Black Sea who were closely related to the Cimmerians, began marauding in Urartu, Mannaea, and Tabal. In 679 B.C.E., a group of Scythians joined the Cimmerians who had entered the region earlier and together they crossed the Taurus Mountains to the south, prompting Assyrian vassals in Tabal and Cilicia to revolt. Esarhaddon immediately invaded Cilicia, suppressed the rebellions, and defeated the Scythian-Cimmerian bands. Many of these marauders decided to move westward, and three years later, they invaded and destroyed the Phrygian kingdom, killing King Mita (Midas). They continued periodic raids into western Anatolia over the next 70 years, but they were finally defeated by the Lydians and were gradually absorbed into the Anatolian population. The kingdom of Lydia took possession of the former Phrygian territory and developed into a power in Asia Minor.

Around the same time, some tribes of Medes seem to have been joining together in alliances or small kingdoms and growing stronger. To halt this growth of Median power and secure the supply of horses previously provided by the Medes, Esarhaddon launched a series of cavalry raids into Iran from 676 to 675 B.C.E. He penetrated central Iran as far as the desert east of Teheran, attacked the Medes and made several of their chieftains into Assyrian vassals, secured allies in the central Zagros Mountains, and most importantly, placed a pro-Assyrian prince on the throne of Elam.

The Levant had remained relatively peaceful after Sennacherib's campaign in 701 B.C.E. except for a revolt by Sidon in alliance with a few north Syrian coastal cities just after the Scythian invasion. In 677 B.C.E., Esarhaddon sacked Sidon, captured (and later executed) the rebellious kings, and established an Assyrian fortress near Sidon to keep the peace. Despite the Assyrian military presence, the ruler of Tyre, secure in his island fortress and incited by the Egyptian pharaoh Taharqa, revolted (probably in 676 B.C.E.). Esarhaddon was busy with his Iranian campaign at that time, but in 675 B.C.E. he determined to punish Egypt, the source of most of the unrest in the west. Ever since the Nubian kings of the Twenty-fifth Dynasty gained control of Egypt around 725 B.C.E., they had stirred up revolts in the Levant in hopes of expelling Assyria from an area traditionally considered an Egyptian sphere of influence. Esarhaddon's first invasion of Egypt was thwarted by a sandstorm, but the following year he returned and captured the major fortified sites in the Delta. He also secured his flank and rear by winning the support of the Arabs and initiating the siege of Tyre. Then, in 671 B.C.E., he struck Egypt again, taking Memphis, the Egyptian capital, and forcing Pharaoh Taharqa to flee to the south. Esarhaddon reorganized the country, removing old officials and putting new ones in place. For the first time in history, both Egypt and Mesopotamia were ruled by the same person (see Map 9.1). However, Assyrian control over Egypt was only temporary. Two years later, Taharqa retook Memphis and stirred up rebellion throughout the Delta. Esarhaddon was leading another campaign to reconquer Egypt when he took ill and died in Syria.

In 672 B.C.E., Esarhaddon had proclaimed his son Asshurbanipal as crown prince of Assyria and another son, Shamash-shum-ukin, as crown prince of Babylon. Though it was clear that Shamash-shum-ukin was to be subordinate to his brother, such an arrangement might have led to a disputed succession and open conflict between the brothers. But it did not, at least not for some time; both men peacefully assumed their posts soon after their father's death. After making sure everything was in order at home and securing the submission of the king of Tyre, Asshurbanipal (668 to c. 627 B.C.E.) sent an army to regain control of Egypt. The Assyrians defeated Taharqa again and recaptured Memphis, but as before, the wily pharaoh avoided capture and took refuge in his native Kush (Nubia). Asshurbanipal made Nekau (Necho in Greek), ruler of the city of Sais in the Delta, his viceroy in Egypt. Taharqa died in 664 B.C.E., and his successor as king of Kush, Tanutamun, took up the crusade to liberate Egypt from Assyrian domination. Tanutamun gained control of all the major Egyptian centers from Aswan to Memphis and killed Nekau, but his victories were short-lived. Asshurbanipal's large army, stationed in the Delta, counterattacked and marched all the way to Thebes. The Assyrians sacked the ancient Egyptian religious center and burned it to the ground. Asshurbanipal named Nekau's son, Psamtik I (Psammetichus in Greek), as vassal king of Egypt, initiating the Saite Dynasty (Dynasty 26).

For seven years after Asshurbanipal's suppression of Egypt, the empire was relatively calm, with only a couple of minor campaigns against the Mannaeans, Medes, and Elam (whose Assyrian-appointed king had proved faithless). However, in 655 B.C.E., the storm broke. Tept-Humban-Inshushinak (Teumman in Assyrian texts), the new king of Elam, aided by an Aramaean tribe of the southern Zagros Mountains, attacked Mesopotamia. The invaders were driven back, and the Elamite king was killed in battle. His head was cut off,

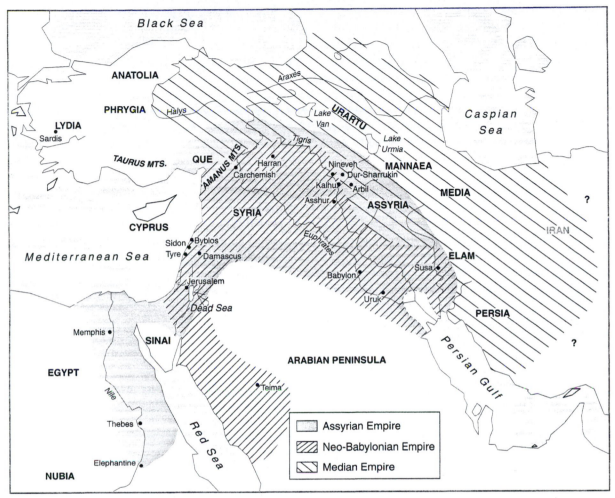

MAP 9.1   The Assyrian, Neo-Babylonian, and Median Empires at Their Greatest Extent (671–655 B.C.E.)

paraded through several cities, then taken to Nineveh. While Asshurbanipal was occupied with this conflict, Psamtik rebelled in Egypt and, aided by Ionian and Carian mercenaries, drove the Assyrian troops out of the country. Asshurbanipal was unable to respond, for almost as soon as he had settled affairs in Elam and punished the Zagros tribes, his brother led a revolt in Babylonia. It took four years for Asshurbanipal to quell the rebellion, but in 648 B.C.E., he retook Babylon. Shamash-shum-ukin committed suicide, throwing himself into the flames of his burning palace.

The Elamites, despite their recent defeat, had supported Shamash-shum-ukin's rebellion, so Asshurbanipal brought Elam back under control in 648 B.C.E. Nevertheless, he was unable to keep a pro-Assyrian ruler on Elam's throne, and the Elamites continued to stir up the Chaldean tribes in Babylonia. His patience at an end, Asshurbanipal invaded Elam once more, and between 642 and 639 B.C.E., he totally devastated the land. He looted and leveled all the major cities, including Susa. He burned Susa's temples and carried off or destroyed the statues of its gods. He even desecrated the tombs of earlier Elamite rulers and carried their bones to Assyria to subject their spirits, deprived of food and drink offerings, to eternal restlessness and torment. He sowed salt over Elam's agricultural land, magically cursing it so that nothing would grow there. Along with vast amounts of booty, he took tens of thousands of Elamites back to Assyria. Elam was so thoroughly destroyed that it would never again threaten Mesopotamia. Ironically, however, it also could no longer threaten the Medes who were being unified by a chieftain named Khshathrita, known as Phraortes to the Greeks (c. 647 to 625 B.C.E.). During the remainder of Asshurbanipal's reign, the power of the Medes continued to grow, and there was no longer a strong Elamite kingdom standing between them and Mesopotamia's eastern border.

Asshurbanipal's annals do not go beyond 639 B.C.E., so little is known of the last decade or so of his reign. Even the date of his death is not certain, though calculations based on an inscription indicate that it occurred in 627 or 626 B.C.E. Probably because of Asshurbanipal's preoccupation with Babylonia and Elam, he made no attempt to regain Egypt. Psamtik seems to have been allowed to become an ally, probably by promising not to interfere in Levantine affairs. Herodotus, a fifth-century B.C.E. Greek historian, indicates that in the latter part of Asshurbanipal's reign, Assyria was invaded by Medes and then by Scythians, with the Scythians reaching all the way to Palestine. Whether this account is accurate or not, Assyria seems to have experienced a serious decline during Asshurbanipal's final years. He doesn't seem to have had much time to relax and enjoy the luxurious palace he had erected at Nineveh.

NEO-ASSYRIAN SOCIETY AND CULTURE

The King, Crown Prince, and Queen

The Neo-Assyrian king, like earlier Mesopotamian rulers, was the viceroy of the gods, their representative on earth and the intermediary between them and human beings. Despite his great power, the Assyrian king was not deified as was the Egyptian pharaoh. However, the king embodied god-like attributes, enabling him to make the proper decisions and fulfill the will of Asshur, the Assyrian national deity, and the rest of the gods. His emulation of the gods was essential, for the country's well-being depended upon the king's personal virtues and his proper execution of the rituals associated with kingship.[5] Thus, in theory, the king was the state—an absolute ruler whose decisions could not be questioned and whose advisors and ministers were just his "servants."

In practice, though, the king's authority was partially limited by tradition, the power of the Assyrian landed nobility, and the necessity of having his major decisions approved by the gods. A king was expected to honor customary individual and group property rights, previous grants of tax exemptions, and other legal precedents. If he failed to respect such traditions, he would have had a difficult time convincing the people that he was administering the god Asshur's justice, one of the obligations of Asshur's chosen one. Also, the king ignored or offended the Assyrian nobles at his own peril. The growth of the empire during and after the time of Tiglath-pileser III (744 to 727 B.C.E.) necessitated the appointment of many new governors and officials, somewhat lessening the authority of the noble families that had held many of the highest offices as their hereditary right. Nevertheless, since army officers, governors, high officials, and queens came from the landed nobility, this class remained a power to be reckoned with. Members of this group engineered or supported the revolutions and coups that often bedeviled Assyrian monarchs. Moreover, the nobility had to approve the person the king chose to succeed him. So, the king could not afford to alienate too many members of this potent class. Finally, Assyrian kings made no important decisions and undertook no significant actions without first consulting the will of the gods as expressed through omens. There was a council of 16 expert astrologers and diviners of all types whose job it was to advise the king on meaning of the omens. Thus, omens (or those who interpreted them) could theoretically direct the actions of the king. However, the Assyrian king was not a puppet to be manipulated by those who interpreted the omens. There was no single high priest who could use his power over omen-taking to create a theocracy like the high priest of Amun did in Upper Egypt during the Third Intermediate Period. Not only did the Assyrian king usually consult his 16 primary religious advisors (who frequently disagreed with one another), but he also knew something of the art and could tell if the diviners were twisting their readings of the portents to their own ends. Moreover, as Georges Roux has remarked, usually "astrologers and diviners gave the king a general set of circumstances within which he felt free to 'do as he wished', and there were even cases when he asked for several omens in succession until he obtained one that fitted his plans."[6]

Like the Egyptian pharaoh, the Assyrian king preserved the divinely ordered world against chaos and enforced the principles of law handed down by the gods. However, the king not only ruled in place of the gods on earth, he also represented humans before the deities. When the gods were displeased, the king had to perform propitiatory rites, and every year during the New Year Festival, he underwent ritual humiliation as a kind of scapegoat for his people. When omens concerning the king were especially bad, he probably had to "die" to placate the heavenly powers. At such times of crisis, a substitute king was chosen and "reigned" for as long as one hundred days, participating in rituals of atonement while the real king and his sons were confined to the palace. At the end of this time, the substitute king seems to have been killed and the real king reestablished on his throne. The possible existence of this practice in Early Dynastic times was mentioned previously in Chapter 2, but it is well attested during the Neo-Assyrian era.

The ancient concept that the king was chosen by Asshur and the other gods prevented the Assyrians from developing a system of succession whereby a king's oldest son automatically ascended to the throne. The king probably could choose *any* of his sons to be crown prince, but the choice had to be approved by the gods (through omens), by other members of the royal family, and by the Assyrian nobles. Esarhaddon and Asshurbanipal (and possibly Sennacherib) were younger sons who were chosen as crown prince ahead

of their older brothers. This custom, however, produced some instability in the Assyrian monarchy, for resentful brothers and their supporters often revolted when the crown prince ascended to the throne. Moreover, a usurpation created its own legitimacy. In Mesopotamian thought, victory proved that the usurper was really the person chosen by the gods to be king. Since a new Assyrian king not only would be occupied for a time with installation and other rituals of office, but also often with suppressing rebellions by his brothers, unhappy vassals often chose the time of transition from one reign to another to revolt. Once the king's choice for crown prince was approved by the gods and by the Assyrian nobility, the designated heir went to live in his own palace, the *bit reduti* ("House of Succession") just north of Nineveh. There, he had a court similar to his father's and underwent training for the future administrative and military obligations he would have as king. He also assumed additional responsibilities, such as ruling the homeland while the king was away on military campaigns.

Though Assyrian rulers had several wives, only one was designated as the queen (the *sekallu*, "[lady] of the palace"). How she was chosen is unknown, though there are indications that queens were usually drawn from the principal noble families. The queen was also usually the mother of the crown prince. However, it is not clear whether she became queen because she was the mother of the person chosen to be crown prince or whether because she was the designated queen, only one of her sons could be named crown prince. Some Assyriologists argue that the first wife to bear the king a son became the queen.[7] The queen had special quarters in the royal palaces and had a large household and estates of her own. To administer these holdings, she even had her own bureaucracy headed by a wealthy and powerful female official called the *shakintu*. The queen's high position at court and prestige among the people were sometimes important factors during the succession, especially if the king died suddenly and she had to rally support for the designated heir. On occasions when the new king was still a minor, the former queen (now the queen-mother) often served as regent until her son came of age. Most queen-mothers remained respected members of the court, and some, such as Sammuramat (mother of Adad-nirari III) and Naqi'a (mother of Esarhaddon) became influential advisors to their sons. In fact, Naqi'a was almost a co-ruler; she had a palace of her own, received reports on religious and military matters, and composed royal inscriptions. She outlived her son, and her influence continued into the early years of her grandson Asshurbanipal's reign.

Non-Royal Social Classes

Beneath the royal family, the free Assyrian population seems to have been divided into three classes: nobility, practitioners of various professions, and "peasants." The nobles (*mar banuti*), members of princely houses, were wealthy and powerful owners of large estates. This small privileged class supplied the empire's governors, army officers, chief priests, and often, queens. The king also selected his principal advisors from their ranks. Obviously, members of noble families would have been well educated in preparation for their eventual roles in the governing bureaucracy. Interestingly, even the women of these families seem to have been educated, for they not only served as chief priestesses and queens, but Sargon II and his successors sometimes appointed noble women as provincial governors.

The much larger professional class (known as *ummane*) consisted of bankers, scribes, physicians, farmers, merchants, and all sorts of artisans. The great majority of those who practiced these various professions were male, but a few women are known to have owned businesses, and there were even some female scribes. Generally, though, the status of middle- and lower-class women in Assyrian society was low; they were usually dependent upon their male relations and restricted to caring for the household. The *ummane* were organized into trade guilds similar to those of the medieval era in Western Europe. However, Assyrian guilds not only maintained professional standards and quality, but also made sure that their members fulfilled their obligations to the state (such as tax payments, forced labor, and military service). Though much Assyrian

trade was still conducted by temples and the crown, many members of the *ummane* also engaged in free market trade, increasing the commerce that was the lifeblood of the Assyrian state. The empire's growth expanded Assyrian trade to such an extent that a Judean prophet could complain that Assyria had multiplied its merchants "more than the stars of the heavens" (Nahum 3:16). The position of the farmers within the *ummane* class is not clear, but most of them probably owned their own land. It is possible, though, that some leased their land or managed estates belonging to the state or nobles.

The poorly documented "peasants" (*hubshi*) must have constituted the bulk of the Assyrian population and provided most of its soldiers and colonists. The vast majority were probably tenant farmers on the lands of the crown, temples, or nobles, though some worked as hired laborers in cities and towns. The commoners were poor, but they had many rights that elevated them above the ranks of slaves. For example, the state provided at least two years' sustenance for the wife of a peasant who was killed or captured while serving in the army. The fertility of Assyria's soil and the prosperity of the empire probably made the life of Neo-Assyrian *hubshi* better than that of any contemporary Near Eastern peasants except those of Egypt.

Below these classes of free citizens were the slaves who were state, temple, or personal property. Most were prisoners of war, though some came from impoverished individuals who had been forced to become debt slaves or family members (usually children) of paupers who had sold them into slavery. Foreign captives had few rights and were assigned the most menial or dangerous jobs. Debt slaves, though, could own property, marry a free person, conduct business, and appear in court. In theory, they could pay off their debts and obtain their freedom, but high interest rates made that course extremely difficult, if not impossible. However, skilled slaves who worked as artisans were usually allowed to keep some of their wages, and occasionally they succeeded in purchasing their freedom. In a few instances, gifted slaves even managed to obtain important positions in the government.

The Army

The Assyrians were hardy, resilient people who made excellent soldiers. The growth and dominance of their empire was due primarily to their fighting capabilities and military organization. The Neo-Assyrian state had a standing army consisting of professional soldiers (some native Assyrians, but most drawn from the subject peoples, especially the Aramaeans) and Assyrian citizens performing their obligatory term of military service. In theory, all Assyrian males seem to have been subject to a period of military service. However, wealthy individuals appear to have been able to pay for exemptions or to supply others to serve in their place. Those adult male citizens who were not performing their service in the regular army were part of the militia. These Assyrian troops were supplemented by contingents drawn from the various conquered peoples.

Earlier armies had consisted of two components, chariotry and infantry, but the Assyrian army had three, chariotry, infantry, and cavalry. Chariots were still significant weapons in Iron Age battles, though their importance declined as mounted cavalry became more efficient in the seventh century B.C.E. Like the Egyptians, the Assyrians divided their chariot force into squadrons of 50 chariots each. Also as in Egypt, ninth- and early eighth-century B.C.E. Assyrian chariots generally carried two men, a driver and an archer. Quivers of arrows were attached to the body or carriage of the chariot along with an axe for use in close quarters. There was also a shield and long spear kept inside the carriage. The king's chariot usually carried an extra man, a shield carrier, to better protect the king. However, Tiglath-pileser III (744 to 727 B.C.E.) made the chariots heavier, increased the size of the wheels and changed the number of spokes from six to eight. This change may have been necessary to compensate for the heavier equipment or armament carried by his chariot warriors. The normal number of men in a chariot increased over time as well, to three in the era of Sargon II (721 to 705 B.C.E.) with the addition of a shield-bearer, and four in the time of Asshurbanipal (668 to c. 627 B.C.E.)—a driver, archer, and *two* shield-bearers to protect them. As Yigael Yadin has pointed out, "this virtually con-verted the charioteers into a mounted infantry unit."[8] By this time, though, the chariot was not as useful a striking force as the cavalry.

The Assyrian infantry consisted of archers, slingers, and spearmen. The archers provided covering fire for the assault forces during a battle in open terrain or when besieging a city (see Figures 8.1 and 9.2). From the time of Tiglath-pileser III onward, during sieges, archers were usually protected by tall, thick wicker shields behind which they knelt and fired their arrows (see Figure 9.2, lower central section). Like other Assyrian soldiers, they wore bronze or iron helmets and sometimes also donned protective **mail** shirts consisting of a mesh of small interlocked metal rings (known as chain mail) or small overlapping plates of bronze or iron. Slingers also usually wore helmets and mail shirts and provided covering fire by stones from their slings (see Figure 9.2, lower left side). The spearmen were the army's assault troops in both hand-to-hand battles and during a siege. They wore helmets, were armed with long spears, and occasionally wore long coats of leather or mail. In open battle, spearmen had to be able to move swiftly and freely. Then, their torsos were usually protected only by crisscrossed leather bands holding circular metal plates over their chests. Their main protection came from light wicker shields strengthened with a covering of leather. The shape and size of the shield varied over time, from small rectangular or circular ones to a large curved shield that covered much of the body. The discipline, training and armament of Assyrian spearmen influenced the development of Greek armies in the seventh and sixth centuries B.C.E.

The most significant military innovation of the first millennium B.C.E. Assyrians was the integration into the army of true cavalry, a highly mobile force with warriors mounted on horseback. They may have learned the effectiveness of mounted warriors from some of their seminomadic opponents in the northern Zagros Mountains, but the earliest depictions of mounted cavalry are in the reliefs of Asshurnasirpal II (883 to 859 B.C.E.). The cavalrymen rode bareback; saddles and stirrups had not yet been invented. At first, they rode in pairs, one rider holding both sets of reins and guiding the horses while the other fought, using either a compound bow or a long spear. By the time of Sargon II, cavalrymen were managing their own horses, even when their hands were engaged using bows and arrows. Mounted cavalry was even more effective than chariots in outflanking the enemy and attacking it from the side or rear. Like chariots, spear-carrying horsemen could also launch direct frontal attacks on enemy forces and break through their ranks. The most important advantage of cavalry over chariots, though, was that it could carry out these maneuvers in mountainous and wooded terrain where chariots could not be used.

The Assyrian army was accompanied by efficient auxiliary units of specialists trained for specific tasks such as crossing rivers or besieging cities. Miners and sappers dug tunnels and undermined walls (see Figure 8.1, lower left section). The engineer corps constructed wheeled battering rams with wicker or, later, leather-covered superstructures to protect the operators (see Figures 8.1 and 9.2). They built tall siege towers to raise archers to the level of defenders on the battlements. They also erected ramps to allow the battering rams and assault troops to reach and attack vulnerable parts of city walls (see Figure 9.2). Moreover, the engineers built pontoon bridges across small streams and constructed boats or rafts to carry equipment across larger ones, while the troops swam to the other side on inflated goatskins. All in all, the Assyrian army, including its auxiliary branches, was the best trained, best supplied and most efficient that the world had yet seen.

Administration of the Empire

The Assyrians' administration of their vast empire was also more efficient than any previously known. The king (or, in his absence, the crown prince) oversaw the administration of the Assyrian heartland, including the four major cities of Asshur, Kalhu, Nineveh, and Arbil (Arbela) and their surrounding fields. These cities had special privileges such as exemption from taxation and from the military draft. The king had a group of major advisors who helped him make

important decisions, and since Assyria was a militaristic state, the members of this advisory body were usually high-ranking army officers and often, provincial governors. Chief among these officials was the *turtanu* (tartan in the Bible) who was commander-in-chief or "field marshal" of the armies (after the king) as well as the governor of the important district of Harran. He also served a year's term as *limmu*. The *limmu* was an Assyrian official who gave his name to the year, and he probably also conducted religious ceremonies at the New Year's Festival for that year. The king was almost always the *limmu* for his second year on the throne. After him would follow the *turtanu*, then other district governors in order of their rank. Other members of the king's inner group of advisors and administrators were the Chief Cup-Bearer (*rab shaqê* in Akkadian and *rabshakeh* in the Bible), the Great Chancellor, the Palace Herald, and the Superintendent.

Outside Assyria proper, the empire was divided into states bound to the Assyrian king by treaties and provinces ruled for the king by appointed governors. Provinces were in turn divided into districts, each centered on a city or large town and presided over by a district chief. Some governors who held dual positions, such as the *turtanu* or *rab shaqê*, must have had deputy governors to oversee their provinces while they were elsewhere advising the king or participating in military campaigns. The treaties between Assyria and its subject states assured Assyrian support for the vassals, but in exchange required obedience to the Assyrian king, support for his choice as crown prince, yearly payment of tribute, contributions of men to the Assyrian army when requested, and usually that royal or noble hostages be sent to the Assyrian court.

Quick and reliable communication between the king and his governors or vassal rulers was vital in such a large and diverse empire. So the Assyrians created a more advanced version of the messenger system used by the Third Dynasty of Ur more than a millennium earlier (see Chapter 3). Royal messengers traveled by horse or mule along the main thoroughfares of the empire (called "royal roads") between the provinces and Assyria. Along the various routes, at intervals equaling about one day's journey (20 to 30 miles), there were garrisoned posts with provisions and changes of horses and mules for messengers and their military escorts. This efficient communication system presaged that of the later Achaemenid Persians who are usually given credit for first developing it.

The Assyrians have become famous for their use of torture, mutilation, and other acts of what has been called "calculated frightfulness"[9] to keep their subjects in line. However, the Assyrians highly valued loyalty, and violation of an oath of allegiance to the king was regarded as a grave offence against the gods whose viceroy he was and in whose names the oath was sworn. Thus, meting out swift and harsh punishment to rebellious vassals was not just politically or militarily desirable, but a religious obligation, as well. When rebellious cities or states surrendered quickly and turned over their seditious leaders to the Assyrians, the population was usually treated leniently. Only the leaders were punished (usually by torture and then execution) and replaced by others friendly to Assyria. When a city or country refused to surrender, generally a much harsher policy was followed. Once the Assyrians triumphed militarily, they would make an example of a portion of the population, usually members of the upper classes. Some were staked to the ground and skinned alive. Others were mutilated by having their eyes put out or their hands, feet, or tongues cut off. Still others were beaten and tortured in various ways before being impaled on sharpened stakes erected around the city. Such atrocities served as warnings and deterrents to others who might think about rebelling in the future. In addition, the horrible punishments, as well as the depictions of them within Assyrian palaces, testified that the king was upholding the gods' honor and enforcing their justice.

The second part of the punishment for a rebellious people was the deportation of a selected portion of the population, usually the nobles, merchants, and artisans. When Asshurnasirpal II began deporting defeated peoples to Assyria early in the ninth century B.C.E., the practice seems to have been primarily intended to resettle depopulated parts of the country. Subsequent inscriptions show that the foreigners were treated the same as the Assyrians and became Assyrian citizens. After mentioning how many deportees he had carried off, a king usually claims: "I settled them, as Assyrians I counted them; the yoke of Asshur, my lord, like the Assyrians, I laid on them; tribute and tax like the Assyrians I laid on them."[10] However, the deportations carried out from the late eighth through the seventh century B.C.E. by Sargon II and his successors were quite different. These kings treated many of the deportees as "booty" to provide labor on state building projects or to be given as slaves to temples, nobles, or Assyrian cities. Instead of resettling Assyria, large numbers of deportees were just shifted from one part of the empire to another. For example, Sargon II settled Israelite deportees in Assyria (2 Kings 17:6), while Babylonians and Elamites were relocated to the area that had once been the Kingdom of Israel (2 Kings 17:24). During the heyday of their empire, the Assyrians uprooted several hundred thousand people in this way. They hoped that the deportees, far from their native lands and traditions and living among people with different languages and customs, would have little incentive or ability to revolt. However, the growing number of foreign, discontented people in and around Assyria itself probably contributed to the rapid demise of Assyrian power and helps to explain the failure of Assyria to rise again after its collapse.

Art, Literature, and Science

People often think of Assyria only as a nation of cruel but efficient warriors, but Assyria also produced many superb artists and scholars. Though Assyrian artistic, literary, and intellectual traditions were based on those of Babylonia, in sculpture, at least, the pupils surpassed their teachers. The Assyrians carved colossal limestone human-headed winged bulls and lions to guard palace doorways. They lined palace walls with beautiful limestone panels sculpted in bas-relief (see Figures 8.1 and 9.3). The reliefs from the Palace of Asshurbanipal at Nineveh, discovered in the 1850s and now in the British Museum, are generally considered the apex of Assyrian art. The most exquisite of all are the hunting scenes, which exhibit an expressive realism and a generally sympathetic understanding of animal suffering. The portrayal of a wild ass hampered in her flight by concern for her foal or that of a lion suddenly checked in his charge by an arrow piercing the back of his neck or of a dying lioness roaring her defiance while dragging her paralyzed hind legs (see Figure 9.3) are all masterpieces of animal sculpture.

The Assyrians also treasured and added to earlier Mesopotamian literary, religious, and scientific works. The final editions of key Mesopotamian compositions such as *The Creation Epic* (called *Enuma elish* in Akkadian) and the *Epic of Gilgamesh* come from the Neo-Assyrian era. The same is true for the major astronomical/astrological texts. Moreover, Asshurbanipal's scribes compiled several medical textbooks from earlier texts and traditions. Within his magnificent palace, Asshurbanipal collected a superb library of approximately 20,000 cuneiform tablets copied from archives, schools, and temples throughout Mesopotamia. These texts ranged in date from Sumerian times to his own era and included examples of almost every type of written material: literary works, king lists, annals, vocabulary lists (some of them bilingual), medical tablets, and lists of omens, rituals, and magical incantations. Asshurbanipal claimed to be an exceptional scholar, able to read and understand all of the diverse material in this library:

> I learned the craft of the sage Adapa, the hidden secrets of the entire scribal profession. . . . I have read sophisticated texts in obscure Sumerian and Akkadian difficult to comprehend, and have studied inscriptions on stone from the time before the flood with elite companions.[11]

It is likely that this was just an idle boast, for texts in his library that contained archaic terms or obscure words or signs were commonly annotated with a more current equivalent. Nevertheless, Asshurbanipal deserves the gratitude of modern scholars for amassing this great collection of Mesopotamian lore. Its tablets have been the source of much of our knowledge of ancient Mesopotamia.

FIGURE 9.3 The Dying Lioness

This relief is from Asshurbanipal's palace at Ninevah.

Source: The British Museum London.

Photo: Werner Forman/ Art Resource, New York.

THE NEO-BABYLONIAN (OR CHALDEAN) EMPIRE (625–560 B.C.E.)

Destruction of Assyria (627–605 B.C.E.)

Asshurbanipal seems to have died in 627 B.C.E., and Kandalanu, the vassal king he had placed on the throne of Babylon, died the same year. Almost immediately, civil war broke out in Assyria, with two of Asshurbanipal's sons fighting over the succession. At the same time, after a year in which there was no recognized king of Babylon, Nabopolassar (Nabu-aplausur, 625 to 605 B.C.E.), probably a Chaldean who had formerly been governor of the Sealand, claimed the throne. His rule was not universally accepted, so there was fierce warfare in Babylonia, as well. The sources for these years of conflict are somewhat contradictory, and the chronology is problematic. Fortunately, a series of Babylonian chronicles record the events after 616 B.C.E.

It is clear that by 616 B.C.E., Nabopolassar had gained control of Babylonia. He then proceeded to launch an attack against Assyria. His invasion led Assyria to made an alliance with Egypt, probably by abandoning all Assyrian claims to the Levant. In 615 B.C.E., Nabopolassar failed in an attempt to conquer the city of Asshur and was forced to retreat. But when the Assyrian army followed him southward, the Medes, probably with Babylonian instigation, took advantage of the situation and invaded the Assyrian heartland. The Medes had recently been unified and without Elam to check them, had quickly grown in strength and boldness. Under Huvakshatra, a ruler known to Herodotus as Cyaxares (c. 625 to 585 B.C.E.), they captured Tarbisu, a city near Nineveh, looted Kalhu, and destroyed Asshur in 614 B.C.E. Nabopolassar marched north to join them, and outside the ruins of Asshur, the Babylonians and Medes entered into a treaty of friendship. This alliance seems to have been sealed later through the marriage of Nabopolassar's son Nebuchadnezzar to a daughter or granddaughter of the Median king.

The armies of the Medes and Babylonians now worked in tandem. In 612 B.C.E., the combined forces, joined by a contingent of Scythians, laid siege to Nineveh. The city held out for three months, but finally was overwhelmed and turned into a heap of rubble. The allies also destroyed Kalhu (which had torn down major sections of its walls to repair the damage inflicted in 614 B.C.E.) and several other Assyrian cities. As the news of Nineveh's fall spread through the empire, many former Assyrian subjects must have reacted with the joy expressed by the Judean prophet Nahum (3:7b, 19, New Revised Standard Version):

> "Nineveh is devastated; who will bemoan her?" . . .
>
> There is no assuaging your hurt, your wound is mortal.
>
> All who hear the news about you clap their hands over you.
>
> For who has ever escaped your endless cruelty?

The remaining Assyrian forces fled westward to Harran under the leadership of a new ruler, since the former king had perished at Nineveh. There, they were joined by a small force of their Egyptian allies. The Babylonians and Medes did not follow immediately. Instead, Nabopolassar spent the next year making sure all of the Assyrian heartland and the western provinces along the middle Euphrates were firmly under his control while the Medes spread their power into the territory of Urartu. However, in 610 B.C.E., the Babylonians and Medes attacked Harran, forcing the Assyrians and Egyptians to flee, first to Syria, and then, after an abortive counterattack on Harran in which the final Assyrian king died, to Carchemish. There, the tattered remnants of the former Assyrian army were joined by the main Egyptian army led by Pharaoh Nekau II (better known as Necho, 610 to 595 B.C.E.), who was intent on stopping any further Babylonian expansion. Josiah, king of Judah, may have tried to prevent the Egyptian forces from aiding the Assyrians, but Necho killed him at Megiddo (c. 609 B.C.E.). In 605 B.C.E., led by Nebuchadnezzar, the Babylonian crown prince, the joint Babylonian-Median army launched a surprise attack on Carchemish and decisively defeated the Egyptian forces just outside the city. The Egyptians fled southward in disorder with the Babylonians and Medes on their heels. But Nebuchadnezzar broke off the pursuit when he was notified that his father had died. He had to return immediately to be crowned king of Babylon. In little more than 20 years, the once-mighty Assyrian Empire had collapsed, and Assyria itself had been almost totally destroyed. Most of Assyria's major cities lay in ruins, never to rise again, and its people, depleted by almost constant fighting, were taken off in slavery by the Medes or absorbed by the former captives in their midst. Seldom in history has a nation, especially one previously so powerful, vanished so quickly and completely.

Formation of the Neo-Babylonian and Median Empires

The Medes and Babylonians seem to have divided up the areas that had been part of the Assyrian Empire with little animosity or conflict. Babylon's trade was with the west, so it needed control over the Phoenician ports and Syria up to the Taurus Mountains (especially Carchemish with its crossing over the Euphrates). The Neo-Babylonian (or Chaldean) kings also held Elam, and of course, Mesopotamia. The Medes took the eastern portions of Assyria, probably made the closely related Persians their vassals, and began gradually extending their control over Urartu, Tabal, and most of eastern Anatolia (see Map 9.1).

Almost immediately after his coronation, Nebuchadnezzar II* (604 to 562 B.C.E.) returned to Syria to make sure that the resurgent Egyptian power in the Levant had been destroyed and that the region was firmly under Babylonian control. For the next three years, he campaigned in Syria and Palestine, collecting tribute from Damascus, Sidon, Tyre, Judah, and other states and destroying those, like Ashkelon, who resisted. In 601 B.C.E., Nebuchadnezzar marched against Egypt, hoping to finish the

conquest he had been compelled to abort earlier. This time, the Egyptians fought fiercely, and both sides suffered heavy casualties. Nebuchadnezzar was forced to retreat to Babylon to regroup, but the Egyptian army had also been so bloodied that it could not pursue the Babylonians. However, Nebuchadnezzar's defeat convinced Jehoiakim, the king of Judah, against the advice of the prophet Jeremiah, to stop paying tribute to Babylon and return to an Egyptian alliance. It took Nebuchadnezzar a couple of years to build up his strength before responding. Just as the Babylonian armies marched westward in 598 B.C.E., Jehoiakim died (or possibly was murdered), leaving his 18-year-old son, Jehoiachin, to experience Babylon's wrath. Nebuchadnezzar descended on Jerusalem in 597 B.C.E. and, after a brief siege, forced the city to surrender. He seized the treasures of Solomon's Temple and the royal palace as tribute, carried off Jehoiachin, most of the royal family, and thousands of the upper classes, and placed Zedekiah, Jehoiachin's uncle, on Judah's throne. Most of the Judean exiles, including the prophet Ezekiel, were settled near Nippur, but their king was kept as a hostage in Nebuchadnezzar's palace in Babylon. There, archaeologists found cuneiform tablets listing the rations given to Jehoiachin (called "Ya'ukina, king of the land of Yahudu"[12]) and his family.

Though the Babylonians conducted several campaigns in Syria-Palestine during the next few years, they do not seem to have prevented Judah and other Levantine vassals from contemplating rebellion. After an uprising in Babylon in 595 B.C.E. that forced Nebuchadnezzar to execute many of his troops, Zedekiah discussed revolt with envoys from Tyre, Sidon, Ammon, Moab, and Edom, but the conspiracy collapsed when the Babylonian army returned to the area. However, soon after Psamtik II (Psammeticus II, 595 to 589 B.C.E.), successor of Nekau (Necho) II, showed Egyptian strength by a march into Palestine in 591 B.C.E., Zedekiah was again moved to revolt. Psamtik died in 589 B.C.E., but his son and successor, Wahibre (Apries to the Greeks and Hophra in the Bible, 589 to 570 B.C.E.), supported the rebellion by capturing Gaza and attacking Tyre and Sidon. When

---

*Because of biblical references to him, this king is one of the best-known ancient rulers. His name is usually written Nebuchadnezzar in the Bible (with Nebuchadrezzar as a variant), so the more familiar spelling has been used here. However, the actual Akkadian name, Nabu-kudurri-usur ("Nabu will protect my offspring"), shows that Nebuchadrezzar is closer to the original.

Nebuchadnezzar's armies approached, though, the Egyptians retreated to their own country and the Babylonians seem to have regained control of most of Phoenicia and Philistia. Then, in 587 B.C.E., the Babylonians began an 18-month-long siege of Jerusalem which ended with the city's almost complete destruction in the summer of 586 B.C.E. Zedekiah's sons were killed before his eyes, then he was blinded and taken to Babylon. Thousands of Judah's citizens were deported to Babylonia where they joined their countrymen, beginning the famous "Babylonian Exile." Many others escaped the Babylonians and fled to Egypt.

Meanwhile, the Medes had been engaged in a five-year-long war with Lydia for control of central Anatolia. According to Herodotus, a major battle between the two armies was interrupted by a solar eclipse (which astronomers date to May 28, 585 B.C.E.). After this sign of divine displeasure, Nebuchadnezzar mediated a peace treaty between the Medes and Lydians, making the Halys River the boundary between their respective kingdoms. Though the Medes and Babylonians had remained friendly during the early part of his reign, Nebuchadnezzar may have begun to fear the growth of Median power. In the latter part of his reign, he followed the example of the much earlier Third Dynasty of Ur and built a great defensive wall across Mesopotamia where the Tigris and Euphrates are closest together. He constructed another fortification wall just north of Babylon between the Euphrates and one of its branches. These walls protected Babylonia from invasion from the north and probably were intended primarily as protection against the Medes.

Nebuchadnezzar may have bypassed Tyre from 588 to 587 B.C.E., or it may have been briefly pacified and then revolted again. In any case, three years after the fall of Jerusalem, the Babylonians besieged Tyre. It held out for 13 years, but was finally forced to surrender in 571 B.C.E. Continued unrest in Judah, including the assassination of the governor the Babylonians had installed, caused further deportations of people from 582 to 581 B.C.E. But for the last ten years of his reign, the Levant was firmly in Nebuchadnezzar's hands. Ezekiel 29:19–21 and a fragmentary Babylonian tablet indicate that Nebuchadnezzar attempted another invasion of Egypt in 568 B.C.E., but he does not seem to have penetrated beyond the eastern Delta area if, indeed, he got that far. On the other hand, he does seem to have conquered the Arab tribes of northwestern Arabia before he died in 562 B.C.E. and was succeeded by his son, Amel-Marduk (the biblical Evil-Merodach).

Nebuchadnezzar's Babylon

The ruins of ancient Babylon, still called Babil in modern times, were extensively excavated from 1899 until 1917 by a German expedition led by Robert Koldewey. Iraq's Directorate General of Antiquities has conducted further excavations and extensive restorations at the site since 1958. Though some of the remains the archaeologists have uncovered may derive from Esarhaddon and Asshurbanipal's rebuilding of Babylon, most reflect the widespread activities of Nebuchadnezzar who thoroughly enlarged and reconstructed the city. The Babylon of the Chaldean rulers continued to astonish visitors in later times, so impressing the Greeks that they recognized two of its monuments (the "Hanging Gardens" and the city's huge fortification walls) as wonders of the ancient world.

In ancient times, the Euphrates, which now flows to the west of the ruins, ran through the middle of this large city of about 100,000 people. Babylon was roughly a rectangle, with the Euphrates cutting through its long sides and dividing it in two with a slightly larger portion of the city on the eastern side of the river (see Figure 9.4). It was protected by a 40-foot-wide moat connected to the Euphrates and a double set of walls separated by about 24 feet (7 meters), each strengthened by towers spaced 60 feet (18 meters) apart. The outer wall was about 12 feet (3.7 meters) thick and the inner wall 21 feet (6.5 meters) thick. Eight great fortified gateways (including the ceremonial Ishtar Gate) and several smaller entrances gave access into the city. Beyond the old city's walls on the west bank of the river, Nebuchadnezzar built another great double wall and moat about 17 miles long protecting his grand summer palace (known as the "Northern Palace") and some of the suburbs that had developed outside the old city (see Figure 9.4).

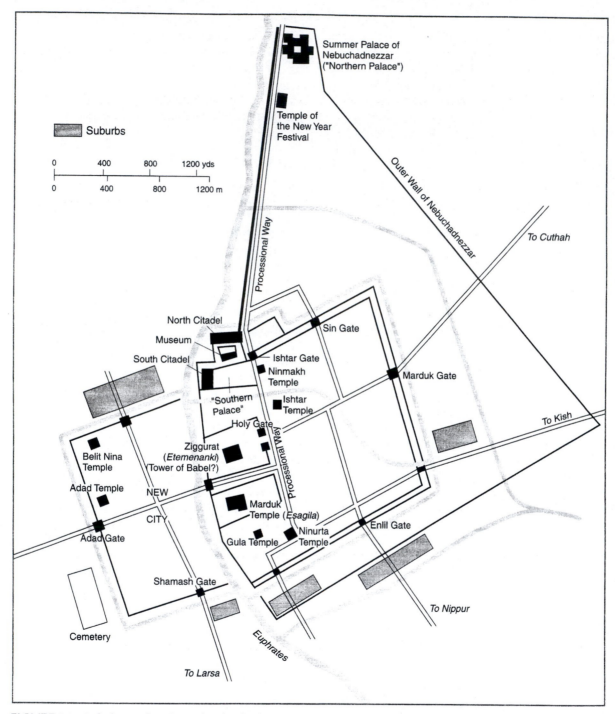

FIGURE 9.4   Babylon at the Time of Nebuchadnezzar (604–562 B.C.E.)

Source: Adapted from Harry Thomas Frank, ed., *Hammond's Atlas of the Bible Lands* (Maplewood, NJ: Hammond Inc., 1977), B-17.

Nebuchadnezzar also extensively restored Babylon's older palaces. The largest was the so-called "Southern Palace" on the Euphrates (see Figure 9.4) protected by two fortresses, the North Citadel and South Citadel. He enlarged and almost totally rebuilt this palace, replacing the older sun-dried brick buildings with ones made of baked brick and using imported cedar beams to support the roof. He created a large new throne room decorated with colorful glazed bricks forming figures of lions, garlands of palmettos, rosettes, and other motifs accented with gold, silver, and precious stones. Nearby were the king's luxurious private quarters and the harem. The palace included five large courtyards and quarters for administrators and the garrison. In the northeastern corner of the palace, the German excavators uncovered the foundations of a large structure identified by Koldewey as the famous "Hanging Gardens." Ancient Greek and Roman writers described this massive tiered building (supposedly created to please a concubine who missed her native hills) and claimed that it had equipment to raise water from the river to irrigate the gardens planted on its different levels. However, though the structure the Germans excavated had thick lower walls and vaulted chambers that could have supported a high superstructure, it was too far from the river to make irrigation an easy process. Thus, most modern scholars question Koldewey's identification, and recent excavations at the site indicate that it was a storage building for administrative tablets.

Esarhaddon and Asshurbanipal had rebuilt *Esagila* (the great temple of Marduk), *Etemenanki* (its ziggurat), and Babylon's many other temples. However, Nebuchadnezzar embellished the eight-tiered ziggurat (whose name means "House of the Foundation Platform of Heaven and Earth") with decorations and covered the temple at its top with blue glazed bricks. This great ziggurat, about 300 feet square at its base and probably about as high, may have been the inspiration for the biblical story of the Tower of Babel (the Hebrew name for Babylon) in Genesis. Nebuchadnezzar provided even more lavish decoration for some of the chapels within *Esagila*. He plated the interior walls of the chapel of Marduk with gold and decorated the bases of its columns with alabaster and lapis lazuli. He also provided the god with a gold-plated wooden bed and throne as well as a ceremonial chariot and barge made of wood plated with gold and silver set with precious stones. The Babylonians later told the visiting Herodotus that 800 talents (about three tons) of gold had been used in this chapel alone. Nebuchadnezzar also plated the walls of other shrines with gold, silver, and precious stones.

The greatest surviving example of Nebuchadnezzar's monumental structures is the Ishtar Gate near the original northern entrance into the city (see Figure 9.4). This huge gateway, through which ran a wide road known as the Processional Way, was actually a series of gates with protective battlements above and guard chambers at ground level. The towers at its northern end were 70 feet high; the vaulted opening was 15 feet wide and 35 feet high (see Figure 9.5). The towers at the southern end of the gateway were much taller, but they were not preserved to their full height. The gateway's walls were covered with blue glazed bricks with alternating pairs of red and white dragons (sacred to Marduk) and bulls (sacred to Adad) standing out in bas-relief. The walls north of the gate on either side of the Processional Way (lower center and right of Figure 9.5) were also lined with blue enameled bricks decorated with a procession of large white bas-relief lions (sacred to Ishtar) with red and yellow manes. Since this gateway was the most spectacular find the early-twentieth-century German excavators made, they dismantled it, carefully numbering each brick, and shipped the remains to Berlin. There they were reassembled in the Vorderasiatisches Museum, where visitors can see them today.

The Processional Way (see Figure 9.4), along which major religious and military pageants proceeded, ran from Nebuchadnezzar's summer palace and the Temple of the New Year Festival through the Ishtar Gate, past the entrance of the Southern Palace to a point between the enclosure for the ziggurat and the *Esagila* temple. It then turned westward and ran between the two sacred enclosures (with entrances into both) and ended at a bridge across the Euphrates.

FIGURE 9.5
Reconstruction of Babylon's Ishtar Gate

Just inside the gate on the right is the Southern Palace and the traditional site of the "Hanging Gardens." The ziggurat *Etemenanki* can be seen in the distance in the upper right.

Source: The Oriental Institute of the University of Chicago.

This large avenue was 30 to 50 feet wide and paved with limestone slabs brought from Lebanon. The central part of the road (about 20 feet wide) was bordered with red breccia stone from the middle Euphrates region. It is no wonder that visitors like Herodotus who viewed this road and the magnificent structures lining it were awed by the grandeur of Chaldean Babylon.

The End of the Neo-Babylonian Empire

Almost nothing is known of the brief reigns of Amel-Marduk (561 to 560 B.C.E.) and his successor Neriglissar (Nergal-shar-usur, 559 to 556 B.C.E.). The Hellenistic Babylonian historian Berossus claimed that Amel-Marduk ruled in an overbearing and unlawful fashion, prompting his murder and replacement by Neriglissar, his brother-in-law. Neriglissar's inscriptions indicate that he undertook some public works projects and won a battle against a ruler from western Cilicia who had raided into the Babylonian-held territory in eastern Cilicia and northwestern Syria. He reigned for four years then died, leaving the throne to his son, who was still only a child. However, only a couple months into the new reign, the leading officers of the state decided to replace Neriglissar's heir with Nabonidus, a Babylonian noble and son-in-law of Nebuchadnezzar who had held high military posts under his father-in-law and Neriglissar.

Nabonidus (Nabu-na'id, 556 to 539 B.C.E.) was the son of a former governor of Harran and a woman who probably was a priestess in Harran's temple of the moon god, Sin. However, it is not known if his parents were of Chaldean origin. He seems to have been devoted to his mother, Adad-guppi, and he buried her with royal honors when she finally died at the age of 104 in 547 B.C.E. Because of her, Nabonidus developed a deep reverence for the deity she had served throughout her life. He restored the ruined ziggurat and temples of Ur, one of the moon god's cities, and rebuilt Ehulhul, Sin's temple in Harran. Nabonidus was very interested in the past, searching out earlier foundation deposits whenever he restored the great temples of Sumer and Akkad. He also made his daughter priestess of Nanna (Sin) in Ur, following the precedent Sargon of Agade had established some two millennia earlier. During his repair work at various sites, Nabonidus uncovered inscriptions, monuments, even statues of his predecessors and kept these antiquities in a "museum" in the residence of his daughter in Ur. There they were excavated in the 1920s by the famous archaeologist, Sir Leonard Woolley. Because of Nabonidus' fascination with ancient customs and his search for antiquities, sometimes he is dubbed "the first archaeologist."

While Nabonidus also added to the temple of Marduk in Babylon, his emphasis on the god Sin and the city of Harran angered the priests of Marduk and other conservative elements in Babylonia. So, when plague, famine, and high inflation struck southern Mesopotamia, Nabonidus regarded the misfortunes as punishment for the treasonous murmurings of the priests and people of Babylon, Borsippa, Nippur, Ur, Uruk, and Larsa. Fed up with the Babylonians' grumbling and inspired by a dream, around 549 B.C.E., Nabonidus installed his son Bel-shar-usur (biblical Belshazzar) as regent in Babylon and took up residence in the oasis of Teima in northwest Arabia. Some have discerned economic motives for this move, for Teima was the point where the caravan trade route from southern Arabia diverged to go in different directions to Damascus, Egypt, and Mesopotamia. Others have favored a religious explanation, noting that Teima was a center for the worship of the moon god, as Harran was. Still others argue that his enemies must have prevented Nabonidus from returning to Babylon. Whatever his reasons, Nabonidus stayed in Teima for most of the rest of his reign, and during that time, the New Year Festival could not be celebrated in Babylon, for it required the king's presence.

Angered by Nabonidus' earlier slights and the constant postponements of the New Year Festival, many priests and high officials in Babylon secretly supported Cyrus II, the Persian king. They spread propaganda accusing Nabonidus of being a madman and a heretic. These charges continued to circulate in much later times, and are reflected in Hellenistic works such as the biblical Book of Daniel (where Nebuchadnezzar is erroneously identified as the mad king) and in a legendary account found among the Dead Sea Scrolls. Cyrus (Kurash) II had risen to the throne of Persia in 560 or 559 B.C.E., probably as a vassal of Astyages (Ishtumegu in cuneiform sources), king of the Medes (c. 585 to 550 B.C.E.). At that time, the Medes controlled Harran, so when Nabonidus became king of Babylon three years later and wanted to rebuild Sin's temple there, he encouraged Cyrus to rebel against the Medes and help the Babylonians capture the city. Cyrus accepted the alliance, and a war with the Medes ensued. In 550 B.C.E., Astyages was betrayed by his own generals and captured by Cyrus. Thus, overnight, the roles were reversed—the Persians became the masters and the Medes became their vassals. During the following decade, while Nabonidus stayed in Teima and work proceeded on Sin's temple in Harran, Cyrus extended his power into

Asia Minor and further into Iran (see Chapter 10). By 539 B.C.E., the Persian king was ready to take on Babylon. Nabonidus finally returned to the city and directed its defense, but it was too late. Assyria went over to the Persian side and Belshazzar was killed while trying to prevent Cyrus' invasion of Babylonia. Nabonidus fled and Babylon fell to Cyrus without resistance. Soon afterward, the Persians captured Nabonidus and probably killed him, though different stories about his fate circulated in later times. Thus ended not only the Neo-Babylonian Empire, but also the last native dynasty to govern Babylon.

THE EMERGENCE OF BIBLICAL MONOTHEISM

The Triumph of the Reform Movement

In the eighth century B.C.E., many, if not most, citizens of Israel and Judah still seem to have thought of Yahweh as another name for El, the head of the Canaanite pantheon, with the goddess Asherah as his consort. Archaeologists have found inscriptions from this time blessing individuals by "Yahweh and his Asherah,"[13] and the temples of both kingdoms contained the goddess' sacred poles or trees. Also, in every excavated Israelite and Judean city of this time, including Jerusalem, archaeologists have uncovered fertility figurines that probably represent Asherah. But the "Yahweh Only" party led by prophets continued in both the north and the south, probably as a minority movement.

When Israel was destroyed in 722–721 B.C.E., many of its people took refuge in Judah, doubling the southern kingdom's population. Some of these refugees brought writings and traditions that Judean editors would begin to merge with their own southern accounts and lore. The Judean reform party, probably strengthened by the addition of some of its counterparts from the north, blamed the destruction of Israel primarily on that kingdom's religious practices, especially its worship of other deities in addition to Yah-

weh. Their movement gained royal support when the death of the Assyrian king Tiglath-pileser III (727 B.C.E.) and the admonitions of the prophet Isaiah probably influenced the new Judean King Hezekiah (c. 727 to 697 B.C.E., see Table 9.2)[14] to initiate a series of reforms. He tried to centralize worship in Jerusalem. To this end, he destroyed many of the high places where Yahweh had been worshipped in Canaanite fashion, pulling down their standing stones or pillars and cutting down Asherah's sacred poles or trees. He also purified the Temple of Solomon in Jerusalem, smashing the bronze serpent supposedly made by Moses. At Beersheba, Hezekiah's agents seem to have demolished a large horned altar upon which animal sacrifices had been burned. Archaeologists found its sandstone blocks, one of which had the figure of a snake carved into it, reused in a later limestone wall. This altar and that in a small temple at Arad (probably destroyed by Josiah) show that until late in the Judean monarchy, religious ritu-

TABLE 9.2
Chronology of the Last Kings of Israel and Judah, 747–586

(All dates are B.C.E. and are probably correct to within about ±10 years or less. The names of the most important rulers are printed in boldface.)

The Kingdom of Isreal	The Kingdom of Judah
Zechariah & Shallum (c. 747)	**Uzziah** (c. 767–739)
Menahem (c. 747–742)	
Pekahiah (c. 742–740)	
Pekah (c. 740–731)	Jotham (c. 739–734)
Hoshea (c. 731–722)	Ahaz (c. 734–727)
	Hezekiah (c. 727–697)
	Manasseh (c. 697–642)
	Amon (c. 642–640)
	Josiah (c. 640–609)
	Jehoahaz (c. 609)
	Jehoiakim (c. 609–598)
	Jehoiachin (c. 598–597)
	Zedekiah (c. 597–586)

als, including animal sacrifices, were conducted in places other than Jerusalem.

Hezekiah probably died c. 697 B.C.E., only a few years after his unsuccessful rebellion against Sennacherib, leaving to his son Manasseh (c. 697 to 642 B.C.E.) a kingdom reduced in size, impoverished, and partly depopulated by the Assyrians. Manasseh learned a lesson from his father's defeat, and (despite the suggestion of rebellion in 2 Chronicles 33:11) seems to have remained a loyal Assyrian vassal throughout his long reign, which lasted into that of Asshurbanipal (668 to 627 B.C.E.). He rebuilt the high places his father had destroyed, made new sacred poles for Asherah and, possibly in imitation of Mesopotamian practices, worshipped the stars and planets ("all the host of heaven," 2 Kings 21:3). The later biblical authors therefore blamed his backsliding evil ways for the eventual destruction of Judah. As P. Kyle McCarter, Jr. pointed out, however, Manasseh's restoration of the old cultic practices probably should be characterized as "a counter-reformation, involving a wholesale rejection of the innovative religious policies of Hezekiah, which, as Manasseh probably saw it, had not succeeded in protecting Judah from Assyria."[15]

Manasseh's son and successor, Amon, was assassinated after a brief reign (c. 642 to 640 B.C.E.), leaving the throne to his eight-year-old son, Josiah (c. 640 to 609 B.C.E.). Josiah was one of Judah's most important kings, for events that occurred during his reign marked a turning point in the development of biblical religion. In Josiah's eighteenth year on the throne, while undertaking repairs on the Temple, the high priest found a scroll called "the Book of the Law." A female prophet named Huldah verified that the book did indeed contain the words of Yahweh and Josiah then initiated a series of reforms based on the book's demands. Almost all modern biblical scholars agree that this "Book of the Law" was essentially the work we know as Deuteronomy. Deuteronomy is the only book in the Pentateuch to use the term "Book of the Law," and Josiah's reforms correspond closely to Deuteronomy's requirements (which sometimes differ from those in other parts of the Pentateuch). Like the "instructions" earlier Egyptian wisdom teachers

had produced for their pharaohs, Deuteronomy presents itself as a "testament" from Moses providing rules to guide future actions, especially those of kings. It stresses the concept of a covenant (or agreement) between Yahweh and the Israelites in which they pledged that they would not worship any god but Yahweh. This work probably had been written by a Levite a generation or two before it was found in order to champion reforms like those of Hezekiah and to condemn the cultic practices from earlier times that were reinstated by Manasseh.

Following the commands of the Book of the Law, Josiah centralized all worship in the Temple of Yahweh in Jerusalem from which he eliminated Canaanite cult objects and foreign idols.[16] Throughout Judah he once again destroyed high places, both those Manasseh had rebuilt and those (probably including the temple in Arad) that somehow had survived Hezekiah's reform. He also slaughtered the priests who had officiated at the high places and eliminated all mediums and magicians. Moreover, Josiah extended his reforms into areas that once had been part the Kingdom of Israel. As we have seen, when Asshurbanipal died in 627 B.C.E., civil war had broken out in Assyria and Babylonia. This turmoil had allowed Josiah, then in his early twenties, to seize some of the northern territory that had been turned into Assyrian provinces. Thus, he was able to purge pluralistic Yahwism and foreign worship practices from much of the north as well as from Judah. It has been noted, though, that these reforms in Judah and the former Israelite territory probably had political and economic as well as religious motivation. Josiah's centralization program concentrated power in Jerusalem and aided his desire to recreate the kingdom of David. By eliminating the small shrines scattered throughout the country, he also was able to obtain the dues and offerings that previously had supported these high places and the Levites who had officiated at them.

One of Josiah's contemporaries was so inspired by the ideals of the Book of Deuteronomy and by Josiah's reforms that he made them the standard for judging the past. He compiled many older traditions and accounts into a long history of Israel and Judah which modern biblical scholars call the **Deuteronomistic History**. This exceptional work of biblical historiography consists of the books of Joshua, Judges, First and Second Samuel, and First and Second Kings, plus a narrative bridge connecting the book of Deuteronomy to its beginning.[17] Throughout the Deuteronomistic History, rulers are judged by how well or poorly they followed the commands laid down in Deuteronomy, especially those forbidding worship of other gods and prohibiting worship anywhere but in the Jerusalem Temple. Naturally, it depicts Josiah as the only truly righteous king ever to rule Judah or Israel, the greatest figure since Moses, and the initiator of a golden age.

But the Deuteronomistic historian's high hopes for the future were soon dashed. As Assyrian power collapsed, Pharaoh Necho II of Egypt, intent on preventing Babylonian seizure of the Levant, marched north in 609 B.C.E. It is usually assumed that Josiah tried to prevent Necho from aiding the Assyrians and that the Judean army met the Egyptians in battle at Megiddo. However, Josiah doesn't seem to have objected when Egyptian forces passed through his territory in 616 and 610 B.C.E. So it has been argued that Josiah might have gone out of his fortress at Megiddo intending to support Necho's march into Syria. Presumably, problems developed only after Josiah met the pharaoh. Perhaps Necho demanded that Josiah become a vassal or cede territory such as Megiddo that controlled communications and supply lines between Syria and Egypt.[18] Whatever the prelude, a battle or a meeting gone bad, Josiah was captured and executed by the Egyptians, undoubtedly raising questions about God's justice in the minds of many Judeans.[19]

The Babylonian Exile

Judah was now forced to become a vassal of Egypt, and though Josiah's son Jehoahaz briefly became king, he was deposed by Necho. The Egyptian ruler put Eliakim, a younger son of Josiah, on the throne and renamed him Jehoiakim (c. 609 to 598 B.C.E.). After Nebuchadnezzar's defeat of Necho at Carchemish and Hamath (605 B.C.E.) and his campaign in Syria and Palestine (604 B.C.E.), Jehoiakim was forced to become a Babylonian vassal. However, after Nebuchadnezzar's setback in Egypt in 601 B.C.E., Jehoiakim renounced his allegiance to Babylon, but died or was murdered in 598 B.C.E. The Babylonians invaded Judah and conquered Jerusalem twice, carrying off King Jehoiachin in 597 B.C.E. and his uncle Zedekiah in 586 B.C.E. On both occasions, many Judeans were deported, and in 586 B.C.E., the Temple was burned and the city largely destroyed. Still more people were taken away in 582 after the assassination of Judah's Babylonian governor.

However, the exiles were not treated badly in Babylonia. Jehoiachin and his family were imprisoned for a time in Babylon, but in 561 B.C.E., Amel-Marduk, Nebuchadnezzar's successor, released them. They became royal wards in Babylon and had some freedom of movement, though they were not allowed to return to Judah. Most of the other Judean exiles were settled near Nippur as tenants on land depopulated by wars and Assyrian deportations. They were allowed to own property and go into business, and a few seem to have become quite wealthy. Some clearly assimilated the local culture and religion, for texts show that sometimes within the same family some individuals had names referring to Babylonian gods while others had Yahwistic names.[20]

On the other hand, inspired by the nearby presence of Jehoiachin, whom they hoped to see restored to his throne in Judah, as well as by prophets, priests, and elders, many of the exiles did not abandon their nationality or syncretize their religion. Instead, these Judeans experienced a kind of religious revival that produced extraordinary results. During the next half-century, previously written materials were brought together, edited, and added to Deuteronomy to form the Pentateuch (or *Torah* as it came to be called from references to the "Book of the Law [*Torah*]" in Deuteronomy). A second edition of the Deuteronomistic History was retained behind Deuteronomy. This new version, possibly by the same person who wrote the original, continued Judah's story up to the Exile, which it explained as the necessary punishment for Judah's past disobedience to its covenant with Yahweh and its failure to obey his commandments. This history originally had climaxed with the reign of Josiah, but now slight changes were introduced to indicate that even Josiah had not been good enough to make up for the sins of Manasseh and some of his predecessors. Thus, during the Exile, the core of the Hebrew Bible (Genesis through 2 Kings) was put essentially into the form it has today.[21] The sayings of the prophets also began to be collected and edited, a process that would continue through the Persian Period.

Many of later Judaism's customary features such as prayer three times a day and the rules and specific dates for fasting seem to have developed during the Exile. These Jewish customs later passed into Christianity and Islam. Though there is no direct evidence for their existence until much later, synagogues also may have originated at this time as at least partial substitutes for Solomon's Temple as places for communal meetings and prayer. Their later existence, even after the Temple in Jerusalem had been rebuilt and sacrificial cultic worship resumed, indicates that synagogues continued to meet a need for people to gather together for prayer and religious study. The most likely time for the beginning of such traditions was during the Exile. However, some refugees, either believing that Deuteronomy 12 applied only to worship within Palestine or not accepting Deuteronomy as normative to their Yahwism, continued to perform sacrifices in places other than Jerusalem. Judean mercenary soldiers who settled at Elephantine in Egypt built a temple to Yahweh some time before 525 B.C.E., possibly even before the fall of Jerusalem to Nebuchadnezzar. However, such practices would be anathema to the former exiles who returned to Judah from Babylonia.

The most important Judean religious development of the sixth century was the change that occurred in the conception of Yahweh. The eighth- and seventh-century prophets had already stressed that Yahweh demanded ethical conduct more than religious rituals such as offerings or sacrifices—in fact, if individuals did not treat one another fairly, God would not accept their formal worship. The author of Deuteronomy had echoed the prophets' message of Yahweh's holiness and righteousness, presenting an ethereal view of a deity who lived in the heavens and could not be contained in an earthly habitation, not even in the Jerusalem Temple. Earlier sources had described the

Temple as the place where Yahweh lived and its Holy of Holies as the place where he was invisibly enthroned above the cherubim. But Deuteronomy considers the Temple to be the place where only Yahweh's *name* dwells (Deuteronomy 12:5, 11, 21; 14:23–24, etc.). Moreover, the prophets, especially Isaiah and Jeremiah, had emphasized that Yahweh used the Assyrians and Babylonians as his instruments to punish Israel and Judah, so he was in control of history. These views were adopted by the Judean leaders during the Exile, especially the editors who began creating the Bible out of earlier sources. Consequently, Nebuchadnezzar's destruction of Jerusalem and the Temple was seen as Yahweh's will, not as a sign of his defeat by foreign gods. Earlier reformers (and even the covenant stressed by Deuteronomy) had insisted only on henotheism or monolatry, the exclusive worship of one god (in this case, Yahweh) without denying the existence of others. But the exaltation of Yahweh's power and majesty that accompanied the destruction of the Israelite kingdoms transformed what had been, at best, a kind of implicit monotheism, into explicit ethical monotheism. In the teachings of the unknown exilic prophet scholars call Deutero-Isaiah ° (or "Second Isaiah"),[22] the existence of other gods is not only denied, but their worshipers are derided for believing that idols have divine power:

> Those who lavish gold from the purse,
> and weigh out silver in the scales—
> they hire a goldsmith, who makes it into a god;
> then they fall down and worship! . . .
> If one cries out to it, it does not answer
> or save anyone from trouble.[23]

Thus, from the ruins of two of the smallest and weakest kingdoms of the Near East emerged the basic belief of later Judaism, Christianity, and Islam—that there is a single, all-powerful deity whose righteousness and justice require that individuals live upright, moral lives.

°For unknown reasons, this prophet's oracles were later attached to those of Isaiah, who had lived a century earlier. Deutero-Isaiah was responsible for chapters 40 through 55 of the Book of Isaiah.

SUGGESTIONS FOR FURTHER READING AND INFORMATION

Internet Sites

Assyria—See the web site for the Oriental Institute of the University of Chicago listed at the end of Chapter 1 and that of the British Museum's Mesopotamian collection listed at the end of Chapter 2.

Books and Articles

The Assyrian and Neo-Babylonian Empires

Barnett, R. D. *Assyrian Sculpture in the British Museum.* Toronto: McClelland and Stewart, 1975.

Beaulieu, Paul-Alain. *The Reign of Nabonidus, King of Babylon, 556–539 BC.* New Haven, CT: Yale University Press, 1989.

Brinkman, J. A. *Prelude to Empire: Babylonian Society and Politics, 747–626 BC.* Philadelphia: Babylonian Fund, 1984.

Frame, Grant. *Babylonia 689–627 BC: A Political History.* Istanbul: Nederlands Historisch-Archaeologisch Instituut te Istanbul, 1992.

Grayson, A. Kirk. *Assyrian and Babylonian Chronicles.* Locust Valley, NY: J. J. Augustin, 1975.

Healy, Mark. *The Ancient Assyrians.* London: Osprey Publishing, 1991.

Oded, Bustenay. *Mass Deportations and Deportees in the Neo-Assyrian Empire.* Wiesbaden: Reichert, 1979.

Porter, Barbara N. *Images, Power, and Politics: Figurative Aspects of Esarhaddon's Babylonian Policy.* Philadelphia: American Philosophical Society, 1993.

Reade, Julian. *Assyrian Sculpture.* Cambridge, MA: Harvard University Press, 1999.

Russell, John M. *Sennacherib's "Palace Without Rival" at Nineveh.* Chicago: University of Chicago Press, 1992.

Saggs, H. W. F. *The Might That Was Assyria.* London: Sidgwick and Jackson, 1984.

Wiseman, D. J. *Nebuchadnezzar and Babylon.* London and New York: Oxford University Press, 1986.

Cimmerians, Scythians, and Egypt

Gorelik, M. V., E. N. Cernenko, and E. V. Gerneko. *Scythians, 700–300 BC.* Men at Arms Series, No. 137. London: Osprey Publishing Company, 1983.

Morkot, Robert G. *The Black Pharaohs: Egypt's Nubian Rulers.* London: The Rubicon Press, 2000.

Rolle, Renate. *The World of the Scythians.* Translated by F. G. Walls. Berkeley: University of California Press, 1989.

Welsby, Derek A. *The Kingdom of Kush: The Napatan and Meroitic Empires.* London: British Museum Press, 1996.

Yamauchi, Edwin M. *Foes from the Northern Frontier: Invading Hordes from the Russian Steppes.* Grand Rapids, MI: Baker Book House, 1982.

Israel, Judah, and the Emergence of Monotheism

Gallagher, William R. *Sennacherib's Campaign to Judah, New Studies.* Leiden: Brill, 1999.

Gnuse, Robert K. *No Other Gods: Emergent Monotheism in Israel.* Journal for the Study of the Old Testament Supplements 241. Sheffield, UK: Sheffield Academic Press, 1997.

Hadley, Judith M. *The Cult of the Goddess in Ancient Israel and Judah: The Evidence for Asherah.* New York and Cambridge: Cambridge University Press, 1999.

Niditch, Susan. *Ancient Israelite Religion.* New York: Oxford University Press, 1997.

Olyan, Saul M. *Asherah and the Cult of Yahweh in Israel.* Atlanta: Scholars Press, 1988.

Patai, Raphael. *The Hebrew Goddess.* Detroit: Wayne State University Press, 1990.

Pettey, Richard. *Asherah: Goddess of Israel.* New York: Peter Lang Publishing, 1991.

Smith, Mark S. *The Origins of Biblical Monotheism: Israel's Polytheistic Background and the Ugaritic Texts.* London and New York: Oxford University Press, 2001.

Sweeney, Marvin A. *King Josiah of Judah: The Lost Messiah of Israel.* London and New York: Oxford University Press, 2001.

Ussishkin, David. *The Conquest of Lachish by Sennacherib.* Tel Aviv: Tel Aviv University, Institute of Archaeology, 1982.

NOTES

1. The Bible (2 Kings 18:14) claims that Hezekiah had to pay 30 talents of gold and 300 talents of silver. Sennacherib's annals claim the amount was even higher—30 talents of gold and 800 talents of silver, precious stones, and other treasures.

2. For arguments supporting this view, see John Bright, *A History of Israel*, 3rd ed. (Philadelphia: Westminster

Press, 1981), pp. 298–309, and William H. Shea, "Jerusalem Under Siege: Did Sennacherib Attack Twice?" *Biblical Archaeology Review*, vol. 25, no. 6 (November/December 1999), pp. 36–44, 64.

3. See Mordecai Cogan and Hayim Tadmor, *II Kings*, The Anchor Bible 11 (Garden City, NY: Doubleday, 1988), pp. 223–251, especially pp. 246–251, and William R. Gallagher, *Sennacherib's Campaign to Judah, New Studies* (Leiden: Brill, 1999).

4. This translation is based on those by D. D. Luckenbill, *The Annals of Sennacherib* (Chicago: The Oriental Institute, 1924), and *Ancient Records of Assyria and Babylonia* (Chicago: The Oriental Institute, 1926–27), vol. II, sections 233 ff., D. J. Wiseman in D. Winton Thomas, ed., *Documents from Old Testament Times* (New York: Harper and Row, 1958), p. 67, and A. Leo Oppenheim in James B. Pritchard, ed., *Ancient Near Eastern Texts Relating to the Old Testament*, 2nd ed. (Princeton, NJ: Princeton University Press, 1955), p. 288.

5. Some scholars emphasize this aspect of Assyrian kingship so much that they see the king as a semidivine being. See Simo Parpola, "The Assyrian Tree of Life: Tracing the Origins of Jewish Monotheism and Greek Philosophy," *Journal of Near Eastern Studies*, vol. 52 (1993), pp. 161–208, especially pp. 167–168 and "Sons of God: The Ideology of Assyrian Kingship," *Archaeology Odyssey*, vol. 2, no. 5 (November/December 1999), pp. 16–27, 61.

6. Georges Roux, *Ancient Iraq*, 3rd ed. (London and New York: Penguin Books, 1992), p. 344.

7. See, for example, A. Kirk Grayson, "Mesopotamia, History of (Assyria)" in David N. Freedman, editor-in-chief, *The Anchor Bible Dictionary* (New York: Doubleday, 1992), vol. 4, p. 750. This view assumes, though, that the eldest son automatically became crown prince (as Grayson claims on the same page), which does not seem to be the case.

8. Yigael Yadin, *The Art of Warfare in Biblical Lands* (New York: McGraw-Hill, 1963), vol. II, p. 300.

9. Grayson in Freedman, editor-in-chief (1992), vol. 4, p. 748.

10. B. Oded, *Mass Deportations and Deportees in the Neo-Assyrian Empire* (Wiesbaden: Reichert, 1979), p. 81–84.

11. Simo Parpola, "Sons of God: The Ideology of Assyrian Kingship," *Archaeology Odyssey*, vol. 2, no. 5 (November/December 1999), p. 24.

12. H. W. F. Saggs, *The Greatness That Was Babylon* (New York: Hawthorn Books, 1962), p. 144.

13. See the works listed in Note 36, Chapter 8.

14. The Bible provides two contradictory synchronisms with Assyrian chronology for the reign of Hezekiah. 2 Kings 18:9 says that the siege of Samaria (724 to 722 B.C.E.) began in Hezekiah's fourth year, indicating that he came to the throne in 727 B.C.E. However, 2 Kings 18:13 states that Sennacherib's 701 B.C.E. invasion of Judah occurred in Hezekiah's fourteenth year, placing the start of his reign in 714 B.C.E. Those who accept the theory that Sennacherib invaded Judah twice support the second of these dates, so that Hezekiah would still have been on the throne in 688 B.C.E.

15. In McCarter's revision of Siegfried Horn's chapter on the Divided Monarchy in Hershel Shanks, ed., *Ancient Israel From Abraham to the Roman Destruction of the Temple*, rev. ed. (Washington, D.C. and Upper Saddle River, NJ: The Biblical Archaeology Society and Prentice Hall, 1999), p. 185. The quote was not in the first edition of this work.

16. The Bible contains two different versions of the course of Josiah's reforms. 2 Chronicles 34:3–5 claims that he began a series of cultic reforms in his twelfth regnal year and then initiated an even greater reform in his eighteenth year after finding the Book of the Law. 2 Kings 22–23 mentions only the reforms begun in Josiah's eighteenth year. Most historians have accepted the version in Kings as the more historical account as we have here.

17. For an overview of the concept of and arguments for the existence of a Deuteronomistic History, see Richard E. Friedman, *Who Wrote the Bible?* (New York: Summit Books, 1987), pp. 103–135 and Steven L. McKenzie, "Deuteronomistic History" in Freedman, editor-in-chief (1992), vol. 2, pp. 160–168.

18. See R. D. Nelson, "*Realpolitik* in Judah (687–609 B.C.E.)" in W. W. Hallo, J. C. Moyer, and L. C. Perdue, eds., *Scripture in Context II* (Winona Lake, IN: 1983), p. 188, and McCarter's revision of Horn's chapter on the Divided Monarchy in Shanks, ed. (1999), p. 192.

19. God supposedly rewarded good and punished evil in this world. If so, then why did evil people often succeed and bad things happen to good people like Josiah? Questions of this kind engendered by Josiah's death and/or the destruction of Jerusalem and Judah a generation later probably led someone to produce the Book of Job sometime during the sixth century B.C.E.

20. See Nahman Avigad, "Seals of Exiles," *Israel Exploration Journal*, vol. 15 (1965), pp. 228–230.

21. For a more complete description of this process, see a standard introduction to the Old Testament such as Bernhard W. Anderson, *Understanding the Old Testament*, 4th ed. (Upper Saddle River, NJ: Prentice Hall, 1986), especially pp. 427–466.

22. For a summary of the arguments for the existence of Deutero-Isaiah, see Richard J. Clifford, "Isaiah, Book of (Second Isaiah)" in Freedman, editor-in-chief (1992), vol. 3, pp. 490–501 and the bibliography given there.

23. Isaiah 46:6, 7b, New Revised Standard Version. See also Isaiah 41:21–24 and 44:9–17.

10
The Persian Empire

THE ORIGINS AND GROWTH OF THE ACHAEMENID EMPIRE

The Fluorescence of the Lydian Kingdom (c. 685–547 B.C.E.)

The Lydians were an Indo-European speaking people of western Asia Minor who primarily occupied the territory in and around the Hermus (modern Gediz Çay) and Cayster (modern Küçük Menderes) River valleys. Their language was related to Hittite and Luwian, so they were probably descendants of the people who had lived in this area in the second millennium when it was known to the Hittites as Assuwa, later part of the Arzawa Lands. Lydia's main city was Sardis in the Hermus River valley at the foot of Mount Tmolus. No native Lydian accounts of their history have survived, so most of what we know about them comes from Herodotus and other Greek writers.

While there may have been a small kingdom centered on Sardis earlier, the first information we have about Lydia concerns the rise of the Mermnad dynasty, founded by Gyges (c. 685 to 652 B.C.E.). This king expanded Lydian control westward, initiating conflict with Greek settlements on the Aegean coast of Asia Minor. However, he had difficulty maintaining his territory when the Cimmerians and Scythians began raiding into western Anatolia after destroying the Phrygian Kingdom in 676 B.C.E. Assyrian sources indicate that sometime between 668 and 665 B.C.E., Gyges (called Guggu of Ludu by the Assyrians) sought Asshurbanipal's aid against the frequent Cimmerian attacks. Gyges seems to have been temporarily successful against the Cimmerians, and may have become overconfident about his own strength, for in 654 B.C.E., he supported Egypt's revolt against Assyria. Thus, he had no one to call upon when Cimmerians again invaded Lydia two years later. They partially destroyed Sardis and killed Gyges, but the kingdom survived. Despite further sporadic Cimmerian raids, Gyges's successors, Ardys (c. 652 to 615 B.C.E.) and Sadyattes (c. 615 to 605 B.C.E.), were able to resume Lydia's territorial expansion. They conquered several of the Greek cities of Ionia to the west and took control of much of the former Phrygian territory to the east.

Lydia became a small empire and entered its era of greatest prosperity and power during the reign of Alyattes (605 to 560 B.C.E.). He drove the Cimmerians out of Lydia and ended their incursions once and for all. As he extended his territory eastward into the old Hittite heartland, however, he encountered another foe. The Assyrian Empire had just been destroyed and the Medes had taken control of Armenia (Urartu) and were pressing westward. For five years, Alyattes fought against the Medes with neither side being able to gain the upper hand. As previously mentioned in Chapter 9, in the sixth year of this war (585 B.C.E.), a battle was interrupted by a total solar eclipse which Herodotus says was predicted by Thales of Miletus, the first Greek philosopher. This omen led Alyattes and Cyaxares, king of the Medes, to accept a peace treaty brokered by Nebuchadnezzar of Babylon. The boundary between the two kingdoms was fixed at the Halys River, and to seal the agreement, Alyattes's daughter married Astyages, heir to the Median throne. When Alyattes's long reign ended in 560 B.C.E., he was buried north of Sardis in a marble burial chamber covered by the largest tumulus, or mound, in Anatolia (a type of burial borrowed from the Phrygians).

Alyattes's son and successor, Croesus (560 to 547 B.C.E.), enlarged the Lydian empire to its greatest physical extent. He brought all of the Greek city-states in Asia Minor under Lydian control, becoming deeply influenced by Greek culture in the process. He imported Greek ceramics and hired Greek builders and sculptors to work on his buildings in Sardis. As a result, there was a tendency to blend elements of the two cultures, especially their religions. The Lydian mother goddess Kybele (Cybele) was identified with the Greek goddess Artemis and became the main deity worshipped at Ephesus. The Lydian god Leus was recognized as equivalent to Greek Zeus, and the Lydian god of wine, Baki, was adopted by the Greeks as Bacchus (which became another name for Dionysos, a fertility god derived from Thrace). Greeks regarded Croesus as extremely wealthy and extravagant, an impression created, in part, by his lavish donations to the Oracle of Apollo at Delphi and to the archaic temple of Artemis/Kybele at Ephesus. Lydia's reputation for unlimited wealth may also have been due to its introduction of coinage, its most important contribution to later civilization. Alyattes seems to have minted the first true coins

(which were made of electrum). But the use of coins became more common during the reign of Croesus, so much so that Herodotus credited him with their invention. Greeks quickly recognized that these bits of electrum, gold, or silver (and later, bronze) whose purity and weight were guaranteed by the official stamp they bore greatly facilitated trade. Miletus and other Ionian cities began minting coins of their own during the sixth century, and the practice quickly spread to the Greek mainland and beyond. Despite his wealth and glory, Croesus was the last Lydian king. In 547 B.C.E., his small empire fell to the Persian armies of Cyrus the Great.

The Creation of the Persian Empire

The Indo-European-speaking Persians were closely related to the Medes. When they are first mentioned in an inscription of Shalmaneser III in the 840s B.C.E., they were living in northwestern Iran in close proximity to the Medes. At least some of them were still in this region through the reign of Sargon II (721 to 705 B.C.E.) whose inscriptions associate them with the Medes and the Mannaeans. Later, Sennacherib states that during his eighth campaign (692 to 691 B.C.E.) Persians were allies of Elam and Anshan in southwestern Iran, and in 640 B.C.E., Asshurbanipal mentions a king of Parsua named Cyrus (Kurush in Persian, Kurash in Akkadian). So many scholars believe that groups of Persians began migrating southward after 800 B.C.E., reaching Parsa sometime between 692 and 640 B.C.E. Others believe that the Assyrian records are referring to two or three different groups of Persians who had migrated into western Iran from the northeast rather than through the Caucasus. That theory, though, is based on the older view that southern Russia was the homeland of the Indo-European speakers rather than the more recent evidence that they arose in Armenia and the Caucasus (see Chapter 3). However they arrived there, by about 650 B.C.E., a group of Persians had made themselves masters of the southern part of the old Elamite kingdom, and their early rulers adopted the old title, "King of Anshan" (see Table 10.1). Because of Persian dominance, this southeastern section of the Zagros

TABLE 10.1
Probable Chronology of the Median, Lydian, and Persian Rulers

(All dates are B.C.E.*)*

Media	Lydia	Persia
Deiokes (*c.* 700–647)	Gyges (*c.* 685–652)	
Phraortes (*c.* 647–625)	Ardys (*c.* 652–615)	Teispes (*c.* 650–620)
Cyaxares (*c.* 625–585)	Sadyattes (*c.* 615–605)	Cyrus I (*c.* 620–590)
Astyages (*c.* 585–550)	Alyattes (605–560)	Cambyses I (*c.* 590–559)
	Croesus (560–547)	Cyrus II (559–530)
		Cambyses II (530–522)
		Bardiya (Smerdis) (522)
		Darius I (522–486)
		Xerxes (486–465)
		Artaxerxes I (465–424)
		Darius II (424–405/4)
		Artaxerxes II (405/4–359)
		Artaxerxes III (359–338)
		Artaxerxes IV (338–336)
		Darius III (336–330)

chain came to be known as Parsa (Persis to the Greeks, Persia in English), and today it is called Fars in Iranian, the modern descendant of the ancient Persian language. The Persian kings of Anshan/Parsa traced their descent from an ancestor named Hakhamanish (better known in the Greek form, Achaemenes), so they are called Achaemenians or the Achaemenid Line.

Though there is no evidence to support his claim, Herodotus says that the Persians were forced to become vassals of the Medes by Phraortes, the king who unified the Medes (see Table 10.1), and that they remained Median subjects until the reign of the Persian king Cyrus II, generally known as Cyrus the Great (559 to 530 B.C.E.). Herodotus and other Greek historians preserved several legendary accounts of Cyrus' origins and rise to power, some of which treat him as a royal castoff raised by shepherds in the tradition of Sargon of Akkad, Moses, Romulus and Remus, and Snow White. Others claim he was a poor commoner who rose by stages to become cup-bearer of the king and, finally, king himself. However, Cyrus

was probably a member of the Persian royal line as he stated on the Cyrus Cylinder, a Babylonian inscription from 539–538 B.C.E., which claims that he was the son of Cambyses, the son of Cyrus, the son of Teispes, each of whom bears the title "Great King, King of Anshan" (see Document 10.1). This genealogy seems to be confirmed by a royal seal whose Elamite inscription reads "Kurash (Cyrus) of Anshan, son of Chishpish (Teispes)." Herodotus claims Cyrus was also related to the royal lines of Lydia and Media. His mother, Mandane, supposedly was the daughter of the Median king Astyages and the Lydian princess he married as part of the peace agreement between the two peoples. However, the information and chronology used by Herodotus is hopelessly confused at this point. Cyrus II was an adult when he came to the throne in 559 B.C.E., but the Median-Lydian marriage had taken place only in 585 B.C.E., the date of the solar eclipse that ended the war between the two kingdoms. The 26 years that elapsed between those dates is not enough time for the birth and maturation of Cyrus' mother and of Cyrus himself. It is possible

DOCUMENT 10.1
The Cyrus Cylinder

This Akkadian text was inscribed around 538 B.C.E. on a nine-inch-long baked clay barrel. It presents Cyrus' claim that Marduk had chosen him to replace the impious Nabonidus and contains a statement of his policy of allowing groups that had been deported to return to their homelands if they wished and of supplying funds for rebuilding their ruined temples.[1]

Nabonidus made the worship of Marduk, the King of the Gods, into an abomination, and daily he used to do evil against Marduk's city. . . . He tormented Babylon's people with the yoke (of corvée labor) without relief; he ruined them all.

Because of the people's complaints, (Marduk,) the Lord of the Gods, became furious and departed from their region. The other gods living among them also left their mansions, angry that Nabonidus had brought them into Babylon. But, Marduk. . . relented, his anger abated and he had mercy upon the people. He scanned all the countries, searching for a righteous ruler willing to lead him in the annual procession. Then he spoke the name of Cyrus, King of Anshan, declaring him to be the ruler of the entire world. . . . Marduk, the great lord, protector of his people, beheld with pleasure Cyrus' good deeds and upright heart. Therefore he ordered Cyrus to march against Marduk's own city of Babylon. . . . Marduk allowed Cyrus to enter Babylon without a battle, sparing Babylon any calamity. He delivered Nabonidus, the king who didn't worship him, into Cyrus' hands. . . .

I am Cyrus, King of the World, Great King, Legitimate King, King of Babylon, King of Sumer and Akkad, King of the Four Corners of the Earth, son of Cambyses, Great King, King of Anshan, grandson of Cyrus, Great King, King of Anshan, descendant of Teispes, Great King, King of Anshan, of a family which always exercised kingship, (a monarch) whose rule Bel and Nebo love and whom they want as king to please their hearts. All the kings of the entire world from the Upper to the Lower Sea—those seated in throne rooms or living in other types of buildings as well as all the sheikhs of the tent dwellers of the West land—brought me their heavy tribute and kissed my feet in Babylon. To (regions). . . as far as Asshur and Susa, Agade, Eshnunna, the towns of Zamban, Me-Turnu, Der and the region of the Gutians, I returned the divine images which used to live there and restored the sanctuaries which had been in ruins for a long time. I also gathered all the former inhabitants of these places and returned them to their homes. Furthermore, at the command of Marduk, the Great Lord, I resettled in their former chapels, the places that make them happy, all the gods of Sumer and Akkad whom Nabonidus, to the anger of the Lord of the Gods, had brought into Babylon. . . . Moreover, I endeavored to repair their dwelling places.

that the battle could be pushed back to 603 B.C.E., the date of an earlier eclipse, but the evidence makes it very unlikely that the Medes controlled Urartu and eastern Anatolia by that date. So it does not seem likely that Cyrus was related to the kings he would later overthrow.

Phraortes and Cyaxares had organized the Median army along Assyrian lines, separating it into divisions of archers, infantry, and cavalry. In turn, Cyrus copied the Median military structure. According to the Greek writer Xenophon, Cyrus developed the famous Persian cavalry, training Persians to fight from horseback in the Assyrian and Median manner. He also copied Median organizational patterns for the court, government, and treasury. As we saw in Chapter 9, Nabonidus encouraged Cyrus to revolt against Astyages in order to drive the Medes out of Harran, though it doesn't seem to have taken much persuasion to convince Cyrus that he should expand his realm at the expense of his overlord. In 550 B.C.E., while the armies of the Medes and Persians were preparing to do battle, the generals and troops of Astyages mutinied. They handed their king over to Cyrus and accepted him as their ruler. Cyrus took much of the treasure of the Median capital, Ecbatana (modern Hamadan), back to Persia, but the real prizes he obtained were Media's horses and grazing lands as well as its manpower reserves. Instead of treating the Medes as slaves or captive labor, he integrated their upper classes into the Persian ruling class, appointing many Medes to high governmental positions and giving some of their generals similar positions within his own army. This caused the Medes to regard Cyrus as their valid king, and outsiders later found it difficult to distinguish Medes from Persians. In fact, the Greeks eventually used the two ethnic designations as synonyms.

Cyrus then seems to have extended his empire to the northeast, conquering Bactria and the Oxus region (which probably had not been part of the Median Empire) before an attack by Lydia turned his attention to the west. Croesus, king of Lydia, probably saw the demise of the Median Empire as an opportunity to renew Lydian expansion into eastern Anatolia. According to the well-known story by Herodotus, Croesus asked the Oracle of Delphi in Greece whether he should attack the Persians and was told that if he did, he would destroy a mighty empire. Thinking this oracle promised him victory, Croesus led his forces across the Halys River in 547 B.C.E. Cyrus quickly responded, driving back the Lydian army and, after a brief siege, capturing Sardis, Lydia's capital. Too late, Croesus realized that the mighty empire his attack had destroyed was his own. Cyrus returned to Ecbatana with Croesus as his prisoner, leaving an army to finish the conquest of western Asia Minor by subduing the Greek city-states along the coast.

During the next few years, Cyrus seems to have spent most of his time conquering central and eastern Iran. By 539 B.C.E., he felt strong enough to move against the Neo-Babylonian Empire. He defeated Belshazzar and Nabonidus in battle (see Chapter 9) and met little resistance when he marched into the great city of Babylon. Herodotus claims, probably correctly, that Babylon surrendered so easily because Cyrus diverted most of the Euphrates' flow north of the city, allowing the Persian army to wade along the riverbed and enter the city through its water gates. When Babylon fell, all of the territory it had ruled came under Persian control, making Cyrus master of almost the entire Near East (see Map 10.1).

Cyrus's propaganda depicted him as a good king, selected by Marduk to oust the impious Nabonidus, restore order, and reconstruct Mesopotamia's temples (see Document 10.1). He also had cultivated the support of the Judean exiles, being hailed as Yahweh's "anointed one" (messiah) by Deutero-Isaiah (Isaiah 45:1–4) in language reminiscent of Cyrus's own proclamation (see Document 10:1, paragraph 2). To maintain this Judean backing (and possibly to gain allies for a future attack on Egypt), in 538 B.C.E., Cyrus issued a decree allowing the exiles to return to Judah and ordering the rebuilding of the Temple of Yahweh in Jerusalem. Thus, the "Babylonian Exile" officially came to an end, though many Judeans, especially younger ones who had grown up in Babylonia, chose not to return to their ancestral homeland. Cyrus

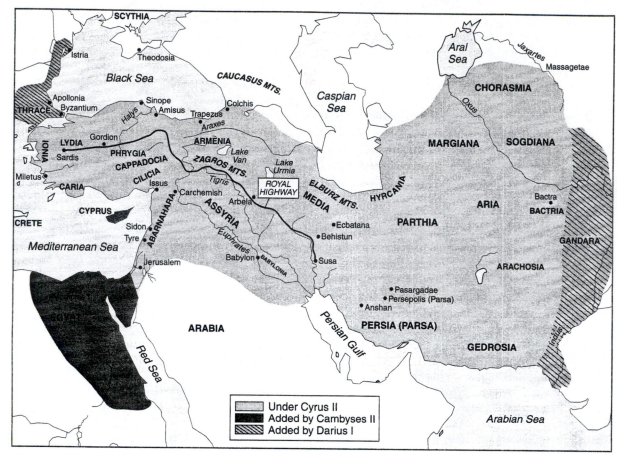

MAP 10.1 The Achaemenid Persian Empire

followed a similar lenient policy elsewhere (see Document 10.1), preserving most of the earlier governmental units of subject peoples and supporting local religious establishments. He decided to administer his territories through appointed governors rather than vassal kings, but whenever possible, these officials were natives of the areas they ruled. As a result, Medes, Babylonians, Elamites, Judeans, and probably Lydians accepted him as their legitimate ruler.

As previously mentioned, Cyrus's Achaemenid predecessors had designated themselves kings of Anshan, and the city of Anshan, part of the ancient kingdom of Elam, seems to have been their capital. It

is natural then, that Elamite culture exerted a strong influence over the Persians. The Elamites taught the Persians how to use chariots in warfare and influenced to some extent the way they dressed. The Persians also used the Elamite language and its cuneiform script for their early inscriptions. After the conquest of Babylon, Persian kings also made inscriptions in Akkadian, and they probably used Aramaic for correspondence, since it had become the common language of trade and commerce throughout the Near East. Nevertheless, Elamite continued to be used for writing in addition to these other languages. On the other hand, Persian seems to have remained only a spoken language until the time of Darius I.

After creating an empire, Cyrus decided to establish a new capital at Pasargadae (probably at the site now known as Murgab) in Persia. While he continued to use earlier palaces at Babylon, Susa (the old Elamite capital), and Ecbatana (the Median capital), he built an elegant palace for himself at Pasargadae. He also had his tomb constructed nearby. The plan of his palace reflects influences from the Elamite pre-Persian population of Anshan and from the Medes, but its doorways exhibit the work of Greek and Lydian stonemasons, and its reliefs were based on Assyrian and Babylonian models. There are even some Egyptian elements in Pasargadae's sculptures, probably derived from earlier Egyptian influence on Phoenician and Syrian art. Thus, Cyrus began the practice of blending the artistic styles of previous cultures, a convention continued by his successors.

Cyrus spent the last nine years of his reign consolidating his hold over the lands he had conquered and building forts in the northeast to keep out marauding central Asian nomads. It was while campaigning against one of these nomadic tribes in 530 B.C.E. that he fell in battle, making his son, Cambyses (Kabujiya in Persian), king. Despite his death, Cyrus's final military campaign seems to have been successful, for Cambyses II (530 to 522 B.C.E.) inherited a stable kingdom that suffered no territorial losses along its northeastern frontier. The only remaining trouble spot was Egypt, which had taken control of Cyprus after the fall of the Neo-Babylonian Empire. So, Cambyses began making preparations for the conquest of Egypt, a project Cyrus seems to have planned but had not lived to accomplish. Cambyses built a large fleet whose ships and men were supplied mainly by the vassal Phoenicians and Ionian Greeks, and he made arrangements with the Arabs to supply his army with water skins during the march across northern Sinai. Then, in 525 B.C.E., the Persian forces invaded the eastern Delta. A contingent of Greek mercenaries hired by the Egyptians defected to the Persians and the rest of the Egyptian army was routed. Pharaoh Psamtik (Psammeticus) III and his remaining forces fled to Memphis, but the city fell after a very brief siege by Cambyses's army and fleet. Herodotus depicts Cambyses as a ruthless, egotistical, paranoid tyrant who, following his conquest, showed no regard for Egyptian religion and culture. However, contemporary Egyptian evidence tells a different story. After sending the captive Psamtik off to Susa, Cambyses adopted pharaonic titles and took care to respect Egyptian temples and religious customs, thus winning the acceptance of most of the Egyptian people.[2] He quickly established his dominion over all of Egypt and even seems to have extended his rule into northern Nubia just south of the Nile's first cataract. The rulers of Libya and Cyrene to the west hastened to send Cambyses tokens of submission, and Cyprus also surrendered voluntarily. For the first time in history, the entire Near East was unified into a single vast empire.

THE PERSIAN EMPIRE AT ITS HEIGHT

Crisis and Restoration

Though Cambyses was probably not as despotic as Herodotus claimed, he must have done something to anger many of the Persian nobles, for in 522 B.C.E. a revolt broke out in favor of Bardiya, Cambyses's younger brother. Cambyses immediately began the trek back to Persia, but on the way home he died, possibly (as Herodotus claims) from an accidental leg wound from his dagger while he was mounting his horse. Both of our ancient sources, Darius I's inscription at Behistun and Herodotus's narrative (which probably derived ultimately from Darius's account), claim that Cambyses had previously murdered his real brother, Bardiya (whom Herodotus calls Smerdis). Supposedly a Median look-alike named Gaumata pretended to be the dead prince and incited revolt. Supported by six prominent nobles (and probably by Cambyses's army), Darius, a high-ranking army officer who claimed to be a relative of Cyrus, opposed the rebels. In a relatively short time, he killed the usurper and ascended the throne as Darius I (Persian Darayawush I, 522 to 486 B.C.E.). Darius's account of these events, of course, was meant to support his claim to the throne, and many scholars doubt its accuracy. His genealogy is especially suspicious. Elsewhere he stated that his father and grandfather were both still alive when he became king. So, if they were really descended from Teispes as he asserts (his great-grandfather was supposedly a brother of Cyrus I), both his grandfather and father would have had a more direct claim to the throne than he did. Moreover, it is difficult to believe that the murder of Cambyses's younger brother could have been kept secret for three years (as Darius's account claims it was) or that Persian nobles would have been fooled by a Median imposter. Thus, many (if not most) historians today believe that Darius was the usurper and that the man he overthrew was in fact Bardiya, the son of Cyrus the Great and brother of Cambyses.[3] Another possible indication that Darius was not the legitimate successor is the fact that after becoming king, he quickly married Cyrus's surviving daughters and grand-daughters to assure that his children would be the only legitimate descendants of Cyrus. Unfortunately,

the truth concerning Darius' background and rise to power will probably never be known.

However, the crisis was not over when Darius became king. When news of his accession spread through the empire, a new series of revolts occurred, especially in Media, Babylonia, Elam, the Iranian plateau, and within Persia itself. The fact that much of the Persian heartland rose against Darius is another indicator that many of the Persian nobles did not accept his claim to be the legitimate successor of Cambyses. However, his supporters and their armies fought on several fronts against the rebel forces. Only after more than a year of hard fighting were most of the rebellions quelled, and Egypt was not brought back under control until 518 B.C.E. To celebrate his victory, Darius had a relief depicting his triumph over Gaumata and the other rebels carved high upon a cliff at Behistun (or Bisitun) overlooking the main road from Ecbatana to Babylon (see Figure 10.1). Origi-

FIGURE 10.1   Relief and Inscription of Darius I at Behistun

Source: Deutsches Archaeologisches Institut, Berlin.

nally, this monument in the heart of the former rebel territory was accompanied by cuneiform inscriptions in Akkadian and Elamite, presenting Darius's version of the events surrounding his assumption of kingship. However, just before it was completed, Darius seems to have decided that its message should be proclaimed in his native tongue as well. So, he declared, "according to the will of [the god] Ahuramazda I have made the writing of a different sort, in Aryan, which did not exist before."[4] His scribes, probably influenced by Aramaic writing, adapted the cuneiform script to write Old Persian, creating a simplified syllabic writing system that is almost like an alphabet—there are only 46 signs of which six are seldom-used ideographs. They then added an Old Persian version of the text to the Behistun monument and smoothed the cliff below and on the sides of the relief so it could not be reached and defaced. In the mid-nineteenth century, the British scholar Henry Rawlinson was able to copy and decipher the Old Persian inscription, and its cuneiform script helped him and other scholars eventually decipher the Akkadian and Elamite inscriptions, as well. Because of this breakthrough, philologists gained the ability to read the voluminous Mesopotamian inscriptions and tablets that were being uncovered at the same time.[5]

Reorganization of the Empire

Once Darius had suppressed all the revolts against his rule, he began to reorganize the empire. The system he created remained strong and vibrant through the reign of Artaxerxes II (405 to 359 B.C.E.) and even survived into the reign of Alexander after he conquered the Persian Empire in 330 B.C.E. Darius continued to use Ecbatana, Babylon, and Pasargadae as royal residences, but he made the old Elamite capital of Susa his administrative center. He built a grand new palace at Susa, expanded the city, and erected new fortifications there. However, later in his reign he also built a palace at a new location and named it Parsa, the same word that was applied to his country (Persia) and people (Persians). This site is generally known, though, by the designation the Greeks gave it—Persepolis ("City of the Persians"). Darius chose

to be buried there, and instead of constructing a tomb like that of Cyrus, he had his sepulcher cut into the cliffs at Naksh-i Rustam, just north of Persepolis. After the construction of Persepolis, there were five royal residences. Susa and Babylon remained the administrative centers of the empire; Pasargadae was the site of coronations; Persepolis was the place where the important New Year Festival was celebrated and where Darius and three of his successors were buried; and Ecbatana was a summer retreat to get away from the heat of Susa and Babylon.

Cyrus and Cambyses had appointed governors for sections of the empire and assessed tribute, but Darius made the administrative structures much more uniform and systematic. He divided the empire into 20 districts called **satrapies** (though the number increased over time), each of which was assessed a fixed annual tax (tribute) valued in silver (except for the Indian satrapy, whose tribute was valued and paid in gold). The amount each satrapy paid was determined by the productivity of its land and the wealth of its people. Persia, the only region of the empire that had not been conquered, was not part of a satrapy. It was ruled directly by the king and paid no taxes, though Persian landowners had to supply infantry, cavalry, or chariot troops to the army depending on the extent of their holdings. The semi-nomadic pastoral tribes that lived in the Zagros Mountains and the Arabs were the only other groups not fully integrated into the empire; they were treated as allies. Darius (and his successors) gave gifts to the chieftains of these difficult-to-conquer semi-nomadic groups and in exchange, they helped the Persians in various ways. The Zagros chieftains protected the major roads through the mountains, and the Arab sheikhs helped the Persian army find routes through the desert.

Each satrapy was governed by a Persian or Median aristocrat known as a **satrap**, and each contained a garrison of Persian troops to keep order, enforce the king's edicts, and collect taxes. Most of the satrapies were very large, and some contained several different ethnic groups or nations who were allowed to manage their own local affairs and maintain their traditional religions and customs. Such subunits of the satrapy were usually governed by local rulers appointed by the Persian king. So, for example, within the satrapy called Abarnahara ("Beyond the [Euphrates] River," that is, the Levant and Cyprus), the city-states of Syria and Phoenicia had their own local governments, as did the regions of Cyprus, Ashdod (the entire area of Philistia), Judah, Samaria, Ammon, Moab, and Idumaea (Edom). Within the Lydian and Carian satrapies of western Asia Minor, the Ionian Greek cities continued to be governed by their own tyrants as they had been before the Persian conquest.

The satraps usually lived in cities that had once been capitals of earlier states or empires and had courts that were modeled on the royal court. They usually owned large estates and possessed tremendous wealth. Darius appointed many of his closest and most trusted relatives to these posts, but he also created several safeguards to keep these powerful officials in check. Most important was the fact that just as in the system devised by Sargon of Agade, the commander of each Persian garrison was directly responsible to the king who appointed him, not to the satrap in whose satrapy he served. On one occasion, when a satrap in western Anatolia began acting too independently and was suspected of treason, Darius sent an envoy to present several edicts to the satrap and his court. This royal officer noticed that during the reading of a couple of minor administrative orders, the guards were attentive and seemed to respect Darius and his authority. He then presented royal orders that the Persian soldiers cease serving the satrap and kill him—orders which they promptly obeyed. Each satrap also had a treasurer and a secretary appointed by the king who were responsible to him. In addition, special officials called "the king's eyes" and "the king's ears" often descended upon the capitals of satrapies without warning. These bureaucrats reviewed official records, audited the books, questioned the satrap's staff and members of the public, and reported their findings directly to the king. Moreover, the king had many informants throughout the empire. All of these independent sources of information and the speed of communica-

tion between the satrapies and the king discouraged disloyalty and conspiracy.

Darius' reforms brought prosperity as well as peace to the empire. The Persians improved agriculture throughout the empire by supporting the introduction of new crops and technologies. From India, they brought rice into Mesopotamia and sesame into Egypt. They introduced pistachio nuts into Syria from Anatolia. During their invasion of Greece, the Persians planted alfalfa, a common crop in Media, to provide fodder for their horses. For thousands of years, the Mesopotamians had grown flax primarily to obtain oil from its seeds, but the Persians encouraged more extensive use of its fibers to make cloth. Darius and his successors also increased the arable land within Persia through irrigation. To prevent evaporation, the water had to be brought from the mountains in underground channels whose construction was probably modeled on the mining tunnels of Urartu. Eventually similar irrigation channels were created in other parts of the empire, as well.

Trade and commerce also benefited from Darius's actions. He standardized weights and measures and, though Lydian coins continued to be used, he introduced the first Persian royal coinage. Persian gold *darics* (probably named after Darius) became the gold currency of choice within Greece as well as the Near East. Darius also upgraded the overland routes and waterways along which trade moved. The Persians became noted for building roads and ensuring the safety of those who traversed them. They maintained, straightened, and improved the major roads that already crisscrossed the empire west of the Zagros, and they built new roads to connect the eastern provinces to one another and to the western portion of the empire. In places where conditions were not ideal, the king's engineers cut ruts into the roadbeds at the standard width of wagon and chariot axles. These deep grooves kept wheeled vehicles from going off the road. The king stationed troops at river crossings, mountain passes, and other key points along the roads so that traffic could be monitored and controlled. These guard posts not only deterred and limited the extent of revolts, they also made the roads safer for peaceful travel and trade by suppressing banditry. The Royal Highway, the most famous of the Persian roads, ran over mountain chains, across rivers, and through valleys from Susa in Elam to Sardis in Lydia (with an extension to Ephesus on the Aegean coast), a distance of almost 1,700 miles (see Map 10.1). To aid waterborne trade, Darius completed construction of a 90-mile-long canal that had been begun but abandoned by the Egyptian Pharaoh Necho around 600 B.C.E. This 150-foot-wide channel connected the Bitter Lakes at the edge of the eastern Delta to one another and to the Pelusiac Branch of the Nile on the north and to the Gulf of Suez (a branch of the Red Sea) on the south. The entire route was about 125 miles long, compared to the modern 107-mile-long Suez Canal which it anticipated by 2,350 years.

For almost instantaneous communications, principally warnings of revolts or invasions, the Persians used fire signals from one hilltop station to another. However, the Persians' excellent transportation network also made it possible for them to use a "pony-express" system to rapidly carry more complex messages to and from the farthest reaches of their vast empire. Darius copied this system from the Assyrians, setting up way stations with supplies, horses, and trusted messengers at about 15-mile intervals along major roads. Only royal messengers or other individuals bearing sealed authorization could use these stations and their supplies. Herodotus claims that messages, passed from rider to rider, each utilizing several fresh horses and continuing night and day, took only seven days to go from Sardis to Susa via the Royal Highway, normally a three-month trip for a caravan. To accomplish this feat, the royal messengers would have had to average almost 250 miles every 24 hours! Thus, they earned Herodotus' encomium, which has been taken as the motto for the United States Postal Service:

> Nothing human travels as fast as these Persian messengers. . . . Neither snow, nor rain, nor heat, nor darkness of night prevents these couriers from completing their designated stages with utmost speed.[6]

Wars With the Greeks

Around 514 B.C.E., Darius led an expedition against the Scythians north of the Black Sea. He crossed the Hellespont on a bridge of ships, advanced through Thrace and across the Danube, using another floating bridge. The Persians may have been attempting to punish the Scythians for past raids into Anatolia and weaken them so they could not conduct future ones. However, these seminomadic people retreated into the steppes of the Ukraine, destroying forage and fouling wells as they went. Unable to bring the Scythians into battle, Darius had to backtrack to Thrace where he organized the conquered territory south of the Danube into a satrapy that would act as a buffer state against the seminomads. Then he returned to Susa. Ionian Greeks, who provided many of the ships for the bridges and most of the men who guarded them, regarded this campaign as a defeat and were probably shocked to discover that the feared Persian army was not invincible after all.

Despite Persian acceptance of local autonomy and support for local cults and temples, in 499 B.C.E., the Ionian cities revolted against Darius. Herodotus claims that the personal frustrations and fears of Aristagoras, tyrant of Miletus, led him to promote the revolt after his failure to conquer the island of Naxos. There must have been considerably more behind it than this, for in addition to the Ionian Greeks, the Greeks in Cyprus joined the revolt. Under Persian rule, the tyrants of the various eastern Greek city-states had not been able to expand their territories or take radical measures to ease economic discontent, practices often followed by tyrants on the Greek mainland. Thus, their popularity and influence had declined. These factors probably led some eastern Greek cities to depose their tyrants, an act of rebellion against Persia (which had appointed them). In self-defense, other tyrants took up leadership of the revolt.

The Ionians appealed to their fellow Greeks on the mainland for help, but only Athens (which sent 20 ships) and Eretria (which sent 5) responded positively. Athenian and Eretrian contingents joined the Ionian forces when they marched against Sardis in

498 B.C.E., captured it and, for some unknown reason, burned it to the ground. When Darius heard about this action, he was infuriated that mainland Greeks had participated in this destruction of a great city, and he vowed he would take revenge against Eretria and Athens after he had suppressed the Ionian revolt. He first subdued Cyprus with the help of a Phoenician fleet, then he sent several armies to attack different Ionian cities at the same time. In 494 B.C.E., the Persian army besieged the city of Miletus, the leader of the revolt, while a fleet of 600 Phoenician, Egyptian, Cilician, and Cypriot ships arrived to blockade it by sea. The large Persian fleet met 353 Greek ships in battle at Ladê, off the coast near Miletus, and, after several Greek contingents sailed home when they were promised leniency, the remainder of the Ionian fleet was almost totally destroyed. Miletus was taken, its surviving population deported to the shores of the Persian Gulf near the mouth of the Tigris river, and the revolt collapsed.

Except for Miletus, the Persians treated the defeated Ionian cities tolerantly. The aristocrats and wealthy merchants seem to have been the leading adherents of independence and aggressive foreign policy, ideas that promoted revolt, while the small-scale farmers who constituted the bulk of the citizenry primarily desired peace in which to tend their crops. So the Persians installed democratic governments in most of the recaptured cities in place of their earlier tyrannies. These democracies gave at least some power to the lower classes who tended to be more amenable to Persian overlordship. The Ionians also had to agree to settle future disputes between their cities by arbitration rather than warfare. Darius's envoy reassessed their tribute payments on the same scale used previously and the assessment remained unchanged during the next two generations.

Darius could now turn his attention to the mainland Greek states that had participated in the Ionian revolt. In 492 B.C.E., he sent an expedition commanded by his son-in-law, Mardonius, to secure Thrace and Macedonia. Perhaps this force also intended to attack Athens and Eretria as Herodotus says, but we will never know. Many of its ships were destroyed in a storm while rounding the Mt. Athos

promontory in Chalcidice and the survivors had to return to Asia Minor. Two years later, Darius sent a fleet carrying a 15,000 to 20,000-man force directly across the Aegean to punish the two Greek states. It captured Eretria on the island of Euboea with minimal difficulty, then landed near Marathon on the eastern shore of Attica. The Persians brought with them Hippias, the former tyrant of Athens, in hopes that his supporters and many of Athens' poorer farmers (who, like their equivalents in Ionia, tended to be pro-Persian) would rise up and support the Persian cause. However, though Cleisthenes, the creator of Athens' relatively new democratic constitution, had favored an alliance with Persia, the anti-Persian aristocrats, merchants, and artisans controlled the state and composed the army. Thus, approximately 10,000 Athenian hoplites (heavy-armed infantry soldiers), supplemented by a 600-man contingent from the city of Plataea, marched to Marathon to repel the Persian invasion. The Greeks took a position in the hills overlooking the plain at Marathon, awaiting the arrival of Spartan reinforcements. They were afraid that if they ventured down onto the flat ground the Persian mounted archers would decimate them. On the other hand, the Persians did not want to fight in the hills where the effectiveness of their cavalry would be reduced. After a few days, the Persians tired of waiting and decided to sail around Attica and attack from the other side. They began loading the horses aboard the ships, leaving the infantry to guard the plain. Even though the Spartans had not yet arrived, when the Athenians realized that the cavalry threat was gone, they charged down onto the plain and engaged the more lightly armored Persian infantry in battle. The Persians supposedly suffered more than 6,000 casualties as opposed to only 192 Greek dead. The Persian fleet sailed around Attica, but the leaders of the still-considerable force decided against landing in the face of the Greek army that had marched all night across Attica to get into position. The fleet sailed home and the first Persian attempt to conquer Athens ended in failure.

Darius began planning a larger-scale invasion of Greece, but before the preparations were complete, he died in 486 B.C.E. Subsequently, revolts broke out in

Egypt and Babylon. His son and successor, Xerxes I (486 to 465 B.C.E.), crushed these revolts by 481 B.C.E., then turned his attention to the conquest of Greece. In 480 B.C.E., he led a huge army of probably between 100,000 and 200,000 men across the Hellespont and into Greece. This formidable force was supported by a fleet of about 1,000 ships that sailed along the Aegean coast, protecting the army's left flank. The Greek city-states in Thessaly and central Greece decided against resistance, sending earth and water (symbols of submission) to Xerxes, but many southern cities, led by Athens and Sparta, committed themselves to fight. The Persian army quickly destroyed the small Greek force that was sent to delay them at the pass of Thermopylae and the Persian fleet forced the outnumbered Greek fleet to withdraw from Cape Artemisium at the northern end of Euboea. Xerxes advanced into Attica and burned the city of Athens. But the Athenian population had taken refuge on the island of Salamis just off Attica's western coast, protected by the Greek fleet stationed in the narrow straits between Salamis and the mainland. When the Persian fleet arrived, its admirals crowded too many ships into the narrow waterway, making it impossible for them to maneuver properly when the Greek vessels rowed out to attack. Fire broke out in part of the Persian fleet and quickly spread through the congested ships, adding to the chaos and confusion. The Persian fleet was forced to withdraw. Despite its losses, it still outnumbered the Greek fleet, but its officers and men were so demoralized that its fighting effectiveness had been destroyed. Xerxes sent it home to refit and reorganize and he soon followed with the bulk of his army.

Xerxes left a strong detachment under Mardonius to hold the conquered portions of Greece until the following spring when the entire Persian force would return. However, the Greeks struck first. Early in the spring of 479 B.C.E., a Greek army consisting mostly of Spartans and Athenians defeated Mardonius's troops near the city of Plataea. Mardonius was killed and the remnants of his army fled from Greece. Soon afterward, the Greek fleet destroyed a large portion of the Persian fleet at Mycalê on the coast of Asia Minor when many of the Ionians in the Persian force changed sides. During the following decades, Greeks drove the Persians out of their satrapy in Thrace, Greek fleets raided Lycia in southwestern Asia Minor, and destroyed another Persian fleet at the mouth of the Eurymedon River in southern Asia Minor. Athens also supported a revolt in Egypt, but suffered great losses when the Persian forces brutally crushed the rebellion. In the midst of this ongoing struggle, Xerxes and his crown prince, Darius, had been assassinated (465 B.C.E.) by three courtiers who made a younger prince, Artaxerxes I, king (465 to 424 B.C.E.). By 448 B.C.E. both sides were tired of the conflict and generally agreed to terms, though no formal treaty seems to have been signed. The Greek Delian League, led by Athens, agreed to stay out of Persian affairs and not to interfere with Persian possessions, while Artaxerxes I granted complete internal autonomy to the Ionian city-states and promised that the Persian fleet would stay out of the Aegean. Nevertheless, the Persians still claimed dominion over the Ionians and probably continued to collect tribute from them for a time. Thus, the so-called "Peace of Callias" was more a temporary truce than permanent cessation of hostilities between Greeks and Persians. It does mark a turning point, however. The failure of the Persians to conquer Greece ended the expansion of the Persian Empire and presaged the beginning of its slow decline.

PERSIAN CULTURE

The King and Court

As in most Near Eastern cultures, at the head of Persian society was a king whose position was hereditary. Like most rulers of earlier Mesopotamian kingdoms, the Persian king was not considered divine—he was the chosen viceroy of the god Ahura Mazda, creator of the world. Thus, it was believed that all people throughout the earth owed him obedience and tribute. To stress the fact that the king's authority was sanctioned by divine power, Darius introduced royal costumes and court ritual even more elaborate than those of earlier empires. Over a striped tunic, crimson trousers and boots, the king wore a full-sleeved long purple robe embroidered with designs in gold. He was also distinguished by his high flat-topped fluted felt cap (and on special occasions, a gold tiara), golden scepter, and the multitude of golden jewelry at his ears, neck, and wrists. Servants whose duties took them near the king had to be muffled so their breath would not touch him, and any person who approached him had to prostrate himself on the ground. He sat on a throne beneath a purple canopy supported by four columns, and in the palace he walked on purple carpets, which no other feet were allowed to touch.

In theory, the king's power was absolute, but in practice, like Assyrian kings, he was expected to confer with important nobles and officials and behave in traditional ways. For example, though the king's word was law, the ruler usually consulted royal judges ("lawbearers") who informed him about previous laws and traditions. The king usually adhered to such laws and customs, but when he wished to deviate from them, it is clear that the royal judges could not (and would not) stand in his way. Herodotus says that when Cambyses wanted to marry his sister, the royal judges informed the king that they could not find a law permitting such a union (which violated custom). On the other hand, they pointed out, Persian law clearly stated that the king could do as he pleased. So, Cambyses went ahead with the marriage.

The succession to the throne was hereditary, but not by primogeniture (that is, the oldest son did not automatically become crown prince). In theory, Ahura Mazda chose the future king, but in practice the god's selection was indicated by the reigning monarch. Like Assyrian kings, a Persian ruler could designate a younger son as his successor, as Darius I did when he chose Xerxes as crown prince. Xerxes was not Darius's eldest son, but he was the son of Cyrus' daughter Atossa and the first prince born after Darius became king. Most of Darius's successors do not seem to have followed his example of having several wives, though they did have a multitude of concubines. Even those who had only one wife still usually had several legitimate sons (as opposed to the children of concubines) from which to select a successor. The belief that Ahura Mazda could choose a prince other than the firstborn to become king tended to foster harem intrigues and often civil wars over the succession, just as a similar belief had done in Assyria.

Persian princes were schooled in the company of boys from prominent noble families by Magi, members of a special priestly tribe or class among the Medes. Though the Persians used Elamite, Akkadian, and Old Persian for their inscriptions and Aramaic for commerce and correspondence, reading and writing do not seem to have been part of a Persian education. The king and his officials dictated to scribes whatever they wanted recorded, and they had scribes read written matter to them. Upper class boys, in addition to military skills that were common to all Persian males, learned court etiquette and royal law while being steeped in the traditions and heroic legends of their ancestors. The Magi also emphasized loyalty to the king and taught their students the precepts and practices of the court religion (probably Zoroastrianism)—especially the necessity of telling the Truth and opposing the Lie (see following section "The Religion of Zoroaster"). This education prepared the boys for their future roles as kings, satraps, or other high officials.

From the time of Darius I onward, Persian kings married only women from the families of the six nobles who had made Darius king. Persian women, especially queens, were usually kept sheltered in harems and are rarely mentioned or depicted. Nevertheless, queens, and by extension the women of the noble families from which they came, were often dynamic and forceful individuals who were wealthy and powerful in their own right. They often had considerable influence with their husbands, and (if we may trust Herodotus) some seem to have been more aggressive than their royal spouses. Queens controlled large estates in Egypt, Syria, and other lands that were administered by officials who reported to the Chief Eunuch of the harem. The women of the harem were protected and served by many eunuchs (usually drawn from among the subject peoples), but in addition, some queens were given their own personal armies as gifts from their husbands.

The main official at court, second only to the king, was the *Hazarapatish* ("Commander of a Thousand," called the Chiliarch by the Greeks), a kind of prime minister chosen from the highest Persian nobility. He commanded the king's bodyguard, supervised the pages, ushers, and others at court, personally delivered messages to the king, and controlled the royal audiences. Other members of the nobility with titles such as "King's Spear Carrier" and "King's Bow Carrier" also held high positions at court. In addition to the nobility, eunuch chamberlains and cup-bearers also became very influential at court from the time of Artaxerxes I onward.

The king customarily rewarded the loyalty of his relatives and nobles by granting them large estates in various parts of the empire. From the revenues of these estates, the holders had to pay money for the services and equipment of soldiers for the royal armies. Originally, in Persia, landowners seem to have had to supply men for military service, but as the empire grew, the nobles were allowed to substitute monetary payments. The payments ranged from the amount required for an archer to that necessary to provide and support a chariot, driver, and either two or four horses. Bondsmen (serf-like individuals who were bound to the land), slaves, or free tenant farmers worked these estates for the usually absentee landowners.

The Persian Army

Initially, the Persian military was extremely efficient and powerful, but its effectiveness decreased in time due to the sheer size of the empire it had to control and failure to integrate its many ethnic components into one unified structure. The core of the army consisted of 10,000 each of cavalrymen and "Immortals," a band of elite infantry whose name derived from the fact that whenever a member died, a new member immediately took his place, keeping the number always constant. One thousand of the Immortals made up the royal bodyguard. All members of these two select regiments were Persians and professional soldiers, sworn directly to the king. There also probably were two similar elite 10,000-man regiments consisting entirely of Medes.

Persian infantrymen are usually depicted carrying both a bow and a spear, and inscriptions indicate that they were skillful with both. Cavalrymen also seem to have used both bows and spears. So there was no separate "archer" contingent in the Persian portion of the army, though military units from subject peoples might contain such specialists. The army also contained a squadron of chariots, famous for the vicious scythes attached to their wheel-hubs, but these vehicles seem to have been used more for show than as a major military weapon. Rarely did they play a significant part in crucial battles, though toward the end of the empire they were occasionally used to disrupt and scatter bands of infantry or foragers. Likewise, camels and elephants were used by the Persian army, but generally not during battle. Except for a contingent of camel-riding Arab cavalry in Xerxes' host, the Persian army used camels only as pack animals. The Persians also knew about Indian war-elephants, but they usually avoided taking these huge beasts on military campaigns because they consumed too much food and water. Elephants were used on occasion to perform heavy work in the homeland areas such as uprooting trees or demolishing walls.

The main components of the army were the infantry and cavalry, and each branch was divided into 50-man units. Each of these units probably consisted of ten five-man squads (though some think that two five-man squads were first joined into a ten-man platoon, five of which made up the basic 50-man unit). Two 50-man units constituted a *drafsha* ("flag"), probably named for the standards that distinguished these companies from one another on the battlefield. "Flags" were grouped into larger divisions of 1,000 and 10,000 men. Persian infantrymen wore soft felt caps, trousers, and long-sleeved embroidered tunics, usually over a shirt of mail armor. Each had a quiver of arrows slung over his shoulder and a dagger hanging at his right thigh, while he carried a skin-covered wicker shield, a spear, and a bow. Members of the cavalry dressed in a similar fashion, except that they frequently wore metal helmets instead of soft caps. A cavalryman also carried a dagger, spear, bow, shield, and quiver, but he also often had an iron club and two javelins. In the latter part of the Achaemenid Period, the bodies of cavalry horses were also protected with mail coverings. The cavalry was the most feared portion of the Persian military forces and was unmatched until the time of Alexander the Great.

From childhood, Persian boys learned how to ride, shoot arrows, and fight on foot and on horseback. They competed against one another in strenuous cross-country foot races and learned how to forage for food and other supplies. When they reached the age of 20, Persian males became eligible for service in the standing army, and many chose to make the military their career. Like the later Roman legionaries, Persian soldiers were well trained, highly motivated, and extremely mobile. They could cover great distances in remarkably short periods of time and proved to be extremely effective warriors in battle. These Persian troops were supplemented with contingents from the subject peoples, dressed and armed in many different ways. These forces added manpower, but naturally they were not as highly trained, dedicated, or loyal as the Persians were. As time went on, the Persians began to rely more and more on such levies rather than on Persian troops, thus reducing the quality and effectiveness of the Achaemenid armies.

The Religion of Zoroaster

The religion embraced by the Persians and most other Iranians of the Achaemenid Period was founded by an early teacher named Zarathustra (Zoroaster in Greek). He was a priest of the old Iranian religion which was closely related to that of Vedic India. However, he was also a prophet who believed that he had revelations from God concerning the way to salvation. It used to be accepted that Zoroaster lived from the late seventh through the early sixth century B.C.E. based on a later Persian tradition that placed his career 258 years before Alexander's conquest of Persia in 330 B.C.E.[7] However, almost all scholars specializing in Zoroastrian studies now agree that the prophet must have lived much earlier, some-

time between c. 1400 and 900 B.C.E. This is the era that produced the Hindu *Rig-Veda*, a work whose language is very similar to the *Gathas*, poetic compositions that scholars generally agree derive from Zoroaster himself. Such antiquity is also necessary to explain the difference in language between the *Gathas* and later portions of the *Avesta* (the Zoroastrian sacred book) that were developed to explain the *Gathas* and incorporate them into worship. Moreover, Greek writers of the fourth century B.C.E., basing their accounts on those of Persian informants, placed Zoroaster thousands of years before their own time, a tradition that is unlikely to have developed if he had really been a sixth-century B.C.E. contemporary of Cambyses I and Cyrus the Great. On the other hand, domesticated camels had begun to be used for transport by Zoroaster's time, so we are probably not too far wrong if we place his activity around 1000 B.C.E. (give or take a century). Later traditions about his life may include some valid information (such as his father's name and the claim that he lived for 77 years), but they are largely vehicles for recounting miracles about his birth, childhood, and career. The *Gathas*, Zoroaster's 17 hymns or prayers, written in a difficult-to-understand eastern Iranian dialect, provide the only reliable information on his life and teachings.

Before Zoroaster's time, Iranians seem to have been polytheists whose religion was a form of animism. They worshiped cosmic gods and beings whose presence was manifested in feelings, qualities, and states as well as in physical objects and natural phenomena. As in the Indian Vedic religion, there were probably two classes of deities, *ahuras* (called *asuras* in India) who were heavenly and remote from humans and *daevas* (*devas* in India) who were nature deities and war gods more intimately associated with humans. The Iranians believed that the creation of the world had occurred in seven successive stages: sky, water, earth, plants, animals, humans, and fire. Worship consisted largely of daily open-air ritual offerings to fire and water with occasional animal sacrifices during which the participants became ritually intoxicated by drinking the fermented juice of the *haoma* plant (*soma* in India). The people seem to have believed that after death, souls went to an underworld where they were sustained by food and drink offerings from their descendants. A few fortunate souls of heroes were allowed to ascend to heaven to live with the gods.

During Zoroaster's lifetime, the peaceful agricultural and cattle-breeding group to which he belonged seems to have been under frequent attack by well-armed groups of chariot-using nomadic marauders. The violence and bloodshed caused by these predatory raids probably led Zoroaster to meditate about *asha*, the principle of Truth, Justice, and Righteousness that should govern everything in the world, and its opposite, *druj*, the Lie, Wickedness, and Disorder. The contrast and conflict between these two principles probably had been already a part of the old Iranian religion, but it became central to Zoroaster's ethical dualism. He proclaimed that the uncreated and eternal god, Ahura Mazda ("Wise Lord" or "Lord of Wisdom"), was totally good, wise and beneficent. But this benevolent deity was opposed by another uncreated being, Angra Mainu (the "Evil" or "Destructive Spirit"), who was wholly evil, obtuse, and malevolent. (In later Zoroastrianism, the names of these deities were contracted into Ormazd and Ahriman.)

Supporting Ahura Mazda were the *Amesha Spentas* ("Holy" or "Bounteous Immortals"): the Holy Spirit (*Spenta Mainu*, which later was sometimes seen as just another name for Ahura Mazda), Desirable Dominion, Wholeness (or Health), Immortality, Holy Devotion, Good Purpose, and Best Truth (or Best Righteousness). These beings were both independent deities and aspects of Ahura Mazda himself, but they also could enter into human beings who choose to follow the Wise Lord. Zoroaster also acknowledged the existence of the old *ahuras* ("Lords") as beneficent angel-like beings sent out by the *Amesha Spentas*. On the other hand, the prophet claimed that the *daevas* were malicious servants of Angra Mainu who, like their master, were to be denounced and opposed. Thus, in Zoroastrianism, *daeva* came to mean "demon." In India, the opposite development occurred, with the *asuras* in time being regarded as demons, while the *devas* became the only true gods. Five times a day followers of Zoroaster were supposed to pray while standing in the presence of Fire (the sun,

moon, or a hearth fire), the symbol of Truth, Justice, and Righteousness.

Zoroaster claimed that Ahura Mazda created the world as a perfect place, but he foresaw that Angra Mainu would corrupt it and that it would become the place where the battle between Good and Evil would be fought. Even though Ahura Mazda and Angra Mainu are both uncreated, they were not equal in power according to Zoroaster. He proclaimed that Ahura Mazda and his forces will win the struggle against Evil, and Angra Mainu and his followers will be punished in a Last Judgment. Humans have a free will, so they must choose whether to support Ahura Mazda or Angra Mainu, to be *ashavans*, "followers of Truth (or Righteousness)" or *dregvants*, "followers of the Lie." By choosing to live by the principle of Righteousness and to fight against Evil, humans can be *saoshyants* ("future saviors") and help bring about *Frasho-kereti* ("Making Wonderful"), the restoration of the world to the perfection it had when first created. The choices people make in this world will determine their ultimate fate. Three days after death, the soul's good thoughts, words, and deeds will be weighed against its bad ones and it will either cross "The Bridge of the Requiter" to "best existence" (heaven) or be plunged into a chasm and condemned to "worst existence" (hell) where it will be tormented and oppressed. Souls will remain in either heaven or hell until *Frasho-kereti*, the end of this world as we know it, when they will rejoin their bodies during a general resurrection. The resurrection will be followed by a Last Judgment in which everyone will have to walk through a fiery river of molten metal. Despite the river's heat, no harm will befall the good who will pass through it to live forever on the renewed and perfected earth which will be like a beautiful garden (or "paradise," the Persian word for "garden"). On the other hand, the bodies and souls of the unrighteous will be completely consumed by the burning river. Then the molten metal will flow into hell, destroying Angra Mainu and the *daevas*. These ideas of Zoroaster constitute the earliest known systematic **eschatology**, that is, teachings about "final things" or the end of the world.

Zoroaster not only assailed the *daevas* worshiped during his time (the most important of which was Indra), but also attacked animal sacrifice (or at least the cruel way it was performed) and the use of the *haoma* beverage during sacrificial rites. These ideas caused him to be rejected and persecuted by his own people. He fled to another eastern Iranian tribe where he managed to convert the chieftain named Vishtaspa (who should not be confused with a later namesake, the father of Darius I). Protected and supported by Vishtaspa, Zoroaster's religion began to spread, probably reaching the western Iranian Medes and Persians sometime during the eighth century B.C.E.

During the period after Zoroaster's death, several changes occurred in his religion. Light and Darkness came more and more to be symbols respectively of Truth and the Lie, Good and Evil, and each of the Bounteous Immortals was though to dwell within and guard one of the seven elements of creation. When western Iran accepted Zoroastrianism, the Median Magi gradually made themselves the priests and arbiters of doctrine within the Zoroastrian religion. They preserved the oral traditions brought from the east, but also introduced many of their own customs into Zoroastrianism, especially the use of tower temples in which fires were constantly kept burning. Also, though Zoroaster had opposed the use of representations or images of the divine, the Achaemenid rulers depicted Ahura Mazda in the same way that the Assyrians had portrayed their chief god Asshur—as a human figure within a winged solar disk. (See Figure 10.1. The winged figure facing the king is Ahura Mazda.) Coupled with this development was a growing emphasis on another aspect of sun worship in the person of an old Iranian deity named Mithra (Mitra in India), a god Zoroaster had ignored. Within Zoroastrianism, this solar deity came to be regarded as a guardian of contracts and god of justice, war, and victory. At times he became as popular as Ahura Mazda and was invoked by Achaemenid kings after the time of Artaxerxes II along with the Wise Lord (usually written as one word, Ahuramazda, in Achaemenid inscriptions). Anahita, an old fertility goddess, is also mentioned in these later inscriptions. Old purity laws were strengthened as a result of Zoroastrian dualism, with pollution by contact with corpses and blood being particularly abhorrent. As a result, instead of burying or cremating the dead, Zoroastrians exposed corpses until their bones were picked clean by animals or birds so that they would not contaminate the earth or fire. Strict laws were created to confine and isolate women during menstruation so their blood could not contaminate others. Other customs of the old religion such as offering food and clothing to the dead and even the use of *haoma* in some rites also made their way back into Zoroastrian practice. Finally, though Zoroaster had challenged all people to be *saoshyants* or agents of the world's redemption, after his death his followers adopted the belief that during the End Times, *the Saoshyant*, a miraculously born savior, would lead the forces of Good to victory in a final battle against Evil.

The reader will almost certainly have noticed the correspondence between many Zoroastrian beliefs and aspects of Judaism and Christianity. Most assuredly, this similarity is not accidental. Zoroastrianism probably had become widespread in western Iran during the eighth and seventh centuries B.C.E., for an Assyrian tablet in Asshurbanipal's library seems to include Ahura Mazda (written Assara Mazas) in a list of gods. Though we have no evidence for Cyrus and Cambyses, Darius I and subsequent Achaemenid rulers almost certainly accepted the Zoroastrian faith. In his Behistun inscription, Darius characterizes his opponents as followers of the Lie and credits his victories to a god named Ahuramazda, while on his tomb he declared that he was a friend to good and an enemy to evil. Inscriptions of Xerxes I and Artaxerxes I are even more clearly Zoroastrian in character. Thus, though the *Gathas* and the rest of the *Avesta* were preserved only orally for more than a thousand years (they were not written down until sometime between the third and fifth centuries C.E.), Zoroastrian ideas were almost certainly present in Persia and Mesopotamia early enough for Judean exiles to be influenced by them.

Persian Architecture and Art

Just as the Persian empire embraced the entire Near East, their architecture and art were also international, utilizing artisans and blending styles from all parts of the empire. The Persians, being primarily a herding people before the time of Cyrus, had few native architectural or artistic traditions. Their artistic genius lay not in their originality, but rather in their ability to combine elements of different artistic styles into one harmonious whole.

It has already been mentioned that Cyrus's palace at Pasargadae exhibited Median, Elamite, Mesopotamian, Egyptian, Lydian, and Greek elements, and Darius's palaces at Susa and Persepolis reflect the same mixtures. Darius's palace at Susa, for example, combined a series of courtyards like those in Nebuchadnezzar's palace at Babylon with columned porticos and halls like those of Pasargadae. The wide, columned entrances and porticos that the Persians utilized in their palaces were based on Median structures, but the multicolumned audience hall, called an *apadana*, with its soaring, open interior supported by widely spaced graceful columns seems to be a largely Persian innovation. Some scholars think it may have been inspired by large tents used in earlier times. Others think the plan may be based in part on Egyptian hypostyle halls, but utilizing slender columns in place of the massive ones used by the Egyptians. The most beautiful of these audience halls was constructed by Darius I (with additions by Xerxes I) on a 46-foot-high terrace at Persepolis (see Figure 10.2). It had wide, columned porticos on three sides, two of which could be approached by monumental double

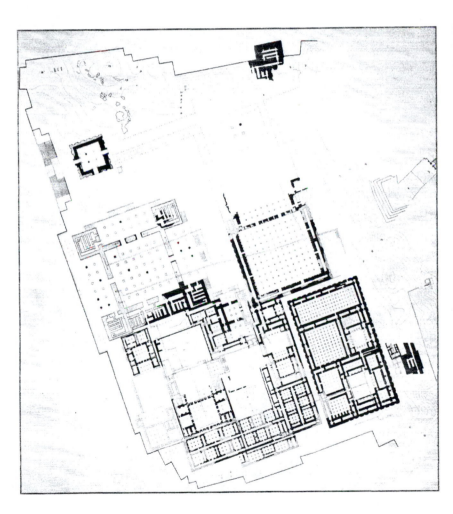

FIGURE 10.2   Plan of Persepolis

Source: Courtesy of the Oriental Institute of the University of Chicago.

staircases decorated with reliefs of the Immortals, lions attacking bulls, and processions of tribute bearers. Each portico had 12 slender 65-foot-high columns on Egyptian-like bases that were fluted in Ionian Greek style. The capitals of the east and west porticos were in the shape of the joined foreparts of two bulls, while those of the north portico and interior had double-bull or double-lion figures surmounting elongated double-Ionic capitals. These, in turn, stood atop Egyptian-like flower-capitals (see similar ones in the Gate of All Lands, Figure 10.3). The columns supported heavy cedar beams from Phoenicia, which in turn supported smaller roof tim-

bers. Probably the roof beams, decorative elements of the columns, and bas-relief carvings on the staircases were all originally painted in bright colors.

Other buildings at Persepolis also featured columned interiors and entrances flanked by large Mesopotamian-style carved bulls (see Figure 10.3). Most of these structures were erected by Darius I, but Xerxes I and Artaxerxes I also added "palaces," halls, and other features (see Figure 10.2). These grand structures probably were used only for formal receptions and ceremonial purposes rather than as living quarters. There are no kitchens with ovens or food preparation areas, no source of running water, and no

FIGURE 10.3 Doorway of the Gate of All Lands

Two 18-foot-high human-headed limestone bulls flank the official entrance to Persepolis.

Source: The Art Archive/Dagli Orti

provisions for sanitation. Undoubtedly, the real palace where the king, harem, and entourage dwelled while at Persepolis was on the plain in front of the monumental terrace. At that location, archaeologists have found the remains of grand buildings and a garden with an ornamental lake. Other dwellings may have been scattered across the plain as well, but this area has not been extensively excavated.

Persian sculpture, metalwork, and other arts exhibit the same eclectic blending of various motifs, styles, and techniques seen in their architecture. Bas-relief carvings and sculpture in the round are generally in Assyrian style, but many of the sculptors seem to have been Ionian Greeks, and a few Greek features (such as the drapery folds in robes) can be noted. However, Persian reliefs are much more static than Assyrian ones. Instead of battles or hunting scenes, the Persians glorify the king by depicting processions of soldiers and tribute bearers, the king in triumph over his enemies (see Figure 10.1), or worshiping Ahura Mazda before a fire altar. Persian metalwork, mostly gold and silver vessels, jewelry, and ornaments through which the Persians displayed their wealth, also reflected the eclectic style. These objects, created primarily by Median and Egyptian artisans, were often decorated with winged ibexes, winged lions with horns, griffins, and other fantastic creatures in addition to normal animals such as lions, ibexes, or wild rams. These animal figures are a blend of traditional Iranian, Scythian, Mesopotamian, and Greek styles and motifs. The amazing thing is how gracefully and naturally these disparate elements have been merged into beautiful works of art.

JUDAH DURING THE PERSIAN PERIOD

The Restoration of Judah

Though Cyrus seems to have given permission for the Judean exiles to return to their homeland in 538 B.C.E., the actual resettlement took place in two major waves almost two decades apart. The first group to be repatriated was led by Sheshbazzar, who (despite his Babylonian name) was described as a "prince of Judah" (Ezra 1:8)[8] commissioned by Cyrus to be governor of Judah and to rebuild the Temple of Yahweh. These people faced a formidable and disheartening task upon their return home. The city of Jerusalem was in ruins, squatters occupied the property which legally belonged to those who had been in exile, finances were not yet organized, Idumaeans (Edomites) had taken control of much of the Negev, and some neighboring peoples and leaders did not want to see a restored Judah. The conflicts between "the people of the land" (those Judeans who had not been taken off into exile) and "the sons of the exile" (those returning from exile) were especially severe, for "the sons of the exile" considered themselves the only true Yahwists. Despite the fact that "the people of the land" claimed to worship Yahweh, the returnees considered them impure like the people of Samaria, many of whom were descended from foreigners settled there by the Assyrians. So, although Sheshbazzar began rebuilding the Temple's foundation, the work did not progress very far; most of Jerusalem remained in ruins. The former exiles, perhaps made overly optimistic by the wonderful visions of the restoration presented by Deutero-Isaiah (such as Isaiah 43:18–21; 49:8–21), seem to have sunk into despair and lethargy when confronted by the multitude of problems that faced them in Judah.

In 520 B.C.E., Zerubbabel, probably a grandson of the former king Jehoiachin[9] and the new governor appointed by Darius I, and Jeshua (Joshua), the High Priest, led another group of former exiles back to Judah from Babylonia. Encouraged by the prophets Haggai and Zechariah, they rebuilt the Temple's foundation (which had never been finished or had suffered damage since the time of Sheshbazzar) and completed work on the Temple itself by 516–515 B.C.E. However, around this time, Zerubbabel disappears from the record. There is no indication what, if anything, happened to him, but some think it probable that Darius removed him from office or allowed his term to expire because his Davidic lineage was reviving Judean nationalistic sentiment and hopes for a reestablishment of the monarchy (see Haggai

2:20–23). He was probably the last member of House of David to govern Judah.

Problems continued to beset the Judeans, especially those instigated by the Samaritans who lived in the area that formerly had been the Kingdom of Israel. Zerubbabel had rebuffed their offer to help rebuild the Temple, and in Bernhard Anderson's words, "the hand extended in friendship curled into a fist."[10] Economic and political rivalries undoubtedly aggravated this religious quarrel between the peoples of Samaria and Judea. Large portions of Jerusalem were like a ghost town, and large sections of its walls remained in ruins until the reign of Artaxerxes I (465 to 424 B.C.E.), when Ezra and Nehemiah supposedly arrived to reorganize the community. However, the order in which these two men accomplished their missions remains in question.[11] According to the Bible, Ezra arrived first (in the seventh year of Artaxerxes) and Nehemiah came later (he was governor between Artaxerxes I's twentieth and thirty-second years and had a second term sometime before Artaxerxes I's death). However, for a variety of reasons, from the nineteenth century until relatively recently, most historians and biblical scholars argued that Nehemiah's mission had preceded that of Ezra. Some thought that Nehemiah had been governor of Judah during the reign of Artaxerxes I and that Ezra had been sent to Jerusalem a couple of generations later during the reign of Artaxerxes II. Others emended the passage that claimed that Ezra arrived in the "seventh" year of Artaxerxes to "thirty-seventh" year. But in recent years, the biblical order—Ezra, then Nehemiah—has been defended, and new reconstructions of the period have been suggested. At the present time, there is no consensus on this issue, but now many (perhaps even a majority) of biblical scholars seem to support the traditional order in which Ezra arrived in Judah in 458 B.C.E. and Nehemiah in 445 B.C.E.

Ezra was not a governor or political authority, but rather a priest and a scribe. Persian kings often promoted harmony by restoring and supporting local religious cults and traditions, so Artaxerxes (I or, possibly, II) sent Ezra to Judah to stabilize the province's social and religious situation. He was given vessels for use in the temple and funds to buy sacrificial animals,

drink offerings, and other materials for the cult. But the most important object he carried back to Jerusalem was a copy of a work called the book of the *torah* ("law" or "instruction") of Moses. He gathered the citizens of Jerusalem together and read to them from this book throughout the week-long Feast of Tabernacles. Levites interpreted the readings (or possibly paraphrased them in Aramaic) so the people could understand them. While there has been some debate about the identity of this "book of the law" (Deuteronomy? the Priestly Code? the Holiness Code?), most biblical scholars have (probably correctly) assumed that it was the Pentateuch, the Torah of the present Hebrew Scriptures. The readings were concluded with a dramatic covenant renewal ceremony in which the people pledged "to walk in God's law, which was given by Moses" and "to observe and fulfill all the commandments, rules and statutes of Yahweh" (Nehemiah 10:29). To ensure the unity of the family, the basic institution that would have to carry out these laws, and to guard against future apostasy, Ezra prohibited marriages between Jews ("sons of the exile") and non-Jews (including "the people of the land"). He especially opposed marriages between Jewish men and non-Jewish women, demanding that all such marriages be ended by divorce (Ezra 10). Many scholars see Ezra's reforms as the real beginning of Judaism as a religion of "The Book," with the Law as the fundamental guide for Jewish life. They, therefore, regard Ezra as the father or architect of Judaism (which is viewed as a distinct entity that developed out of the earlier Israelite/Judean religion).[12] Others point to Josiah as earlier having promulgated a written law code (Deuteronomy) and to the traditions surrounding Moses as a lawgiver in early Israel. They also note that when the second-century B.C.E. Jewish sage Jesus Ben Sirach praised the great heroes of Judaism, Ezra was not included in the list.[13] Nevertheless, the editor who put together the books of Ezra and Nehemiah clearly considered Ezra the greater of the two men and one of the towering figures of Jewish history. Most later Jewish tradition agreed with this assessment.

The career of Nehemiah is described in the biblical book of Nehemiah, which (with the exception of chapters 8 through10) is essentially derived from a first person narrative (called the Memoirs of Nehemiah), probably written by Nehemiah himself. He was a cup-bearer to the Persian king Artaxerxes I, but when he heard about the problems afflicting Judah, he persuaded the king to send him there as governor. He found himself opposed by Sanballat, governor of Samaria, and a coalition of other neighboring peoples who constantly complained about him to the Persian king, tried to undermine his authority, and threatened to attack him. Despite this opposition, soon after his arrival in Judah, Nehemiah organized the rebuilding of Jerusalem's gates and walls and repopulated the city by a lottery that selected one-tenth of Judah's population to become new residents of Jerusalem. He also instituted economic reforms concerning mortgages, loans, and interest to protect people who were losing their lands and being forced into slavery because of debt. Presumably he was a wealthy man, because he also canceled the taxes that previous governors had imposed to support themselves and their staff. In addition, he implemented some economic requirements of the biblical Law, demanding strict observance of the Sabbath and making sure that the people supported the priests and temple staff with their tithes. Finally, he enrolled citizens according to genealogy, allowing only those from families who had experienced the Exile to be considered Jews, and either instituted or enforced (depending on whether he preceded or followed Ezra) a prohibition of intermarriage. Many scholars consider these reforms necessary prerequisites for those of Ezra,[14] though, as indicated, the chronological relationship between the two men is still uncertain.

While we cannot be sure of the date for Ezra's mission, a group of Aramaic letters found at Elephantine in Egypt indicate that Nehemiah's governorship belonged to the time of Artaxerxes I. These letters, part of an archive called the Elephantine Papyri, belonged to a community of Jewish mercenary soldiers serving in the garrison at Yeb (Elephantine). Their temple, dedicated to Yahu or Yaho (Yahweh), was destroyed in 410 B.C.E. by Egyptian priests supported by the local garrison commander.

They wrote to Bagoas, the governor of Judah, and to the High Priest Jehohanan (Johanan), urging them to support their petition to rebuild the Temple. Then, when they received no answer, they wrote again in 407 B.C.E. to Bagoas and sent a copy to the sons of Sanballat (Nehemiah's adversary), the former governor of Samaria (see Document 10.2). Thus, Nehemiah and Sanballat must have served as governors a generation earlier, during the reign of Artaxerxes I (465 to 424 B.C.E.).

Religious Developments During the Persian Era

Whether or not the reforms of Ezra and Nehemiah created Judaism out of Israelite/Judean religion is debatable, but it is clear that their measures began a new era in the religion. Though the prophets Haggai, Zechariah, Obadiah, Malachi, and Joel were active during the Persian Period, they are minor figures. Clearly the role and influence of prophets declined in the post-exilic period. Once the Jews had a written Word of God, they did not expect God to speak directly through prophets, as he was believed to have done in the past. By the end of the Persian Period, Jews generally believed that prophecy had ended with Ezra and no new prophets were expected until the Last Days. Coupled with this decline of prophecy was the development of oral traditions interpreting the Law and applying it to new situations. Thus, though they theoretically went back to the time of Moses, the real roots of the later rabbinical tradition were established during the Persian era.

A major effect of the Ezra-Nehemiah reforms was the exclusivism they introduced by forbidding marriages between Jews and non-Jews. This prohibition was not based on nationalism or ideas of racial superiority, but arose from the fear of religious syncretism and cultural assimilation. Some Judeans who had married Ammonites, Moabites, or other foreigners had abandoned the Hebrew language, presumably speaking only Aramaic. Inspired by teachings of Deuteronomy, the "sons of the exile" believed that allowing foreign spouses to worship their own deities

DOCUMENT 10.2

Elephantine Papyri Concerning the Egyptian Temple of Yaho (Yahweh)

This is a copy of the second letter (407 B.C.E.) sent to Jerusalem to obtain support for rebuilding the Elephantine temple of Yaho (Yahweh) that had been destroyed and a memorandum of an oral response given to the person carrying the letter. Interestingly, the memorandum indicates that Bagoas and Delaiah, son of Sanballat, probably unwilling to commit themselves in writing, orally authorized the temple's reconstruction (but called it only a "house of offering") and did not specifically give permission for performing animal sacrifices there. According to Deuteronomy, blood sacrifices were only permitted at the Temple in Jerusalem. Another letter from Elephantine, probably addressed to Arsames, the satrap of Egypt, indicates that the Elephantine Jews agreed that if the temple were rebuilt, no burnt offerings would take place there, only incense, grain, and drink offerings. The letter below, though, makes it clear that animal sacrifice *had* been practiced at the temple before its destruction.[15]

To our lord Bagoas, governor of Judah, your servants Yedoniah and his colleagues, the priests who are in the fortress of Elephantine. May the God of Heaven seek after the welfare of our lord at all times and give you favor before King Darius [II] and the nobles a thousand times more than now. May you be happy and healthy at all times. Now, your servant Yedoniah and his colleagues depose as follows: In the month of Tammuz in the 14th year of King Darius [= 410 B.C.E.], when Arsames departed and went to the king, the priests of the god Khnub [Khnum], who is in the fortress of Elephantine, conspired with Vidaranag, who was commander-in-chief here, to wipe out the temple of the god Yaho from the fortress of Elephantine. So that wretch Vidaranag sent to his son Nefayan, who was in command of the garrison of the fortress of Syene [Aswan], this order, "The temple of the god Yaho in the fortress of Yeb is to be destroyed." Nefayan thereupon led the Egyptians with the other troops. Coming with their weapons to the fortress of Elephantine, they entered that temple and razed it to the ground. . . . Now, our forefathers built this temple back in the days of the kingdom of Egypt, and when Cambyses came to Egypt he found it built. They [Cambyses and the Persians] knocked down all the temples of the gods of Egypt, but no one did any damage to this temple. . . . We have also sent a letter before now, when this evil was done to us, (to) our lord and to the high priest Johanan and his colleagues the priests in Jerusalem and to Ostanes the brother of Anani and the nobles of the Jews. Never a letter have they sent to us. . . . From then to now, in the year 17 of King Darius, no meal-offering, in(cen)se, nor burnt offering have been offered in this temple. Now your servants Yedoniah, and his colleagues, and the Jews, the citizens of Elephantine, all say thus: If it please our lord, take thought of this temple to rebuild it, since they do not let us rebuild it. Look to your well-wishers and friends here in Egypt. Let a letter be sent from you to them concerning the temple of the god Yaho to build it in the fortress of Elephantine as it was built before; and the meal-offering, incense, and burnt offering will be offered in your name, and we shall pray for you at all times, we, and our wives, and our children, and the Jews that are here, all of them, if you do thus, so that that

---

DOCUMENT 10.2, CONTINUED

Elephantine Papyri Concerning the Egyptian Temple of Yaho (Yahweh)

temple is rebuilt. . . . We have also set the whole matter forth in a letter in our name to Dela-iah and Shelemiah, the sons of Sanballat the governor of Samaria.

Memorandum of what Bagoas and Delaiah said to me: Let this be an instruction to you in Egypt to say before Arsames about the house of offering of the God of Heaven which had been in existence in the fortress of Elephantine since ancient times, before Cambyses, and was destroyed by that wretch Vidaranag in the year 14 of King Darius: to rebuild it on its site as it was before, and the meal-offering and incense to be made on that altar as it used to be.

---

within Judah would be anathema to Yahweh. Such toleration might even lead to the acceptance of foreign deities in the temple as had occurred in the time of King Solomon. Thus, the move to prevent mixed marriages primarily was intended to preserve the religious purity of the Jewish people. Nevertheless, it produced a closed community that largely lost sight of the universalist mission to be a "light to the gentiles" espoused by Deutero-Isaiah. The book of Jonah, a short story containing a lot of folk humor, seems to have been written to protest the new narrow vision of Judaism's scope and mission. The story is set during the era when the Assyrian Empire was at its height, and after several humorous turns in the plot, Jonah winds up in Nineveh proclaiming that God was going to destroy the Assyrians because of their evil ways. They suddenly repent, however, and God decides to forgive them, whereupon Jonah becomes furious. Jonah feels that the people of Nineveh deserve to be destroyed, and he complains that God's soft heart was exactly why he didn't want to be a prophet in the first place—he knew that God "was a gracious and merciful God, slow to anger, and abounding in steadfast love" (Jonah 4:2). When the angry Jonah pouts and refuses to preach anymore, God has to teach him that the divine creator of the world has a right to be concerned about the welfare of all people, including non-Jews, even Judah's enemies. This humorous yet eloquent plea for a more universal outlook did not succeed, though, in reversing the exclusivism of post-exilic Judaism.

The Persian Period also seems to have seen the development of Jewish eschatology (beliefs about the Final Things). Earlier prophets such as Hosea, Jeremiah, Ezekiel, and Second Isaiah had promised that a new "golden" age would dawn in the future when Israel and Judah recommitted themselves to Yahweh or returned to Palestine after the exile. These ideas seem to have been supplemented and expanded during the Persian Period, probably primarily by Jews who remained in Babylonia. There, they seem to have been influenced by Zoroastrian concepts that answered a basic question raised by monotheism. If there is only one God and he is good, why is there evil in the world? Much of the world's wrongs can be blamed on the choices and actions of human beings, but clearly humans do not cause all of this planet's injustice. For example, why did a good and just God create a world where natural disasters strike down innocent people? Some Jews decided that a rebellious angel had become God's enemy and, like Angra Mainu in Zoroastrianism, was responsible for all the evil and injustice in the universe. Accompanying this belief was the idea that God had a multitude of angels to do his bidding while the Evil One commanded hordes of demons. The concept of the messiah, God's anointed king, also began to change as hopes for a restoration of the Judean monarchy under Zerubbabel or another member of the line of David faded. The belief arose that, like the Zoroastrian Saoshyant, the Messiah would lead God's angelic legions against the demonic forces and destroy them in a great battle at the End Time. Then there would be a resurrection of the dead and a final judgment after which evil doers would be either destroyed or forever punished in hell while the righteous would enjoy the glories of eternal life in God's everlasting kingdom.

These ideas appear in Jewish writings for the first time during the Hellenistic Age, but they must have been incubating for some time during the Achaemenid Period in Jewish communities that were in close contact with Zoroastrians. But for a long time, perhaps two or three centuries, they were most likely accepted by only a small minority of Jews. Most Jews continued to believe, as Israelites and Judeans had in pre-exilic times, that there was no afterlife—God rewarded and punished within this world. The good were supposed to prosper, and the evil were supposed to receive great misfortune. Only gradually would reality intrude, leading more and more devout Jews to recognize that the real world did not work that way. Eventually, some, like the author of Ecclesiastes (written about 200 B.C.E. and possibly influenced by Greek Epicurean philosophy), abandoned belief in God's direct involvement in human affairs. Others, especially during the persecution of their faith by the Seleucid king Antiochus IV between 168 and 165 B.C.E., took solace in the Persian-inspired eschatological beliefs expressed in the biblical book of Daniel, written during those dark days of oppression. Following the success of the revolt against the Seleucids, what probably had been a minority view through the latter part of the Persian Period and the early part of the Hellenistic Age became the dominant view within Judaism. And it was this eschatological Judaism that, in turn, gave birth to Christianity and later strongly influenced Islam.

THE END OF THE ACHAEMENID PERSIAN EMPIRE

Decline of the Empire (424–330 B.C.E.)

When Artaxerxes I died in 424 B.C.E., his son (by a concubine), Ochos, claimed the throne and took the name Darius II (424 to 405/404 B.C.E.). But two of his brothers, Xerxes (a legitimate son and probably the designated successor) and Sogdianus (another son of a concubine) also asserted their right to the throne. This three-way civil war raged for a year before Xerxes and Sogdianus were killed and Darius II became undisputed ruler. During Darius's reign, the Peloponnesian War between Athens and Sparta was raging in Greece (431 to 404 B.C.E.), and Persia took advantage of the situation to reassert its control over Ionia, which had come under Athenian domination. Athenian imperialism was clearly a threat to Persian interests, so when Athens lost a fleet attempting to conquer Syracuse (413 B.C.E.), Darius began sending funds to Sparta so it could build a fleet and challenge Athens' control of the seas. This policy hastened Athens' ultimate defeat, which came soon after Darius died.

Darius' eldest son and crown prince, Arsaces, succeeded him and took the throne name Artaxerxes II (404 to 359 B.C.E.), but the new king was plunged into crises almost immediately. Egypt had revolted and established its independence under Pharaoh Amyrteus (404 to 399 B.C.E.), founder of Dynasty 28. Before Artaxerxes could adequately respond to the Egyptian rebellion, his brother Cyrus, the satrap of Lydia, attempted to make himself king. In 401 B.C.E., Cyrus marched on Babylon with an army that included some 10,000 Greek mercenaries. Artaxerxes met his brother in battle at Cunaxa, north of Babylon, and though the Greeks acquitted themselves well, Cyrus was killed in the battle. Their cause lost, the Greek mercenaries marched north along the Tigris River and fought their way through western Armenia to the Black Sea whence they returned to Greek lands. Xenophon, one of the leaders of the Greek mercenaries, wrote *Anabasis* or *March of the Ten Thousand*, an account of the Greeks' experiences that later convinced Alexander of Macedon that Persia was ripe for conquest.

Despite the inauspicious beginning of his reign, Artaxerxes achieved some success after his brother's death. Though he was not able to reconquer Egypt, he managed to keep it from spreading its rule over the Levant. Possibly as part of his policy to pacify Syria-Palestine and limit Egyptian influence there, he sent Ezra to Jerusalem in 398 (assuming that the Artaxerxes of Ezra 7:7 is Artaxerxes II and not Artaxerxes I). Furthermore, continuing conflict in Greece between Sparta, on the one hand, and Thebes, Athens, and other cities on the other, allowed Artaxerxes to impose a settlement called the King's Peace in 387/386 B.C.E. Under the terms of this agreement, the Greek city-states were forbidden to form large alliances (or "Leagues") and had to recognize Persian control over the Greek cities in Asia Minor. Thus, in many ways, the ultimate winner of the Peloponnesian War was not Sparta, but Persia!

Artaxerxes II enjoyed a long reign of 46 years, but prior to his death, he had to execute his oldest son and crown prince, Darius, for conspiring to seize the throne. His next oldest son was tricked into committing suicide. So, when Artaxerxes died in 359 B.C.E., he was succeeded by his ruthless son Ochus who, according to the Greek writer Plutarch, had skillfully engineered the deaths of his older brothers. Ochus took the name Artaxerxes III (359 to 338 B.C.E.) and assured his position by murdering all of his relatives who might claim the throne—not a minor undertaking, since Artaxerxes II supposedly fathered 115 sons. Artaxerxes III was the last of the strong Achaemenid kings, crushing revolts in Syria and Phoenicia c. 345 B.C.E. and reconquering Egypt in 343 B.C.E. In 338 B.C.E., as Philip II of Macedon was establishing his control over Greece, Artaxerxes and all of his sons except one were poisoned by Bagoas, the chief eunuch. The surviving son, Arses, was made puppet king with the name Artaxerxes IV (338 to 336 B.C.E.), but Bagoas killed him, too, when he tried to establish his independence. Bagoas then made a distant relative of the royal family king as Darius III (336 to 330 B.C.E.), but once in power, Darius had Bagoas eliminated.

Conquest by Alexander the Great

While the Persian monarchy was being weakened by intrigues and constant assassinations, a new power had arisen across the Aegean Sea. Philip II (359 to 336 B.C.E.) had reorganized the Macedonian army, modifying the equipment and fighting style of the infantry phalanx, and with this new force he greatly extended Macedonian dominion. His expansion culminated with control over most of Greece in 338 B.C.E., when he and his 18-year-old son Alexander defeated an army of Thebans and Athenians at Chaeronea. Philip then turned his attention to "liberating" the Greek cities of Ionia, but before he undertook his planned invasion of Asia Minor, he was assassinated by a disgruntled nobleman in 336 B.C.E. Alexander III (336 to 323 B.C.E.) thus became king in the same year as Darius III, the man he would challenge for control of the Near East.

After consolidating his power within Macedon and Greece, in 334 B.C.E., Alexander led his well-trained army and superb cavalry into Asia Minor. He was almost killed in his initial battle with Darius's forces at the Granicus River, but he survived to inflict a stinging defeat on the Persians, killing large numbers of them. Alexander gained control of Anatolia (including the ports and their Phoenician fleets) and won the support of his new subjects. In Caria, he restored power to Ada, a queen who had been deposed by her brother, and had himself adopted as her son. This action legitimized his claim to Caria and won him unstinting support from his new "mother." As he advanced, he continued this policy of placing local rulers in charge of satrapies (whose organization he maintained) while keeping military forces under Macedonian command.

Darius and his army (which included many Greek mercenaries) met the Macedonian forces in 333 B.C.E. at Issus, a relatively narrow spot along the north Syrian coast. Alexander led the Companions, his heavy cavalry that had been stationed on the right flank, in an angled charge against the Persian center, breaking through almost to the position of Darius himself. Darius fled from this onslaught, disheartening many of the Persian soldiers who also turned and ran, turning the battle into a rout. Soon afterward, Alexander captured the Persian baggage train, which not only had the treasure Darius had carried with him but also the women of the court, including Darius's wife, mother, and children. He treated them courteously, continuing to lay a foundation for Persian acceptance of him as rightful ruler.

While Darius fled eastward to rebuild his army, Alexander seized most of the Phoenician ports, initiated a siege of Tyre (which would not surrender), and was welcomed as Pharaoh by the people of Egypt. Then in 331 B.C.E., he advanced into Assyria to confront Darius again at Gaugamela, not far from the ruins of Nineveh. Darius had arrayed his forces on a level plain, which would allow him to make the best use of his cavalry and the 200 scythed chariots he had gathered. During the battle, however, the chariots proved worthless against the Macedonian infantry that allowed them to charge through gaps in the formation which closed up again after their passage. Once in the rear, the chariots were set upon by light infantry whose soldiers killed the horses with long spears. Meanwhile, the Macedonian cavalry, again led by Alexander, made straight for the position of Darius, who once more fled from battle, initiating another rout. Afterward, Alexander systematically took possession of the Persian capitals—Babylon, Susa, Pasargadae, Persepolis, and Ecbatana—whose treasuries contained 180,000 talents (more than 7,400 tons) of gold! In the spring of 330 B.C.E., he allowed his army to loot Persepolis, the symbol of Persian power and grandeur. Then, possibly while drunk, he burned it to the ground, supposedly in revenge for Persian devastation in Greece. Some scholars think, though, that the destruction was a calculated action to indicate the end of Achaemenid rule. Soon afterward, Darius, still fleeing, was murdered by one of his own satraps. When Alexander found the body he had it returned to Persepolis and given a royal burial. Then, with the support of Darius's family, Alexander proclaimed himself the legitimate ruler of Persia and avenger of Darius. What he had created (and continued to expand), however, was a Macedonian Empire—the Persian Empire died in 330 B.C.E. with its last Achaemenid king.

SUGGESTIONS FOR FURTHER READING AND INFORMATION

Internet Sites

General information on ancient Persia (Iran): http://www.art-arena.com/history.html

Texts from ancient Persia: http://www.fordham.edu/halsall/ancient/asbook05.html

A paper on "Changing Perceptions of Achaemenid Art": http://www.oakland.edu/_jkristen/html/ahpapers/pers/persian.htm

Books and Articles

Persian History and Culture

Brosius, Maria. *Women in Ancient Persia, 559–331 BC.* Oxford and New York: Oxford University Press, 1996.

The Cambridge History of Iran, Volume II: *The Median and Achaemenian Periods.* Cambridge and New York: Cambridge University Press, 1985.

Cook, J. M. *The Persian Empire.* New York: Schocken Books, 1983.

Curtis, John. *Ancient Persia.* Cambridge, MA: Harvard University Press, 1990.

Dandamaev, M. A. *Political History of the Achaemenid Empire.* Translated by W. J. Vogelsang. Leiden and New York: E. J. Brill, 1989.

———, and V. G. Lukonin. *The Cultural and Social Institutions of Ancient Iran.* Cambridge: Cambridge University Press, 1989.

Frye, Richard N. *The History of Ancient Iran.* Munich: C. H. Beck, 1984.

Hoglund, K. G. *Achaemenid Imperial Administration in Syria-Palestine and the Missions of Ezra and Nehemiah.* Society of Biblical Literature Dissertation Series 125. Atlanta: Scholars Press, 1992.

Hole, Frank, ed. *The Archaeology of Western Iran.* Washington, D.C.: Smithsonian Institution Press, 1987.

Roaf, Michael. *Sculptures and Sculptors at Persepolis.* London: British Institute for Persian Studies, 1983.

Sancisi-Weerdenburg, H., and Amélie Kuhrt, eds. *The Greek Sources: Achaemenid History Workshop.* 3 vols. Leiden: Netherlands Organization for Scientific Research, 1987–1988.

Schmandt-Besserat, Denise, ed. *Ancient Persia, the Art of an Empire.* Malibu, CA: Undena, 1980.

Sekunda, N., and S. Chew. *The Persian Army, 560–330 BC.* Osprey Military Elite Series, No. 42. London: Osprey Publishing Company, 1992.

Zoroastrianism

Boyce, Mary. *A History of Zoroastrianism.* 3 vols. Leiden: E. J. Brill, 1975–1991.

———, ed. and translator. *Textual Sources for the Study of Zoroastrianism.* Texts and Sources for the Study of Religion. Totowa, NJ: Barnes & Noble, 1984.

———. *Zoroastrianism: Its Antiquity and Constant Vigour.* Costa Mesa, CA: Mazda, 1992.

Malandra, William W., ed. and translator. *An Introduction to Ancient Iranian Religion: Readings from the Avesta and Achaemenid Inscriptions.* Minneapolis: University of Minnesota Press, 1983.

Nigosian, S. A. *The Zoroastrian Faith: Tradition and Modern Research.* Montreal: McGill-Queen's University Press, 1993.

Greece and Judah

Cohn, Norman. *Cosmos, Chaos and the World to Come: The Ancient Roots of Apocalyptic Faith.* New Haven, CT: Yale University Press, 1993.

Davies, D., and L. Finkelstein, eds. *The Cambridge History of Judaism,* Volume I: *The Persian Period.* Cambridge and New York: Cambridge University Press, 1984.

Demand, Nancy. *A History of Ancient Greece.* New York: McGraw-Hill, 1996.

Pomeroy, Sarah B., Stanley M. Burstein, Walter Donlan, and Jennifer Tolbert Roberts. *Ancient Greece: A Political, Social, and Cultural History.* Oxford and New York: Oxford University Press, 1999.

Stern, Ephraim. *Archaeology of the Land of the Bible,* vol. II: *The Assyrian, Babylonian and Persian Periods (732–332 B.C.E.),* The Anchor Bible Reference Library. New York: Doubleday, 2001.

———. *Material Culture of the Land of the Bible in the Persian Period.* Warminster, UK: Aris and Phillips, 1982.

NOTES

1. This translation by the author is based on A. Leo Oppenheim's translation in James B. Pritchard, ed., *Ancient Near Eastern Texts Relating to the Old Testament,* 2nd ed. (Princeton, NJ: Princeton University Press, 1955), pp. 315–316 as well as that in Victor H. Matthews and Don C. Benjamin, *Old Testament Parallels: Laws and Stories from the Ancient Near East* (New York/Mahwah, NJ: Paulist Press, 1991), pp. 147–150.

2. See the evidence cited in J. M. Cook, *The Persian Empire* (New York: Schocken Books, 1983), pp. 48–49 and Amélie Kuhrt, *The Ancient Near East, c. 3000–330 BC* (London and New York: Routledge, 1995), vol. II, pp. 662–664.

3. See, for example, Cook (1983), pp. 50–53; Michael Roaf, *Cultural Atlas of Mesopotamia and the Ancient Near East* (Oxford and New York: Equinox and Facts on File, 1990), p. 207; Kuhrt (1995), pp. 664–666.

4. Cook (1983), p. 68.

5. For information on the decipherment of cuneiform and the rediscovery of ancient Mesopotamia see Brian M. Fagan, *Return to Babylon: Travelers, Archeologists and Monuments of Mesopotamia* (Boston and Toronto: Little, Brown and Company, 1979); William H. Stiebing, Jr., *Uncovering the Past: A History of Archaeology* (Buffalo, NY: Prometheus Books, 1993; paperback: Oxford University Press, 1994), pp. 85–118; C. B. F. Walker, "Cuneiform," *Reading the Past: Ancient Writing from Cuneiform to the Alphabet* (New York: Barnes and Noble, 1998), pp. 58–62 (Walker's section of this book was originally published in 1987 by the British Museum as a separate work entitled *Cuneiform*).

6. *Histories,* VIII. 98. This translation is based on those of George Rawlinson, *The History of Herodotus* (New York: Tudor Publishing Co., 1956), p. 461; Jim Hicks, *The Persians* (New York: Time-Life Books, 1975), p. 57; and Cook (1983), p. 108.

7. See, for example, R. C. Zaehner, *The Dawn and Twilight of Zoroastrianism* (New York: G. P. Putnam's Sons, 1961), p. 33.

8. It was once thought that Sheshbazzar was identical with Shenazzar, a descendant of Jehoiachin, mentioned in I Chronicles 3:18, but that identification has been challenged on linguistic grounds and is now rejected by most scholars. See Peter Ackroyd, "Israel in the Exilic and Post-Exilic Periods," in G. W. Anderson, ed., *Tradition and Interpretation* (Oxford: Clarendon Press, 1979), p. 331 and note 35. In Hebrew, the word translated "prince" means "leader," not necessarily a member of the Davidic line.

9. In the books of Ezra (3:2, 8; 5:2), Nehemiah (12:1), and Haggai (1:1, 12, 14; 2:2, 23), Zerubbabel is designated the son of Shealtiel, while I Chronicles 3:19 states that Pedaiah was his father. However they solve this discrepancy,

most scholars have been willing to accept the premise that Zerubbabel *was* of Davidic lineage. See, for example, Bryan E. Beyer, "Zerubbabel," in David N. Freedman, editor-in-chief, *The Anchor Bible Dictionary* (New York: Doubleday, 1992), vol. 6, p. 1085. On the other hand, a few argue that he probably was not of the royal line and that the two different genealogies were created to give him Davidic lineage and connect him directly with pre-exilic Judah. For this view, see J. Maxwell Miller and John Hayes, *A History of Ancient Israel and Judah* (Philadelphia: Westminister Press, 1986), p. 456.

10. Bernhard Anderson, *Understanding the Old Testament*, 4th ed. (Englewood Cliffs, NJ: Prentice Hall, 1986), p. 517.

11. For a discussion of the three major positions and the arguments for and against each, see John Bright, *A History of Israel*, 3rd ed. (Philadelphia: Westminster Press, 1981), "Excursus II: The Date of Ezra's Mission to Jerusalem," pp. 391–402. See also Ralph W. Klein, "Ezra-Nehemiah, Books of" in David N. Freedman, editor-in-chief, *The Anchor Bible Dictionary*, vol. 2, pp. 735–737, and Eric M. Meyers' revision of James D. Purvis, "Exile and Return: From the Babylonian Destruction to the Reconstruction of the Jewish State" in Hershel Shanks, ed., *Ancient Israel*, rev. ed. (Washington, D.C. and Upper Saddle River, NJ: Biblical Archaeology Society and Prentice Hall, 1999), pp. 221–229.

12. See, for example, Anderson (1986), pp. 527–530.

13. See Eric M. Meyers's revision of Purvis in Hershel Shanks, ed. (1999), pp. 223–224. The list of Judaism's "famous men" is found in Sirach 44–50 (note especially 49:11–13).

14. See, for example, Miller and Hayes (1986), p. 468–469.

15. The translation is by H. L. Ginsberg in Pritchard, ed. (1955), pp. 491–492. Explanatory material in square brackets was added by W. Stiebing.

11

The Legacy of the Ancient Near East

FOOD, DRINK, AND ANIMALS

Though the discovery of agriculture and domestication of animals also occurred in other areas, the Near Eastern agricultural revolution produced most of the domesticated crops and animals still used in the West today. The basic varieties of wheat, barley, peas, and lentils, as well as many nuts (such as almonds, pistachios, acorns, and walnuts) and fruits and berries (including grapes, apples, apricots, dates, lemons, figs, pomegranates, mulberries, and juniper berries) had been domesticated in the Near East by c. 6000 B.C.E. Furthermore, ancient Near Easterners developed many of the food products made from these plants, especially bread, cakes, raisins, soups, and porridges. The Near East also passed to the West some crops like rice and cotton originally domesticated in India or points further east.

Two of the most important food products made from domesticated plants were intoxicating beverages—beer and wine. The discovery of fermentation probably happened accidentally from observation of food stored in damp conditions that fostered this process. Nevertheless, from very early times people were using grain to produce beer and grapes to make wine. Ancient Near Eastern beer was made by grinding barley or wheat into flour, leavening it, and kneading it into loaves that were heated until fully risen. The loaves were then broken apart and placed in a jar, water was added, and the two were mixed until the liquid was the right consistency. It was then allowed to ferment. Malt was not used in making Near Eastern beer. Eventually the fermented liquid would be carefully poured off, leaving most of the dregs in the bottom of the jar. Even so, enough sediment usually remained in the final product that the beer was drunk with a straw (a metal tube) or filtered through a strainer (usually built into the spout of the beer jug). Wine was produced much as it is today, by stomping grapes in a tub to mash them and produce liquid, then pouring off the liquid and allowing it to ferment. Wine also was strained before being drunk in order to remove any grape residue. In Egypt, wine jars were labeled with the source and date of the vintage, just as today.

Ancient Near Eastern peoples also first domesticated the animals most commonly used in the West. These domesticated animals include our primary pets—cats and dogs—food animals such as cattle, pigs, sheep, goats, ducks, and geese; and working animals such as horses, donkeys, mules, and oxen. Early Near Eastern farmers and herders also derived milk and eggs from their domesticated animals and learned to make cheese, butter, and yogurt from cow and goat milk. Moreover, they domesticated bees to produce honey for sweetening beverages (including some types of beer), cakes, and other products.

MATHEMATICS AND SCIENCE

Some of the most crucial contributions of the ancient Near Eastern civilizations were in the area of mathematics and science (including technology and engineering). The contributions of ancient Greece in these fields are usually recognized, but Greek mathematics and science were based on elements borrowed from the Near East, especially Mesopotamia. As we saw in Chapter 2, the Mesopotamians used a mathematical system based on 60, so they divided the day into 12 "double hours" of equal length (60 "double minutes" each). In the Hellenistic Period (the era after Alexander the Great's death), Greek astronomers borrowed the idea of dividing the day and night into hours of equal length, but instead of 12 "double hours" they used 24 "single" hours of 60 "single" minutes each. Mesopotamians also divided circles into 360 degrees, another element borrowed by the Greeks. We still use these divisions, even though our mathematical system is a decimal system, based on 10 rather than 60.

Mesopotamian mathematicians knew the principle of the Pythagorean Theorem a millennium before Pythagoras, and they could solve the problems of Euclidian geometry more than a thousand years before Euclid. They did not, however, devise abstract theorems the way the Greeks did. On the other hand, as mentioned in Chapter 2, they created tables of square roots, cube roots, reciprocals, and cubic equations, as well as more common multiplication and division tables. The most important aspect of Mesopotamian mathematics was the fact that, unlike Greek and Roman numerical systems, it utilized a place notational system. In Roman numerals, placing the sign for 1 before the sign for 10 (IX) indicated "9"

(10 − 1), and 1 after a 10 (XI) equals "11" (10 + 1). It is very difficult to multiply and divide with such a system, especially when the numbers are large. In the Mesopotamian system, the sign for 1 and for 60 are the same, so a 1 before a 10 would be 70, not 9. The signs for 2, 4 and 9, written in that sequence (II IV IX), could not be read as a single number in the Roman system—it would not make sense. In the Mesopotamian system, though, the signs 2, 4, 9 would stand for $(2 \times 60) + (4 \times 60) + 9 = 7,449$. This system seems to have been taken to India during the Persian Period, and the Indians converted it to a base-ten system and added the sign for zero. Because of their place notational system, Mesopotamians were able to solve many complex algebraic equations, and this aspect of mathematics seems to have been taken east as well. The Arabs later borrowed the Indian notational system, further developed algebra (to which they gave its name, *al-jebr*, "the reunion of broken parts"), and passed both on to the West along with Arabic numerals. We are still using them today.

Mesopotamian mathematical astronomy and horoscopic astrology have also had a great impact on Western thought. Babylonians were keeping astronomical records of the movements of heavenly bodies before 1600 B.C.E., and by Assyrian and Neo-Babylonian times they were predicting solar and lunar eclipses. They used a lunar calendar with alternating months of 29 and 30 days, making the year only 354 days long. In early times, though, they recognized that the solar year was some 11 days longer, so once every three years or so they added an extra month to keep their lunar year somewhat synchronized with the solar year. By the mid-eighth century B.C.E., Babylonian astronomers had worked out the exact length of the solar year and created a calendar that required adding an extra lunar month sometimes after three years and other times after two years, so that seven months were added every 19 years. By the fourth century B.C.E., this intercalation was being done automatically using a mathematical formula instead of having to be ordered by the king. This extremely accurate Mesopotamian lunar calendar was borrowed by the Jews during the Exile and is still the basis for both the Jewish and Christian religious calendars.

At the same time, Egyptians were creating a 365-day-long solar-year calendar. During the Hellenistic Age, Greek scholars in Alexandria, using astronomical data developed in Babylonia, recognized that the solar year was just slightly less than 365¼ days long. So, they added a leap year to the Egyptian calendar, making every fourth year 366 days long. This calendar was introduced into Rome by Julius Caesar in 45 B.C.E., and with only a small change made by astronomers for Pope Gregory XIII in the sixteenth century C.E., it is the calendar we use today.°

Mesopotamian astronomy arose out of the need to understand celestial omens relating to the future of the country or king, so it was always bound up with astrology. Babylonians eventually created the astrological zodiac with its 12 divisions, and by Persian times, they were using the signs of the zodiac and the positions of certain stars at birth to chart horoscopes for individuals. The Magi, members of the Median priestly class who became Zoroastrian priests, learned astronomy and astrology from the Babylonians and became very proficient in these subjects during the Persian Empire. After the Macedonian conquest of the Near East, Hellenistic Greek scholars grew to respect the expertise of the Magi and from them learned Mesopotamian astronomy and astrology. The Greeks continued to advance both these fields and passed them on to the West. They also borrowed the words *magos* (singular) and *magoi* (plural), using them to refer to astronomers or astrologers in particular, or to very wise or learned men in general. Thus, the Gospel of Matthew refers to *magoi* (or Magi, using the Latinized spelling), individuals in the East (Mesopotamia or Persia?) who see a new star at Jesus' birth and recognize its significance. Our words "magic" and "magician" also derive from the Greek use of *magos/magoi*.

Near Eastern technology and engineering were also influential. Plows and other agricultural implements were first developed in the Near East, as were the techniques for throwing pottery on a potter's wheel and firing it in a kiln, producing bronze (and later iron) artifacts, and making and dyeing wool cloth. This technology quickly spread throughout the Mediterranean world. People in neighboring regions also learned the surveying and engineering skills necessary for creating elaborate irrigation systems from Near Eastern societies. Other techniques for producing glass, perfumes, and special dyes were more closely guarded, so their influence outside the region where they were created is difficult to determine. One often-ignored Near Eastern export is military techniques and equipment. The armament, training, and tactics of the Assyrian infantry was borrowed by peoples in Asia Minor who passed them on to the Greeks. There, these elements were used to create the Greek hoplite armies that played a significant role in overthrowing aristocracies and replacing them with tyrants within Ionia and Greece. Tyrannies, in turn, eventually gave way to oligarchies and, in some instances, democracies.

The engineering and building achievements of the Egyptians and Babylonians amazed and inspired the Greeks and Romans. Many ancient writers considered the great walls of Babylon and the "Hanging Gardens" wonders of the world. In addition, the Pyramids of Giza were on *all* the Greco-Roman lists of wonders of the ancient world. These huge walls, buildings, and stone structures, as well as the monumental temples at Thebes in Egypt, spurred other ancient cultures to strive to emulate Near Eastern greatness when constructing their own buildings and monuments.

LANGUAGE AND LITERATURE

Modern Hebrew, Arabic, and Iranian are living descendants of ancient Near Eastern languages (though Hebrew had to be revived as a common spoken tongue). Aramaic and Coptic (a derivative of ancient Egyptian) are still used for religious rites in some communities. Other languages, including Sumerian, Akkadian, Elamite, Hittite, and Hurrian, died out in antiquity or during the Middle Ages and had to be

---

°Since the solar year is actually 365 days, 5 hours, 48 minutes and 42 seconds long instead of the 365 days, 6 hours of the Julian calendar, adding an extra day every four years over centuries got the calendrical date ahead of the solar year. The Gregorian calendar solved this problem by dropping ten days in 1582 and then decreeing that years ending in hundreds be leap years only if divisible by 400.

rediscovered in modern times. Nevertheless, the impact of Near Eastern thought and culture on the West can be gauged in part by the large number of words from these early cultures that have been passed down into our modern speech. The derivation of "magic" and related words from the Iranian Magi has already been mentioned. Our word "abyss" comes from Greek *abussos*, which derives from *absu* (or *abzu* or *apsu*), the Sumerian and Akkadian term for the "Deep," the waters on which the earth floats. In addition, as one might suspect, many current names for places and geographical features in the Near East are derived from their Near Eastern originals, usually through Greek versions of the earlier names. For example, Tigris comes from the Greek version of Sumerian *Idiglat* and Euphrates from the Greek attempt to represent the Akkadian *Purattu*, which in turn goes back to Sumerian *Buranun*. Other words were borrowed along with the objects or materials they represented: adobe (from the Spanish for "mud-brick" through Arabic *at-tub* from Akkadian *tub* and Sumerian *dub*); ebony (through Greek *ebenos* from Egyptian *hebni*); jasper (through Greek *iaspis* from Akkadian *yashpu*); myrrh (through Greek *murra* from *murru*, a word common to most Semitic languages); naphtha (through *naphthos*, a Greek word for petroleum from Persian *naft* from, in turn, Akkadian *naptu*); natron (through Greek *nitron* from Egyptian *netri*); saffron (through Arabic *za'faran* from Sumerian and Akkadian *azupiranu*). This list is only a sample of the many words (and products) we have borrowed from the ancient Near Eastern cultures.

Naturally, the literature produced in these ancient languages has had considerably more impact than the languages themselves. The Bible, of course, stands head and shoulders above all other ancient works in terms of its influence on later cultures even when its religious importance is ignored and it is considered only as a literary work. Some knowledge of the Bible is necessary for proper appreciation of many works of Western literature because they make frequent allusions to its phrases or stories. Many expressions or idioms such as "the face of the earth," "valley of the shadow of death," or "am I my brother's keeper?" have become part of the English language

from the seventeenth century King James (or Authorized) translation of the Bible.

Many other Near Eastern works continued to affect later thought through the Bible (which they had influenced). Some, though, had a more direct effect on later cultures. The Mesopotamian flood story was borrowed not only by the biblical tradition, but also probably lies behind the ancient Greek traditions about Deucalion's flood. The accounts of Gilgamesh's exploits in the Mesopotamian *Epic of Gilgamesh*, passed on to Hittites and others, probably influenced Greek traditions about Heracles (Hercules). Mesopotamian accounts of the origins of the gods, filtered through Hurrian and Hittite versions, influenced the Greek poet Hesiod's *Theogony* (written c. 700 B.C.E.).

Finally, the element that makes all literature possible—writing—the West owes to the ancient Near East. The alphabet used in most Western countries goes back to the Latin alphabet, which was borrowed from the Etruscans who got it from the Greeks. The Cyrillic alphabet used in some eastern European nations descends directly from Greek. The Greeks got their alphabet from the Phoenicians who received it from their Canaanite ancestors who developed it from Egyptian hieroglyphs. Egyptian hieroglyphs may themselves have been partially inspired by Sumerian cuneiform, the first known writing system.

MUSIC, ART, AND ARCHITECTURE

We have few details about ancient music, but what we do know indicates that the roots of Greek and other Western scales and music theory were fed from the ancient Near East. The reconstructed harps and lyres from the "royal tombs" of Ur and representations of similar instruments in art seem to indicate that even in Early Dynastic Sumer (c. 2900 to 2300 B.C.E.), seven-tone and eight-tone scales were known. The modern major scale was known by at least the Old Babylonian Period (c. 2000 to 1600 B.C.E.) and probably earlier. Two Mesopotamian tablets provide the names for the lyre strings and numbers for the intervals between them. Thus, the mathematical relationships between the notes of the scale were already recognized in the Near East before 500 B.C.E. It is now clear that Pythagoras was speaking nothing but the plain truth when he claimed that he learned his mathematics and music (as well as the relationship between them) in the Near East. Two other tablets give instructions for tuning stringed instruments and the names of seven different tunings or scales. So it is probable that even the various Greek scales or modes had already developed in the Near East before taking root in Greece. Moreover, a c. 1400 B.C.E. tablet found at Ugarit has proved to be a piece of "sheet music" recording the melody, harmony, and words of a Hurrian cult song.[1] Before this discovery, it was thought that the practice of noting both the tone for the melody and one for the harmonic accompaniment arose only during the Middle Ages.

Greek art and architecture, major influences on later Western cultures, borrowed many elements from the Near East. The Ionic style capital for columns was derived from "Proto-Aeolic" capitals used in Palestine and Syria around 900 B.C.E. The derivation of Greek fluting (the grooves cut into the sides of columns) from Mesopotamian or Egyptian bundles of reeds used in early buildings, however, is questionable. The Greek Corinthian "orientalizing" style of pottery (c. 750 to 650 B.C.E.) used motifs borrowed from Asia Minor, Syria, Phoenicia, and Mesopotamia. At the same time, Greek statues were being modeled on those of Egypt. The Archaic Greek depictions of young men stand rigidly, one leg stepping forward, arms straight down at the sides and the fists clenched against the thighs just as in Egyptian portrait statues. These poorly proportioned, stiff imitations gradually developed into the beautiful naturalistic Greek sculptures of classical times.

RELIGION AND SPECULATIVE THOUGHT

All of the above are significant contributions of the ancient Near East to modern civilization, but with the possible exception of writing, the Near East's greatest impact, by far, has been in the realm of religion and speculative thought. The Near East produced the three great monotheistic faiths of modern times—Judaism, Christianity and Islam., The roots of all three go back into antiquity. As we have seen, Judaism was in large part a product of its ancient Near Eastern environment, and it was influenced by the concepts, stories, and practices of other cultures, especially those of Mesopotamia and Canaan. The Zoroastrian-influenced eschatological Judaism of late Persian and Hellenistic times, in turn, gave rise to Christianity.

Not only was Zoroastrian eschatology incorporated into early Christianity through Judaism, but also through Mithraism, a Roman-era religion developed out of the earlier Persian faith that became Christianity's chief rival in the first three centuries C.E. From Mithraism, the Church borrowed the concept of Purgatory (which is not found in the Bible), as well as December 25th as the date for Jesus' birthday and the tradition that he was born in a cave. The solar cycle was an important part of sun worship in antiquity, and thus came to be central to Mithraism. The Divine Sun (Mithras) reaches the peak of its power at the summer solstice, June 21st, then begins to wane in the fall. It succumbs to its enemies at the winter solstice, December 21st, and dies. The period of daylight is shortest at this time of year and the night is longest. Darkness has triumphed over light. For about three days, the sun seems to rise and set in about the same place and the days remain short. Then, from December 25th onward, the sun seems to regain its vigor. It gradually gets higher each day and the hours of daylight lengthen until they once again reach their peak at the summer solstice. Thus, December 25th was the day on which Mithras, also known as *Sol Invictus* ("the Unconquerable Sun"), was born. Since the myth is cyclical, it is also the day on which he rose from the dead after dying on December 21st. Moreover, Mithras supposedly came into existence in a cave by springing directly from a rock, attended only by Persian shepherds. When the emperor Constantine became a Christian in the fourth century C.E. and placed Christianity in a favored position, Christians did what they could to destroy or replace the previous religions. One way they accomplished that goal was by appropriating pagan places of worship. Christian churches were built over many formerly pagan shrines, especially ones used for the worship of Mithras. Archaeologists have found several Mithraic "caves" under early Christian churches in Rome. Christians also borrowed the birthday of Mithras to commemorate the birthday of Jesus. By so doing, they made the birthday of the Sun into the birthday of the Son (of God) whom they regarded as the true "sun of righteousness" mentioned in Old Testament prophecy (Malachi 4:2).

Though Islam did not come into being until the seventh century C.E., during the Western medieval period, Muhammad and his followers recognized the continuity between Islam and the Judeo-Christian tradition. The god who revealed himself to Muhammad was the same god worshipped by Jews and Christians. Muslims believed Muhammad's revelations to be the last, most complete, and perfect ones delivered to humans by God, but they did not deny that he had given earlier revelations to Abraham (the father of both Jews and Arabs), Moses, and Jesus. Today the majority of the world's population either practices one of these three religions or exists in a culture that has been largely shaped by one or more of them.

Finally, it has been customary to associate a logical, rational approach to the world with the Greeks and a mythopoeic ("myth-making") view that understands the world only through myth or religion with the earlier Near Eastern civilizations. While there is some truth to this distinction, it has often been overemphasized and made too absolute. Most Greeks and Romans retained mythopoeic thought patterns long after the development of Greek philosophy and its offshoot, science—for that matter, so do modern Christians, Jews, Muslims, and other believers in revealed truth. Even Greek philosophers did not totally abandon myth in their quest to understand the world. "All things are full of gods" is one of the only statements attributed to Thales of Miletus, the first Greek philosopher, who seems to have used the concept of a world-soul to explain change and motion.[2] Other pre-Socratic philosophers saw strife or attraction and repulsion as the means by which the world came into being and functioned, ideas that may have developed from contact with Zoroastrian dualism. Even Plato used myths in many of his dialogues to introduce concepts that could not be presented otherwise. On the other hand, while the people of the ancient Near East explained the world in terms of myth, they could also be logical and rational in their approach to individual problems. Their scientific observations of the motion of heavenly bodies, the rise of the Nile and other natural events, and their logical approach to mathematics and engineering provided the foundation upon which Greeks could construct their theories and generalizations. In the end, the two opposing forces in modern thought, logic and science on the one hand and religions which rely on revealed truth on the other, are both rooted in the ancient Near East, the cradle of Western civilization.

SUGGESTIONS FOR FURTHER READING AND INFORMATION

Hallo, William W. *Origins: The Ancient Near Eastern Background of Some Modern Western Institutions.* Leiden: E. J. Brill, 1996.

Mitchell, T. C., ed. *Music and Civilization.* British Museum Yearbook 4. London: British Museum Press, 1974.

Neugebauer, Otto. *The Exact Sciences in Antiquity.* New York: Harper and Row, 1962.

———. *A History of Ancient Mathematical Astronomy.* 3 vols. Studies in the History of Mathematics and Physical Sciences 1. Berlin: Springer Verlag, 1975.

Van der Waerden, F. *Science Awakening.* London and New York: Oxford University Press, 1961.

NOTES

1. See "World's Oldest Musical Notation Deciphered on Cuneiform Tablet," *Biblical Archaeology Review*, vol. 6, no. 5 (September/October 1980), pp. 14–25. The song was recorded using replicas of ancient instruments on *Sounds from Silence,* BIT ENKI Publications and Records, Berkeley, CA.

2. See F. M. Cornford, *From Religion to Philosophy* (New York: Harper Torchbooks, 1957), pp. 127–129.

Glossary

Absolute chronology—A dating system in which years are counted forward and backward from a specific event. The absolute chronology used in the West is based on the supposed year when Jesus of Nazareth was born.

Afro-Asiatic—A designation for a family of languages that includes Berber, ancient Egyptian, Cushite, and other generally North African languages in addition to the Semitic languages such as Hebrew and Arabic.

Akh—The Egyptian term for a transfigured or glorified spirit of light in the afterlife. A person who through burial rites is transformed into an *akh* is an effective being in the other world just as he or she was in this one. The word was also used to describe a son who performed rites to transform his dead father into a blessed spirit or for a person who performed pious rites for the good of the gods.

Akhet—Normally translated "horizon," this Egyptian word means much more. It is the home of light located between the horizon and the underworld, and the place where a dead person becomes an *akh*, a potent inhabitant of the world beyond death. Each day, the sun is transformed this way as it rises and sets.

Akkadian—A term used for the dynasty of Sargon of Akkad and its era, and for the Semitic language of ancient Mesopotamia that Sargon spoke. The principle dialects of the Akkadian language were Babylonian and Assyrian.

Amarna—The modern name for the location of the Egyptian king Akhenaton's capital city, Akhetaton ("Horizon of the Aton," or better, "Place of the Transformation of the Solar Orb"). As an adjective, it refers to anything having to do with the reign of Akhenaton and his immediate successors.

Amarna Letters—A collection of letters written in Akkadian on clay tablets found in the ruins of Akhenaton's city at El-Amarna in central Egypt. These documents are correspondence to the Egyptian pharaoh from the rulers of other major powers and from vassal rulers of city-states in Syria and Palestine. Most of the letters belong to the reign of Akhenaton, but a few come from the last years of Amenhotep III, and a few extend into the reign of Tutankhamun.

Amorites—People speaking a West Semitic language who originally seem to have been seminomads settled primarily in southern Syria along the western fringes of Mesopotamia. Around 2000 B.C.E. large numbers of them moved into Mesopotamia, western Syria, and Palestine.

Anatolia—Another term for Asia Minor.

Arabah—The valley that runs from the southern end of the Dead Sea to the northern end of the Gulf of Aqaba.

Artifact—Anything that has been made, altered, or used by humans or which owes its position in space to humans.

Aryans—This is the native Iranian and Indian (Vedic) term the Indo-European speakers who invaded Iran and India after (or, some would say, in conjunction with) the collapse of the Indus civilization applied to themselves. In fact, it is the source of the place name "Iran" which means "land of the Aryans." Like "Indo-European," it is a linguistic term, not a racial or ethnic one, despite its misuse by nineteenth- and twentieth-century racists.

Asia Minor—The large peninsula that is the Asiatic part of modern Turkey. It is bounded on the north by the Black Sea, on the west by the Bosporus, Sea of Marmora, Dardanelles, and Aegean Sea, and on the south by the Mediterranean Sea.

Assemblage—In archaeology, this term designates a group of objects found in association with one another and believed to be of the same date and to belong to one group of people.

Ba—In Egyptian belief, a spiritual element of a person that expressed his personality and power. After death, the *ba* could move about freely, even beyond the tomb.

C.—An abbreviation for the Latin word *circa* meaning "about" or "approximately."

Carbon-14 dating—See **Radiocarbon dating**.

Cartouche—An oval design surrounding each of the last two of the five names of Egyptian pharaohs. Cartouches were also sometimes placed around the names of queens and gods.

Cataract—A term used for a place in the Nile where there are rapids or small waterfalls.

Cenotaph—An empty tomb or other monument created to honor the memory of a dead person whose remains are buried elsewhere.

Co-regency—A period when two rulers shared the throne. Co-regencies were often utilized during the Egyptian Middle and New Kingdoms. When a pharaoh was growing old or feeble he might name someone (usually his son) as co-regent (or co-ruler) to help maintain control and make the succession easier.

Corvée—A term (derived from pre-revolutionary France) that refers to temporary forced labor which citizens had to perform for the state. Corvée labor was used to build most ancient Near Eastern monuments such as Mesopotamian ziggurats or Egyptian pyramids.

Cosmology—Stories and/or ideas relating to the structure and origins of the universe.

Cuneiform—A writing system consisting of signs composed of "wedge-shaped" elements. It was first developed in southern Mesopotamia to write Sumerian, but it was adapted to write other languages as well, including Akkadian, Elamite, Hittite, and Persian. It was generally written on clay tablets, but could be carved into stone, as well.

Cylinder seal—A carved or engraved small stone or metal cylinder that was rolled over wet clay to leave an impression of its design. It was usually used in place of a signature on documents or to indicate ownership of objects.

Dendrochronology—Tree-ring dating. By comparing groups of wide and narrow tree rings, scholars have been able to connect modern sequences of rings with those in old stumps and even older logs and beams to create a tree-ring sequence that stretches back more than 6,000 years.

Determinatives—"Silent" signs in ancient cuneiform and hieroglyphic writing systems that were meant to clarify the meaning of a word, often by indicating its category ("god," "man," "wooden object," "action verb," etc.).

Deuteronomistic History—This work of biblical historiography by an unknown author consists of the books of Joshua, Judges, First and Second Samuel, and First and Second Kings, plus a narrative bridge connecting the book of Deuteronomy to its beginning. It was inspired by the book of Deuteronomy and judges Judean and Israelite rulers by how well or poorly they followed the commands laid down in Deuteronomy, especially those forbidding worship of other gods and prohibiting worship anywhere but in the Jerusalem Temple.

Divination—The act of determining a god's will by interpreting omens or signs (such as lightning flashes in the sky, directions of flights of birds, folds in an animal's liver, etc.).

Dry Farming—Farming that is dependent upon rainfall alone to water the crops.

Dynasty—A succession of rulers from the same bloodline or family. This term can also be used for the period during which one such family ruled (as is often true for references in Egyptian history).

El-Amarna—See **Amarna**.

Electrum—An alloy of gold and silver that was highly prized in antiquity. It was harder and stronger than pure gold.

Eschatology—Doctrines or teachings about "the End" or "Final Things" (*eschaton* in Greek). These teachings usually include concepts of the end of this world and an afterlife in a world to come.

Eunuch—A castrated male. In the ancient Near East, eunuchs usually served as harem attendants or palace officials.

Golden Horus name—The third of an Egyptian king's names. Its significance is not known.

Hatti—The designation generally used by ancient Near Eastern peoples for both the Hittite kingdom and the Hittite people. Scholars use it today primarily for the Hittite territory in central Anatolia around Hattusas and also as a designation for the entire Hittite Empire.

Heb-sed—An Egyptian rite usually translated "Jubilee Festival." It was usually celebrated by a pharaoh after he had been on the throne for 30 years. It renewed his vitality and magically repeated both the creation of the world and pharaoh's enthronement as ruler of Upper and Lower Egypt.

Hieroglyphic—A writing system developed in Egypt that primarily uses pictures of objects as its signs for words or sounds. This term is also applied to other forms of picture-like writing, such as that which the Hittites developed in Asia Minor.

Horus name—The first of five names usually used by ancient Egyptian rulers. It presented the pharaoh as the earthly incarnation of Horus, a sun god who avenged his dead father Osiris and became the legitimate ruler of Egypt.

Hypostyle hall—A colonnaded roofed room, usually quite large, that stood between an open court and the main shrine in an Egyptian temple. The papyrus and lotus-shaped columns represented the plants of the primeval marsh from which the first mound of earth (the higher land under the temple's shrine), the source of all creation, had emerged.

Ideogram—A written sign or symbol that represents a complete word or idea. Such characters are also sometimes called logograms or ideographs. When the sign is a drawing of the object represented, it is usually called a pictograph.

Incipient cultivation—A term used for the practice of saving and planting seeds of wild plants that once had been simply gathered and consumed. It is thought that this practice preceded and led to the domestication of plants in the Near East.

Incipient herding—This term is used for the assumed practice of driving groups of wild animals into pens and keeping many of them there for some time before killing and eating them. It is thought that people selected the young to eat, thus allowing the older animals to breed in captivity. The familiarity between humans and animals resulting from this practice may have led to domestication of animals.

Indo-European—A designation for a family of languages that includes Vedic, Sanskrit, Hindi (and many other languages of India), Persian (and other Iranian languages), Hittite (and several other ancient languages of Asia Minor), as well as the various groups of European languages. It is a linguistic, not a racial or ethnic, term.

Inundation—The term used for a Nile flood in Egypt. It also denoted a season in the Egyptian calendar: the time when the Nile was in flood, usually July through October.

Ka—In Egyptian thought, the "life-force" or "animating spirit" of an individual. The *ka* was an individual's spiritual double that gave his body motion and vitality.

Kush—The name for the area and kingdom on the Nile in Nubia, south of the second cataract. Its kings ruled Egypt as the Twenty-fifth Dynasty.

Lapis lazuli—A beautiful royal-blue stone found mainly in Afghanistan. It was the most desired "precious" stone in the ancient Near East and was used for jewelry and decorative inlay, especially in Mesopotamia.

Levant—A term for the Mediterranean's eastern coastal region between Egypt and Turkey. This geographical area comprises Syria west of the Euphrates River, Lebanon, Israel, and western Jordan.

Limmu—An official in Assyria who gave his name to the year and probably conducted religious rites as well. There was a different *limmu* for each year, and lists of these officials formed a chronology for Assyria.

Logogram—See **Ideogram.**

Lower Egypt—The Nile Delta area north of Cairo.

Ma'at—The ancient Egyptian word for "truth, order, balance, harmony," that is, "everything in its rightful place." The Egyptians personalized *Ma'at* as a goddess, the daughter of Re, maintained and supported by pharaoh and the other deities.

Magi—Members of a special priestly tribe or class among the Medes who eventually became the priestly class within the Zoroastrian religion.

Mail—A type of body armor, usually a shirt, made either of small interlocked metal rings or overlapping metal plates.

Matriarchy—Literally, "mother-rule." This term is applied to a society or family dominated or ruled by a woman or women.

Me—In Mesopotamia, these were the divine powers or rules that allowed the gods' perfect plan or design for every activity, office, institution, piece of equipment, and even each attitude and belief to be implemented or realized in the world.

Mesopotamia—Greek for "between the rivers." This name is used for the Tigris and Euphrates River valleys and the region between them, essentially modern-day Iraq and eastern Syria.

Nebty **name**—The "two Ladies" name of an Egyptian pharaoh. It was usually the second of five names used by a king and represented him as the embodiment of the patron goddesses (the "two Ladies") of Upper and Lower Egypt.

Negev—The dry southern part of Palestine that stretched from just north of Beersheba to the Gulf of Aqaba and the desert of Sinai on the south. This word is also sometimes written Negeb.

New Year Festival—A spring celebration held annually in Mesopotamia during which it was believed that the gods established the destinies of individuals and states for the coming year. This festival also came to include the originally separate *Akiti* or *Akitu* agricultural celebrations and the Sacred Marriage ceremony in which the ruler "wed" the fertility goddess to guarantee fruitfulness to the land and its people. In first millennium celebrations of the New Year Festival, the Epic of Creation was recited (and perhaps acted out) to ensure that the gods would continue to triumph over chaos, and the king underwent rites of atonement for himself and his people. The Persians later adopted this festival, and it may have influenced rites connected with the Israelite Day of Atonement and rabbinic interpretations of the Jewish New Year celebration.

Nomarch—The administrator or governor of a nome or district of Egypt.

Nome—One of the traditional administrative districts of ancient Egypt. There were 22 nomes in Upper Egypt and 20 nomes in Lower Egypt.

Nomen—The final name (of five) used by ancient Egyptian pharaohs, and generally the one used by modern scholars (Thutmose, Amenhotep, Ramesses, etc.). It was usually the name a pharaoh had received at birth.

Obsidian—A shiny dark green to black natural glass produced during volcanic eruptions. It was a desirable trade object and came primarily from Anatolia.

Omen—A phenomenon or occurrence regarded as a sign or message sent by a deity.

Pantheon—Collectively, all of the deities worshiped by a given culture or nation.

Patriarchy—Literally, "father-rule." This term is applied to a family ruled by its leading (usually its oldest) male or to a society dominated or ruled by men.

Pharaoh—A title for kings of Egypt derived from the Hebrew Bible. The Hebrew term was an attempt to reproduce the Egyptian word *per'o* (or *per'aa*), which meant "great house." This word was originally a term for the royal palace, but during the Eighteenth Dynasty it came to be used to refer to the king himself.

Phonograms—Written symbols that represented *sounds* rather than individual words. Alphabetic characters are phonograms, but so also were many of the signs used in ancient cuneiform and hieroglyphic writing systems. Cuneiform and hieroglyphic phonograms usually represented syllables rather than single consonant or single vowel sounds.

Pictograph—Literally, "picture writing." See **Ideogram.**

Pottery sherds—or **potsherds.** See **Sherds**.

Praenomen—The fourth of five names an Egyptian pharaoh assumed upon ascending to the throne. It was preceded by the title usually rendered "King of Upper and Lower Egypt." A pharaoh's praenomen and nomen were usually written in oval symbols called cartouches. If an ancient text or inscription referred to a pharaoh by only one name, it was usually the praenomen that was used.

Pylon—The Greek word for "gate." It is used for the fortress-like gateways of Egyptian temples.

Radiocarbon dating—A dating method that indicates how long organic matter has been dead by measuring its ratio of radioactive carbon (^{14}C or carbon-14) to normal carbon.

Redistributive economy—A managed economic system in which a central institution (such as a temple or government) controls all or most of the society's production, collecting it and redistributing it to the society's members.

Relative chronology—A method of dating things in relation to one another: event "B" took place before event "C," but after event "A." Such dating is used when fixed or absolute dates are not known. Relative chronologies can be derived from many sources, including archaeology and texts such as king lists.

Satrap—The governor of a major division of the Persian Empire.

Satrapy—One of the major divisions of the Persian Empire. Under Darius I, there were 20 satrapies, but the number increased in later times.

Scarab—An Egyptian amulet carved in the shape of a scarab beetle (also known as a dung beetle). Egyptian scarabs usually had inscriptions on their flat undersides.

Sed Festival—See **Heb-sed.**

Semitic—A designation for a group of languages that includes Akkadian (ancient Babylonian and Assyrian), Arabic, Aramaic, Hebrew, and many other languages, both ancient and modern. It is a linguistic term, not a racial or ethic one. Semitic languages are part of the larger Afro-Asiatic family.

Shabti——An Egyptian magical burial figurine (also known as an *ushabti* or *shawabti*). From the Middle Kingdom onward, Egyptians deposited such figurines in tombs to magically perform work in the afterlife in place of the dead.

Sherds—Pieces of broken pottery vessels (variation is "shards"). They are the most common remains at most Near Eastern archaeological sites. Archaeologists usually use pottery sherds to identify and date the individual layers of archaeological sites and as characteristic objects for distinguishing many ancient cultures.

Stele—(plural, **stelae**) An upright commemorative stone slab with at least one inscribed and/or sculptured surface.

Stratigraphy—The study of the sequence of layers (strata) uncovered by archaeological excavation. Stratigraphical analysis produces a relative chronology of the material in question.

Gamkrelidze, T. V., 100, 102 (n. 40)
Gandhara, 2, 298
Ganges river, 81
Ganj Dareh. *See* Tepe Ganj Dareh
Ganweriwala, 40, 81
Gardiner, Alan, 160 (n. 1), 191 (n. 3, 7), 192 (n. 25)
Gath, 245, 252
Gathas, 308, 310
Gaugamela, 320
Gaumata, 299, 300
Gauri, K. L., 138 (n. 28)
Gaza, 2, 250, 252, 257, 264, 269, 280
Geb, 120
Gebauer, A. B., 27
Gedikli, 60
Gedrosia, 298
Genesis, Book of, 49, 121, 251, 283, 289
German(s), 281, 283
Germanic languages, 96
Gerneko, E. V., 290
Gezer, 175, 209, 244, 247, 250
Ghalioungui, Paul, 135
Gibeon, 243
Gibson, M., 26, 63 (n. 12)
Gilead, 264
Giles, F. J., 191 (n. 15, 19)
Gilgamesh, 42, 43, 45, 47
Gilgamesh and Agga of Kish, 43, 54
Gilgamesh and the Bull of Heaven, 54
Gilgamesh and the Land of the Living, 54
Gilgamesh, The Death of, 45, 54
Gilgamesh, Enkidu and the Nether World, 54
Gilukhepa, 171
Gimbutas, Marija A., 28 (n. 18)
Ginsberg, H. L., 260 (n. 15), 322 (n. 15)
Girsu (Telloh), 30, 51
Gitin, S., 220
Gittites, 246
Giza, 113, 126, 127, 128, 130, 170
Gla, 212
Gnuse, Robert K., 261 (n. 28), 290
Godin Tepe, 32
God's Wife of Amun, 162, 163, 164–165
Goedicke, Hans, 136
Goetze, A., 192 (n. 33)
Goodison, Lucy, 28 (n. 18)
Gordias, 229
Gordion, 218, 229, 298
Gorelik, M. V., 290
Gorny, R. L., 222 (n. 48)
Gottwald, Norman, 244, 261 (n. 33)
Granicus River, 319
Grayson, A. Kirk, 258, 290, 291 (n. 7, 9)

Greece, Greek(s), 3, 4, 7, 19, 46, 61, 73, 74, 96, 97, 98, 103, 126, 128, 130, 147, 153, 158, 174, 176, 177, 178, 204, 205, 212–213, 217, 218, 219, 227, 229, 233, 235, 236, 237, 240, 241, 252, 253, 270, 272, 275, 280, 281, 293, 294, 295, 299, 301, 302, 303–305, 307, 311, 312, 313, 318, 319, 320, 325, 326, 327, 328
Green, Anthony, 61
Greenberg, Moshe, 191 (n. 9)
Greene, Joseph A., 260 (n. 18, 19)
Greene, Kevin, 26
Gregory XIII (Pope), 325
Grimal, Nicolas, 135
Groom, Nigel, 259
Gubal, Gubla (Byblos), 40, 59, 69, 98, 147, 148, 169, 175, 194, 224, 227, 234, 235, 237, 239, 241, 267
Gudea, 68, 75
Gugunum, 86
Guichard, F., 100 (n. 8)
Gulf. *See* Persian Gulf
Gurgum, 265
Gurney, O. R., 219, 220 (n. 4, 10, 11)
Güterbock, Hans, 220 (n. 5)
Guti, Gutian(s), 68, 72–73, 75, 98, 296
Gyges, 293, 295

Habuba Kabira, 32, 34, 107
Habur river, 69, 97, 223
Hacilar, 12, 16
Hadad, 232–233, 239, 253
Hadadezer, 226, 231
Haddock, B. A., 26
Hadley, Judith M., 261 (n. 36), 290
Hadramawt, 256, 257
Haggai, 313, 315
Hajji Muhammad, 19, 20
Halaf culture, 19, 20
Haldi, 228, 265
Hallager, Erik, 221 (n. 27)
Halligan, John M., 191 (n. 9)
Hallo, William W., 26, 63 (n. 10), 260 (n. 4), 291 (n. 18), 328
Halpern, Baruch, 259
Halys river, 2, 230, 271, 281, 294, 297, 298
Hama, 59, 60
Hamath, 224, 226
Hamazi, 41, 60
Hamilton-Paterson, James, 137 (n. 15)
Hammer, C. U., 161 (n. 30)
Hammurabi (Hammurapi), 9, 71, 86, 87–89, 90, 91, 94, 241

Hanfmann, George M. A., 258
"Hanging Gardens." *See under* Babylon
Hanigalbat, 97, 196
Hanson, D., 102 (n. 39)
Haoma, 308, 310
Hapiru, 175
Harappa, Harappan(s), 40, 81–84
Harbottle, Garman, 161 (n. 19)
Harden, Donald, 259, 260 (n. 12, 13)
Harding, A. P., 222 (n. 50)
Harran, 69, 257, 271, 279, 285
Harrell, James, 138 (n. 27)
Harris, J. R., 192 (n. 28, 31)
Harris Papyrus, 210
Harrison, R. G., 192 (n. 31)
Harrison, Timothy P., 259
Hart, George, 136
Hasanlu, 40, 228
Hassek Hüyük, 32
Hassan, Fekri A., 101 (n. 12)
Hassuna culture, 19, 20
Hathor, 119, 152, 167, 172
Hatshepsut, 162, 163, 164, 165–168, 171
Hatti, 94, 173, 174, 193–194, 196, 197, 198, 208, 210, 219
Hattian(s), 94, 204
Hattusas, 2, 40, 69, 94, 95, 193, 194, 197, 198, 199, 201, 204, 213, 214, 218
Hattusilis I, 95–96, 97, 193
Hattusilis III, 193, 196–198, 202
Hawass, Zahi, 135, 138 (n. 29)
Hawkes, Nigel, 101 (n. 13)
Hayes, John H., 262 (n. 47), 322 (n. 9, 14)
Haynes, Joyce L., 135
Hazael, 231–232, 251
Hazor, 148, 235, 244, 247, 249, 250
Healy, John F., 190, 191 (n. 11)
Healy, Mark, 290
Hebrew(s), 111, 115, 175, 176, 177, 230, 231, 233, 243, 253, 283, 289, 314, 321 (n. 8), 325
Heb-sed (Jubilee Festival), 122, 123, 124, 144–146, 173, 181
Heider, George C., 262 (n. 46)
Heliopolis, 2, 113, 120, 126, 130, 171, 172, 180
Hellenistic Age, 242, 251, 284, 285, 318, 325
Hellespont, 303, 305
Heltzer, M., 221 (n. 26)
Hendel, Ronald S., 261 (n. 25)
Hendrickson, Elizabeth F., 27
Henry, Donald O., 27
Hepat, 202
Heracles (Hercules), 204, 326

Heraclitus of Ephesus, 27 (n. 3)
Herakleopolis, 113, 139, 143
Herem ("ban"), 255
Herm, Gerhard, 259
Hermonthis (Armant), 152
Hermopolis, 156, 171, 187
Hermus River, 293
Herodotus, 5, 103, 127, 147, 212, 218, 272, 281, 283, 284, 293, 295, 297, 299, 303, 306
Herr, Larry G., 259
Heshbon, 243, 250, 254
Hesiod, 204
Hezekiah, 267, 269, 286–287, 290 (n. 1), 291 (n. 14)
Hiebert, Fredrik, 84
Hierakonpolis, 106, 108, 109, 113, 118
Hieroglyph(s), Hieroglyphic writing. *See under* Writing
Hillman, G. C., 27
Himelfarb, Elizabeth J., 191 (n. 10)
Hindu Kush mountains, 40
Hinz, Walther, 62
Hippias, 304
Hiram I, 235, 246–247
Hissarlik. *See* Troy
Historical study, the nature of, 3–5
Historical writing(s), 204–205, 242, 251, 287–289
Hittite(s), 49, 88, 96, 98, 116, 119, 169, 170, 174, 175, 176, 188, 219, 227, 229, 230, 293, 294, 325, 326
  kingship, 200
  law, 199–200
  New Kingdom, 193–205, 207, 210, 211, 212, 213–215
  Old Kingdom, 94–95
  religion and ritual, 201–203
Hodder, Ian, 26
Hoffmann, Michael A., 136
Hoffmeier, James K., 259, 261 (n. 26)
Hoffner, Harry A., 219, 221 (n. 28)
Hoglund, K. G., 320
Hole, Frank, 320
Homer, Homeric, 178, 198–199
Hood, Sinclair, 160
Hooker, J. J., 222 (n. 38)
Hophni, 243
Horemheb, 163, 188–189
Horn, Siegfried, 260 (n. 5), 262 (n. 44), 291 (n. 15, 18)
Hornung, Erik, 135, 160 (n. 12), 190, 191 (n. 13), 192 (n.24)
Horse(s), 83, 96, 98, 247, 270, 297, 307

Horus, 109, 113–114, 116, 117, 119, 120, 121, 128, 130, 167, 172
Hosea, 251, 317
Hoshea, 263, 286
Huffmon, H. B., 102 (n. 39)
Huldah, 287
Huni, 124, 126, 133
Hunt, Lynn, 26
Hurri, Hurrian(s), 49, 68, 71, 74, 95, 97–98, 170, 176, 194, 202, 203, 204, 209, 214, 228, 230, 325, 326
Hussein, Fawzia, 192 (n. 31)
Huvakshatra. *See* Cyaxares
Hyksos. *See under* Egypt
Hypostyle hall(s), 121, 206, 311
Hyrcania, 298

Ibal-pi-El, 88
Ibbi-Sin, 68, 79
Ibiza, 237
Icosium, 237
Ideogram (ideograph), ideographic, 34–37, 71, 111, 112, 202, 203
Idumaeans. *See* Edom
Ikram, Salima, 137 (n. 16)
Iliad, 198
Ilium. *See* Troy
Illyrian(s), 253
Imhotep, 123–124
Inanna, 46, 48, 50,
Incipient cultivation, 11, 12
Incipient herding, 11, 22
Indar/Indra, 98
India, 81, 83, 96, 97, 235, 308, 309, 310, 323, 324
Indo-European(s), 36, 83, 94, 95–97, 98, 170, 204, 213, 229, 252, 253, 293, 294
Indo-Iranian(s), 36, 85, 96, 98, 203
Indus (Harappan) civilization, 3, 40, 61, 81–84, 85
Indus river (and valley), 2, 3, 34, 40, 52, 61, 81, 83, 85, 298
Inanna, 46, 66
Infant sacrifice. *See* Sacrifice, infant
Instruction for King Merikare, 141
Instruction of a Man for His Son, 149
Instruction of King Amenemhet I, 147, 149
Intermediate Period. *See under* Egypt
Inundation. *See under* Nile
Iolkos, 212
Ionia, Ionian(s), 271, 298, 299, 302, 303–304, 305, 312, 313, 319, 325
Ionian Islands, 212
Ionian Sea, 237

Iran, Iranian(s), 12, 20, 32, 33, 34, 37, 40, 52, 61, 69, 72, 77, 81, 84, 85, 96, 97, 257, 269, 270, 271, 286, 294, 295, 300, 308, 310, 325
Iraq, 12, 20, 281
Iron Age, 84, 243, 244, 253, 275
Irqanata, 226
Irra-imitti, 86
Irrigation, 20, 21, 53, 57, 79, 302
Irhuleni, 224, 226
Isaiah, 256, 267, 286, 289, 292 (n. 23), 313
Ishbi-Erra, 86
Ishme-Dagan, 87, 88
Ishtar, 46, 66, 90, 202, 239, 254, 283
Ishtar Gate. *See under* Babylon
Isin, 30, 37, 45, 86, 88
Isis, 116, 117, 170
Isisnofret, 207
Islam, 289, 318, 327, 328
Israel, Israelite(s), 1, 12, 116, 176, 184, 199, 200, 203, 205, 209, 209, 214, 217, 224, 226, 227, 231, 232, 233, 241–251, 252, 254, 255
  Divided Monarchy, 90, 243, 248–251, 263, 277, 286–289, 314
  religion, 242–243, 249–251, 286–289, 315–318
  United Monarchy, 244–247
Isserlin, B. S. J., 259, 262 (n. 40, 41)
Issus, 298, 319
Istanbul, 1, 12, 40
Istria, 298
Isuwa, 194
Italic languages, 96
Italy, 212, 236
Ithoba'al, 235, 249
Itjtawy-Amenemhet, 146
Ivanov, V. V., 100, 102 (n. 40)

J (the Yahwist narrative), 242, 251
Jabbok River, 253
Jacob, Margaret, 26
Jacobsen, Thorkild, 62, 64 (n. 28), 100 (n. 4, 7)
Jahaz, 255
Janssen, J. J., 221 (n. 30)
Jarmo, 10, 12, 15
Jaxartes (Syr Darya) river, 2, 40,
Jehoahaz, 248, 286
Jehoash, 248, 251
Jehoiachin, 280, 286, 321 (n. 8)
Jehohanan (Johanan), 315, 316
Jehoiakim, 280, 286, 288
Jehoram (Joram), king of Israel, 231, 248, 251, 254, 262 (n. 43)

Jehoram, king of Judah, 248, 249
Jehoshaphat, 248, 249, 256
Jehu, 224, 231, 248, 251
Jeitun (Djeitun), 40, 84
Jemdet Nasr, 29, 30, 31, 32, 34, 36, 37, 76, 107
Jeremiah, 240, 256, 317
Jericho, 12, 13–14, 15, 16, 40, 59, 243
Jeroboam I, 248
Jeroboam II, 248
Jerusalem, 2, 40, 69, 148, 175, 240, 244, 246, 247, 248, 250, 251, 257, 267, 268, 269, 271, 280, 281, 286, 287, 288, 289, 297, 298, 313, 314, 315, 319
Jesus of Nazareth, 6, 327, 328
Jesus Ben Sirach, 314
Jew(s), Jewish. See Judaism
Jezebel, 249, 251
Jezreel, 251
Jezreel Valley, 247, 252
Job, Book of, 256, 291 (n. 19)
Joel, 315
Johnson, D. L., 222 (n. 49)
Jonah, Book of, 317
Jones, Tom B., 63 (n. 10)
Joppa, 253
Joram. See Jehoram
Jordan (Transjordan), 1, 12, 14, 231, 235, 243, 251, 253, 255
Jordan river (and valley), 13, 231, 251, 252, 253
Jordan, Paul, 128, 136, 137 (n. 23, 24, 25, 26), 138 (n. 28, 29)
Joshua, 175
Joshua, Book of, 243, 251, 288
Josiah, 279, 286, 287–288, 289, 291 (n. 16, 19), 314
Jotham, 286
Joukowski, Martha S., 220, 221 (n. 28)
Judah, Judean(s), 227, 231, 240, 241, 242, 245, 246, 248–251, 255, 256, 263, 267, 279, 280–281, 286–289, 297, 302, 313–318
Judaism, Jew(s), Jewish, 289, 310, 314, 315, 324, 327
Judges (shophetim), 242, 243, 245, 248
Judges, Book of, 243, 251, 288
Judgment. See Final judgment

Ka, 117, 122, 124, 128, 151, 168
Kabul, 2, 40
Kadashman-Enlil, 171
Kadesh Barnea, 243, 250, 255
Kalabsha, 113

Kalhu (Calah), 224, 271, 276, 279
Kamm, Anthony, 259
Kammenhuber, Annelies, 102 (n. 45)
Kamose, 156, 157
Kamp, K., 63 (n. 13)
Kandahar, 2, 40
Kandalanu, 264, 279
Kanesh (Kültepe), 40, 60, 69, 85–86, 90, 94, 95, 194
Kaptara. See Crete
Karachi, 40
Karageorghis, V., 161 (n. 32), 220
Karduniash. See Babylonia
Karnak, 9, 113, 144, 152, 162, 163, 164, 166, 167, 172, 197, 206, 208
Karum, 85
Kaska, Kaskan(s), 194, 205, 214, 216
Kassite(s), 9, 94, 95, 98–99, 216, 217
Katz, S. H., 27 (n. 8)
Kay, P. A., 222 (n. 49)
Kazallu, 30
Keftiu. See Crete
Kemosh (Chemosh), 254, 255
Kemp, Barry J., 135
Kempinski, Aharon, 161 (n. 26)
Kengir League, 50–51
Kenyon, Kathleen, 13,
Kephallenia, 212
Kerioth, 255
Kerma, 153, 154
Kerr, Richard, 101 (n. 14)
Khaba, 133
Khafajeh (Tutub), 30, 41
Khafre (Chephren), 128–130
Khalifa, Haya Ali Al-, 100
Khamadi, 140
Khan, 84
Khania, 158
Kharga Oasis, 154, 169
Khartoum, 34, 103
Khasekhem, 106, 114
Khasekhemwy, 106, 114
Khayan, 140
Khentkawes, 130, 131, 165
Khepri, 120
Khinamun, 85
Khirbet al-Mudayna, 255
Khnum, 151, 316
Khons, 167, 172, 226
Khorsabad. See Dur-Sharrukin
Khshathrita. See Phraortes
Khufu (Cheops), 126–128, 133
Khurab, 85
Khuzistan. See Susiana
Ki, 48

Killebrew, Ann E., 221 (n. 22)
Kings, Books of, 242, 251, 263, 264, 267, 277, 288, 289, 291 (n. 14, 16)
King's Highway, 235, 249, 254, 256
King's Peace, 319
Kir (Kir-hareseth), 254
Kish, 30, 37, 38, 41, 42, 43, 45, 50, 51, 65, 66, 69,
Kitchen, Kenneth A., 197, 220 (n. 2), 221 (n. 15), 258, 259
Kition, 236, 240
Kiya, 186, 187
Kizzuwatna, 97, 194
Klein, Jacob, 64 (n. 28)
Klein, Ralph W., 322 (n. 11)
Klengel, Horst, 26
Knapp, A. Bernard, 26
Knossos, 158, 178, 212, 218
Koldewey, Robert, 281, 283
Kramer, Samuel N., 62, 63 (n. 10, 17), 64 (n. 20–22, 30), 101 (n. 23)
Kraus, Fritz R., 99
Krishna, 66
Kroll, Stephan, 258
Kronos, 204
Kubaba, 230
Kubeila. See Kybele
Kudur-Mabuk, 86–87
Kudurru, 99
Kuhrt, Amélie, 26, 38, 63 (n. 14), 100 (n. 1, 5), 101 (n. 21), 102 (n. 37), 137 (n. 7), 222 (n. 37), 260 (n. 7), 262 (n. 47), 320, 321 (n. 2)
Kukla, George, 99, 100 (n. 8), 101 (n. 9, 12, 16, 18)
Kulli, 40
Kültepe. See Kanesh
Kumarbi, 97, 204
Kummuhu, 265
Kuniholm, P. I., 161 (n. 31), 222 (n. 50)
Kurunta, 198
Kush. See Nubia
Kussara, 69, 94, 95
Kybele (Cybele, Kubeila), 229, 294

Labarnas, 95
Labor, specialization of, 16, 19–20, 22, 24, 52, 106
Lachish, 246, 251, 267, 268
Ladê, 304
Laffineur, R., 161 (n. 32)
Lagash (Al-Hiba), 29, 30, 37, 41, 43–44, 66, 68, 75, 86
Lahun, 147, 149
Lake Nasser, 103, 207, 208

Lake Sevan, 227, 228
Lake Urmia, 2, 40, 69, 214, 225, 227, 228, 265, 271, 298
Lake Van, 2, 40, 69, 97, 214, 227, 245, 263, 271, 298
Lamb, H. H., 222 (n. 48, 50)
Lamberg-Karlovsky, C. C., 27 (n. 10), 28 (n. 14), 63 (n. 6), 101 (n. 26, 28, 29)
Lapis lazuli, 23, 40, 44
Larsa, 20, 30, 37, 86–87, 88, 89, 285
Latin, 96
Law code(s), 78, 91–93, 116, 199–200
Lazpa (Lesbos), 194
League of Delos. *See* Delian League
Lebanon, 1, 12, 127, 195, 205, 224, 231, 235, 284
Lees, G. M., 62 (n. 1)
Lefkowitz, Mary R., 135, 136 (n. 2)
Legge, A. J., 27
Lehmann, Johannes, 219
Lehner, Mark, 136, 138 (n. 29, 30)
Leick, Gwendolyn, 260 (n. 13)
Lemche, Niels Peter, 259
Lemnos, 61
Lentopolis, 227
Lesbos, 61
Lesko, Barbara S., 26, 135
Leus, 294
Levant, Levantine, 1, 11, 13, 58, 59, 60, 156, 158–159, 175, 217, 224, 225, 232, 251, 257, 267, 272, 279, 281, 302
Leviathan. *See* Lothan
Levite(s), 243, 287, 314
Libby, Willard, 8
Libya, Libyan(s), 1, 104, 105, 112, 113, 115, 146, 147, 163, 173, 205, 208, 209, 215, 227, 237, 299
Lichtheim, Miriam, 135, 160 (n. 3, 15), 192 (n. 25)
Lichtman, Allan J., 26
Limassol, 236
Limmu official (and lists), 9, 276
Linear A or B. *See under* Writing
Lindenberger, James M., 259
Lipit-Ishtar, 90
Lipodystrophy, 181
Literature, 54, 90, 149, 204–205, 251, 278, 287–289, 326
Littauer, Mary A., 102 (n. 43)
Liverani, Mario, 99
Lixus, 237
Liwak, Rüdiger, 161 (n. 21)
Lloyd, Seton, 62, 259 (n. 1)
Lothal, 40, 81

Lothan (Leviathan), 64 (n. 24)
Lower Land, 194, 214, 230
Luckenbill, D. D., 291 (n. 4)
Luft, Ulrich, 137 (n. 18)
Lugal, 44, 45, 51, 53
Lugalbanda, 43
Lugalzagesi, 44, 65–66, 68
Lukka (Lycia, Lycians), 194, 208, 210, 211–212, 213
Lukonin, V. G., 320
Lullubi, 68, 69, 70, 71, 98
Luwian(s), 95, 96, 204, 212, 213–214, 229, 230, 293
Luxor. *See* Thebes
Lydia, Lydian(s), 2, 237, 252, 270, 271, 281, 293–294, 295, 297, 298, 299, 302, 311, 318

Maadi, 106
Ma'at, 114–115, 116, 117, 139–143, 149, 150, 151, 168, 172, 181
Macedon, Macedonian(s), 304, 319, 320
MacDonald, Burton, 259
MacDonald, M. C. A., 262 (n. 49, 51)
Machinist, Peter, 221 (n. 20)
Macqueen, J. G., 220 (n. 12)
Magan, 40, 67, 68, 69, 256
Mahdy, Christine El, 190
Magi, 1, 306, 310, 325
Magzaliya, 12
Maharith, 255
Ma'in, 256, 257
Maisels, Charles K., 27, 28 (n. 17), 30
Malamat, Abraham, 102 (n. 39)
Malachi, 315, 328
Malandra, William W., 321
Malek, Jaromir, 135, 136, 137 (n. 5, 6), 192 (n. 30)
Mallia, 158
Mallory, J. P., 100
Malqata, 171
Malta, 236, 237
Manasseh, 286, 287
Mandane, 295
Manetho, 5, 9, 108, 112, 131, 139, 147, 152, 153, 154, 155
Manishtusu, 67, 68
Mannaea, Mannaean(s), 263, 265, 269, 270, 271, 294
Manning, Stuart W., 160, 161 (n. 30, 31)
Marad, 30
Marathon, 304
Mardonius, 304, 305
Marduk, 46, 64 (n. 23), 90, 265, 267, 283, 285, 296, 297

Marduk-apil-iddina. *See* Merodach-baladan
Marfan's Syndrome, 191 (n. 19), 192 (n. 22)
Margiana, 40, 84, 298
Mari, 2, 40, 41, 51, 60, 67, 68, 69, 75, 86, 87, 88, 89, 90, 91, 94, 97, 241
Marius, Richard, 27 (n. 2, 5)
Markoe, Glenn E., 135, 259, 260 (n. 9, 10, 11, 12, 14, 20)
Marrassantiya (Halys) River, 194
Martin, Geoffrey T., 190
Master, Daniel, 262 (n. 39)
Martu. *See* Amorites
Maryannu, 98, 170
Massalia, 237
Mastaba, 107, 119, 123–124, 130, 144
Master, Sharad, 101 (n. 13)
Mathematics, 55–56, 204, 324
Matriarchy, 25
Matthew, Gospel of, 325
Matthews, Robert, 101 (n. 13)
Matthews, Victor H., 26, 321 (n. 1)
Matthiae, Paolo, 62, 99
Maysar, 81
Mazar, Amihai, 26, 74, 101 (n. 15, 17), 220, 262 (n. 39)
Mazar-i-Sharif, 40
McBride, S. D., 102 (n. 39)
McCall, Henrietta, 62
McCarter, P. Kyle Jr., 249, 260 (n. 5), 261 (n. 25), 262 (n. 44), 287, 291 (n. 15, 18)
McDermott, John J., 259
McGovern, Patrick E., 161 (n. 19)
McIntosh, Jane, 26
McKenzie, Steven L., 259, 291 (n. 17)
Me, 49, 51
Meadow, R., 100 (n. 8)
Medeba, 254
Media(n), Medes, 2, 96, 225, 257, 265, 270, 271, 272, 279–281, 294, 295, 297, 298, 299, 300, 306, 307, 310, 311, 325
Medicine, 56–57, 93, 94, 134, 278
Medina, 2, 257
Medinet Habu, 164, 210, 211, 217
Mediterranean Sea, 1, 2, 12, 40, 69, 103, 113, 194, 210, 214, 215, 217, 218
Meek, Theophile, 191 (n. 8)
Megiddo, 168, 244, 245, 247, 250, 253, 264, 279, 288
Meidum, 113, 126
Meketaton, 185, 186
Mellaart, James, 16, 17, 28 (n. 13), 101 (n. 10)
Melos, 252
Melqart, 239, 249, 253

Melos, 61

Meluhha, 40, 67, 72, 81–84

Memphis, 2, 40, 69, 108, 110, 113, 119, 123, 139, 146, 154, 157, 163, 169, 181, 189, 206, 214, 257, 270, 271, 298, 299

Memphite theology, 121

Menahem, 286

Mendenhall, George, 244, 261 (n. 33)

Menes (Meni), 108–110

Menkaure (Mycerinus), 126, 130, 133

Mentuhotep II (Nebhepetre Mentuhotep), 140, 144–146, 164, 167

Mentuhotep III, 140

Menua, 228

Merari, 243

Merhav, Rivka, 258

Merimde, 22–23, 113

Meritaton, 186

Meritneith, 112, 165

Meritre Hatshepsut, 165

Merodach-baladan (Marduk-apal-iddina) II, 264–265, 267, 268

Merneptah, 205, 208, 209, 243

Mersin, 12, 40

Mesannepadda, 42, 43

Mesha, 231, 251, 254, 255

Mesha Stele, 254, 255

Meshel, Ze'ev, 261 (n. 36)

Mesilim (Mesalim), 41, 43

Meskalamdug, 44, 45

Mesopotamia, Mesopotamian(s), 1, 2, 7, 8–10, 13, 24, 30, 40, 60, 61, 65–94, 96, 97, 98, 99, 107, 108, 112, 115, 116, 119, 120, 141, 158, 176, 195, 203, 204, 216, 223, 225, 238, 239, 240, 249, 256, 257, 258, 265, 266, 268, 270, 272, 278, 285, 301, 310, 311, 312, 313, 324, 325, 326
Akkadian Empire, 65–75
Early Dynastic Period, 32, 40–58
kingship, 44–45, 50–51, 68–71, 272–273, 297
prehistoric cultures, 19–22; Uruk/Jemdet-Nasr era, 29–39

Messenger(s), 77, 276–277

Messiah, 297, 318

Metal(s), metallurgy, 23, 57, 60, 68, 78, 81, 155, 171, 178, 199, 227, 229, 236, 252, 256

Meteor(s), meteorite(s), 74, 101 (n. 13)

Me-Turnu, 296

Meyers, Eric M., 26, 322 (n. 9, 13)

Michael, H. N., 161 (n. 31)

Midas. See Mita

Midas City, 229

Middle East, 1–2

Midea, 218

Midian, 244

Mikasa, Prince Takahito, 220

Miletus (Milawata), 178, 194, 198, 213, 294, 298, 303, 304

Milid, 265

Military organization, 57, 72, 173, 217–218, 274–276, 297, 307–308

Milkom, 253

Millard, Alan R., 25, 260 (n. 4, 13), 261 (n. 26), 262 (n. 49)

Miller, J. Maxwell, 259, 261 (n. 35), 262 (n. 47), 322 (n. 9, 14)

Miller, P. D., 102 (n. 39)

Min, 121, 152, 172

Minoans. See Crete

Mita (Midas), 229, 270

Mitanni, Mittanian(s), 97–98, 168, 169, 170, 171, 173, 174, 194–195, 199, 203

Mitchell, Larkin, 137 (n. 8)

Mitchell, T. C., 328

Mithra/Mitrasil, Mithraism, 98, 310, 327–328

Mitinti, 269

Moab, Moabite(s), 246, 249, 251, 253–255, 256, 263, 267, 280, 302, 315

Moabite Stone. See Mesha Stele

Mohenjo-Daro, 40, 81, 82, 83, 84

Molech (Malik), 253, 262 (n. 46)

Montet, Pierre, 220

Montu, 152, 172

Monotheism, 178, 181–185, 243, 251, 286–289, 327

Moore, A. M. T., 27

Moorey, P. R. S., 62, 63 (n. 19)

Moortgat, Anton, 62

Moran, William L., 64 (n. 28), 100 (n. 4), 190, 191 (n. 16, 17, 18)

Morkot, Robert G., 290

Morley, Neville, 26

Morocco, 236

Morris, Christine, 28 (n. 18)

Moscati, Sabatino, 259

Moses, 178, 242–243, 286, 287, 314, 315, 328

Mot, 176, 239

Mother goddess, 13, 16, 24–25

Motya, 237, 240

Mount Athos, 304

Mount Gilboa, 246

Moyer, J. C., 291 (n. 18)

Muhammed, 328

Muhly, James D., 220 (n. 9)

Mummification, mummy, 117, 118, 163, 187

Munhata, 12

Munro, M. A. R., 161 (n. 30)

Mureybit. See Tell Mureybit

Murghab river, 84

Murnane, William J., 137 (n. 6), 190, 192 (n. 25, 26), 220 (n. 1)

Mursilis I, 95, 193

Mursilis II, 193, 194, 204–205

Mursilis III. See Urhi-Teshub

Musasir, 228, 265

Mushkênum, 91–93

Music, 54–55, 326–327

Muski, 214–215, 216, 229

Mut, 167, 172, 181, 226

Mutemwiya, 170, 172

Muwatallis II, 193, 195–196, 198

Myrrh. See Menkaure

Mycalê, 305

Mycenae, Mycenaean(s), 178, 198, 210–211, 212–213, 217, 218, 252

Mycerinus. See Menkaure

Myrrh, 256–257

Na'aman, Nadav, 262 (n. 39)

Nabonassar (Nabu-nasir), 264

Nabonidus (Nabu-na'id), 264, 285–286, 296, 297

Nabopolassar (Nabu-apla-usur), 264, 279

Nadab, 248

Naditum, 90

Nahal Hemar, 12, 15

Nahal Oren, 11, 12

Nahum, 274, 279

Namazga, 40,

Nammu, 48, 75

Nanna, 46, 66, 76, 77, 86, 285

Napata, 169, 170

Naqada I (Amratian) period, 23, 106, 110, 117

Naqada II (Gerzian) period, 105–108, 110, 117, 118, 119

Naqada III period, 106

Naqi'a, 274

Naram-Sin, 67, 68–72, 73, 77, 204, 205

Narmada river, 81

Narmer, 109–110, 111, 115

Nasatyas/Nasattyana, 98

Natron, 118,

Natufian culture, 11–13

Navali Cori, 16, 17

Nebo, 255, 296

Nebuchadnezzar II, 264, 279, 280–284, 288, 289, 294, 311

Necho (Nekau) I, 270

Necho (Nekau) II, 236, 279, 280, 288, 303
Nefayan, 316
Nefertari, 207
Nefertiti, 165, 180, 181, 182, 183, 185–186
Neferure, 164, 166, 168
Negev (of Judah), 59, 73, 74, 235, 244, 246, 313
Nehemiah, 314–315, 321 (n. 9)
Nekau. *See* Necho
Nelson, A. R., 137 (n. 3)
Nelson, R. D., 291 (n. 18)
Neo-Assyrian Period. *See under* Assyria
Neo-Babylonian Period. *See under* Babylonia
Neo-Hittite(s), 213–214, 224, 229, 230, 235
Neolithic era and groups, 13–25, 84
Neolithic Revolution, 10, 95
Nergal, 226, 254
Neriglissar (Nergal-shar-usur), 264, 284–285
Nerik, 194
Nesha. *See* Kanesh
Nesian. *See* Hittite
Neugebauer, Otto, 328
Neumann, J., 221 (n. 33, 34), 222 (n. 35)
New Delhi, 81
New Year Festival(s), 49–50, 121–122, 265, 273, 276, 282, 283, 285, 301
Nicholson, Paul, 136
Niditch, Susan, 290
Niermeier, B., 161 (n. 26)
Niermeier, W.-D., 161 (n. 26, 32)
Nigosian, S. A., 321
Nile river (and valley), 2, 12, 40, 103–104, 105, 106, 107, 113, 114, 115, 116, 147, 154, 169, 214, 215, 219, 257, 271, 298, 303, 328
  cataract(s), 103, 113, 114, 115, 144, 146
  delta. *See under* Egypt
  inundation(s), flood(s), 9, 73, 104, 114–115, 123, 129, 131, 140
Ninbanda, 44
Nineveh (Kuyunjik and Nebi Yunus), 2, 32, 40, 67, 69, 169, 214, 216, 225, 266–267, 269, 272, 276, 279, 317, 320
Ningal, 80
Nippur, 30, 31, 37, 38, 43, 51, 71, 75, 77, 78, 86
Nissen, Hans J., 27, 28 (n. 16, 17), 62 (n. 2), 63 (n. 4), 79, 100 (n. 6), 101 (n. 22)
Nitiqret (Nitocris), 131, 148, 165
Nobles, 52, 53, 91, 131–132, 139, 143, 149, 194, 200, 274, 300, 301, 304, 306, 307
Nome(s), nomarch(s), 106, 109, 112, 139, 146
Nora, 236, 237
Notre Dame Cathedral, 206
Noush000, 85

Nubia (Kush), Nubian(s), 2, 3, 34, 40, 103–104, 105, 107, 112, 113, 144, 146, 147, 148, 153, 154, 157, 162, 163, 164, 168, 169, 170, 171, 172, 173, 187, 188, 205, 207, 267, 270, 271, 299
Nuhasse, 194
Numbers, Book of, 242, 243, 251
Nun, 120, 124
Nur, Amos, 222 (n. 47)
Nut, 120
Nützel, W., 62 (n. 2)
Nuzi, 97

Oasis hypothesis, 10
Oates, David, 27
Oates, Joan, 27, 62, 63 (n. 11), 64 (n. 29), 100 (n. 7)
Obadiah, 315
Obsidian, 8, 11, 23
Ochos (son of Artaxerxes I), 318
Ochos (son of Artaxerxes II), 319
O'Connor, David, 135, 137 (n. 12), 160 (n. 13), 161 (n. 16)
Oded, Bustenay, 290, 291 (n. 10)
Olyan, Saul M., 261 (n. 36), 290
Oman, 2, 22, 40, 68, 74, 81, 256
Omari, 23, 106
Omen(s), 67, 203, 272–273, 278, 325
Omri, 231, 248, 249, 250, 251, 254, 255
Onomasticon of Amenope, 252
Ophir, 235, 246, 256, 257
Oppenheim, A. Leo, 62, 63 (n. 16), 100 (n. 1), 260 (n. 2), 321 (n. 1)
Opet-festival, 122, 167–168, 172
Oracle of Delphi. *See* Delphi, Oracle of
Oren, Eliezer D., 160 (n. 13), 161(n. 16, 17, 19, 22, 24, 25, 27, 29, 31)
Orion, 128–129
Orlin, Louis, 99
Orontes River, 194, 196, 224, 226
Osiris, 112, 116, 117, 125, 143, 206
Ouranos (Uranus), 204
Oxus civilization, 40, 61, 84–85
Oxus (Amu Darya) river, 40, 81, 84, 297, 298
Özdogan, Mehmet, 27

Padi, 269
Paduhepa, 202
Pakistan, 1, 19, 40, 61, 81, 85
Palaic, 96, 229
Palermo Stone, 9, 108
Palestine, Palestinian(s), 3, 7, 11, 13, 22, 23, 58–60, 73, 74, 98, 105, 107, 112, 115, 140, 147, 148, 152, 153, 156–157, 162, 164, 168, 169, 173, 174–176, 179, 188,

190, 201, 208, 209, 210, 211, 215, 217, 218, 224, 227, 233, 235, 242, 243, 244, 252, 253, 272, 280, 317, 319, 327
Palmer, Leonard R., 102 (n. 41)
Papyrus, 104–105, 108, 109, 175, 237
Parker, Simon B., 190
Parkinson, Richard B., 160
Parpola, Simo, 221 (n. 33, 34), 222 (n. 35), 291 (n. 5, 11)
Parr, Peter, 161 (n. 20)
Parsa. *See* Persia
Parthia, 298
Pasargadae, 2, 298, 299, 301, 311, 320
Patai, Raphael, 290
Patriarch(s), patriarchy, patriarchal, 25, 53, 194, 199, 241, 242
Peace of Callias, 305
Peckham, Brian, 260 (n. 11)
Pedaiah, 321 (n. 9)
Peet, Thomas Eric, 220, 221 (n. 31)
Pekah, 286
Pekahiah, 286
Peleset. *See* Philistines
Peletites, 246
Peloponnese, 213
Peloponnesian War, 318, 319
Pendlebury, J. D. S., 192 (n. 27)
Pentateuch. *See* Torah
Pepi II, 131, 133
Perdue, L. C., 291 (n. 18)
Peregrine, Peter N., 26
Peribsen, 106, 114
Per-Ramesses. *See* Pi-Ramesse
Persepolis, 2, 298, 301, 311–313, 320
Persia (Parsa, Persis), Persian(s), 2, 9, 40, 96, 228, 233, 236, 239, 242, 271, 280, 285, 289, 294–320, 325
  art and architecture, 310–313
  imperial administration, 301–302
  kingship, 305–306
  military organization, 307, 308
  religion and ritual, 308–310
Persian Gulf, 1, 2, 3, 22, 29–31, 37, 40, 52, 61, 67, 69, 75, 79, 81, 86, 169, 214, 271, 298
Persis. *See* Persia
Pettey, Richard, 290
Pettinato, Giovanni, 62, 99
Phaistos, 158
Phalanx, 319
Pharaoh(s), 9, 115, 121, 128, 130, 131, 132, 140, 143, 163, 164, 165, 167, 174, 175, 178, 179, 181, 183, 187, 208, 267, 272, 273, 288, 303, 318, 320
Philip II, 319

Philistia, Philistine(s), 210–211, 212, 217–218, 231, 235, 245, 246, 251–253, 263, 267, 302

Philosophy, 328–329

Phinehas, 243

Phoenicia, Phoenician(s), 2, 162, 176, 177, 196, 204, 224, 229, 230, 231, 233–241, 242, 249, 253, 256, 280, 299, 302, 312, 319, 320, 326

Phonogram(s), phonetic sign(s), 71, 111–112

Phraortes (Khshathrita), 272, 295, 297

Phrygia, Phrygian(s), 2, 215, 228, 229, 265, 270, 271, 298

Phylakopi, 61

Piracy, pirate(s), 61, 208, 211, 218, 219

Pi-Ramesse, 113, 197, 206, 243

Pitard, Wayne T., 260 (n. 5)

Pitassa, 194

Pithanas, 94

Pithom, 152

Pitman, Walter, 64 (n. 27)

Plague. *See* Disease and plague

Plataea, 304, 305

Plato, 328

Poliochni, 61

Pollard, A. M., 26

Pollock, Susan, 62, 64 (n. 19)

Pomeroy, Sarah B., 321

Pontic Mountains, 227

Porter, Barbara N., 290

Postgate, J. N., 62

Postgate, Nicholas, 62

Pottery, 17–19, 20, 21–22, 31–32, 39, 106, 178, 210–211, 243, 244, 252

Pottery wheel, 19, 23, 325

Potts, D. T., 100

Potts, Timothy, 62

Pouyssegur, Patrick, 25

Predynastic period. *See under* Egypt

Pre-Pottery Neolithic cultures, 13–15

Price, T. D., 27

"Primitive democracy" in Mesopotamia. *See* Democracy

Pritchard, James B., 26, 63 (n. 16), 100 (n. 1), 101 (n. 23, 36), 160 (n. 2), 260 (n. 2), 262 (n. 47), 321 (n. 1), 322 (n. 15)

Prophecy, prophet(s):
    Aramaean, 91, 233
    Israelite and Judean, 91, 248, 249–251, 286, 287, 288, 289, 315
    Mesopotamian, 90–91
    Persian, 308–310
    Phoenician, 91, 241

Prophecy of Neferti, 146, 149

Prostitution, cultic, 90, 240

Protests of the Eloquent Peasant. See Eloquent Peasant

Proto-Aeolic capitals, 249

Proto-Elamite, 34, 39, 61

Proto-Hittite(s), 94

Protoliterate Period, 34

Proto-Vedic, 98

Psalms, Book of, 104, 184, 256

Psamtik (Psammetichus) I, 270, 271

Psamtik (Psammetichus) II, 280

Psamtik (Psammetichus) III, 299

Ptah, 120, 121, 171, 183, 207

Puabi, 44

Pulu Pul. *See* Tiglath-Pileser III

Punjab, 81

Punon, 256

Punt, 147, 168, 235, 256, 257

Purvis, James D., 322 (n 11–13)

Puzrish-Dagan. *See* Drehem

Puzur-Inshushinak, 72

Pylon(s), 121, 171, 172

Pylos, 212, 219

Pyramid(s), 114, 123–124, 126–128, 129, 130, 131, 134, 147, 149–150, 152, 325

Pyramid Texts, 118, 124, 125

Pythagoras, 324, 327

Qade, 256, 257

Qadesh, 98, 168, 169, 174, 188, 194, 195–196, 206, 217

Qala buildings, 84

Qal'at Bahrain, 80

Qarhoh, 254, 255

Qarqar, 224, 226, 249, 265

Qataban, 256, 257

Qatar, 2, 3, 20, 21, 40, 79

Qatna, 88, 97, 194, 195

Qaus (Qos), 256

Qedar, 257, 258

Qode (Cilicia), 210

Quarrel of Apopi and Seqenenre, 155

Que (Cilicia), 226, 247, 265, 271

Queen of Sheba. *See* Sheba, Queen of

Quirke, Stephen, 117, 121, 136, 137 (n. 14, 19), 160 (n. 9, 10)

Qurayya, 257

Raamses. *See* Pi-Ramesse

Rabbath-Ammon (Amman), 250, 253

Rab shaqê, 276

Race(s), 105

Radiocarbon dating, 8

Rainey, Anson F., 161 (n. 21)

Ramesses I, 165, 189, 205

Ramesses II, 10, 167, 171, 189, 195–196, 197, 205, 206–208, 243

Ramesses III, 205, 209–210, 211, 215, 217, 251

Ramesses IV, 205

Ramesses VII, 215

Ramesses IX, 205, 215

Ramesses X, 215

Ramesses XI, 215

Ramesseum, 164, 197, 207

Ramoth–Gilead, 231

Rampolla, Mary Lynn, 3, 27 (n. 1)

Rapiqum, 88

Ratnagar, S., 100

Rawlinson, George, 321 (n. 6)

Rawlinson, Henry C., 301

Re, 114, 116, 120, 121, 125, 128, 130, 142, 143, 163, 167, 171, 172, 183, 196

Reade, Julian, 62, 100, 290

Redford, Donald B., 135, 136 (n. 1), 161 (n. 17, 24), 190, 191 (n. 14), 192 (n. 27), 221 (n. 17, 19), 222 (n. 42)

Redford, Susan, 220

Redistributive economy, 31, 52, 72, 78

Redman, Charles L., 27, 28 (n. 17)

Red Sea, 2, 40, 154, 168, 169, 235, 256, 257, 271

Reeves, Nicholas, 190, 192 (n. 28, 29, 31)

Rehoboam, 227, 248

Relay stations, 77

Religion and cultic practices, 12–13, 14–15, 16–17, 46–50, 98, 119–123, 128, 152, 176, 200–203, 228, 229, 232–233, 239–241, 242–243, 249–251, 252, 253, 256, 258, 272–273, 286–289, 308–310, 315–318

Rendtorff, Rolf, 261 (n. 23)

Renfrew, Colin, 26, 100, 102 (n. 41)

Report of Wenamun, 226–227, 237, 241, 252

Resheph, 239

Rhodes, 2, 158, 178, 198, 212, 236, 237

Rice, Michael, 100, 136

Richard, Suzanne, 62, 99, 100 (n. 9), 101 (n. 15)

Rig-Veda, 83, 97, 308

Rim-Sin (I), 87, 88, 89

Rim-Sin II, 94

Ritual sex. *See* Prostitution, cultic

Rimush, 68

Road(s), 77, 276–277, 298, 302–303

Roaf, Michael, 62, 320, 321 (n. 3)

Robb, J., 137 (n. 3)

Robins, Gay, 135, 138 (n. 33), 160, 165, 191 (n. 1, 2, 6)

Rogers, Guy MacLean, 135
Rogerson, John, 259, 261 (n. 25)
Rolle, Renate, 290
Rollefson, Gary, 15, 28 (n. 12)
Roman(s), 240, 241, 308, 325, 327
Romer, John, 190, 221 (n. 31)
Rosen, A. M., 26
Rosen, Arlene, 74, 101 (n. 18)
Rosen, Steven, 261 (n. 32)
Roth, Martha T., 62, 99
Roux, Georges, 62, 63 (n. 11), 100 (n. 3),
    101 (n. 30, 32, 33), 273, 291 (n. 6)
"Royal heiress" theory, 164–165
"Royal Tombs" of Ur, 44–46, 47, 55, 56. 86
Rusa I, 265
Russell, John M., 290
Russia, Russian(s), 83, 95, 96, 265, 269, 294
Ryan, William, 64 (n. 27)
Ryholt, K. S. B., 160

Saba (Sheba), 247, 256, 257, 258
Sabbath, 315
Sabium, 88
Sabloff, Jeremy A., 14, 27 (n. 10), 28
    (n. 14), 63 (n. 6), 101 (n. 26, 28, 29)
Sacred Marriage ceremony, 45, 49–50, 51, 70
Sacrifice, infant, 240–241
Sadyattes, 293, 295
Saggs, H. W. F., 26, 39, 62, 63 (n. 14), 101
    (n. 20), 290, 291 (n. 12)
Sahara Desert, 103
Sahure, 130
Sais, Saite, 270
Salamis, 305
Salitis, 140, 154
Samal, 230
Samaria, 249, 250, 264, 291 (n. 14), 314,
    315, 317
Samarkand, 2, 40
Samarra culture, 19
Sammuramat (Semiramis), 225, 274
Samothrace, 237
Sams, G. Kenneth, 258, 260 (n. 3)
Samsat, 32
Samson, Julia, 190, 192 (n. 28)
Samsu-ditana, 88
Samsu-iluna, 88, 94, 98
Samuel, Books of, 242, 245, 251, 288
Sanakhte, 123, 133
Sanakhtenre Tao I, 140
Sanballat, 315, 317
Sancisi-Weerdenburg, H., 320
Sandars, Nancy K., 220, 221 (n. 26), 222
    (n. 43)
Sanskrit, 96

Santorini. See Thera
Saoshyant(s), 309, 310, 318
Sapallitepe, 40
Saqqara, 9, 113, 119, 123, 124, 126, 146, 171
Sardinia, Sardinian(s), 212, 235, 236, 237,
    240
Sardis, 2, 237, 271, 293, 294, 297, 298, 303
Sarepta, 234, 235
Sargon of Agade, 44, 65–67, 68, 70, 72, 95,
    204, 285, 302
Sargon II, 264, 274, 275, 276, 277, 294
Sarna, Nahum M., 261 (n. 27)
Sasson, Jack M., 26
Satioh, 165
Satire of the Trades, 149
Satrap(s), satrapy, satrapies, 301–302, 319,
    320
Saul, 245, 251
Scarab(s), 150, 151, 152
Schliemann, Heinrich, 198
Schloch, Robert, 129, 137 (n. 26)
Schmandt-Besserat, Denise, 62, 63
    (n. 7, 12), 320
Schmidt, Heike C., 220
Schmidt, John D., 220
Schools. See Education
Schneider, Thomas, 117, 137 (n. 12)
Schulman, Alan R., 137 (n. 4), 161 (n. 18)
Schulz, Regine, 136, 137 (n. 12, 18)
Scribe(s), 36, 53, 60, 111, 112, 140, 173, 179
Scorpion king, 108–109, 115, 116
Scythia, Scythian(s), 269–270, 272, 279,
    293, 298, 303, 313
Seal(s), 32–33, 80, 81, 82, 84, 85, 204, 253
Sealand, 94, 217, 268, 279
Sea of Galilee, 250
Sea of Marmara, 194
Sea Peoples, 173, 208–212, 213, 214, 215,
    217, 227, 251–252
Second Isaiah. See Deutero-Isaiah
Sedeinga, 172
Seha River Land, 194, 198
Seidel, Matthias, 136, 137 (n. 12, 18)
Sekallu, 273
Sekhemib, 106, 114
Sekhmet, 119
Sekunda, N., 321
Seleucid(s), 318
Seminomad(s), seminomadic, 38, 61, 73,
    74, 85, 91, 216, 243–244, 253, 256,
    257, 258, 303
Semite(s), Semitic, 36, 38, 39, 58, 60, 97,
    174, 175, 176, 203, 230, 253
Senenmut, 166
Senior, L., 100 (n. 8)

Sennacherib, 264, 266–268, 269, 273, 291
    (n. 14), 294
Senusret I, 140, 146–147
Senusret II, 140, 147
Senusret III, 9, 140, 147–148
Sepseskaf, 130, 133
Seqenenre Tao II, 140, 155–156
Serabit el-Khadim, 148, 176, 243
Serapeum, 171
Seth, 114, 116, 152, 155
Seti I, 174, 195, 205–206
Seti II, 205
Shabako, 267
Shabti(s), 150, 151, 186
Shadad, 61, 85
Shafer, Byron E., 136, 137 (n. 12)
Shakintu, 273
Shallum, 286
Shalmaneser I, 196, 215
Shalmaneser III, 224–225, 226, 230, 231,
    235, 249
Shalmaneser IV, 224
Shalmaneser V, 263–264, 265
Shamash, 46, 89
Shamash-shum-ukin, 264, 270, 271
Shamshi-Adad I, 86, 87–88, 90
Shamshi-Adad V, 224, 225
Shanks, Hershel, 259, 261 (n. 25, 27, 35,
    38), 262 (n. 39, 44), 291 (n. 15, 18),
    322 (n. 11, 13)
Shardana, 208, 210, 212, 252
Shar-i-Sokhta, 40, 61
Shar-kali-sharri, 68, 73, 87
Sharer, Robert J., 26
Sharuhen, 154, 156–157, 161 (n. 21), 162
Shasu, 243
Shaushka, 202
Shaw, Ian, 136
Shea, William H., 291 (n. 2)
Shealtiel, 321 (n. 9)
Sheba, Kingdom of. See Saba
Sheba, Queen of, 247, 258
Shebitqu, 267
Shechem, 148, 244, 250
Shekelesh, 208, 210, 212
Shelemiah, 317
Shenazzar, 321 (n. 8)
Sherihum, 68, 69
Sheshbazzar, 313, 321 (n. 8)
Sheshi (Salitis?), 140
Shimashki, 39, 69
Shinnie, P. L., 136
Shipwrecked Sailor, The, 149
Shiwini, 228

Tell—The Arabic word for a mound formed by the construction, occupation, and destruction of buildings over time. A site occupied for hundreds or thousands of years will have many layers, or strata, of occupational debris.

Tell el-Amarna—See **Amarna**.

Upper Egypt—The portion of the Nile Valley from the first cataract to the beginning of the Delta around modern Cairo.

Uraeus—An image of a rearing cobra worn on the brow of an Egyptian pharaoh. It was thought to magically protect him from enemies.

Ushabti—See **Shabti**.

Vizier—An administrative official in the ancient Near East second only to the king. The vizier was much like a modern prime minister.

Votive objects—Statues, weapons, or other objects dedicated to a deity or deities in fulfillment of a vow or as an act of worship. Such objects were usually placed in shrines or temples or ceremonially buried.

Yahweh—The personal name of the god of Israel and Judah, written with just the consonants equivalent to YHWH. Yahweh was probably originally a creator god whose name derived from the causative form of the Hebrew verb "to be," meaning "He brings into being [all that exists]."

Ziggurat—An Anglicized form of the Akkadian *ziqqurratu*, the term for a high platform with several stages or levels, like a stepped pyramid, on top of which major Mesopotamian temples were built. The word is also sometimes written ziqqurat.

OUTLINE OF ANCIENT NEAR EASTERN CHRONOLOGY, 4000–330 B.C.E.*

Date	Mesopotamia & Iran	The Levant	Egypt	Anatolia & the Aegean
4000	Cities begin developing in Mesopotamia	Chalcolithic ("copper and stone") Period	Farming villages throughout Egypt	Chalcolithic ("copper and stone") Period
3600	Uruk "colonies" established, Ideographic tablets appear in Mesopotamia & Elam			
3400			Separate kingdoms develop in Upper and Lower Egypt	
3200	Proto-Elamite culture develops and expands in Iran			
3000	Sumerians develop syllabic cuneiform writing Beginning of the Early Dynastic Period (c. 3000–2330)	Early Bronze Age urbanization	Hieroglyphic writing developed "Menes" unifies Egypt, c. 3050 Dynasties 1 & 2 (c. 3000–2686)	Early Bronze Age Urbanization in Anatolia
2800				
2600			Old Kingdom, Dynasties 3–6 (c. 2686–2180) Pyramids erected at Giza **Khufu** (c. 2589–2566)	Minoan civilization begins on Crete
2400	**Sargon of Agade** (c. 2330–2279) Akkadian Empire (c. 2330–2193)	Ebla flourishes in Syria		
2200		Early Bronze Age cities destroyed; semi-nomadic interlude (c. 2200–2000)	1st Intermediate Period (c. 2200–2060) Middle Kingdom, Dynasties 11–13 (c. 2060–1780)	Cities destroyed; Indo-Europeans move in? (c. 2200–2000)
2000	Third Dynasty of Ur (c. 2112–2004) Invasion of Amorites	Middle Bronze Age (c. 2000–1500) Proto-Canaanite alphabet developed		Minoan palaces arise in Crete Assyrian merchant colonies in Anatolia (c. 1920–1750)
1800	**Shamshi-Adad** (c. 1809–1776) **Hammurabi** (c. 1792–1750)		Second Intermediate Period (c. 1720–1540) Hyksos Rule (c. 1650–1540)	Earthquakes destroy Minoan palaces? (c. 1800) Thera explodes in Aegean (c. 1625)
1600	Hittites destroy Babylon (1595) Kassite rule (c. 1590–1157)	Mitanni a major power Late Bronze Age (c. 1500–1150)	New Kingdom, Dynasties 18–20 (1550–1150)	

(continues)

OUTLINE OF ANCIENT NEAR EASTERN CHRONOLOGY, 4000–330 B.C.E., continued

Date	Mesopotamia & Iran	The Levant	Egypt	Anatolia & the Aegean
1500		Egyptian control of the Levant	Thutmose III (c. 1479–1425)	Mycenaeans conquer Crete (c. 1500) Hittite Empire at its height
1400	Kurigalzu I Burnaburiash II	Hittites conquer northern Syria	Akhenaton (c. 1350–1334)	Suppiluliumas I (c. 1344–1322) Mursilis II (c. 1321–1295)
1300			Ramesses II (c. 1279–1212)	Muwatallis II (c. 1295–1272) Hittite Empire destroyed;
1200	Aramaean attacks	Sea Peoples invade Aramaean states created		Mycenaean palaces destroyed; Dark Age in Greece
1100	Zoroaster reforms Iranian religion? Chaldeans move into Babylonia	Israel created (c. 1150–1025) David (c. 1005–960)		Neo-Hittite kingdoms flourish
1000		Solomon (c. 960–931) Divided Monarchy in Palestine	Libyan rule (Dynasties 22–23, 945–747)	Urartu flourishes in eastern Anatolia Phrygia flourishes in central Anatolia
900	Neo-Assyrian Empire			Greek Dark Ages end, alphabet introduced into Greece
800	Asshurnasirpal II (883–859)	Aram-Damascus is powerful		Lydian kingdom flourishes in western Anatolia (c. 685–547)
700	Sargon II (721–705) Assyrian Empire at its height Asshurbanipal (668–627)	Phoenicians establish colonies around Mediterranean	Nubian rule (Dyn. 25, 747–656)	
600	Neo-Babylonian Empire (625–539) Nebuchadnezzar (604–562)	Jerusalem destroyed by Nebuchadnezzar (586)	Saite Period (Dyn. 26, 664–525)	
500	Cyrus II creates Persian Empire (550); Darius I (522–486)		Persian conquest (525)	Persians conquer Lydia & Ionian cities (547)
400	Xerxes I (486–465)	Ezra (458?); Nehemiah (445?)		
330	Conquest by Alexander (331)	Conquest by Alexander (333/2)	Conquest by Alexander (332)	Conquest by Alexander (334/3)

*The most import rulers' names are printed in boldface.

Index

A-annepadda, 41
Abarnahara, 298, 302
Abi-eshuh, 88
Abijam (Abijah), 248
Abraham, 328
Abu Gosh, 12
Abu Hureyra. *See* Tell Abu Hureyra
Abu Rawash, 128
Abu Salabikh, 30, 38
Abu Simbel, 113, 174, 207, 208
Abydos, 2, 9, 106, 111, 113, 139, 143, 146, 152, 154, 155, 171, 176, 206
Abzu (or *apsu*), 46, 48
Acco, 235, 247, 250
Achaea, Achaean(s), 178, 198–199, 212
Achaemenes, Achaemenian(s), Achaemenid, 295, 298, 308, 318, 320
Achish, 245
Ackroyd, Peter, 321 (n. 8)
Acre, 148
Ada, 319
Adab, 41
Adad, 226, 283
Adad-idri. *See* Hadadezer
Adad-guppi, 285
Adad-nirari I, 196, 215
Adad-nirari II, 224
Adad-nirari III, 218, 224, 225, 232, 274
Adams, Robert McC., 28 (n. 16), 62, 63 (n. 3)
Adams, W. Y., 135
Administrative organization, 71–72, 77–78, 112, 146, 148, 200, 228, 237–239, 252, 257–258, 301–302, 307
Admonitions of Ipuwer, 149, 152, 160 (n. 14)
Adonis, 239
Adriatic Sea, 237
Aegean cultures and kingdoms, 3, 61, 73, 173, 176–178, 211
Aegean Sea, Aegean area, 1, 61, 158, 169, 210, 211, 212–213, 236, 237, 251, 252, 253, 293, 304, 305
Aegina, 61
Afghanistan, 1, 23, 34, 40, 61
Africa, 1–2, 10, 13, 235, 236, 256, 257

Afrocentrism, 136 (n. 2)
Afterlife, 47, 117–119, 141–143, 150, 151, 309, 318
Agade (Akkad), 38, 65, 66, 67, 68, 69, 70, 72, 73, 75, 81, 89, 285, 296
Agga (Aka), 42, 43, 54
Agricultural Revolution, 10, 13–16, 22–23, 323
Aha (Hor-Aha), 108, 110, 111
Ahab, 226, 231, 244, 248, 249–251, 254
Ahaz, 286
Ahaziah, king of Israel, 248, 251, 262 (n. 43)
Ahaziah, king of Judah, 248, 251
Ahhiyawa (Ahhiya), 194, 195, 198, 212
Ahmose, 156, 162, 163, 165, 167
Ahmose Nefertari, 162–163, 164
Ahura Mazda (Ormazd), 305, 306, 309–310, 313
Ahuras, 308, 309
Ai, 243
Ain Ghazal, 12, 14–15
Ain Mallaha, 12
Aitken, M. J., 26
Akalamdug, 44
Akawasha, 208, 210
Akh, 118, 119, 124, 125, 143, 150, 182
Akhenaton (Amenhotep IV), 163, 165, 175, 178–187, 189, 194
Akhet, 119, 125, 126, 182, 184
Akhetaton (El-Amarna), 94, 178, 181, 182, 184
Akiti (Akitu) festival(s), 49–50,
Akkad. *See* Agade
Akkadian(s), 36, 38, 39, 46, 54, 60, 65, 69, 71, 77, 80, 90, 98, 174–175, 178, 197, 203, 204, 278, 301, 306, 326
Akkadian Empire, 65–75, 76, 79, 81, 97, 205
Akurgal, Ekrem, 219
Alaca Hüyük, 40, 60, 213
Alalakh, 59, 97, 159, 178, 194, 212, 218
Alalla, 237
Alasiya. *See* Cyprus
Albright, William Foxwell, 63 (n. 10, 11), 262 (n. 47)

Aldred, Cyril, 135, 190, 191 (n. 19), 192 (n. 21, 29)
Aleppo, 8, 40, 68, 69, 88, 95, 97, 194, 226, 257
Alexander III, the Great, 301, 308, 319–320
Alexandria, 113, 325
Algaze, Guillermo, 62, 63 (n. 5)
Algebra, 324
Algeria, 237, 240
Ali Kosh, 12, 15
Alishar, 60, 213
Alksandus (Alexandros?), 198
Allen, James P., 191 (n. 13), 192 (n. 25)
Alphabet. *See under* Writing
Altin Tepe, 228
Altyn Tepe, 40, 84
Alyattes, 293–294, 295
Amada, 113, 170
Amanus Mountains, 67, 69, 271
Amarna. *See* Akhetaton
Amarna Letters, 94, 175, 186, 188, 208
Amar-Sin, 68, 77, 78
Amaziah, 248
Amel-Marduk (Evil-Merodach), 264, 281, 284, 288
Amenemhet I, 140, 146–147, 152, 163
Amenemhet II, 140, 147
Amenemhet III, 140, 147, 148
Amenemhet IV, 140, 148
Amenhotep I, 9, 163
Amenhotep II, 163, 169–170, 174
Amenhotep III, 117, 163, 165, 167, 170–173, 175, 178, 179, 180, 181, 182, 189
Amenhotep IV. *See* Akhenaton
Amenmose, 205
Amesha spentas, 309
Amka, 194, 195, 205
Amman, 14, 253
Ammiditana, 88
Ammisaduqa, 88
Ammon, Ammonite(s), 226, 246, 250, 253, 254, 263, 267, 280, 302, 315
Ammurapi, 213
Amon, 286, 287

Amorite(s) (Amurru, Martu), 58, 60, 74, 78–79, 86, 88, 242

Amos, 251

Amri, 40

Amun, 117, 144, 151–152, 163, 164, 165, 167, 168, 172, 179, 180, 181, 182, 183, 187, 189, 195, 207, 226, 227, 241, 273

Amun-Re, 120, 121, 163, 168, 227

Amurru (place), 175, 194, 196, 210

Amut-pi-El, 88

Amyrteus, 318

An (Anu), 46, 48, 49, 66, 80, 204

Anahita, 310

Anat, 233, 239

Anatolia (Asia Minor), 1, 3, 15–17, 21, 22, 40, 47, 52, 60–61, 67, 68, 69, 72, 73, 74, 85–86, 90, 94, 95, 96, 97, 98, 158, 174, 193, 195, 201, 204, 210, 212, 213, 214, 216, 217, 218, 219, 227–230, 233, 257, 265, 271, 280, 286, 293, 294, 297, 302, 303, 305, 319, 320

Anau, 40, 84

Anderson, Bernhard W., 260 (n. 22), 292 (n. 21), 314, 322 (n. 10, 12)

Anderson, G. W., 321 (n. 8)

Andreu, Guillemette, 136

Andrews, Carol, 137 (n. 15)

Angel(s), 317, 318

Angra Mainu (Ahriman), 309, 317

Anittas, 94

Ankara, 40

Ankhesenamun (Ankhesenpaaton), 186–188

Ankhkeperure Neferneferuaton, 186–187, 192 (n. 30, 31)

Anshan, 39, 40, 68, 69, 75, 294, 295, 296, 298, 299

Antiochus IV, 318

Anu. See An

Anubis, 167

Apadana, 311

Apasa. See Ephesus

Aphek, 148

Apil-Sin, 88

Apis bull(s), 171, 207

Apollo, 239

Apollonia, 298

Apopi (Apophis), 140, 155, 157

Appleby, Joyce, 26

Aqaba, Gulf of, 235, 246, 247, 250, 255, 256

Arab(s), Arabia, Arabian(s), 1, 2, 12, 21, 40, 69, 79, 81, 104, 113, 119, 178,

226, 233, 235, 236, 246, 247, 255, 256–258, 270, 271, 281, 298, 299, 324, 325, 326

Arab Gulf. See Persian Gulf

Arabah, 235

Arachosia, 298

Arad, 59, 243, 286

Aral Sea, 2, 40, 298

Aram, Aramaean(s), Aramaic, 214, 216, 223, 230–233, 234, 242, 246, 247, 249, 251, 263, 264, 298, 314, 315, 325

Ararat. See Urartu

Aratama, 170

Arbil (Arbela), 216, 271, 276, 298

Archaeology, archaeological, archaeologist(s), 4–5, 6–7, 13, 14, 15, 17, 20, 21, 22, 23, 34, 45, 51, 59, 60, 61, 72, 80, 81, 83, 84, 85, 87, 106, 127, 158–159, 174, 176, 178, 179, 204, 210, 216, 218, 220 (n. 13), 235, 240, 242, 243, 245, 246, 253, 280, 281, 285, 286, 313

Archeomagnetic dating, 8

Ardys, 293, 295

Aria, 2, 298

Aristagoras, 303

Aristocrats. See Nobles

Ark of the Covenant, 248

Armenia, 2, 12, 40, 74, 96, 97, 98, 227, 294, 298

Army. See military organization

Arnon River, 253, 254, 255

Arnuwandas II, 193

Arnuwandas III, 193

Aroer, 254, 255

Arrapha, 97

Arsaces. See Artaxerxes II

Arsames, 316

Arses, 319

Art(s), 12, 55, 155, 227, 277–278, 294, 310–313, 327

Artaxerxes I, 295, 305, 310, 312, 314, 315, 318, 319

Artaxerxes II, 295, 301, 310, 314, 319

Artaxerxes III, 295, 319

Artaxerxes IV, 295, 319

Artemis, 294

Artifact(s), 5, 17, 106, 108

Artisan(s), 24, 52, 55, 85, 106, 153, 215, 227, 236–237, 310, 313

Arvad, 226, 235, 236, 237, 250, 267

Aryan(s), 36, 83, 85, 97

Arzawa, Arzawan(s), 95, 174, 194, 195, 204, 210, 293

Asa, 248

Asante, Molefe Kete, 136 (n. 2)

Asha, 309

Ashavans, 309

Ashdod, 246, 250, 252, 267, 269, 302

Asherah, 152, 176, 240, 244, 249, 286, 287

Ashkelon, 148, 209, 250, 252, 267

Ashmore, Wendy, 26

Ashtar-Kemosh, 254

Ashtart (Astarte), 233, 239, 240, 241, 252, 254

Asia, Asiatic(s), 2, 16, 19, 79, 84, 85, 98, 157, 170, 171, 175, 188, 209

Asia Minor. See Anatolia

Asiab. See Tepe Asiab

Aşikli Hüyük, 12

Askitario, 61

Asshur, 40, 41, 67, 69, 75, 85, 86, 87, 214, 216, 224, 225, 226, 264, 271, 272, 276, 279, 296, 310

Asshurbanipal, 264, 270–272, 273, 274, 275, 277, 278, 279, 281, 287, 294, 310

Asshur-dan III, 224

Asshur-nadin-shumi, 264, 268

Asshurnasirpal I, 216

Asshurnasirpal II, 223–224, 225, 235, 275, 277

Asshur-nirari V, 224

Asshur-uballit I, 215

Assman, Jan, 135

Assuwa, 293

Assyria, Assyrian(s), 9, 20, 45, 67, 68, 69, 85, 86, 87, 88, 94, 98, 99, 169, 170, 175, 194, 195, 196, 213, 214, 215–217, 223–225, 226, 227, 228, 229, 230, 231, 232, 233, 245, 249, 253, 256, 257, 258, 298, 303, 306, 313, 317, 320, 325

    art, literature and science, 277–278

    imperial administration, 276–277

    kingship, 272–273, 297

    military organization, 275–276

    Neo-Assyrian Period, 263–278, 279, 286, 287, 288, 294

    Old Assyrian Period, 85–86

    social structure, 272–274

Astour, Michael, 221 (n. 28, 29)

Astrology, astrologer(s), 56, 128, 272–273, 278, 324, 325

Aström, Paul, 26

Astronomy, astronomical observation(s), 8–9, 56, 128–129, 133–134, 278, 324–325
Astyages (Ishtumegu), 285, 294, 295, 297
Aswan (Syene), 103, 113, 127, 149, 154, 207, 316
Asyut, 144, 154
Ataroth, 255
Atbara river, 103, 154, 257
Athaliah, 248, 249, 251
Athens, Athenian(s), 212, 237, 303, 304, 305, 319
Athribis, 171
Aton, 171, 172, 173, 179, 180, 181–185
Atonement rites, 45, 46–47, 273
Atossa, 306
Attica, 61, 212, 304, 305
Atum, 120, 121, 125, 128, 182
Avaris (Tell ed-Dab'a), 113, 152, 154, 156, 157, 162, 206
Avesta, 308, 310
Avigad, Nahman, 291 (n. 20)
Awan, 39, 40, 41, 67
Awayli. *See* Tell Awayli
Awêlum, 91–93
Ay, 163, 165, 180, 184, 187, 188–189
Azores, 236

Ba, 118–119, 124, 141, 142, 143
Ba'al, 152, 155, 232, 233, 239, 240, 241, 244, 249, 253
Ba'al-zebub (Ba'al-zebul), 252
Baasha, 248
Babylon, 2, 9, 30, 40, 46, 66, 69, 71, 87, 87, 88, 89, 97, 169, 175, 176, 193, 194, 214, 256, 257, 263, 265, 267, 268, 269, 271, 272, 279, 280, 281–284, 285, 296, 297, 298, 299, 300, 301, 311, 318, 320;
    "Hanging Gardens," 281, 282, 283, 284, 325
    Ishtar Gate, 99, 282, 283, 284
    Northern Palace, 281, 282
    Processional Way, 282, 283–284
    Southern Palace, 282, 283
    Temple of Marduk (*Esagila*), 282, 283
    Ziggurat (*Etemenanki*), 282, 283, 284
Babylonia, Babylonian(s), 2, 5, 30, 98, 99, 169, 171, 203, 207, 223, 225, 230, 239, 257, 268, 269, 277, 300, 305, 317, 324
    Kassite period, 98–99, 215–217
    Neo-Babylonian Period, 264, 279–286, 287, 288–289, 294, 295, 297, 298, 299
    Old Babylonian Period, 85–94, 95

Babylonian Chronicle, 264
Babylonian Exile, 242, 245, 281, 288–289, 315, 317
Bacchus, 294
Bactra, 2, 298
Bactria, 2, 40, 84, 297, 298
Badarian culture, 23
Badawy, Alexander, 159
Bad-tibira, 30
Baghdad, 19, 20, 30, 41, 79
Bagoas (governor of Judah), 315, 316, 317
Bagoas (chief eunuch of Artaxerxes III), 319
Bahn, Paul, 26
Bahariya Oasis, 154
Bahrain, 2, 21, 40, 79, 80
Baillie, M. G. L., 161 (n. 30), 222 (n. 50)
Baines, John, 135, 137 (n. 9), 192 (n. 30)
Baki, 294
Balearic Islands, 237
Balikh river, 97, 223, 224
Baltic languages, 96
Baluchistan, 40
Ban (sacrificial offering). *See* Herem
Banning, E. B., 26
Bardiya (Smerdis), 295, 299–300
Barnett, R. D., 290
Bar-Yosef, Ofer, 26, 27
Barnett, R. D., 221 (n. 26)
Bar-Yosef, Ofer, 27 (n. 10)
Basgelen, Nezih, 27
Basta, 12
Bastam, 228
Beckman, G., 219
Beer, 11, 323
Beersheba, 250, 286
Behistun (Bisitun), 298, 300–301
Beidha, 12
Beisamoun, 12, 15
Beketaton, 172
Bell, Barbara, 138 (n. 32)
Bell, Lanny, 137 (n. 12)
Belshazzar (Bel-shar-usur), 285, 286
Ben-Hadad (Bir-Hadad), 231, 232, 251
Beni Hasan, 113, 147, 154
Benjamin, Don C., 321 (n. 1)
Beqaa, Valley, 231, 235
Berlin, 283
Bermant, Chaim, 62, 99
Bernal, Martin, 136 (n. 2)
Berossus, 5, 284
Berytus (Beirut), 235, 250
Bes, 123
Betancourt, P. P., 161 (n. 31, 32), 222 (n. 43)
Bethel, 244, 248, 250
Bethlehem, 245

Beth Rehob, 231
Beth-shean, 235, 250
Beth Shemesh, 148
Betyl(s), 240
Beycesultan, 60
Beyer, Bryan E., 322 (n. 9)
Beyerlin, Walter, 25
Bia, Biainili. *See* Urartu
Bible, biblical, 49, 66, 78, 97, 115, 176, 178, 200, 210, 221 (n. 20, 21), 224, 227, 230, 231, 232, 233, 237, 240, 241, 242, 243, 244, 245, 246, 247, 249, 250, 251, 252, 253, 254, 256, 264, 266, 267, 276, 280, 281, 288, 289, 290 (n.1), 291 (n. 14, 16, 19), 314, 315, 326
Bienkowski, Piotr, 25, 260 (n. 13), 262 (n. 49)
Bietak, Manfred, 26, 156, 159, 161 (n. 23, 27, 29, 32)
Biggs, Robert, 26
Binger, Tilde, 258
Biran, Avraham, 260 (n. 6)
Biridashwa, 98
Bit-Adini, 223–224, 230
Bit-Bahyani, 230
Bit-Halupe, 230
Bit-reduti, 273
Bittel, Kurt, 219
Bit-Yakin, 265, 268
Bit-Zamani, 230
Black, Jeremy, 61
Black Obelisk, 226
Black Sea, 1, 2, 12, 40, 49, 69, 96, 194, 195, 214, 237, 265, 269, 271, 298, 303, 318
Blue Nile, 103, 154
Boeotia, 212, 213
Bogucki, Peter, 27
Book of the Dead, 143, 151
Borsippa, 30, 285
Bottéro, Jean, 61
Bouqras, 12
Bourriau, J. D., 159
Boyce, Mary A., 321
Bozrah, 256
Braidwood, Robert, 10, 15
Brandt, K., 137 (n. 3)
Breasted, James, 168, 178, 191 (n. 12), 221 (n. 14)
Breton, J. F., 259, 262 (n. 50)
Brier, Bob, 190, 191 (n. 13), 192 (n. 31, 32)
Bright, John, 64 (n. 26), 258, 290 (n. 2), 322 (n. 11)
Brinkman, J. A., 222 (n. 36), 290

Brittany, 236

Bronze Age, 57, 96, 198, 217, 218, 219, 233, 239, 240, 241
  Early Bronze Age, 58–61, 72–74, 84, 147, 158, 253
  Late Bronze Age, 173, 174–176, 199–219, 243, 244, 253
  Middle Bronze Age, 147, 159, 174, 246, 253

Brosius, Maria, 320

Brothwell, D. R., 26

Bryant, Edwin, 100

Bryce, Trevor, 199, 219, 220 (n. 1, 3, 4, 8), 221 (n. 26), 222 (n. 46, 52)

Bryson, R. A., 222 (n. 48)

Buccellati, Giorgio G., 99

Bullae, 34

Burial practices, 11–12, 15, 16, 17, 23, 47, 114, 117–119, 149–150, 153, 182, 183, 229, 252, 294, 310

Burney, Charles, 25

Burutas, 230

Butzer, Karl W., 101 (n. 16), 135, 138 (n. 32), 222 (n. 49)

Byblos. *See* Gubal

Cadiz. *See* Gadir

Caesar, Julius, 325

Cahill, Jane, 262 (n. 39, 42)

Cairo, 22, 40, 103, 106, 113, 189

Calah. *See* Kalhu

Calendars, 9–10, 56, 104, 133, 324–325

Callaway, Joseph A., 261 (n. 34, 35)

Cambyses I, 295, 296

Cambyses II, 295, 298, 299, 300, 301, 308, 310, 316, 317

Camel(s), 226, 233, 257, 260 (n. 8), 307, 308

Campbell, Edward F. Jr., 190

Canaan, Canaanite(s), 49, 58, 60, 119, 147, 152, 154, 155, 156–158, 168, 170, 174–176, 177, 184, 187, 196, 206, 209, 210, 215, 217, 218, 230, 233, 239, 240, 241, 242, 243, 244, 248, 249, 250, 252, 253, 286, 326, 327

Cape Artemisium, 305

Capel, Anne K., 135

Cappadocia, 298

Carbon-14 dating. *See* Radiocarbon dating

Carchemish, 2, 32, 40, 69, 97, 169, 194, 195, 210, 213, 214, 224, 229, 230, 254, 265, 271, 279, 280, 298

Carpenter, Rhys, 222 (n. 48)

Carter, Elizabeth, 61, 99

Carter, Howard, 188

Carthage (Qart-hadasht), 236, 237, 238, 239, 240, 241

Cartouche, 116, 123, 183

Caspian Sea, 1, 2, 37, 40, 69, 84, 96, 169, 214, 271, 298

Casson, Lionel, 135

Caste system, 83

Çatal Hüyük, 12, 16–18

Cataracts. *See under* Nile

Caubet, Annie, 25

Caucasus, 1, 74, 96, 97, 227, 265, 294, 298

Cavalry, 217, 226, 270, 275–276, 297, 307–308, 319, 320

Çayönü Tepesi, 12, 15–16

Cayster River, 293

Celtic languages, 96

Cernenko, E. N., 290

Černy, Jaroslav, 220, 221 (n. 30)

Chadwick, John, 190, 220 (n. 7)

Chadwick, Robert, 137 (n. 25)

Chaeronea, 319

Chagar-Bazar, 97

Chakrabarti, Dilip K., 100

Chalandriani, 61

Chalcidice, 304

Chalcolithic Period, 23

Chaldean(s), 223, 225, 263, 264, 265, 267, 268, 271, 279, 280, 281, 284

Chanhu-Daro, 40, 84

Chariot(s), 57–58, 85, 96–97, 155, 173, 196, 203, 217, 226, 247, 275, 276, 298, 307, 320

Cheops. *See* Khufu

Chephren. *See* Khafre

Cherethites, 245

Cherubim, 248

Chew, S., 321

Child sacrifice. *See* Sacrifice, infant

Childe, V. Gordon, 10, 13, 31

Chios, 61

Choga Mami, 20

Christian(s), Christianity, 289, 310, 318, 324, 327–328

Chronicles, Books of, 263, 291 (n. 16), 321 (n. 8, 9)

Chronology (and dating), 6–7, 8–10, 29, 68, 88, 106, 133, 140, 158, 159, 161 (n. 30, 31, 32), 163, 193, 224, 248, 264, 279, 286, 291 (n. 14), 295

Cilicia, Cilician(s), 2, 210, 212, 213, 214, 230, 269, 285, 298, 304

Clapp, Nicholas, 259

Class differences, origins of, 22, 24, 31

Clausen, H. B., 161 (n. 30)

Clay tablets, 33, 34, 36, 59, 60, 71, 78, 85, 90, 95, 99, 175, 176, 179, 203, 254, 278, 280, 281, 310

Clayton, Peter A., 135, 137 (n. 10)

Cleisthenes, 304

Clifford, Richard J., 292 (n. 22)

Climatic change, 10–11, 13, 31, 73–74, 96, 218–219

Cline, Eric H., 190, 222 (n. 47)

Code of Hammurabi, 78, 91–93

Cogan, Mordecai, 291 (n. 3)

Cohen, Raymond, 190

Cohn, Norman, 321

Coins, coinage, 294

Colchis, 298, 302

Coleman, John, 136 (n.2)

Collon, Dominique, 25, 61

Colossi of Memnon, 164, 171

Comet(s), 74, 101 (n. 13)

Communal property, 20, 24, 199

Complaints of Khakheperre-sonbe, 149

Composite bow, 57, 155, 173

Constantine, 327

Coogan, Michael, 25

Cook, J. M., 320, 321 (n. 2, 3, 4, 6)

Cooper, Jerrold S., 38, 63 (n. 12)

Coptos, Coptic, 121, 152, 325

Co-regency, co-regent(s), 146, 148, 179–180, 186, 187, 189, 206

Corinth, 237

Cornford, F. M., 328

Coronation rite(s), 117, 121–122

Corsica, 237

Corvée labor, 53, 127, 247

Cosmology, 48–49, 120–121

Court History of David, 242

Covenant, 200, 243, 287

Craft specialization. *See* Artisans

Crawford, Harriet, 62, 100

Crete (Caphtor, Kaptara, Keftiu), Cretan(s), 2, 3, 67, 147, 153, 156, 158–159, 174, 176, 178, 210, 212–213, 214, 217, 235, 236, 237, 298

Croesus, 294, 295, 297

Crouwel, J. H., 102 (n. 43)

Cultic prostitution. *See* Prostitution, cultic

Cumae, 237

Cunaxa, 318

Cuneiform. *See under* Writing

Curnow, A., 100 (n. 8)

Curse of Agade, 72

Curtis, John, 320

Cuthah, 30

Cyaxares (Huvakshatra), 279, 294, 295, 297

Cybele. *See* Kybele

Cylinder seal(s), 32–33, 44, 45

Cyprus, 2, 3, 12, 40, 67, 69, 174, 175, 178, 198, 210, 211, 212, 213, 214, 227, 235, 236, 237, 240, 252, 253, 257, 267, 271, 298, 299, 302, 303, 304

Cyrene (Cyrenaica), 237, 299

Cyrus I, 295, 296, 300

Cyrus II, 285–286, 294–299, 300, 306, 308, 310, 313

Cyrus (son of Darius II), 318

Cyrus Cylinder, 295, 296

Daevas, 308, 309

Dagan, 91

Dagon, 252

Dahshur, 126, 127, 149

Dakhla Oasis, 154

Dalfes, H. Nüzhet, 99, 100 (n. 8), 101 (n. 9, 12, 16, 18)

Dalley, Stephanie, 61

Damascus, 2, 40, 196, 224–225, 226, 230–232, 233, 235, 236, 249, 250, 251, 257, 263, 271, 280, 285

Dan, 231, 232, 235, 248, 249, 250, 252

Dandamaev, M. A., 320

Daniel, Book of, 285

Danube River, 303

Danuna. *See* Denyen

Dardany (*Dardanoi?*), 198

Darius I, 295, 298, 299–304, 305, 306, 310, 311, 312, 313

Darius II, 295, 316, 318

Darius III, 295, 319–320

Darius (son of Artaxerxes II), 319

Dashli Oasis, 40

Daviau, P. M. Michèle, 262 (n. 48)

David, 231, 244, 245–246, 251, 253, 254, 255, 256, 287, 313

David, Rosalie, 135

Davies, D., 321

Davies, Philip R., 261 (n. 38)

Davies, Vivian, 135

Davies, W. D., 135

Dead Sea, 69, 250, 253, 271

Dead Sea Scrolls, 285

Dearman, Andrew, 259

Death of Gilgamesh. See Gilgamesh, The Death of

Dedan, 2, 257

Deiokes, 295

Deir el-Bahri, 144, 145, 163, 164, 166–167, 172

Deir el-Medina, 164

Deities:

Ammonite, 253

Arabian, 258

Aramaean, 232–233

Canaanite/Phoenician, 152, 176, 239–240

Edomite, 256

Egyptian, 116–117, 119–123, 181–185

Hittite, 201–202

Israelite, 244, 286–289

Lydian, 294

Mesopotamian, 46–49

Mitannian, 98

Moabite, 254–255

Neo-Hittite, 230

Phrygian, 229

Urartian, 228

Delaiah, 316, 317

Delian League, 305

Delphi, Oracle of, 294, 297

Delta. *See under* Egypt

Deluge. *See* Flood

Demand, Nancy, 321

Democracy, democracies, 50, 51, 304

Demon(s), 47, 317

Den, 112

Dendera, 113

Dendrochronology (tree-ring dating), 8

Denyen (Danuna), 210, 217, 252

Deportation(s), 195, 199, 263, 264, 267, 272, 277, 288

Der, 30, 296

Derry, Douglas, 192 (n. 31)

Determinatives (in writing), 36, 111, 112

Deutero-Isaiah (Second Isaiah), 289, 297, 313, 317

Deuteronomy, Deuteronomist(ic), 90, 199, 287, 288, 289, 314, 315, 316

Deuteronomistic History (Joshua-2 Kings), 287–289

Dever, William G., 258, 261 (n. 30, 33), 262 (n. 39)

Diakonoff, I. M., 102 (n. 45)

Dibon, Dibonite, 231, 243, 250, 251, 254, 255

Dickson, Oliver, 222 (n. 43)

Dilbat, 30

Dilmun, 40, 67, 69, 72, 79–81, 256

Dion, Paul-Eugène, 262 (n. 48)

Disease and plague, 23–24, 83, 140, 186, 195, 205, 225, 263, 285

Dispute of a Man With His Ba, 141, 142

Divination, 47, 203

Divine kingship, 45, 68–71, 72, 77, 86, 115–117, 167, 172–173, 182–183

Diyala river, 2, 30, 41

Djedefre, 128, 133

Djeitun. *See* Jeitun

Djer, 112, 119

Djoser, 123–124

Dodson, Aidan, 135, 137 (n. 16)

Domestication of animals, 11, 12, 14, 15, 22, 23

Donley, D. L., 222 (n. 48)

Dor, 210, 227, 235, 250, 252, 264

Dorian(s), 217

Dornemann, Rudolph H., 259

Dossin, Georges, 101 (n. 32, 34, 35)

Dothan, Moshe, 221 (n. 22)

Dothan, Trude, 211, 221 (n. 22, 23, 24)

Doumas, Christos G., 160

Dra Abu el-Naga, 163, 164

Dravidian(s), 39, 83

Dregvants, 309

Drehem (Puzrish-Dagan), 30, 78

Drews, Robert, 97, 98, 100, 102 (n. 40, 42, 43, 44, 45), 217–218, 221 (n. 26), 222 (n. 39, 40, 41, 44, 45, 46, 51)

Drought, 73, 74, 79, 96, 140, 216, 218–219, 244

Druj, 309

Dry farming, 20, 73,

Duma, 2, 257, 258

Dumuzi (Tammuz), 43, 48, 50, 239

Dunstan, William E., 25

Dur-Sharrukin (Khorsabad), 265, 266, 271

Dur-Yakin, 265

Eannatum, 43, 44

Early Bronze Age. *See* Bronze Age

Early Dynastic Period in Egypt, 74, 112–123, 125

Early Dynastic Period in Mesopotamia, 36, 37, 40–58, 70, 273

Earthquake(s), 218, 219

Ebla (Tell Mardikh), 8, 40, 59–60, 67, 68, 69, 254

Ecbatana, 297, 298, 299, 300, 301, 320

Ecclesiastes, 318

Economy, economic system, 22, 31, 51–52, 57, 72, 78, 93–94, 199, 218, 227–228, 230, 233, 235–236, 252, 256–258, 274, 302, 307, 315

Eden, 43, 49

Edfu, 2, 113

Edom (Se'ir), Edomite(s), Idumaeans, 231, 246, 250, 253, 255–256, 257, 263, 267, 280, 302, 313

Education, 53–54, 60, 306

Edwards, I. E. S., 26, 135, 137 (n. 20), 221 (n. 26)

Egypt, Egyptian(s), 1–3, 7, 8–9, 12, 13, 22–23, 34, 40, 41, 45, 52, 59, 60, 103, 108–112, 113, 115, 116, 117, 148, 153, 156, 162, 171, 194, 205, 214, 215, 217, 234, 235, 239, 241, 242, 243, 244, 252, 253, 257, 264, 267, 270, 271, 285, 288, 297, 298, 299, 304, 305, 306, 311, 312, 315, 318, 319, 320, 325, 326
   Amarna period, 178–190
   burial and afterlife, 117–119, 183
   delta, 22–23, 103, 104, 105, 106, 108, 109, 110, 114, 139, 140, 151, 154, 155, 158, 206, 208, 209, 215, 226, 227, 235, 236, 237, 270, 281, 299
   Early Dynastic Period, 112–123, 125
   Hyksos, 140, 153–158, 159, 162
   intermediate period(s), 139–143, 152–158, 159, 225–227, 273
   kingship, 115–117, 149, 167, 172–173, 182
   Middle Kingdom, 9, 140, 143–152, 153, 160 (n. 14), 167, 172, 176
   New Kingdom, 9, 10, 147, 160 (n. 14), 162–189, 195–198, 205–208, 215
   Old Kingdom, 59, 118, 123–134, 139, 140, 141, 146, 147
   predynastic era, 22–23, 105–112, 116, 118, 119
   religion and ritual, 119–123, 181–185
Ehrich, Robert W., 26
Ekallatum, 87
Ekron, 210, 252, 267, 269
El, 176, 244, 249, 286
Elah, 248
Elam, Elamite(s), 2, 39–40, 41, 42, 43, 67, 68, 69, 216, 217, 230, 264, 265, 268, 270–272, 277, 279, 294, 298, 300, 301, 306, 311, 325
Elba, 237
Elburz Mountains, 298
Elephantine, 2, 69, 105, 113, 155, 257, 271, 289, 315, 316
Elephantine Papyri, 315, 316–317
Elephants, 307
El-Hiba, 226
Eliakim. See Jehoiakim
Elijah, 249
El Kab, 113
Ellipi, 225
Eloquent Peasant, Protests of the, 132, 149
Eltekeh, 267
Emar, 59, 60, 90, 216
Emporio, 61
En, 51, 53

England, 236
Enheduanna, 66–67, 71
Enki, 46, 48, 49,
Enlil, 43, 46, 48, 49, 51, 64 (n. 23), 66, 71, 80, 90, 205
Enlil-bani, 86
Enmebaragesi, 42–43
Enmenanna, 71
Ensi, 51, 53, 75, 77
Entum (high priestess?), 65, 66
Enuma elish. See Epic of Creation
Eph'al, Israel, 259
Ephesus (Apasa?), 2, 194, 229
Epic of Creation (Enuma elish), 90, 278
Epic of Erra, 216–217
Epic of Gilgamesh, 47, 54, 278
Epicurean philosophy, 318
Eretria, Eretrian(s), 303, 304
Eridu, 19, 21, 22, 29, 30, 31, 37, 46, 49, 51, 86
Erra, 217
Esarhaddon, 258, 264, 268–270, 273, 274, 281, 283
Eschatology, eschatological, 309, 317, 327
Eshba'al, 245, 246
Eshmun, 239
Eshnunna, 30, 41, 88, 89, 90, 296
Esna, 113
Estes, J. Worth, 135
Ethiopia, Ethiopian(s), 103,
Etruria, Etruscan(s), 212, 236, 237, 241, 326
Euboea, 235, 304, 305
Euclid, 324
Eunuch(s), 90, 147, 306
Euphrates river, 1, 2, 12, 13, 20, 21, 29–31, 37, 40, 47, 49, 58, 67, 69, 79, 86, 94, 97, 169, 194, 205, 214, 215, 216, 219, 223, 224, 225, 257, 271, 280, 281, 297, 298, 302
Europe, 19
Eurymedon River, 305
Evil-Merodach. See Amel–Marduk
Execration Texts, 148
Exile, the. See Babylonian Exile
Exodus, 241, 242–243
Exodus, Book of, 243, 251
Eyre, Christopher, 138 (n. 34)
Ezekiel, 280, 381, 317
Ezion-geber, 235, 250, 256
Ezra, 314–315, 319, 321 (n. 9)

Fagan, Brian, 26, 27, 138 (n. 32), 259 (n. 1), 321 (n. 5)
Failaka Island, 79

Fairservice, Walter, 83, 101 (n. 25)
Faiyum Oasis, 22–23, 113, 147, 151, 226
Falcon, N. L., 62 (n. 1)
Famine, 79, 140, 208, 216, 263, 285
Fantar, M'hamed Hassine, 260 (n. 16, 17)
Farafra Oasis, 154
Fars, 39
Faulkner, R. O., 136, 137 (n. 21), 160 (n. 4–8, 11)
Feder, Kenneth L, 27 (n. 4)
Feinan, 256
Feldman, Steven, 191 (n. 10)
Filer, Joyce M., 192 (n. 31)
Final judgment, 141, 143, 309, 318
Finkelstein, Israel, 243, 259, 261 (n. 25, 30, 31, 37), 262 (n. 38)
Finkelstein, L., 321
Finley, M. I., 73, 101 (n. 11)
Finn(s), Finnish, 83
Fission-track dating, 8
Flood (the Deluge), 42, 49, 278
Flood(s), 21, 47, 49, 83–84
Forman, Werner, 136
Fortification(s), fortress(es), 13–14, 20, 24, 59, 60, 75, 79, 84, 106, 115, 146, 147, 153, 155, 156, 168, 178, 194, 212, 217, 224, 228, 230, 235, 236, 246, 247, 249, 266, 267, 281, 282, 283, 299, 316
Foster, Benjamin, 62, 99, 100 (n. 2), 222 (n. 37)
Foster, John L., 135
Frame, Grant, 290
Frankel, D., 258
Frankfort, Henri, 100 (n. 3), 101 (n. 23), 137 (n. 11, 12, 13, 17)
Frankfort, H. A. G., 101 (n. 23), 137 (n. 17)
Frankincense, 256–257
Frasho-kereti, 309
Frayne, Douglas R., 99
Freedman, David N., 26, 101 (n. 43), 161 (n. 21), 191 (n. 9), 221 (n. 26), 260 (n. 4, 5, 8, 11, 22), 261 (n. 30, 36), 291 (n. 7, 9, 17), 292 (n. 22), 322 (n. 9, 11)
French, Valerie, 26
Friedman, Renée, 135
Friedman, Richard Elliott, 260 (n. 22), 262 (n. 45), 291 (n. 17)
Friedrich, W. L., 161 (n. 30)
Frye, Richard N., 320

Gad, 255
Gadd, C. J., 101 (n. 19)
Gadir (Cadiz), 236, 237, 239
Galilee, Galilean, 235, 263
Gallagher, William R., 290, 291 (n.3)

Shophet(im), 239, 245
Shortugai, 40
Shu, 120, 182
Shu-Ilushu, 86
Shulgi, 68, 77–78, 86
Shuruppak, 30, 31
Shu-Sin, 68, 78–79
Shuttarna II, 171
Sicily, Sicilian(s), 212, 240
Sidon, Sidonian(s), 224, 234, 235, 236, 237,
    239, 250, 263, 267, 270, 271, 280
Silberman, Neil Asher, 259, 261 (n. 25, 30,
    31, 37), 262 (n. 38)
Sillibel, 269
Silsileh, 113
Silverman, David P., 136, 137 (n. 6, 12),
    138 (n. 34)
Simpson, William Kelly, 26, 63 (n. 10),
    136, 260 (n. 4)
Sin (moon god), 46, 285
Sinai, 73, 74, 104, 105, 113, 148, 169, 176,
    200, 214, 243, 271, 299
Singer, Itamar, 221 (n. 26, 32)
Sin-muballit, 88
Sinuhe, Story of, 147, 149
Sippar, 30, 46, 71, 86, 88
Siptah, 205
Sirius (*Sepdet*, Sothis), 9, 133
Sitamun, 170
Slave(s), slavery, 52–53, 72, 91, 132–133,
    199, 274
Slavic languages, 96
Smenkhkare, 163, 186–187, 189, 192
    (n. 30, 31)
Smerdis. *See* Bardiya
Smith, Edwin, 134
Smith, Grafton Elliot, 192 (n. 31)
Smith, Mark S., 290
Smith, Tyson, 136 (n. 1)
Snefru, 126, 127, 133, 147
Snell, Daniel C., 26, 38, 63 (n. 13)
Sobek, 119, 151–152
Sobekneferu, 140, 148, 165
Social stratification, 11, 24, 31, 52, 91, 106,
    132–133, 272–274
Sogdianus, 318
Soggin, J. Alberto, 259
Soleb, 172
Solomon, 235, 237, 242, 244, 246–247,
    256, 317
Soma, 98,
Somalia, 168, 256
Song of the Harper, 140, 141
Soviet Union, 84
Spain, 236

Sparta, Spartan(s), 304, 305, 319
Speiser, Ephraim A., 101 (n. 36)
Spence, Kate, 137 (n. 22)
Spencer, A. J., 136, 137 (n. 4)
Sphinx(es), 128–130, 170, 172
Spice(s), 256, 257
Stager, Lawrence E., 260 (n. 18, 19, 21)
Steiner, Margreet, 262 (n. 38, 42)
Steinkeller, Piotr, 64 (n. 28)
Stele, stelae, 68, 70, 89, 91, 99, 156, 157, 162,
    170, 208, 209, 226, 231, 232, 240, 254
Step Pyramid, 123–124, 126
Stern, Eliezer, 220, 221 (n. 17), 222 (n. 48)
Stern, Ephraim, 321
Stiebing, William H. Jr., 27 (n. 4), 101 (n. 20,
    32, 33, 34, 35), 102 (n.38), 125, 142,
    157, 160 (n. 15), 209, 221 (n. 18),
    222 (n. 38, 48), 259, 260 (n. 2, 15),
    261 (n. 27, 29, 30), 321 (n. 1, 5),
    322 (n. 15)
Stolper, M. W., 61
Story of King Neferkare, 149
Story of Sinhue. See Sinhue
Stratigraphy, stratigraphical, 6–7, 63 (n. 18)
Strouhal, Eugen, 136, 138 (n. 33)
Strudwick, Helen, 190
Strudwick, Nigel, 136, 190
Subar, Subarian(s), 39
Suberde, 12, 16
Substitute king rite, 45, 86, 273
Sudan, 103, 168
Suffete. *See* Shophet
Sumer, Sumerian(s), 29, 36, 37–39, 40–58,
    66, 71, 75, 76, 77, 86, 89, 90, 176,
    203, 216, 278, 285, 296, 326
Sumerian King List, 38, 40, 41, 42, 43, 44,
    45, 73, 75
Sumerian Renaissance. *See* Ur, Third
    Dynasty of
Sumu-abum, 88
Sumu-la-El, 88
Sun Goddess of Arinna, 200–201, 202
Sun temple(s), 130, 180
Suppiluliumas I, 188, 193–195, 205. 230
Suppiluliumas II, 193, 213
Susa, 2, 21, 34, 39, 40, 67, 68, 69, 85, 86, 214,
    271, 296, 298, 299, 301, 303, 311, 320
Susiana (Khuzistan), 21, 22, 24, 39
Sweeney, Marvin A., 290
Syllabic writing, 36–37, 60, 111, 112
Syracuse, 318
Syria, Syrian(s), 1, 2, 3, 11, 12, 13, 20, 21, 32,
    44, 52, 58–60, 68, 69, 73, 74, 97, 98,
    112, 140, 148, 152, 156, 168, 169, 170,
    173, 174–176, 179, 188, 190, 193, 194,

195, 196, 205, 206, 208, 209, 213, 214,
    215, 217, 218, 224, 225, 227, 230–241,
    242, 253, 257, 258, 263, 264, 265, 270,
    271, 280, 285, 288, 299, 302, 306, 319,
    327
Systems collapse, 218, 219

Tabal (Tubal), 214, 230, 265, 269, 280
Tablets. *See* Clay tablets
Tabuk, 257
Tadmor, Hayim, 291 (n. 3)
Tadukhepa, 171
Taharqa (Tirhaka), 267, 270
Tales of King Khufu, 149
Tammuz, *See* Dumuzi
Tanis, 226, 227
Tanit. *See* Ashtart
Tanutamun, 270
Tarsus, 60
Taruisa, 198, 212
Tauber, H., 161 (n. 30)
Tauret, 123
Taurus and Anti-Taurus Mountains, 16, 67,
    68, 69, 194, 229, 280
Tawosret, 205, 210
Taxes and/or tribute, 44, 53, 72, 77–78,
    174, 200, 230, 235, 247, 258, 264,
    267, 276, 307, 317
Taylour, Lord William, 191
Tefnut, 120, 182
Tehenu. *See* Libya
Teheran, 270
Tehom ("the Deep"), 49, 64 (n. 24)
Teima, 2, 257, 271, 285
Teisheba, 228
Teispes, 295, 296, 300
Telepinus, 202
Tell (Tel), 7
    Abu Hurere, 161 (n. 21)
    Abu Hureyra, 11, 12
    Agrab, 30, 41
    Amal, 235
    Aswad, 30
    Awayli, 19, 20, 21
    Brak, 32, 34
    ed-Dab`a. *See* Avaris
    ed-Der, 30;
    el-Ajjul, 154, 161 (n. 21)
    el-Far'ah, 161 (n. 21)
    el-Maskhuta. *See* Pithom
    el-Wilayah, 30
    es-Sawwan, 19, 20
    Harmal, 30
    Kabri, 159
    Keisan, 235

Khuera, 41
Kuyunjik. *See* Nineveh
Leilan (Shubat-Enlil), 73, 74, 87, 90, 100 (n. 8)
Masos, 235
Mureybit, 12, 13
Nebi Yunus. *See* Nineveh
Qasile, 252
Ramad, 12, 15
Sahab, 253
Taya, 41
Ubaid, 30
Ugair, 30
Umeiri, 253
Temple(s) and shrines, 20, 31, 46, 52, 53, 59, 70, 72, 76, 77, 80, 84, 99
  Canaanite/Phoenician, 240, 241
  Egyptian, 117, 121–122, 128, 130, 144, 145, 146, 153, 155, 163, 164, 166–167, 168, 171–172, 179, 180, 181, 187, 207
  Israelite, 246, 248, 280, 286–287, 288, 289, 297, 313, 314, 316
  Mesopotamian, 32, 33, 265, 283, 296, 297
  Moabite, 255
  Neolithic, 16–17, 21, 22, 24
  Persian, 310
  Philistine, 252
  Uruk/Jemdet-Nasr era, 32, 33
Tenant farmers, 52, 72, 132, 274
Tepe:
  Asiab, 12, 15
  Ganj Dareh, 12, 15
  Gawra, 22
  Guran, 12
  Hissar, 40, 85
  Sarab, 12
  Sialk, 40
  Yahya, 39, 40, 61, 85
Tept-Humban-Inshushinak (Teumman), 270
Terqa, 91
Teshub, 202, 204, 228, 232
Tetisheri, 164
Teucrians (*Teukroi*), 212
Teumman. *See* Tept-Humban-Inshushinak
Thales of Miletus, 294
Tharros, 237, 240
Thasos, 237
Thebes (in Egypt), 2, 40, 69, 113, 143, 144, 152, 154, 155, 156, 163, 164, 167, 172, 176, 180, 181, 206, 215, 226, 270, 271, 298
Thebes (in Greece), 212, 319
Theodosia, 298

Thera (Santorini), 158, 159, 161 (n. 30, 31, 32), 176, 177, 178, 181, 189
Thermi, 61
Thermoluminescence dating, 8
Thermopylae, 305
Thessaly, 212, 305
Thinis. *See* This
Third Dynasty of Ur. *See under* Ur
This (Thinis), 112, 113
Tholfsen, Trygve R., 26, 27 (n. 2)
Tholoi, 20
Thomas, Carol G., 27 (n. 5), 220 (n. 7)
Thomas, D. Winton, 291 (n. 4)
Thompson, Thomas L., 261 (n. 25)
Thoth, 119
Thrace, Thracian(s), 2, 215, 229, 298, 303, 304, 305
Thutmose I, 163–164, 165, 167, 170, 174, 182
Thutmose II, 163, 167
Thutmose III, 10, 163, 165, 166, 167, 168–169, 170, 174, 178, 189, 230
Thutmose IV, 163, 165, 170
Tiamat, 48, 49
Tiglath-pileser I, 214, 216
Tiglath-pileser III, 263, 265, 272, 275, 286
Tigris river (and valley), 1, 2, 12, 20, 21, 29, 30, 31, 40, 47, 69, 79, 87, 169, 194, 214, 219, 223, 224, 225, 264, 266, 267, 271, 298, 304, 318
Til-Barsip, 224
Tiryns, 212, 218
Tiy, 170, 172, 173, 179, 180, 181
Tjeker (Tjekel?), 210, 212, 217, 227, 237, 252
Tokens, 34, 112
Tophet(s), 240–241
Torah (Pentateuch), 242, 287, 288, 314
Tower of Babel, 283
Toynbee, Arnold, 21, 28 (n. 15)
Tracer, D. P., 137 (n. 3)
Trade, 3, 11, 14, 16, 22, 23, 32, 39, 40, 52, 59, 60–61, 67, 72, 77, 78, 81, 85–86, 107, 132, 140, 144, 147, 153, 158–159, 174, 213, 218, 226–227, 229, 230, 233, 234, 235–237, 246–247, 252, 256–258, 274, 280, 285, 298, 302–303
Transjordan, Transjordanian. *See* Jordan
Trapezus, 298
"Treasure of Priam," 60
Treaty, treaties, 196–198, 200, 201, 204
Trigger, Bruce G., 136, 137 (n. 3)
Tripolitania, 237
Trireme(s), 236
Troy (Ilium, Hissarlik), Trojan(s), 2, 40, 60, 69, 194, 198–199, 212, 213, 218

Tubb, Jonathan N., 191, 261 (n. 34)
Tudhaliyas I, 193
Tudhaliyas IV, 193, 198
Tukulti-Ninurta I, 215, 216
Tukulti-Ninurta II, 224
Tummal Text, 43
Tunip, 97
Tunis, Tunisia, 236, 240
Turin Canon, 108, 131, 146
Tureng Tepe, 40
Turkey, 12, 20, 31, 32, 34, 68, 94, 96
Turkmenistan, 40, 61, 84
Tursha, 208, 210, 212
Turtanu (tartan), 276
Tushhan, 224
Tushpa, 228, 263
Tushratta, 98, 171, 179, 180, 194, 195
Tutankhamun (Tutankhaton), 163, 175, 179, 187–188, 189, 195
Tyldesley, Joyce, 136, 166, 190, 191 (n. 4, 5, 6), 192 (n. 25), 220
Tyre, Tyrian(s), 148, 175, 224, 234, 235, 236, 237, 238, 239, 240, 241, 246–247, 249, 250, 263, 267, 270, 271, 280, 281, 298, 320
Tyrrhenians (*Tursenoi*), 212

Ubaid. *See* Tell Ubaid
Ubaid Period, 19, 20–22, 29, 31, 37, 38, 76, 79–80
Uganda, 103
Ugarit (Ras Shamra), 2, 12, 40, 97, 175–176, 194, 196, 213, 214, 218, 234, 239
Ukraine, 95, 265, 303
Ululaua. *See* Shalmaneser V
Umma, 30, 31, 43–44, 65, 66, 69, 78
Underworld, 45, 47, 119
United Arab Emirates, 2, 22, 68
Ur, 2, 22, 29, 30, 31, 37, 40, 41, 42, 43, 46, 50, 66, 67, 69, 75, 78, 80, 85, 86, 285;
  "Royal Tombs" of, 44–46, 326
  Third Dynasty of (Ur III), 9, 75–79, 80, 81, 85, 86, 89, 97, 276, 281
  Ziggurat at, 75–76, 285
Urartu, Urartian(s), 97, 225, 227–228, 263, 265, 268, 269, 279, 280, 294, 297
Urban Revolution, 29–31
Urbanism, urbanization, 31, 41, 59, 60, 74
Urhi-Teshub (Mursilis III), 193, 196
Urkesh, 97
Ur-Nammu, 68, 75–76, 78
Uruinimgina, 43–44, 78
Uruk, 2, 30, 31, 34, 38, 41, 42, 43, 44, 46, 50, 66, 67, 75, 86, 88, 285

Uruk Period, 29–33, 34, 36, 37, 38, 52
Urzababa, 65
Userkaf, 130
Ushabti. See Shabti
Ussishkin, David, 290
Utu, 46, 47, 70
Utuhegal, 68, 75
Uzziah (Azariah), 248, 251, 286

Valla, F., 27
Vallat, François, 100
Valley of the Kings, 113, 163, 164, 187, 188, 206, 208
Valley of the Queens, 164
Van Beek, G. W., 259
Van De Mieroop, Marc, 62
Van der Waerden, F., 328
Van Sertima, Ivan, 136 (n. 2)
Van Seters, John, 160 (n. 14), 161 (n. 20), 261 (n. 23, 25)
Varuna/Arunasil, 98
Vidaranag, 316, 317
Vishtaspa, 310
Vizier(s), 65, 123, 131, 148
Voigt, Mary M., 27 (n. 8), 258
Von Soden, Wolfram, 26

Wachsmann, Shelley, 221 (n. 25)
Wahibre (Apries), 280
Walker, C. B. F., 36, 62, 63 (n. 8, 9), 321 (n. 5)
Warad-Sin, 87
Ward, William A., 160, 220, 221 (n. 28)
Warren, P. M., 161 (n. 32)
Wasshukanni, 97, 194
Watanabe, Kazuko, 64 (n. 28)
Watterson, Barbara, 136, 190, 191 (n. 20)
Weather God of Hatti, 201–202
Weeks, Kent R., 192 (n. 23), 220, 221 (n. 13)
Wegner, Josef, 160
Weiss, B., 222 (n. 48)
Weiss, Harvey, 73, 74, 99, 100 (n. 8), 101 (n. 9, 12, 16, 18)
Weitzman, Michael, 62, 99
Welsby Derek A., 290
Wenamun, 226–227, 237, 241
Wenke, Robert, 11, 13, 27 (n. 7, 9, 11), 105, 136 (n.3)
Wente, Edward, 136
Weshesh, 210, 212
Westbrook, Raymond, 190

Wetterstrom, W., 100 (n. 8)
White Nile, 103
Wick, D. P., 27 (n. 5)
Wilford, John Noble, 137 (n. 8, 9)
Wilhelm, G., 100
Wilkinson, T. J., 259, 262 (n. 50)
Willeitner, Joachim, 220
Wilson, John A., 131, 138 (n. 31), 192 (n. 25, 27), 209, 221 (n. 16, 18)
Wilusa, 194, 195, 198, 212
Wiseman, D. J., 290, 291 (n. 4)
Wolff, Samuel R., 260 (n. 21)
Wood, Michael, 220 (n. 6)
Woolley, Sir Leonard, 44, 45, 49, 62, 63 (n. 18), 64 (n. 25), 161 (n. 28), 285
Women in:
  Arabia, 258
  Egypt, 112, 130, 131, 132, 165–168
  Hatti, 199, 200
  Mesopotamia, 44–45, 50, 51, 53, 54, 273–274
  Oxus culture, 85
  Persia, 306, 320
  prehistoric times, 24–25
Writing:
  Aegean (Linear A, Linear B), 178, 199, 253
  alphabetic, 112, 176, 177, 229, 233, 241, 256, 301, 326
  cuneiform, 33–37, 112, 175–176, 202, 203, 227, 233, 234, 278, 298, 301, 326
  Egyptian hieroglyphs, 34, 110–112, 155, 176, 326
  Hittite, 203, 204, 227, 229, 230
  Indus script, 82–83
  Oxus script?, 84
  Urartian, 227

Xenophon, 297, 318
Xerxes (king of Persia), 295, 305, 306, 310, 311, 312
Xerxes (son of Artaxerxes I), 319

Yadin, Yigael, 275, 291 (n. 8)
Yahweh, 233, 243–244, 246, 248, 249, 250, 251, 255, 286, 287, 288, 289, 297, 313, 314, 315, 316, 317
Yahwism, Yahwist(s), 249, 313

Yahwist Narrative. *See J*
Yakar, J., 62
Yamauchi, Edwin M., 290
Yamhad. *See* Aleppo
Yamm, 176
Yanoam, 209
Yaroch, L. A., 137 (n. 3)
Yasmah-Adad, 87–88, 101 (n. 32)
Yathrib (Medina), 257
Yazilikaya, 198, 202
Year names, 9, 71, 99, 112
Yedoniah, 316
Yemen, 256
Yoffee, N., 63 (n. 13)
Young, Gordon D., 100
Young, Peter A., 136 (n. 2)
Younger, K. Lawson Jr., 26
Yurco, Frank J., 136 (n. 2)

Zab River (Upper), 224
Zaccagnini, Carlo, 222 (n. 43)
Zaehner, R. C., 321 (n. 7)
Zagros Mountains, 15, 34, 52, 68, 71, 77, 78, 98, 223, 227, 229, 233, 263, 265, 270, 271, 294, 298, 301, 302
Zakarba'al, 237
Zakros, 158
Zamban, 296
Zangger, Eberhard, 222 (n. 44)
Zarathustra. *See* Zoroaster
Zarins, Juris, 260 (n. 8)
Zawi Chemi, 12, 15
Zawiyet el-Aryan, 128
Zechariah (king of Israel), 286
Zechariah (prophet), 315
Zedekiah, 280–281, 288
Zered River, 254, 255
Zerubbabel, 313–314, 318, 321 (n. 9)
Zeus, 204, 294
Ziggurat(s), 32, 75–76, 282, 283, 285
Zimansky, Paul E., 258
Zimri, 248
Zimri-Lim, 88, 89, 91
Zincirli, 60, 230
Zobah, 231, 246
Zodiac, 128, 325
Zoroaster (Zarathustra), 306, 308–310
Zoroastrian(s), Zoroastrianism, 310, 317, 318, 325, 327, 328